A REGIONAL GEOGRAPHY OF
THE UNITED STATES
AND CANADA

Toward a Sustainable Future

Second Edition

LISA BENTON-SHORT
JOHN RENNIE SHORT
CHRIS MAYDA

ROWMAN & LITTLEFIELD

Lanham • Boulder • New York • London

Executive Editor: Susan McEachern
Editorial Assistant: Katelyn Turner
Senior Marketing Manager: Kim Lyons
Interior Designer: Barbara Werden

Credits and acknowledgments for material borrowed from other sources, and reproduced with permission, appear on the appropriate page within the text.

Unless otherwise indicated, photographs are by Chris Mayda and maps, graphs, and charts by Don Lafreniere, Doug Rivet, Jennifer Mapes, Miriam Hill, Reed Hall, Hugh Semple, and Zachary Napier.

Published by Rowman & Littlefield
An imprint of The Rowman & Littlefield Publishing Group, Inc.
4501 Forbes Boulevard, Suite 200, Lanham, Maryland 20706
www.rowman.com

Unit A, Whitacre Mews, 26-34 Stannary Street, London SE11 4AB, United Kingdom

British Library Cataloguing in Publication Information Available

Library of Congress Cataloging-in-Publication Data

Names: Benton-Short, Lisa, author. | Short, John R., author. | Mayda, Chris, 1948 – author.

Title: A regional geography of the United States and Canada: toward a sustainable future / Lisa Benton-Short, John Rennie Short, Chris Mayda.

Description: Second edition. | Lanham, MD : Rowman & Littlefield, [2018] | Includes bibliographical references and index.

Identifiers: LCCN 2018004649 (print) | LCCN 2018006432 (ebook) | ISBN 9781442277199 (electronic) | ISBN 9781442277182 (cloth : alk. paper)

Subjects: LCSH: United States—Geography. | Canada—Geography. | Human geography—United States. | Human geography—Canada. | Sustainable development—United States. | Sustainable development—Canada. | United States—Environmental conditions. | Canada—Environmental conditions. | United States—Economic conditions. | Canada—Economic conditions.

Classification: LCC E161.3 (ebook) | LCC E161.3 .M343 2018 (print) | DDC 917.3—dc23

LC record available at https://lccn.loc.gov/2018004649

♾™ The paper used in this publication meets the minimum requirements of American National Standard for Information Sciences—Permanence of Paper for Printed Library Materials, ANSI/NISO Z39.48-1992.

Printed in the United States of America

Brief Contents

Detailed Contents

14   **The Great Plains and Canadian Prairie: Land of Opportunity, or Where the Buffalo Roam?**   **307**

15 The Rocky Mountains: High in Elevations, Aspirations, and Appreciation   339

16 Intermontane: Baked, Beguiling, and Booming   367

Illustrations

Charts

Maps

Photos

Tables

Preface

We took over as authors for this second edition in 2016 due to a sad circumstance. The book's first author, Chris Mayda, a professor in the department of geography and geology at Eastern Michigan University, a champion for sustainability and alternatives ways of thinking and living, passed away in March 2016 after a long-term illness.

The first edition of *A Regional Geography of the United States and Canada: Toward a Sustainable Future* was the result of her passion for sustainability. It was also the result of a ten-year investment of her time. In the course of researching this book, she visited all fifty US states and the provinces of Canada, looking at rural and agricultural geography, and also undertook a six-week, six-hundred-mile trek along the US-Canadian border. This book remains the only regional geography text with a focus on sustainability.

So it was with great humility and some trepidation that we agreed to write this second edition. It was difficult to see how we could "improve" the book. The book had been developed while Chris taught a regional course, and it integrated her personal, teaching, and research interests in sustainability. It was a massive and comprehensive book and a significant accomplishment of which she must have been extremely proud.

We settled for making the second edition "different" and aligning it with our expertise, which is more oriented to human geography. To this end, we have expanded discussions on urbanization, migration, and diversity. We feel this change nicely complements her comprehensive coverage of the physical and historical geography of the region.

In addition, we have integrated six overarching themes that we hope will unify the book. In nearly ever chapter, we present these themes as box case studies. These themes are as follows:

- National parks
- Urban sustainability best practices
- Climate change or critical environmental challenges
- Geospatial technologies applied to a regional issue
- Global connections
- Iconic images or cultural festivals

It has been a privilege to work on this second edition.
—Lisa Benton-Short and John Rennie Short

Part One

MOVING TOWARD SUSTAINABILITY

THEMES

PHOTO 1.1. Lower Colorado River Valley in Arizona and California. Transitions in nature are usually gradual, but along this valley they have been dramatic. In this dry hot desert area the few natural plant and animal habitats are threatened. Water management of the river basin has been contested between the riparian vegetation and agriculture.

1
FUNDAMENTAL CONCEPTS
Regions and Ecoregions

Chapter Highlights

After reading this chapter, you should be able to:

- Understand the concepts of regions and ecoregions
- Explain the importance of ecoregions in this book
- Discuss the limitations of using ecoregions
- Define ecoregional transitions
- Compare the regions and ecoregions of the United States and Canada

Terms			
	ecosystem	holistic system	sustainable geography
bioregion	(or ecological system)	region	unintended consequences
ecology	ecotone	subregion	watershed
ecoregion	geography		

Introduction

In this chapter we will consider two fundamental themes of **region** and **ecoregion** that constitute essential building blocks of this book.

The book draws on two disciplines: **geography** and **ecology**. Geography is a bridging discipline between the humanities, the arts, and the sciences. Geography is the study of humans and their interactions with the environment, and as such, championing a sustainable biosphere is a natural part of the discipline. Throughout history, humans have interacted with and affected the places they inhabit, impacting **ecosystems**.

Sustainable geography studies the **holistic systems** relationship between the human, biologic, and physical environments. Its main premise is that everything is connected. Sustainable geography adds to our understanding of the workings of the world.

Ecology is the interdisciplinary science that studies the interactions of living organisms (including humans) with each other and with the surrounding physical world. Ecology studies whole ecosystem components and has been applied to the study of human interactions with the rest of the natural world. Ecological systems are the foundation for studying sustainable geography. Ecosystems interact with the surrounding areas at multiple scales. Changes at one level will affect the surrounding levels, often in the form of **unintended consequences.**

Ecosystems range in size from the molecular level to Gaia (whole earth) systems. Every biotic being has a specific range where it can live. Exceeding the range results in habitat shifts or alters land configurations and can cause the loss of a species because of deforestation or the loss of coastal zones because of rising sea levels. Human activity has consequences that include the loss of species, deforestation, altered water supplies, and loss of agricultural output.

Regions and Ecoregions

By using the concept of region, a specified area that has distinct qualities that differ from the surrounding areas, this portion of North America (Mexico is also part of North America but is not covered in this book) can be arranged in any number of ways. For example, Joel Garreau wrote a book in 1981 called *The Nine Nations of North America*. He based his regional classification on culture and values, not on state or national boundaries or physical geography.

But in this book, the regions presented are based on physical and ecological relationships. To move towards a more sustainable future, humans need to better understand the consequences of their activities on the physical environment. This approach will reach beyond the typical political divisions of both countries.

Ecoregions are ecologically coherent and defined by landforms, climate, **watersheds** (the drainage basin for a geographical area of a river and its tributaries), and ecosystems. Ecoregions are regional-scale ecosystems that are closely related to **bioregions**, which are more closely defined by living beings.

Over the past century, the regional geography of the United States and Canada has been mapped following a variety of physical rather than political or cultural divisions. Maps of the regional physical divisions of the United States were defined by Nevin Fenneman in 1917 and 1928 (map 1.1). In 1995, Robert G. Bailey created an ecoregion map of the United States (map 1.2). In Canada, the Department of Agriculture and Agri-Food Canada and the Nature Conservancy have created maps of Canadian ecoregions (map 1.3). The Fenneman map has many close relationships with the ecoregion map because landforms are one of the elements in an ecoregion map, which also is shaped by climate, vegetation, soil, and watersheds. We have used these maps as guidelines for the ecoregion map of the United States and Canada used in this book.

In this book, the North American subcontinent of the United States and Canada is further divided into **subregions**, which share general characteristics of the larger region but have unique features that differentiate them. The physical and ecological patterns of the subregions are related to the whole region and therefore will share some regional elements. For example, in the Great Plains region, low precipitation and grasslands are common, but several subregions characterize the variety in the Great Plains landscape. Most of the Great Plains has an almost overwhelming expanse of level topography, yet in western

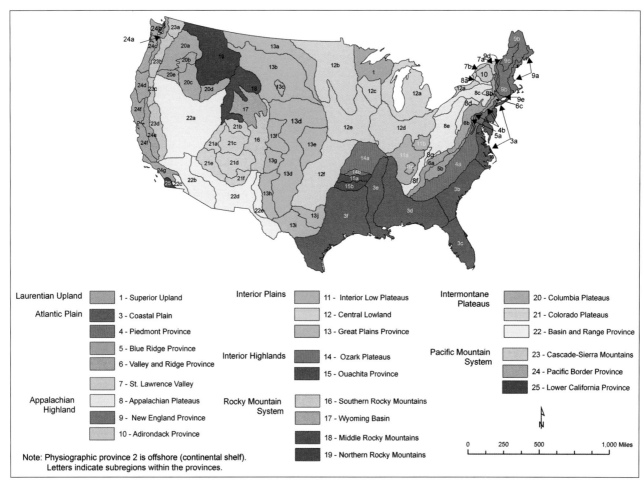

MAP 1.1. Map after Fenneman, "Physiographic Divisions of the United States."

Source: Nevin M. Fenneman, "Physiographic Divisions of the United States," Annals of the Association of American Geographers 18, no. 4 (December 1928): 261–353

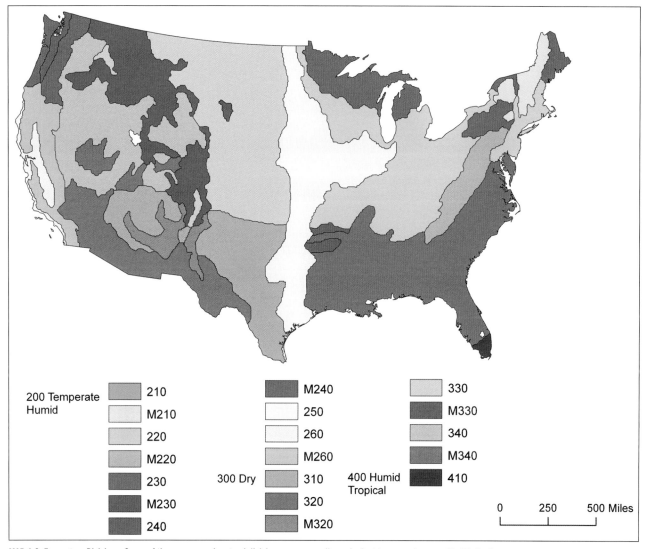

MAP 1.2. Ecosystem Divisions. Some of the more prominent subdivisions are generally equivalent to ecoregions used in this book:

230: Subtropical division (Atlantic and Gulf coastal plain)

220, 250: Prairie, including the prairie peninsula (Central Lowlands)

260: Mediterranean (California)

310, 330: Temperate steppe division (Great Plains)

320, 340: Temperate desert division (Basin and Range)

Source: Robert G. Bailey, Description of the Ecoregions of the United States. 2nd ed. (map). Miscellaneous Publication No. 1391. Washington, D.C.: U.S. Department of Agriculture, U.S. Forest Service, 1995, at http://www.fs.fed.us/land/ecosysmgmt/colorimagemap/ecoreg1_divisions.html

South Dakota, the Dissected Missouri Plateau subregion has uplifted topography, featured in the Black Hills, where the climate and vegetation differ from the surrounding plains. The uplift has caused a microclimate of increased precipitation that has also shifted the vegetation from one of grasslands to pine-covered hills. The Dissected Missouri Plateau is still part of the semiarid Great Plains, but it has its own unified theme of uplift and pines that distinguish it from the surrounding area.

It should also be noted that by using ecoregions and privileging physical and environmental patterns, the cultural character of a place may not fit neatly. For example, consider Birmingham, Alabama. The physical geography and ecological systems are aligned with Appalachia. Its economy is similar to Appalachia: mineral extraction and steel manufacturing. But culturally, we could make the case that Birmingham equally belongs in the Gulf Coast region, with the rest of the state of Alabama. As predominately African American, the city embraces a deep South culture, and was home to the birth of the Civil Rights Movement. This example shows there is not always a clear line between ecoregions and the places that constitute them.

Borders

On one side of the 49th parallel is the United States; on the other side is Canada. The division is arbitrary, unless you are living by the laws of the land on either side, where borderland farmers of each country use their land based on national policy.

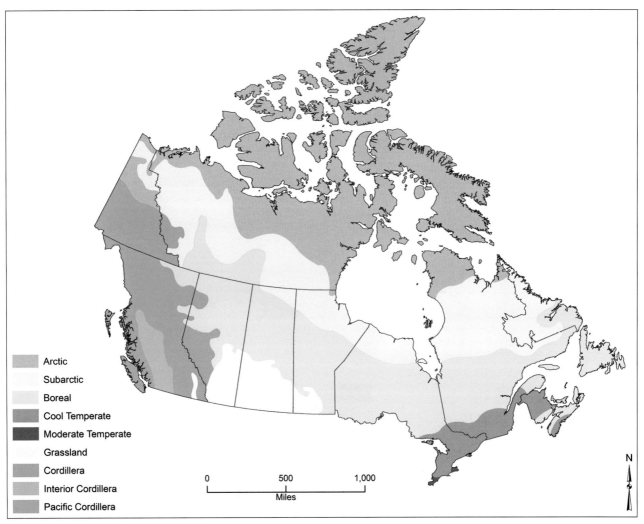

Legend:
- Arctic
- Subarctic
- Boreal
- Cool Temperate
- Moderate Temperate
- Grassland
- Cordillera
- Interior Cordillera
- Pacific Cordillera

0   500   1,000
Miles

N

MAP 1.3. Ecoregions of Canada.

Source: Agriculture and Agri-Food Canada, at http://www.agr.gc.ca/index_e.php

Current borders are overwhelmingly shaped by politics. Most recognized political borders—such as the geometric outline of Colorado—bear no relationship to the surrounding ecological systems or watersheds. Ecoregions imagine borders that are defined by natural systems.

Borders between natural systems are not usually abrupt (photo 1.1) but transitional. While some natural borders are decisive, most borders may be better served by frontier zones, transitional areas between regions. A frontier zone border can be equated to an **ecotone**, a transition between ecological communities.

Sometimes physical features, especially rivers, define state or national borders—the Red River between Oklahoma and Texas, the Colorado River dividing Arizona and California, the Rio Grande separating the United States and Mexico—but these borders do not always reflect watersheds or ecological boundaries (photo 1.2). Rivers are the core of a watershed. A river's watershed boundaries extend to the headwaters of its tributaries and are encompassed by drainage basins. A few state and county boundaries along the East Coast are watershed based, and the border of Labrador is defined by the Atlantic watershed; the Rocky Mountain Continental Divide defines the Pacific and Atlantic watersheds, as well as portions of Idaho, Montana, Alberta, and British Columbia; however, most borders run through the core of a watershed and therefore create more problems than solutions.

Disregarding natural transitions, as artificial political borders do, results in dividing ecosystems and watersheds between two or more states or provinces. Few states or provinces as they exist today are contained within one region. Multiple governmental bodies usually act autonomously and competitively and rarely practice interjurisdictional cooperation, which exacerbates regional and ecosystem needs. The overall health of the ecosystem or watershed is neglected for the short-term betterment of the political unit.

For example, national water policies vary east and west of the Mississippi River. In Canada and east of the Mississippi in the United States, riparian rights are connected to land ownership and cannot be sold outside the watershed, but the western United States is under the principle of prior appropriation, where water is unconnected to land ownership and is considered a commodity.

BOX 1.1   NATIONAL PARKS IN THE UNITED STATES AND CANADA

In 1872, the US Congress passed legislation creating the first national park, Yellowstone. In the United States, the movement to create national parks arose from an increased understanding of natural systems and human impact on them. The overriding purpose of the national parks is to protect resources of significance to the nation and also to convey the meanings of these resources to the public. National parks have been, from the beginning, about public use and enjoyment. Some have called them "the best idea America ever had."

Since Yellowstone, new parks have been added so that currently the national park system in the United States comprises 417 areas covering more than 84 million acres in every state, and the District of Columbia. Parks have served as a barometer of society's changing attitudes and perceptions about what they are, or should be. They are a collection of both *natural* and *cultural* heritages. The US national park system includes the monumental areas of Yellowstone, Yosemite, and Grand Canyon as well as historic sites such as Abraham Lincoln's birthplace, Gettysburg,

the Aztec Ruins in New Mexico, the Statue of Liberty, and the National Mall in Washington, D.C.

Canada designated its first national park, Banff, in 1885. The national park system in Canada is similar to that in the United States and comprises both natural and cultural heritage sites. There are 224 locations including large nature parks such as Banff, Glacier, and Jasper as well as cultural sites such as the historic district of Westmount in Quebec.

We highlight national parks for several reasons:

- They represent the most distinctive and unique ecosystems;
- They represent some of the most important historical sites;
- They require stewardship of both natural and cultural heritage;
- They are subject to political, economic, and environmental pressures; and
- They contribute to regional and national identity.

PHOTO 1.2. The Colorado River, along the California–Arizona border, is the largest river in the driest part of America. The border divides the states and the watershed. Therefore, the states fight for water rights. Rather than working with the river, they work against it, and they have overallocated the river's water.

These are two very different ways to allocate water use. As we shall learn, these artificial water policies have been implemented without regard to dependent watersheds and the ecological communities. In the Basin and Range subregion, cities grow beyond their carrying capacity and claim as much water as possible without regard for the surrounding areas. There has been talk of shipping water from the Great Lakes to water-starved areas as if it were as simple as just moving water, ignoring the multiple ecosystems that would be affected, perhaps even destroyed.

Regions of Canada and the United States

In this book, physical, human, and ecoregional components have been considered in creating each of the chapters. In some cases, physiographic characteristics were paramount (as in the Intermontane), in some, ecological (as in the Gulf Coast or Florida), and in others, human culture (as in Megalopolis). The book follows many traditional geographic patterns of

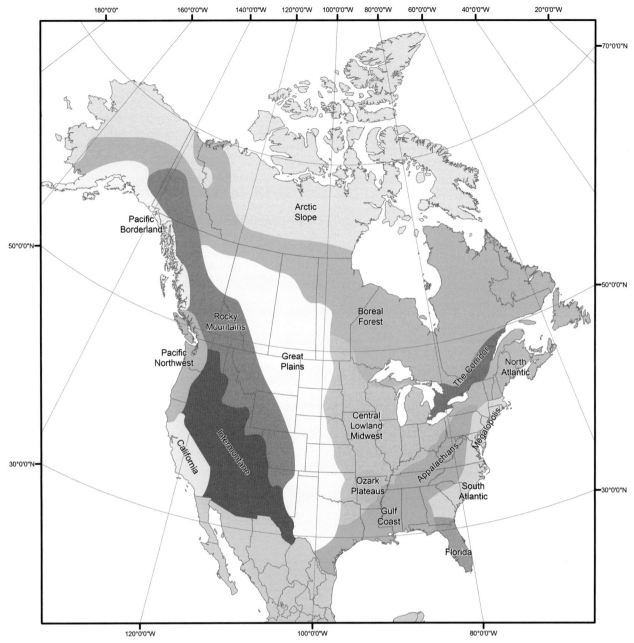

MAP 1.4. The Ecoregional Divisions of the United States and Canada as Used in This Book.

regional boundaries but places more emphasis on sustainable relationships within ecoregions and their surroundings.

The regions as defined in the book are shown in map 1.4 and are discussed in Part II, one per chapter, in the following order:

- Canadian Corridor
- North Atlantic
- Megalopolis
- Appalachia and the Interior Plateau
- South Atlantic
- Florida
- Gulf Coast
- Ozarks
- Midwest
- Great Plains and Canadian Prairie
- Rocky Mountains
- Intermontane
- Pacific Northwest
- Alaska, the Pacific Borderland, and Arctic Boreal Canada
- California
- Hawai`i

Questions for Discussion

1. How do ecoregional boundaries differ from political boundaries?

2. What is the difference between studying geography anthropocentrically and ecologically? Explain the advantages and disadvantages of each.

3. The modern world chose to conquer the landscape. How would a sustainable world differ from the modern approach?

4. How do nation-state borders differ from ecoregional borders? Which is more sustainable? Explain.

Suggested Readings

Anderson, J. R. "Major Land Uses" [map]. *The National Atlas of the United States of America.* Reston, Va.: U.S. Geological Survey, 1970.

Ayers, Edward L., ed. *All over the Map: Rethinking American Regions.* Baltimore, Md.: Johns Hopkins University Press, 1996.

Bailey, Robert G. *Description of the Ecoregions of the United States.* 2nd ed. [map]. Miscellaneous Publication No. 1391. Washington, D.C.: U.S. Department of Agriculture, U.S. Forest Service, 1995, at http://www.fs.fed.us/land/ecosysmgmt/colorimagemap/ecoreg1_divisions.html

———. *Ecoregion-Based Design for Sustainability.* New York: Springer, 2002.

———. *Ecosystem Geography.* New York: Springer, 2009.

Bradshaw, Michael. *Regions and Regionalism in the United States.* Jackson: University Press of Mississippi, 1988.

Brown, Lester. *State of the World.* New York: Norton, annual since 1984.

Commission for Environmental Cooperation (CEC). *Ecological Regions of North America: Toward a Common Perspective.* Montreal: Commission for Environmental Cooperation, 1997.

Fenneman, Nevin M. "The Circumference of Geography." *Annals of the Association of American Geographers* 9 (1919): 3–11.

———. "Physiographic Divisions of the United States." *Annals of the Association of American Geographers* 18, no. 4 (December 1928): 261–353.

Garreau, Joel. *The Nine Nations of North America.* Boston: Houghton Mifflin, 1981.

McGinnis, Michael Vincent, ed. *Bioregionalism.* London: Routledge, 1999.

Omernik, James M. "Map Supplement: Ecoregions of the Conterminous United States." *Annals of the Association of American Geographers* 77, no. 1 (March 1987): 118–25.

Sale, Kirkpatrick. *Dwellers in the Land: The Bioregional Vision.* Athens: University of Georgia Press, 2000.

Andruss, Van, Christopher Plant, Judith Plant, and Eleanor Wright, eds. *Home! A Bioregional Reader.* Gabriola Island, British Columbia, Canada: New Society Publishers, 1990.

Warkentin, John. "Canada and Its Major Regions: Bouchette, Parkin, Rogers, Innis, Hutchinson." *Canadian Geographer* 43, no. 3 (Fall 1999): 244–48.

Zelinsky, Wilbur. "North America's Vernacular Regions." *Annals of the Association of American Geographers* 70, no. 1 (March 1980): 1–16.

Zimmerer, Karl S. "Human Geography and the 'New Ecology': The Prospect and Promise of Integration." *Annals of the Association of American Geographers* 84, no. 1 (March 1994): 108–25.

Internet Sources

Atlas of Canada, at https://www.nrcan.gc.ca/earth-sciences/geography/atlas-canada

Parks Canada. Terrestrial Ecozones of Canada, at parkscanadahistory.com/publications/fact-sheets/eng/ecozones.pdf.

Reliable Prosperity: A Project of Ecotrust, at http://tribalp2.org/reliable-prosperity-a-project-of-ecotrust/

Systems Thinking, at http://www.thinking.net/Systems_Thinking/systems_thinking.html

U.S. Department of Agriculture. 2012. Census of Agriculture: Maps and Cartographic Resources, at https://www.agcensus.usda.gov/Publications/2012/Online_Resources/Ag_Census_Web_Maps/index.php

U.S. Environmental Protection Agency. Ecoregions, at https://www.epa.gov/eco-research/ecoregions

PHOTO 2.1. Wind Turbines near Rock Springs, Wyoming. Wind power provides only 1 percent of America's energy. Ninety-two percent of energy in the United States is nonrenewable and polluting.

2
FUNDAMENTAL CONCEPTS
Sustainability

Chapter Highlights

After reading this chapter, you should be able to:

- Define sustainability
- Understand the "Three Es" of sustainability
- Explain the importance of the United Nations Sustainable Development Goals
- Define and discuss environmental justice

Terms

anthropocentric
Brundtland Report

carrying capacity
ecological footprint
environmental justice
external costs

life cycle analysis
nonrenewable resource
renewable resource
sustainable development

sustainable development
goals (SDGs)
"three Es"
triple bottom line

Introduction

The idea of **sustainability** coalesces around the three issues of environment, economic development, and social equity. Importantly, sustainability is not concerned only with the environment: at its root it is concerned with the quality of human life. The concept of sustainability has emerged from long and rich intellectual evolution of ideas (photo 2.1).

In the United States, many writers, thinkers, and scholars have reconceptualized nature–society relationships. The writings of Henry David Thoreau's *Walden* published in 1854 remains a classic read about the transformative power of nature. George Perkins Marsh, who published *Man and Nature* in 1864, argued that human impact on the environment could have significant effects. He drew attention to the unforeseen consequences of human actions; floods and landslides, for example, were often the result of overgrazing.

During the 1960s and early 1970s, numerous writers and thinkers expanded discussions about the impact of human activities on the natural environment. In 1962, Rachel Carson published *Silent Spring*. It was a pivotal moment in the US

environmental movement. *Silent Spring* begins with the image of a birdless spring, a result of pesticides such as DDT (dichlorodiphenyltrichloroethane) destroying birdlife. Her book chronicled the growing use of chemicals like DDT, deildrin, endrin, and parathion, detailing their deleterious effects on humans, plants, and animals. Her book helped to launch the environmental movement that raised public consciousness about the relationship of humans and Earth. It challenged us to rethink our relationship with the natural world.

Donella Meadows led the Club of Rome, a group of scholars, who in 1972 published *Limits to Growth*. The book used computer models to understand how unchecked economic and population growth impacts finite resources. Ecological economist Herman Daly's 1973 book *Steady State Economy* argued that economic activity degrades ecosystems and interferes with natural processes that are critical to various life support services.

These writers and thinkers—along with many others—raised concerns that there are limits to economic growth and resource use. Three themes—environment, equity, and economy—have been discussed and debated for more than a century.

BOX 2.1 AN ENVIRONMENTAL MOVEMENT EMERGES IN THE UNITED STATES

The year 1969 was one of environmental disasters. Lake Erie was declared "dead," so polluted that it was devoid of fish and aquatic life. In the nation's capital, the Potomac River was clogged with blue-green algae blooms that were both a nuisance and a public health threat, and the local rivers were little more than open sewers. Off the shores of Santa Barbara in California, a large oil spill contaminated miles of shoreline, killing sea otters, birds, and other marine animals, while television crews filmed frantic volunteers trying to wash the oil off the dying animals and birds. On June 22, railroad sparks set fire to the Cuyahoga River in Cleveland. The river, saturated with oil, kerosene, debris, and other flammable chemicals, was engulfed in a five-story-high blaze of flames. The fire burned for five days. The Cuyahoga became the symbol of urban water pollution and the need for the federal government to become involved in cleanup and regulation. Jonathan H. Adler, associate professor of law at Case Western Reserve University, remarked on the legacy of the Cuyahoga:

The Cuyahoga fire was a powerful symbol of a planet in disrepair and an ever-deepening environmental crisis, and it remains so to this day. That a river could become so polluted to ignite proved the need for federal environmental regulation. Following on the heels of several best-selling books warning of ecological apocalypse and other high-profile events such as the Santa Barbara oil spill, the 1969 Cuyahoga fire spurred efforts to enact sweeping federal environmental legislation. The burning river mobilized the nation and became a rallying point for the passage of the Clean Water Act.[*]

These and other episodes around the United States served as a rallying point for the emergence of the modern environmental movement and the passage of the 1969 National Environmental Policy Act. This watershed legislation established the Environmental Protection Agency (EPA) and charged the agency to study pollution and recommend new policies.

The environmental movement signaled the start of a new era: the age of sustainability.

*Jonathan H. Adler, "Smoking Out the Cuyahoga Fire Fable: Smoke and Mirrors Surrounding Cleveland," *National Review*, June 22, 2004, at https://www.nationalreview.com/2004/06/smoking-out-cuyahoga-fire-fable-jonathan-h-adler/

Defining Sustainability

In 1987, the United Nations World Commission on Environment and Development issued a report called *Our Common Future*. The report was the product of a commission of foreign ministers, finance and planning officials, economists, and policymakers in agriculture, science, and technology. The report is often referred to as the **Brundtland Report**, after Gro Harlem Brundtland, chair of the commission. The report defined sustainable development as "development that meets the needs of the present without compromising the ability of future generations to meet their own needs." Seen as the guiding principle for long-term global development, sustainability consists of three pillars: economic development, social development, and environmental protection. These are often referred to as the "**three Es**"—economy, ecology, and equity.

Since *Our Common Future*, international discussions and debates about sustainability continued with Agenda 21 in 1992. The preamble to Agenda 21 notes,

Humanity stands at a defining moment in history. We are confronted with a perpetuation of disparities between and within nations, a worsening of poverty, hunger, ill health and illiteracy, and the continuing deterioration of the ecosystems on which we depend for our well-being. However, integration of environment and development concerns and greater attention to them will lead to the fulfillment of basic needs, improved living standards for

all, better protected and managed ecosystems and a safer, more prosperous future. No nation can achieve this on its own; but together we can—in a global partnership for sustainable development.

Sustainability is now the guiding agenda for the protection of both the local and the global commons.

Implementing Sustainability

Sustainability aims for an ecological equilibrium of Earth's interconnected ecosystems that maximizes efficiency, minimizes waste, and spends interest but not principal.

In 2015, after three years of negotiations and debate, 193 countries agreed to to adopt the **Sustainable Development Goals (SDGs)**. The SDGs build on the success of the 2000 United Nations Millennium Development Goals and aim to go further to end all forms of poverty. The new goals are unique in that they call for action by all countries—poor, rich, and middle-income—to promote prosperity while protecting the planet (chart 2.1). They recognize that ending poverty must go hand-in-hand with strategies that build economic growth and address a range of social needs including education, health, social protection, and job opportunities, while tackling climate change and environmental protection. The SDGs set an agenda for investment in advancing sustainability.

The seventeen SDGs set out to tackle a whole range of issues including ending hunger, improving health, combating

BOX 2.2 PROTECTING AND REGULATING THE ENVIRONMENT

The Environmental Revolution resulted in dramatic legislative and regulatory changes in both the United States and Canada. In the United States, the government responded quickly, passing dozens of environmental policies and creating new institutions such as the EPA, which merged environmental responsibilities previously scattered among dozens of offices and programs. New departments, agencies, and boards for protecting the environment proliferated at the federal, state, and city levels. A flurry of congressional activity produced a flood of legislation. Within a few years of establishing the EPA (1969), Congress passed the Clean Air Act (1970), the Clean Water Act (1972), and the Endangered Species Act (1973). These three pieces of legislation still form the backbone of twenty-first-century environmental regulation.

Canada created the Department of Environment in 1971 with a similar set of responsibilities as the US EPA. Like the United States, Canada also passed key environmental legislation that includes the Canadian Environmental Assessment Act, the Pest Control Products Act, the Canada Shipping Act, the Arctic Waters Pollution Prevention Act, the Fisheries Act, and the Transportation of Dangerous Goods Act.

The Environmental Revolution and the resulting legislation of the 1970s marked an important shift in the role of government as a consensus developed around the proposition that environmental problems are public problems that cannot be solved only through private action and an unregulated market.

CHART 2.1. The 2030 Sustainable Development Goals.

climate change, and protecting oceans and forests. These targets help focus efforts to implement the "three Es" of sustainability. Importantly, these seventeen SDGs were a reminder to developed countries such as the United States and Canada that there is work to do to achieve sustainability. Sustainable development is not just for developing countries.

Sustainable practices are being adopted globally. Europe has led the way. North America has been slower to respond, but there are many local, municipal, and regional initiatives underway, which we will explore throughout the book.

Achieving a sustainable lifestyle will not be easy. It will require changing agricultural methods and environmental, energy, and urban planning practices. It will require changing the **anthropocentric** mindset that has dominated the developed world for the past several hundred years.

The modern age worked on only an economic, profit-based model, while the Age of Sustainability recognizes limits and the **external costs** of environment and social equity, such as waste, pollution, and social injustice. Including environmental and social equity within the cost of goods reflects the full cost to the consumer and is called the **triple bottom line (TBL)**, "planet, people, and profit."

The TBL promotes corporate social responsibility and sustainable development as equally important as profit. The traditional economic model used by both the United States and Canada endorses a bottom line consisting of revenues, minus costs and expenses. This bottom line measures economics alone. The environmental and social costs are passed along to the consumer, whereas the TBL includes these external costs.

The TBL measures more than economic profit; it calculates the environmental and social values added or erased by companies. The TBL champions sustainable development transitions including new societal and environmental values, transparency, and **life cycle analysis** (following a product from raw material to disposal).

The shift to sustainability is not about giving up what we have, but about answering these challenges with innovation, creativity, and a shift in thinking that is more holistic. To have a sustainable mindset is to see that everything is connected and that there are limits to our world, and then to act accordingly.

BOX 2.3 CARRYING CAPACITY

Carrying capacity is defined as the maximum population size of a species that an area can support without reducing the area's ability to support the same species in the future. The carrying capacity can be measured for any biological life-form, but this discussion concerns humans living in an ecologically balanced world. Long-term sustainability depends on how people live on the planet. There are two standards for measuring carrying capacity with regard to humans: biophysical and social.

The biophysical carrying capacity describes the maximum number of people that can live on Earth within technological capabilities. The biophysical carrying capacity has a higher maximum population than the social, but the standard of living is lower.

The social carrying capacity is based on how many people can live on Earth under a specific social system. The level of technological development determines the carrying capacity; the social carrying capacity is below the biophysical survival number. For example, if the entire world were to live at the Afghan standard of living, the carrying capacity would be considerably higher than if the entire world lived as Americans. Which brings up the question, how many people could the world hold if all people were to live as an average American?

If the world population were to live as Americans or Canadians now do, the global population would have to be less. According to the ecological footprint, at least five Earths would be necessary to provide the world population with the American or Canadian living standard. Therefore, the social carrying capacity for the North American standard of living would support 1.3 billion people (one-fifth of the current population). Any more people living at this standard would be unsustainable over the long term; it would rob future generations of resources.

To maintain a sustainable carrying capacity at current population levels requires increasing the use of **renewable resources**, decreasing the use of **nonrenewable resources**, and conserving energy use.

Living within the limits, recognizing impact, and understanding the complexity and unintended consequences of our actions will bring humans closer to a sustainable existence necessary for a sustainable future. This text will cover sustainability challenges and practices from a variety of angles and highlight examples of best practices. Sustainable goals will be discussed in numerous ways, including confronting climate change, reducing automobile dependence, combating poverty, and reducing per capita use of resources and waste while improving livability.

The Ecological Footprint

A sustainable life requires living within the limits of global resources. Population experts do not consider the consumption levels of the current population sustainable.

The populations of the United States and Canada live well beyond their available land resources, which is measured by an equation called the **ecological footprint**—calculating human consumption of resources in relation to Earth's renewable capacity. The ecological footprint approximates how much productive land and water are needed to provide for a population. The ecological footprint can be measured at any scale, from individual to global. The land used is then compared to the land occupied. In the United States and Canada, the ecological footprint is much larger than the land it occupies and, therefore, unsustainable on a global scale.

On average, there are 4.5 acres of productive land per person in the world. The average productive land needed for developed countries is 15.8 acres, for middle-income countries 5 acres, and for low-income countries 2 acres, but Americans require 24 acres and Canadians require 22 acres. The number of acres multiplied by the population gives the number of Earths necessary (as if we had more than one) to live in that fashion. For example, if everyone on Earth were to consume at the American rate, there would need to be 5.3 Earths; to consume as the average Canadian would require 4 Earths.

The ecological footprint does not propose that all people live exactly the same, but it does allow people to see where they are in relation to the rest of the world population. For example, if everyone (seven billion people) lived at the same level, dividing up all resources equally, the standard of living on Earth would be something like the following:

- strict vegetarian, eggs a few times a week;
- no processed food;
- two people living in 500 square feet;
- no running water;
- no electricity;
- public transportation or bicycle; and
- no flying.

While the footprint equation has been criticized because of some of its assumptions, it is a rough measure of the demands on nature caused by a large population consuming resources. The human consumption of natural resources by the current world population is approximately 140 percent more than Earth can sustain. The current ecological footprint of world population is unsustainable. Another way to say this is: Earth is spending its principal rather than only its interest. If the principal is continuously spent there will be no interest, no principal, and Earth will soon be bankrupt to maintain a healthy quality of life standard of living for the human population.

The ecological footprint can be reduced by limiting population and consumption. The countries that can conserve most are the developed countries, where population growth is small but consumption continues to grow. The countries where population growth rates are high are usually the less developed countries, where consumption is stagnant or dropping.

BOX 2.4   POPULATION AND CONSUMPTION

While we tend to think of "population" as being an issue of too many people for the carrying capacity of Earth, in fact many experts argue that it is how much a given population consumes that is the real issue. Consumption is a global problem but differs in the developed and developing worlds. The developed world consumes global resources at unsustainable rates that deplete supply. Globally, 20 percent of the world's people in the highest-income countries account for 76 percent of total private consumption expenditures, the poorest 20 percent a minuscule 1.5 percent. More specifically, the richest fifth

- consume 45 percent of all meat and fish, the poorest fifth 5 percent;
- consume 58 percent of total energy, the poorest fifth less than 4 percent;
- have 74 percent of all telephone lines, the poorest fifth 1.5 percent;
- consume 84 percent of all paper, the poorest fifth 1.1 percent; and
- own 87 percent of the world's vehicle fleet, the poorest fifth less than 1 percent.

Although the United States constitutes about 5 percent of the world population, the country consumes about one-third of all processed minerals, 25 percent of nonrenewable energy, and creates about one-third of global pollution. The United States remains the world's largest producer of garbage and industrial waste. Americans use 159 gallons of water daily, while more than half of the world's population lives on 25 gallons.

American consumption degrades resources worldwide because of its dependence on imported goods, often exporting its raw materials overseas to be processed in countries with low wages and fewer environmental regulations than the United States. This practice is the ultimate fragmented thinking of the status quo economy: exploit and pollute elsewhere, because pollution in one place is treated as disconnected from any other place—but everything is connected.

Becoming responsible consumers is a major challenge to sustainability, and there are several goals around improving consumption patterns in SDG #12.

Environmental Equity

Most Americans know something about water pollution, air pollution, climate change, and the use of fossil fuels. However, there is more to sustainability than simply minimizing our environmental impact, developing policies that promote recycling, or passing legislation to prevent environmental degradation. It is important that we pay equal attention to the third "E" of sustainability: equity. The distribution of environmental "goods" such as parks and street trees, and environmental "bads" such as polluting industries and waste facilities, should be just.

Sadly, many environmental "bads" such as toxic facilities are predominately concentrated in lower income and minority-dominated areas of cities, and major infrastructure projects with negative environmental impacts such as highways are more commonly found in poorer and more minority neighborhoods. Study after study reveals a correlation between negative environmental impacts and the presence of racial/ethnic minorities. Race continues to be the most significant variable associated with the location of hazardous waste sites and the greatest number of commercial hazardous facilities is located in areas with the highest composition of racial and ethnic minorities. One study showed that three out of every five Black and Hispanic Americans lived in communities with one or more toxic waste sites. Although socioeconomic status was also an important variable in the location of these sites, race was the most significant.

In the United States and Canada, and around the world, the poor and the marginal more often than not live in the areas of the worst environmental quality. In the United States, among the counties that have three or more pollutants, 12 percent are majority white, 20 percent are majority African American,

and 31 percent are majority Hispanic. Race and ethnicity intertwine with access to power to produce an uneven experience of environmental quality at home and in the workplace. Environmental inequality is large and pervasive.

Socioeconomic status also plays a major role in the environmental quality of living. Poorer communities have less pleasant urban environments and often bear the brunt of negative externalities. It is through their neighborhoods that motorways are constructed; it is in their neighborhoods where heavy vehicular traffic can cause elevated lead levels in the local soil and water. There is a direct correlation between socioeconomic status and the quality of one's environment.

Poor people get dumped on because they are poor, and they are poor because they lack the wealth to generate political power and bargaining strength. In many cities and suburbs, the best and safest areas have gone to those with the most money and those with the least get what is left.

Environmental inequalities occur not only through the presence of environmental "bads"; they are also found in the absence and lack of access of environmental "goods." One example: geographers have mapped trees and found an inequitable distribution of trees in the city of Milwaukee. The more affluent white areas had more extensive urban tree canopy than the poorer and blacker areas of the city. Because trees can positively effect the quality of neighborhoods, through aesthetic and pollution-diminishing properties, the distribution of uneven green space reproduced uneven social space. The city's shift from a public to a more private funding of the urban tree canopy, part of a more general urban neoliberalization, thus marks a regressive social policy, as the wealthier areas can afford the funds more than the poorer areas.

BOX 2.5 MAPPING ENVIRONMENTAL JUSTICE

In 2015, the EPA released EJSCREEN, an environmental justice mapping and screening tool that allows Americans to identify sources of pollution and contamination near their homes. EJSCREEN users choose a geographic area; the tool then provides demographic and environmental information for that area.

EJSCREEN lets you compare a community to the rest of the state, EPA region, and nation by using percentiles. The national percentile tells you what percent of the US population has an equal or lower value, meaning less potential for exposure/ risk/ proximity to certain facilities, or a lower percent minority (map 2.1).

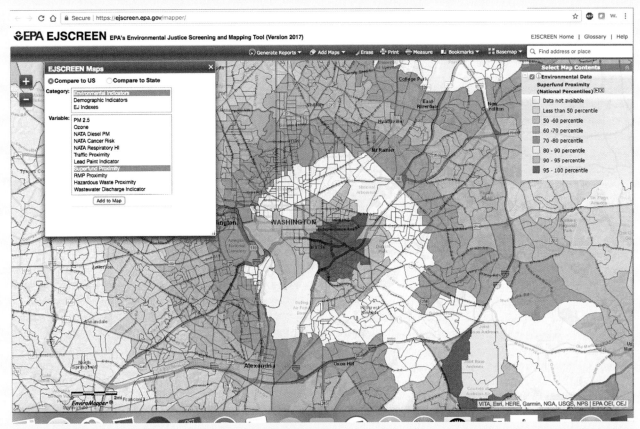

MAP 2.1. Washington, D.C., Neighborhoods near a Superfund Site. The map shown was made using the EJScreen data for Washington, D.C., and selected for proximity to a Superfund site. The map shows that residents in Wards 6, 7, and 8 are more vulnerable to Superfund sites than other wards in the District. These are wards that are predominately African American.

Environmental Justice

The existence of environmental inequalities, whither in terms of siting of waste plants or the absence of green spaces, raises the issue of **environmental justice**. The US EPA defines environmental justice as the "fair treatment and meaningful involvement of all people regardless of race, color, national origin, or income with respect to the development, implementation, and enforcement of environmental laws, regulations, and policies."

This is a narrow definition that restricts the issues to one of a relationship with public policies. "Fair treatment" implies that no single group should bear a disproportionate share of negative environmental consequences or a disproportionate lack of positive environment consequences. "Meaningful involvement" implies that people should have the opportunity to participate in environment decisions and effect regulatory bodies.

Environmental justice was given legislative existence in the United States in 1994 when President Clinton signed Executive Order 12898 that initiated an environmental justice program within the EPA. The aim was to raise awareness of environmental justice issues, identify and assess inequitable environmental impacts, and provide assistance to local areas and community groups. The promotion of environmental justice essentially disappeared under the Bush administration, but under Obama's presidency it made something of a comeback. Under the environmental justice 2014 Program, the EPA devised strategies to protect health in polluted neighborhoods, empower communities to take action, and establish partnerships with local and state governments to promote healthy sustainable communities. Several mapping tools have been developed and used by EPA, including EJSCREEN.

Environmental justice issues arise from the obvious fact that there is a correlation between the siting of hazardous facilities and low-income communities and/or minority communities. However, legal redress is difficult if procedures are correctly followed or permits are legally obtained. In many cases it is the everyday operation of the market or the civic society wherein environmental injustices are created and maintained. If the aim of sustainability is to produce more equitable outcomes, we need more positive interventions. Environmental impact statements, for example, need a more explicit assessment of equity and justice issues. Low-income communities facing environmental challenges should also receive greater resources from the government, not simply equal treatment under the law. Unless more positive outcomes are engineered, the system will continue to produce inequitable results.

Genuine sustainability requires us to consider our actions in relation to others and to pursue a more democratic civic politics. It involves ensuring environmental and economic benefits are distributed equitably among all citizens. This could be one of the biggest challenges to a more sustainable future.

A Sustainable World

A sustainable future includes the following elements:

- creating societies that allow individuals to realize their potential;
- reducing poverty;
- ensuring social justice;
- educating holistically;
- minimizing nonrenewable resource consumption;
- maximizing resource and energy efficiency;
- minimizing polluting toxins;
- respecting and working with the natural environment rather than against it;
- cradle to cradle industry;
- ecological balance and integrating ecosystems;
- including humans aligned with nature as part of the many ecosystems;
- living with sustainable agricultural practices;
- controlling population growth; and
- reducing material consumption.

Questions for Discussion

1. Can we have economic success and still fail as a country?

2. How would business change if the triple bottom line were adopted?

3. How would your world change if sustainability became the norm? How long would it take?

4. Which of the seventeen new SDGs are the biggest challenge in your community?

5. What, in your opinion, will happen to the United States and Canada in the next twenty-five years if sustainability does not become the norm?

6. Why do you think most people overlook the "equity" aspect to sustainability?

Suggested Readings

Adams, B. *Green Development: Environment and Sustainability in a Developing World.* 3rd ed. London: Routledge, 2008.

Carson, R. *Silent Spring.* New York: Houghton Mifflin, 1962.

Dresner, S. *The Principles of Sustainability.* 2nd ed. New York: Roultedge, 2008.

Edwards, A., and D. Orr. *The Sustainability Revolution: Portrait of a Paradigm Shift.* British Columbia, Canada: New Society Publishers, 2005.

Heynen, N., H. Perkins, and P. Roy. "The Political Ecology of Uneven Urban Green Space," *Urban Affairs Review* 42 (2006): 3–25.

Oreskes, N., and E. Conway. *Merchants of Doubt: How a Handful of Scientists Obscured the Truth on Issues from Tobacco Smoke to Global Warming.* New York: Bloomsbury Press, 2011.

Portney, K. *Sustainability.* Cambridge, Mass.: MIT Press Essential Knowledge Series, 2015.

Risse, M. *On Global Justice.* Princeton, N.J.: Princeton University Press, 2012.

Sachs, J. *The Age of Sustainable Development.* New York: Columbia University Press, 2015.

Sarkar, S. *Environmental Philosophy: From Theory to Practice.* Oxford: John Wiley & Sons, 2012.

United Church of Christ Commission for Racial Justice. *Toxic Wastes and Race in the United States: A National Report on the Racial and Socio-economic Characteristics of Communities with Hazardous Waste Sites.* New York: Public Data Access, 1987.

United Nations, World Commission on Environment and Development. *Our Common Future,* 1987.

Internet Sources

Ecological Footprint calculator: The footprint calculator is available online at http://www.footprintnetwork.org/en/index.php/GFN/page/calculators/ It should be noted that the ecological footprint does not represent all environmental impacts, but it is a representative measure.

Carbon Footprint, at http://www.carbonfootprint.com

United Nations Sustainable Development Goals, at http://www.un.org/sustainabledevelopment/sustainable-development-goals/

United States EPA on environmental justice, at https://www.epa.gov/environmentaljustice

PHOTO 3.1. Arches National Park, Utah. More than two thousand natural sandstone arches, spires, and pinnacles highlight the dramatic setting. The formations are the result of salt, erosion, and uplift exposed to wind and water.

3
REGIONS
The Physical Context

Chapter Highlights

After reading this chapter, you should be able to:

- Describe the relationship between physical systems
- Outline the creation of US and Canadian landforms
- Describe basic shared physical features of the United States and Canada
- Identify critical issues associated with water systems
- Distinguish between point and nonpoint pollution
- Understand the basic science of climate change and how human activity impacts climate change

Terms

aquifer	continental shelf	groundwater	pocosin
basalt	dome mountain	ice age	point source pollution
biome	drainage basin	karst	Precambrian
bog	erosion	marsh	precipitation
boreal forest	fault	Mediterranean climate	rain shadow
caldera	fault-block mountain	Moraine	shield
carbon cycle	fjord	nonpoint source pollution	swamp
climate change	folded mountain	orographic precipitation	taiga
continental climate	glacial drift	pedalfer	tundra
continental glaciation	glacier	pedocal	volcanic mountain
	global warming	platform	wetland
	greenhouse gases (GHGs)	Pleistocene	xerophytic

Introduction

In Canada and especially in the United States, many residents no longer relate to or understand the landforms, climate, and ecological communities they live in.

Understanding how unique physical regions and distinct landforms may be affected by human intervention requires a basic knowledge of the complex physical and ecological landscape and an appreciation of its natural beauty (photo 3.1).

Each regional chapter will focus on three interrelated physical geography themes:

- physical geography, which includes ecology and major landforms;
- water; and
- climate.

This chapter will introduce these three themes in more detail. It will outline the basic concepts in physical and ecological environments. It will also introduce critical issues including water supply, water quality, **climate change**, and increased hazards.

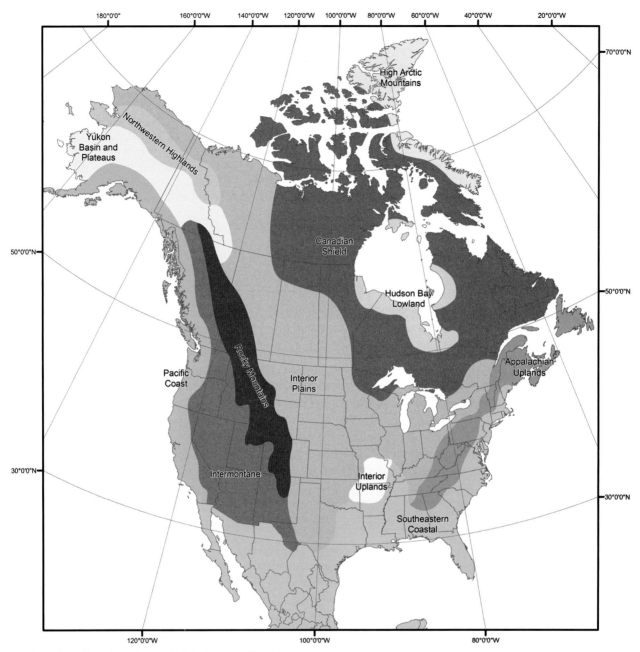

MAP 3.1. The Basic Physical Landforms of the United States and Canada.

Physical Geography

On a broad scale, the United States and Canada have different physical landscapes and ecological systems, although a physiographic map reveals some shared patterns (map 3.1). **Boreal forest** occupies almost half of Canada, and another quarter is **tundra**. Most of the United States outside of Alaska has a temperate climate. Only 1 percent of Canada's land is urban, whereas urban settlement in the United States occupies 6 percent of the land. Latitude accounts for some of the reasons the land cover and settlement patterns differ, but knowing the geologic history of the two countries reveals a more complete tale.

A Brief Geologic History of the United States and Canada

The story begins more than four billion years ago along the edge of Hudson Bay, where small drifting landmasses collided and formed the Canadian or Laurentian Shield. At that time, the continental crust was about 25 percent of the continent's current size. The **shield** formed when volcanic magma (liquid rock) cooled, solidified, and rose above sea level. Sedimentary deposits covered and extended the shield to form a **platform.**

The Canadian Shield extends from the edges of the Rocky Mountains to the Appalachian Uplands. The platform overlies much of the shield. Glaciated and eroded multiple times, the once mountainous shield is now a low-lying, rocky, bare,

BOX 3.1 DID YOU KNOW . . . GLACIERS

- There are two kinds of **glaciers**: continental and alpine.
- Continental glaciers spread from a central mass of ice over continents.
- Continental glaciers comprise over 90 percent of all glacial ice.
- Alpine glaciers are found in mountains ranges and descend from high valleys.
- Alaska has more than a hundred thousand glaciers.
- Seventy-seven percent of all freshwater is in the form of ice, mostly locked in glaciers.
- When the last ice age peaked about eighteen thousand years ago, glaciers covered 30 percent of the land. Today, they cover about 10 percent.

- During the most severe ice age (about eight hundred million years ago), glaciers were present in tropical latitudes and may have reached within degrees of the equator.

While glacial activity has been a natural part of the physical cycle, the current melting may be the result of human activity. The current melting of glaciers has affected river flows, decreased hydropower generation, and caused species migration, as well as affected forestry and agriculture-based livelihoods.

---

and gouged landscape, littered with **wetlands** and millions of lakes. The **Precambrian** volcanic action was during the oldest geologic period, during which volcanic magma heated and pressurized metals, forming mineral resources. Canadian Shield ores are important twenty-first-century resources.

By 1.5 billion years ago, the continental crust had grown to about 80 percent of its current size. During the next six hundred million years, the North American landmass was part of Rodinia, one of the first supercontinents formed by continental drift. New land accreted to today's east coast, forming the roots of the Appalachian Mountains. However, at this time the continent straddled the equator. The warm climate produced the first forms of life. This period was followed by a significant "snowball Earth" (there have been several) about 650 million years ago.

North America then spawned a vast inland sea; oceans widened and then closed as Gondwana and Laurasia formed supercontinents. About five hundred million years ago, new life forms were established on the equator-centered continent. As the tropical plants of this period died, they were buried and pressurized, forming some of America's many coal basins. Small skeletal organisms deposited on the oceanic floor became limestone. Portions of Africa attached to the east coast, forming Massachusetts and Atlantic Canada.

During the geologic Mesozoic era (250 to 65 million years ago), Pangaea formed and an interior seaway across the Great Plains region divided North America. Another period of heat and pressure transformed more tropical plants to coal or natural gas. Then about 250 million years ago, the Pacific Plate on the west coast began to subduct beneath the North American Plate, and much of the coastal states accreted to the continent. California remained an offshore island, and a submerged Florida broke off from Africa and attached to the continent.

About two hundred million years ago, Pangaea broke up and the east coast of the continent attained a more recognizable shape. As South America moved south, the empty space evolved into the Gulf of Mexico; North America drifted away from Africa, opening up the Atlantic Ocean. Along the Atlantic

coast the Appalachians, as tall as today's Rockies, began to erode. Their soil built up the Atlantic Coastal Plain. Inland, the Keweenaw Rift helped form Lake Superior and left a volcanic mineralized belt of copper ore.

The next step in the continental formation was the rise of the Rocky Mountains, the shaping of volcanoes and mountains in the far west and the accretion of land to form the Alaskan peninsula. The Great Plains and the Atlantic and Gulf coasts were still submerged, but the United States was beginning to take a recognizable shape about 100 million years ago.

In the next thirty million years, the Atlantic and Gulf coastal plains emerged from the seas as sediment washed down from the inland. After another thirty million years, the Pacific Plate isle of California accreted to the North American Plate, becoming part of the mainland. The plate margins are defined by the San Andreas Fault.

From fifteen to five million years ago, the Columbia River Plateau was flooded with magma that hardened into **basalt**, which was then ravaged many years later by the Missoula Floods, leaving the Channeled Scablands. Northern Florida emerged from the sea.

Over the past seventy million years, three major **ice age** periods flattened vast portions of Earth with massive miles-deep ice sheets (**continental glaciation**). The most recent ice age arrived two million years ago and scoured the northern continent, until about twelve thousand years ago. The past twelve thousand years, the Holocene, has been an interglacial warm period and the ice has receded, although there have been at least twenty occurrences of minor recessions and advances.

North American **Pleistocene** glaciations covered and reshaped the landscape from Canada south through the Central Lowlands. For example, the Ohio and Missouri river systems were formed as the glaciers melted. Today, their channels roughly mark the southern extent of the ice sheets (map 3.2). Fertile **glacial drift** was deposited over the scoured surface, and the physical landscape was pockmarked with millions of glacially formed kettle lakes. Along coastal areas, such as in

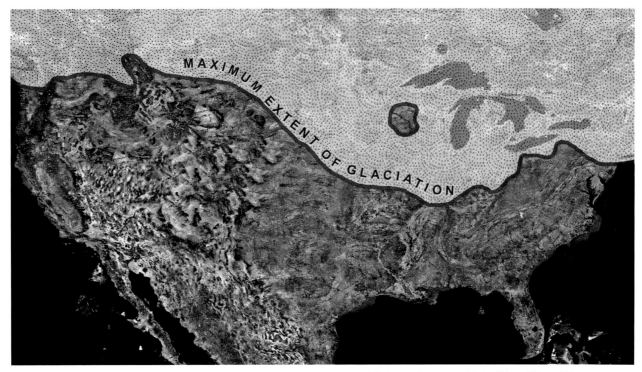

MAP 3.2. Maximum Extent of Glaciation. The southern extent of glaciation from the last round of Pleistocene ice was roughly the Ohio and Missouri Rivers.

Newfoundland, retreating glaciers carved the long steep **fjords** that finger out to the sea.

Characteristic glacial landscapes over Canada and the northern United States include the following:

- bare rock scoured of soil (e.g., the Canadian Shield);
- drained glacial lakes, leaving behind deposits of fertile sediment. Lake Agassiz, straddling the US-Canadian border, became the fertile Red River Valley;
- boggy soils, such as those found throughout the Great Lakes region;
- **Moraines** found throughout the Great Lakes and Northern Atlantic coastal regions, including Cape Cod, Long Island, Nantucket, and Martha's Vineyard; and
- the scoured Puget Sound mainland and islands.

The **continental shelf** emerged and then was submerged once again as the glaciers retreated, leaving behind islands and capes: Martha's Vineyard, Nantucket, Long Island, and Cape Cod. The ice age retreat left the two countries' landscapes close to what they are today. The Great Lakes Basin and the millions of glacial lakes left Canada and the United States with plentiful supplies of freshwater. The continental margin took shape as sediments were deposited along the Atlantic coast. Along the Pacific coast, uplift occurred. Glaciers shrank.

Humans made their way to the Americas. Another minor ice age occurred between 1400 and 1800 CE. And then the climate began to warm about 150 years ago, when fossil fuels that had been trapped in Earth's lithosphere began heating the atmosphere as carbon dioxide was released.

Landforms and Processes

There is a complex range of landform features in the United States and Canada.

- In the United States, lowlands constitute about half the land area, occupying the east coast and interior prairie from the Appalachians to the Rocky Mountains.
- The most recent continental ice sheets covered most of Canada and the northern US lowlands until about twelve thousand years ago. The glacial retreat left a prime agricultural landscape of flat land and fertile soil.
- Plateaus are uplifted, flat-topped tablelands and comprise about one-quarter of the US land area. The premier plateaus are in the Appalachian, Ozark, and Intermontane regions. The Cumberland and Ozark Plateaus are often called mountains, but their geology reveals plateaus dissected by waterways. In Canada, the major plateau region is in interior British Columbia.
- Mountains occupy about one-quarter of the land area in both countries; we explore these below.

Mountains

The oldest mountains in North America and perhaps the oldest in the world are the Appalachians, formed almost five hundred million years ago. The Rocky Mountains and the Cascade–Sierra Nevada mountain systems formed at the western margins of the continent about sixty-five million years ago. Active mountain building continues today in Hawai`i and the Cascades.

TABLE 3.1. Major Mountain Systems in the United States and Canada

	Location	Highest peak	Extent
Eastern mountains			
Torngat	Labrador, Quebec, Nunavut	5,420 ft.	182 miles north–south 125 miles east–west
Laurentians	Quebec	3,825 ft.	267 miles north–south 459 miles east–west
Appalachians	The United States and Canada, from Newfoundland to Mississippi	Mt. Mitchell 6,684 ft.	1,896 miles north–south 2,114 miles east–west
Western mountains			
Rocky Mountains	Along British Columbia/Alberta border at Yukon south to New Mexico (including Idaho, Montana, Wyoming, Colorado, and Utah)	Mt. Elbert 14,433 ft.	1,709 miles north–south 1,097 miles east–west
Sierra Nevada	California, Nevada	Mt. Whitney 14,491 ft.	389 miles north–south 231 miles east–west
Cascade Mountains	Washington, Oregon, California, and British Columbia	Mt. Rainier 14,411 ft.	725 miles north–south 194 miles east–west
Coastal Mountains	British Columbia, Washington, Oregon, and California	Mt. Eddy 9,025 ft.	1,455 miles north–south 752 miles east–west
Alaska and Canadian coastal ranges	Alaska, British Columbia, and Yukon	Mt. McKinley 20,320 ft.	1,393 miles north–south 11,901 miles east–west
Brooks (northern extension of the Rocky Mountain system)	Alaska/Yukon	Mt. Chamberlin 9,020 ft.	336 miles north–south 740 miles east–west

Mountain systems are composed of many ranges. The Rocky Mountain system contains about thirty ranges, such as the Wasatch, Teton, and Bitterroot ranges. The west coast linear backbone—from the Brooks Range to Tierra del Fuego—includes the Sierra-Cascade ranges (table 3.1).

Geologic processes build the four mountain types—folded, dome, volcanic, and fault-block. Examples of each are found in the United States and Canada, although in various states of erosional development. **Erosion** wears down mountains, changing their original shape and exposing core rocks.

Folded mountains are the most common; they are formed when two plates collide, compress the rock, and having nowhere to go but up, elevate the mountains in folds like a rug pushed against a wall. The Appalachian Ridge and Valley subregion and the White Mountains of New Hampshire (photo 3.2) are folded mountains, as is the Rocky Mountains' Bighorn Range.

Stress can fracture rock and result in crustal movement called faulting. Displaced rock layers structure **fault-block mountains**—Wyoming's Tetons, Basin and Range, and California's Sierra Nevada—with one gently sloping side and one steep side.

When plates collide, one plate thrusts upward while the other plate plunges into the mantle, where heat and pressure melt the plate and form magma. A **dome mountain** develops when the magma rises from the mantle, creating pressure that warps or folds the crust but does not reach the surface. The rounded magma "dome" is only revealed when the crust cracks, splits, and erodes. The Black Hills of South Dakota are characteristic dome mountains.

When magma rises to the surface and erupts (at which point it becomes lava), the mountain is a volcano, which is formed separately and is usually much higher than surrounding mountains (photo 3.3).

Volcanic mountains consist of stratovolcanoes (such as those in the Cascades) and shield volcanoes (such as those in the Hawaiian Islands). Stratovolcanoes are steep-sided, symmetrical cones formed by explosive ejections of lava, which can tear mountains down or build them up. For example, Washington's Mount Saint Helens exploded in 1980, causing the stratovolcano to lose thirteen hundred feet of elevation. The Hawaiian Islands are an example of gently sloping shield volcanoes. As the Pacific Plate moved over the mid-Pacific hot spot, the successive accumulation of fluid lava flows created the islands.

Water

Water is another critical theme examined in each chapter. The United States and Canada are endowed with freshwater, especially in formerly glaciated areas; however, freshwater remains a precious resource. Ninety-seven percent of all water is found in oceans and is therefore saline; freshwater is either locked in glaciers (2 percent) or in surface or **groundwater** systems (1 percent). Of the 1 percent of accessible water, only one-quarter is located on the surface in rivers, lakes, and streams, which are all divided into watersheds.

Watersheds and Rivers

A watershed defines the total geographical area of numerous individual **drainage basins,** which drain a river to a single termination point, usually from mountains to lowlands and out

PHOTO 3.2. Mount Washington, in the Appalachian White Mountains of New Hampshire, is the highest point in the Northeast at 6,288 feet. It has been a popular tourist destination and hiking area since the mid-nineteenth century, despite a reputation for erratic weather.

PHOTO 3.3. Volcanic Mount Hood is the highest mountain in Oregon at 11,240 feet, rising above the clouds and the Cascade Mountains. Volcano formation is separate from and usually higher than the surrounding mountains.

to sea. Watershed divides are typically perceived as located along high mountain ridges, but other divides are found along slight increases of elevation, such as the Great Lakes Basin and the Mississippi drainage. Political borders, however, seldom follow or respect watersheds, resulting in fragmented policies regarding the use and sharing of water resources. Managing water requires a wide-ranging ecological understanding of the landscape, including watersheds, erosion, deposition, and the effects of water use and pollution.

Water follows the path of least resistance, usually to the ocean. Along its path, water erodes or deposits sediment, causing beneficial or adverse effects. Sediment deposited on floodplains leaves behind fertile soils, provides natural flood and erosion control, and recharges groundwater. Rivers build natural levees in relation to the river flow, but often human intervention with artificial levees meant to facilitate economic growth has caused environmental degradation that has worsened flooding. Dams, levees, and roads have altered drainage basins and increased their vulnerability to hazards. For example, areas that are prone to flooding should not be built upon. The massive 1993 flood of the Mississippi and Missouri river confluence was due to artificial levees that did not allow the floodplains to accept the water and caused more flooding than if the artificial levees had not been built. The costs for the flooding were the loss of about a hundred thousand homes, millions of acres of farmland, and $15–$20 billion in damages. Flooding again in 2011 resulted in additional damages to the same area, when levees were intentionally ruptured in one less-populated area in order to save more-populated areas. Damages were in the billions.

The United States and Canada have seven major watershed drainage areas, along with major rivers (map 3.3):

- Atlantic (Hudson River, Delaware River)
  - Saint Lawrence/Great Lakes (Saint Lawrence River)
- Pacific (Columbia, Snake, Sacramento, Yukon, and Fraser rivers)
- Gulf of Mexico (Mississippi, Ohio, and Missouri rivers, and the Rio Grande)
- Gulf of California (Colorado River)
- Arctic (Mackenzie River)
- Hudson Bay (Nelson River, La Grande Rivière)
- Great Basin (Humboldt River, interior drainage)

Major American rivers are the Mississippi along with its primary tributaries, the Ohio and Missouri; the Colorado; the Columbia and its major tributary, the Snake River; and the Yukon. Both the Columbia and Yukon rivers have their headwaters in Canada. Canada's major rivers are the Mackenzie, the Fraser, and the Saint Lawrence (table 3.2). Rivers and streams are often connected to lakes and human-made reservoirs.

Lakes

Glacial, structural, and artificial processes form lakes. Glacial lakes are the most numerous. They are remnants of the last ice age, and they are found in Canada and the northern tier of the United States. The Great Lakes, linking the borders of both countries, are the largest glacial lakes; they contain the largest single lake within the United States, Lake Michigan, and the largest lake, which is shared by both countries, Lake Superior. The Canadian Shield has more than a million lakes in Quebec alone, while Minnesota, Wisconsin, and Michigan each contain thousands of glacial lakes. Kettle or pothole lakes are formed when ice calves from a glacier and sets in the land, while other lakes are the result of glacial scour, such as the Finger Lakes of upstate New York or the Mission Bay district of Michigan.

In the Intermontane, former ice age lakes have either dried up or are ephemeral, adjusting their size annually according to weather conditions—smaller in the spring and summer when water flow declines, and larger during the cooler autumn when water flow exceeds evaporation. In the Great Basin, evaporation exceeds **precipitation**, resulting in high-salt-content lakes with no exterior drainage.

Structural lakes may be formed by any one of several geologic processes. Oregon's Crater Lake **caldera** was formed when ancient Mount Mazama collapsed after a volcanic eruption emptied the magma chamber. Other structural lakes include **fault** valleys (e.g., Lake Tahoe) and cut-off meander oxbow lakes, which form during flood events. Sinkholes form in **karst** areas, when chemical and mechanical weathering dissolves limestone. Sinkhole lake levels rise and fall periodically in response to subsurface water levels. Karst lakes are found in humid environments, such as the Ozarks and Florida.

Artificial lakes and reservoirs store river and stream runoff for urban, recreational, hydroelectric, and irrigational uses. Some of the largest artificial lakes are Lake Mead on the Nevada–Arizona border, Lake Powell in Utah and Arizona, and Lake Eufaula in Oklahoma. Most artificial lakes and reservoirs were built without considering the ecological consequences, and have caused massive aquatic imbalances.

TABLE 3.2. Major US and Canadian Rivers

World rank by drainage	River	Drainage area (000 sq. mi.)	Length (miles)
5	Mississippi–Missouri	2,001	3,740
12	Mackenzie	1,144	2,635
14	St. Lawrence	909	2,485
19	Nelson	666	1,600
23	Columbia	415	1,249
24	Rio Grande	336	1,900

Source: Environment Canada, at http://www.ec.gc.ca/eau-water/default.asp?lang=En&n=45BBB7B8-1#canada; US Geological Survey, at http://pubs.usgs.gov/of/1987/ofr87-242/

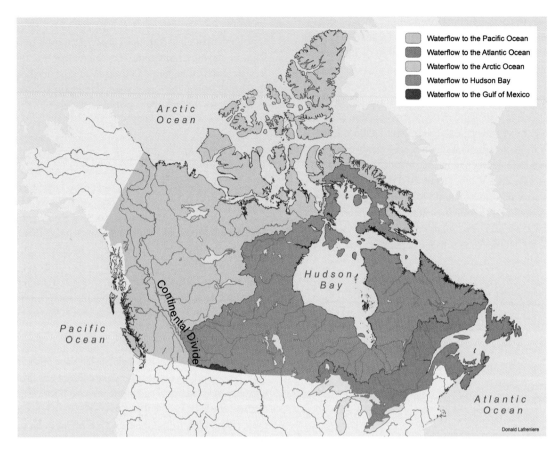

Waterflow to the Pacific Ocean
Waterflow to the Atlantic Ocean
Waterflow to the Arctic Ocean
Waterflow to Hudson Bay
Waterflow to the Gulf of Mexico

Arctic Ocean

Continental Divide

Hudson Bay

Pacific Ocean

Atlantic Ocean

Donald Lafreniere

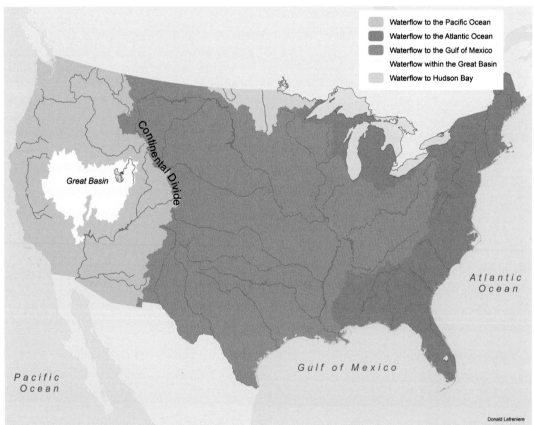

Waterflow to the Pacific Ocean
Waterflow to the Atlantic Ocean
Waterflow to the Gulf of Mexico
Waterflow within the Great Basin
Waterflow to Hudson Bay

Continental Divide

Great Basin

Atlantic Ocean

Pacific Ocean

Gulf of Mexico

Donald Lafreniere

MAP 3.3. Major Canadian and US Watershed Drainage Areas.

BOX 3.2 SWAMPS, BOGS, POCOSINS, MARSHES, BAYOUS, AND FENS

The numerous wetland types in the world are often simplified and called swamps. But swamps are only one type of wetland; there are bogs, **pocosins**, marshes, bayous, and fens. A swamp specifically is a wetland with saturated soils and standing water during the growing season. Swamps proliferate because of low elevation, numerous floodplains, and tidal surges. Typical vegetation is shrubs and trees, but swamps do not contain cattails and other nonwoody plants. Many swamps are found in formerly glaciated lands. For example, there are 219 named swamps in Michigan. About one-third of Michigan's swamps have been drained.

Bogs are wet and spongy waterlogged ground, covered usually by sphagnum moss and characteristic shrubs. Bogs are usually found in formerly glaciated areas and in former lake bottoms, as in Michigan, Minnesota, Ontario, and Quebec. Bogs do not take well to draining and therefore tend to be sparsely populated. A few examples are

- Minnesota's Big Bog, found at the southern end of former Lake Agassiz;
- Eastern Ontario's Mer Bleue sphagnum bog, near the Ottawa River; and
- Pennsylvania's Tannersville Cranberry Bog, a sphagnum bog. Although this bog is not known for its cranberries, many bogs are.

Pocosins are found along the mid-Atlantic coastal plain, especially in North Carolina. Pocosins are usually saturated, though

they can be dry during prolonged droughts. They are deficient of nutrients, especially phosphorus, and are often pine flatwoods or what is known as shrub bogs. They are often drained, and this has led to their loss and the destruction of the ecosystems aligned with them.

Marshes are shallow water, wet most of the year, and contain grasses and nonwoody water-loving plants such as cattails and water lilies. They may be either freshwater or salt marshes. Many former pothole lakes have naturally drained and evolved into marshes. When an area has more open water, it is then called a swamp. Marshes are important reproductive areas for aquatics. Some marsh areas include estuaries and waterways along the barrier island of the Atlantic South. In the Canadian Shield and along the Great Lakes are many freshwater marshes.

Bayous are found in the Gulf Coastal region, a flat region that has slow-moving, almost stagnant secondary watercourses of rivers. A bayou is similar to a swamp, except that it is slow moving. A bayou has both trees and nonwoody vegetation.

Fens are similar to bogs, except that fens are neutral or alkaline and fed by groundwater. Vegetation favors alkaline-loving plants that are more diverse than bogs, such as grasses, sedges, and wildflowers. The major fen in the United States is the Geneva Creek Iron Fen in Colorado; it is rich in iron oxide deposited by the groundwater.

As ecosystem interactions are understood, the focus has changed to maintaining healthy ecosystems and creating compatible water-release programs for spawning fish and shellfish. Since 2002, the Nature Conservancy and the Army Corps of Engineers have formed the Sustainable Rivers Project to protect river ecology while maintaining human services. Many environmental organizations have begun to support dam removal projects when the dam is doing more harm than good.

Groundwater

Groundwater is stored in the cavities and spaces between subsoil layers beneath plant root zones. Most soil has moisture within it, but groundwater soil is saturated. The upper level of the saturated ground, the water table, can occur at any depth, fluctuating in relation to use and climatic conditions. About 50 percent of Americans and 25 percent of Canadians rely on groundwater for drinking, and 65 percent of groundwater is used for irrigated crop production.

Groundwater has traditionally been a source of uncontaminated water. The soil filters out contaminants and pollutants before they reached the water table. However, the amount of contaminants now entering the soil often far outweighs the

soil's filtering capability. The major contaminants include gasoline, oil, road salts, chemical fertilizers, and sewage from ill-maintained septic systems. There are concerns over groundwater pollution caused by unregulated water quality in septic systems in Washington, Texas, and California. Groundwater pollution due to extensive agricultural and residential runoff has affected supplies in Wichita, Miami, Los Alamos, San Antonio, and Spokane, as well the Ogallala Aquifer, the largest aquifer in the nation.

An **aquifer** is an underground, water-soaked layer of rock and sand, which can be accessed by pumping or pressure. Across the Great Plains, thousands of windmills pump water from shallow aquifers, but the Ogallala is more than two hundred feet below the surface. Groundwater in deep aquifers is accessed with a well and a gasoline pump. Aquifers recharge (replenish) when rainwater seeps down through the soil, but sometimes more water is withdrawn than replenished. For example, the Ogallala Aquifer fossil water (water sealed in the aquifer for millions of years) has a low recharge rate, and overpumping and low precipitation have caused the water table to decline. Groundwater and aquifer abuse has reduced available water and lowered water tables.

Wetlands

Wetlands—**swamps**, **bogs**, and **marshes**—are ecotones, or transitional zones between dry land and permanent water bodies. Wetlands filter impurities before surface water reaches the groundwater. However, many wetlands have been destroyed or impaired, which has increased groundwater pollution.

Throughout American history, wetlands were disparaged and drained for conversion to agricultural or residential use. But in the 1950s, a semantic shift began to redefine "smelly" swamps and marshes as "useful" wetlands. Still, although the importance of wetland ecology was noted throughout the twentieth century, only since the 1980s has wetland removal been regularly challenged and the ecological benefits of wetlands—flood buffers, erosion control, water filtration, recreation, and wildlife habitation—been promoted.

Removing wetlands increased water pollution and destroyed coastal buffer zones that protected inland areas. For example, the Louisiana coastal wetlands buffered the mainland against storm surges; therefore, wetland loss increased the destruction caused by Hurricane Katrina. Most states have lost a majority of their wetlands (map 3.4). California has lost 91 percent of its limited wetlands; in the wetland-rich Great Lakes states, 50–90 percent are drained.

Critical Water Issues

Both the United States and Canada face challenges associated with water supply and water quality.

Water Supply

While most populations in the United States and Canada take safe drinking water for granted, there remain a number of threats to drinking water. Virtually all freshwater requires some form of purification process for human consumption. Even water from high-elevation mountain streams requires water filtration to eliminate disease-causing bacteria. Possible contaminants include lead, arsenic, and chromium. Improperly disposed-of chemicals, animal and human wastes, wastes

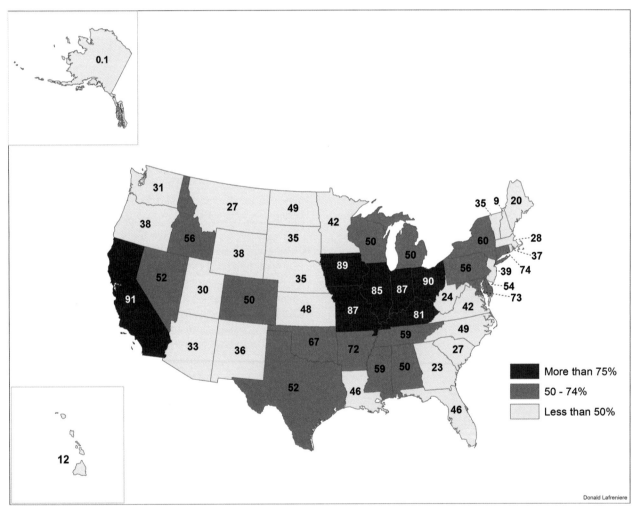

MAP 3.4. Percentage of Wetlands Acreage Lost, 1780s–1980s. Twenty-two states have lost at least 50 percent of their original wetlands. Seven states—Indiana, Illinois, Missouri, Kentucky, Iowa, California, and Ohio—have lost more than 80 percent of their original wetlands. Since the 1970s, the most extensive losses of wetlands have been in Louisiana, Mississippi, Arkansas, Florida, South Carolina, and North Carolina.

injected underground, and naturally occurring substances also have the potential to contaminate drinking water. Drinking water that is not properly treated or disinfected, or that travels through an improperly maintained distribution system, poses a health risk. In a post-9/11 world, drinking water utilities find themselves facing new responsibilities due to concerns over water system security and threats of infrastructure terrorism.

Allocating water to satisfy economic or political interests is a challenge. For example, political borders divide watersheds arbitrarily. As population and water use have increased, serious disputes have arisen over allocations, causing conflicts over the divisions in the watersheds. Water wars occur in expected regions, such as the deserts of Arizona and Nevada, but also in unexpected regions, such as the humid southeastern states, where recent population growth, suburban development, and a lack of water conservation have depleted supplies.

Adding to the water worries is the decline in fresh water quantity and quality. Increasing agriculture demands and growing urban populations have put tremendous strain on fresh water supply systems, particularly in the United States. Canadians have abundant freshwater and do not have the water shortages of the United States, and while they have been happy to sell their oil and gas, they have drawn the line at selling water.

Water Quality and Pollution

Water pollution has been a long-standing problem in both countries. Approximately 40 percent of US freshwater is polluted, and Canada continues to dump raw sewage into the open sea. Water quality may be affected by either **point source pollution** or **nonpoint source pollution**. Point sources are identified in specific locations, such as industrial plants or agricultural feedlots. Government regulations have mitigated many point sources. However, diffuse nonpoint sources, such as crops and urban runoff, are difficult to control and remain the largest source of water-quality issues. The most common nonpoint pollutants are nutrients and sediment. In rural areas, agricultural runoff contains nitrogen and phosphorus that contaminate rivers and streams. In urban areas, runoff from pesticides and fertilizers applied to lawns and gardens, and salts, antifreeze used to treat road surfaces, and even garbage enter into the waterways as nonpoint pollutants.

As the United States and Canada industrialized throughout the twentieth century, water quality degraded and became a subject of public concern. In 1970, the Canada Water Act addressed water- quality standards, while in 1972, the United States passed the Clean Water Act to restore integrity to the nation's waters. There were significant improvements as a result, but the results are mixed. Point source pollution from industrial sources has been reduced. In many rivers and lakes, oxygen levels have recovered due to the filtering out of organic wastes. Some pollutants have declined, but others are on the increase. In 1972, two-thirds of US lakes were too polluted for swimming or fishing; today, two-thirds of the lakes, rivers, and waterways are safe for swimming and fishing. In 1970, more

than 70 percent of industrial discharge was not treated at all; today, 99 percent is. Lake Erie, declared "dead" in 1969, has recovered. And in the Cuyahoga River, once a stark symbol of the plight of America's rivers, the blue herons have returned, and the city now boasts new marinas lining a river walk and upscale sidewalk cafes.

However, much remains to be done. Almost half of US waters are still impaired—too polluted to serve as sources of drinking water, or to support good fish and wildlife. Wetlands continue to be lost to pollution and development. Nonpoint source pollution—runoff from farms and from cities is inadequately addressed by existing regulation.

Climate

The Canadian and United States climatic range varies from Florida's southern tip to the Arctic tundra. Most US inhabitants live in the temperate zone of the lower forty-eight states. North of the 38th parallel, residents generally enjoy a four-season climate, while those to the south have less seasonal variation. Most of Canada is north of the 49th parallel (about the latitude of Frankfurt, Germany), but Canadian weather is usually colder than European cities at equivalent latitudes for two reasons:

1. Canada's high western mountains block the oceanic warmth of the westerly winds.
2. Canada lacks the warm North Atlantic Drift that moderates the western European climate.

Wind patterns across the United States and Canada blow from the west and carry weather systems from the West Coast to the east. The Pacific Northwest has a wet climate, because westerly winds are subject to pressure systems bringing sunshine in summer and rain the rest of the year. The leeward (eastern) side of the West Coast spine of mountains is in the **rain shadow** and therefore drier.

The Arctic jet stream and the warm, humid Gulf weather influence weather east of the Rocky Mountains. The jet stream is a narrow band of high-speed winds moving from west to east five to ten miles above the surface, and fluctuating north or south depending on air pressure. The jet stream brings more cold weather in the winter when it moves south; in the summer, the jet stream tends to retreat north into Canada. The jet stream has commercial value and energy possibilities. Pilots seek out the time- and fuel-saving west-to-east stream to decrease fuel consumption and shorten flying times. Scientists have been studying how to harness the power of the jet stream wind to meet world electricity needs.

The Gulf of Mexico transports moisture-laden winds into the central and southeastern United States and generates climatic events. Fronts occur when cold, heavy polar air collides with the Gulf's tropical air. When warm, moist air collides with a polar air mass, powerful thunderstorms and tornadoes can develop. The cold air stays close to the surface, while the

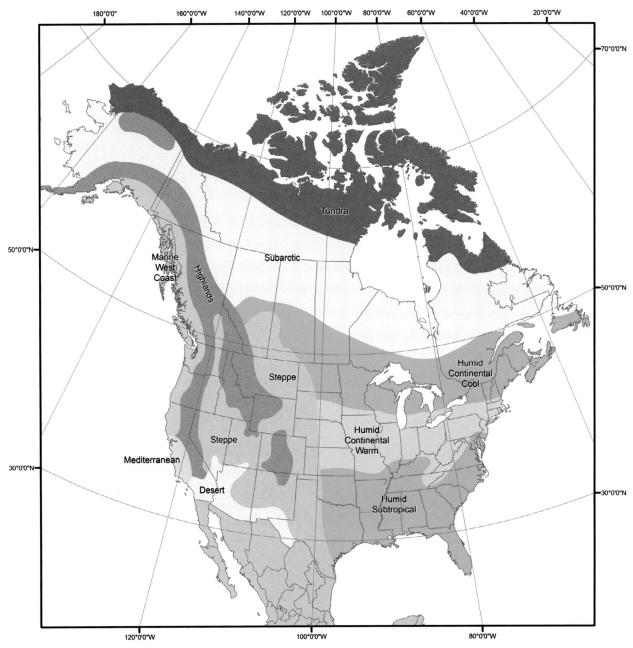

MAP 3.5. Basic US and Canadian Climate Regions.

warmer air is pushed upward, cools, and forms clouds and precipitation. Hurricanes often enter into the belly of North America by way of the Gulf.

Precipitation is scattered over the physical landscape. The southeastern low relief allows rainstorms to spread over wide areas, whereas along the western coast the narrow rain bands are forced up mountains, producing **orographic precipitation**. Moisture condenses as the ascending air cools, delivering rain and snow in higher elevations. Upon reaching the mountains' summit, the air descends and warms, and the rains cease, leaving the leeward slopes in the rain shadow found in the Intermontane and east of the Rockies.

Climate Regions

The 100th meridian is a general divide between the wet and humid eastern half of the continent and the drier steppe to the west (map 3.5). The 38th parallel (just north of San Francisco on the West Coast and just south of Washington, D.C., on the East Coast) separates the southern mild winters from northern "real" winters with snow even at low elevations. The Southwest is very dry, even desert, whereas the Gulf of Mexico influences the much more humid and wet Southeast, although it lies at the same latitude as the Southwest.

The Northeast has four distinct seasons. The interior areas of the Northeast experience a **continental climate** with its more

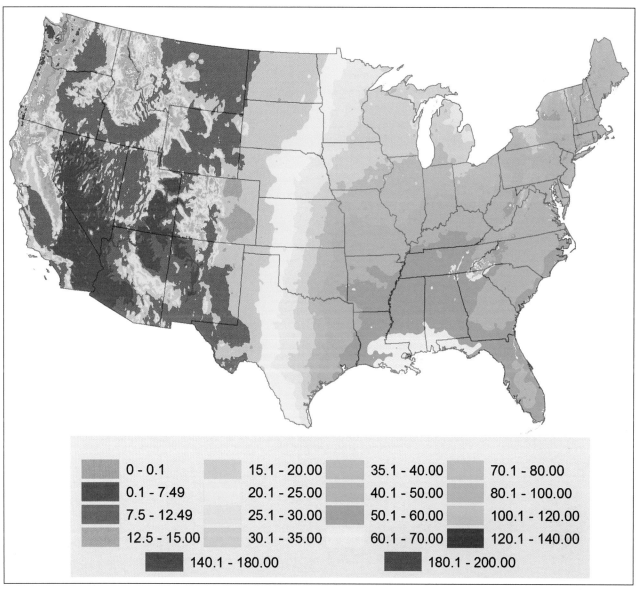

MAP 3.6. US Precipitation. Notice how the twenty-inch line falls at about the 100th meridian (the eastern edge of the Oklahoma Panhandle).

Range	Range	Range	Range
0 - 0.1	15.1 - 20.00	35.1 - 40.00	70.1 - 80.00
0.1 - 7.49	20.1 - 25.00	40.1 - 50.00	80.1 - 100.00
7.5 - 12.49	25.1 - 30.00	50.1 - 60.00	100.1 - 120.00
12.5 - 15.00	30.1 - 35.00	60.1 - 70.00	120.1 - 140.00
140.1 - 180.00		180.1 - 200.00	

seasonal variation in temperatures, the result of land losing heat more rapidly than water. The Northeast is generally colder, with an annual temperature below 65°F (18°C), although it is often divided between a warmer region to the south with long summers, and a colder region at the 42nd parallel north into Canada along the Saint Lawrence lowlands. Annual precipitation averages 30–60 inches (75–150 cm) distributed throughout the year (map 3.6).

The humid, subtropical Southeast has a long growing season enhanced by more than 30 inches (75 cm) of annual rain, mostly during the summer months. The average annual temperature is above 67°F (19°C), and frost is infrequent. In the southernmost region, trade winds influence the subtropical to tropical weather.

The Northwest can be wet or dry, depending on its location in relation to the Cascades. The westerly winds of the marine west coast bring moisture from the Pacific Ocean, making this small region from the coast to the Cascades the wettest in the two nations. Most precipitation falls between October and March. The greatest precipitation in the continental United States occurs on the Olympic Mountains, which receives over 150 inches (380 cm) annually. British Columbia's Vancouver Island is the wettest in Canada, receiving 80–100 inches (200–250 cm) annually. Most of the region, though, receives around 38 inches (95 cm) of annual rainfall, enough to keep the evergreen forests green, but not enough to deter population growth.

Moving beyond the Cascades, the northern Intermontane and interior prairie of Canada are a climatic world apart from the western shore. Most moisture falls on the windward side of the Cascades. The leeward, drier side of the mountains falls within the rain shadow. Warmer summers and colder winters characterize the Intermontane continental climate.

The Southwest's desert and steppe are the nation's driest and warmest. Seasons vary subtly, with few days below freezing. Most of the region receives less than 20 inches (51 cm) of rain annually; desert areas receive less than 5 inches (13 cm). The **Mediterranean climate** of the southern Pacific Coast differs from the rest of the United States. Mild but moist winter months average a semiarid 15 inches (38 cm) of rain annually, but summers are hot and dry. The year-round growing season was a prime attractor for initial settlement.

Extending from the Atlantic to the Pacific and roughly from the 52nd parallel to the 60th parallel, the subarctic region boreal forest continues to the Arctic tree line. A long, dark, cold winter and brief, dry summer dominate the subarctic seasons. The region has little precipitation, as the cool air's tenuous hold on moisture forms less rain or snow. Mountains block warmer Pacific air, and the region is too far north to be influenced by the Gulf of Mexico's warm, moist air.

North of the 60th parallel, the tundra region supports fewer trees, lichen, and plant life. Temperatures rarely exceed 50°F (10°C) at any time during the year, and winter temperatures average −30°F (−34°C). The tundra region receives little precipitation and is often referred to as a polar desert. The ground is covered with mosses, peat, and permafrost.

Climate Change

One of the most pressing challenges to sustainability is climate change and in many of the chapters we will examine how climate change could impact that ecoregion in a specific boxed text. It is important to understand the basic science behind climate change, as this is an issue that we discuss in many chapters.

Climate change is linked to **greenhouse gases (GHGs)**. There are four principle GHGs: carbon dioxide, methane, nitrous oxide, and fluorinated gases. Carbon dioxide, methane, and nitrous oxides are continuously emitted into and removed from the atmosphere by natural processes on Earth. Anthropogenic (man-made) activities cause additional quantities of these and other GHGs to be emitted or sequestered, thereby changing their global average atmospheric concentrations. Most anthropogenic emissions come from the combustion of carbon-based fuels, principally wood, coal, oil, and natural gas (photo 3.4). According to the US Environmental Protection Agency, the primary sources of these gases are the following:

- Carbon dioxide (CO_2): Carbon dioxide enters the atmosphere through burning fossil fuels (coal, natural gas, and oil), solid waste, trees, and wood products,

PHOTO 3.4. South Carolina Lowcountry Marsh.
Source: iStock/KeithBriley

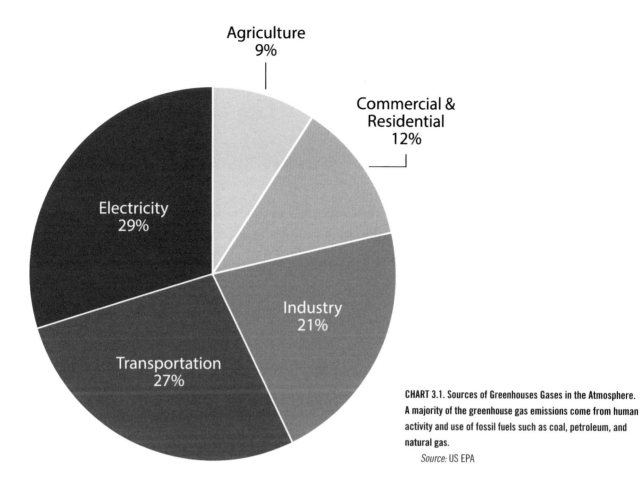

Agriculture
9%

Commercial &
Residential
12%

Electricity
29%

Industry
21%

Transportation
27%

CHART 3.1. Sources of Greenhouses Gases in the Atmosphere.
A majority of the greenhouse gas emissions come from human
activity and use of fossil fuels such as coal, petroleum, and
natural gas.
Source: US EPA

and also as a result of certain chemical reactions (e.g., manufacture of cement). Carbon dioxide is removed from the atmosphere (or "sequestered") when it is absorbed by plants as part of the biological **carbon cycle**. Currently, CO_2 accounted for about 82 percent of all US greenhouse gas emissions from human activities.

- Methane (CH_4): Methane is emitted during the production and transport of coal, natural gas, and oil. Methane emissions also result from livestock and other agricultural practices and by the decay of organic waste in solid waste landfills.
- Nitrous oxide (N_2O): Nitrous oxide is emitted during agricultural and industrial activities, as well as during combustion of fossil fuels and solid waste.
- Fluorinated gases: Hydrofluorocarbons, perfluorocarbons, and sulfur hexafluoride are three synthetic, powerful GHGs that are emitted from a variety of industrial processes (chart 3.1).

These four gases absorb some of the energy being radiated from Earth's surface and trap it in the atmosphere, essentially acting like a blanket that makes Earth's surface warmer than it would be otherwise be (chart 3.2).

GHGs are necessary to life as we know it, because without them the planet's surface would be about 60°F cooler than present. However, as the concentrations of these gases continue to increase in the atmosphere, Earth's temperature is climbing above past levels. According to NOAA and NASA data, Earth's average surface temperature has increased by about 1.2–1.4°F since 1900.

So is there a genuine "climate debate"? Yes and no. Scientists are certain that human activities are changing the composition of the atmosphere, and that increasing the concentration of GHGs will change the planet's climate. But they are not sure by how much it will change, at what rate it will change, or what (and where) the exact effects will be. This level of uncertainty about impact is what climate change deniers have focused on in their effort to prevent regulation of energy use or to sign important international treaties to limit emissions. Extreme climate change deniers also question whether anthropogenic emissions are significant, and point to Earth's history of fluctuating climate patterns. However, climate scientists and experts have proven that anthropogenic emissions are significant and that these concentrations do affect global average temperatures.

In the United States and Canada, reliance on fossil fuels explains why these countries contribute significantly to climate change. For example, coal-burning power plants produce about half of US electricity and are responsible for 40 percent of emitted CO_2, two-thirds of SO_2, and almost a quarter of NO_x emissions. These power plants have contributed to climate change. Another major source is transportation: planes, trains, and cars all use petroleum.

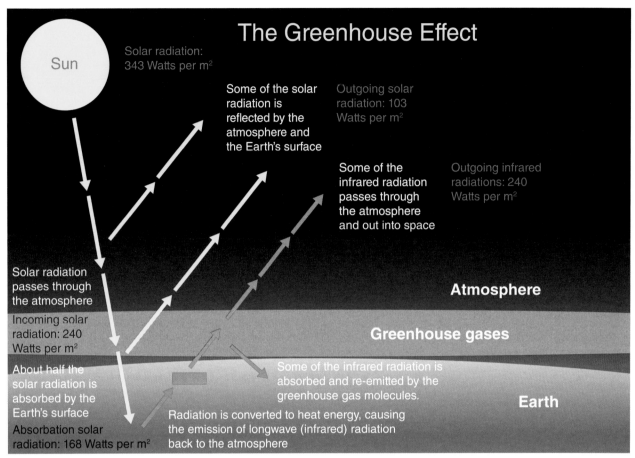

The Greenhouse Effect

Sun

Solar radiation: 343 Watts per m²

Some of the solar radiation is reflected by the atmosphere and the Earth's surface

Outgoing solar radiation: 103 Watts per m²

Some of the infrared radiation passes through the atmosphere and out into space

Outgoing infrared radiations: 240 Watts per m²

Atmosphere

Solar radiation passes through the atmosphere

Incoming solar radiation: 240 Watts per m²

Greenhouse gases

About half the solar radiation is absorbed by the Earth's surface

Some of the infrared radiation is absorbed and re-emitted by the greenhouse gas molecules.

Earth

Absorbation solar radiation: 168 Watts per m²

Radiation is converted to heat energy, causing the emission of longwave (infrared) radiation back to the atmosphere

CHART 3.2. The Greenhouse Effect.

There is some good news, however. Emissions from fossil fuel combustion has decreased as a result of multiple factors including substitution from coal to natural gas consumption in the electric power sector, warmer winter conditions that reduced demand for heating fuel in the residential and commercial sectors, and a slight decrease in electricity demand.

Climate change has been the subject of numerous international efforts. Many countries agree on the need to stabilize GHG emissions; however, the US federal government has been lax in its commitment to accepting and arresting global climate change.

Fortunately, the US federal government's lack of political will to reduce emissions has been countered at the local level. In 2005, several hundred majors met in Seattle to sign the Mayors Agreement on Climate Change. To date, more than 1,100 mayors have signed on. This is important because it shows that despite the lack of progress on the national level, cities and towns throughout North America are taking action on climate change.

The most recent international effort to address climate is the 2015 Paris Agreement. The Paris Agreement will work towards making sure Earth's temperature does not rise above 2°C; this degree change is usually agreed upon as being the tipping point to preventing massive effects of climate change. The Paris Agreement requires that ratifying nations "peak" their greenhouse gas emissions as soon as possible and pursue the highest possible ambition that each country can achieve. In all, 195 nations—including the United States—signed the Paris Agreement, the first time that the world has agreed on a path forward.

In the spring of 2017, President Trump announced he was withdrawing the United States from the Paris Agreement, turning its back on the fight against climate change. Currently, the United States is the only country to have rejected or withdrawn from the Paris Agreement.

Despite this controversial decision, many climate experts say that carbon dioxide emissions will likely continue to decrease as cities, states, and even companies have pledged to uphold the Paris Agreement. A coalition of Mayors from Pittsburgh, San Diego, Austin, and Charlotte promised they will continue to lead in achieving climate treaty goals. States like California and New York will keep pursuing their own programs to reduce emissions and the private sector is already shifting toward cleaner energy. Former New York City mayor Michael Bloomberg stated, "It is important for the world to know, the American government may have pulled out of the Paris agreement, but the American people are committed to its goals, and there is nothing Washington can do to stop us." In the end, leadership on climate change may come from the bottom up, rather than the White House or Congress.

BOX 3.3 SEA-LEVEL RISE

Climate change leading to **global warming** has taken center stage in the twenty-first century. Scientific evidence and on-the-ground analysis reveal physical changes that will continue to affect both the United States and Canada. One of the most serious, sea-level rise, will have increasing environmental and human costs. Sea-level rise will affect wetland resources, recreational opportunities, coastal development, and coastal habitats for all forms of life. While all coastal areas will be affected, the Atlantic and Gulf coasts are the most threatened because of their wide and low coastal plains.

Global climate weather models have consistently predicted increased sea levels of 0.6 and 2 feet (0.18–0.59 meters) by 2100, which will have a disastrous impact on coastal communities, especially where the coastal plain is widest and lowest,

such as along the Chesapeake Basin to the barrier islands off the South Atlantic coast and the Louisiana coastline. These regions are especially vulnerable because of low-lying topography, the possibility of intense and frequent storms, and because they are one of the most populated and built-up areas in the United States.

Along the Atlantic and Gulf coastal areas, sea-level rise could inundate up to 22,000 square miles (35,000 km) of land and force cities such as New York, Washington, D.C., Miami, and New Orleans to upgrade their flood defenses and drainage systems or face adverse consequences.

The Pacific coast is not as vulnerable, except for the heavily populated and low-lying areas in San Francisco Bay and Puget Sound.

Soils

Soil is a fundamental physical element. Healthy soil grows food, sequesters carbon, maintains biodiversity, holds moisture, and fights off wildfires. Healthy food production depends on maintaining healthy soil rich in organic material that both feeds crops and builds soil structure. Synthetic fertilizers may feed plants short-term but will break down soil structure and biotic activity.

Soils are composed of organic matter, living organisms, and weathered layers of rock transported over time by water, wind, or glaciers. Fertile, porous, and structurally sound soil includes stable minerals and organic compounds. Although more than twenty thousand soil types are found in the United States, for the purpose of this book, we will only look at the basic soils of eastern and western United States and the basic soils of Canada and Alaska.

The 100th meridian also divides eastern and western North American soils and vegetation types. Eastern soils are aluminum- and iron-rich and called **pedalfer** (Greek *ped* [soil] + *al* [aluminum] + *fer* [ferrous oxide, which is iron]); western soils are calcium- and lime-rich and called **pedocals** (*pedo* [soil] + *cal* [calcium]) (map 3.7).

Pedalfer soils receive more precipitation and can be productive soils because the clay content holds water near the surface. But the precipitation may also leach nutrients and diminish soil fertility. Pedocal soils are quite fertile because precipitation rarely reaches the water table and soil nutrients are recycled, but the lack of water limits agricultural productivity.

Many Canadian boreal soils are acidic due to the lack of leaf litter. In the grasslands, soils tend to be black and rich in calcium carbonate. In the north, peat forms in poorly drained, waterlogged permafrost ground.

Organic material and soil organisms make up the nutrient-rich topsoil, which forms slowly—about one inch every five hundred to one thousand years. In the United States,

topsoil erosion is about eighteen times faster than formation. Protecting the topsoil from erosion is the first step toward sustainable soil and agricultural production. Topsoil erosion during the 1930s' Dust Bowl was caused by tilling, drought, and ill-managed land. Subsequent soil management programs introduced conservation tillage, contour plowing, and terracing.

Natural processes form soil types specific to place. For example, prior to European settlement, the Great Plains grasslands had the necessary tillage (soil organisms and bison hooves) and fertilizer (bison manure and decomposed grasses) for maintaining healthy soils. Soil erosion accelerated when the dense Plains grasslands were replaced by cultivation and the livestock shifted from bison, whose diet is based on perennial grasses, to cattle, whose diet requires more processed feed. In addition, bison hooves break up the ground and allow water penetration, while cattle hooves pack soil and cause more soil erosion.

Anything done to change soil, such as changing fauna, draining wetlands, or irrigating crops, disturbs existing ecosystems.

Ecological Communities

An ecosystem is not merely a group of organisms that share space, but a community of organisms that cooperate and compete for resources, resulting in a whole that is more than the sum of the parts. Each ecosystem member has some functions in common with the others, such as recycling nutrients, using the sun's energy, creating soil, and maintaining a healthy environment. As part of the ecosystem structure, humans depend on ecosystem health. A healthy system benefits humans; a sick ecosystem degrades the quality of life.

Ecological communities influence one another and are never static. Energy flows continually between the producer, consumer, and decomposer levels. Most ecosystem energy

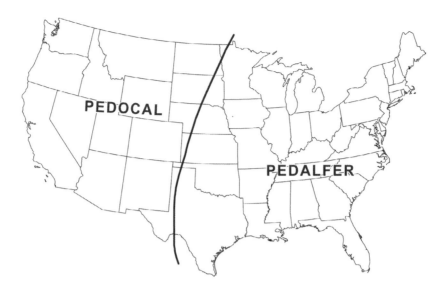

MAJOR VEGETATION REGIONS OF NORTH AMERICA

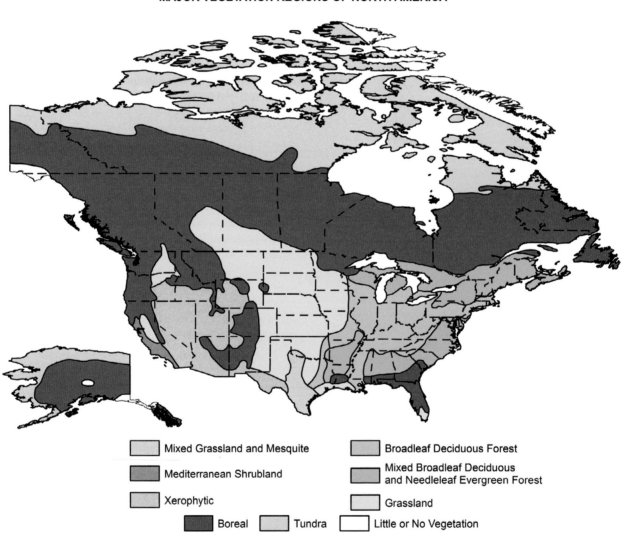

Mixed Grassland and Mesquite

Mediterranean Shrubland

Xerophytic

Boreal   Tundra   Little or No Vegetation

Broadleaf Deciduous Forest

Mixed Broadleaf Deciduous and Needleleaf Evergreen Forest

Grassland

MAP 3.7. Soil Type (top) and Major Vegetation Regions (bottom). Vegetation type is related to climate, precipitation, altitude, and latitude. The soil type is also related to each of these variables and helps determine what grows where. Pedocal soils are drier and have a layer of calcium carbonate that lessens leaching, whereas pedalfer soils receive more precipitation and many nutrients are leached from the soil.

flows produce little, if any, waste. Although many early cultural groups lived symbiotically with ecological communities, modern humans have often lost this dynamic equilibrium, causing waste, pollution, and species loss.

Since ecological communities are living, dynamic systems, it is difficult to establish a "natural" reference. Pre-European settlement is usually chosen as the baseline, but studies have revealed that the landscape was not pristine before European arrival: Native American tribes had altered the landscape to fit their needs and cultures.

What follows is a basic division of ecological communities on a semicontinental scale that includes vegetation and wildlife in relation to landforms, climate, and soil. The three major divisions are eastern (wet, forest), western (dry, grassland), and boreal (cool, coniferous forest).

Eastern Community

European settlers encountered the eastern ecological community upon arrival from Europe. Eastern ecological communities' ample precipitation patterns support broadleaf deciduous hardwoods in the lowlands and conifers at higher elevations and latitudes or on poor soils. In the northern regions, deciduous hardwood forests have added organic leaf litter that enriched agricultural soil. The midwestern deciduous forests do best in rich loamy soils. Pines grow best in nutrient-deficient sandy soils, as in the Pine Barrens of New Jersey or the Atlantic and Gulf coastal plains.

From the coast to the Midwest, the presettlement landscape was forested, but few native forests survived agricultural settlement. However, some land was abandoned and new forests emerged or were planted. In New England, the cutover forests were often abandoned because of the stony soil remnants of ice age drift. The settlers either turned away from agriculture and toward the sea or moved west as the land opened for settlement. In the Tidewater South, lands were cut over but often abandoned later because of poor soil management. Forests, often tree plantations, now occupy much of the land again.

Large carnivores such as bison retreated from the eastern community after European settlement. Deer, raccoons, and squirrels remain and even thrive despite dense human settlement.

Western Community

The drier western grasslands have the potential to evaporate more moisture than what they gain from precipitation. Seasonal rains support grasses but inadequately support forests. Most native grasslands have been converted to abundant agricultural production, which benefits for a limited time from recycled nutrients and irrigation. However, the loss of the long, rooted grasses that maintained moisture and held the soil in place has caused erosion. Crops forced to yield beyond natural limits have become unsustainable due to fossil fuel–based inputs.

The Intermontane is the driest region. In the Basin and Range desert, **xerophytic** plants (cactus, yucca, and creosote) have adapted to the dry conditions by limiting water loss and storing moisture in their stems.

Since the 1960s, the Great Plains and Intermontane have depended on irrigation to increase agricultural production. However, irrigation has caused land degradation, which alters vegetation, soils, and water distribution. Irrigation has encouraged farmers to grow crops that are inappropriate for this arid region, such as corn or cotton. Irrigation may be sustainable if the land grows appropriate crops for the region.

Pre-European settlement grasslands supported bison and antelope. Most native wildlife has been killed. Only a few species—coyotes, rattlesnakes, and a variety of lizards and other reptiles—survive today.

Boreal Forest

The continent-wide boreal forest, or **taiga**, ranges from Labrador to the Bering Sea and extends in latitude from the northern Prairie to the tundra. The boreal forest also extends across Asia and Europe and is the world's largest **biome**—a geographic area defined by its climate, soil, plants, and animals. Boreal trees include coniferous needle-leaf evergreens, including firs, spruces, and pines, and small-leaved deciduous trees such as birches and willows.

The boreal ecosystem receives little precipitation but is inundated with wetlands due to low evaporation rates and underlying discontinuous permafrost. The appearance of continuous permafrost marks the transition to tundra.

Some of the denizens of the boreal region are black bears, gray wolves, moose, and beavers. Black bears are found throughout North America but especially in the boreal forest. Gray wolves have occupied the entire boreal forest area. Moose live in the boreal forest of Canada and the Atlantic Northeast. The beaver is an environment-influencing animal that builds systems of dams and canals, resulting in ponds where they live. Most are found in the boreal forest today, although during the early nineteenth century they were hunted almost to extinction across the United States and Canada.

North of the boreal forest, mosses, lichens, and the shallow-rooted black spruce constitute the permafrost tundra vegetation.

Disasters and Hazards

Natural disasters, such as earthquakes, hurricanes, tornadoes, and volcanic eruptions, are radical disruptions in physical systems. But understanding the interrelations of the multiple variables is a complex science still in its infancy. Adding to the complexity is how human activity may be exacerbating these events.

For example, levees, human-made lakes, dams, and numerous other human contrivances have temporarily contributed to economic success, they have also added to desertification, erosion, deforestation, depletion of the fisheries, loss of biodiversity, excessive energy consumption, and destruction

BOX 3.4 GEOSPATIAL TECHNIQUES AND ENVIRONMENTAL CHANGE

In many chapters we introduce ways that geospatial techniques are being used to better understand environmental change. Geospatial techniques together with remote sensing, geographic information science, global positioning system (GPS), cartography, geovisualization, and spatial statistics are being used to capture, store, manipulate, and analyze complex situations. These techniques have been applied in various fields including the following:

- meteorology;
- forestry;

- environmental management;
- agriculture;
- health;
- climate change and sea-level rise;
- monitoring of natural resources (air, water, land, etc.);
- ground-level ozone; and
- soil erosion.

Geospatial techniques are also being applied to predict and manage environmental hazards such as wildfires, hurricanes, and earthquakes.

of coastal environments. Ameliorating these effects will require learning to live more in tune with nature. Many of these subjects will be the focus of regional environmental topics in the coming chapters.

Many disturbances in the natural environment have been indirectly caused or exacerbated by human intervention or the stresses placed on the environment by continued population growth. Some of these "natural" disasters that we explore in subsequent chapters include the following:

- Drought: Abnormally dry weather in regions that depend on precipitation to provide food and water for the entire biotic community. Major drought conditions throughout the Great Plains in the 1930s created the Dust Bowl, caused by farmers leaving the dry topsoil exposed to the wind. While lessons were learned from the Dust Bowl, continued droughts are still a problem. Continued droughts throughout the Southeast hindered growing populations, fisheries, and energy usage. California's vegetation is often dry due to long-term drought, and is susceptible to lightning strikes which erupt into fires.
- Fire: Lightning and volcanic eruptions are fires caused by other than human intervention. Organisms have adapted to fire as part of their life cycle. In the Great Plains' grasslands or California's sequoia forests, the effect of wildfire on native vegetation has been positive, clearing invasive species, adding nutrients to soil, and germinating seeds. Fire is a natural part of many cycles of plant life, but human intervention has caused major fires and interrupted these cycles. Western culture has traditionally viewed wildfire as negative and attempted to prevent wildfires and extinguish them when they occur. The US policy toward fires has changed since the 1960s from total suppression to controlled burns, such as in Yellowstone National Park in 1988. Within months of the burn, the vegetation began to regrow and the forest became healthier.

- Severe storms: Massive storms such as tornadoes, flash floods, and hurricanes impact the North American continent. Tornadoes, which occur when massive fronts collide, are most common in the United States, especially in Tornado Alley, where they are now watched closely. Early warning systems have saved lives and reduced property losses. However, severe tornadoes in the spring of 2011 killed hundreds despite early warning systems. The increased intensity of tornadoes, flash floods, and hurricanes is linked to climate change.
- Earthquakes formed by the grinding of plate boundaries release energy measured on the Richter scale. Most earthquakes occur along the Pacific Ocean Ring of Fire. Major earthquakes have struck Alaska and California in the past century. In 1964, Alaska had one of the largest earthquakes ever recorded (9.2). California has had several major quakes: the San Francisco earthquakes of 1906 (6.9 estimate) and 1989 (7.1) and the Northridge earthquake of 1994 (6.7). The fact that few lives have been lost has been attributed to higher building standards in the United States. But building standards aside, the cost of a "big one" in California, where one in eight Americans resides, may be more than what the United States can afford.

Earthquakes, meteorite impacts, landslides, or volcanic eruptions cause the massive displacement of water that creates tsunamis. Tsunamis caught the world's attention in late 2004, when an offshore earthquake in Indonesia generated a devastating wave that destroyed shoreline communities across the Indian Ocean basin, killing hundreds of thousands and reducing entire villages to rubble. Tsunamis were once again destructive in 2011, when Japan was struck by major earthquakes and resulting tsunamis. The United States has also been the recipient of tsunamis on the Atlantic and Pacific coasts, as well as Hawai`i and Alaska. Tsunami prediction can now occur after a wave is generated, but it gives little time to protect life and property.

Questions for Discussion

1. Are humans a part of nature or apart from nature? Justify your answer.
2. Where are the most active physical landforms on the North American continent and why is it so?
3. Discuss the importance of water to ecoregions.
4. Discuss the difference between point and nonpoint water pollution and what progress has been made in each.
5. How might climate change affect various climate regions?
6. How are soil and other ecological communities interconnected?
7. How are natural disasters or hazards impacted by human activity?

Suggested Readings

Ahrens, C. D. *Meteorology Today*. 6th ed. St. Paul, Minn.: Brooks/Cole, 1999.

Atwood, W. W. *The Physiographic Provinces of North America*. Boston: Ginn, 1940.

Briggs, D., et al., eds. *Fundamentals of the Physical Environment*. London: Routledge, 1997.

Bulkeley, Harriet. *Climate Change and the City*. London and New York: Routledge, 2012.

The Canadian System of Soil Classification. *Agriculture and Agri-Food Canada Publication 1646*. 3rd ed. Ottawa: NRC Research Press M-55, Soil Classification Working Group, 1998.

Christopherson, R. *Geosystems*. Upper Saddle River, N.J.: Prentice Hall, 2005.

Condie, K. C. *Plate Tectonics and Crustal Evolution*. 4th ed. Burlington, Mass.: Butterworth-Heinemann, 1997.

Gersmehl, P.J. "Soil Taxonomy and Mapping." *Annals of Association of American Geographers* 67, no. 3 (1977): 419–28.

Grossman, D. H., et al. *International Classification of Ecological Communities: Terrestrial Vegetation of the United States*. Vol. 1, *The National Vegetation Classification System: Development, Status, and Applications*. Arlington, Va.: The Nature Conservancy, 1998.

Hunt, C. B. *Natural Regions of the United States and Canada*. San Francisco: Freeman, 1973.

Mackenzie, F. T., and J. A. Mackenzie. *Our Changing Earth: An Introduction to Earth System Science and Global Environmental Change*. Upper Saddle River, N.J.: Prentice Hall, 1995.

Rogers, J. J. *A History of the Earth*. New York: Cambridge University Press, 1993.

Solomon, S. *Water*. New York: Harper Perennial, 2010.

Sedjo, R. A. *The Forest Sector: Important Innovations*. Discussion Paper 97-42. Washington, D.C.: Resources for the Future, 1997.

Thornbury, W. D. *Regional Geomorphology of the United States*. New York: Wiley, 1965.

Trenhaile, A. S. *Geomorphology: A Canadian Perspective*. Toronto: Oxford University Press. 1997.

Wilson, E. O. *The Diversity of Life*. New York: Norton, 1992.

Internet Sources

The Nature Conservancy: Rivers and Lakes, at http://www.nature.org/initiatives/freshwater/

Geological History of Jamestown, Rhode Island, at www.jamestown-ri.info/geological_history.htm

Intergovernmental Panel on Climate Change, at http://www.ipcc.ch/

National Aeronautics and Space Administration (NASA), Natural Hazards, at http://earthobservatory.nasa.gov/NaturalHazards/

Peakbagger.com, at http://www.peakbagger.com/

U.S. EPA. 2016. "Overview of Greenhouse Gases and Sources of Emissions" at https://www.epa.gov/ghgemissions/inventory-us-greenhouse-gas-emissions-and-sinks

U.S. Geological Survey, History of Wetlands in the Conterminous United States, at http://water.usgs.gov/nwsum/WSP2425/history.html

The Atlas of Canada, at http://atlas.nrcan.gc.ca/site/english/index.html

PHOTO 4.1. Monterey, California. In the early 1850s, Monterey's Cannery Row was the center of Chinese fishing and export industry to China. Chinese enclaves flourished until the 1882 Chinese Exclusion Act stopped immigration until 1943. Today, Chinese New Year is a celebration of tradition and the Chinese community.

4
REGIONS
The Human Context

Chapter Highlights

After reading this chapter you should be able to:

- Describe general patterns of historical geography and settlement
- Identify important ethnicities and races that impact the cultural landscape
- Describe contemporary population dynamics in the United States and Canada
- Outline the demographic transition as it impacts the United States and Canada
- Discuss immigration trends and patterns in the United States and Canada
- Discuss urbanization trends in the United States and Canada
- Describe how economic restructuring impacts internal migration patterns
- Describe the three sectors of the economy
- Discuss how changes to each of the three economic sectors has impacted regions and metropolitan areas

Terms

allophone	death rate	natural increase	sprawl
Anglophone	deindustrialization	primary sector	Sun Belt
baby boom	Francophone	replacement level	tertiary sector
birthrate	globalization	rural	total fertility rate (TFR)
	metropolitan area	Rust Belt	urbanization
	migration	secondary sector	

Introduction

The previous chapter introduced the physical processes that help create regions. Regions are also created through human activity; in turn these activities have impacts on the natural and built environments. This chapter discusses the critical ways humans influence the places in which they live by introducing the following five themes that will be covered in each regional chapter:

- Historical Geography and Settlement
- Cultural Perspectives
- Population, Immigration, and Diversity
- Urban Trends
- The Economy

Historical Geography and Settlement

The historical geography and settlement of each region is critical to understanding how people have used natural resources to develop economies, altered the physical environment, and established land use patterns, all of which lay the foundation for the contemporary period.

The first humans to settle in North America came from Asia between twelve thousand and seventeen thousand years ago, at the time of the last ice age. Evidence suggests that their population grew rapidly and that they settled throughout Canada, the Great Plains, and the Eastern Woodlands. Then, beginning in the sixteenth century, settlers from Europe arrived. Generally, until the late twentieth century, Europeans dominated the ethnic makeup of Canada and the United States. However, in each region, countries of origin for immigrants were different, resulting in different land use patterns, architecture, and cultural legacies. These are important to understanding contemporary regional geography.

Canada

After Native Peoples, the first immigrants were a significant French-speaking population occupying Quebec and the Maritimes; then came migrants from the British Isles. The historical legacy can be seen today in the percentage of Europeans in Canada:

- Canadian, 32 percent;
- English, 21 percent;
- French, 15 percent;
- Scottish, 14 percent;
- Irish, 13 percent; and
- German, 9 percent.

Canadians divide themselves linguistically into **Francophones**, **Anglophones**, and **allophones** (those who speak a language other than French or English). Most Francophones occupy Quebec and New Brunswick, Anglophones in the other provinces, but allophones are becoming a larger segment of the population. Most allophones live in the most populated provinces: Ontario, British Columbia, Alberta, and Quebec.

The United States

The initial American immigrants were Spanish and settled in St. Augustine, Florida (1565), and Santa Fe, New Mexico (1610). However, Spanish settlement within the United States in the succeeding years was sparse and not the major thrust of the Spanish Empire. Beginning in the seventeenth century, the thirteen British colonies established the dominant Anglo culture along the eastern seaboard.

Today, the combined populations of United Kingdom ancestry (English, Irish, Scottish, and Scots-Irish) comprise 23 percent, and Germans comprise 16 percent. Settlement of the United States was east to west, but the Great Plains region was usually bypassed and settled after the west and after the transcontinental railroad enabled transport of crops to markets.

Ethnic group settlement varies throughout the United States. For example, Irish have favored New England, Iowa, and Montana, while Mexicans are predominately in the southwest and west (photo 4.1).

Cultural Perspectives

The diverse people that make up the United States and Canada influence the cultural landscape and create distinctive regional characteristics and perspectives, which we explore in each chapter. Briefly, we highlight the more dominant ethnicities.

Native Americans and Canadian Aboriginals

The forefathers of North American Aboriginals began to migrate and spread throughout the continents from Asia about twelve thousand to seventeen thousand years ago. Native Americans (or First Nations or Aboriginal peoples, as they are called in Canada) were scattered in their settlements and were members of numerous linguistic and cultural groups. The estimates for the pre-Columbian indigenous population of Canada and the United States have varied widely (from two to eighteen million north of Mexico).

Contact with Europeans was traumatic for the natives, who lacked immunity to European diseases. Within a century, 90–95 percent of the indigenous population had died. The population has never recovered. However, their cultural imprint on the landscape remains strong in many areas: in place names, in local art and architecture, and in the culture found on many reservations.

In 2016, 5.4 million Americans claimed American Indian or Alaska Native ancestry. About one-third of Native Americans live on reservations, across the Southwest and in South Dakota, and the remainder live outside the reservation system, mostly in Oklahoma (former Indian Territory) and California.

In 2016, the Canadian Aboriginal and Métis population was 1.6 million (about 5 percent). About one-half the Aboriginal population live on reservations. More Canadian Aboriginals claim native blood than a century ago, when only 127,000 claimed ancestry. Some of the "growth" in those claiming Native American or First Nation ancestry is that it is now more acceptable to belong to this group.

Indigenous populations in both countries have higher **birthrates** than their respective national populations. In Canada, the Inuit have the highest growth rate. Life expectancy for Native Americans and Canadian Aboriginals remains lower than that of the general population and poverty rates tend to be higher.

African American Blacks

The involuntary immigration of Africans began early in the colonization period. While some northern colonies participated in the slave trade, the southern plantations required a large labor pool, and nine out of ten slaves were in the South by the time of the American Revolution. Emancipation came after the Civil War and changed life in the South for both plantation owners and former slaves.

By 1900, nine million blacks lived in the South, but within a short period many left the South and its racist Jim Crow laws for jobs and opportunities in northeastern and midwestern industries. Fully one-third of blacks lived in the North, Midwest, or West by the late twentieth century; one in four lived in three states: New York, Florida, and Georgia.

But after 1995, a new migration pattern was established, as blacks began to repopulate the South. Approximately three hundred thousand returned to the South between 1995 and 2000, about three times the number who returned from 1965 to 1970. They left their northern homes and returned to southern

BOX 4.1   ICONIC IMAGES AND CULTURAL FESTIVALS

In many chapters, we highlight either an iconic image or a cultural festival as a way to better illustrate the ways in which people, places, and moments have shaped a region's history and identity.

For example, festivals were started to pass the legends, knowledge, and traditions onto the next generation. Festivals are a way many celebrate heritage, culture, and traditions, and they can be place specific. For example, Mardi Gras is associated with New Orleans. Festivals play an important role to add structure to our social lives, and connect us with our families, communities, and backgrounds. There are many types of cultural festivals such as national, religious, and seasonal. Cultural festivals and events are increasingly becoming arenas of discourse enabling people to express their views on wider cultural, social, and political issues.

Iconic images can be photographs, art work, statues, or structures. Iconic images are often associated with with emotional impact for people in a given time, place, or culture. For example, the raising of the flag at Iwo Jima, Andy Warhol's can of soup, or the photograph of Martin Luther King, Jr. standing on the steps of the Lincoln Memorial during his "I Have a Dream" speech still resonate powerfully today.

cities, especially Atlanta. Most of the blacks who returned had achieved middle-class prosperity and chose to return to neighborhoods where they felt they had roots. While many blacks have prospered, African American economic progress has lagged in relation to other groups.

For four hundred years, the black population size in Canada was modest in size; some arrived as slaves brought by Loyalist refugees, and some as free people. In 1901, there were 17,400 blacks in Canada, or 0.3 percent of the population. In 2016, the black population was 1.2 million, or 3.5 percent of the Canadian population. Forty-five percent of the blacks living in Canada are Canadian-born, but since the 1990s almost half are immigrants who arrived from Africa, the Caribbean, and Central and South America. While blacks populate most Canadian cities, a higher percentage live in Brampton, Montreal, and Toronto.

Hispanic Population

The Spanish arrived in New Mexico at the beginning of the seventeenth century. Since that time, Hispanics have been a major settlement and cultural force within the entire Southwest. Prior to the immigration laws of 1920, Mexicans (and Canadians) had unrestricted access to the states. Since restriction quotas were enforced, the largest contingent of legal immigrants into the United States has been from Mexico, with additional immigrants from other Latin American and Caribbean countries. About ten million illegal Hispanic immigrants have also arrived.

Every state has a Hispanic population; however, two-thirds live in California, Texas, Florida, and New York. The states with the highest percentage of Hispanics are those bordering Mexico (Arizona, California, New Mexico, and Texas); New Mexico leads the nation with 48 percent Hispanic population.

Today about half a million Hispanic Canadians constitute 1.3 percent of the total population, with the largest proportions living in Manitoba and Ontario, followed by British Columbia and Quebec. About half live in Toronto or Montreal. The majority of Canadian Hispanics are foreign born and arrived during the past twenty years. The largest groups of Hispanic immigrants are from El Salvador and Mexico.

Asian Population

Asians have been a part of the United States population since the settlement of the West Coast; however, their numbers were few until after the 1960s. The Chinese Exclusion Act, which stopped Chinese immigration in 1882, was not repealed until 1943.

California had the earliest contingent of Asians. Chinese and some Japanese males mined gold or worked in constructing the railroad. Most Asian immigrants lived along the West Coast, or later in Hawai`i, but some settled in Chicago and New York. Japanese immigrants were few in number prior to strict quotas after World War I.

After 1960, immigration policies opened the door to Asian immigrants. The first immigrants were Filipinos and Chinese from Taiwan and Hong Kong, but later immigrants came from many other Asian countries. Since the 1990s, Asians have constituted more than one-third of total US immigrants. Thirty-five percent settled in California: Chinese in the San Francisco area and South Asians, mostly from India, along the southeastern shore of San Francisco Bay. Although Hawai`i's total percentage of Asians within the United States is small—4.4 percent—42.8 percent of all Hawaiians are of Asian ancestry.

In 2016, more than 18.4 million Asians lived in the United States (5.7 percent of the population). The largest contingent are from China, India, the Philippines, Korea, Vietnam, and Japan.

Asians began to arrive in Canada during the late nineteenth century. Small groups of Chinese and South Asians migrated to Vancouver. Many arrived from California, but later arrivals emigrated from China. The Chinese Immigration Act of 1923 restricted immigration until the 1940s, when a contingent of Hong Kong Chinese began to arrive, along with Asians from Vietnam, India, and the Philippines.

The largest visible ethnic group continues to be South Asians, followed by Chinese and blacks. A majority of Canada's Asians have immigrated in the past twenty years. The vast majority of Asians live in the urban areas of Ontario or British Columbia.

Population, Immigration, and Diversity

Population dynamics, migration, and diversity continue to significantly impact the United States and Canada, although these processes vary regionally. Each chapter will explore contemporary trends in population, migration, and diversity.

Population Dynamics

The United States is home to 323 million people. Each year, there are about two million more births than deaths. Overall, the US population is growing slowly with a **natural increase** (growth in population by births over deaths) of 0.81 percent as of 2017. These numbers indicate national growth without taking migration into account. Each year, the United States grows by approximately 1 million new immigrants. Table 4.1 highlights population trends for the United States and Canada compared to other regions of the world.

Canada is home to thirty-seven million people, and like the United States, it too is growing slowly, with a natural increase of 0.73 percent as of 2017. In the United States, the **total fertility rate (TFR)**—the number of children born to a woman—is 1.8, while Canadians are at 1.6. The US and Canadian TFRs are below the **replacement level** of 2.1, yet the populations continue to grow because of immigration.

Population growth is certainly an important issue in sustainability, but for the United States and Canada, it not population growth that presents the biggest challenge. Rather, it is what is happening to population structure: an aging population.

Aging Population

In affluent countries, such as the United States and Canada, population is aging because of low birthrates and long life expectancies (low **death rates**). Life expectancy has continued to increase and Americans and Canadians are living longer than in the past. Life expectancy in the United States is seventy-nine, and in Canada it is eighty-two.

Aging **baby boomers** are already shifting the age structure the United States and Canada. The number of Americans aged sixty-five and older is projected to more than double from forty-six million today to over ninety-eight million by 2060, and the sixty-five-and-older age group's share of the total population will rise to nearly 24 percent from 15 percent. In 2015, Canada passed a milestone: the population of people sixty-five and older is now larger than the number of children under fifteen.

A range of issues confronts a "graying" society including transit accessibility, physical accessibility to buildings, and the need to provide more in-home and community health care services. The consequences for Canada and the United States will be social, financial, and political. Financially, the ratio of the

TABLE 4.1. Population of the World and Its Major Areas, 1750–2050

Population Size (millions)

Major area	1750	1800	1850	1900	1950	2000	2010	2015	2050(est)
World	791	978	1,262	1,650	2,521	6,115	6,892	7,336	8,909
Africa	106	107	111	133	221	819	1,030	1,171	1,766
Asia	502	635	809	947	1,402	3,698	4,157	4,397	5,268
Europe	163	203	276	408	547	727	739	742	628
Central and South America	16	24	38	74	167	521	544	630	809
North America	2	7	26	82	172	319	344	357	392
Oceania	2	2	2	6	13	31	37	40	46

Percentage Distribution

	1750	1800	1850	1900	1950	2000	2010	2050
World	100	100	100	100	100	100	100	100
Africa	13.4	10.9	8.8	8.1	8.8	13.4	14.9	19.8
Asia	63.5	64.9	64.1	57.4	55.6	60.5	60.3	59.1
Europe	20.6	20.8	21.9	24.7	21.7	11.9	10.7	7.0
Central and South America	2.0	2.5	3.0	4.5	8.5	8.5	7.8	9.1
North America	0.3	0.7	2.1	5.0	5.1	5.2	5.0	4.4
Oceania	0.3	0.2	0.2	0.4	0.5	0.5	0.5	0.5

Source: United Nations Population Division, *The World at Six Billion,* at http://www.un.org/esa/population/publications/sixbillion/sixbillion.htm

working population to those over sixty-five was 12:1 in 1950, but in 2050 it will be about 3:1 in both the United States and Canada. This will have implications for Social Security taxes, retirement plans, and health care. For example, whether by choice or necessity, many baby boomers are choosing to work beyond the age of sixty-five, thereby decreasing jobs for the younger population, who would ordinarily fill the positions of the retired.

The shifting age structure will alter policies in both countries. The retired population requires more health care, does not consume at the same levels as the younger population, and therefore affects the gross domestic product (GDP). As the baby boomers age, many will relocate from the northern to southern cities, accenting already stressed environmental conditions in these areas.

Migration and Diversity

The United States and Canada are diverse societies built on a long history of immigration. Immigration continues to be a critical factor in population growth and in the increasing diversity of those who live in both the United States and Canada.

Historic Waves of Immigration

There were five waves of immigration in the United States, and Canada had two intense waves that occurred at approximately the same time (table 4.2). During the seventeenth and eighteenth centuries, the first wave of immigrants came from England, Scotland, or Ireland, although a few were Dutch or German. In Canada, the earliest immigrants were from France and settled in Nova Scotia or Quebec. These waves of immigration contributed predominately European stock to the population, although recent waves have expanded diversity.

The first wave in the United States consisted of perhaps a million mostly British settlers, who became the backbone of the nation's hearths and cultural mores. After the American Revolution, the British no longer immigrated in great numbers; they were replaced by Scots-Irish and then German settlers.

As the War of 1812 and the Napoleonic era raged in America and Europe, immigration to the Americas almost ceased, but it began to increase again in 1820.

The second wave of settlers, from 1820 to 1860, was estimated at six million. Most immigrants were from Northern Europe, including Ireland, Germany, the Netherlands, France, Switzerland, and Scandinavian countries. Most were seeking new opportunities or fleeing religious or political persecution.

Immigration continued until the 1890s, interrupted only by the Civil War. The one exception to the halt of immigration during the Civil War was a flow of immigrants into the United States from Canada. The robust US economy contrasted to a depressed Canadian economy where many, especially those from Quebec, choose to migrate into northeastern US textile towns. Many towns in Massachusetts, Vermont, and New Hampshire still have large French Canadian populations. Toward the end of this wave, the Canadian Prairies were opened to settlement, and many German Mennonite, Swedish, and Ukrainian farmers moved into the region.

The most significant immigration period occurred from 1890 to the onset of World War I (1914), when an average of one million immigrants, from Russia and from southern and eastern Europe, came to America. Between the world wars, 1918–1941, both the United States and Canada impeded immigration and discriminated against both southern Europeans and Asians. For a short period after World War II (1945–1950), the Displaced Persons Act authorized admission of refugees escaping persecution. They arrived from England, Germany, Italy, and Eastern Europe, but the number of immigrants declined as the Soviet Iron Curtain tightened its grip on Eastern Europe.

Immigration Today

Patterns of immigrations are far different today from those of the 1960s. The US Immigration Nationality Act (1965) and revisions to Canada's Immigration Act (1967–1968) removed quotas of immigration from countries in the developing world,

TABLE 4.2. Waves of US and Canadian Immigration

	Who	Why	Where
First wave (1600–1750)	British (US) French, British (Canada)	Religious persecution, economic opportunities	Eastern seaboard
Second wave (1820–1860)	Irish, German, Welsh, Scots-Irish, Northern Europeans	Pushed by political and economic factors (crop failure, famine)	East Coast cities, Ohio, and Appalachia
Third wave (1865–1873)	Belgian, Czech, Scandinavian	Pulled by political stability, economic growth, agricultural land	North Central US
Fourth wave (1878–1890)	Southern and Eastern European (Canada: Eastern European from 1890 to 1921)	Religious persecution, access to land, rise of industrialization	Used transcontinental rail access to Great Plains, Canadian Prairie, Midwestern cities
Fifth wave (1890–1914)	Russian, Southern and Eastern European	Religious persecution, political unrest	New York, large cities
Sixth wave (1960–)	Latin American, Asian	Economic opportunity	West coast of both countries, large cities

TABLE 4.3. Foreign Born in the United States and Canada, 1960–2015

Canada	1960	1970	1980	1990	2000	2005	2015
Foreign born (in millions)	2.76	3.251	3.8	4.3	5.55	6.1	7.2
Total population (in millions)	17.9	21.7	24.5	27.7	30.7	32.2	35.2
Percent foreign born	15.4	14.9	15.5	15.6	18	18.9	20.7

The United States	1960	1970	1980	1990	2000	2005	2015
Foreign born (in millions)	9.7	9.7	14.2	23.25	34.8	38.3	45.78
Total population (in millions)	186	210	230	255	284	298	320
Percent foreign born	5.2	4.6	6.2	9.1	12.2	12.8	14.3

Source: US Census Bureau and Canadian Census

radically changing the source of immigrants. With the removal of restrictive immigration quotas and ongoing improvements in global transportation and communications, immigrants to the United States and Canada come from increasingly diverse backgrounds. European immigration dropped from 50 percent in the 1950s to 10 percent by 2000. In the United States, the largest groups were Latin Americans, accounting for about one-half of all immigrants, and Asians, constituting about one-third of the total. Immigration rates have increased in both Canada and the United States and both countries have received immigrants from more than 190 countries. In the United States, about one million immigrate annually; the Canadian goal allows the equivalent of 1 percent of its total population to immigrate annually. In 2015, the US foreign-born population stood at more than 45.7 million, or 14.3 percent, while Canada's foreign-born accounted for more than 20 percent of the total population, the highest percentage of any G8 country (table 4.3).

And unlike mid-century conceptions of immigrants as factory workers and ghetto residents, present-day newcomers bring financial capital and technological know-how that is transforming North America.

With birthrates declining in both Canada and the United States, immigration is the most significant contributor to population growth. This process has led to increased ethnic and racial diversity in the past twenty years.

In North America, long an established region of immigrant settlement, the rates of immigration are among the highest in the world. Each year, more than one million people migrate legally to the United States; however, an additional five hundred thousand migrants (approximately) enter illegally. Canadian immigration is about 250,000 annually, and another 8 percent arrive or stay illegally. In the United States, the documented and undocumented immigrant birthrate is higher than that of the native-born citizens, which raises the overall birthrate. For example, about 1.38 million foreign-born individuals moved to the United States in 2015, countering the below–replacement level fertility rates.

A majority of Canadian immigrants arrive from Asia; China, India, and the Phillipines are the largest sources. More than 90 percent of Canada's foreign-born population lives in four provinces: Alberta, Ontario, Quebec, and British Columbia. Canadian immigration patterns have undergone considerable changes in the late twentieth century. Both the immigrants and their destinations have changed. The largest immigrant group into Canada has been South Asian Indians, followed by Mainland Chinese, followed by Filipinos. The overwhelming immigrant gateway has been Toronto, where 51 percent of all residents are foreign born. Immigrants who speak French often choose to migrate to Quebec, while many Asians, especially Chinese, have chosen to migrate to Vancouver, British Columbia.

Mexicans accounted for approximately 27 percent of immigrants in the United States, making them by far the largest foreign-born group in the country. India was the next largest country of origin, with close to 6 percent of all immigrants, followed by China (including Hong Kong but not Taiwan) and the Philippines, at close to 5 percent each. El Salvador, Vietnam, and Cuba (about 3 percent each), as well as the Dominican Republic, Korea, and Guatemala (2 percent each), rounded out the top ten. Together, immigrants from these ten countries represented 58 percent of the US immigrant population in 2015.

More than half of the undocumented immigrants to the United States arrive from Mexico; others arrive from Central and South America or overstay their visas. Two-thirds of the undocumented immigrants settle in one of eight states: California, Texas, Florida, New York, Arizona, Illinois, New Jersey, and North Carolina.

Immigrant Settlement

While we tend to think of immigrants as coming to and from countries, most immigrants actually go to cities. Immigrant gateway cities are growing in number because of **globalization** and the acceleration of migration driven by income differentials, social networks, and various state policies to recruit skilled and unskilled laborers as for both temporary and permanent.

As large numbers of foreign-born residents mix with more established populations, North American cities become the places where global differences arc both celebrated and contested. Immigrants can add to a city's global competitiveness by enhancing cross-border business connections, linguistic capabilities, and attractiveness to tourists. Although the three largest immigrant destinations in North America are New York City, Toronto, and Los Angeles, there are sixty other metropolitan regions with more than one hundred thousand foreign-born residents. In Canada, immigrants go primarily to one of its three largest cities: Vancouver, Montreal, and Toronto. But even in smaller Canadian cities such as Ottawa and Calgary, over 20 percent of the population is foreign born. In the United States, immigrants are targeting newer gateways such as Washington, D.C., Phoenix, Charlotte, and Atlanta, where the proportional increase in the foreign-born population is much higher than in traditional gateways.

Yet, crude measurements of the foreign-born populations tell us little about the composition or distribution of immigrants within cities. Some cities are home to a "hyperdiverse" foreign-born population; others are home to large numbers of foreign-born residents, but are not particularly diverse. Two of the most hyperdiverse cities in the world are New York and Toronto (chart 4.1). Together, they are home to millions of foreign-born residents who have come from every country of the world.

In Toronto, 51 percent of the city's population is foreign born, one of the highest percentages for any major **metropolitan area**. About seventy thousand immigrants from approximately 170 countries arrive in the city annually. No one group dominates Toronto's immigrant stock. Nine countries account for half of the foreign-born population, led by China, then India, the United Kingdom, Italy, the Philippines, Jamaica, Portugal, Poland, and Sri Lanka. Other hyperdiverse metropolitan areas in North America include Vancouver, Washington, D.C., San Francisco, and Seattle. Due to the globalization of migration, there is a growing tendency for immigrants to come from a broader range of sending countries and for North American cities to be more racially and ethnically diverse.

New York's Foreign-Born Population

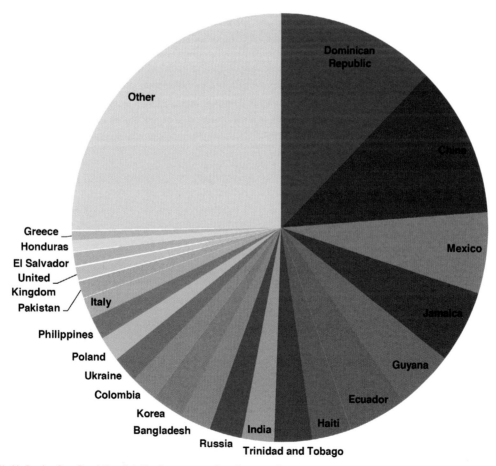

CHART 4.1. New York's Foreign-Born Population. Note the diverse range of sending countries.

Source: Globalization, Urbanization and Migration data set (http://gstudynet.org/gum/)

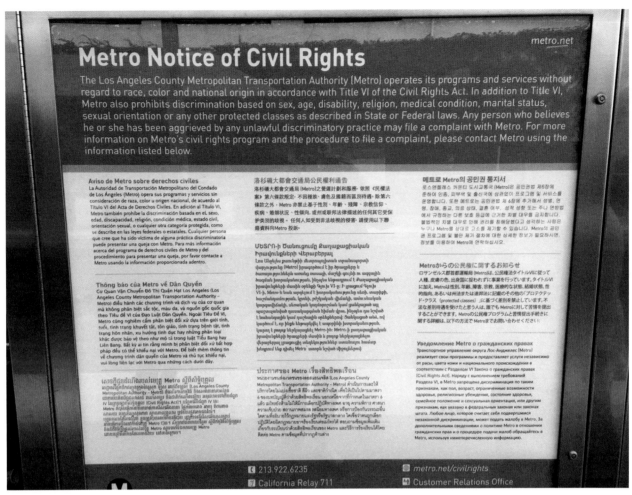

PHOTO 4.2. Los Angeles Metro sign Cities like Los Angeles have significant numbers of residents for whom English is a second language and have policies that require important public information be communicated in multiple languages.

Source: Lisa Benton-Short

Not all immigrant gateways are hyper-diverse. Mexican immigrants account for about half of the foreign-born population in Los Angeles, Chicago, Houston, and Dallas. These millions of Mexicans have affected US cities in unexpected ways. For example, four of the top ten television shows in the Los Angeles market are Spanish-language broadcasts. Yet, Los Angeles recognizes its growing diversity by offering important information in multiple languages (photo 4.2). In Miami, foreign-born Cubans dominate. Immigrants from mainland China and Hong Kong account for over 25 percent of the foreign-born population in Vancouver. It is fair to say that North American cities will continue to be home to many of the world's immigrants well into the twenty-first century.

Diversity

The increasingly diverse streams of immigration have created issues of identity for many newcomers. Immigrants are no longer ghettoized, low-skilled manual labor; they are creating new identities as revitalizers, innovators, and businesspeople. Yet, the identities that older Americans and Canadians ascribe

to this group sometimes remain stuck in the past—seeing immigrants as "others."

New forms of diversity have also emerged in other cultural contexts. North America has experienced an increase in the visibility and culture of people who are lesbian, gay, bisexual, transgendered, and queer (LGBTQ). In 2005, Canada legalized gay marriage, and more recently, many US states have followed the same path. The past decade has been a formative time for the advancement of gay and lesbian rights, and identities. The city is a focal point: early gay and lesbian life in cities helped to create gay villages (for example, the Castro in San Francisco, Church Street in Toronto) (photo 4.3). Today, in some places, gay villages are heavily branded and marketed by business associations and municipal governments. Yet, some gay neighborhoods have lost out to gentrification: rent increases, property speculation, and denials of applications for LGBTQ events have lost out to the upwardly mobile mainstream.

Far from adopting some kind of cosmopolitan mega-identity, women, immigrants, racial minorities, and gay men and lesbians continue to experience life in the United States and Canada in vastly different ways.

PHOTO 4.3. The Castro District's Rainbow Crosswalk Intersection. The Castro District in San Francisco is synonymous with gay culture. In the 1960s and 1970s, gay men began buying charming old Victorians at relatively low prices ($20,000–$40,000), and the neighborhood was soon named for its busiest thoroughfare, Castro Street, and the neighborhood became a vibrant and cohesive community with sizable political and economic power. The district celebrates its thriving gay and lesbian population.

Source: iStock/diegograndi

MAP 4.1. Major Urban Agglomerations of the United States and Canada.

Source: United Nations, Department of Economic and Social Affairs, Population Division (2014), World Urbanization Prospects: 2014 Revision, http://esa.un.org/unpd/wup/

Urbanization and Urban Trends

Another theme explored in each regional chapter is **urbanization**, defined as the complex process of urban growth in demographic, social, political, behavioral, and economic terms. It is now a fact that in many areas of the world, a majority of the population lives in urban areas and this trend is only growing. In the United States and Canada, a majority of the population has been urban throughout most of the twentieth century and into the first decades of this century. Currently, more than 85 percent of the US and Canadian populations lives in urban areas (map 4.1).

BOX 4.2 URBAN TERMS

- *City*: a political designation that refers to a large, densely population place that is legally incorporated as a municipality. Today we use the term "urban area" as it better describes the spatial forms of the twenty-first century.
- *Metropolitan area*: a metropolitan area includes a center city plus all surrounding territory (urban and **rural**) that is somehow integrated into the urban core. In the United States, the term "Metropolitan Statistical Area" (MSA) is the official moniker designated by the US Census Bureau and is defined as an area that has an urban core of at least fifty thousand people. In Canada, the official term is "Census Metropolitan Area" (CMA), which must have an urban core of at least one hundred thousand people.

- *Urban area*: as cities have expanded, the boundary between urban and rural is less distinct. In both the United States and Canada, automobile transportation has allowed suburbanization and **sprawl**. The urban area thus includes the city and its suburbs.
- *Sustainable city*: the "three Es" applied in the urban context. Herbert Giradet, a leading urban sustainability scholar, defines a sustainable city as "a city that works so well that all its citizens are able to meet their own needs without endangering the well-being of the natural world or the living conditions of other people, now or in the future."

Nearly three out of four of North Americans live in cities, and experts predict that by 2050 this percentage could be greater than 90 percent. In Canada, half of the population lives in the three largest urban areas: Toronto, Montreal, and Vancouver. Yet despite the urban nature of these two countries, North American cities vary in size, form, and fortune. The New York metropolitan region has twenty-two million people, Los Angeles has eighteen million, and Chicago has ten million. Atlanta, Houston, Miami, Philadelphia, Toronto, and Washington, D.C., have five million or more, while Baltimore, Denver, Ottawa, Portland, and Vancouver have about two million people. There are some forty-eight cities that have one million people.

In the United States, recent urban population growth has been robust in western and southwestern cities, while many cities in the East and the Midwest such as Detroit and Buffalo have seen economic and demographic decline. In Canada, the fastest growing metropolitan areas are the Prairie cities of Calgary and Edmonton.

One spatial outcome of urbanization in North America has been the emergence of metropolitan areas. As metropolitan areas grow larger and merge into each other, they can form **megapolitan** areas. The largest one in the United States is the urbanized Northeastern seaboard, a region named Megalopolis by the geographer Jean Gottmann in the 1950s. Megalopolis stretches from south of Washington, D.C, north through Baltimore, Philadelphia, New York, and north to Boston. This region is responsible for 20 percent of the nation's GDP. In 1950, Megalopolis had a population of almost thirty-two million people; by 2010, it had increased to almost fifty million, about 15 percent of the US population, almost one in six of the population. Today, Megalopolis consists of 52,300 square miles stretching across twelve states, the District of Columbia, and 124 counties (see chapter 7).

In addition to the obvious demographic significance, Megalopolis reminds us of the environmental impact of such population growth: more people, more suburban development and loss of farm land; more people driving cars, running dishwashers, flushing toilets and showers, living in bigger houses. It is estimated that Megalopolis generates approximately one hundred thousand tons of garbage each day.

North American megalopolitan regions are defined as clustered networks of metropolitan regions that have at least ten million. Geographically, they comprise at least two contiguous metropolitan areas, which include city centers and their surrounding suburbs. In North America, there are eleven megalopolitan regions (table 4.4). Collectively, megalopolitan regions constitute only 20 percent of the nation's land surface yet comprise 67 percent of the population. On a smaller population scale, geographer Stanley Brunn has identified numerous urban regions in the United States (map 4.2).

TABLE 4.4. Megalopolitan Areas of the United States and Canada

Area	Anchor Cities
Cascadia	Vancouver, Seattle, Portland, Eugene
NorCal	San Francisco, San Jose, Oakland, Sacramento
Southland	Los Angeles, San Diego, Las Vegas
Valley of the Sun	Phoenix, Tucson
I-35 Corridor	Kansas City, Oklahoma City, Dallas, San Antonio
Gulf Coast	Houston, New Orleans, Mobile
Piedmont	Birmingham, Atlanta, Charlotte, Raleigh
Peninsula	Tampa, Miami, Orlando
Midwest	Chicago, Madison, Detroit, Indianapolis, Cincinnati
Northeast	Richmond, Washington, D.C., Philadelphia, New York, Boston
Main Street	Windsor, Toronto, Montreal, Quebec City

Source: Adapted from the Metropolitan Institute at Virginia Tech University

BOX 4.3 URBAN SUSTAINABILITY BEST PRACTICES

The fact that three out of four of North Americans live in cities means that what cities are doing to plan for sustainability will be absolutely critical in the coming decades.

There is good news. One of the biggest developments in the last ten years is that nearly all US and Canadian cities have established sustainability offices and created sustainability plans. Many of these plans are comprehensive in that they address a range and diversity of issues that include the following:

- food;
- climate change;
- water quality;

- water supply;
- parks and recreation;
- social justice and equity;
- green economy/green jobs;
- transportation;
- energy use;
- housing;
- garbage and recycling; and
- risk and resilience to hazards.

In many chapters we will highlight some of the best practices because the reality is: without sustainable cities, there will be no sustainable future.

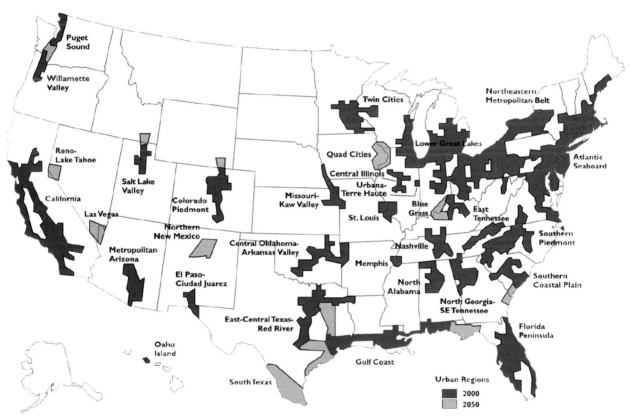

MAP 4.2. Possible Urban Regions in 2050.

Source: Stanley D. Brunn, Maureen Hays-Mitchell, and Donald J. Zeigler, eds. *Cities of the World: World Regional Urban Development*, 5th ed. (Lanham, MD: Rowman & Littlefield)

The Economy

In each regional chapter we examine the economy by looking at the three sectors of economic activity. These are primary, secondary, and tertiary (table 4.5).

The **primary sector** includes agricultural, forestry, mining, and fishing and is very much influenced by geography. Mining is a function of mineral distribution, while fishing takes place beside rivers, lakes, and coasts. The type of agriculture depends on climate and weather, and soils and water availability, and this too varies across the United States and Canada. Overall, the role of the primary sector is less important in contemporary regional economic growth, although in some ecoregions, agriculture and mining still play an important role.

TABLE 4.5. The Three Sectors of the Economy

	Primary	Secondary	Tertiary
What the sector does	Obtaining raw materials from natural resources	Processing raw materials into goods	Wholesale and retail, banking, insurance, tourism, health, education, inventing new products, research, science, information manipulation
Examples	Mining Fishing Agriculture Logging	Automobiles Steel Furniture Clothing Housing	Stores Hotels Transportation Schools Science labs University research Computers

The manufacturing of goods constitutes the bulk of the **secondary sector**. The large-scale manufacturing of goods as a major component of an economy is associated with the Industrial Revolution and has been a key part of economic growth and development in the United States and Canada since the nineteenth century. In the late nineteenth century, Pittsburgh became a center for coal and steel production. In the early twentieth century, Detroit became the center for the manufacturing of cars. The rise of the manufacturing led to tremendous economic growth and rapid urbanization, but industrialization depended on coal and created unhealthy pollution. Today, manufacturing still contributes to economic growth and many jobs rely on this sector, but there have been major changes.

In the mature economies of the United States and Canada, there has been a shift from manufacturing to services, the **tertiary sector**. In the United States, for example, service employment now accounts for one in every three US workers and almost 30 percent of GDP. Services include selling, assistance, and expertise, rather than making a tangible product. The term tertiary or service sector covers a wide range of activities from teaching to health care, financial consultation, and computer information.

The tertiary sector consists of a range of differing job experiences and pay. At one end are high-paid Wall Street brokers with numerous benefits; at the other end are waiters in restaurants who work for minimum wage and may not have health or retirement benefits.

One dynamic sector of services is the knowledge-based industries that include advertising, banking services, financial services, and information technology. Since 1980, these have been the most important job growth areas, and regions in the United States and Canada have deliberately attempted to attract these types of companies in order to grow their economies.

Historically, we can see a trend: most people worked within the primary economy; the secondary economy dominated the Industrial Revolution, and the tertiary since the mid-twentieth century. All continue to operate but in varying

degrees. The primary economy employed about 95 percent in 1800 but only 7 percent work in the primary sector today. The secondary sector dominated from the nineteenth into the mid-twentieth century but has declined in the United States and Canada; it now accounts for less than 20 percent of the jobs.

The impact of globalization on North America has affected economic restructuring. A critical economic shift has occurred due to **deindustrialization** that began in the 1970s and has continued for nearly forty years. Many corporations began moving out of North America to developing countries lured by lower labor costs and tax breaks that promised higher profit margins. Starting in the 1970s, but increasing during the 1980s and 1990s, in cities such as Pittsburg, Syracuse, Buffalo, Cleveland, Windsor, and Detroit, companies fired or relocated workers, closed factories, and left the region or country. These cities were transformed from vibrant manufacturing centers to "**Rust Belt**" cities of despair. This decline marked a critical shift in the North American economy and these impacts reverberate today. Detroit, for example, was once home to both GM and Ford and was dubbed "Motor City" or "Motown." At its peak, Detroit was home to 1.8 million residents in 1950. Today, its population is around seven hundred thousand.

While many industrial regions and cities have experienced deindustrialization and economic decline, the rise of the **service sector** has offset some of this decline but often in other cities and regions. Florida, California, the Pacific Northwest and the Canadian Corridor, and cities such as Seattle, Orlando, Miami, Phoenix, Calgary, and Vancouver have grown primarily through the expansion of the service sector. Increased jobs in wholesale and retail trade, finance, insurance, real estate, information and communication technologies, education, and medical services have driven growth. The Midwest and Ozarks, however, have struggled to attract the service sector.

The twin processes of deindustrialization and the growth of service sector have fundamentally restructured the economies

BOX 4.4   GLOBAL CONNECTIONS

North America operates within a system of networks and flows that connect places in profound ways. The United States and Canada have been fortunate in that both countries are key globalization arenas.

The impact of globalization has affected economic restructuring and social polarization and these processes have had profound affects. Many North American regions and their major cities have not only transformed their economies and their fortunes, they have transformed the lives of those who live in them.

In many chapters we feature ways in which the region is globally connected—politically, economically, socially, or environmentally.

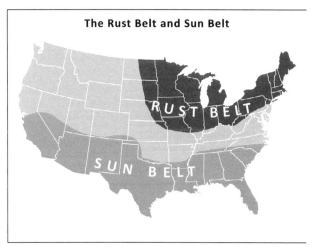

The Rust Belt and Sun Belt

MAP 4.3. The Rust Belt and the Sun Belt.
Source: Lisa Benton-Short

of North America. There has been a geographic shift from the so-called Rust Belt to the **Sun Belt**—an area south of the 38th parallel (map 4.3). The Rust Belt is characterized by economic and population loss and today is challenged to rebuild the economic base. The Sun Belt has tended to benefit from robust growth in the service sector and has seen population growth, all of which has impacted internal migration.

Internal migration (migration between states) is one outcome of deindustrialization and the shift in economic job growth sectors. More than half of those under forty live in a state other than their birth state. Relocation varies regionally. During the last twenty years, the Northeast and the Midwest lost population, while the South and West gained population. In Canada, internal migration concentrates into Ontario and Alberta, where young adults move to follow job opportunities in the Golden Horseshoe of Ontario and Alberta's booming oil-based economy.

Push and pull factors affect migration patterns. California's jobs and warm climate were the pull factors that encouraged people to move there in the 1950s. Later in the twentieth century, people were pushed from their homes by age, cold weather, and industrial pollution for the warmer but air-conditioned southern urban areas. In Canada, population also migrated south. Many retirees chose to settle in the mild and sunny Okanagan Valley of British Columbia.

Another major factor generating change is the link of places and cities to global trends. Globalization has also restructured North America in numerous ways. Many places focus on attracting international investment as much as regional or national investment and making stronger global connections in trade, travel, and tourism. Cities in both the United States and Canada have been fortunate in that key globalization arenas have been concentrated in Europe, North America, and East Asia. As we will see throughout the book, these economic transformations continue to play pivotal roles in shaping North America.

Questions for Discussion

1. Why does historical geography and settlement matter in contemporary United States and Canada?

2. What are examples of ways that different ethnicities and racial groups affect the cultural landscape?

3. What are population challenges facing the United States and Canada?

4. How is population distribution and movement affected by economic changes?

5. How does urbanization present both challenges and opportunities for sustainability?

6. How have the three economic sectors changed in importance in the United States and Canada over time?

Suggested Readings

Allen, J., and E. Turner. *We the People: An Atlas of America's Ethnic Diversity*. New York: Macmillan, 1988.

Bailey, A. *The Rise of a Modern Population Geography*. London: Hodder Education, 2005.

Benton-Short, L., ed. *Cities of North America: Contemporary Challenges in U.S. and Canadian Cities*. Lanham, MD: Rowman & Littlefield, 2014.

Brunn, St., Hays-Mitchell, M., Ziegler, D. and J. K. Graybill, eds. *Cites of the World, (6th Edition)*. Lanham MD: Rowman & Littlefield, 2016.

Chappell, N. and M. Hollander. *Aging in Canada*. Dons Mills, Ontario: Oxford University Press, 2013.

Ehrlich, P. *The Population Bomb*. New York: Ballantine, 1968.

Kinsella, K., and D. R. Phillips. "Global Aging: The Challenge of Success." *Population Bulletin* 60, no. 1 (March 2005).

Noble, A. G., ed. "To Build a New Land: Ethnic Landscapes in North America." Baltimore, Md.: Johns Hopkins, 1992.

Portes, A., and R. Rumbaut. *Immigrant America: a Portrait*. 4th ed. Oakland, Calif.: University of California Press. 2014.

Roy-Sole, M. "Keeping the Métis Faith Alive." *Canadian Geographic* 115 (March–April 1995): 36–46.

Schaefer, R. *Race and Ethnicity in the United States*. 8th ed. Boston, Mass.: Pearson, 2015.

Statistics Canada. "South Asians in Canada: Unity through Diversity." *Canadian Social Trends* 78 (Autumn 2005).

———. "Canada's Ethnocultural Mosaic, 2006 Census," Catalogue no. 97-562-X, 2006.

Uitto, J. I., and A. Ono, eds. *Population, Land Management, and Environmental Change*. Tokyo: United Nations University, 1996.

Weeks, J. *Population: an Introduction to Concepts and Issues*. 12th ed. Boston, Mass.: Wadsworth Publishing, 2015.

Internet Sources

U.S. Census, at www.census.gov/.

The U.S. Census has maps at: https://www.census.gov/geo/maps-data/.

Canadian Census, at www.statcan.gc.ca/

Population Pyramids, at https://www.populationpyramid.net/world/2017/

Canada's Population Clock, at http://www.livepopulation.com/country/canada.html

Central Intelligence Agency, World Factbook, at https://www.cia.gov/library/publications/the-world-factbook/

Population Reference Bureau. *World Population Data Sheet*, 2017, at http://www.prb.org/

U.S. Census Clock, at https://www.census.gov/popclock/

Part Two

MOVING TOWARD ECOREGIONS

PLACES

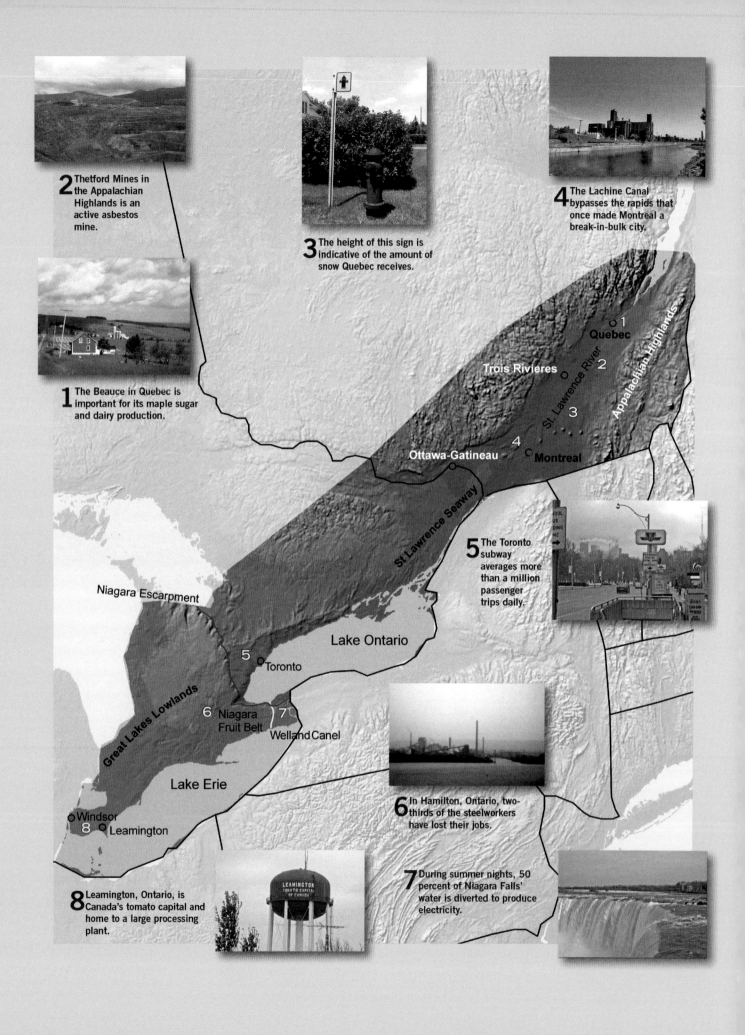

2 Thetford Mines in the Appalachian Highlands is an active asbestos mine.

3 The height of this sign is indicative of the amount of snow Quebec receives.

4 The Lachine Canal bypasses the rapids that once made Montreal a break-in-bulk city.

1 The Beauce in Quebec is important for its maple sugar and dairy production.

5 The Toronto subway averages more than a million passenger trips daily.

6 In Hamilton, Ontario, two-thirds of the steelworkers have lost their jobs.

8 Leamington, Ontario, is Canada's tomato capital and home to a large processing plant.

7 During summer nights, 50 percent of Niagara Falls' water is diverted to produce electricity.

Quebec 1
Trois Rivieres
2
St. Lawrence River
3
Appalachian Highlands
4
Ottawa-Gatineau
Montreal
St Lawrence Seaway
Niagara Escarpment
Lake Ontario
5 Toronto
Great Lakes Lowlands
6 Niagara Fruit Belt
7
Welland Canel
Lake Erie
Windsor
8 Leamington

5
THE CANADIAN CORRIDOR
A Shift in Core Value

Chapter Highlights

After reading this chapter you should be able to:

- Discuss Inner and Outer Canada and how the relationships may be changing
- Identify francophone and anglophone Canada
- Describe how the Canadian manufacturing sector evolved
- Discuss Montreal and Toronto and their place in Canada
- Explain how Quebec emerged into the twentieth century with the Quiet Revolution

Terms

break-in-bulk point
British North America Act
Canadien
cap and trade
Confederation
Corridor
Crown Land
cultural hearth
equalization payment

escarpment
General Agreement on Tariffs and Trade (GATT)
Golden Horseshoe
habitant
Inner Canada
locks
long lot
Lower Canada
Loyalist

Main Street
maîtres chez nous
National Policy
North American Free Trade Agreement (NAFTA)
Outer Canada
portage
Québécois nationalism
Quiet Revolution
rang system

Reciprocity Treaty of 1854
rift valley
Royal Proclamation of 1763
seigneur
seigneurie
tariff
Treaty of Paris (1763)
Upper Canada
vernacular

Places

Appalachian Uplands
Frontenac Axis
Great Lakes Lowlands

Hamilton, Ontario
Lake Erie
Lake Ontario
Leamington, Ontario

Niagara Escarpment
Niagara fruit belt
St. Lawrence Lowlands
St. Lawrence River

St. Lawrence Seaway
Trois-Rivières, Quebec
Welland Canal

Cities

Montreal, Quebec
(2016 CMA 4.1 million)

Ottawa–Gatineau
(2016 CMA 1.3 million)

Quebec City, Quebec
(2016 CMA 800,000)

Toronto, Ontario
(2016 CMA 5.9 million)

PHOTO 5.1. A Sugar Maple Tree in Ontario. The sugar maple is a species of maple native to the hardwood forests of eastern Canada. The shape of the leaf is well known—it is found on the Canadian flag and the sugar maple is the national tree of Canada. In the fall, the sugar maple's leaves turn yellow, brilliant orange, or red.

Source: iStock/mirceax

Introduction

"If some countries have too much history, Canada has too much geography," said Prime Minister William Mackenzie King in 1936 describing Canada, the second largest country on Earth. Canada is a country where its vast land mass obscures the fact that it has a relatively small population: it is the second largest country in the world, but its 35 million inhabitants make Canada only the thirty-ninth most populated country.

While expansive in land area, 90 percent of the population is within 100 miles (161 km) of the US border. The narrow 700-mile-long (1,127 km) **Corridor**, along the St. Lawrence River and Great Lakes is home to 61 percent of the entire country's population. The Corridor land area is about the size of England and Wales, or two-thirds the size of France. And although six of Canada's ten largest cities are situated along this southeastern border, most of the Corridor is open farmland and cities are hours apart (photo 5.1).

"The Corridor" is one of several terms that define this elongated region; others include "**Main Street,**" "axis," "heartland," and "Central Canada." Canada's core–periphery divide places the Corridor in **Inner Canada** and the rest of the country as periphery, **Outer Canada**. The Corridor is also the political, economic, demographic, and cultural core—the home of its two distinct European cultures.

Quebec remains francophone (French-speaking), and it is a distinct cultural region, especially along the St. Lawrence Lowlands area. Ontario and most of the other provinces are predominantly anglophone, English in language and culture.

In 1867, the nation formed, with its core and authority in the St. Lawrence and Great Lakes Corridor. The Corridor, Inner Canada, has been accused of exerting its might over the rest of the country, Outer Canada. Toronto, Ottawa, and Montreal dominate the eastern part of the country.

Canadian identity has been shaped by four basic factors: geographic extent, northern climate, cultural history, and natural resources. Each continues to redefine Canada, and most especially the Corridor. Climate change and shifting commodity economies have partially destabilized and redefined the twenty-first-century Canadian physical landscape.

The Corridor's once dominant manufacturing economy has been replaced by the growth of the raw material resource economy in the northwest. With resources in the temperate zones depleted, people are looking to the abundant resources in the untapped north, but in the process creating more greenhouse gas (GHG) emissions and reconfiguring the Inner Canada and Outer Canada economies.

Despite these changes, Canada has been more progressive than the United States in addressing its sustainable future. Corridor cities such as Toronto lead the way in embracing diversity, dealing with climate change and planning for a more sustainable future.

Physical Geography

Ninety-five percent of Quebec and Ontario, the Canadian Shield, is sparsely populated, but the other 5 percent, the lowlands Corridor, is the most densely populated region in Canada. Sandwiched between the Appalachian Uplands to the south and the Canadian Shield to the north, the Corridor strip is divided into the St. Lawrence Lowlands to the northeast and the Great Lakes Lowlands to the southwest. Separating the two subregions is the Frontenac Axis, which connects the massive Canadian Shield with the Adirondack outlier across the border in New York (map 5.1). The Corridor region is within the St. Lawrence River watershed (inclusive of the Great Lakes watershed), but it is not the entire watershed. The entire watershed of this ecoregion is divided by the US–Canada border.

BOX 5.1   DID YOU KNOW . . . INNER AND OUTER CANADA

Politically and culturally, Canada has bifurcated between Inner Canada (lowlands of Ontario and Quebec) and Outer Canada (the rest of the country). Inner Canada, the Corridor, has been the core of the country industrially, politically, and demographically.

The two distinct linguistic and cultural histories punctuate the Inner Canada favoritism. Quebec, once called **Lower Canada**, is mostly French-speaking and Roman Catholic, while Ontario, **Upper Canada**, is English and initially settled by **Loyalist** Protestants. (The lower and upper designations are in relation to the St. Lawrence River, where Upper Canada is at the upper reaches of the river.) Despite their differences, the heavily populated portions of Ontario and Quebec have had political, economic, and demographic control of Canada since **Confederation**.

Ottawa, the capital, positioned on the border between the provinces of Quebec and Ontario, is often accused by other Canadians of favoring the Corridor with an apparent monopoly on population, political clout, manufacturing, service, and research and development that leaves the rest of the country—98 percent

of the territory and 40 percent of the population—discontented. With a majority of the population, the Corridor is also disproportionately represented in the House of Commons, which reinforces the Corridor's dominance.

However, the balance of power within Canada is shifting. Robust economic growth in Alberta and British Columbia have given them new economic leverage. And power has shifted as well. No longer is the prime minister necessarily bound to the Corridor. Quebec's secession attempt, phrased as cultural separatism, has now been matched by Alberta's geographic separatism, where oil sand money has given them power to speak up about such matters as limiting the federal government's authority and such issues as "forced" bilingualism, gun control, and energy policy. Newfoundland has also challenged the Inner Canada dominance with its offshore oil deposits that have pumped new life into what had been a moribund economy.

Despite western and Maritime alienation, Canadian policies still favor economic, cultural, and political unification.

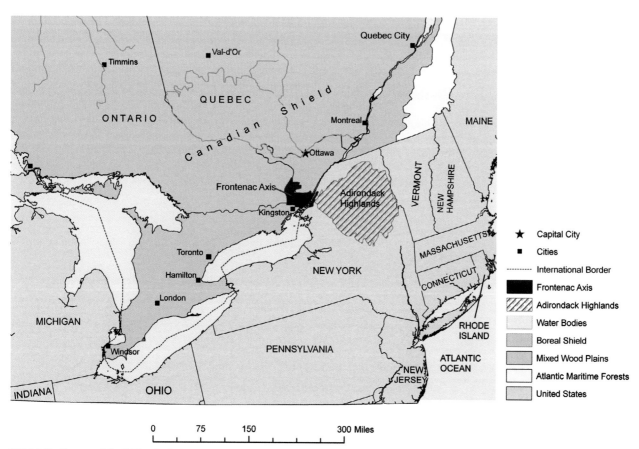

MAP 5.1. The Frontenac Axis, Dividing the St. Lawrence Lowlands (north of the axis) from the Great Lakes Lowlands (south of the axis). The Frontenac Axis connects the Canadian Shield with the New York Adirondacks. The Corridor Lowlands was a mixed wood forest prior to its current agricultural and urban use. Small portions of the forest remain and are protected.

Corridor Lowlands

The Corridor, the southernmost part of Canada, is in the same ecoregion as the American Midwest, but to the north it is a sub-region of colder climate.

The Corridor ecozone is the smallest in Canada, and although now populated and cleared, it was entirely forested when Europeans arrived. The Corridor deciduous mixed wood plain contained many sugar maples (Canada's national symbol) and moving north evolves into a boreal mixed and then coniferous forest.

The St. Lawrence Lowlands live up to their name, except for the igneous intrusion of the Monteregian Hills, rising 800 feet (250 m) above Montreal. The earthquake-prone St. Lawrence Lowlands are part of a **rift valley** (a valley formed by the sinking of land between two faults) that has registered about ten earthquakes each century.

The Champlain Sea, of which Lake Champlain is a remnant, inundated the St. Lawrence Lowlands plain for about two thousand years at the end of the last ice age. Fertile sediment from the sea unevenly covers the flat plain between Montreal and Quebec City. The plain is widest at Montreal and along the south side of the St. Lawrence.

Continuing southwest, hugging the northern shores of lakes Erie and Ontario, the Great Lakes Lowlands' glacially derived clay deposits cover all, except the exposed Niagara Escarpment limestone. The Great Lakes Lowlands is both an important agricultural area and one of the most densely populated in Canada (map 5.2).

Niagara Escarpment

The Niagara Escarpment is a geographic anomaly that begins in New York State, enters Canada at Niagara Falls, and then continues around the Michigan Basin (map 5.3). Separating lakes Ontario and Erie, the limestone and dolomite outcrop rises 200 feet (60 m) above the Ontario Plain. Several gorges cleave the **escarpment**, the most notable being the 7-mile (11 km) Niagara Gorge, where Niagara Falls has eroded the escarpment at a rate of 4 feet (1.2 m) a year. In seventy-five thousand years, the two Great Lakes will merge. But meanwhile, the escarpment creates a warming microclimate where fruit trees and wineries have flourished, although they now have given way to an increasingly suburbanized landscape.

Water

Canada has abundant freshwater. Much of that water feeds the St. Lawrence River, one of the continent's main natural transport routes, which connects the Atlantic and the interior. Both Natives and fur traders once **portaged** the river's two major obstacles, the Lachine Rapids and Niagara Falls. Later, the St. Lawrence Seaway bypassed the obstacles.

The St. Lawrence River begins near Kingston, Ontario, and courses along the ancient rift valley, draining into the Gulf of St. Lawrence estuary. The watershed includes the Great Lakes and reaches north into the Canadian Shield. Towns are positioned at river confluences, such as Kingston located at the northeastern end of Lake Ontario and Trois-Rivières located at the three mouths of the St. Maurice River.

Explorers LaSalle and Cartier sailed up the St. Lawrence River, hoping they had found the Northwest Passage. Cartier, obsessed with finding a route to China, followed the river and named the Lachine (China) Rapids in 1535.

Montreal, the head of ocean navigation, was founded at the rapids as a **break-in-bulk** city—all goods had to be portaged around the rapids to continue their journey. In 1825, the Lachine Canal bypassed the rapids and became the heart of Montreal's factory-laden industrial sector. The Lachine Canal launched the Corridor economy with lumber and wheat from the interior.

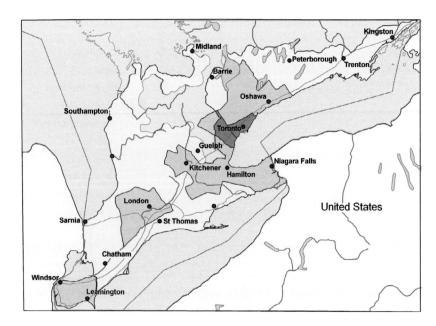

MAP 5.2. The Great Lakes Lowlands occupy the fertile region of Ontario from Lakes Ontario and Erie to the Canadian Shield. It is also the most densely populated part of Canada, with several large cities.

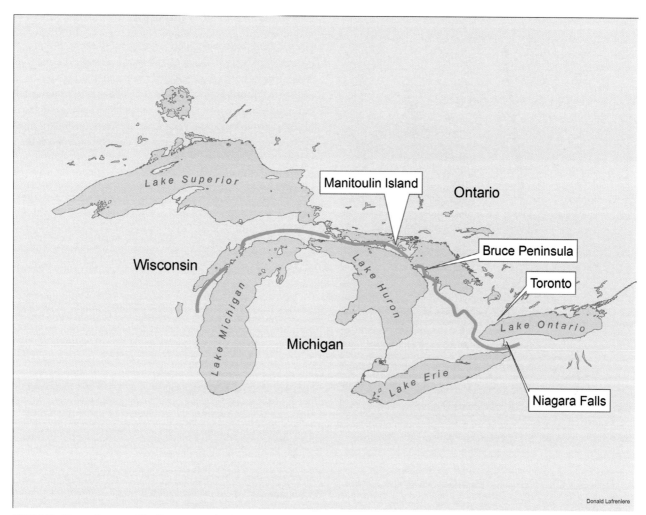

MAP 5.3. The Niagara Escarpment is a limestone cap that has eroded much more slowly than the surrounding rock. An obstacle for both the Erie and Welland canals, the escarpment was traversed by a series of locks.

But in 1959, the St. Lawrence Seaway opened and eroded the importance of the Lachine Canal. The canal closed for thirty-two years because of toxic sediment from years of industrial contamination. Since 1988, a prevention plan has eliminated the discharging of many industrial and agricultural chemicals into the river, and the canal reopened in 2002 as a pleasure boat waterway.

The Niagara Falls presented a physical obstacle to transport. The falls were bypassed by a series of five **locks** called the Welland Canals. The locks and the falls have become a lynchpin for tourism and hydropower economies. However, the challenges of climate change include maintaining energy and shipping economies.

The Niagara River falls into the glacially formed Niagara Gorge and in the process generates 2.4 million kilowatts (enough power to light twenty-four million 100-watt bulbs) of hydroelectric power for the Eastern United States and Canada. In order to maintain both the tourism economy and generating hydropower, Niagara's flow was cut in half during the nighttime hours of the April–October tourist season. Hydropower's

importance as an energy source has grown during the twenty-first century, as energy shortfalls and the pollution of coal-burning power plants become major impediments to reducing GHG emissions. Private Canadian companies built hydropower generators on **Crown Land** (government-owned land) in order to expand waterpower production and reduce the carbon footprint.

The St. Lawrence Seaway system stretches 2,038 nautical miles, connecting all the Great Lakes to the St. Lawrence River and the Atlantic Ocean. The first link in the chain was built in 1829, when the first of four sequential Welland Canals circumvented Niagara Falls. The canal was rebuilt each time to satisfy the ever-larger ships passing through the canal, much as today the system is once again under the same threat (photo 5.2). The St. Lawrence Seaway opened in 1959.

The Seaway, a joint Canadian and US project, opened the Great Lakes to ocean-going vessels during the ice-free season (usually March to December) and also enhanced power generation. The system allowed bulk carriers of the post–World War II era to pass from one lake to another, to the Atlantic, and back.

PHOTO 5.2. Welland Canal, St. Catherine's, Ontario. Since 1829, ships have been raised a total of 327 feet between Lake Ontario and Lake Erie. The canal has been rebuilt four times to accommodate ever-larger ships. It helped support a large manufacturing workforce in Welland until the 1990s, when globalization closed many companies and forced others to downsize.

Since the late twentieth century, supertankers and ocean-going container ships have been too large to fit in the Seaway locks. These large ships must unload to smaller ships at Montreal or Atlantic port, which increases the cost of shipping. Seaway shipping tonnage has declined over the past twenty-five years. About 80 percent of the Seaway traffic is bulk cargo from the interior—grain, iron ore, and Powder River Basin low-sulfur coal—which is popular with European utilities. The remainder is smaller containerized "feeder" ships carrying manufactured goods.

Since 2000, the Seaway and Great Lakes have experienced a decrease in carrying capacity, an increase in the cost of moving cargo, and an increase in ship sizes. Suggestions to improve the Seaway include conserving water, shifting energy production, reducing sprawl, and cleaning up industrial practices.

The St. Lawrence water levels have always fluctuated, but climate change has exacerbated fluctuations and caused shipping problems. For example, lower water levels in the western portion of the river require increased dredging. Additional problems include invasive species and the system's aging infrastructure, which requires maintenance.

Climate

Most of Canada lies north of the 49th parallel, about the latitude of Frankfurt, Germany, but Canadian weather is usually colder than European cities at equivalent latitudes because the North Atlantic Drift and wind circulation patterns warm the European plains. Lower Canadian temperatures are due to the high western mountains blocking oceanic warmth, and the lack of large bodies of water to moderate the temperature leaves the region with the more extreme temperature fluctuations of a continental climate.

The Corridor seasonal climate of long, harsh winters and shorter warm, humid summers progresses north along the St. Lawrence Lowlands, where winters become extreme. Precipitation is ample, about sixty inches annually, much of it as snow. On the leeward side of the Great Lakes, the water moderates the climate, including heavy lake-effect snow; some areas average one hundred inches annually.

Along the St. Lawrence Corridor area, winter sets in by mid-December, when the river freezes leaving Montreal icebound. Unstable Gulf and Arctic winter weather systems can spawn major storms, blizzards, and ice storms.

Historical Geography and Settlement

Prior to European arrival, sixty thousand to eighty thousand Aboriginals lived in the Corridor lowlands. Algonquin lived along the St. Lawrence waterway; the Iroquoian Confederacy lived near the Great Lakes. The small Algonquin bands lived as nomadic hunters and fishers, while the Iroquoian agriculturalists lived in concentrated communal villages composed of up to three thousand residents. Today, about eleven thousand Algonquin live in small communities across Quebec and eastern Ontario, and part of the Iroquoian Confederacy settled north of lakes Erie and Ontario.

The French and Algonquins established early fur trade relations, but this lasted only as long as the Natives were of use to the Europeans and the Europeans to the Natives. Land loss for the Natives accelerated after the American Revolution, when many Loyalists migrated to Canada, necessitating land acquisitions from the Lake Ontario Aboriginals.

In 1867, the **British North America Act** created the Dominion of Canada, consisting of Nova Scotia and New Brunswick, Quebec (Lower Canada), and Ontario (Upper Canada). Soon after, Manitoba (1870), British Columbia (1871), and Prince Edward Island (1873) joined the decentralized federation called Confederation. In order to keep peace within the linguistically split country, Canada adopted a federalist government that granted political authority to the central government for foreign affairs and national and interprovincial communications and transportation, while provinces had authority over land use, education, and language.

BOX 5.2 NATIONAL PARKS: THE SAGUENAY–ST. LAWRENCE MARINE PARK

Shortly after the United States designated its first national park (Yellowstone, 1872), Canada designated its first national park, Banff, in 1885. Today, national parks are administered by Parks Canada under whose stewardship rests a wide range of protected areas, encompassing National Historic Sites, National Park Reserves, and National Marine Conservation Areas.

The National Marine Conservation Areas are a relatively new creation in the park system. There are only three such parks currently. One of them is in Quebec: the Saguenay–St. Lawrence Marine Park. It is the first national park in Quebec to protect a purely marine environment. The park is located at the confluence of the Saguenay and the St. Lawrence Rivers. The area draws significant numbers of whales, seals, and sea birds who come for the rich food supply stirred up by the mixing of waters.

Historically, the beluga whale (or white whale) was abundant in this area (photo 5.3). However, intensive commercial whaling in the early twentieth century almost led to its extinction. There were an estimated eight thousand to ten thousand belugas in the waters of the Saint Lawrence in 1900. Today, there are about nine hundred. The need to protect the beluga and a large part of its summer habitat prompted the creation of the Saguenay–St. Lawrence Marine Park in 1998.

Despite the designation as a national park, there are challenges: the sheer volume of shipping traffic means a higher risk of oil spills, and the speed of ships can cause collisions with the whales. Use of personal watercraft, like jetskis, can also cause problems. The quick and irregular movements of these jetskis are problematic for whales and seals, particularly the belugas and their young, since they have difficulty evaluating their trajectory and avoiding them, which increases the risk of collision.

At the initiative of Parks Canada and Fisheries and Oceans Canada, the pilots of merchant and passenger vessels have been asked to adapt their sailing in areas frequented by whales. In addition, all ships must stay a minimum of 440 yards (400 meters) distance from any threatened or endangered species and the use of jetskis and hovercraft are prohibited within the park boundaries.

PHOTO 5.3. Beluga Whales. The beluga whale is an Arctic and sub-Arctic cetacean that has adapted to its Arctic environment. They are distinguished by their all-white color and the protuberance at the front of its head that houses an echolocation organ.
Source: iStock/Navidim

Quebec

The French were the first Europeans to colonize Canada. The initial French immigrants traded copper kettles and beads for furs to satisfy the European beaver felt hat fashion of the time. Most Quebec settlers were Catholic, an imprint that remains visible on the landscape to the present day.

Fur traders eschewed agriculture, but the French Crown decided that permanent settlers would strengthen the French New World position and began encouraging families and women to emigrate. Few French were naturally inclined to immigrate to the hostile, harsh New France. Immigration was also hampered by the cost; the French lacked the subsidized

BOX 5.3 GREAT LAKES INVASIVE SPECIES AND SYSTEMS THINKING

Invasive species are introduced to a habitat and thrive because they lack predators or parasites. What we call invasive species are part of the dynamic nature of ecology. Nature is not steady state. Change happens in the world, and humans are often the agent of this change, though other animals and weather can also be agents of change. Invasive species have existed before human intervention, but humans have accelerated the changes. Many invasive species are transported by humans, often with unintended consequences.

Unintended Consequences

The largest and most evident unintended consequence of invasive species is their pushing out native species, thereby upsetting the ecological order. For example, the introduction of plants, such as purple loosestrife, in the Great Lakes was intentional, but the full impact of the plant in its new habitat was not understood. This nonindigenous plant became invasive largely because it is a prolific seed producer of up to 2.7 million seeds annually.

The introduction of invasive species has accelerated since the globalization of trade. More than a third of the invasive species in the Great Lakes have arrived since the opening of the St. Lawrence Seaway. Most invasive species arrived via ballast water discharged from ships, such as the zebra mussel, which was released into the Great Lakes from a Caspian Sea tanker's ballast water in 1988. Regulations requiring exchanging ballast water prior to entering the Great Lakes have been ineffectual.

Local and Ecoregional Impacts

Species brought into new ecosystems lack predators and proliferate far beyond their native habitat abilities, resulting

in species that overrun native species. The Great Lakes have received more than 140 exotic species since the 1800s. The most recent Great Lakes invasive species threat, the Asian carp, is being held back by artificial means along the Chicago River. When a nonindigenous species flourishes in a new habitat, it upsets the ecosystem energy flow. The Asian carp could quickly become invasive because of their mobility and their voracious appetites. The effect of an invasive species on food supply was demonstrated when the zebra mussel reduced the available food and spawning habitat for local fish populations. The Asian carp entry into the Great Lakes ecosystems could result in a reinforcing feedback loop. With no controls to stop their entry, the carp begin to upset the ecosystem, resulting in more carp. Without government intervention before the carp's entry, the fish will destroy the ecosystem and the fishing and tourist industry tied to the existing system.

The following are a few of the significant invasive species:

- Zebra mussel
- Sea Lampry
- Purple loosestrife
- Asian carp

Invasive species reduce the complexity and diversity of an ecosystem, making it less resilient. The economic and ecological impact of these invasive species has been significant, including reduction in the fishery and damage to water supplies. Control mechanisms run into the billions, although means of effective control or eradication of many of these species have not been found.

---

passage practiced by the British. Indentured servants who immigrated worked for three years to pay their passage, but they were rewarded after with land, something they had no access to in France.

In the seventeenth century, the North American colonies had far more French immigrants than British. But the hard life, hostile Natives, and cold weather disenchanted many French settlers. About two-thirds returned to the mother country.

New France settlers were divided socioeconomically into a two-class model, the *seigneurs* and *habitants*. The *seigneurs* were aristocrats appointed by the king and given *seigneuries*, which were large swaths of land (the Seigneury of Beaupré, for example, was forty-eight miles long and eighteen miles deep). The *seigneurs* subgranted their land to the *habitants*, who were expected to pay rent with a portion of their crop. A wide cultural gap separated the *seigneurs* and the *habitants* from the beginning. The *seigneurs* were enlightened by the new modern Baroque outlook. The *habitants* were peasants or lower-middle-class Roman Catholics from Normandy, and more conservative. A few other settlers were minor government officials and a

small merchant middle class, hoping that time spent in Canada would pay off in the future.

Most of the *seigneuries* were located fronting the St. Lawrence and its tributaries. The French Canadians initially settled riverfront land in the distinctive long-lot style imported from Normandy (photo 5.4). **Long lots** are about one-tenth as wide as they are long and consist of about seventy to ninety acres. The narrow width maximized the number of farmers with river frontage and created a village-like community. The lot depth encompassed a variety of uses: arable land, pasture, and timber for building material and fuel. As waterside lots filled, further *rangs* or rows were created away from the water, in what is known as the ***rang* system**.

In 1713, the British gained access to the Maritimes and the eastern seaboard. British and French both claimed land, with Natives caught between the two but usually siding with the British. Both French and British sent troops, and military engagements led to the Seven Years' War. The war was ended by the **Treaty of Paris (1763)**, when the French relinquished their New World holdings to the British. The British and Scots

BOX 5.4   CLIMATE CHANGE IN THE CORRIDOR

Since the 1970s, Environmental Canada, the US Environmental Protection Agency (EPA) and numerous state and local agencies have been actively improving the water quality in the Great Lakes via the identification of point source polluters and nonpoint source pollution.

However, climate change remains a looming issue. There are many possible impacts.

For example, more mid-winter snow melts and rainstorms—and more frequent heavy rainfalls, especially in spring—may lead to higher soil-erosion rates, meaning that the Great Lakes Rivers are likely to carry more soil into harbors. One study found that higher air temperatures are already warming the Great Lakes, blocking ice from forming, and increasing rates of evaporation that may lead to lower lake levels.*

Another impact is on invasive species. Some researchers are concerned that invasive or non-native species may dominate the Great Lakes aquatic ecosystem due to forecasted increases in water temperature. Still other researches note that climate change could allow coldwater species to thrive, pushing out invasive species. Freshwater species at all trophic levels may be impacted by temperature change and apex dynamics.

A third impact could be on the shipping industry itself. The shipping industry may be at risk as large cargo vessels will have less draft due to lower lake levels. Lower lake levels will be created by the increased melting of ice, increased lake temperatures, increased evaporation, and diminished ice. Lower water levels in the Great Lakes may increase operating costs because cargo companies will have to carry less tonnage to increase ship draft. Long distance carriers depend upon the economies of scale and often work within very thin margins. With a modest lowering of the Great Lakes, shipping costs are projected to increase between 5 and 22 percent by the year 2030. Shorter freeze periods were once thought of as a positive component of climate change, but researchers note that longer shipping times will not translate to more economic productivity.†

It is difficult to predict exactly what changes will occur with precipitation patterns due to climate change. The future may include periods of both too much and too little precipitation. With increased precipitation and too much water in the system it will be impossible to release enough to prevent flooding. But with too little, there will not be enough for shipping.‡

While the impacts of climate change impacts are uncertain, one thing is certain: the Great Lakes and St. Lawrence Seaway are complex ecosystems that we do not yet fully understand, making it even more difficult to predict changes that may occur.

---

*Keith Schneider, "Great Lakes Ports and Shipping Companies Counfounded by Climate Changes and Water Levels," Circle of Blue, August 17, 2012, at http://www.circleofblue.org/2012/world/great-lakes-ports-and-shipping-companies-confounded-by-climate-changes-and-water-levels/

†Phillip G. Levasseur and Dane McKinney, "Introduction: The Great Lakes-The St. Lawrence River: Under Climate Change," April 22, 2010, at http://www.ce.utexas.edu/prof/mckinney/ce397/Topics/StLawrence/StLawrence(2010).pdf

‡Alana Bartolai, Lingli He, Ardith Hurst, Linda Mortsch, Robert Paelke, and Donald Scavia, "Climate change as a driver of change in the Great Lakes St. Lawrence River Basin," Journal of Great Lakes Research 41, no. 1, 45–58, January, 2015, at http://www.sciencedirect.com/science/article/pii/S0380133014002378

PHOTO 5.4. The Long Lots of the Original French Settlers. The *rang* or range system differentiates Quebec from English grid pattern settlements. Long lots were narrow strips of land that allowed many farmers to have river frontage. As river frontage filled, another set of long lots would be made along a road parallel to the first, establishing a second *rang*, and later, a third, fourth, and so on.

established townships along the outer edges of the southern *seigneuries*, south to the American border and west following the Ottawa River. Over time, English, French, and Aboriginals occupied the region.

While French immigration ended after the war, a high birth-rate supported rapid population growth. The French expanded settlements onto British land or to the adjacent American Northeast. From 1840 until the twentieth century, push and pull factors prevailed, pushing many French Canadians away from the dominant agricultural life and pulling them to mill jobs in the burgeoning Industrial Revolution in the United States. Québécois heritage continues to influence many northeastern towns.

The Treaty of Paris also established Aboriginal "rights" to the New World, through the **Royal Proclamation of 1763**, which would later be used to determine the definition of Aboriginal title and rights in the territory west of Quebec. The proclamation, actually a strategic tool to retain Native and Aboriginal allies during the colonial wars, recognized prior Aboriginal occupancy and permitted self-government and compensation for their land. However, over the ensuing years, immigrants acquired land at the expense of the Aboriginals. In 1982, Canadian Aboriginals fought back and used the Royal Proclamation as the basis for Aboriginal title. They gained constitutional protection for fishing, logging, and hunting rights, as well as an inherent right of self-government.

Ontario

Aboriginals and nomadic French fur traders inhabited Ontario's dense forests until the American Revolution, when ten thousand Tory Loyalists became the first permanent European settlers. With their land confiscated in the United States, Loyalists sought refuge in the remaining British colonies. They moved to Nova Scotia and New Brunswick, but most chose Quebec. Cultural differences—anglophone and Protestant versus francophone and Catholic—were enough impetus to carve a new, western colony, Upper Canada, located southwest of Kingston along Lake Ontario. Based on their Loyalist participation in the Revolution, the British gave the settlers provisions and land.

During the War of 1812, Americans, thinking Canadians desired liberty from British rule, attacked Canada and were thwarted. Although the war itself was a stalemate, it demonstrated an early sense of an independent Canadian nationhood. Canadian immigration shifted from Americans to a wave of British and Irish settlers fleeing difficult economic conditions in Europe. The best agricultural land was settled by 1830. By Confederation, some 1.4 million migrants had settled in Upper Canada; another 1.2 million were split between Quebec and Atlantic Canada.

Upon Confederation, Upper Canada, renamed Ontario, occupied only the lowlands area, but it would expand four times in the succeeding years to incorporate newly acquired lands in the wild, rough-hewn Canadian Shield. However, the best farmland was along the Corridor, so when good Corridor land was no longer available, the sons and daughters of the large rural families migrated to the rich prairie farmland of Manitoba, while others populated the growing cities of Ontario. By the time of Confederation, Ontario had the largest population and had established a national industrial economy.

Cultural Perspectives

The Corridor has two distinct cultural landscapes. To the northeast, Quebec's landscape reflects French settlement patterns, from long lots to cultural artifacts. Although the culture has changed significantly since the 1960s' **Quiet Revolution**, the artifacts remain and are cherished as an important part of the province's French history.

Southwest of the Frontenac Axis are the Great Lakes Lowlands, similar in physical landscape but anglophone culturally. The **Golden Horseshoe**—the agglomerated urban area surrounding the southwest end of Lake Ontario—highlights the Great Lakes Lowlands, which has become the most multicultural region in Canada.

The French Canadian presence along the St. Lawrence River has remained strong for more than two hundred years. Of the thousands of French who had migrated to New France, less than ten thousand remained by 1763. They became the seed stock for the eight million Francophones who live in the province today.

French-speaking Canadians from Quebec will often refer to themselves as Québécois. Through the 1990s, the term *Québécois* also indicated a preference for the Parti Québécois or separatist notions of **Québécois nationalism**, but that meaning has diffused into one indicating a more general and proud reference to the people, society, and nation. In November 2006, Prime Minister Stephen Harper supported the recognition of several Quebec cultural nations within a united Canada, including the Métis, the Canadian Aboriginals, and the Québécois. Today the term *Québécois* is more likely to mean a proud descendant of the original settlers in New France. The terms *French Canadian* or **Canadien** also refer to New France ancestry but without the separatist innuendos of *Québécois*.

The French **cultural hearth** is in Quebec, where more than 80 percent of the population is francophone. However, the French influence reaches beyond Quebec. In New Brunswick, 34 percent are francophone, mostly along its eastern shore. Ontario's eastern counties bordering Quebec also have a large French-speaking population.

The French have maintained their language despite the rest of Canada becoming English-speaking. Montreal—the world's second-largest francophone city—is bilingual. It is possible to live one's entire life speaking English while living in the francophone hearth. Anglophones have congregated in Montreal, while Quebec's rural lowlands and Quebec City are generally francophone.

The French language in Quebec is quite different from Parisian French. The original French inhabitants came to Quebec in the seventeenth and early eighteenth centuries, and after 1760 the settlers had little contact with the motherland, so the language has evolved from the northern French dialect of the early settlers. The surrounding English-speaking populace, the Aboriginal contact, and Quebec's environment influenced the development of a francophone Canadian vocabulary. Idioms and slang developed independently in both France and Quebec. The words and pronunciation of Quebec French and Parisian French differ more than the pronunciation of American English and British English.

Quebec City is the center of the francophone hearth. Almost everyone has been a unilingual francophone, but slowly in the twenty-first century even this is changing, much to the chagrin of those who feel that bilingualism will be the downfall of the francophone landscape. For example, when entering a shop in Quebec City, one will be greeted initially with a friendly "Bonjour!" but if the customer proves to be less than fluent in French the college-age storekeepers will immediately break into an almost flawless English. The youth seem to be both proud of their native language yet aware that speaking English opens

PHOTO 5.5. Ville de Quebec, founded in 1608, was built in the style of a medieval walled French city, with steep-roofed and dormered sturdy fieldstone buildings. It is the only walled city in the United States and Canada. The homes in the city are also reminiscent of northern French architecture, and the influence of northern France extends even to the language and the food. Visiting Ville de Quebec is an inexpensive way to feel like you are in France, only better, because the people are friendly and gracious in their acceptance of less-than-perfect French.

TABLE 5.1. Population Density, 2017

	Canada	United States	Ontario	Quebec	New York City	Los Angeles	Toronto	Montreal
Per square mile	9.27	90	5.33	2.25	28,000	8,300	1,300	1,295
Per square kilometer	3.9	35.3	14.8	5.9	72,519	21,496	3,368	3,356

Source: US Census; Statistics Canada

many opportunities. Only time will tell whether the French language will be diluted throughout the lowlands.

The French Canadian culture can be seen in the **vernacular** (common style using local building materials) landscape which has evolved to suit the countryside and includes steep roofs with flared eaves, porches, and colorful twin-gabled homes (photo 5.5). Roman Catholic artifacts dot the countryside—life-size crucifixes, monasteries, and silver-towered churches—although all are slowly disappearing on the rural landscape, as both rural culture and the Church's influence diminish.

The Roman Catholic Church has been the most powerful social and cultural institution in Quebec. The Church regulated society and its social services, so it became the de facto state during the late nineteenth century until the 1960s, when dramatic changes occurred and the Church's influence declined. Multiple reasons for the decline of the Church include its failure to embrace birth control, the insular and limited educational system, and the emphasis on an agrarian lifestyle. But this all changed after World War II and the Quiet Revolution.

Population, Immigration, and Diversity

Canada is a sparsely populated country, far less densely populated than the United Kingdom or France, and its neighbor the United States. Within Canada, both Ontario and Quebec are more densely populated than the country as a whole, and the majority live within the narrow Corridor (table 5.1). Fully 61 percent of Canada's total population lives in the area from Windsor to Quebec City (map 5.4).

In 2016, the Quebec provincial population surpassed eight million and was the second largest in Canada. Until the twentieth century, two-thirds lived in rural areas. Most of the riverside counties were Roman Catholic and francophone, while Appalachian Upland counties usually were anglophone and Protestant. Although the Quebec population had grown rapidly by natural increase, the English in Quebec grew more by immigration. According to Canada's most recent census (2016), 4 million of the 8 million living in Quebec said they spoke only French, while 3.5 million residents said they spoke both French and English.

The total population of Ontario is about 13.4 million. Ontario's Golden Horseshoe is the most densely populated, economically prosperous, and industrialized zone in Canada (map 5.5). With more than eight million people, the Golden Horseshoe contains one-quarter of Canada's population, and 75 percent of Ontario's.

Immigration and Diversity

Historically, many Canadians have immigrated to the United States, especially prior to the beginning of US immigration inspections in 1894. Up until this point, some Canadians and many European immigrants escaped stringent immigration

BOX 5.5 THE QUIET REVOLUTION

Quebec was an insular rural province until World War II exposed many veterans to new places and ideas that took shape politically during the 1960s. During this period, the social, political, industrial, and population dimensions of Quebec changed radically, resulting in a modern urban society with two major urban centers: Montreal and Quebec City.

Quebec had always been a Roman Catholic province, where religion dominated society. But the Quiet Revolution secularized the province, and following the slogan of *maîtres chez nous* ("masters of our own house"), shed its dependence on religious education, its ideas of birth control, and its rural folk culture. The birth of an assertive French Canadian nationalism replaced Catholicism, favoring francophone business over anglophone, and supporting the ascendancy of the separatist Parti Québécois.

But as the province industrialized and grew economically, its birth rate plummeted from one of the highest to the lowest in the nation. The Québécois feared losing francophone culture and possibly political power. Instead, the revolution spawned separatist ideals.

Over the ensuing years separatism spread, and through the 1990s the Parti Québécois gained Parliamentary representation and power. The separatist movement was split between those who favored federalism and those who favored secession from Canada.

In 1976, Canada officially became a bilingual country, in order to appease those separatists who feared that the French language would be lost both because of their lower birth rate and because of an increase in immigrant populations. Despite the bilingual victory, the Quebec government enforced the almost exclusive use of French in Quebec. Today, provincial documents are in French alone, while national documents are bilingual. Many Canadians, including anglophone Quebecers, continue to grumble at the enforcement of French within the classroom and the strict use of French within Quebec.

In 1995, the Québécois separatist movement reignited a province-wide vote on succession. The province voted to remain within Confederation by a slim margin. Since that time, occasional bursts of separatism still erupt.

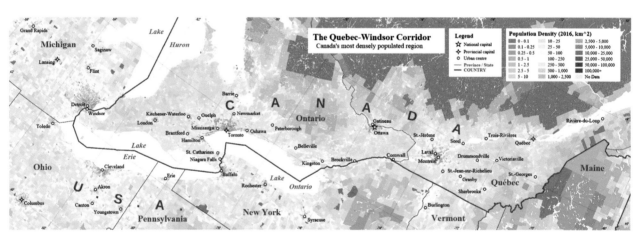

MAP 5.4. Fully 60 percent of Canada's total population lives in the area from Windsor to Quebec City.

inspections at US ports of entry and freely crossed over from Canada into the United States. Many Canadians continue to emigrate from Canada to the United States today.

Another emigrating group has been the Québécois; since 1960, an estimated 610,000 have left Quebec for other provinces (namely Ontario) and US cities. Reasons for Québécois emigration range across Quebec's language laws, policies, and economic health. First Anglophones left the province during the separatist regimes of the 1970s and 1980s, but francophone Quebecers have also pursued opportunity in Ontario or the United States. The émigrés are often in their prime earning years, leaving behind the aging, which increases the tax burden for those who remain. The more that leave, the higher the taxes for the remaining populace.

Today, however, it is immigration, not emigration that is the dominant demographic trend. Recent immigration has fueled regional population growth, although the sources of migrants have changed markedly since the 1980s. Asian and African immigrants have increased, and Europe and North American immigrants have decreased. And, as is true of migration settlement patterns in North America, immigrants are settling primarily in cities. Immigrants to Canada favor the five largest urban centers: Toronto, Vancouver, Montreal, Calgary, and Ottawa–Gatineau.

The primary immigrant city is Toronto, where eighty-five thousand migrate annually. In Toronto, 150 languages are spoken and 50 percent of the residents are immigrants—the highest proportion of immigrants in either the US or Canadian

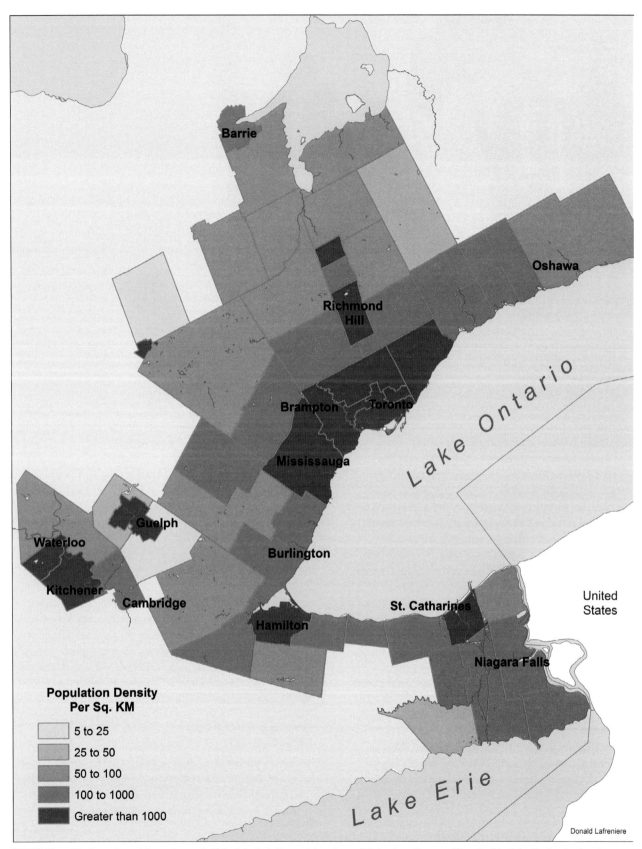

Population Density Per Sq. KM

	5 to 25
	25 to 50
	50 to 100
	100 to 1000
	Greater than 1000

Barrie

Oshawa

Richmond Hill

Brampton   Toronto

Mississauga

Lake Ontario

Guelph

Waterloo

Burlington

Kitchener

Cambridge

Hamilton   St. Catharines

United States

Niagara Falls

Lake Erie

Donald Lafreniere

MAP 5.5. The golden horseshoe, at the western end of lake Ontario, is the most densely populated and wealthy area of Canada. It includes the Greater Toronto Metropolitan Area. Twenty percent of Canada's and more than half of Ontario's population lives in the Golden Horseshoe.

Source: Statistics Canada, at http://geodepot.statcan.ca/diss/highlights/page9/page9a_e.cfm

PHOTO 5.6. Sponsors, family, and others welcome Syrian refugees at Toronto's Pearson International Airport.

Source: iStock/stacey_newman

cities. Many cities have tried to parlay the diversity of their populations into identities as "global cities" or "cosmopolitan cities." In 1998, Toronto—known for its "hyperdiverse" population including 44 percent foreign-born residents from South and East Asia, Latin America, and the Caribbean—adopted the motto "Our Diversity, Our Strength" (photo 5.6).

Cities in Canada are becoming more ethnically diverse, largely because of Canada's connection with the British Empire. During the nineteenth century, Irish Catholics migrated, but by the twentieth century the immigrant population was global and often outside of the British Empire, including Eastern Europeans, Caribbean, and Asian immigrants. For those living in countries once part of the former British Empire, "Commonwealth of Nations" status gives someone priority criteria for applying to immigrate. This is one difference between the US and Canadian migration policies.

The primary city for French-speaking immigrants is Montreal. Haiti is the largest source, but others have arrived from Africa and South America. More than 50 percent of Canadian immigrants enter the economy at below the poverty level. Even those with good linguistic abilities and education are only slowly assimilated into the general populace and job market.

Since the defeat of the 1995 separatist vote, Quebec has redefined its immigrant identity from one of political separatism, a resistance identity as a nation, to one of accommodating distinct societies within greater Canada.

Urban Trends

Eighty percent of Canada's population is now urban, and eight of Canada's twelve largest cities, including the largest—Toronto and Montreal—are within the Corridor.

The Corridor includes four major cities:

- Quebec City, the French Canadian cultural hearth;
- Montreal, the break-in-bulk city at the Lachine Rapids;
- Ottawa–Gatineau, the capital city, located on the border between Ontario and Quebec; and
- Toronto, located at a shortcut to reach the interior.

Other cities of note in the Corridor include Trois-Rivières in Quebec and Hamilton, Kitchener–Waterloo, and London in Ontario. Trois-Rivières, whose economy is based on the pulp and paper industry, proved to be well situated for two reasons: (1) Trois-Rivières marks the sea level for the St. Lawrence and tidal fluctuations affect points east, and (2) lumber could be easily transported down the subsidiary rivers to the St. Lawrence.

Hamilton, Kitchener–Waterloo, and London form a squat triangular area in the Great Lakes Lowlands south of Toronto and are in the most populated area of the province outside of Toronto. Hamilton is the former steel town of Canada, while Kitchener is a blue-collar, automobile-oriented city. Waterloo is a university town with high-tech industry. London is home to Western Ontario University and is a manufacturing city.

Quebec City, Ville de Quebec
(2016 CMA 800,000)

In 1608, Samuel de Champlain established the first permanent settlement of Quebec (*qebec* is a Micmaq word for "the narrows") on a defensive bluff overlooking the narrows of the St. Lawrence.

Originally established as a fur-trading outpost, Quebec City became the administrative and cultural center for New France. However, the city's importance waned for two reasons: (1) the fur trade moved farther west, making Montreal the main outpost, and (2) the British gained control of Quebec in 1759. For a while, the province almost had a majority British population,

but Quebec City has once again reclaimed its place as the cultural and political center for Québécois society. More than 90 percent of the residents speak French.

Quebec City is distinctive because of its European appearance. Quebec was built as a typical early-seventeenth-century medieval French city and is the only preserved walled city in North America. Quebec City has grown well beyond the medieval walls, in the form of a typical North American suburban landscape, but the walled city remains intact after a rehabilitation effort in the 1960s (albeit thoroughly tourist-oriented) and has been declared a UNESCO World Heritage site (photo 5.7).

Tourism and regional seasonal activities have provided the city with an economic base, as has its role as a government town. Estimates are that one in five jobs is with the federal government, and over the last several years, the federal government has added twenty thousand jobs in the capital region. Other industries revolve around its transportation network and resource processing. It also boasts the largest technology park in Canada. The 2016 Census showed that the metro area is home to more engineers, scientists, and PhDs per capita than any other city in Canada.

As with many Canadian cities, Quebec City has been a leader in sustainability for more than two decades. For example,

- In 1992, it actively participated in the Earth Summit in Rio de Janiero.
- In 1996, it produced a report for the international community listing its sustainable development actions.
- In 2002, it participated in the World Summit on Sustainable Development in Johannesburg for which it prepared and presented Quebec's Report on Sustainable Development.
- It has organized summits, forums, and symposiums to encourage civil society and governments to commit to sustainable development.

Montreal
(2016 CMA 4.1 million)

Montreal was founded in 1642 on an island at the break-in-bulk point where the Lachine Rapids impeded travel on the St. Lawrence River. (Montreal takes its name from the best-known of the island hills, "Île de Mont-réal.") Originating as a mission to convert the Natives, Montreal developed as a fur trade port. For the first hundred years, Montreal's growth was inhibited by fierce battles with neighboring Iroquois. The city walls protected Vieux-Montreal, although unlike Quebec City's, the walls were torn down in the first decades of the nineteenth century as the city grew.

Montreal's nineteenth-century economy concentrated on finance, transportation, and manufacturing, most of it dominated by the majority anglophone population. But geography shaped another aspect of the growing city in the early twentieth century. Canada did not endorse Prohibition as did the United States, so Montreal—being close to the border—served as a convenient getaway for alcohol and raucous nightlife; its reputation continued after Prohibition was repealed.

During the 1950s, the city cleaned up its rowdy image. The city was further enhanced with the opening of the St. Lawrence Seaway in 1959, the 1967 Montreal Expo, and the 1976 Summer Olympics, all of which brought visitors to the province. Montreal is also an important rail and port city connecting the Great Lakes and the St. Lawrence Seaway.

During the first half of the twentieth century, Montreal was the largest city in Canada, but it lost that designation to Toronto during the 1970s when the separatist movement threatened the stability of Quebec. During this time, new language laws gave primacy to the French language and prompted many Anglophones to leave, including corporate headquarters that relocated to Toronto. Montreal remains the second city of Canada and has continued to grow, but at a slower rate

BOX 5.6 ICONIC IMAGES: THE MONTREAL OLYMPIC GAMES

The Summer Olympic Games of 1976 was held in Montreal. A specially designed brand new complex was built, Olympic Park/Parc Olympique, to hold many of the main events.

The new buildings and elaborate Games cost a great deal of money, almost $1.5 billion at a time when Games revenues were limited. The Montreal Games took place before the lucrative television contracts. The result was a huge loss and major debt for local taxpayers. The debt was only finally paid off in 2006.

In subsequent years, the park was little used, deteriorating and crumbling-- an iconic image of failed dreams and expensive ambitions (photo 5.8). But in 2016, more money was devoted to revamping the grounds and enlivening the site with events and festivals. In 2017, the stadium was also used as a welcome center for refugees, mainly Haitians, into Canada.

After decades of lying idle, yet still costing more than $1 million a year to maintain, the Olympic Park may be finding a new role.

PHOTO 5.8. Montreal's Crumbling Olympic Venue. The deteriorating structure highlights that investing in specialized sports infrastructure for a two-week event can be financially risky as the venue may not continue to be used.
Source: John R. Short

than either Toronto or Vancouver, both of which receive more immigrants.

The economy grew slowly during the 1980s and into the 1990s, but has since reemerged based on aerospace, electronics, pharmaceuticals, entertainment, and telecommunications, while maintaining a strong service sector and several educational institutions. Three cities in the world lead the way in aeronautics: Seattle, Toulouse (France), and Montreal. Companies like Bombardier, Bell Helicopter, and Pratt & Whitney benefit from Montreal's research universities, technical labor pool, and tax breaks from the Quebec government.

Montreal has pursued sustainability, especially the development of public transit and a high overall rating for sustainable transport. Almost 30 percent of the work force now leaves their cars at home when traveling to work. The carbon emissions are also low because of Hydro-Québec's water-generated energy.

Montreal was one of the first cities to sign the Geotourism Charter of the National Geographic Society and continues to move towards sustainability. It has eco-friendly metro cars, green buildings like the popular La Tohu, Maison du Développement Durable, and talks of rolling out the first "solar highway" in Canada. Sustainability is becoming a tourist draw: there are numerous eco-tourist things to do within the city, such as the Montreal Biodome, Biosphere at Parc Jean-Drapeau, and Mont Royal, along with plenty of Made in Montreal sustainable souvenirs.

In 2016, the city released its third five-year sustainability plan (the first plan was in 2005), the result of collaboration with more than 230 partner organizations and representatives from central municipal departments and local municipal administrations. The tagline "Together toward a sustainable metropolis" effectively sums up Montreal's commitment to sustainability planning.

PHOTO 5.9. Toronto City Hall. An ice rink full of skating people in front of City Hall.
Source: iStock/bukharova

Toronto, Ontario
(2016 CMA 5.9 million)

Toronto is located at the mouth of the Humber River, the accustomed indigenous overland shortcut (instead of through the Great Lakes and Detroit) to Ontario's northern lakes and rivers.

In 1792, Upper Canada established York as its conservative, Protestant, and puritanical capital. In 1834, the town name was changed to Toronto. It had become the commercial and agricultural center for the English colony.

Toronto is the largest city in Canada. Within the Greater Toronto Area are several other cities including Brampton, North York, fast-growing Richmond Hill, and Mississauga. Greater Toronto is the most ethnically diverse city in Canada, and the fifth-largest city in the United States and Canada (photo 5.9). Toronto is the only major Canadian city where British or French are not in the majority. More than 60 percent of the population is non-British.

Currently, some 48 percent of the city's population are foreign-born, one of the highest percentages for any major metropolitan area. About seventy thousand immigrants from approximately 170 countries arrive in the city annually. No one group dominates Toronto's immigrant stock. Nine countries account for half of the foreign-born population, led by China, then India, the United Kingdom, Italy, the Philippines, Jamaica, Portugal, Poland, and Sri Lanka.

Toronto grew into an international financial center and home of the national stock exchange. Toronto was second only to Montreal until the 1970s, when it became the primary city. It developed a manufacturing economy in the nineteenth century but began to deindustrialize in 1950.

Toronto's high-tech service sector and tourism industries have propelled its economy into the twenty-first century. Toronto's good public transportation system and environmentally protected underground shopping area allows the populace a place to mingle despite weather conditions.

Toronto's urban sprawl spreads across the flat plain and is a challenge to sustainability efforts. Not surprisingly, its traffic congestion is the worst in Canada: bottlenecks cost drivers 11.5 million hours and 5.8 million gallons (22 million liters) of fuel each year. The city has also dealt with a lack of landfill space, due to the geologic structure of the Canadian Shield, which lacks a soil barrier to protect groundwater. For decades, Toronto shipped its garbage to Michigan. Dissent by Michiganders has forced Toronto to rethink its garbage policy, and in 2010 it stopped shipping waste to the United States. While waste is now processed and stays within Ontario, its landfill will close by 2030 if the city does not significantly reduce, reuse, and recycle, thereby diverting trash from landfills. With the adoption of a progressive sustainability policy, Toronto now diverts 50 percent of its waste but aims to get that to 70 percent. Every year, the City of Toronto manages over a million tons of waste each year. One way it is doing so is through its ReUseit web site, which provides information on community donation organizations and links to popular reuse sites (such as Craig's list, UsedToronto.com, and Freecycle).

The city has also been a leader in lowering CO_2 emissions, establishing a step-by-step plan to reduce emissions by 50 percent by 2050. There is wide support of energy conservation and renewable energy projects, which include Canada's largest solar photovoltaic installation.

Ottawa–Gatineau
(2016 CMA 1.3 million)

Ottawa–Gatineau sits on the border of Ontario and Quebec, at the confluence of three rivers: the Gatineau, the Rideau, and the Ottawa. The lumber industry drove the economy during the nineteenth century using the rivers for rafting logs to mills.

In 1832, the Rideau Canal connected Ottawa with Kingston and Lake Ontario and the economy grew (photo 5.10). In 1858, Ottawa was chosen as the national capital, elevating the lumbering town to a position of international importance.

Today, Ottawa is the fourth-largest city in Canada. Ottawa's robust economy centers on high technology and the federal government. The federal government is the largest employer in the region, although technology is a close second. A cooperative arrangement between government and industry helped to refashion the city-region as a tech-pole now known as "Silicon Valley North." The Ottawa–Gatineau high-tech sector, which focuses on information technology, telecommunications, and nanotechnology, has employed anywhere between fifty thousand and eighty-five thousand workers per year during the past decade and includes well-known firms such as Corel, Nortel, and Adobe. Although the "government town" is usually seen as the antithesis of an open-market environment fostering technology and innovation, the Canadian federal government has actually been central in the development of the region's tech-pole. The government is not only the largest user of information technology in the region, but it has also actively funded high-tech research and innovation in the laboratories of the National Research Council. Other public–private bodies, such as the Ottawa-Carleton Research Institute and the Ottawa Capital Network, provide the funding and programming to ensure that local innovations can be leveraged into the creation of local startup firms. By capitalizing on these networks and Ottawa's highly educated talent pool (30 percent have university degrees), Ottawa has developed its own version of Silicon Valley—one committed to local research, development, and reinvestment. Finance, insurance, and real estate have been other major growth industries.

However, Ottawa shares many of the same challenges facing other cities, including high youth unemployment and a proportional rise in part-time and low-paying service-sector jobs. A recent reported found that the number of workers earning minimum wage jobs increased from 2.4 percent in 1997 to 12 percent in 2014. Ottawa is also the least diverse urban economy in Canada. Counterbalancing the concern about low diversity is the fact that federal government employment and spending provides a buffer against economic downturns.

Ottawa began as an unplanned, organic city, but when the city was designated the capital, it developed open green spaces and a greenbelt to limit urban sprawl. The city currently has

BOX 5.8 GEOSPATIAL TECHNOLOGIES: MEASURING URBAN SPRAWL

In order to assess the effectiveness of city planning, researchers at the University of Toronto used GIS to analyze fifty years' worth of land-use data. They found little evidence of the vast suburban sprawl common to many North American city regions. The strong control of planning, which allowed planners to limit new residential construction and direct it toward exiting settlements rather then green field sites, led to the desired goals of compact and contiguous development. In contrast to the sprawl of many North American metro areas, the Toronto metro region succeeded in creating a smarter urban growth.

PHOTO 5.10. The Rideau Canal. The Parliament buildings can be seen in the background.

Source: iStock/PaulMcKinnon

the largest number acres in parkland per thousand residents in Canada. Bike paths crisscross the city at a higher rate than most cities in Canada or America. Land use codes now require bike parking in many facilities. Ottawa's first zero-waste grocery store, Nu, opened in 2017. It sells a variety of products—dry food, fresh produce, cleaning and beauty supplies—without any packaging. Instead, people are encouraged to bring their own reusable containers or to borrow or purchase them from the store.

The Economy

Historically, the Canadian economy has been based on trade with Britain and the United States. But British adoption of an open-trade policy in the mid-nineteenth century removed the preferential **tariffs** granted to the British protectorates, and Canada then focused on trade with its southern neighbor. The **Reciprocity Treaty of 1854** (also known as the Elgin-Marcy Treaty) reduced tariffs on natural resources between Canada and the United States in exchange for granting Americans navigational rights to the Great Lakes and fishing rights on the Grand Banks. Economically, the treaty enriched Canada, providing a market for its abundance of timber and wheat. But the Americans canceled the treaty in 1865 for a variety of reasons, in part because the states were indebted by the Civil War and wanted to protect their industries by imposing high tariffs. Canada balked, and the cancellation of the treaty provided an impetus for Canadian Confederation.

Confederation came with challenges: to create a national economy and remain independent of the United States. But its vast geography created economic and political competition between the distant Canadian regions.

The natural attraction between Canadian regions and their US complements made Canadian unity more difficult. The Atlantic Provinces shared a trading history with New England. The Corridor had an industrial affinity with the nearby American industrial core. The Prairie region was geographically an extension of the Great Plains, and British Columbia's population aligned mostly within the Pacific Northwest Puget Sound Basin. Each region often identified with its neighboring US state more than it identified with Canada. Despite repeated attempts to renew a reciprocity agreement in the ensuing years, the United States was adamant in its trade demands, and Canada's response was to create the **National Policy**.

In 1879, the National Policy of high tariffs on imported manufactured goods effectively divided inner (core) from outer (periphery) Canada economically and politically. The National Policy was meant to build and protect Canada and to reduce reliance on the United States. Canadian firms declared independence in response to the high tariffs the United States had imposed on Canadian goods. From the late nineteenth century until the 1930s, the two countries assigned each other least-favored nation status, and trade fell off between the neighboring countries.

BOX 5.9 GLOBAL CONNECTIONS: THE NORTH AMERICAN FREE TRADE AGREEMENT

In 1944, after World War II, the world economy began restructuring. At Bretton Woods (New Hampshire), the International Monetary Fund (IMF) and the World Bank were formed to oversee monetary systems. The introduction of the General Agreement on Tariffs and Trade (GATT), first introduced in 1947, was heralded as the beginning of a New World Economic Order. A series of eight GATT agreements over the next few decades liberalized trade and reduced tariffs in order to extend commercial advantage for the United States.

In 1994, the United States, Canada, and Mexico created a regional trading bloc, the North American Free Trade Agreement, NAFTA, to promote the freer flow of goods and services across international borders. NAFTA was established to encourage greater trade among the three principal countries of North America by reducing and eventually eliminating tariffs between the countries.

One result has been the concentration of industry north and south across the border. Toronto, which has traditionally been the focus of an East–West Canadian economy, has increasingly turned its attention to the North–South economic opportunities created by NAFTA.

But as the United States and Canada experienced a steep decline in manufacturing jobs, there was growing discontent that this was caused by NAFTA. In addition, impoverished Mayan famers in the southern Mexican state of Chiapas saw globalization

in the form of NAFTA as negatively impacting their culture and way of life. They worried cheap corn from the Midwestern region of the United States would flood Mexico, making it impossible for Mayans to continue farming for a living.

While it is true that many jobs relocated from the United States or Canada to Mexico, the effects of NAFTA were mitigated when China entered the World Trade Organization (WTO) in 2000, shifting jobs from countries like Mexico to the lower-cost labor market in China.

One of the results of NAFTA and the WTO in Canada has been the loss of jobs in Ontario's automobile industry. Following in the trudging footsteps of the American Big Three manufacturers, the effect has devastated the local Ontario economy. The economy of Canada is tied not only to the auto industry but to the US economy in general.

The United States remains Canada's largest trade partner, with more than 80 percent of all Canadian goods going to the States (21 percent of US goods go to Canada). Questions abound about Canada's dependence on the United States, as Canada continues to seek new trading partners (Europe, Latin America). The mood is vulnerable though, as the end-of-the-millennium economy turned for the worse. Deregulation, lumber disputes, and oil in the Beaufort Sea and Alberta could bring Canada into protectionism or a further alliance with new trading partners.

Tensions were also high between Inner Canada and Outer Canada because of the perceived economic and political favoritism toward the Corridor. Those favoring Inner Canada's strength believed in a strong federal government and industrial core located in the Corridor, while those favoring Outer Canada favored a more equitable division of power and decentralized trade, which empowers the provinces. The government continued the National Policy into World War II, but the policy was slowly dismantled after the war. A series of agreements—the **General Agreement on Tariffs and Trade (GATT)** and the Auto Pact of 1965, among others—reduced tariffs until the **North American Free Trade Agreement (NAFTA)** opened up free trade in 1995.

Although the National Policy focused on protecting Canadian goods, it affected all aspects of the Canadian economy. Ontario's manufacturing grew, along with an urban workforce. While good for Ontario's economy, buying Canadian goods was more expensive than purchasing in the nearby American regions for two reasons: economies of scale, and geography (long transit routes increased transportation costs). For example, farmers in the western provinces now had to buy Canadian equipment at higher prices than American goods, which kept the Canadian economy strong. But the farmers were at the mercy of the global economy, having to sell on a fluctuating commodity market.

The story continued in 2007, when the Canadian dollar reached parity with the US dollar; the Canadian dollar had been at 60 percent of the US dollar previously. Upon parity, Canadians visited the States for deals on everything from shoes to cars. The response from Canadian companies was to establish rules and regulations to halt the flow of capital into the States. For example, many people chose to buy their cars in the States, where they are less expensive, but Canadian dealerships retaliated by not honoring the warranties of US-purchased cars. Today, one US dollar equals 1.25 Canadian dollars. But the US/Canadian dollar relationship is always in flux: often when the US dollar is strong, the Canadian dollar is weaker.

The Primary Sector

The traditional primary sector economy in this region includes agriculture, furs, fish, lumber, and mineral resources, and these have remained important exports.

Agriculture

The Corridor is a substantial Canadian agricultural region located near a majority of the population, thereby assuring an available market. The Quebec and Ontario agricultural areas developed independently and specialized in crops and livestock that related to their distinct cultural and climatic conditions.

TABLE 5.2. Size of Canadian Farms, 2017

Province	Average Size in Acres
Quebec	279
Ontario	233
Canada	728

Source: Statistics Canada

While the average size of an Ontario and Quebec farm is the smallest in the nation, the farms practice more intensive production than Prairie farms (table 5.2).

Ontario agriculture has two distinct regions. The more productive is west of Toronto and produces grains, specialty crops, and livestock. East of Toronto is less productive. Quebec's agriculture is along the Lowlands Corridor, chiefly along the southern shore between Montreal and Quebec City. The short growing season limits crop growth, and so the region specializes in livestock production.

The Ontario Farm   Ontario's agriculture is dominant between Toronto and Windsor. The region is involved in specialty crops, livestock, and a growing organic market. The Ontario farm is much smaller than the average Canadian farm, but the Ontario farm is an appropriate size for the regional specialty crops—tobacco, tomatoes, stone fruits, and hemp. Crop production has ebbed and flowed over time in relation to changing agricultural laws, preferences, and styles.

Ontario grows more than a third of all Canadian vegetables, many grown in greenhouses. Leamington, located on Lake Erie's north shore, has the largest concentration of greenhouses in Canada and a nine-hundred-employee Heinz factory for processing its chief crop, tomatoes. North of Leamington, along the Niagara Escarpment, is the Niagara fruit belt, located between lakes Erie and Ontario. The fruit belt benefits from the warmer air off the lakes and can therefore grow more crops than usually found at this latitude. Niagara Escarpment fruit has been a staple until the late twentieth century, when labor costs escalated and it became less economical to grow stone fruits. Vineyards capitalized by wealthy individuals became popular.

Ontario livestock production had been a staple for the region, but it contracted after 1996 when the century-long federally funded Crow Rate corn subsidy ended.

In 1998, legislation legalized industrial hemp. Industrial hemp is grown for fiber, food oil, meal, paper, and biomass. Many small companies are producing hemp food, health products, and clothing. Canadian exports of hemp seeds and oil are primarily in foods, but there is increasing demand for hemp in building and car-part manufacturing. In recent years, Canadian hemp exports have generated some $45–50 million in revenue.

The Quebec Farm   Prior to World War II, French Canadian Quebec remained a predominantly rural farming population but has since become more specialized, intensive, and technologically developed. Quebec farms are also far smaller than the Canadian average.

Most agricultural pursuits were in the Lowlands area, especially along the flat and fertile right bank of the St. Lawrence. Other agricultural areas include the eastern townships and along the Montreal Laurentians. Production choices are limited in Quebec because of a brief growing season, from a miniscule three months in the Montreal Laurentians to up to five months on the Montreal Plain.

Through the nineteenth century, Quebec grew grains, but as western Canada's more favorable growing conditions opened up, Quebec switched to forage and livestock. Livestock production, mostly dairy and hogs, remains the most important agricultural activity, accounting for almost half of all farming operations. Quebec produces the most hogs in Canada. Most of these are destined for the export market, especially to the United States.

Quebec accounts for more than half of Canada's cheese production, and four companies account for more than 90 percent of Quebec's production. The remainder is divided among ninety specialty cheese makers who produce quality handmade cheeses, which are more sustainable and protect small farms.

Mineral Resources

The Canadian Shield is the most mineral-rich region of Canada; however, the Appalachian Uplands and the St. Lawrence Lowlands area are also mineral resource areas. Ninety percent of Canadian aluminum has been mined in Quebec, making Canada the fourth-largest producer in the world and second largest exporter behind Russia. Aluminum production thrives on the inexpensive and available hydroelectric power of Quebec. However, a lack of processing and dependence on importing semifinished products, largely for the aircraft industry, have led Canada to begin developing an aluminum manufacturing sector to supply Montreal's aerospace industry.

Asbestos has been mined since 1847 in the eastern township towns of Asbestos and Thetford Mines. Production has continued, even as other mines have shut down due to health concerns with asbestos manufacturing. Most asbestos uses have been banned across the developed world, so most sales are to less developed countries. The health risks of asbestos found in Quebec mines—chrysotile—is played down within the towns.

The Secondary Sector

The Corridor shares manufacturing enterprises with neighboring US industry. Until the 1990s, 50 percent of all jobs in the Golden Horseshoe were in the manufacturing sector, but there have been an estimated loss of 212,000 manufacturing jobs in Ontario and 97,000 in Quebec since 2004. Many of the manufacturing jobs that Canada has lost are low-skill and low-paid; Canada can not compete on labor costs with countries such as China or Vietnam. Still, the government has launched programs to encourage manufacturing investment, such as the automotive innovation fund to invest between 250 and 500 billion dollars between 2008 and 2016, and it has cut corporate tax rates.

The loss of so much of the manufacturing sector qualified Ontario in 2009, for the first time ever, to receive $347 million from the federal government as an **equalization payment**. Canada's Equalization Program transfers federal funds from wealthier to less affluent provinces and has caused continual discord between the wealthy and poorer provinces. The economic failure of primary industry has caused Canada's equalization payments to the Atlantic provinces to be disproportionately large. For example, in 2017, the equalization payments to Quebec were $11 billion and $1.4 billion to Ontario, while robust growing provinces such as Alberta, Saskatchewan, and British Columbia received none.

Auto Production

Manufacturing in Southern Ontario and Quebec developed hand in hand with the financial industry. Auto manufacturing developed as a crucial segment of the Corridor economy and was allied with industrial growth in neighboring Detroit. Until 1965, the Canadian auto industry developed with much smaller independent plants and smaller branch plants of US companies. The United States opened Ontario branches and enjoyed reduced tariffs.

The signing of the 1965 Auto Pact was a major step that eliminated tariffs between the two countries. American and Japanese carmakers and car part manufacturing grew in the core region in alliance with Detroit industry. The industry profited on the low-valued but stable Canadian dollar. The car industry flourished from 1965 into the 1990s, when foreign competition began to affect the industry in both countries. By 2006, following the decline in American auto production and

the escalating worth of the Canadian dollar, Canadian production also declined.

Steel

Canada's steel town is Hamilton, Ontario, situated at the west end of Lake Ontario within the Golden Horseshoe. Available coal and Great Lakes iron ore created an auto production market. The greater Toronto market complemented the growth of industry and heavy manufacturing in the second decade of the twentieth century.

However, as with so many American and Canadian manufacturing industries, the steel companies hit hard times, and many steel mills have declared bankruptcy. A takeover and consolidation within American and Canadian steel companies followed. The two major steel companies—Dofasco and US Steel Canada (formerly Stelco)—emerged from bankruptcy proceedings. Overall, steel manufacturing remains a $14-billion industry, but it is challenged by volatile steel prices, global overcapacity, struggling energy and resource sectors, and the massive dumping of illegally subsidized steel from China.

Energy Production

Quebec and Ontario are both replete with energy options. Ontario's provincial electricity is produced by coal-burning power plants, hydropower, and nuclear energy. Ontario became the first province to replace coal-produced electricity with conservation, natural gas, and wind power. Ontario fully phased out its coal plants with the last one closing entirely in 2014. Today, renewables are responsible for 66 percent of Canadian electricity, with 60 percent of all power in Canada coming from hydropower. Northern Quebec has extensive hydropower sources. Hydro-Québec provides power to the province and to the northeastern United States (Alaska and the Canadian North Chapter) (photo 5.11).

PHOTO 5.11. Hydroelectric Dam in Ontario.
Source: iStock/martellostudio

In 2005, Canada produced almost no solar power at all. In 2015, it produced more than three thousand gigawatt hours. Ninety-eight percent of all Canadian solar production is in Ontario, where financial incentives have driven the installation of new solar power plants.

A cap-and-trade program aims to reduce GHG emissions in Canada. A cap-and-trade program involves capping GHG emissions by large companies, or purchasing credits from companies under the cap limits. Provincial government programs set caps on emissions and tradable allowances. British Columbia was the first province to introduce cap-and-trade legislation, followed a few months later in 2008 by Quebec and Ontario, who agreed to continue integrating their economies. Ontario's cap-and-trade program is designed to help fight climate change, and reward businesses that reduce their GHG emissions. The **cap and trade** is mandatory for a facility or natural gas distributor that emits twenty-five thousand tons or more of GHG emissions per year; it is voluntary for any other facility or company. Cap and trade is projected to generate about $2 billion per year in proceeds. The Ontario government says it plans invest this into programs that save homeowners energy and money, to enhance public transportation, provide electric vehicle incentives, and fund solar housing retrofits.

Canada seemed poised to favor a continent-wide cap-and-trade program, but oil sands exports have stymied improving the cap-and-trade policy. Oil sands production from Alberta threatens Corridor aims for cap and trade and continues the long-standing tension between the core and periphery.

The Tertiary Sector

Ontario's economy is one of the more diverse in Canada. Although manufacturing plays an important role, in fact the service sector accounts for more than 76 percent of its economy. In 2014, the section of Highway 401 between Toronto and Waterloo became the world's second largest innovation corridor after California's Silicon Valley, employing nearly 280,000 tech workers from around the world and containing over 60 percent of Canada's high tech industry.

Financial services are also a growth area. Toronto serves as Canada's financial services capital and headquarters and is home to the largest banks in the country. It is also home to the Toronto Stock Exchange (TSX), which leads globally in mining listings. Ontario's financial services sector generates approximately $63 billion in GDP and employs about 365,000 people in some 12,000 financial services firms. Ontario is also home to regional banking headquarters for Goldman Sachs, Bank of America, Deutsche Bank, and Bank of China.

In Quebec, aerospace, finance, and information technology have grown in importance.

Canada also aggressively pursues tourism. The most visited places in the Corridor include Toronto, Montreal, Quebec City, and the outdoor tourist–based economy in the nearby Laurentian Mountains in the Canadian Shield. In Quebec, tourism represents 2.5 percent of the province's GDP and nearly four hundred thousand people are employed in the tourism sector.

Montreal and Quebec City tourism are attractive because of their francophone appeal and Old World feel. The walled city of Quebec is unsurpassed in North America for its location, European architecture, and cuisine. Even during the winter the city shines, with an annual February ice festival with snow sports and a unique ice hotel built for the Mardi Gras festival and melted on April 1 each year.

A Sustainable Future

The Corridor region will remain a center of Canadian power because of its population dominance, large cities, and capital. In many ways, the Corridor parades the essence of the bicultural and steadily more multicultural country. Canada feels it must continue to grow economically to prosper, and a large immigrant population augments Canada's low birthrate growth.

Canada is is finding its own way in the twenty-first century, without guns, with health care, favoring same sex marriage, legalizing marijuana production, and recognizing the importance of sustainability. However, frustrated cries for equality from Outer Canada are being heard, as Alberta with its oil sands and Newfoundland with its offshore oilfields gain more power, more control, and more of the export economy, even as manufacturing slows in the Corridor.

Many of the challenges to a more sustainable Canadian Corridor include the following:

- invasive species in the waterways;
- water quality;
- water consumption;
- urban air pollution;
- threatened species;
- organic farming;
- volatile organic compound (VOC) emissions; and
- municipal waste generation and weak recycling rates.

In general, the average Canadian is more aware and active in environmental sensibility than the average American. Many provincial and municipal governments have sustainable development plans and strategies. Cities such as Toronto and Quebec are leading efforts around crafting a diverse range of sustainability projects that address many of the challenges listed above.

Questions for Discussion

1. What is the traditional rivalry between Inner Canada and Outer Canada?

2. In what ways is Inner Canada now being challenged by Outer Canada?

3. Explain the shifting of population between Toronto and Montreal during the 1970s.

4. Why were there four Welland Canals built, and why might there be a fifth?

5. How is the Niagara Escarpment significant in the Corridor region?

6. How has the National Policy affected trade in Canada?

7. Why did the St. Lawrence Valley and not Acadia become the French cultural hearth of Canada?

8. What site and situation features made Montreal a prime center? Why did it become the economic center of Canada under British rule?

9. What was the effect of the Quiet Revolution? What grew from it?

10. What was Ontario called prior to Confederation, and who settled there?

11. What are the religious differences between Ontario and Quebec? When did it start and how did it evolve? How has it changed since the 1960s? Why?

12. What are some of the trends around population, immigration, and diversity?

13. What are the major cities of the Corridor doing in regards to sustainability?

14. Why is there the possibility of a shift in power between the Corridor and other Canadian regions in the twenty-first century? What other region challenges the hegemony of the Corridor?

Suggested Readings

Bonnell, J. *Reclaiming the Don: An Environmental History of Toronto's Don River Valley*, Toronto: University of Toronto Press, 2014.

Bourne, L. S., and R. D. MacKinnon, eds., *Urban Systems Development in Central Canada: Selected Papers* Toronto: University of Toronto Press, 1972.

Chapman L. J., and D. F. Putnam. *The Physiography of Southern Ontario*. 3rd ed. Toronto: Ontario Ministry of Natural Resources, 1984.

Craig, G. M. *Upper Canada*. Toronto: McClelland and Stewart; New York, Oxford University Press, 1963.

Dickinson, J., and B. Young. *A Short History of Quebec*. Montreal: McGill-Queen's University Press, 2000.

Gayler, H. *Niagara's Changing Landscapes*. Ottawa: Carleton University Press, 1994.

Greenberg, J. *A Natural History of the Chicago Region*. Chicago: University of Chicago Press, 2004.

Greenwald, M., A. Levitt, and E. Peebles. *The Welland Canals: Historical Resource Analysis and Preservation Alternatives*. Toronto: Historical Planning and Research Branch, Ontario Ministry of Culture and Recreation, 1979.

Grenier, F., ed. *Québec*. Toronto: University of Toronto Press, 1972.

———, ed. *Quebec Studies in Canadian Geography*. Toronto: University of Toronto Press, 1972.

Guindon, H., ed. *Quebec Society: Tradition, Modernity, and Nationhood*. Toronto: University of Toronto Press, 1988.

Harris, C. *The Reluctant Land: Society, Space, and Environment in Canada before Confederation*. Vancouver: University of British Columbia Press, 2008.

———. *The Seigneurial System in Early Canada: A Geographical Study*. Madison: University of Wisconsin Press, 1966.

Kaplan, D. H. "Population and Politics in a Plural Society: The Changing Geography of Canada's Linguistic Groups." *Annals of the Association of American Geographers* 84, no. 1 (March 1994).

Levine, A. *Toronto: Biography of a City Madeira Park*, British Columbia: Douglas and McIntyre, 2015.

Louder, D., ed. *The Heart of French Canada: From Ottawa to Quebec City*. New Brunswick, N.J.: Rutgers University Press, 1992.

Louder, D., and E. Waddell, eds. *French America: Mobility, Identity, and Minority Experience across the Continent*. Translated by Franklin Philip. Baton Rouge: Louisiana State University Press, 1993.

Martin, V. *Changing Landscapes of Southern Ontario*. Toronto: Boston Mills Press, 1989.

McIlwraith, T., and E. K. Muller (eds). *The Historical Geography of a Changing Continent*. 2nd ed. Lanham, MD: Rowman & Littlefield, 2001.

Ray, D. M. "Dimensions of Canadian Regionalism," Geographical Paper no. 49. Ottawa: Department of Energy, Mines, and Resources, 1971.

Yeates, M. *Main Street: Windsor to Quebec City*. Toronto: MacMillan, 1975.

Zubrzycki, G. *Beheading the Saint: Nationalism, Religion and Secularism in Quebec*. Chicago: University of Chicago Press, 2016.

Internet Sources

Great Lakes Commission, at http://www.glc.org/

A Report Card on Canada, at http://www.conferenceboard.ca/hcp/default.aspx

The City of Ottawa, Sustainability Plan, at http://ottawa.ca/calendar/ottawa/citycouncil/ec/2012/02-21/03-Document%203%20-%20CoF_Sust%20Plan_FINAL%5B1%5D.pdf

Toronto's Environmental Progress Report, at https://www1.toronto.ca/City%20Of%20Toronto/Environment%20and%20Energy/Action%20Plans,%20Policies%20&%20Research/PDFs/City_of_Toronto_EPR_2015_FINAL_ACC.pdf

InvestinOntario, "Financial Services", 2017, at https://www.investinontario.com/financial-services#intro

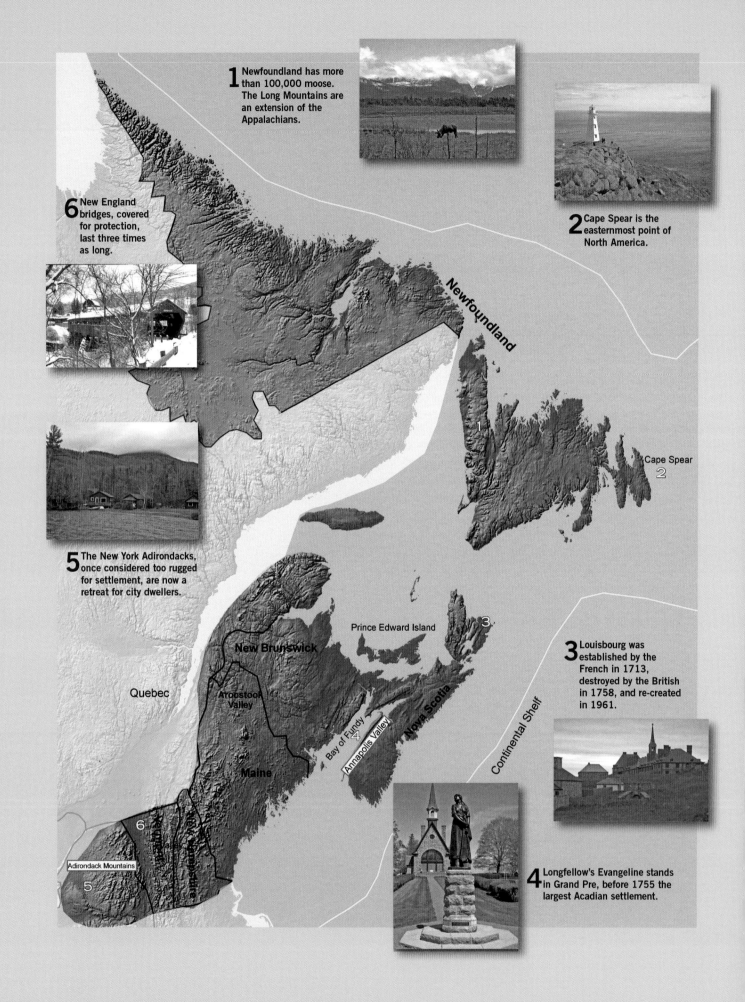

1 Newfoundland has more than 100,000 moose. The Long Mountains are an extension of the Appalachians.

2 Cape Spear is the easternmost point of North America.

6 New England bridges, covered for protection, last three times as long.

5 The New York Adirondacks, once considered too rugged for settlement, are now a retreat for city dwellers.

3 Louisbourg was established by the French in 1713, destroyed by the British in 1758, and re-created in 1961.

4 Longfellow's Evangeline stands in Grand Pre, before 1755 the largest Acadian settlement.

Newfoundland

Cape Spear

Prince Edward Island

New Brunswick

Quebec

Aroostook Valley

Bay of Fundy

Annapolis Valley

Nova Scotia

Continental Shelf

Maine

New Hampshire

Adirondack Mountains

6

THE NORTH ATLANTIC PROVINCES AND NORTHERN NEW ENGLAND
New Economic Hopes

Chapter Highlights

After reading this chapter you should be able to:

- Distinguish between the Maritime Provinces and Atlantic Canada
- Explain the collapse of the cod fishery
- Discuss how Northern New England interacts with Megalopolis
- Describe the resettlement of Newfoundland
- Give an overview of the importance of the Grand Banks
- Define the tragedy of the commons
- Describe the geographic limitations of the region

Terms

bank (geology)
brewis
capelin
cod
cultural preadaptation
Exclusive Economic
   Zone (EEZ)

flake
Green Mountain Boys
maritime influence
milkshed
monadnock
North Atlantic Ocean Conveyor
outport

phytoplankton
polders
postindustrial economy
privateer
quaternary sector
resettlement
resource hinterland

short sea shipping
smart growth
thermohaline circulation
tidal bore
tragedy of the commons
trawler

Places

Acadia
Adirondacks
Annapolis Valley
Appalachian Uplands
Aroostook Valley

Atlantic Canada
Bay of Fundy
Continental Shelf
Flemish Cap
Georges Bank
Grand Banks

Gulf Stream
Hibernia oil field
Labrador
Labrador Current
L'Anse aux Meadows

Maritime Provinces
Newfoundland
North Atlantic Drift
Northern New England
Scotian Bank

Cities

Bangor
   (2016 MSA 153,000)
Burlington
   (2016 MSA 214,000)

Fredericton
   (2016 CMA 105,000)
Halifax
   (2016 CMA 403,000)
Manchester

   (2016 MSA 406,000)
Moncton
   (2016 CMA 144,000)
Portland
   (2016 MSA 519,000)

St. John
   (2016 CMA 126,000)
St. John's
   (2016 CMA 205,000)

Introduction

The North Atlantic includes the northeastern United States, the Maritime Provinces of Canada, and Newfoundland. The northeastern United States area lies north of Megalopolis and includes Vermont, New Hampshire, Maine, Massachusetts outside of the Boston metro area, and the Adirondacks and upstate New York. The four provinces of Atlantic Canada are Prince Edward Island, Nova Scotia, New Brunswick, and Newfoundland. New Brunswick and the two smallest provinces, Prince Edward Island and Nova Scotia, are the Maritime Provinces. Newfoundland and its territory, Labrador, have a very different history, and are seldom included within the Canadian Maritime Province culture, but form their own cultural region.

The North Atlantic region is as breathtakingly beautiful as it is economically and ecologically struggling. The dramatic beauty both invites and rejects human activities. The rock-strewn surface, the fjords, the bare, windswept summits, and the mile upon mile of nothing but rock, sea, and trees are glacial legacies. With poor agricultural soils, only two natural resources make this region economically attractive: the fishery and lumber. The fishery provided both a food source and an income. Fish were once so plentiful that it was said that a bucket thrown in the sea emerged filled with fish (photo 6.1). But the fishery

collapsed in 1992. Only water fills the bucket today. Lumber, while plentiful, has been exploited in the past and then abandoned as regional manufacturing shut down, largely because of the region's isolated location. The loss of the fishery and lumbering industries left the Atlantic Provinces and Northern New England without their main sources of income.

Once upon a time, the Atlantic Provinces—Nova Scotia, New Brunswick, Prince Edward Island, and Newfoundland—were important economically. They were the major shipping ports to Europe and shared a reciprocity agreement with the adjacent New England states. Today, the regional economy depends on limited natural resources, and Atlantic trade has become secondary to Pacific trade.

The Atlantic Provinces cling to political and economic stability as they lose population to Canada's urban centers. Tourism has become the economic base, but it affords meager recompense in relation to the national economy. With the loss of the **cod** fishery, their greatest source of income, the provinces floundered, until offshore oil production increased along with oil prices. But offshore drilling is a short-term answer to continued economic security, and so some, such as Prince Edward Island, have turned to alternative energy sources.

Northern New England is in similar economic shape. The once dominant shipbuilding industry and the fishery that gave its name to Cape Cod have both disappeared. The

PHOTO 6.1. Lobster boats and traps are an iconic image of the region.

Source: iStock/Atlantic_Adv

TABLE 6.1. Critical Environmental Challenges

- Geographic isolation from the rest of the continent. Distance from major markets, especially the distance of the Atlantic Provinces from the Canadian Corridor.
- A limited resource base. The dramatic glacial landscape has rocky soils, limiting the ability to support large populations and industry.
- A formidable climate. The region is prone to natural weather extremes such as ice storms and nor'easters
- Declining fish stocks.
- Warming sea temperatures.

current economy relies on wealthy Megalopolis residents seeking solace in a scenic northern New England coastal home. However, a second-home economy based on retirement or vacations may not provide enough for the permanent populations.

The region's chief export, arguably emigrants—especially the vital young—hinders rebuilding the economy. Its small town and rural nature attracted some population growth from urban areas in the respective countries, but most were retirees or second-home residents. The small population makes for small internal markets, dependent on vulnerable primary industries—fishing, forestry, and mining. In addition to economic challenges, the region faces considerable environmental challenges (table 6.1).

Physical Geography

The North Atlantic has two distinct onshore physiographic regions, the Appalachian Uplands and the Canadian Shield, and one offshore region, the Continental Shelf. The North Atlantic coastal plain is all but submerged.

From Atlantic Canada down through northern New England, the Appalachian Uplands is a fjord-indented coastline with a rolling interior—the result of repeated glaciations. The rolling foothills of the Canadian Appalachian Uplands skirt the US border, extending to the Gaspé Peninsula before terminating in Newfoundland. The portion between Lake Champlain and Maine is known as the Estrie or eastern townships. In the United States, the Appalachians are called the Green and White Mountains.

Shaped by glaciers, the Uplands' rock-strewn fields and scraped-bare mountains are clothed in hardwood and coniferous forests. About 90 percent of Maine and New Brunswick remain a roadless second-growth boreal forest.

The Labrador Canadian Shield is part of the ancient North American craton, upon which newer (only one to two billion years old!) crusts have accreted. In Labrador, glaciers sculpted the coastline fjords and exposed bedrock; inland remains forested. Tectonic forces embedded resource minerals into the shield rock. For example, Northern Labrador's Voisey's Bay nickel ore was intruded between two ancient and collided craton crusts. The site has become an important twenty-first-century mining site.

The North Atlantic Continental Shelf ranges between 200 and 350 miles from the shore and is called the Grand Banks.

Sunlight penetrates the relatively shallow, six-hundred-foot-deep **banks**, supporting abundant plant and sea life. The prolific fishery has attracted fishers from around the globe. The edge of the Grand Banks marks the end of the North American continent; beyond, the continental slope plunges two miles to the ocean floor abyss.

Regions

Nova Scotia

Virtually surrounded by the sea, Nova Scotia, originally named Acadia by the French, consists of a peninsula and island. The narrow Isthmus of the Chignecto land bridge connects the peninsula to New Brunswick; Cape Breton Island, separated from the mainland by the two-mile-wide Strait of Canso, has been connected to the mainland by a causeway since 1955 (photo 6.2). The causeway also caused ecological imbalances within the Gulf of St. Lawrence, including changes in the tidal regime, sediment deposition, and upsetting ecosystems. For example, nonnative bobcats entered Cape Breton after the causeway was completed and forced relocation of the native but less aggressive lynx into the more isolated highlands.

The rugged Atlantic coastline is indented with countless bays, inlets, and coves. Marine sediment covers the straighter Fundy coastline and the low-lying and stone-free Annapolis Valley, one of the few places with fertile soil to support the province's agriculture.

Prince Edward Island

From mud flats to marshes, a variety of red sand beaches border the coastal margins of the smallest province (2,185 square miles), the crescent-shaped Prince Edward Island, where one is never more than ten miles from the sea. The fertile seacoast prairies of Prince Edward Island are reclaimed from the sea and now utilized as farmland. Prince Edward Island, called the "Garden Isle," has had most of its forest cover converted to agriculture.

Tourism was inconvenient until the nine-mile-long Confederation Bridge linked the island to the New Brunswick mainland in 1997. The bridge's environmentally sensitive engineering respects local terrestrial and aquatic environments. Following the environmental theme, the island province has recently adopted the name "the Green Province," has endorsed wind turbine and biomass energy production, and practices a high rate of recycling.

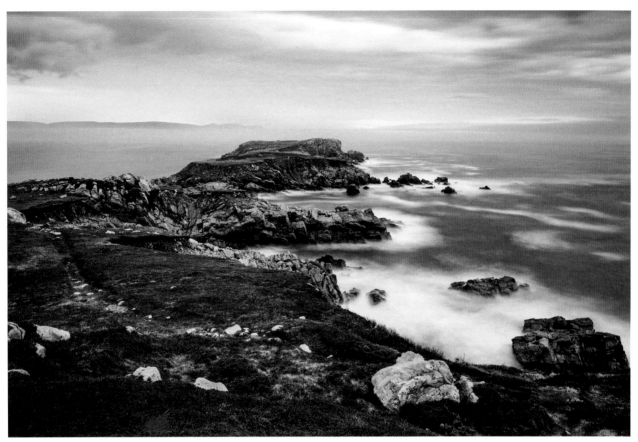

PHOTO 6.2. Whitepoint, Cape Breton.
Source: iStock/rachelmcgrath

New Brunswick

New Brunswick is divided into two general regions: a flat to undulating maritime plain occupies one-third, and the remaining area is the thickly forested Appalachian Uplands. The St. John River cuts through the highlands and flows alongside the larger cities: Edmundston, Fredericton, and St. John, a city famous for its reversing waterfalls caused by Fundy tides.

Newfoundland

The island of Newfoundland, affectionately called "The Rock," and its mainland territory, Labrador, compose Canada's most easterly province. Fjords and deep harbors indent the coastline; moss and lichens populate the tree-laden inland, while people populated the coastline. Inland, a hundred thousand nonnative moose have overrun the native caribou. Hunting moose is a popular and legal sport that provides meat for the subsistent Newfoundlander's diet.

A series of peninsulas divides the island. The most prominent are Avalon, home to the capital, St. John's, and the 180-mile-long Northern Peninsula, crested by the two-thousand-foot-high barren plateaus of the Long Mountains. On the west coast of the Northern Peninsula, the mountains drop to a small coastal plain, whereas the mountains along the east coast fjords plunge directly into the ocean.

Lying at a similar latitude, Newfoundland is colder than Vancouver, because the cold Labrador Current flows down from the Arctic and surrounds Newfoundland (photo 6.3).

Northern New England

Over the past million years the White and Green Mountains of New Hampshire and Vermont (*vermont* means "green mountain" in French) have lost elevation to erosion. Today, the elevation averages 2,500 feet; Vermont's Green Mountains top out at 4,500 feet, and Mount Washington in the White Mountains reaches 6,288 feet. Another type of peak is the stand-alone geological remnant **monadnock**. The best known is 3,165-foot Mount Monadnock in New Hampshire, where 1887 fires scarred the rocky summit, leaving it treeless despite its low peak (photo 6.4).

The United States (Vermont and New York) and Canada (Quebec) share the fertile Lake Champlain Valley. The Lowlands hold Lake Champlain, North America's sixth-largest lake, which some proclaim as the sixth Great Lake. The lake has served as a commercial highway between Montreal and the Northeast. Along its shore are several regional cities: Ticonderoga and Plattsburgh in New York and Burlington in Vermont. Water features—lakes, ponds, and wetlands—pockmark the Lake Champlain ecosystem, protected by a microclimate that

BOX 6.1 DID YOU KNOW . . . LABRADOR

One of the few instances that a watershed marks a political division is where the Atlantic watershed divides the territory of Labrador from Quebec to the west. Located entirely within the Canadian Shield, Labrador's rugged, ragged, and fjorded coastline is capped at its northern margin by the Torngat Mountains. The original inhabitants of Labrador are Inuit and a few hardy English, who fish and trap.

Labrador was originally part of New France. Quebec still claims Labrador as its own. However, in 1927 Labrador was granted to Newfoundland as part of its fishing grounds, though Quebec has claimed mineral rights in Labrador.

Newfoundland and Labrador residents are touchy about Quebec's claims, because Quebec includes Labrador within its economy. Why? Labrador projects have been profitable for Quebec but have seldom profited Newfoundland and Labrador. One of the few shared investments is the hydroelectric power station at Churchill Falls in Labrador, the second-largest hydroelectric plant in North America, which is jointly owned by Newfoundland and Labrador Hydro Company and Hydro-Québec. The Hydro Company produces 80 percent of Newfoundland and Labrador electricity

PHOTO 6.3. An Iceberg at Fort Amherst, St. John's.
Source: iStock/NancyAZeglen

extends the growing season. The fertile agricultural soils are marred by residential and commercial developments that have polluted runoff and diminished air and water quality. Habitat reductions, fire suppression, invasive species, and fragmented aquatic and terrestrial habitats have resulted. Numerous non-profit groups are restoring riparian lands, managing erosion, and reducing phosphorus loads from agricultural runoff.

The Frontenac Axis cuts across the St. Lawrence Lowlands and connects the primeval Adirondacks and the Canadian Shield. The Adirondacks are part of the Canadian Shield, but for millions of years the igneous rock core was covered and deformed by sediment before emerging as a dome about sixty-five million years ago. The Adirondack wilderness contains two thousand glacial lakes and the headwaters of the Hudson River,

PHOTO 6.4. Mount Monadnock, New Hampshire. This isolated peak has a rocky summit that was severely glaciated and then eroded. Nineteenth-century fires left the peak bare and with an artificially low treeline.

which along with thin eroded soils formed a formidable barrier to settlement and exploitation.

Water

The lumber, farming, and tourist economies profited from the glacial waterways and lakes, including Lake Champlain and Lake Placid, home to the 1932 and 1980 Winter Olympics.

While generally unnavigable, Atlantic Province waterways have played an important part in economic development. The waterways provided regional transportation and easy access to food and fresh water.

River power supported northern New England's initial Industrial Revolution. The smaller regional rivers were the perfect size for the technological capabilities of the nation's nascent saw and textile mills.

The Appalachian Plateau topography was critical to the movement of timber on Maine's largest rivers—the Penobscot, Saco, Androscoggin, Kennebec, and St. John. From the mountain flanks these swift-moving rivers carried timber from the westernmost corners to the sea, supplying ship builders and pulp and paper manufacturers.

The lumber industry depended on waterpower harnessed by dams, but not without consequences. Power generation grew and blocked salmon spawning grounds and created pollution. In 1800, an estimated eighty thousand salmon returned to

spawn in the Penobscot, whereas in 2000, the salmon numbered less than two thousand. The Penobscot River became one of the most polluted in the nation by 1996, due to the paper industry's use of the toxic carcinogen dioxin.

By the second half of the twentieth century, dams along the Penobscot and Maine's smaller rivers were technologically obsolete but still blocked fish runs. Implementation of the 1972 Clean Water Act affected discharge of water by dams and resulted in cleaning up many riverine pollutants and the return of salmon runs. The Penobscot no longer occupies the most endangered list; however, salmon runs are still limited.

The Bay of Fundy was initially settled in 1604 by the French, who called the land Acadia. They settled and diked tidal marshlands for farming and pasture. The Bay has the highest tidal fluctuations in the world (photo 6.6). Twice a day, seawater surges in and out of the funnel-shaped bay, carving cliffs along the shoreline. The Bay of Fundy tides erode, transport, and deposit sediment, forming tidal marshes along the Maritime prairies.

The tidal movement differs within areas of the bay. At the six-mile-wide mouth near the Atlantic, the fluctuations are slight, but further north the Minas Basin fluctuations are the largest, normally around fifty feet). The Minas Basin is also the location of the **tidal bore,** where the incoming tide meets the outgoing freshwater, thereby changing the flow of the river. Spectacular peaked-wave tidal bores can form when one force meets the other.

BOX 6.2   THE ADIRONDACK STATE PARK

The Adirondack Park was created in 1892 by the state of New York. Containing six-million acres, the Park is the largest park in the contiguous United States. It covers one-fifth of New York State, is equal in size to neighboring Vermont, and is nearly three times the size of Yellowstone National Park (photo 6.5). The Adirondacks are not part of the national park system, but we highlight it here because it is an excellent example of ways that individual states have protected and preserved natural areas. Unlike most national parks, Adirondack Park contains not only public lands but also private lands where people live year-round. More than half of the lands are private and home to 105 towns and villages, farms, working forests, businesses, and communities. The integration of both public and private lands is a unique model for conservation.

The Adirondacks remained forested while most of the East Coast was stripped of its wood. Known as the "Great Northern Wilderness," these mountains were not settled by either the Native Americans or Europeans until the late nineteenth and early twentieth centuries, when artists and writers discovered its natural beauty. Because of their relatively pure nature, the mountains were a perfect setting for the incipient conservation movement that began with George Perkins Marsh's *Man and*

Nature (1865). By 1885, the Adirondacks emerged relatively intact and protected. The largest unlogged tract in the eastern United States is the forty thousand acres of virgin forest in the Five Ponds Wilderness Area.

Large-scale logging in other areas left bare, eroded slopes and sediment-filled streams, which taught those involved with the park's creation about environmental devastation and the actions necessary to protect the mountains. Ecologically tied to the Erie Canal and indirectly to New York City, the health of Adirondack waterways was imperative. The Adirondack Park declaration assured the Adirondacks would never be sold as timberland, its waterways would be protected, and the forests would remain "forever wild."

However, the park is beset with problems for its future. Many diverse groups depend on the region, and each group has a different set of priorities. Some need the natural resources, the wood; others rely on the same woods for tourism; developers want to build more; and conservationists want no building at all. Across America, the forest, often called the "land of many uses" and unfortunately nicknamed the "land of many abuses," cannot be everything to everyone.

PHOTO 6.5. Adirondack Park, New York.
A View of Lake George in autumn.
Source: iStock/RickSause

Tidal power has been a partial source of energy since the nineteenth century, and interest in decreasing fossil fuel dependence has renewed interest. Since 1984, experiments in electrical generation have focused on bay area tidal power—perfecting underwater power by using the rising and falling tides. Tidal power may generate an instream potential of 300 megawatts—enough to power about a hundred thousand homes. Underwater turbines in the Bay of Fundy began operating in 2016; it currently generates enough electricity to power

500 homes. The turbine is part of a large-scale demonstration project to test the technology in the powerful tides of the Bay of Fundy over the next several years.

The Gulf Stream and the Labrador Current

The Gulf Stream originates in the Gulf of Mexico and then follows the wind north along the Gulf Coast through the Straits of Florida and up the East Coast continental slope (map 6.1). The stream is 10°F warmer than the surrounding waters. Near

PHOTO 6.6. The Bay of Fundy is known today as having the highest tidal range in the world, up to fifty feet twice a day as these two photos of the same boat illustrate. The power generated by the tides is now being converted to electricity.

Newfoundland, it turns toward Europe. Mid-ocean the current splits into the **North Atlantic Drift**, which moderates the high-latitude climate of Europe, and the Canary Current, which brings cool water to the Iberian Peninsula and beyond.

The cold Labrador Current (30°F, or 1.7°C) meets the northward-flowing Gulf Stream (68°F, or 20°C) off the coast of Newfoundland at the Grand Banks. The Labrador Current flows from Greenland's glaciers north into Baffin Bay and then south. Salt lowers the freezing temperature of water, so the Labrador Current—receiving freshwater from the Hudson Bay system—freezes more quickly than the saltier Gulf Stream Current. The Labrador Current usually freezes during winter, breaks up in May, and is ice-free by July. The Labrador Current delivers icebergs, which calve from Greenland's glaciers and seldom melt until they encounter the warm Gulf Stream, then melt rapidly, although icebergs have been reported as far south as Bermuda. Icebergs are now closely monitored because of their hazards to shipping—the *Titanic* was the victim of an iceberg.

When the two currents collide, they create advection fog (when warm air flows over cooler air below) and violent weather. The meeting place of the Gulf Stream and Labrador Currents is over the Grand Banks, one of the foggiest places in the world and formerly one of the richest fishing grounds.

Climate

The **maritime influence** along the coast of the North Atlantic moderates regional temperatures throughout the year, but because of prevailing winds it does not reach too much into the interior. Regional temperatures are similar to the Great Lakes and the St. Lawrence but are somewhat lower than similar latitudes of Western Europe. North Atlantic temperatures rarely rise above 90°F (32°C) or drop below 1°F (−17°C). Winters are long with continuous snow cover.

Precipitation is 40–55 inches (100–140 cm) annually, with adequate amounts during the four-month frost-free growing season. The cold climate often freezes the harbors of Atlantic Canada, Maine, and the Gulf of St. Lawrence.

The Gulf Stream–Labrador Current confluence transfers heat between the cold and warm currents, which sometimes results in penetrating fog and intense storms with gale-force winds—nor'easters. Newfoundland has the strongest winds, especially in winter. Low-pressure systems exit from the St. Lawrence River and create cloudy weather over the Atlantic, which can generate winds up to ninety miles per hour. Other conditions associated with the storms include a numbing wind-chill spray and reduced visibility.

Historical Geography and Settlement

The English, Irish, and Scots settled the North Atlantic region, while the French Acadians settled the Maritimes. Their cultural imprint has shaped today's landscape. Native Americans, while populating the region prior to European arrival, are a miniscule part of the current population.

Native American Algonquian and Iroquoian families lived in northern New England. The Iroquois lived in the lowlands near Lake Ontario and the Appalachian Uplands, and on occasion they hunted in the Adirondacks.

The Eastern Woodland Micmac were dominant in the Maritime Provinces, while the Beotuks dominated Newfoundland. The Micmac were among the first Aboriginals to have contact with the Europeans. Many of the Natives began trading with French fishers in the early 1500s. The story of their demise is somewhat different from the devastation of the other local tribes.

Prior to European arrival, the Micmac hunted and gathered during the summer and managed their accumulated food throughout the rest of year. After contact and trade with the Europeans, the Natives quit hunting and began depending on the dried vegetables, hardtack, and alcohol they received for their furs. The furs-for-food trade disrupted traditional winter food storage. Over the years the Micmac began to gorge during the summer, leaving few stores for the winter, because they

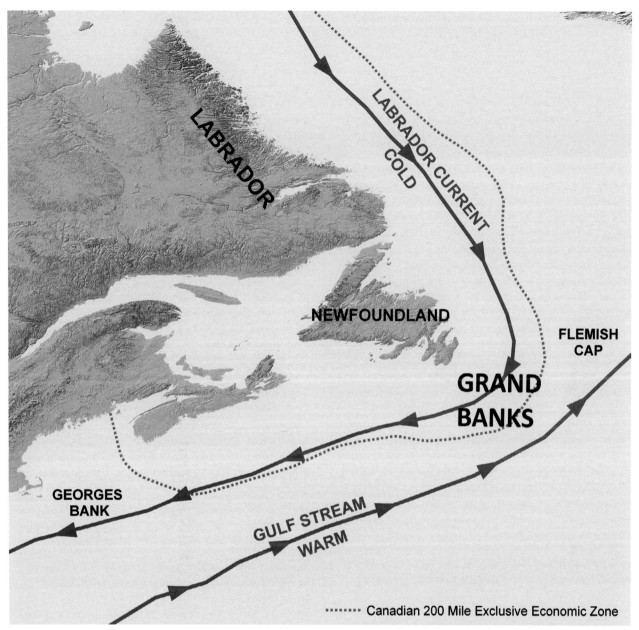

MAP 6.1. The meeting of the cold Labrador Current and the warmer Gulf Stream has numerous effects on the region, among them fog and the perfect conditions to grow phytoplankton. The fishing area includes a series of shallow areas—perfect for sunlight-spawned phytoplankton, the first link in the marine food chain—extending from the Grand Banks off Newfoundland to Georges Banks near Cape Cod. The Labrador Current also brings icebergs down from Greenland. Sometimes the icebergs anchor on the shallow continental shelf below and can become hazardous for shipping, as when the Titanic met its fate. The continental shelf of North America is widest near Newfoundland, where it extends more than three hundred miles.

depended on the European trade to provide winter provisions. Occasionally, the Europeans did not arrive during the year, and the Natives starved. Mismanagement of food supply and the resulting diseases are most probably behind the 90 percent decline in the Micmac population, from thirty-five thousand in 1500 to thirty-five hundred in 1600.

In Newfoundland, the Beotuk caused problems for the European fishers. The European travel pattern in the Atlantic North was migratory through the seventeenth century;

Europeans arrived in the spring and returned to Europe in the fall. They sometimes built camps in Newfoundland and expected to return to them each spring, but the Beotuk scavenged the camps for wood and nails. Nails were so precious that the Beotuk would often burn the camps just to acquire the nails, and so each year the camps had to be rebuilt. While many Native Americans died due to disease exposure, the Europeans viewed them as a hindrance and systematically killed them for sport. By 1829, the last Beotuk died.

BOX 6.3 CLIMATE CHANGE AND THERMOHALINE CIRCULATION

Climate change can be an indirect effect of oceanic and atmospheric interactions. The ocean contains 99.9 percent of the heat capacity of the climate system. Heat is distributed around the globe by way of the **North Atlantic Ocean Conveyor** current, a central part of **thermohaline circulation** in which heat is transferred from the equator toward the poles.

The conveyor circulates warmth and stabilizes weather patterns. The warm water increases evaporation, and the water becomes more saline (saltier). But the farther north it flows the more the water cools, until at a point off the coast of Norway gravity pulls the now salty, cool water (cold water is more dense than hot water) thousands of feet to the ocean bottom. The water is then pushed south within an undercurrent that wraps the world's oceans; it rises again in the Indian Ocean and makes its way back to the beginning of the conveyor along the coast of Africa.

The Gulf Stream is an important part of the conveyor. The ocean conveyor explains why places at the same latitude have different climates. England is at the same latitude as Labrador (54°N), but England's temperature is warmer, because the North Atlantic Drift extension of the Gulf Stream draws warm surface water from the tropical regions to the north. Conversely, the iceberg-filled water of the Labrador Current chills Labrador and Newfoundland. The conveyor is responsible for the warm Gulf Stream where it meets the Labrador Current.

Higher temperatures over the North Atlantic result in more precipitation, melt icebergs, and increase freshwater while decreasing water salinity. Dense water (cold and salty) tends to sink, while less dense water (warm and less salty) stays at the surface. The water in the North Atlantic is now cool and salty and sinks, but if freshwater continues to be added (icebergs melting and increased precipitation), the ocean's salinity will drop (making it less dense) and the water will no longer sink. This could even halt both the ocean conveyor and the Gulf Stream. The loss of salinity caused by additional freshwater (icebergs and increased precipitation) may trigger another ice age or ice event, such as happened during the Little Ice Age between 1300 CE and 1800 CE.

A decade ago this circulation scenario was dismissed as impossible, but scientists continually discover supporting evidence. The result of the shutdown could mean an increase in severe ocean weather, a major food chain disruption, and a rapidly advancing ice age, the duration of which no one can predict. Other effects of a shift in the ocean conveyor include the shift in salinity and warmer surface water temperatures; these could increase the number and intensity of hurricanes.

If these changes were to occur, the East Coast of the United States and Canada would be directly affected. The Atlantic and Gulf coasts have recently experienced more intense hurricane seasons than normal. If the ocean conveyor circulation were to halt, the land, no longer warmed by the Gulf Stream, would grow rapidly colder. The interaction of each part of the climate system is more complex than current computer models can predict, but climate change is happening.

In Maine, the Malecite, Abenaki, and other tribal groups were hunter-gatherers and practiced agriculture. Little remains of their culture except the Maine tongue twister toponyms:

- *aroostook*: "beautiful river"; a county in northern Maine known for its potatoes and bilingual population (French and English).
- *passagassawakeag*: "a sturgeon's place" or "a place for spearing sturgeon by torchlight"; a river that runs through Belfast at Belfast Bay.
- Penobscot: "the rocky part" or "at the descending rock"; the name of a sovereign indigenous people and their language (mispronunciation of *Penawapskewi*), and Maine's longest river.

The Atlantic Provinces

While evidence remains of Viking visits, and many believe that pre-Columbian fishing crews plied the Grand Banks, the first Europeans to permanently settle the Atlantic Provinces were the Acadians. During the early 1600s, English, Scots, and Irish fishers settled in Newfoundland and along the North Atlantic coast.

Newfoundland

Europeans landed on Newfoundland in 988. The Viking Leif Ericsson founded Vinland, named after the wild grapes he found there, and in 1010, Thorfinn Karlsefni settled there for a few years. Archaeological evidence has documented a Viking settlement at L'Anse aux Meadows on the tip of Newfoundland's Northern Peninsula, but this was probably only a staging ground for other coastal forays, perhaps as far as the St. Lawrence River.

Permanent European settlement of Newfoundland began in 1610, and by the mid-eighteenth century, more than seven thousand settlers lived in hundreds of coast-hugging **outports** (out from St. John's). St. John's trading company vessels visited each outport twice annually, exchanging supplies for cod, which was shipped back to St. John's and then exported. The credit system of trade was the only access to the outside world for this otherwise self-sufficient but isolated populace (photo 6.7).

Newfoundland was ceded to Britain after the 1713 Treaty of Utrecht. When Canada confederated in 1867, Newfoundland had little reason to join, because its closest trade ties were with Britain. Newfoundland authorities were unsuccessful in brokering a deal with the United States, so Newfoundland became

BOX 6.4   GEOSPATIAL TECHNOLOGY: CHANGES IN THE FOREST

In precolonial times, most of the northeastern United States was heavily forested. With the coming of the Europeans, much of the forests were cleared and cut down. Since the late 1960s, forestry in much of New England and upper Maine is in the form of large-scale clear-cutting and whole-tree harvesting. Mechanized whole tree harvesting transforms a landscape of trees into a wasteland.

We know that forest cover is much less than it once was. But has there been any change in the composition of the remaining forest. One study looked at four centuries of change. Data was available from 1,280 colonial towns in the form of witness trees, identified at the corner of surveys. The data on species was compared with more recent surveys to understand the changes that occur over the centuries.

Across the region there was a decline in the number of beech trees due to deforestation, and logging. Maple, in contrast, because of rapid ability to regenerate after damage, saw both an absolute and relative increase.

Red maple and poplar replaced beech trees and hemlock and as a result, the forest composition is more homogeneous.

The rich fall colors of the New England fall rather than an unchanging landscape are in fact the result of the increase in maples due to anthropogenic land use changes.

Source: Thompson, J. R., D. N. Carpenter, C. V. Cogbill, and D. R. Foster. "Four centuries of change in northeastern United States forests." *PLoS One* 8, no. 9 (2013): e72540, at http://journals.plos.org/plosone/article?id=10.1371/journal.pone.0072540

PHOTO 6.7. Salvage, Newfoundland. Newfoundland is still home to hundreds of picturesque but struggling outports that depend almost entirely on the sea for their livelihoods. Today, with the cod fishery closed, many are leaving their homes to find other opportunities. Salvage has earned a tourism economy because of its scenic beauty.

PHOTO 6.8. Boatbuilding in Great Harbour Deep. Outports were usually isolated, with their only access by the sea. Isolation made the people self-sufficient, often growing their own crops on the bare soil (using seaweed as fertilizer) and building their own boats.

an independent country in 1855. But it failed to maintain a profitable economy. The island country fell into debt by the 1920s and went bankrupt during the Great Depression, and they rejoined the British Empire. After World War II, Britain, under its own financial stress, released the Newfoundland dominion. Newfoundland had to decide its fate as an independent country, a US territory, or part of the Canadian Confederation. However, World War II had changed life for the poor and formerly insulated islanders (photo 6.8).

During the war, the island became a refueling stopover, and many Newfoundlanders were employed by American and Canadian military forces. The strategic importance of the island during the war fostered a belief in many Newfoundlanders that the island could remain independent.

But more forces were at play than they fathomed. Premier Joey Smallwood was the man responsible for the choice of Newfoundland entering the Canadian Confederation in 1949 and for the still controversial agenda known in Newfoundland as the **resettlement**.

Acadia

In 1604, Northern French settlers arrived in the Bay of Fundy, a land they called Acadia. The land was marshy but similar to the industrious settlers' homeland. Farming along the similar French coast landscape had taught them draining and diking techniques. Their **cultural preadaptation** to the new land gave them survival traits that allowed them to build a farming, fishing, and lumbering economy in the new environment.

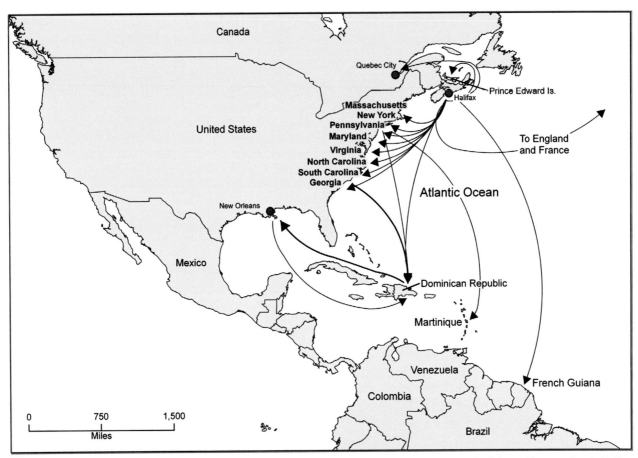

MAP 6.2. Acadian Expulsion (1755–1763). During the French and Indian War, the British deported Acadians from their Nova Scotia homes. They were deported to the American colonies, the Louisiana Territory, Prince Edward Island, and a few to Quebec, Martinique, French Guiana, England, and France.

Because of continued warfare and English **privateer** raids to seize goods, few immigrants settled in Port Royal, located along the well-protected Annapolis Valley harbor. However, the population grew because of a high birthrate. Acadian settlement later spread into New Brunswick, Prince Edward Island, and Maine.

The Maritimes were strategically important to both the French and English. In the first half of the eighteenth century, the two countries battled to control the St. Lawrence trade. The land moved between French and British control, but ultimately the French ceded Acadia to the British in 1713.

The Protestant British were uneasy with the Catholic French Acadians and their respect for, conversion of, and intermarriage with the Micmacs. Additionally, the Acadians refused to trade with or sign an oath of allegiance to the British. The result was the forced removal of the Acadians between 1755 and 1763. More than six thousand Acadians were deported, their homes destroyed, and their lands confiscated. Many Acadians were deported to the American British colonies, others to France or other colonies, such as Quebec or Louisiana (*Cajun* is a corruption of *Acadian*); others became refugees in the inland forests of their former homes (map 6.2).

In the meantime, British and Scots settlers replaced many Acadian farmers in the drained and diked Annapolis Valley,

but their lack of knowledge about **polders** limited their success. The British needed assistance to farm the diked farmlands. Some Acadians returned and taught the new settlers how to manage the diked lands. Even more Acadians returned and resettled after 1763, although not on their old properties. Some were discouraged when they realized their land would not be returned and left again for Maine, the shore of New Brunswick, or Prince Edward Island.

The end of the French and Indian War in 1763 terminated the dream of a French North America. Soon after, the American Revolution impelled about forty thousand British Loyalists to resettle in the Maritimes. The contingent of Loyalists, along with new British, Irish, or Scots settlers, created an English-speaking majority in the 1760s, and Acadia became Nova Scotia. Loyalist settlement extended to the St. John River and New Brunswick in 1794.

In 1783, more than three thousand former slaves left the United States and created small communities in Nova Scotia; Birchtown, with more than fifteen hundred people, was the largest. They had difficulty adjusting to the harsh climate and rugged conditions, so most of the towns were short-lived. Many of the residents immigrated in 1792 to Sierra Leone.

The geographic factors of an embayed coast, narrow coastal land, and poor soil influenced coastal settlement. Fishing along the Grand, Scotian, or Georges banks, trade with Britain (closer than the southern colonies), and shipbuilding also influenced initial settlement. Shipbuilding deforested southern New England after 1750, and the industry relocated to northern New England, where forest resources supported the American ship-building center—building the cheapest and best vessels in the world—until the end of the wooden ship era in the 1850s.

In the 1600s, fishers and disgruntled Puritans from Massachusetts settled the commercial colony of New Hampshire, while French trappers and traders entered Vermont from the north through Lake Champlain. Today, many Vermont towns along the Champlain Valley bear French toponyms. Years later, crop failures and British anti-French discrimination caused more French to resettle from Quebec. Many found employment working in the textile mills.

Both New Hampshire and New York claimed Vermont and agreed to split it along the crest of the Green Mountains. The British prioritized New York claims over those of New Hampshire, and resurveyed New Hampshire land granted to settlers. The conflict agitated the settlers. Ethan Allen and the **Green Mountain Boys** fought the British and meted out vigilante justice upon New York surveyors. After the Revolutionary War, Vermont pursued independence. The Green Mountain Boys' actions and independent attitude led to the formation of the Republic of New Connecticut, then the Republic of Vermont, a safe haven for British and American deserters. The republic lasted from 1777 to 1791, when Vermont became the first state outside the original thirteen to join the United States, its ratification based on balancing its non-slaveholding status against slaveholding Kentucky.

The North Atlantic rural population lives in economically challenged towns. In the States, northeastern towns are often arrayed in the classic village green crowned by a white-spired church, a symbolic pattern rather than a representation of the culture today. Manipulated cultural artifacts include lobster dinners and covered bridges. Almost two hundred covered bridges are in the North Atlantic states and another sixty-one in New Brunswick (photo 6.9). The bridges are functionally obsolete except for their nostalgic significance.

"Lobstah"

Throughout the region, "lobstah" (the local pronunciation) is a common food. A delicacy in today's world, lobster has an indelicate past. Native Americans and early colonists applied the abundant crustacean as fertilizer, or lobster was a monotonous dinner several times a week. This is, of course, no longer the case. Today lobster has benefited by the decline of cod, one of its main predators. The lobster is a regular and high-priced menu item in numerous lobster shacks along the coast (photo 6.10).

During the winter, lobsters retreat to deeper waters and are difficult to catch. To keep stocks of lobster available and provide a more consistent and sustainable market, Maine lobstermen have self-regulated conservation over the years. Many lobsters are "pounded"—caught in the previous peak season and held in blocked-off sections of bays for the winter season. Pounding is most prevalent in Canada. Pounding has become a crucial tool for the northeastern lobster market. A cold spring results in a poor lobster catch, and because of decreased pounding, most Maine lobstermen go wanting, while Canada's pounded catch brings high prices.

Those who continue to fish lobster in Maine have suffered due to depleted stock and competition from mainlanders who

PHOTO 6.9. Wooden Covered bridge in Hartland, New Brunswick.
Source: iStock/gvictoria

PHOTO 6.10. Lobster is an abundant and popular food throughout the region. This is a local lobster restaurant in Antigonish County, at the Strait of Canso, Nova Scotia.

come to fish the waters for sport during the summer season. Small island communities dependent on lobster fishing limit licensing to residents only.

Maine and Northern New England waterfronts have succumbed to high-priced luxury housing, which raises taxes, limits beach access, and regulates what has been self-regulated by the locals for decades. It has been called "Massification," as developers have turned these Northern New England areas into the equivalent of Massachusetts, with elevated prices, ironically compromising the cultural landscape that first attracted tourists and new residents.

Northern New England

The northern New England colonies were imprinted with Puritan values, morals, and frugality. New England's taciturn "Yankee" is a stereotype that contains grains of truth. This harsh land developed into a rooted homeland culture that maximized scant resources, often with picturesque results.

For example, the picturesque rock walls of New England are a valued cultural landscape feature treasured by a romantic urban population—but they were built by settlers to clear their rock-strewn fields (photo 6.11). As time went by, most New England farmers migrated west, fished, or became traders.

PHOTO 6.11. New England Stone Wall. Farmers built walls with stones cleared from their fields. Many farmers chose to leave these stony fields for the better soils of the West. Today, people pay more for homes with these nostalgic old stone walls. Some of the walls are dismantled and used as landscaping and house decoration.

BOX 6.5   CULTURAL FESTIVALS: FIDDLING IN CAPE BRETON

An important part of folk music of Nova Scotia is based on the rich musical traditions that Scottish settlers brought to Canada since the eighteenth century. Like all migrants they brought their culture with them, including their musical forms, the bagpipes, and especially the fiddle.

The duo of fiddle and piano was often played at community halls and social events throughout Nova Scotia, and especially Cape Breton where fiddle players have achieved international renown. Drawing on the rich tradition of Scots-Gaelic mouth music and fiddle playing, the music of Nova Scotia and Cape Breton not only keeps alive a centuries-old musical tradition but also enhances its vitality and extends it range.

The musical tradition that developed into a cultural industry with major stars, record deals, and independent record labels is now used as way to attract tourists.

The Nova Scotia Gaelic Mod is an annual folk festival held in Cape Breton in August that celebrates the Scottish cultural traditions in games, dances, food, and music. The world's largest fiddle sits on the Sydney waterfront in Cape Breton (photo 6.12). There are also smaller festivals held in villages throughout the summer season. The small town of Judique is also known as Baile nam Fonn (Gaelic for Village of Tunes). Names such as Cape Breton and Juduqiue are the **toponymic legacy** of the earlier French settlers.

The Ceilidh Trail runs through Cape Breton linking small towns and villages where folk music is played. Ceilidh is a Gaelic word for a social gathering with music, a party.

A centuries-old musical tradition, alive and thriving, is the basis for a booming tourist industry in the summer months.

PHOTO 6.12. The Largest Ceilidh Kok in the World. Located at the Sydney waterfront.

Source: Spiritrock4u at the English language Wikipedia

Maritimes

Two cultural groups settled Nova Scotia—the Acadians and the Scots. In the early nineteenth century, Scotland's brutal highland clearances stripped tenants of the land they worked. They fled for the familiar feel of the highlands, bogs, and fog of Cape Breton.

Nova Scotia and Prince Edward Island have an abundance of Scottish toponyms, named by Scots who migrated to the provinces. Names such as Inverness, Strathgarney, and Cape Breton abound in the Maritimes. Acadian descendants live along the western Bay of Fundy coast, as well as in towns like Cheticamp along Cape Breton's western coast.

Two of Canada's cultural icons, both women and both in Atlantic Canada, are fictional characters. One was the heroine of the stirring epic poem *Evangeline*, by Henry Wadsworth Longfellow. The poem immortalizes the exile of the Acadians from their Nova Scotia homes. The other, the title character of *Anne of Green Gables*, originated on Prince Edward Island. In

1908, Lucy Maud Montgomery wrote of Anne growing up on a Prince Edward Island farm. The island has become a mecca for those entranced by this childhood classic.

Newfoundland

Newfoundland settlers brought their European culture and dialects to the island. Isolated outports developed their own dialects, which were often unintelligible from one district to another. These distinctive dialects softened or disappeared as communication, transportation, and education equalized speech patterns, but even today, the older inhabitants of outports speak a distinct English dialect that is almost unintelligible to those from outside the outport. Newfoundland language remains sprinkled with eighteenth-century speech patterns and distinctive Newfoundland words. Meanings of words such as *gut* (a narrow passage) and *tickle* (a pass) differ from the rest of English-speaking North America.

Newfoundlanders were an uneducated and poor people who migrated for the fishery opportunities. Most inhabitants seldom left their outport and its fishing grounds except to find a mate. Outports were small affairs populated by few families, and finding a suitable mate often required visiting a neighboring outport, as long as both shared the same religion. Newfoundland outports were divided by denominations, Catholic versus several Protestant sects.

The isolation of Newfoundland and its almost complete dependence on the fishery created a food culture dependent on nonperishables. The traditional Newfoundland meal, **brewis**, includes the nonperishable salted codfish, hardtack, and salted pork. The lack of arable land, expense, and distance from markets make fresh fruit and vegetables rare in the outports even today.

Population, Immigration, and Diversity

The North Atlantic regional population has been stable at best. Decreasing job opportunities and increasing emigration, especially by young adults, has been the standard since the 1920s. Given these economic and demographic challenges, it is not surprising that immigration is not a major trend in this region. However, many of the provinces have attempted to make themselves attractive to immigrants. The Nova Scotia website, for example, boasts that "we are a tolerant, diverse society where everyone is encouraged to build a good life for themselves and become part of their community." Recently, they launched the Nova Scotia Nominee Program, designed to increase immigration to the province by allowing immigration officials to select foreign nationals interested in moving to Canada who have the skills needed in the local provincial economy. These skills include shipbuilding, fishing, and oceanography, among others. This program is designed to expedite the legal immigration process by giving these immigrants a priority. In the last several years, this has attracted about one thousand immigrants to the province. Despite efforts to entice immigration, the main challenges regarding population are emigration and an aging demographic.

The population in the Atlantic Canada and Northern New England states is older than the rest of their respective countries. All rural provincial areas in Canada continue to lose young adults but the Atlantic Provinces have lost the most; Northern New England is also losing its young.

The meager population supports few cities in Northern New England and Atlantic Canada. In Newfoundland and Nova Scotia, four out of five residents live in small dispersed coastal villages, and in Prince Edward Island, almost everyone lives within six miles of the coast. Only in New Brunswick do people live inland in cities along the rivers.

Few job opportunities and a high cost of living cause many young adults to migrate to urban areas. As baby boomers retire, the population will require costly social services, such as health care, but without a strong tax base these services will be underfunded. Older populations also have less discretionary income on which the consumer economy depends and are less inclined to fund school programs.

Maritimes

In 2016, the Maritimes and Newfoundland constituted 6.5 percent of Canada's population, down from 11.6 percent in 1949. Other than the territorial north, Atlantic Canada's 2.3 million population (2016) is the smallest in the nation. Population numbers have stagnated. The collapse of the fishery continued to affect Newfoundland's population until 2007, when there was a slight resurgence of growth due to offshore oil drilling.

Most people in Atlantic Canada claim English, Irish, Scots, or French ancestry. New Brunswick received thousands of Loyalists who fled the United States after the American Revolution. During the latter part of the eighteenth century, fifty-five thousand British, Scots, Irish, and Welsh emigrants settled in Nova Scotia. Most of the immigrants began as farmers, but then turned to the sea.

The French-speaking populations of Nova Scotia, New Brunswick, and Prince Edward Island were Acadian exiles who returned to their homeland and live today in French-speaking towns. New Brunswick is 35 percent francophone; Nova Scotia has eight thousand Acadians who live in francophone villages, and another forty thousand interspersed throughout the general populace. More than twenty-eight thousand Acadian descendants live on Prince Edward Island.

Newfoundland

Generally, the fishing industry and settlement patterns of Newfoundland are intertwined. The fishery collapse left most outport residents unemployed. Few jobs were in commuting distance because many outports are inaccessible by road. The demise of the fishery led to a population loss (580,000 in 1994; 519,000 in 2016), and the high unemployment rate left the province with only 45 percent with full-year employment (the Canada average is about 60 percent). The overall population decline includes almost half of all young adults, who migrated toward areas with jobs. The birthrate is so low that in 2007 Premier Danny Williams offered a $1,000 financial incentive to the parents of every child born in the province.

Almost every small outport lost population, as well as the capital, St. John's (–2.7 percent), and Corner Brook (–8.2 percent). Many working-age residents have immigrated to other parts of Canada. So many Newfoundlanders live in Fort McMurray, Alberta, that they often joke that it (rather than Corner Brook) is the second-largest city in Newfoundland. This leaves the province's aging in place; in 2016, almost 20 percent of the population was over sixty-five, and this percentage will increase. Additional elderly are emigrating "home" when they near retirement (photo 6.13).

In the days when the catch was prodigious and the fishing gear primitive, small fishing villages were strung one next to

PHOTO 6.13. Seniors Dancing Outdoors in Rocky Harbour, Newfoundland. An aging population is a challenge for the North Atlantic Provinces.
Source: iStock/Photawa

one another along the coast. But this has changed. The cod are gone. What remains of the industry is now fished from modern **trawlers**. The remaining quaint towns have become tourist attractions. Today, the structure of society is around economies of scale—bigger is better. The picturesque outports are nostalgic and charming but no longer serve today's economic system. However, the economy has been rebounding as the price of oil escalates and more jobs related to the offshore oil rigs become available.

Oil resources caused the Newfoundland economy to grow by 50 percent between 2000 and 2008, second only to Alberta. Newfoundland, historically the poorest province in the nation profited from increased oil production. Its gross domestic product (GDP) per capita increased from $10,000 below the Canadian average in 1997 to $10,000 above the Canadian average in 2007. By 2016, and after a decline in demand for oil, it was just above the national average. The global recession beginning in 2008 slowed growth in Newfoundland, but it weathered the recession better than most of Canada.

Northern New England

The Northern New England states originated as a British, Yankee Puritan stronghold. Small pockets of Roman Catholicism, such as Québécois French and Irish, are scattered through the Protestant region. In the nineteenth century, two migrations populated Northern New England: the Irish escaping the famine and many Québécois with large families and little arable land migrating toward textile industry jobs. Many towns in Maine, New Hampshire, Vermont, Massachusetts, and upstate New York still have a high proportion of French Canadian families and a high proportion of Irish Americans.

From 1950 until the late 1980s, the Northern New England population increased more slowly than the population of the rest of the nation. Low-density population made education and health care economies of scale difficult to achieve. Most Northern New England states lost some population to emigration, but natural increase and immigration of foreign-born workers to low-paying jobs fueled a modest increase.

The region remains largely non-Hispanic white. For example, in 2016 Vermont was 93 percent non-Hispanic white.

A Growing Demographic

One area of population growth has been in the number of vacation homes. Many second-home areas are in quaint but deprived areas, where the owners of second homes further depress the local economy by outbidding locals for choice second-home locations, then building new and large homes on empty lots or "improving" older homes by investing capital. Second-home owners occupy for only a few weeks a year, which strains the local economy, infrastructure, and public services. The result has negative effects on the local real estate market for the full-time residents. Local shops and community facilities depend on full-time residents to support their economy.

Urban Trends

This region does not have large metropolitan areas compared to many other regions covered in the book. The largest North Atlantic cities are on the coast. In Canada, the coastal cities include Halifax, Nova Scotia; St. John, New Brunswick; and St. John's, Newfoundland. Inland along the rivers of New

Brunswick are Fredericton and Moncton, the latter a city of 120,000 often named as a best place to do business in Canada because of lower tax rates and incentives, all the while touting quality-of-life issues and cost of living. In Northern New England, the largest cities are on water—along the ocean coast, such as Maine's Portland; along rivers, such as Bangor, Maine, or Manchester, New Hampshire; or on lakes, such as Burlington, Vermont.

Halifax, Nova Scotia
(2016 CMA 403,390)

Halifax is situated on one of the largest natural harbors in the world. Nova Scotia's towns were built along the coast for defensive purposes. Louisbourg on Cape Breton protected French fisheries and colonies, whereas Halifax, built in 1749, protected English interests. Halifax remains the largest of the Maritime towns, containing 40 percent of Nova Scotia's population.

Halifax's original peninsula site was unprotected from storms but enabled fishers to be closer to their boats. The defensive peninsular position did protect the towns from Native American conflicts during the first decade of settlement. Later, Halifax became an important military and shipping entrepôt for fish, lumber, and agricultural products. Today, Halifax is the province's commercial core, the region's university center, and the major ice-free container port for the Atlantic north. The larger port of Montreal is icebound during the winter.

Halifax became involved in sustainability prior to the 1992 Rio convention. In 1991, the Halifax Declaration supported universities' pursuit of sustainable development and reversing environmental degradation through education and cooperation. Since that time, the province has continued to seek sustainable development, although it has met opposition (for example, wind power policy favors large corporations over smaller groups or cooperatives). But the Halifax Regional Municipality (HRM) has been one of the most progressive. The HRM reduced its solid waste by 50 percent, and endorsed a clean-burning energy plant that switched from coal oil to natural gas. The HRM chose to endorse more wind energy.

St. John, New Brunswick
(2016 CMA 126,202)

St. John is situated on the Bay of Fundy and is the province's largest city. Loyalists escaping the American Revolution established the town in 1785. Located in the St. John River Valley, the city's economy depends on agriculture, mostly potatoes. St. John also serves as a recreational and scenic tourist area. The harbor and location, although ice-free, are less ideal than Halifax; therefore, it remains a secondary port. In the late nineteenth century, the Canadian Pacific Railroad (CPR) built a line to the port, which remained important until the St. Lawrence Seaway opened in 1959.

St. John's, Newfoundland
(2016 CMA 205,955)

St. John's is situated in a narrow-necked, well-protected deep-water harbor. Founded in 1583, St. John's was the first English colony established in North America. Its economy is based on offshore oil exploration, fish distribution, and Memorial University. The collapse of the fishery caused a loss of population; however, beginning in 2005, offshore gas and oil deposits offered new energy capital and new jobs. The metropolitan area contains about one-third of the island's total population. Newfoundland's rural-urban population and economic divide is defined as anything "beyond the overpass" (city limits) of St. John's (photo 6.14).

Portland, Maine
(2016 MSA 519,900)

Portland, Maine's largest city, cultivates a tourist trade around its historically preserved Victorian mansions along the Western Promenade. The city of Portland has basically stagnated since 1990, but Portland's urban sprawl continues to increase. Lower regional wages influenced technology firms to relocate and the business service economy to expand. Considerable waterfront investment has displaced many local residents and interrupted the commercial fishing economy.

In 2001, the City of Portland's elected officials signed a resolution pledging to participate in the Cities for Climate Protection (CCP) Campaign sponsored by the International Council for Local Environmental Initiatves (ICLEI). By doing so, they joined officials from hundreds of other cities around the world who believe that action at the local level serves as the foundation of the international effort to fight global climate change.

Over the last decade, the city has been very proactive regarding climate change, noting that they have learned from Hurricane Katrina and Superstorm Sandy that Portland is vulnerable to the potentially devastating effects sea level rise and that climate change could have serious impacts on the economy. The city's Old Port, much of it built on fill, is highly vulnerable to sea-level rise and storm surge, and the region's rich fisheries face an uncertain future. Warmer waters are driving Maine's iconic lobsters toward Canada, and ocean acidification is disrupting marine ecosystems. As part of their climate adaptation strategy, they conducted a greenhouse gas inventory, which enabled the city to move forward in the creation of a local action plan for reducing energy use and greenhouse gas emissions. The city has made further commitments to address climate change through participation in the Governor's Carbon Challenge and the US Conference of Mayors' Climate Action Plan.

Recently, the Portland City Council voted unanimously to adopt a goal of powering all of the city's operations and buildings with 100 percent clean energy by 2040. They see this as the first step toward getting the city to commit to 100 percent

BOX 6.6   URBAN SUSTAINABILITY BEST PRACTICES: BURLINGTON, VERMONT

Cities pollute the land in numerous ways—from solid waste (garbage) disposal in landfills to the contamination of soils in industrial and commercial areas. Although the deindustrialization and the closure of polluting factories appears to have left many North American cities cleaner, the derelict structures and polluted landscapes left behind from centuries of manufacturing continue to scar the urban landscape. Commonly referred to as "brownfields," these polluted properties are not only potentially hazardous to human health and the environment, but they also hinder the social and economic vitality of neighborhoods by adding to depressed real estate markets, increased crime rates, and a sense of community despair.

Many abandoned areas that are contaminated are called **brownfield**.

The US Environmental Protection Agency defines a brownfield as "real property, the expansion, redevelopment, or reuse of which may be complicated by the presence or potential presence of a hazardous substance, pollutant, or contaminant." While images of large-scale factories come to mind, many of the most common brownfields are those that we walk, cycle, or drive past every day. These include former gas stations, automotive repair shops, schools and institutions, dry cleaners, print shops, and other service-oriented businesses.

The term *brownfields* came to be used more widely in the mid-1990s in an effort to shift the emphasis away from the contamination issue and towards seeing the land as a resource to redevelop.

The City of Burlington has been proactive in redeveloping brownfields. The city believes cleanup and redevelopment of brownfields spurs economic growth, builds community pride and protects public health and the environment. The state of Vermont and the city of Burlington have incentivized brownfield redevelopments through a statewide Brownfields Revitalization Fund (BRF), tax credits for Downtowns and Village Centers, and Community Development Block Grants. This has led to the successful redevelopment of numerous brownfields in the Burlington area, including the following:

- Architectural Salvage Warehouse: abandoned warehouse into fully redeveloped Architectural Salvage operation;
- River View Apartments: former gas station into affordable housing and office space;
- Multigenerational Center: former drycleaning facility into senior center/daycare/community center facility;
- Thelma Maple Housing Coop: former roofing company site into affordable housing; and
- Metalworks: former offices of Exxon Oil terminal into custom metal fabrication business.

PHOTO 6.14. A View of St. John's Harbour in Newfoundland, Canada.

Source: iStock/Kyle Bedell

clean energy citywide. Currently, there are twenty-six cities in the United States that have pledged to go 100 percent clean energy.

Smaller cities such as those in the North Atlantic may face the additional challenge of being less likely to get much federal or state support as the lion's share of those resources will be focused on big urban centers.

The Economy

The North Atlantic suffers from economic distress for several reasons already mentioned, but the largest problem is the fragmentation dividing the two countries and several non-contiguous landmasses. The Reciprocity Agreement of 1854 protected trade with the United States but was dissolved during Confederation, which led to the region's economic decline. In the twenty-first century, some factions have proposed forming "Atlantica," which would in some ways recreate reciprocity, but perhaps at a price too high for the already distressed region to survive. The region continues to have an economy based on natural resources in rural areas and services in urban areas.

The two countries' rural areas are divided into three basic sectors:

1. Primary industry and resource dependent: Primary industry has been an unreliable source of profit for years. Areas dependent on agriculture, mining, logging, and fishing have declined due to the globalized economy and depleted resources. The collapse of the cod fishery on the Grand Banks hurt Newfoundland's economy for more than a decade.

2. Amenity areas: The coastal sections of Maine, for example, are now drawing second-home owners and retirees who hamper affordable housing for local residents.

3. Transitional: The North Atlantic primary industries are declining, but the area's beauty offers the potential for a service economy. The Adirondacks economy cannot depend on logging interests, but the potential tourist economy can accommodate ecofriendly tourism and some development.

The Primary Sector

As a part of a colonial empire, the Maritimes and Newfoundland were a **resource hinterland** for Great Britain until the markets opened to free trade in 1849. At that time, the Maritimes began a more earnest trade with New England until the Reciprocity Agreement was canceled in 1866. The Maritimes were cut off from US industry, and the fates of Northern New England and the Maritimes became independent of each other for over a century, until the North American Free Trade Agreement (NAFTA).

The 1867 formation of the Canadian Confederation shifted the North Atlantic provincial markets toward the core of the new nation.

The North Atlantic is a peripheral region dependent on natural resources; however, the primary resource industries (fishing, logging, mining, and agriculture) have been in decline, with the exception of oil production in Newfoundland.

While Atlantic Canada welcomes the economic relief from oil production, the region is in need of a long-term sustainable economy. The collapse of the fishery was predicted decades prior to the moratorium, and yet Canadian officials were unable to create a sustainable fishery (photo 6.15). Because oil is a

PHOTO 6.15. Prospect, Nova Scotia. When the cod-fishing industry collapsed in 1992, North Atlantic regional town economies were devastated. Government support to maintain aging infrastructure in small Canadian coastal towns is dwindling.

BOX 6.7 GLOBAL CONNECTIONS: TRADE

During the 1990s, 150 years after the Reciprocity Agreement lapsed, Maine and the Atlantic Provinces reestablished strong trade relations, much of it because of the North American Free Trade Agreement (NAFTA). Exports to Canada, Maine's largest trading partner, have been resources: wood, potatoes, blueberries, and seafood. These commodities are then reimported from the Atlantic Provinces as processed goods, including lobster from New Brunswick or blueberries from Nova Scotia. This export-import market was in many ways similar to the *maquiladora* export-import economy of the United States and Mexico. Exporting raw commodities and reimporting them as finished products takes advantage of inexpensive labor costs. Since NAFTA, Maine alone lost more than twenty thousand manufacturing jobs.

High-tech employment has also shifted to northeastern states, such as Vermont and Maine. The growth is in cost-savings and emerging technologies, such as the many sustainable technological industries welcomed in Vermont. Value-added manufacturing (the higher price obtained after manufacturing), for example, auto suspension and telecommunication equipment, has also increased.

The glacially indented coastline created excellent harbors and access points to the sea, benefiting the Canadian cities of Halifax, St. John, and St. John's, and Bangor and Portland, Maine. In the past, these ports have serviced ships from Mediterranean to Brazilian ports. The Atlantic Provinces were most prosperous during the nineteenth century when they were the center of trade. But Confederation and adoption of the National Policy shifted Canadian trade toward the heart of the Canadian economy. The Atlantic ports lost traffic to Montreal.

In the twenty-first century, conditions have changed. Transportation shifted from water to land routes, harming the water-dependent northeastern regions. Since 2002, in a move related to "**smart growth**," increased shipping has reduced highway traffic. The major twenty-first century ports are in the Pacific or use the Panama Canal and are at capacity. Atlantic trade, through the Suez Canal, could be an economic option, although pirating in the Gulf of Aden is a continual problem. Cities like Halifax, with the necessary infrastructure for large shipping vessels, hope to profit from this, but at the expense of weaker environmental regulations; a continued fear is the loss of sovereignty with integrated trade blocs between Canada, America, and Mexico. Another possible economic boost may come from **short sea shipping**—promoting the use of waterways to ease traffic congestion on national highways.

nonrenewable energy source, it is short-term and will decline. Therefore, investing in renewable energy resources will provide long-term sustainable energy production.

Fisheries

Since the 1400s, the Grand Banks fishery was the catalyst for Atlantic Canada settlement. The original colonial fishery consisted of inshore fishing in small boats. By the 1960s, fishing trawlers changed fishing and the size of fishing vessels. Fishery boats now range from small owner-operated boats to trawlers with processing facilities.

For the past five hundred years, the Grand Banks, extending from the appropriately named Cape Cod to northern Labrador, has been among the world's most productive fishing grounds. Cod, the beef of the sea, was the most consumed fish in Europe.

In the fishing-dependent outports along the coastline of Newfoundland, cod was literally currency. In Europe, dried cod was a preserved food source, and in the West Indies it was an inexpensive food for feeding slaves. Cured and dried cod was a perfect, indestructible international trade commodity. Even after the invention of refrigeration, the favorite catch of fishers was cod—pure white, protein-rich, easy to catch, easy to fillet. Salted cod dried on the Newfoundland **flakes** (a platform for drying cod, built on poles on the foreshore of outports) were a global commodity (photo 6.16). But this wealth of nature was exploited, resulting in a devastated fishery.

Over the past several hundred years, the fishing industry depended on traditional line fishing in small dories along the outport coastline. But the Industrial Revolution and concurrent population growth supported ever larger ships plying the Grand Banks, until mammoth corporate freezer-trawlers from every fish-trawling country were anchored in the Grand Banks. Despite warnings, the cod stock collapsed in 1992. The fishers and the governments failed to act on the recognized changes in the ecosystem. The lack of connect-the-dots systems thinking incurred a classic case of **tragedy of the commons**.

By the 1960s, the government and fishers recognized that collapse was imminent, although little was done to limit fishing. Then in 1977, the **Exclusive Economic Zone (EEZ)** for fishing was extended from twelve to two hundred miles offshore, so maritime countries could control offshore foreign commercial fishing fleets. Canada had almost exclusive jurisdiction over the Grand Banks. However, the Grand Banks extend beyond the two-hundred-mile limit, and foreign trawlers continued to fish the area beyond the EEZ.

By the 1990s, the cod population had dropped by 99 percent from the 1505 estimates. The ineffective regulation of the Grand Banks until it was too late left the region bereft of a recovery. The unintended consequences of industrial technology and greed may have eliminated this ecological niche. The cod have not returned. When there was still a chance to set a quota to regulate and maintain a sustainable catch, it was not done.

PHOTO 6.16. Flakes at St. John's, Newfoundland, 1964. The racks along the coast in the near area and across the neck are flakes, the standard technique for drying fish at the time. Modern refrigeration and the collapse of the fishery ended this traditional way to preserve cod.

Source: Photo by Ed Badura

Local and Ecoregional Impacts Atlantic cod proliferated because of sustained food chain conditions that supported the prey for cod: **phytoplankton**, crab, shrimp, and **capelin** (a small fish similar to a sardine or herring). Each level in the food chain depends on the next, and as the cod disappeared the effect cascaded down the food chain, so that the entire predator-prey relationship shifted. When a top predator, such as the cod, is removed from the food chain, then the predator's food increases—in this case, shrimp and crab. Many fishers turned to catching crab. But once again the food chain became vulnerable to additional imbalances.

Years after the collapse and closing of the cod fishery, the catch remains miniscule. The 2002 catch was only 2 percent of the 1988 catch, and the catch has remained flat in subsequent years. A slight resurgence of capelin has been noted, but cod remain in short supply. The cod may return, but in the meantime the prognosis is not good. Most global fishing zones have since collapsed, and commercial fishing has become problematic. To add to the problems, overfishing is also a victim of climate change, and as the ocean warms, marine ecosystems will be placed under ever greater pressure.

The Atlantic cod disaster was and continues to be horrific, but the process is being repeated in other fishing grounds. The majority of Europe's fishing stocks are reported to be overfished and in need of a moratorium. Several other fishing grounds are also overfished. Placing moratoriums, though, is disastrous for fishing communities.

The North Atlantic region has suffered a dramatic tragedy of the commons by seeking short-term profits while ignoring long-term sustainability in the Grand Banks fishery. Fishing techniques shifted from local outport fisheries to trawlers and factory fishing, which ruined the local economies.

Additional external costs are the socioeconomic issues. Many families in Newfoundland have been dependent on the fishery for their livelihood. However, sad as it is, the livelihood of the individual and their family, whose best interest was to maximize their catch, was not in the best interest of society. The Canadian government's inability to face the unpopular consequences of shutting down the fishery earlier caused tremendous economic disarray in Newfoundland. The immediate effect of the 1992 moratorium was the unemployment of more than thirty-five thousand fishers in hundreds of outports. While the economic and industrial structure has changed, including growth of the snow crab and shrimp catch, it remains to be seen if a sustainable catch can be regulated.

Logging

American logging followed western expansion. The first commercially logged region was the North Atlantic, where settlers logged haphazardly, cutting down nearby forests but bypassing difficult-to-log areas.

For example, the Adirondacks escaped systematic logging because early-nineteenth-century waterpower and technology could only reach the margins of the remote Adirondacks. By the mid-nineteenth century, technology was capable of logging more mountainous terrain, but by that time the center of the logging industry had moved to the Great Lakes states.

Most of today's forests are the result of replanting. Some forests are protected as state parks and remain much as they were historically, although with second-growth trees.

In the past, extensive logging in Atlantic Canadian forests left only small and fragmented virgin forests. Areas that have been particularly threatened are across Newfoundland and Cape Breton, Nova Scotia.

New Brunswick logging flourished throughout the nineteenth century. Much of New Brunswick and western Maine remain forested with second and third growth (only 2 percent remains

BOX 6.8 WOMEN AND THE FISH PLANTS

In Newfoundland, most who fished were male, but women tradition-ally have been part of the fishery. For centuries, they worked at the flakes drying fish, and as technology changed after World War II, they worked in the fish plants of small outports through the 1970s. The plant jobs gave the women a sense of independence and eco-nomic empowerment, although some theorize that the patriarchal economy actually victimized the women in their jobs rather than providing liberty. For example, despite their participation, women were denied the same government benefits as men until 1981. When many plants closed after the 1992 cod fishery moratorium, the consequent job losses overwhelmingly affected women.

When the fishery collapsed, retraining efforts were concen-trated on men, but for women in small outports, retraining was a futile idea because poor transportation networks limit outside opportunities. Losing the plants stripped the women of their jobs. After years of some independence, many women were unable to adjust to unemployment. The destroyed economy was destruc-tive to families and often resulted in increased alcoholism and domestic abuse. Failure of the Canadian government to act on the precautionary principle and protect the people from the collision course of the fishing industry resulted in both the loss of the industry and the destruction of families.

For women, achieving self-reliance required inclusion in the decision-making process, improved access to training and educa-tion, improved gender equity, encouraging women entrepreneurs, and supporting women as they age.*

*Joanne Hussey, "The Changing Role of Women in Newfoundland and Labrador," Royal Commission on Renewing and Strengthening Our Place in Canada, March 2003, at http://www.gov.nl.ca/publicat/royalcomm/research/hussey.pdf

as virgin) in the twenty-first century. In 2002, New Brunswick adopted green environmental standards for the logging industry, the first North American province or region to do so.

The North Atlantic is not an important lumber source region. An exception arose during the early twenty-first century, when disagreements about lumbering in British Columbia shut down that timber area for a few years, resulting in the temporary increase in logging in the North Atlantic region.

Mining

Mining has been significant in the past, but few mines remain open and are inconsequential in the global market. The mining industry is important for the local economies (table 6.2).

Nickel and Copper   Globally important nickel deposits were found in Voisey's Bay, Labrador, in 1993. About thirty million tons of nickel, copper, and cobalt ores have been extracted, worth $10 billion.

Voisey's Bay mining commenced before land claims, work rights, and environmental issues had been addressed. The mining is on indigenous Inuit and Innu land; it was illegal until 1997, when a resolution gave the local Aboriginals rights to some land, royalty payments, a degree of self-government, cash for development, and agreements on employment.

The depressed region has few job opportunities. The histor-ical Aboriginal occupation was seal hunting, but this declined

TABLE 6.2. Mining in the Region

Coal	Cape Breton, Nova Scotia
Nickel	Labrador
Oil and Gas	Newfoundland
Granite and stone	New Hampshire and Vermont

when infrastructure and pollution caused by the mining and without consulting the Natives has destroyed former hunting grounds. The unemployment rate escalated, and Natives were shut out from mining employment during the initial years at Voisey's Bay. The latest and largest mine in Voisey's Bay has had to address Native Innu social equity and environmental justice claims and hire Native workers. By 2005, about 50 percent of the operation workforce was local Inuit.

Oil and Gas   Oil fields were discovered in the Grand Banks in 1878; however, production began in earnest in the 1960s, although still delayed because of offshore engineering problems. For example, the Hibernia oil field halted production until the late 1980s because of floating icebergs, severe storms, and shipwrecks.

Offshore oil and natural gas deposits near Newfoundland can only be profitable when commodity prices are high. The additional jobs and oil revenue accrued to Newfoundland increased provincial investment in infrastructure, education, and medical facilities. Additional income from extensive gas deposits found off the shore of Labrador also benefited the province.

Agriculture

Northern New England   Farming communities populated the earliest Northern New England settlements, but within one hundred years of settlement, farmers either abandoned their stony New England land for farms in the West or abandoned farming altogether and worked in the growing secondary indus-tries of the burgeoning Industrial Revolution.

Prices fell as crop volume grew nationally, and the New England farm became unprofitable. From 1870 to 1920, New England farmers abandoned half of all farmland. From 1870 to 2007 the acres in farmland, in just one county, Rockingham in

New Hampshire, fell from 235,605 to 33,570 acres. The farmers who remained grew specialized crops—potatoes, blueberries, and dairy—for the local market.

In Maine, the Aroostook Valley's soils are set apart from the inhospitable granites surrounding it. The cool, moist climate and sandy loam are ideal for potato growth. Aroostook was once the primary potato-producing area in the United States, but it is now ranked fifth. Maine's potato production is developing crops for more niche-oriented markets, as it must, for it cannot compete with number one Idaho on a commodity basis.

Maine's glaciated landscape and acidic soil happen to be the ideal conditions for winter-hardy blueberries. Ninety percent of the world's wild blueberries are grown along Maine's coastal counties. Small, nonmechanized blueberry farms have been sold to developers, rather than owners investing the necessary capital to continue raising blueberries.

The Lake Champlain Lowlands' proximity to Megalopolis makes it a **milkshed** for the substantial Megalopolis markets. Its high-bulk, low-cost milk, a product with a short shelf-life, has serviced the New York City and Boston markets. Dairies in the Champlain Lowlands were once an economic mainstay for Vermont, and they still provide 90 percent of the state's agricultural income though only a small portion of the total economy. Atlantic North dairies are declining because of rising land values, regulated milk prices, industrial agribusiness, and increased competition from midwestern and western producers.

The Atlantic Provinces Farmland occupies less than 5 percent of the Atlantic Provinces, and less than 0.1 percent of Newfoundland and Labrador. Although many subsistence farmers settled during the nineteenth century, most abandoned their farms during the first half of the twentieth century. In the twenty-first century, the remaining farms are in three small regions: Annapolis Valley in Nova Scotia, St. John River Valley in New Brunswick, and Prince Edward Island. These isolated agricultural areas have been economically stagnant at best.

The growing season, though short, is conducive to apple and potato crops. The warmer climate of the Bay of Fundy protected the fertile farming soils of Nova Scotia's Annapolis Valley. Early in the twentieth century, apples were a staple crop, but they declined after 1950 because of overseas competition and a lack of local markets. The local economy now depends on tourism and the environmentally problematic concentrated animal feeding operations (CAFOs). The CAFO is similar to US chicken or hog farms, a centralized agribusiness that allows farmers to keep their farmland when traditional crops are unprofitable (see chapter 9, Southern Atlantic).

The finest agricultural land on the northeastern coast is Prince Edward Island, which evolved into the picturesque "Garden Isle." The island had fewer stones than glacial till lands, and the red soil was perfect for potato farms, producing one-third of Canada's potato crop. New Brunswick also has a thriving potato-growing and processing industry near the Aroostook Maine border and on its northwestern coast.

American manufacturing and processing of goods began in the Northeast in the beginning of the nineteenth century. Textile mills and pulp and paper mills were located throughout the region.

The first part of the Industrial Revolution in the second decade of the nineteenth century was dependent on harnessing the power of local waterways to run textile mills. The mills thrived until after the Civil War, when the mill industry migrated to the Southern Atlantic states. The migration of the textile industry to cheaper production areas forced the old mill towns to redefine themselves in order to maintain population and economy.

Since the 1990s, the logging industry has also undergone changes. The pulp and paper industry was replaced by increased overseas production. The industrial logging and paper companies have sold their holdings and been replaced by landowners with different objectives. From 2006 to 2008, Katahdin Paper Company blamed high oil prices and globalization when they closed three paper mills in New Hampshire and Maine. Today, many of those manufacturing jobs have gone overseas (photo 6.17).

The Tertiary Sector

The loss of manufacturing has been compensated by a growth of jobs in education, health care, tourism, and business and professional services. However, many of these jobs pay less than the lost manufacturing jobs.

Tourism

Since the end of World War II, tourism has replaced lost industry. The "pastoral" scenes of Maine and Vermont, the beaches of Prince Edward Island, the Bay of Fundy's tidal fluctuations, along with Atlantic Canada's picturesque fishing villages, turned the area into a nostalgic vacationland. Additional cultural attractions include the Acadian past, folk art, fresh seafood, and restored historic landmarks like the fortress at Louisbourg.

The weather can also entice. Cool summers offer a retreat from the hot, humid Megalopolis summers, and winters offer skiing. During nineteenth-century summers, the White Mountains attracted both tourists and artists. The beauty of the northeastern ranges of Appalachia captivated artists, such as Alfred Bierstadt, Asher Durand, and other Luminists of the Hudson River and White Mountains Schools.

Today, the Green Mountains of Vermont are a popular ski retreat, as is Corner Brook, Newfoundland's Marble Mountain, site of the 1999 Canada Winter Games. Northern New England has become a popular second-home location for Megalopolis urbanites. However, while serving the needs of the urban affluent, second-home economies favor the service sector over the higher-paying manufacturing or **quaternary sector** that locals need to support a family.

Tourism is increasingly an important source of economic growth. Nova Scotia's visitor economy is valued at $2 billion and contributes $722 million to provincial gross domestic product. Tourism contributes almost $1 billion in

PHOTO 6.17. Paper Mill at Berlin, New Hampshire, While the Mill Was Still Operating. The wood mill converted to a biomass power plant after the paper mill closed in 2008.

Newfoundland. Almost half of visitors to Nova Scotia and Newfoundland are Canadian; visitors also come from the United States and Europe. Similarly in Vermont, revenue from tourism was $2.5 billion. Visitors under the age of fifty were more likely to hike and backpack, while visitors over the age of fifty were more likely to visit historic sites and museums.

Many tourism businesses are small and medium-sized enterprises and provide the bulk of services to visitors to these provinces while offering employment opportunities to local residents in rural areas and smaller communities (photo 6.18).

Regional Trade Bloc Atlantica

The need for new economies within the North Atlantic is imperative, and a proposed answer is Atlantica: the International Northeast Economic Region (AINER), a trade bloc composed of the four Atlantic Provinces, eastern Quebec, and Northern New England. The proponents believe that

PHOTO 6.18. Chatham, Massachusetts, on Cape Cod. Many small towns and villages draw visitors and tourists.
Source: iStock/Kirkikis

public policy is responsible for the region's lag behind national averages. Some policies Atlantica seeks to change are cross-border interactions, transportation infrastructure, size of government, lowering the minimum wage, and reducing unions. The goal is to use Atlantic Canada shipping ports and highways to transport energy resources and Asian goods to the United States. The proponents cite other successful trading blocs as justification for this trade bloc.

Although some of the ideas are worthy of study, others are less so. Proposals such as lowering the minimum wage and removing the protection of unions from employees are not popular among people in economic doldrums. Opponents worry about workers who stand to lose union protection, receive lower wages, and lose human and environmental rights. Additional protests have been held with concerns over the proposed privately funded $1 billion super-highway planned to cut across New Brunswick and Maine with corridors into Vermont and northern New Hampshire.

The ideals of a healthy Atlantica economy are worthy, but the methods—eradicating traditional trade regulations—favor corporate rather than sustainable interests. There have been numerous trade and networking conferences, but to date, Atlantica remains only a proposal.

A Sustainable Future

If picturesque equaled successful, the North Atlantic would be prosperous. But beauty is becoming accessible only to those who can afford it at the expense of the local population. Large corporate trade blocs that lower wages, or second homes and retirement living are attractions for the region's future.

The last resort for regions dependent on primary industry remains tourism. Historic preservation tourism has become so invasive in the **postindustrial economy** that virtually every city lacking postmodern accomplishments has become a city seeking historic preservation to attract tourists and high-end temporary or permanent residents. What is ironic, though, is that both purchasers of second homes and retirees choose to settle in the region because of the quaint fishing villages but live in high-priced condominiums or McMansions. They drive up the cost of housing and drive out the economy that attracted them.

Being a resource hinterland has been unprofitable within the globalized economy. As long as a region depends on either the primary or tourist economy, in the current globalization it is creating its economic doom. With the future taking shape as a vertically integrated series of subcontracting industries, the losses incurred by the primary economy are subsumed in the larger corporate picture. It spells the end of the unionized worker, the independent farmer, or the fisherman. However, value-added industries are taking advantage of their locations and NAFTA trade opportunities with cross border trade between Canada and the northeastern states. The trade between Maine and the Atlantic Provinces broadened since NAFTA and may expand more if Atlantica proposals are achieve—but the question is, can it be sustainable?

Some of the challenges to a sustainable North Atlantic include the following:

- environmental changes such as climate change or pollution that impact fisheries;
- the continued loss of primary sector employment;
- emigration;
- an aging population; and
- encouraging tourism and vacation homes while maintaining affordability and regional distinctiveness.

Despite these challenges, there is hope on the horizon for an improved economy and a more sustainable region.

The region's greatest geographical advantage may be its coastal location. Regional communities are distinctly different from each other and from the remainder of the respective countries, and sustainable ideas focus on how to profit from the unique nature of the region.

A reliance on land transport is causing industry to improve transportation networks. Short sea shipping may relieve freight congestion and offer transportation advantages.

Both Nova Scotia and Prince Edward Island are in the forefront pursuing sustainable alternative energy. Prince Edward Island has constructed nearly one hundred wind turbines, created an efficient recycling system, and turned to more biomass fuel to free itself of imported fossil fuel energy. Other provinces are beginning to notice and move further in their quest to become more energy efficient.

Nova Scotian politicians have encouraged lower greenhouse gas emissions and solid waste and committing to green land and water use. Sustainability may stimulate the economy rather than devastate it. The government hopes to follow the lead of California and become one of the cleanest and most sustainable environments in the world by 2020. In 2015, Nova Scotia Power achieved a new record in renewable energy, with 26 percent of the electricity used by Nova Scotians coming from renewable resources, exceeding the legislated requirement of 25 percent renewable electricity, and positioning the Province to be on target to meet the 40 percent renewable goal by 2020. Most of the alternative energy is coming from wind power (photo 6.19).

Finally, in another sign of sustainability progress, thirteen organizations across Atlantic Canada came together to mobilize the region to take action on environmental, social, and economic sustainability. The Atlantic Canada Sustainability Initiative (ACSI) was formed with participation and support from local businesses, municipal governments, and non-governmental organizations. It became the first regional, multi-sector sustainability project in North America. These partners, ranging from the major Atlantic telecom provider and a large municipal government to a local coffee shop, have all taken on the challenge of modeling strategic sustainability. The primary goal of the sustainability partners program was to support respected local businesses, NGOs and communities in developing sustainability plans and coordinating around sustainability.

PHOTO 6.19. Picturesque Rural Scene with Water and Windmill on Hillside, in Grand Etang on the Famous Cabot Trail in Cape Breton, Nova Scotia.
Source: iStock/PaulMcKinnon

Questions for Discussion

1. What are possible sustainable growth areas for this region, both geographically and economically?

2. This region has been called the "bypassed east." What are reasons for this name, and why may it not apply today?

3. The population in Northern New England is growing, but how and why? What are the benefits/problems?

4. Explain the evolution of outports in Newfoundland and their relation to fishing.

5. After the collapse of the cod fishery in Newfoundland, the province was in economic decline. What replaced fishing economically?

6. Explain the evolution of Newfoundland from the 1400s to 1949.

7. Explain the controversy between Quebec and Newfoundland over Labrador. What is the agreed upon division?

8. How and why has the economy changed in Newfoundland since 2007?

9. Where did the Acadians first settle and where do they live now? Why has it changed?

10. What did Vermonters and the Green Mountain Boys need to do to get accepted into the United States?

11. Why does this region face challenges of emigration and not immigration?

12. Why is this region home to so few large urban areas?

13. What are examples of sustainability in the region?

14. What economic sectors have dominated the Atlantic North and why have they been declining?

15. In what ways does the tertiary sector promise to stimulate sustainable economic growth?

Suggested Readings

Armstrong, A., and R. C. Stedman. "Culture clash and second home ownership in the US Northern Forest". *Rural Sociology* 78, no. 3 (2013): 318–45.

Bardach, J. E., and R. Santerre. "Climate and the Fish in the Sea." *BioScience* 31, no. 3 (March 1981): 206–15.

Bird, J. "Settlement Patterns in Maritime Canada: 1687–1786." *Geographic Review* 45, no. 3 (1955).

Clark, A. *Acadia: The Geography of Early Nova Scotia to 1760.* Madison: University of Wisconsin Press, 1968.

Copes, P. *The Resettlement of Fishing Communities in Newfoundland.* Ottawa: Canadian Council on Rural Development, 1972.

Corbett, M. J. "We have never been urban: Modernization, small schools, and resilient rurality in Atlantic Canada". *Journal of Rural and Community Development* 9 (2014): 186–202

Cronon, W. *Changes in the Land: Indians, Colonists, and the Ecology of New England.* New York: Hill & Wang, 1983.

Faragher, M. *A Great and Nobel Scheme: The Tragic Story of the Explusion of the French Acadians from Their American Homeland*. New York: W.W. Norton, 2006.

Finch, R. *The Iambics of Newfoundland: Notes from an Unknown Shore*. Berkeley, Calif.: Counterpoint, 2007.

Frideres, J. S. *Native Peoples in Canada: Contemporary Conflicts*. Scarborough, Toronto: Prentice Hall, 1998.

Harris, M. *Lament for the Ocean: The Collapse of the Atlantic Cod Fishery, a True Crime Story*. Toronto: McClelland & Stewart, 1998.

Higgins, P. A. T., M. Mastrandrea, and S. H. Schneider. "Dynamics of Climate and Ecosystem Coupling: Abrupt Changes and Multiple Equilibria." *Philosophical Transactions of the Royal Society* 357, no. 1421 (2002): 647–55.

Holloway, A. "The Best Places to Do Business in Canada." *Canadian Business* 80, no. 18 (September 25, 2006): 26–30.

Hornsby, S. J., and J. G. Reid. *New England and the Maritime Provinces: Connections and Comparison*. Montreal and Kingston: McGill-Queens University Press, 2005.

Innis, H. *The Cod Fisheries: The History of an International Economy*. New Haven, Conn.: Yale University Press, 1940.

Kurlansky, M. *Cod*. New York: Penguin Books, 1997.

Mayda, C. "Resettlement in Newfoundland: Again." *Focus* 48, no. 1 (2004).

McGrath, C., B. Neis, and M. Porter. *Their Lives and Times*. St. John's, NL: Killick Press, 1995.

McReynolds, S. A. "Community sustainability in the year-round islands of Maine". *Island Studies Journal* 9, no. 1 (2014): 79–102.

Mitchell, R. D. "The Colonial Origins of Anglo-America." In *North America: The Historical Geography of a Changing Continent*, edited by T. F. McIlwraith and E. Muller. Lanham, MD: Rowman & Littlefield, 2001.

Miller, V. "Aboriginal Micmac Population: A Review of the Evidence," *Ethnohistory* 23, no. 2 (1976).

Noble, A. *Migration to North America: Before, during, and after the Nineteenth Century*. Baltimore: Johns Hopkins University Press, 1992.

Woodard, Colin. *The Lobster Coast*. New York: Viking, 2004.

Randall, J. E., P. Kitchen, N. Muhajarine, B. Newbold, A. Williams, and K. Wilson. "Immigrants, islandness and perceptions of quality-of-life on Prince Edward Island, Canada". *Island Studies Journal* 9, no. 2 (2014), 343–62.

Reid, J., and J. G. Reid. "The Multiple Deindustrializations of Canada's Maritime Provinces and the Evaluation of Heritage-Related Urban Regeneration." *London Journal of Canadian Studies* 31, no. 1 (2016): 89–112.

Roberts, C. *The Unnatural History of the Sea*. Washington, D.C.: Island Press, 2007.

Tastsoglou, E., A. Dobrowolsky, and B. Cottrell (eds). *The Warming of the Welcome: Is Atlantic Canada a Home Away from Home for Immigrants?* Sydney, Nova Scotia: Cape Breton University Press, 2015.

Tuttle, C. M., and Heintzelman, M. D. "The value of forever wild: an economic analysis of land use in the Adirondacks." *Agricultural and Resource Economics Review* 42 no. 1 (2013): 119–38.

Wallach, B. "Logging in Maine's Empty Quarter." *Annals of American Geographers* 70 (1980): 542–52.

Warkentin, J., ed. *Canada: A Geographical Interpretation*. Toronto: Methuen, 1968.

Wright, M. "Newfoundland and Labrador History in Canada, 1949–1972." Research Paper for the Royal Commission on Renewing and Strengthening Our Place in Canada. March 2003.

Internet Sources

Atlantica: The International Northeast Economic Region, at http://www.aims.ca/site/media/aims/SenateCommittee.pdf

Atlantic Canada Sustainability Initiative at http://www.atlanticsustainability.ca

Burlington, Vermont, sustainability plan at https://www.burlingtonvt.gov/Sustainability

Newfoundland and Labrador Heritage, at http://www.heritage.nf.ca/index.php

Nova Scotia sustainability efforts, at https://novascotia.ca/nse/airlandwater/docs/GreenPlan.pdf

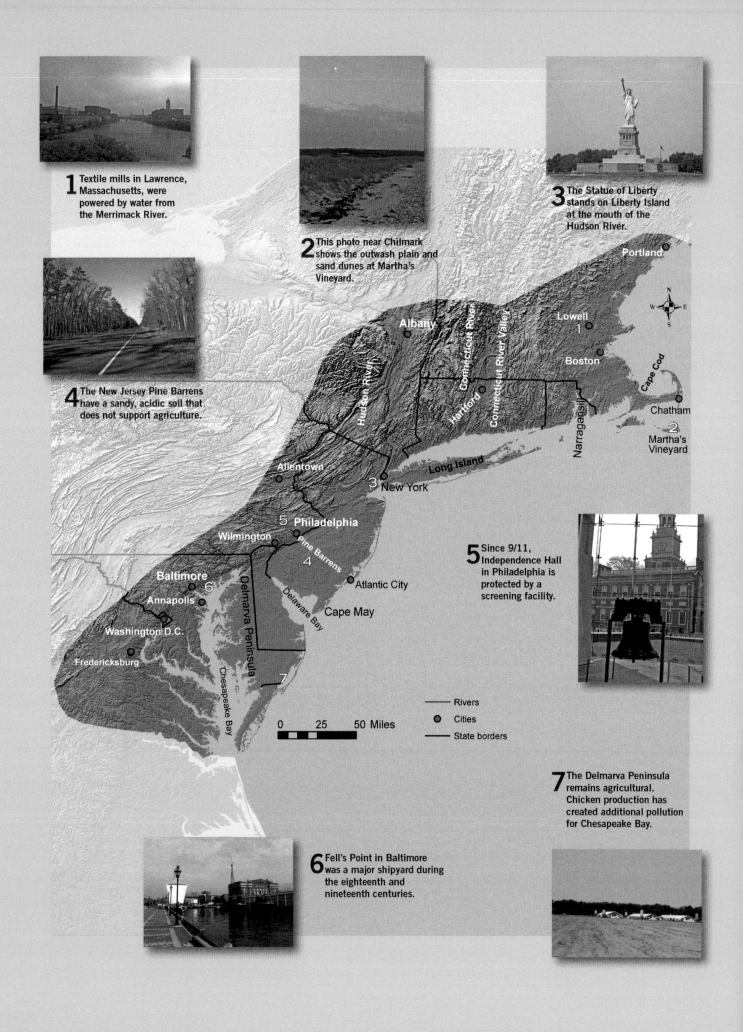

1 Textile mills in Lawrence, Massachusetts, were powered by water from the Merrimack River.

2 This photo near Chilmark shows the outwash plain and sand dunes at Martha's Vineyard.

3 The Statue of Liberty stands on Liberty Island at the mouth of the Hudson River.

4 The New Jersey Pine Barrens have a sandy, acidic soil that does not support agriculture.

5 Since 9/11, Independence Hall in Philadelphia is protected by a screening facility.

6 Fell's Point in Baltimore was a major shipyard during the eighteenth and nineteenth centuries.

7 The Delmarva Peninsula remains agricultural. Chicken production has created additional pollution for Chesapeake Bay.

Portland

Albany

Connecticut River

Lowell **1**

Connecticut River Valley

Hartford

Boston

Cape Cod

Hudson River

Narragansett

Chatham

2 Martha's Vineyard

Allentown

Long Island

3 New York

5 Philadelphia

Wilmington

Pine Barrens

Delmarva Peninsula

4

Atlantic City

Baltimore **6**

Delaware Bay

Cape May

Annapolis

Washington D.C.

7

Fredericksburg

Chesapeake Bay

0   25   50 Miles

—— Rivers
● Cities
—— State borders

7
MEGALOPOLIS
Setting Sustainable Standards

Chapter Highlights

After reading this chapter, you should be able to:

- Describe the Megalopolis region and its largest cities
- Describe some of the region's critical environmental challenges
- Compare urban and suburban growth patterns
- Identify the five boroughs of New York City
- Describe the three cultural hearths
- Explain the success of New York City over its rivals
- Discuss the region's efforts at sustainability

Terms

basement rock
Beltway

borough
BosWash
center of population
Combined Statistical Area

drowned rivers
fall line
LEED
Megalopolis

Pennsylvania Dutch
technopole
transit-oriented
    development (TOD)

Places

Cape Cod, Massachusetts
Cape May, New Jersey

Chesapeake Bay
Connecticut River Valley
Delaware Bay

Delmarva Peninsula
Long Island
Lowell, Massachusetts

Martha's Vineyard
Narragansett Basin
Pine Barrens, New Jersey

Cities (Combined Statistical Areas)

New York-Newark
    (CSA 23.6 million)
Washington-Baltimore-Arlington
    (CSA 9.6 million)

Boston-Worcester-Providence
    (CSA 8.1 million)
Philadelphia-Reading-Camden
    (CSA 7.2 million)

Hartford-West Hartford
    (CSA 1.4 million)

PHOTO 7.1. The Manhattan Skyline as Seen from New Jersey.
Source: Dmitry Avdeev

Introduction

In 1957, Geographer Jean Gottman coined the term **Megalopolis**—Greek for "very large city"—to refer to the region from Boston to Washington, D.C. The "**BosWash**" corridor, populated by fifty million people, is a region where business and finance reign supreme. Regional superlatives include the following:

- generates 20 percent of nation's total personal income;
- fourth-largest economy in the world, ahead of France and the United Kingdom;
- greatest wealth and greatest poverty;
- one-quarter of all US wholesale trade;
- one-quarter of those working in finance and law;
- highest population densities in the nation; and
- business and government center for the nation.

Megalopolis is a small region, encompassing about 1 percent of the continental land, but one out of six Americans (17 percent) reside there. Dense population, connected urban centers, and a postindustrial economy define Megalopolis more than its physical boundaries or watersheds. Its center, New York City, has been the largest city in the United States since the end of the eighteenth century (photo 7.1). Other major cities include Boston, Philadelphia, Baltimore, and Washington, D.C. Although we use the term Metropolitan Statistical Area (MSA) in other chapters, in this chapter we use the term **Combined Statistical Areas** (CSAs) to capture the spatial spread of urbanization in Megalopolis. CSAs refer to the high level of economic interconnection within adjacent cities and urban areas.

Physical Geography

Megalopolis extends from the Atlantic Coastal Plain into the Appalachian Blue Ridge and Piedmont. The rivers may be depressed below sea level, creating **drowned rivers** and converting them to estuaries and bays—Chesapeake, Delaware, and New York bays. Several Megalopolis cities lie near the deep bays of the convoluted coastline.

Megalopolis occupies the Atlantic Coastal Plain. The plain continues offshore, gradually descending on the continental shelf until the continental slope drop-off. The embayed topography, indented coastline, and deciduous forests were a welcome sight to European immigrants. They set about taking the land from the indigenous people and began to farm. In southern Megalopolis, farms expanded into plantations, growing crops that England wanted but could not grow. But in the north, farming was less successful or lucrative; soon northern farms reverted to woodlands, as farmers either moved west toward better land or to the sea or cities of New England. Many non-urban areas of Megalopolis reverted to forest, although exotic species are often more prevalent than native.

The Atlantic Ocean defines the eastern boundary, but the other boundaries are less distinct and change as populations grow and transportation changes. Today, traffic permitting, the Merrimack Valley, once more than a day's ride away, is incorporated into the Boston metropolitan area, as are the coastal areas of New Hampshire and southern Maine. The southern margin expands into counties beyond Arlington, Virginia. The western boundary is the least distinct of all and is best defined as where urban meets rural, seldom more than one hundred miles inland.

Subregions

New England

The Cape Cod to Hudson River portion of New England is a recently emerged part of the continental shelf. Glaciers flattened the land, leaving moraines that shaped the exposed ridge of Cape Cod and the islands of Martha's Vineyard, Nantucket, and Long Island. Climate change has already begun to raise sea levels and erode coastal areas lacking **basement rock**. In Cape Cod, oceanside sand cliffs have no resistance to rising sea level and waves. In Chatham, located on the elbow of the Cape, nine houses were lost to storms, and more are vulnerable to the capricious movement of sand. The Cape's Wellfleet or Chatham shorelines accrete or recede randomly each year, but the continued sea-level rise is washing away the sandy cliffs and threatening habitats and homes.

BOX 7.1 THE METROPOLITAN STATISTICAL AREA (MSA) AND THE COMBINED STATISTICAL AREA (CSA)

We use the term Metropolitan Statistical Area (MSA) when referring to most of the urban areas in this book. For example, the New York–Newark–Jersey City, NY–NJ–PA Metropolitan Statistical Area has a 2016 population of 20.1 million and consists of the following:

- New York–Jersey City–White Plains, NY–NJ Metropolitan Division
- Kings County, NY (*the borough of Brooklyn in New York City*)
- Queens County, NY (*the borough of Queens in New York City*)
- New York County, NY (*the borough of Manhattan in New York City*)
- Bronx County, NY (*the borough of The Bronx in New York City*)
- Richmond County, NY (*the borough of Staten Island in New York City*)
- Westchester County, NY
- Bergen County, NJ
- Hudson County, NJ
- Middlesex County, NJ
- Monmouth County, NJ
- Ocean County, NJ
- Passaic County, NJ
- Rockland County, NY
- Orange County, NY
- Nassau County–Suffolk County, NY Metropolitan Division
  - Suffolk County
  - Nassau County
- Dutchess County-Putnam County, NY Metropolitan Division
  - Putnam County
  - Dutchess County
- Newark, NJ–PA Metropolitan Division
  - Essex County, NJ
  - Union County, NJ

- Morris County, NJ
- Somerset County, NJ
- Sussex County, NJ
- Hunterdon County, NJ
- Pike County, PA
- Northampton County, PA
- Lehigh County, PA

In this chapter, we use the term Combined Statistical Area (CSA) to more accurately represent the region and to highlight that these CSAs are areas with a high degree of economic interconnection. CSAs tend to be larger geographically than MSAs. For example, the New York CSA includes all of the New York–Newark–Jersey City, NY–NJ–PA Metropolitan Statistical Area *and* the following:

- Bridgeport–Stamford–Norwalk, CT Metropolitan Statistical Area
  - Fairfield County
- New Haven–Milford, CT Metropolitan Statistical Area
  - New Haven County, Connecticut
- Allentown–Bethlehem–Easton Metropolitan Statistical Area
  - Warren County, New Jersey
  - Carbon County, Pennsylvania
- Trenton, NJ Metropolitan Statistical Area
  - Mercer County
- Torrington, CT Micropolitan Statistical Area
  - Litchfield County
- Kingston, NY Metropolitan Statistical Area
  - Ulster County
- East Stroudsburg, PA Metropolitan Statistical Area
  - Monroe County, Pennsylvania

Southern Coastal Megalopolis

New York City's landscape has been altered since Henry Hudson landed. The biota were lost under tons of concrete—concrete supported by Manhattan's sturdy schist bedrock (photo 7.2). The look of the land has changed so radically that few could imagine it prior to Anglo American settlement. Just to the south and west of New York City lies New Jersey, the most densely populated state, which contains two anomalous rural areas—Hutcheson Memorial Forest and the Pine Barrens. Southern New Jersey's soil, sandy and acidic, supports miles of pitch pine forests called the Barrens. This poor farmland was never settled to the degree of more productive soils, and today the drive from Atlantic City to Camden remains bucolic. The Pinelands are protected as a national reserve, due to threatening suburban encroachment.

Two major bays define the sites for major Megalopolis cities. The Delaware and Chesapeake bays are two submerged valleys that are now estuaries. The Delaware Estuary stretches from Cape May in New Jersey, inland past Philadelphia, and upstream to Trenton, New Jersey. Three large city ports—Philadelphia; Camden, New Jersey; and Wilmington, Delaware—now support petrochemical shipments and refineries. The Chesapeake Bay estuary is the largest in the nation, incorporating portions of six states and stretching two hundred miles from Havre de Grace, Maryland, to Norfolk, Virginia.

The Fall Line

A major geologic feature of southern Megalopolis is the **fall line**, where the harder rock of the Piedmont ends and the softer coastal soils begin. The inland barrier to navigation, the fall line was once the end of the continental shelf. Over time, sediment from the Appalachians was deposited and built up the coastal plain.

PHOTO 7.2. New York City Skyscrapers. At the tip of the isle of Manhattan sits the financial capital of the United States, and one of the most important cities in the world. It is Manhattan's bedrock geology—a metamorphic rock called schist—that makes the high-rise skyline possible. Where the schist is close to the surface, it provides the structural stability needed for the skyscrapers.

Source: John R Short

The fall line extends from New Jersey to Talladega, Alabama (map 7.1). The Rappahannock River in Chesapeake Bay generally divides the fall line topography; north is a distinct escarpment, south diminishes to rapids with little "fall" but a distinctive soil transition from the harder Piedmont to the sandy coastal alluvium.

Fall line rapids and waterfalls were the end of navigation up or down the rivers and therefore a natural place for break-in-bulk cities to develop as transfer points for portaging goods around the fall line obstructions until bypassed by canals. Megalopolis cities tend to be either at the rapids and waterfalls of the fall line (Trenton, Philadelphia, Baltimore, and Washington) or at harbors (New York and Boston).

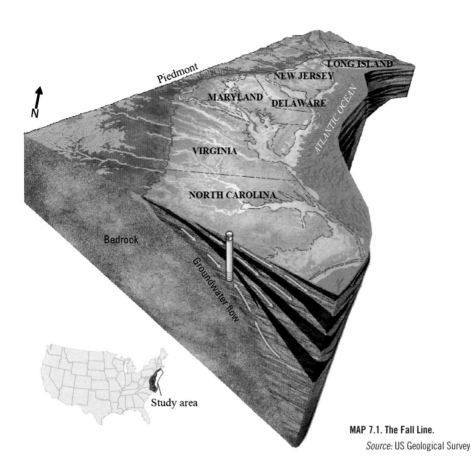

MAP 7.1. The Fall Line.
Source: US Geological Survey

BOX 7.2 THE POSITIVE AND NEGATIVE RESULTS OF DRAINING WETLANDS AND CLEANING ESTUARIES

Seventy percent of Americans now live in coastal counties. Many of these areas, though, were originally tidal swamps, especially along the Atlantic and Gulf coasts. They are habitable today because the swamps were drained. They have been buttressed by billions of dollars of sand dredging and continually rebuilding beaches. The reasons for the draining were both agriculturally and health related.

Draining swamps was intended to create agricultural land, not build sandy beaches and a leisure lifestyle. Along the Atlantic Coast and estuaries, industrious English and Dutch settlers used their knowledge of draining their homeland coastlines to build drainage ditches and create agricultural land in America, such as the extensive reclamation along Delaware Bay. Delaware's drained land was eventually abandoned and reverted back to the tidal marshes when better agricultural lands were found. In Delaware, the abandoned land has been transformed to reduce runoff and increase wildlife habitat, but shopping malls and residential developments are often built on reclaimed land. The far heavier impact on the land destroys the soils of the altered landscape. Restoration of these lands is often impossible.

Another reason to drain the swamps was the so-called fevers of the nineteenth century, which today would go by the modern names of malaria, cholera, and typhoid. Draining the lands and spraying them with pesticides eliminated the causes of the diseases, but it also drastically changed the benefits of a swampy, marshy landscape and caused unintended consequences.

Most people living along the coast are unaware of the prior wetlands. They do not understand how the land has been altered, ecosystems destroyed, and their vulnerability to storms and floods increased. Knowing the history of the land you live on is an important part of becoming sustainable, especially when living in an area that is being affected by climate change. The risk of sea-level rise and flooding in the heavily populated area will increase along with temperatures.

Water

Waterways are plentiful along the Megalopolis coast. Five major rivers—the Connecticut, Hudson, Delaware, Susquehanna, and Potomac—flow from their Appalachian headwaters to the sea. The Delaware and Chesapeake Bays offer safe ports and were the location for Anglo settlements. Barrier beaches extend from Long Island through New Jersey, where the landscape becomes one of drowned valleys or swampy tidal flats. The rivers and bays supported a fishing economy until the late twentieth century, when increased population caused runoff pollution and sea level rise began to threaten coastal areas.

The Appalachian headwater rivers—the Hudson, Connecticut, Delaware, and Potomac—spawned the water-power-dependent cities of the Industrial Revolution and may be a source of future power.

The Hudson River marks the southern extent of the last ice age glaciation. North of the river, the topographic formations—drumlins, moraines, outwash plains, and fjords—are remnants of ice age glaciation. The river follows a fjord that thousands of years ago drained the meltwaters of glacial lakes of Iroquois, Albany, and Vermont. The deep fjord allows the salty Atlantic water to flow as far as Albany.

The Connecticut River, New England's longest river, evolved when glacial Lake Hitchcock drained thirteen thousand years ago after a moraine dam eroded, flooding the valley and blanketing it with fertile sediment. Today, the river flows through the valley, now one of the few regional agricultural areas. Native Americans occupied the valley until they were subjected to diseases brought by the Dutch and English settlers, who began arriving in 1620. By 1670, small Anglo towns extended along the river to Massachusetts.

The Connecticut River has been used and abused over the years. During the Industrial Revolution, the river was used to dump waste, which polluted the water and ruined a once-thriving fishing industry. In the 1960s, deindustrialization, the environmental movement, and legislation such as the Clean Water Act rehabilitated the river. During the 1990s, as sustainability and renewable energy became the new zeitgeist, seventy additional watershed sites were identified as having hydropower potential.

Southern Megalopolis waterways have been less successfully renewed. The Chesapeake, Long Island, and Delaware estuaries continue to house ever-larger populations, while industrial waste, raw sewage, and hypoxia induce fish kills. Tidal action scours the estuaries clean, but pollution now overcomes the tide's ability to cleanse the water. Unsustainable environmental assaults, such as the aborted Broadwater Energy Project to pipe liquefied natural gas, continue to threaten the already contaminated Long Island Sound.

There have been efforts to identify new hydropower energy sources. In New York City, for example, Verdant power established the Roosevelt Island Tidal Energy Project (RITE) in 2012. RITE is located in the East Channel of the East River. The project is a system of underwater turbines—not unlike those used for wind power—that generates enough electricity to power seventy-five thousand homes. A distinct advantage of tidal power over other forms of renewable energy is that it can be easily predicted and monitored. Unlike sunlight and wind flow, the tides of the Earth can be accurately predicted decades in advance.

BOX 7.3   ENVIRONMENTAL CHALLENGES: SOLVING STORMWATER RUNOFF WITH GRAY OR GREEN SOLUTIONS?

Washington, D.C., like many cities in North America, confronts the challenge of nonpoint source pollution in its waterways. It is subject to the requirements set out in the Clean Water Act, and because Washington, D.C. is part of the Chesapeake Bay watershed, it is also subject to the plan for improving water quality for the Bay.

In many cities in Megalopolis, parts of the sewer systems were built between 1870 and 1910 and are combined sewer systems. Combined sewer systems can not handle a large volume of stormwater and a rain event of even one half of an inch causes the combined sewer system to overflow into nearby rivers. In Washington, D.C., there are fifty-three combined sewer outfalls (CSOs) outfalls, the Anacostia and Potomac Rivers, which then flow into the Chesapeake Bay. CSOs can adversely affect water quality by introducing bacteria and trash to the water. The high level of organic debris in the water can also lead to low dissolved oxygen in the water, which can stress or kill fish. In the mid 1990s, D.C. averaged about 3.2 billion gallons per year of CSO overflow. Improvement projects that have included upgrades to various pipes and existing tunnels helped to reduce CSOs to about two billion gallons. But it's not enough, and the Environmental Protection Agency (EPA) has told D.C. to solve the problem.

Solving the problem of stormwater runoff has led to a debate about which type of solutions to implement: gray or green infrastcture?

Gray solutions are man-made, more technological answers to nonpoint source pollution. For example, one gray solution being constructed for D.C. consists of three large concrete tunnels that will serve as storage for stormwater runoff. These tunnels will store combined sewage and when the storm is over, the stormwater will be pumped out of the tunnel and sent to a wastewater treatment plant. The estimated costs is $2.5 billion. When completed, two tunnels will be twenty-three feet in diameter and will hold 157 million gallons of stormwater runoff; a third will be smaller. But is investing $2.5 billion to build concrete storage tanks a good or sustainable solution?

Another possibility is a green solution. A green solution manages stormwater before it enters the city's combined sewer system. Such solutions can include a variety of approaches that use resources to hold, retain, and slowly release the water into the sewerage system. These can include bioretention or rain gardens, which store and filter water. Rain gardens planted with water-loving vegetation can be small—in backyards, parks, or along greenways, for example. Other small scale green infrastructure includes rain barrels, which store water that is running out of gutters on homes and other buildings. Bioswales are another example. A bioswale uses an existing low area to retain water. Finally, green roofs can also retain and store water. The main idea behind green infrastructure is not to eliminate the stormwater runoff, but to slow it down, retain it, and release it slowly over a longer period of time, thus allowing the existing sewage infrastructure to handle the volume of water once the rain event is over.

The challenge in using green infrastructure, however, is that a city will need many different types across many different locations. This may be why the simpler solution of building massive concrete tunnels is appealing. Yet, the benefits of a green solution to stormwater management connects to other types of initiatives such as new requirements for green buildings. Investing in green infrastructure instead of large tunnels and detention tanks is a smarter approach to stormwater management; it can save the city money, and at the same time improve green space and the aesthetic quality of the city.

In addition to issues of water quality, water supply is also a major challenge in the region. Over use of freshwater along the entire eastern shoreline has caused saltwater intrusion that threatens coastal aquifers and results in a depletion of wildlife, aquatic sea life, and lack of water for the growing population. Freshwater supplies have hit crisis levels, and residents of Massachusetts, New York, and New Jersey have been periodically ordered to restrict water use.

The New York City water supply system encompasses three reservoir systems. Much is upstate in the Catskill Mountains on land protected from development. New York City water has been proclaimed as among the best in the world and is one of the last unfiltered drinking water supplies in the nation, although it is treated with chlorine and fluoride to meet disinfection and contamination standards.

Several Megalopolis organizations seek environmental, ecological, and social equity in water use. For example, organizations that support sustainability worked to terminate the Broadwater Project and preserve the waterways for the future by calculating its environmental and social costs, thereby revealing the true cost of modifications.

Chesapeake Bay

Thirty-five millions years ago, a meteor strike formed a crater at the mouth of Chesapeake Bay, creating a drowned estuary in the lower Susquehanna River. The former tributaries of the lower Susquehanna—the Potomac, James, and Rappahannock—now empty into the drowned valley. Much of the area is shallow and a critical nursery habitat for aquatics. The Chesapeake has multiple habitats including forests, wetlands, tidal marshes, and open waters.

Climate change has altered the existing ecosystems and places habitats, beaches, and barrier islands at risk for sea-level rise along the Delaware and Chesapeake bays. An estimated two-foot rise by the end of the century could inundate up to four hundred square miles of the Chesapeake Bay coastline. The low-lying topography and increased population living along the shore make the bay one of the most vulnerable to sea-level rise.

The Chesapeake was once the healthiest estuary for fish and shellfish in the United States, but today, the sixty-four-thousand-square-mile Chesapeake Bay watershed fishery has collapsed. Sixteen million people draining their refuse from the Delmarva Peninsula (Delaware and portions of Maryland and Virginia) and agricultural run-off to the bay has had the unintended consequences of toxicity and loss of aquatic life. The runoff and manure disposal from poultry farms on the peninsula are responsible for causing phytoplankton toxicity. Phytoplankton is food for oysters. In coastal areas known for local seafood, the restaurants sell imported oysters, clams, and crabs.

In addition to agricultural runoff, nonpoint urban runoff has polluted the waters of the Delmarva Peninsula. Runoff from city streets, air pollution, nitrogen- and phosphorus-rich inorganic nutrients from farmlands, and outflows from sewage treatment plants have choked the bay. The excess nutrients block sunlight, hampering grass growth, depleting oxygen from water, and creating a hypoxic zone that kills fish. An oversupply of nutrients causes algae blooms, cutting off the oxygen supply and damaging the clam, scallop, and mussel fishery. The sick ecosystem

has produced sick aquatics. All aquatics are now under strict quotas or limits to preserve the stock.

Today, the Bay's dead zones are estimated to kill seventy-five thousand tons of bottom-dwelling clams and worms each year, weakening the base of the estuary's food chain. This affects the blue crab in particular because they feed on base of the food chain. Crabs are sometimes observed to amass on shore to escape pockets of oxygen-poor water, a behavior known as a "crab jubilee."

The bay's pollution was so egregious that in 1983 the Chesapeake Bay Program was formed, with the goal of reducing nutrients by 40 percent by 2000. The deadline expired unfulfilled, but bay restoration has continued to be a critical investment to improve the environment and restore the ecosystem. For decades, the Chesapeake Bay has been listed among the nation's "impaired waters." Federal and state partnerships have launched programs to reduce nitrogen, phosphorus, and sediment pollution, hoping to get the Bay and its tributaries off the Clean Water Act "Impaired Waters" list by 2025. Experts estimate that it could cost $15 billion to clean up the Bay, and that will need to come from a combination of federal and state investment.

One of the main challenges to cleaning up the Bay is the fragmented watershed shared by several states (map 7.2).

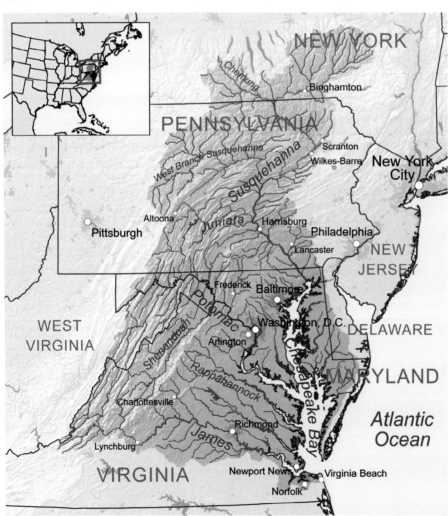

MAP 7.2. States in the Chesapeake Bay Watershed.

Source: Kmusser

BOX 7.4   CLIMATE CHANGE IN NEW YORK CITY

New York City is a city surrounded by water. Historically, its rivers and harbors have been an advantage, facilitating trade and moderating temperatures. In future, climate change will likely increase the city's vulnerability to flooding from hurricanes and storms.

A 2017 study[*] by climate scientists examines how the impact of climate change—higher seas, large storm surge, and more intense hurricanes—will impact New York City over the next three hundred years. The study compares data from three sources: models of storm surge in New York City, probabilistic projections of sea-level rise, and advanced climate models that include high-resolution hurricane simulations.

The study suggests that as global sea levels rise and as a warming atmosphere drives tropical storms, the combination could leave the city facing more frequent and more dangerous flood events. Sea-level rise will make every tropical cyclone that hits New York more likely to cause damaging floods. For example, storm floods of nearly 7.5 feet once occurred only a couple times per millennium. In the next ten to twenty years, 7.5-foot floods

are projected to happen every twenty-five years. By 2030, these floods will occur every five years.

The study also pointed to Hurricane Sandy, which spawned devastating floods in 2012, as an example of extreme weather events the city could face. Superstorm Sandy resulted in ten-foot floods on much of Manhattan, Brooklyn, and Staten Island, inundating thousands of buildings. When slow-moving Sandy made landfall in southern New Jersey, it produced a storm surge for an extended period of time, which amplified the flooding because the storm surge overlapped with a high astronomical tide to produce correspondingly larger flood heights.

These types of impacts of climate change on coastal inundation will require risk management solutions in this highly populated region of millions.

---

*A. Garner, M. Mann, K. Emanuel, R. Kopp, N. Lin, R. Alley, B. Horton, R. DeConto, J. Donnelly, and D. Pollard. "Impact of climate change on New York City's coastal flood hazard: Increasing flood heights from the preindustrial to 2300 CE." *Proceedings of the National Academy of Sciences of the United States of America* 114, no. 45 (2017): 11861–86.

PHOTO 7.3. Chesapeake Bay Bridge. The bridge spans the Chesapeake and links the eastern and western shores of Maryland. It opened in 1952. A parallel span was added in 1973.

Source: John R Short

Although science has drawn a clear road map for saving the Bay, coordinating the various stakeholders has proven very difficult. Under the Clean Water Act, the federal government delegates permits, administration, and enforcement to the states. There are six states and the District of Columbia within the watershed. Each state has numerous counties, cities, and townships; in total there are more than eighteen hundred local governments in the Chesapeake Bay watershed. Getting them all to endorse the science and commit to pollution targets has been a major obstacle to progress. Many

experts say that science has drawn a clear road map for saving the Bay, but it will take tremendous political will to make it happen (photo 7.3).

Climate

Weather in mid-latitude Megalopolis is humid in the summer; winter varies from cold in the north to mild in the south. Winds blowing from the west minimize the ocean's influence. Ample precipitation (forty to forty-five inches) is

BOX 7.5 GEOSPATIAL TECHNOLOGIES: VULNERABILITY TO CLIMATE CHANGE

The US Army Corps of Engineers undertook a two-year study to identify areas of vulnerability to increased storms due to climate change. Their North Atlantic Coast Comprehensive Study used sophisticated geospatial data modeling to identify areas subject to very high and high risk. This map is useful to local communities in order to prepare for and protect against flood risk and damage to ecosystems, property, and vulnerable populations. The subtitle of the report is Resilient Adaption to Increasing Risk.

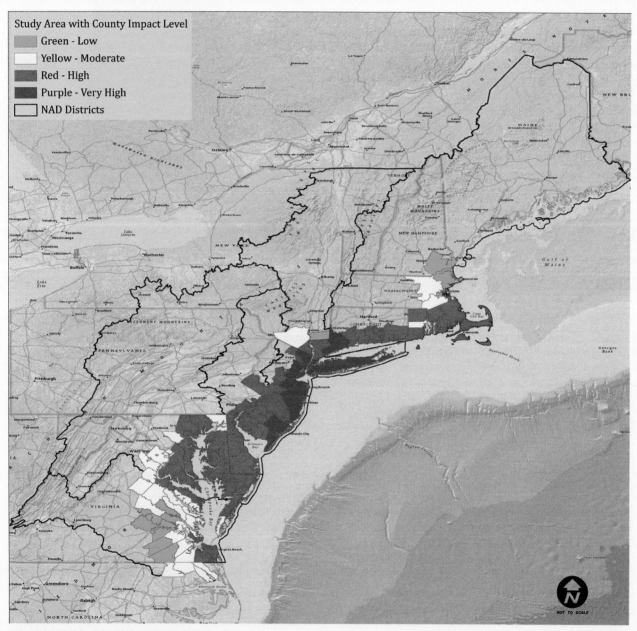

MAP 7.3. Megalopolis: Vulnerability to Climate Change.

Source: US Army Corps of Engineers

distributed throughout the year, with the occasional crippling snowstorm. During the summer, thunderstorms bring considerable precipitation, and the occasional hurricane can damage coastal areas. In 2012, Hurricane Sandy cause considerable damage as it wreaked havoc along the Atlantic coast of Megalopolis and revealed the vulnerability of the region to storm surges and flooding.

Acid Rain (Acid Deposition)

Rain is naturally acidic (pH 5.6) but becomes more so when oversupplies of sulfur dioxide and nitrogen oxides react with the rain and lower the pH. Midwestern coal-burning power plants spew sulfur and nitrogen oxides into the air, which are carried east by the winds and result in acid rain (pH less than 5.6) in the the cities of Megalopolis. While new power plants are equipped with scrubbers to minimize the pollution, older plants are grandfathered in without the pollution mitigation.

Acid rain leaches nutrients from soil, stresses plants, decays building materials, sterilizes lakes, and harms wildlife. Some of the direct consequences have been the death of red spruce trees, loss of sugar maples, and the long-term and life-killing acidification of lakes. Most acid rain is the result of coal-burning power plants, but other causes include automobile emissions, chemical reactions of water in rain, and volcanic eruptions.

Acid rain can be curtailed by reducing car usage and by reducing power plant emissions through technologic devices such as scrubbers, although most power plants will avoid scrubbers due to their half-billion dollar price tag (photo 7.4). Catalytic converters and unleaded gasoline use have decreased atmospheric pollutants. However, catalytic converters have been criticized because they decrease fuel efficiency and increase nitrous oxide, a greenhouse gas. In Megalopolis, the main culprit causing acid rain is midwestern power-plant emissions.

Historical Geography and Settlement

Numerous Native American tribes occupied the region prior to European arrival. They shaped the landscape through the use of fire. Native Americans who hunted game animals were not just taking the "unplanted bounties of nature"; they were using fire to harvest a foodstuff. Few English observers realized that while Native cultures lacked domesticated livestock they nevertheless practiced a different type of animal husbandry.

Diseases contacted from European immigrants diminished their population rapidly, so by 1681 when Penn founded Philadelphia, the decline in the Native population minimized tribal interference with white settlement.

PHOTO 7.4. Cleopatra's Needle near the Metropolitan Museum, New York City. The obelisk had lain in the Egyptian desert for thousands of years before being transported to its current location. When the obelisk arrived in New York, the hieroglyphs were clearly visible, but a hundred years of pollution and acid rain have obscured the inscriptions. Acid rain can destroy irreplaceable cultural artifacts.

Source: Photo by B. Christopherson

Martha's Vineyard, Nantucket, and the Sound

As the glacier retreated ten thousand years ago, Martha's Vineyard and Nantucket, located seven miles south of Cape Cod, were dry, inland hills on the coastal plain. As the ice melted and the water rose, they became islands on the continental shelf. All landscape features and waterways on the islands owe their origin to the glacier, wind, or waves. Sand dunes and beach deposits surround protected, low-barrier beaches and marshes, while wetlands have been filled, drained, and often developed.

Wampanoags settled the islands, perhaps as long as ten thousand years ago. Their diminished numbers occupy a small island reservation. They no longer depend on the fish and shellfish that were once staples of their diet.

Europeans settled the Vineyard in 1642 near the present site of Edgartown. Nantucket was settled in 1795. Settlers farmed and fished the bountiful waters until about 1800; whaling was the primary industry from 1800 until the 1870s, when petroleum replaced whale oil. The tourism economy followed, beginning slowly, with religious camp revival meetings in the Vineyard, while Quakers became the dominant force on Nantucket.

The real growth impetus was World War II and the evolution of mass transport. The Megalopolis population growth and the accessibility of the nearby islands made Martha's Vineyard and Nantucket a summer hideaway for the affluent. In the Vineyard, escalating prices and taxes have caused many of the fifteen thousand year-round local residents to lose their homes. During the summer months, more than a hundred thousand additional residents swell the population, and another twenty-five thousand visit on any summer day.

Cultural Perspectives

Megalopolis was the heart of transplanted European settlement and the home to the three East Coast hearths—Tidewater, New England, and Mid-Atlantic. The influences of these hearths spread across the continent and helped shape how the land was used.

The Tidewater hearth, along the barrier islands from Virginia south, was the first English settlement area. This temperate hearth was settled by a wealthier clientele, who had the king's favor. They were seeking to better their financial circumstances by raising coveted crops—tobacco, rice, indigo, and cotton—that did not grow in England and could be exported there.

The New England hearth in the Massachusetts Bay area was established by twenty thousand Puritans who arrived on the colder and rocky northern coast from 1620 to 1635. The Puritans immigrated because of religious intolerance but were intolerant of others; they even fragmented among themselves, thus beginning other New England colonies. Farming was the presupposed economy, but the poor soils turned many people to trade, shipbuilding, or fishing the Grand Banks. Wood, a plentiful natural resource in New England but rare in deforested England, was the favored material for building ships and homes.

The religiously tolerant Mid-Atlantic cultural hearth was settled by several groups, beginning in 1637 when Swedes and Dutch settled the Delaware estuary south of New York. The changes in the economic system were in full swing by the 1681 settlement of Pennsylvania. Capitalism changed how that hearth was settled. Individuals over groups and speculation over religion shaped the last Atlantic hearth landscape. The Mid-Atlantic hearth became home to various ethnic and religious groups that were unwelcome in their homelands and in New England. English settlers in Pennsylvania were interspersed with Welsh and German Quakers, who settled in separate enclaves. Various religious and utopian sects settled and

continue to occupy the Pennsylvania landscape, such as the Amish in Lancaster County and the Moravians in Bethlehem. The Scots-Irish also arrived through the Philadelphia portal beginning in 1718, but they funneled into the Great Valley seeking more affordable land.

Megalopolis established the settlement and cultural patterns of the eastern half of the nation. The three cultural hearths—Tidewater, New England, and Mid-Atlantic—each had distinctive features and represented ideas that would be copied and modified to fit the westward-moving settlers.

Urban Trends

Megalopolis is the most urban and densely populated region within the United States (map 7.4). The major cities in Megalopolis were established during the colonial period and therefore used traditional site and situation locations. These included defensive and transportation sites and situations in relation to local resources:

- Merrimack Valley: established in relation to water used for manufacturing;
- Boston: established on a defensive site that also was on a good harbor;
- Narragansett Basin: water sites;
- Connecticut River Valley: fertile agricultural land;
- Albany and the Hudson River Valley: waterway into the interior;
- New York City: harbor;
- Philadelphia: between two rivers with access to ocean;

MAP 7.4. Counties and Cities of Megalopolis.
Source: John R Short

- Baltimore: harbor; and
- Washington, D.C.: **center of population**, not north or south.

Some of the cities in Megalopolis—Boston and New York—were built following the feudal organic layout, which is still reflected in the oldest part of the cities. Only later did they adopt the more modern grid pattern that was first practiced in Philadelphia. The cities grew in relation to seventeenth- through nineteenth-century transportation methods—waterways and animal power—and therefore are more compact and more like cities in Europe. This pattern may give them an advantage as we move away from fossil fuel–induced sprawl and toward more sustainable and technologically advanced living patterns.

Merrimack Valley
(2016 pop. Lowell 110,558; Lawrence 80,209)

The first industrialized towns in America, Lowell and Lawrence, were located north of Boston in the Merrimack River valley (photo 7.5). The Merrimack River was the principal energy source for ten cotton and woolen textile mill complexes—Lawrence had the largest worsted wool mill in the world into the 1920s. The buildings still line the river, although they are no longer used as mills. In the early twentieth century, textile and shoe mills moved south in search of cheaper operating costs, which collapsed the regional economy.

Today, the Merrimack populated area extends well beyond the valley into Portsmouth, New Hampshire, and Portland, Maine. In the twenty-first century, the Merrimack region is part of the greater Boston metropolitan region. The Merrimack Valley has attracted immigrants from its founding (the Irish) to the present. Today's immigrants are largely Hispanic and Asian

(Lawrence is 74 percent Hispanic, while Lowell is 17 percent Hispanic and 20 percent Asian).

Industry has focused on renewal as "Innovation Valley," concentrating on technology and green developments. Many of the old textile mills are morphing into retail and loft complexes, including the large green condo development at Wood Mill, which includes a massive geothermal heating and cooling unit. Today, the Merrimack River continues to provide energy for the region, both the traditional dammed power and also innovative undammed hydropower technology such as underwater turbines.

Boston, Massachusetts
(2016 pop. 673,184)

Boston, founded in 1630, remains the economic capital of New England and for a century had the third-largest population in the nation. The Boston CSA is the fifth-largest in the country and includes Cambridge, Quincy, and Rhode Island and extends north along the Massachusetts, southern New Hampshire, and Maine coastal areas. Most of the metropolitan area is urbanized, while western Massachusetts is more rural.

Settlements surrounded Boston's excellent protected harbor. The original landscape was hilly and compact. The original downtown complex contains the twisted, narrow, medieval roads common prior to the adoption of the modern grid (photo 7.6). That pattern, as with other compact US cities, has served it well in its environmental efforts. However, the city continued to grow beyond its peninsula beginnings. The hills were leveled and the fill used to extend the city into the marshes and bay. The result was a tripling in size of the narrow peninsula.

In the seventeenth century, the forests surrounding Boston were a resource for its shipbuilding industry. Boston traders

PHOTO 7.5. Cotton Mill Reborn, Lowell, Massachusetts. Boot Mills processed cotton during the nineteenth century. By the late twentieth century, it was reborn as luxury apartments and condominiums.

PHOTO 7.6. Old State House, Boston, Massachusetts (Brick Building in Center). The oldest surviving public building, built in 1713, was once the tallest structure in the city, but today is dwarfed by the surrounding city. Inner-city Boston streets are medieval in style, laid out prior to the modern gridiron pattern.

roamed the seas from England to the Pacific and China. For example, Boston traders brought the first missionaries to Hawai`i.

But as the Boston hinterlands were tapped, people migrated toward better agricultural land. Traders sought out new enterprises for investment, leading them to create the textile industry during the Industrial Revolution. Later, as industry moved to the southern states, the city went into decline until the 1980s when technologic research at local universities—Harvard, MIT, and a host of other Boston schools—created the Boston **technopole**. Technological industries include electronics, computer, aerospace, and pharmaceuticals. Many major companies are located in both Boston (Liberty Mutual and Houghton Mifflin) and the greater Boston area (Bose, Novartis, and Raytheon).

Boston is the city most identified with the American Revolution. Its many historic buildings and sites include the Old North Church, the Paul Revere House, the Boston Commons, and the Freedom Trail.

Boston is also a cultural center with a strong elitist tradition, especially among those who have longtime roots in the community. The population was white until an influx of African Americans and Latinos in the late twentieth century. In 2016, the ethnic mix was 53 percent white, 24 percent black, 8 percent Asian, and 15 percent Latino. There is a wide discrepancy between socioeconomics and segregated residential areas that correspond with the socioeconomic divisions. While the 2015 median household income was above the US average ($53,900 US; Boston, $55,700 US), almost one-fifth of the population lives below the poverty level (21 percent).

Boston is home to a significant number of foreign born. More than 25 percent of the city was born outside the United States and the number of foreign-born residents increased by nearly 20 percent from 2000 to 2015. The top countries of origin include the Dominican Republic (13 percent), China (10 percent), Haiti (7.5 percent), El Salvador (6 percent), and Vietnam (6 percent). Over the last twenty years, the proportion of Boston's white population decreased almost 20 percentage points. During this time, the black/African American share of the population stayed fairly consistent. The bulk of the change in the racial and ethnic composition of Boston happened in the Latino and Asian communities. And while East Boston by far has the highest concentration of immigrants, most of the city's neighborhoods are home to a substantial population of foreign-born residents.

Boston and nearby Cambridge are national leaders in sustainable development. The city is on the verge of a power revolution, using grass and leaves for methane production, while Cambridge aims to make 50 percent of its homes energy efficient by 2020. It has also been a leader in adopting energy-efficient initiatives, such as providing incentives for increased solar capacity and distributing water-saving kits to residents. Water consumption is one of the lowest in the nation, averaging seventy-four gallons a person daily, versus the US city average of 155 gallons.

Another example has been the rethinking of transportation. In the 1950s and 1960s, many cities built freeways and highways through the center city in an attempt to move goods and people easily (photo 7.7). However, the result was that these roads often destroyed the heart of the city, cutting off pedestrian access to neighborhoods or waterfronts. Since then, many cities have torn down these freeways. One project of note was the "Big Dig," completed in 2005. The Big Dig tunnel through the center of the downtown district replaced the clogged central artery. The Big Dig proved to be a public works project on the scale of the Alaska Pipeline or the English Channel Tunnel. Cost overruns (at $14.6 billion, about seven times the original estimate), corruption, and shoddy construction caused controversy over the Big Dig. Still, the project represented an attempt to take back the city from the car.

Narragansett Basin
(2016 pop. 1,790,219 [Providence]; part of the Boston CSA)

Providence, Rhode Island, is both the second-largest city and second-largest industrial center in northeastern Megalopolis. The Narragansett Basin lowland emerges from the bay of the same name and is composed of Providence, Woonsocket, and Pawtucket and several small islands in Rhode Island, as well as nearby New Bedford and Fall River, Massachusetts.

PHOTO 7.7. A View of Boston and Highway 93. From the 1950s to the 1980s, many cities built freeways or highways or interstates through the center city to improve the efficiency of transportation.

Source: iStock/rabbit75_ist

The dissident Rhode Island colony broke away from Massachusetts and became an important ocean-faring state, dependent on fishing, whaling, rum-making, and the slave trade until it developed a textile industry. The nation's first water-powered textile mill was built in Pawtucket in 1793 (photo 7.8). Other small textile mills allowed the basin towns to develop as mill villages. Larger mills were located on more powerful rivers in Massachusetts.

Cotton and textile mills were the investment standard during the nineteenth century, but from 1920 to 1968, the industry declined and almost half the workforce was unemployed. The current economy relies on trade, finance, and manufacturing of refined goods such as jewelry, silverware, and electrical equipment. The Rhode Island Bay area and its islands are filled with resorts and vacation homes. Sailing and boating are popular, highlighted with the America's Cup yacht race.

Connecticut River Valley

Connecticut's fertile and level land along the Connecticut River Valley is an anomaly in Megalopolis. The coastal and riverine cities—Hartford (2016 pop. 123,423), Bridgeport (145,936), and

PHOTO 7.8. Textile Mill, Pawtucket, Rhode Island. Slater Mill was built in 1793 on the Blackstone River. Modeled after English mills, it was the first water-powered cotton textile mill in America, marking the beginning of the American Industrial Revolution.

New Haven (129,934)—are medium sized in comparison to the Megalopolis metropolitan behemoths.

Each town developed specialties, importing raw materials and producing highly finished products to justify shipment costs. Towns specialized in various textile industries or metal and machinery production. Central Connecticut produced brass clocks, silverware, and cutlery. Bridgeport, New Haven, and Waterbury were famous for hardware, tools, and small machinery. Other towns along the river produced machinery, electrical goods, and precision instruments.

The largest of the Connecticut River Valley cities is Hartford, situated at the head of ocean navigation. Dissenters from the Massachusetts Bay Company settled Hartford in 1635. Hartford became the insurance capital of America, but it also produced typewriters and Fuller brushes.

Challenges to sustainability include the lack of sustainable housing, alternative transportation, and ecology. However, there have been a number of sustainability initiatives. Bridgeport released its sustainability "BGreen2020." The plan outlines policies and actions to improve the quality of life, social equity, and economic competitiveness of the city, while also reducing carbon emissions and increasing the community's resilience to the effects of climate change and increasing energy costs. And the City of New Haven has partnered with Yale University to create a new sustainability plan focusing on climate change.

Albany and the Hudson River Valley
(2016 pop. 98,111)

The Hudson River Valley from New York City to Albany has been a center of transportation since Dutch settlement in the seventeenth century. Albany, the oldest continuously inhabited city in New England, was a Dutch fur-trading post established in 1619. In 1797, Albany replaced Kingston, New York, as the state capital. In 1825, the Erie Canal provided a low-lying continuous passage into the interior via the Great Lakes and elevated Albany's importance.

BOX 7.6   ICONIC IMAGES: THE TWIN TOWERS

On September 11, 2001, two jet planes were purposely flown into the Twin Towers in Lower Manhattan in New York City. Almost three thousand were killed and six thousand wounded in a deadly terrorist attack. Within two hours, the 110 storied towers, set afire by the jet liners, collapsed in a pile of poisonous dust and a heap of twisted metal.

The attack on the nation's largest city inaugurated a new era; it triggered the long war on terror and increased securitization of public space.

The site of the attack was reimagined from crime scene to a place of renewal and commemoration. The site was cleared by May 2002, and construction began on a new 1,776-feet tower; the height is not accidental as it represents the founding date of the Republic. One World Trade Center was completed in 2014.

Where the original two stood is now a place of commemoration (photo 7.9). The 9/11 Memorial that opened in 2014, keeps the footprint of the twin towers as empty spaces filled with water; a place of reflection. Around the edges are inscribed the names of those who lost their lives. A scene of tragedy is transformed into an evocative place of remembrance and contemplation.

PHOTO 7.9. The 9/11 Memorial.
Source: John R Short

Regional towns specialized in specific industries until the middle of the twentieth century. Troy was known for men's shirts and detachable collars. Schenectady grew from Dutch beginnings into the home of General Electric in 1892. Albany was a wood-manufacturing center. The region's manufacturing industries declined after 1950 and have been replaced with trade, services, and government employment.

After years of preparation, Albany drafted its first long-range comprehensive plan, "Albany 2030," in 2012. The plan includes ideas such as neighborhood revitalization, redevelopment, and greenways. The plan is different from other plans because it is comprehensive, including all departments in the city, rather than the typical fragmented plans of the past. Many of the components of Albany's Comprehensive Plan are designed with energy and sustainability in mind. Initiatives such as building a multimodal transportation center, creating livable, vibrant neighborhoods, and revitalizing Albany's downtown and the waterfront all have potential to reduce greenhouse gas emissions and create a more sustainable Albany. In addition, to address climate change, the city plans to take the following actions to reduce greenhouse gas emissions in municipal government operations and the city at large:

- Maintain a greenhouse gas inventory for the city that shows energy use and greenhouse gas emissions from municipal government, transportation and residential, and commercial and industrial sectors.
- Set a target for reducing greenhouse gas emissions.
- Develop a Climate Change Vulnerability Assessment and Adaptation Plan.

New York City
(2016 pop. 8,537,673)

Since 1800, New York City has been the economic, commercial, financial, and cultural center for the nation. New York began in 1624 as a Dutch settlement on the southern tip of Manhattan. Its population bypassed Boston's in 1760 and Philadelphia's in 1800 to become the largest city, because of its deep harbor, coastal position, and access to the interior via the Hudson River and Erie Canal. Other cities competing for the premier position—Montreal, Halifax, Boston, Philadelphia, and Baltimore—all suffered from geographical deficiencies. Montreal is not an ice-free port; Halifax and Boston had lesser ports; and Philadelphia and Baltimore were less accessible, as they were located on narrow estuaries. New York Harbor was

BOX 7.7   DID YOU KNOW . . . THE BOROUGHS

New York City has five administrative units called boroughs (map 7.5). Residents of the boroughs (which were originally independent cities) voted in 1898 to combine and form New York City. Each borough has retained its own personality. Though many Americans have not been to "the city," most people can identify the different boroughs through the many movies and television shows filmed in the city.

Manhattan

Manhattan is the core of the city and has the most skyscrapers in the nation. More than 40 percent of all office space in the nation is found in midtown Manhattan. The island's geologic structure allows the concentration of high-rises. The schist bedrock is close to the surface and provides structural support in the high-rise zones (midtown and Wall Street). In low-rise Greenwich Village and Chelsea, the bedrock lies hundreds of feet below the surface and, therefore, the land cannot support high-rises.

The 1,643,734 (2016) residents of Manhattan are divided into districts that any New Yorker is familiar with: Central Park occupies the center of the island and separates the liberal West Side from the more haute and affluent East Side. To the north, Harlem, historically a Puerto Rican and African American enclave, has become an up-and-coming district in the early twenty-first century. To the south are the gentrified artist areas of Soho (South of Houston), Tribeca (Triangle below Canal Street), and the financial district, where the World Trade Towers once stood. The Lower East Side has historically been home to various ethnic groups and has many of the historic tenement buildings as seen in such movies as *The Godfather*. People who live in Manhattan can often have an elitist attitude about those who live off the island, the so-called B&T (bridge and tunnel) people, who commute to the island daily or for the nightlife.

Manhattan is often referred to as the media capital of the world, with national newspapers (*New York Times*, *Wall Street Journal*), literary magazines (*New Yorker*, *Harper's Weekly*), and advertising agencies, as well as corporate headquarters for such media giants as Time Warner, Condé Nast, and the Hearst Corporation. Major book publishers are also in the city, including Penguin, HarperCollins, Random House, and Simon & Schuster. All three of the major television networks (ABC, NBC, and CBS) are located in the city, as many of the cable networks (HBO and MTV). Many movies have portrayed the city, such as many Woody Allen movies, *Taxi Driver*, and *The Devil Wears Prada*. Depictions of the city vary from violent to glamorous and are a geographic study in itself.

The Bronx

The only mainland borough, the Bronx consists of mostly residential land and commercial interests to service the communities.

Though there are single-family dwellings within the borough, it is known for its numerous housing projects, which have become notorious for drug use and poverty. During the 1980s, many of the housing projects fell victim to arson, for reasons not fully understood. The population in the borough is 1,455,720 (2016) with a density of 11,674 per square mile. The racial makeup is approximately 43 percent black, 45 percent white, and almost 56 percent Hispanic. Most of the Hispanic population is Puerto Rican. About 30 percent of the population lives below the poverty line.

Queens

Queens is a residential borough. Its 2,233,054 (2016) inhabitants, almost 48 percent, are foreign born, and the borough is often considered the most diverse county in the nation. Both La Guardia and JFK airports are in Queens. The economy is based on tourism, the airports, and the headquarters of Jet Blue. Long Island City is a manufacturing and commercial center, with a growing artists' loft community.

Brooklyn

The most populous of the boroughs is Brooklyn, with 2,629,150 residents (2016). The borough has many well-known neighborhoods, such as Bensonhurst, Bedford-Stuyvesant, and Flatbush, along with Coney Island and Brighton Beach. Many Brooklyn neighborhoods are culturally distinct and house specific ethnic groups. In the past, Jewish and Italian immigrants lived in Brooklyn, and today it is home to a large Russian and Pakistani immigrant population. During the first decade of the twenty-first century, the artist community shifted from the now too expensive Soho to Brooklyn neighborhoods, such as Greenpoint and Park Slope. The shift brings a cool factor to the borough, and housing prices have escalated.

Staten Island

Staten Island, the most suburban of the boroughs, has the smallest but fastest-growing population of 476,015 (2016). It was not until 1960 that the island was connected to other boroughs via the Verrazano-Narrows Bridge. Until that time, the southern and central island maintained a rural atmosphere with poultry farms and dairies. Another feature on the island is the Fresh Kills Landfill—the largest landfill in the world at twenty-two hundred acres—the repository of New York City garbage until 2001. It is currently being reclaimed for recreational use and for roads to ease traffic congestion. A regular and free ferry, offering excellent views of the Statue of Liberty, still connects lower Manhattan with Staten Island.

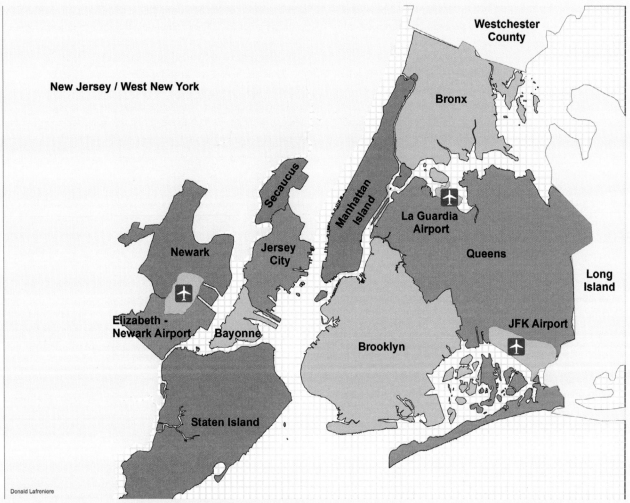

New Jersey / West New York

Secaucus

Newark

Jersey City

Elizabeth - Newark Airport

Bayonne

Staten Island

Westchester County

Bronx

Manhattan Island

La Guardia Airport

Queens

Long Island

JFK Airport

Brooklyn

Donald Lafreniere

MAP 7.5. Borough Map of New York City and Surrounding Area. New York's five boroughs (Manhattan, Brooklyn, Queens, Bronx, and Staten Island) are each an administrative subdivision of New York City. They were created in 1898 when the city consolidated.

the major American port until the twenty-first century, when foreign trade shifted from Europe to Asia.

The waterfront extends over seven hundred miles of well-protected, ice-free piers surrounding Manhattan, Long Island, the East River, and along the northern Jersey shore. The Hudson scours the deep and wide port, enabling ships to come and go with ease. The New Jersey ports of Elizabeth, Newark, and North Bergen are the primary warehouse and intermodal shipping centers for the "Port of New York." As one of the top tier "world cities" (the other two being London and Tokyo), New York anchors its international significance with one of the largest stock exchanges and the world headquarters for the United Nations.

New York City is the financial and corporate national leader. Stock exchanges are located in the Wall Street area, including the New York Stock Exchange (NYSE) and NASDAQ, the largest exchanges in the world (box 7.7). Manufacturing is minimal, but the fashion and garment

industry remains central to the city. One-third of all clothing manufactured in the United States is designed and produced from 34th Street to 42nd Street, although this area's importance is declining because of local high rents and low-cost overseas production.

New York has the second most Fortune 500 corporate headquarters with fifty-five, following Texas's fifty-eight. Most headquarters in the state are in New York City. While many companies maintain a presence in the city, in recent years many others have left for the suburbs or nearby New Jersey because of high tax rates and costs in the city.

New York City is fragmented: two **boroughs** are on islands, two others on Long Island, and one on the New York mainland (map 7.4). The most populated area is Manhattan, a 13.5-mile by 2.3-mile island surrounded by the Hudson, East, and Harlem rivers, its southern tip facing the Upper New York Bay. Staten Island faces New York Bay and is separated from New Jersey by the Arthur Kill, also called the Staten Island Sound. Both

Queens and Brooklyn are located on the southwestern edge of Long Island, while the Bronx is on the mainland just south of Yonkers and Westchester County.

The fragmented nature and population densities of New York City required a supportive transportation network. The city is connected to its boroughs and New Jersey by a plethora of traffic-congested bridges and tunnels. However, there are multiple modes of travel, from autos to buses to local and commuter rail. The city has more miles of public transport than there are miles of city (1.8 miles to each 1 mile), so 37 percent of the workforce commutes by walking, cycling (doubling bike lanes in three years), or the extensive system of subways and hybrid buses.

The metropolitan area extends one hundred miles into four states, including New Jersey (Newark, Jersey City), Pennsylvania (Pike County, the fastest-growing county in Pennsylvania), and Connecticut (Stanford, Greenwich, Westport). North of the Bronx, Westchester County is an elite group of towns where the wealthy own homes in addition to their *pied* à *terre* (literally "piece of ground," apartments or coops) in the city. Beyond Queens, Long Island is now an interwoven mix of suburban communities with the exception of the north shore, which is still somewhat rural, and inhabited as second (third, fourth, or fifth) homes for the past century by the "à la Gatsby" wealthy.

Most of northern New Jersey is incorporated into the metropolitan complex. Since 1980, new luxury high-rises tower where aging piers and warehouses once faced Manhattan. The Jersey shore is a popular weekend haven for many New Yorkers. The south coast of Connecticut has long been a suburban area for wealthy New York rail commuters.

Immigration has been central to both the identity of New York and the individual identities of its neighborhoods. Over twelve million immigrants from Ireland, Germany, Italy, Poland, Greece, and elsewhere arrived in New York City during the late 1800s and early 1900s. During the past three decades, however, newcomers from Latin American and Asia have comprised the bulk of the immigrant population. Despite being one of most ethnically diverse areas in the United States, New York City is still highly segregated. Real estate agents, who serve as gatekeepers to the city's properties, often sort new immigrants toward neighborhoods dominated by their respective ethno-racial groups. Such practices, however, reinforce self-segregating tendencies, ethno-racial ghettos (e.g., Puerto Ricans in the Bronx, Dominicans in Washington Heights), and mutual antipathies between groups. New York thus remains a city of extremes. Within a relatively small area, extreme wealth meets with extreme poverty, global integration encounters local fragmentation, and individualistic economic gain sits side-by-side with the increasing management and regulation of public space.

Among the several challenges to sustainability is the waste situation (a low recycling rate) and the fragmented nature of the city. At the same time, the city has accomplished what seems impossible in a city so large: an excellent water system fed by reservoirs in the outlying counties, where development has been discouraged to protect the water. Water conservation has also been successful. Much the city's environmental and sustainable goals have been because of strong support from local government and multiple environmental awareness campaigns, including a focus on schools and education.

Another innovative project is the Highline. In 1934, an elevated rail line opened in Manhattan, New York, to deliver goods and material to factories and warehouses along its thirteen-mile route through Chelsea and the meat-packing district. When the warehouses and factories closed, the rail line was no longer viable and the last delivery was made in 1980. The narrow railway lay empty. Finally, locals suggested turning the line in to a pedestrian promenade. In 2009, the first section of the linear pedestrian park was opened and the entire park was completed in 2017. Native plant species were planted along its route, growing up beside the old rail tracks (photo 7.10). Today, it is wildly popular among locals and visitors. The conversion of an abandoned railroad track into an urban public space for walking is one of the most successful transformations in the shift from industrial to postindustrial.

In 2007, New York City crafted what many experts considered an ambitious and innovative sustainability plan, PlaNYC. The plan is far-reaching, and includes 127 policy initiatives

PHOTO 7.10. The Highline in New York City. The success of this linear park has inspired other cities to plan for linear parks in old industrial areas.
Source: John R Short

PHOTO 7.11. The Philadelphia Skyline. For many years, the statue of William Penn atop City Hall (in the distance) was the tallest building, but skyscrapers such as One and Two Liberty Plaza, the Mellon Bank Center, and Bell Atlantic Tower are now taller. And yet, the city retains its green space in the squares and circles that date back to Penn's plan.

Source: iStock/f11photo

to achieve ten overarching goals to improve the infrastructure, environment, and quality of life in the city. The plan aims to double the number of green jobs by 2018, improve access to education, and increase demand for green products and services. In addition, the plan aims to clean up brownfields (heavily polluted former industrial sites), encourage public transportation, create more parks and playgrounds, and plant one million trees within the five boroughs. Since the release of the plan, the City has made great strides towards implementing the plan.

Philadelphia, Pennsylvania
(2016 pop. 1,567,872)

Philadelphia was in many ways the nation's first "modern" city. Philadelphia was located for navigational purposes on a narrow peninsula between the Schuylkill and Delaware rivers. It was the first city in America to incorporate right-angle grid streets and several other modern amenities such as house numbering.

Religious and ethnic tolerance differentiated the city from the New England hearth. Most of America's Quakers, Mennonites, Germans, and Scots-Irish entered through the Philadelphia portal. By 1760, Philadelphia was the new nation's capital and the largest city in the new country. As the political center for the American Revolution, Philadelphia's iconic historic sites and features include Independence Hall and the Liberty Bell. Today, the Philadelphia CSA is the eighth largest in America, but its city population is sixth largest and has been declining from its 1950 peak but with a slight uptick in recent years (photo 7.11).

During the nineteenth century, Philadelphia was in the best position to compete with New York for the premier position for culture, population, and trade. However, its dreams of being the number one city in America were dashed with the success the Erie Canal brought to New York City.

Philadelphia remained an important port and historical city because of river access to fertile inland farms and, later, its proximity to coal fields. But the city lacked New York's easy canal route to the west, and so after a failed attempt to compete in the canal arena, it turned its attention to the new railroad industry and became a hub for several rail companies. In the twenty-first century, Philadelphia's economy features manufacturing, food services, medical research, and finance. It is also recognized for its educational and cultural centers.

Philadelphia has been praised for its progressive efforts around sustainability. The city began issuing an annual Greenworks report in 2009. The report measures improvements in five goal areas: energy, environment, equity, economy, and engagement. Within the more than 150 initiatives are comprehensive plans and updating zoning codes. Some of the areas where the city has excelled are in the comprehensive Greenworks program and its many green programs, from energy efficiency to including public input in its plans.

Philadelphia has a comprehensive plan to deal with water quality issues. In 2011, Philadelphia's water department created its "Green Cities, Clean Waters" plan. The city believes that cleaner rivers will increase civic pride in the riverfront areas, result in higher property values and greater potential for valuable riverfront projects. Unlike Washington, D.C., Philadelphia plans to reduce its stormwater runoff and CSO issues by using green infrastructure and the physical reconstruction of aquatic habitats. Developers and designers are using land-based elements such as redirecting runoff from impervious surfaces to green areas and bioswales. They are also encouraging green roofs and adding more trees as a way to reduce demand on the sewer infrastructure. They are also reconstructing and stablizling stream beds and banks, creating aquatic habitat and improving fish passages in the hopes that restoring these waterways will actually make them cleaner. But what makes the

PHOTO 7.12. A View of the Inner Harbor of Baltimore. The lightship Chesapeake and the USS Torsk submarine are docked in front of the National Aquarium. In the background, the old power plant has been re-adapted into retail space for a Barnes and Noble bookstore, the Hardrock Café, and the ESPN Zone bar and grill.

Source: iStock/amedved

plan notable is that many of these approaches have a secondary benefit of protecting open space in the city.

Southeastern Pennsylvania

The industrial cities of Allentown and Bethlehem lie in Lehigh Valley behind a row of ridges in the Ridge and Valley province. Canals and, later, railroads connected the long valley to the seaboard cities. Scranton and Wilkes-Barre anthracite deposits and limestone first attracted steel and cement production, followed by heavy machinery industry. Since the millennium, the southeastern cities have stabilized population despite a loss of manufacturing jobs.

Lancaster and its eponymous county are industrialized, but they have maintained the Amish **Pennsylvania Dutch** farms. This fertile agricultural area near the city has been an important element of Philadelphia's economy.

Baltimore, Maryland
(2010 pop. 614,664)

Baltimore, located on the Chesapeake Bay at the drowned mouth of the Patapsco River, was founded in 1729. Lord Baltimore's barony was meant to be a refuge for English Catholics, although religious toleration allowed many others to settle in the colony.

Baltimore's shipping advantages accelerated growth during the eighteenth century. The city was closer to Caribbean sugar producers than the more northern industrialized cities, and one hundred miles closer to the Ohio Valley than Philadelphia. During the twentieth century, the city's industry grew because of bulk shipping, grain elevators, coal piers, and fertilizer plants.

Baltimore grew to the sixth-largest American city by 1950, but in the 1970s, harbor trade began to decline, and whites fled the city for the new suburbs. The harbor became the focus of redevelopment in the late twentieth century. Since the

gentrification of the narrow streets and brick row houses of Fells Point, the once tawdry harbor has become a tourist attraction and is reclaiming its importance (photo 7.12).

The city of Baltimore remains at two-thirds its 1950 population, but population has stabilized; Baltimore lost 5 percent between 2000 and 2016, while the metropolitan area continues to grow. In the 1970s, Baltimore began to address environmental issues such as reducing air and water pollution, creating efficient land use patterns, and protecting streams, vegetation, and wildlife habitats in the surrounding area. However, sustainable ideals and growth have not infiltrated the city's many pockets of urban crime and poverty.

Washington, D.C.
(2016 pop. 681,170)

Named for the father of the country (although George Washington referred to it as the Federal City), the capital was a planned city. In 1790, the new country needed a capital city, and several cities vied for the title at congressional meetings. The cities with the most justified claims were Philadelphia and New York. However, their northern locations were politically unacceptable for the slaveholding South. James Madison, Alexander Hamilton, and Thomas Jefferson also discussed the need for a federal government and eventually agreed upon a more southern site. George Washington chose the Potomac site, because of its central location to the nation and his own predilection for all things Potomac.

Maryland and Virginia contributed land for America's Versailles, a ten-square-mile city built on a marshy and hilly terrace between the coastal plain and Piedmont. George Washington's friend, Pierre Charles L'Enfant, an American architect of French origin, designed the city. His plan worked within the constraints of the landscape and was considered genius, although his inability to compromise caused the surveyors of the federal district to eventually assume the

BOX 7.8   NATIONAL PARKS: THE NATIONAL MALL

The National Mall is our nation's front yard and its most important public space. It is a place where citizens can contest the ever-changing meaning of the nation, where protests challenge us to rethink what constitutes citizenship, justice, and democracy. It is where memorials and monuments remind us of important events and people that have shaped our national identity. It is where presidents are inaugurated and where the country has commemorated leaders like Lincoln, Jefferson, and King and events with lessons that endure. It is where American society expresses its national ideals of democracy, liberty, and freedom. And it is a national park.

Recent efforts to fortify and secure the Mall reveal a troubling story of barriers in a place that symbolizes freedom. Since 9/11, concerns about the security of public spaces in the United States have preempted those about access.

This was a trend in Washington, D.C., before the fall of the Twin Towers. But after 9/11, the "war on terror" meant there was an urgent imperative to fortress the Mall. Some of the security measures made since are visible (barricades); some, less visible (security cameras); and some, temporary (the double-line fences that surround the Mall for the Fourth of July celebration) (photo 7.13). The fortification of our Independence Day has become so normalized that each year the *Washington Post* publishes a map showing visitors the security checkpoints and public access areas without a hint of irony.

The security on the Fourth of July has never been seriously challenged or overtly resisted. Nor was there much debate about the $20 million spent to construct sunken walkways that now encircle the Washington Monument. The walkways effectively stop trucks or cars carrying explosives from reaching the Monument. They do little to protect against bombs carried in backpacks or by bicycles or the impact from an airplane. The walkways also change the way we approach and experience the Monument. The Washington Monument grounds have historically served as the epicenter of public protests and demonstrations; they are a gathering place where protests often culminate in marches that encircle the Monument and expand outward, filling the grounds in an unbroken chain. While the walkways don't prevent these types of gatherings, they do alter it. The sunken walkways make it difficult for those with strollers, bicycles, or walking disabilities to access the lawn seating area around the monument (the other option is to scale the four-foot wall, not an easy task).

Questions about security on the Mall—and in other public spaces and national parks across America—might not seem as pressing during the war on terrorism. But in the long term, they will determine how we find the balance between needs for security and national conversation. As they stand, public spaces embody an architecture of fear and vulnerability. Since September 11, 2001, security officials seem to have not only the last word but the only word.

PHOTO 7.13. Security on the National Mall in Washington, D.C. This police panopticon keeps watch during the July 4th celebrations.
Source: Lisa Benton-Short

BOX 7.9 URBAN SUSTAINABILITY BEST PRACTICES: CLEANING UP THE RIVER IN D.C.

The sustainability plan for Washington, D.C., is ambitious in many ways. By 2032, the District aims to create five times as many jobs providing green goods and services, cut the citywide obesity rate by 50 percent, eliminate food deserts, reduce green-house gas emissions by 50 percent and cut citywide energy use by 50 percent, and make 100 percent of District waterways fish-able and swimmable.

Improving water quality in the two rivers that surround the District, the Potomac to the west and the Anacostia to the east, is a big challenge. The long-neglected Anacostia River has numerous combined sewer outfalls that discharge untreated waste water when it rains. It is severely polluted by sediment, nutrients, pathogens, and toxins. The river has also been plagued by trash—thousands of plastic bottles and plastic bags are washed into the river yearly from the surrounding suburbs and city sewer systems.

To combat the trash problem, the District launched a "bag fee." The bag fee aims to reduce litter and curb dis-posable plastic and paper bag use by charging five cents for plastic bags at grocery stores and other venues. The bag fee discourages plastic bag use while raising funds to clean the river.

The results are impressive. Since the bag fee took affect, 80 percent of residents are using fewer disposable bags and stream clean up groups report 70 percent fewer bags collected in the Anacostia River. The bag fee has raised about $10 million for the Anacostia River Clean Up and Protection Fund. It has paid for 6 trash traps that have collectively removed more than 25,000 pounds of trash from District waterways, and funded more than 2,300 feet of stream restoration projects, the installation of almost 1,000 trees, 550 rain barrels and 130 rain gardens that help capture polluted stormwater before it reaches the river.

The bag fee has been heralded as one of the nation's most successful "bag laws" and has become a familiar and accepted routine at cash registers across the city. It is also worth noting that this solution has multiple benefits: a reduction of trash destined for landfills also helps to clean up waterways. In combination with other river restoration projects, the future of Washington's "forgotten river" is suddenly looking a little less bleak.

architect function. But L'Enfant's inspired neoclassical ideals continued to influence the capital.

The city's broad boulevards housed only a few federal buildings in the nineteenth century, and few people lived in the city, so it seemed superfluous and grandiose. The city was only populated when Congress convened. Even at the dawn of the twentieth century, large expanses remained a thicket. But over time the city filled in around the federal buildings, until 1943, when the Pentagon became the first federal building built on the other side of the Potomac. In 1964, the **Beltway** circum-ferential highway was built to bypass the crowded streets of the capital city, but soon after the city experienced explosive growth and the Beltway became the primary thoroughfare and congested, which is still an issue today.

The city's 50.7 percent black population (2016) continues to reflect postwar migration. They concentrate in the District, in wards to the east, while whites tend to concentrate in the District to the west. Blacks also live in the suburbs to the east of the District, while whites and immigrants live in the suburbs to the north and west of the District

The booming economy of Washington, D.C. is leaving the city's longtime black residents behind, however. A recent study found that more than half of all new jobs in the District between 2010 and 2020 will require at least a bachelor's degree. The study also noted that the average white household in the region has a net worth of $284,000 while the assets of the average black household are just $3,500. The low assets among black households may be a reflection that housing discrimination years ago kept many from owning homes and building equity.

Although Washington, D.C., was once thought of as black/white, immigration is rapidly changing the city and has become home to hundreds of thousands of new immigrants in the past fifteen years. Despite the economic recession of 2008, Washington, D.C., saw modest economic growth in federal gov-ernment jobs, contract work (government externalities), and the information technology sector. Military-funded aerospace firms such as Northrop-Grumman and Lockheed Martin have established East Coast headquarters in D.C. to be close to the Department of Defense. More recently, the Dulles "High Tech Corridor," which stretches westward from Arlington, Virginia, toward Dulles International Airport, has attracted high-skilled software engineers and other high-technology workers. The firm AOL employs five thousand in its headquarters there. To address a shortage of high-skilled workers in the 1990s, the US Department of Homeland Security created an H1 Visa specif-ically to target foreigners with college degrees in computer-related fields. As a result, many skilled immigrants from India, South Korea, Hong Kong, and mainland China moved to the Washington, D.C., region during this time. Many immigrants from El Salvador, Bolivia, Peru, Brazil, Mexico, and Guatemala have also come to D.C. to work as nannies, landscapers, con-struction workers, and hotel and restaurant staff.

In Washington, many immigrants move directly to the suburbs rather than the central-city. In addition, many immigrants to Washington live in moderate- to high-income neighborhoods, not in the poorest ones. In fact, many are settling in places that only thirty years ago were mostly white and had very few foreign-born residents. Today, the historic image of a city polarized into "Black and White" no longer holds true, and city leaders and residents are grappling with how to include and support increasingly diverse communities.

Washington's economy is based on the federal government. Although only 27 percent of jobs are directly government related, indirectly related jobs include government contractors, nonprofits, lobbyists, and law firms. Nongovernmental employment includes numerous educational and medical institutions and various media enterprises, such as National Public Radio and the *Washington Post*. The National Mall is a stunning tourist attraction that contains national landmarks and monuments (e.g., the Jefferson, Lincoln, and Vietnam memorials, and the Washington Monument) as well as major national museums (e.g., the Smithsonian, National Museum of the American Indian, and National Gallery of Art) (box 7.8).

In 2013, Washington, D.C., launched its Sustainability Plan, an ambitious plan that addresses health and well-being, obesity, green jobs, transportation, water, and climate change.

The Economy

Megalopolis was the birthplace of American manufacturing. The colonial New England economy evolved from the fishery to shipbuilding to water-powered textile mills. The Central Atlantic states of eastern Pennsylvania south to the Washington, D.C., metro area specialized in textiles, clothing, steel, and machinery.

Manufacturing in Megalopolis is no longer an important part of its economy, but it remains the financial heart of America. Sixteen of the top fifty companies are headquartered in the region; however, it is no longer the dominant region for Fortune 500 headquarters.

The Primary Sector

Primary industries are minimal in Megalopolis. Agriculture and fishing linger, but mineral resources and logging are no longer vital. Rural land and forests remain important for Megalopolis and its residents, because they literally provide the breathing space for the urban populations.

Agriculture

Agriculture has historically been a part of Megalopolis, but urban expansion sprawled over many former agricultural lands. Some farming still remains, but it caters to the local market (fruits and vegetables), chicken production (Delmarva Peninsula), or niche markets (mushrooms, organic, Amish).

The Connecticut River Valley, a wheat-producing and dairy area, specialized in tobacco for cigar wrappers in the nineteenth century. After World War II, suburban development sprawled over the former dairies and tobacco fields. Most remaining farmers evolved into truck farmers, but sustaining a small farm is almost impossible today without outside income, so such enterprises cater to an urban family clientele with golf courses, cider mills, and pick-your-own fruit.

The Delaware and Chesapeake Bay estuaries surround the relatively isolated Delmarva Peninsula, a mainstay in agricultural and chicken production. Egg production began in the 1920s, but it evolved into chicken production in the following decade because selling broilers was more profitable than selling eggs. The well-drained soil, low building costs, and proximity to large markets created a thriving chicken industry.

More than six hundred million chickens are grown on the peninsula, supplying 8 percent of American chickens and the majority of local agricultural sales. The chicken industry may be short lived, though, because of urban encroachment and environmental degradation. The peninsula generates more than eight hundred thousand tons of manure annually, which is a source of runoff and excessive nutrient buildup that is a major source of Chesapeake Bay pollution.

Many chicken growers unable to combat rising production costs are selling to developers and moving south, where production costs are lower. Those who remain must deal with the new suburban neighbors who complain about the chicken farm dust and smells.

Some farmers specialize in grain production for specific markets, but historically the most important crop has been tobacco, a crop subsidized so that a small-acreage farmer could realize a profit. Terminating tobacco quotas in 2004 blunted production, and finding replacement crops has been a priority. Organic farming and specialized crops, such as mushrooms, figs, and blueberries have been possible sustainable alternatives for the tobacco farmer.

The Amish settled and farmed the fertile land in Lancaster County west of Philadelphia, which brought prosperity to the city. The principal agricultural output of Amish farms is livestock and dairy products, but they also grow corn, hay, grain, and vegetables. The Amish are known for their old-fashioned, nonelectric ways, but little is known of their leadership in solar and wind power. Solar panels grace Amish barns, and wind power energizes their dairies, while compressed air runs machine shop tools and kitchen appliances.

Amish still live and farm in the county, drawing a large tourist population who come to view their quaint technology and attire. Other residents of Lancaster and the surrounding counties capitalize on the tourist trade, although the Amish do not, and dislike how they have become the center of tourist attention.

The Pressures on Agricultural Land

Within Megalopolis the amount of land devoted to agriculture has a very distinct pattern. At a regional scale, it reflects climatic conditions and the differential length of the growing season. The more northerly, colder counties such as Hillsborough in New Hampshire have only 6.7 percent of land in agriculture as more land is given over to forest cover. Agriculture land use increases as you move south. Rural counties such as Lancaster in Pennsylvania and Carroll and Queen Anne's, both in Maryland, have 64.8 percent, 55.6 percent, and 70.5 percent, respectively, of land in agriculture. In the more urban and suburban counties, less land is devoted to agriculture. The most urban areas such as the Bronx have no agriculture and even suburban counties have little: Suffolk County in eastern Long Island has only 6.1 percent of its land acreage in agriculture. Suburban sprawl is also spreading non-agricultural land uses across the landscape, turning fields into subdivisions and orchards into parking lots. The extent of land devoted to agricultural production has been dwindling since 1950.

Land closer to the cities is much more expensive than land on the periphery of Megalopolis. If farmers do locate in the areas closer to the city they need to engage in intensive high-yield farming, such as the market gardening of fruit and vegetables. In some cases it is not so much distance as time of transportation that is important. Large cities require quick and immediate supplies of fruit and vegetables and other specialized agricultural products. Restaurants, for example, require daily supplies for their diners. Proximity to the city provides swift access but at the price of high land values, which in turn means that only intensive farming with high yields makes economic sense. Organic fruits and vegetables is another emerging market that yields a high dollar return per acre. Affluent consumers are willing to bear the greater costs associated with these products.

High-yield counties are located around New York City, Philadelphia, and Boston. There are other areas of relatively high yield such as New Jersey, giving credence to the state motto of Garden State, Rhode Island, and southern Connecticut. In part, these high yields are a function of proximity to the cities as well as of varying soil fertility.

The Secondary Sector

Early Manufacturing in Southern New England

Early New England manufacturing was decentralized because of a dependence on waterpower. Towns specialized in producing one particular commodity and became known as one-industry towns or mill towns. They were seldom "company towns," as most towns had competitive companies producing the same ware. During the manufacturing era, New England and Mid-Atlantic towns were noted for their distinct specialties, such as Danbury, Connecticut, for felt hats, and silk and rayon goods in Mid-Atlantic towns (table 7.1).

Water-powered mills were built in the late eighteenth century, but during the second decade of the nineteenth century New England's cotton and woolen textile mills dominated American industry. Towns sprang up along streams with sufficient waterpower to support mills—Waltham, Lowell, and Lawrence in Massachusetts; Manchester in New Hampshire; Providence in Rhode Island; and along the Connecticut River Valley.

The technological limitations of building dams and harnessing power determined the geographic situation of the mills. The first water-powered plants developed in New England were accessible to coastal transport. Falls were common, due to the granites of New England's bedrock; the south was far less accessible for transport because of the fall line, and so the early mills were located near the coast and in New England. During the initial industrial phase, harnessing and transporting the power was limited technologically on larger rivers, so falls at smaller streams dominated; hence the inland locations of many early textile mills. By mid-century, steam became the new form of power, and city growth reflected the new source.

Steam plants were coal-powered, but heavy, bulky coal was most inexpensively delivered to ocean ports. The next generation of mills and factories were built along the coal delivery routes, such as Lowell, Salem, and Portsmouth. The mills remained important in the New England area until the 1880s, when electricity became a power source and cotton textile mills began to migrate closer to their southern commodity, where labor and land were less expensive. By World War I, the New England textile economy had severely declined.

Mid-Atlantic Manufacturing

Southern Megalopolis is dominated by the inland fall line cities—Philadelphia, Trenton, Wilmington, Baltimore, and Washington, D.C.—all situated on the two major estuaries. The Delaware River follows the fall line for fifty miles and contains the major cities of Philadelphia, Wilmington, and Trenton. Baltimore and Washington, D.C., are on Chesapeake Bay. With the exception of Washington, these cities developed as access points to both inland and ocean transport. With time, the waterpower advantage succumbed to coal-producing regions. Fall line cities were at first dependent on ocean access for shipping and importing, but in time railroads connected the cities to the interior. The cities evolved into distribution centers

TABLE 7.1. Late-Nineteenth- and Early-Twentieth-Century New England Cities and Their Specialized Industries

City	Commodity produced
Danbury, Connecticut	Felt hats
Woonsocket, Rhode Island	Handkerchiefs
Bridgeport, New Haven, and Worcester, Connecticut	Corsets
Peabody, Danvers, and Woburn, Massachusetts	Leather goods
Brockton, Haverhill, and Lynn, Massachusetts	Shoes
Hartford, Springfield, Waterbury, New Haven, and New Britain, Connecticut	Brass, hardware, electrical goods

for manufactured goods. Both Philadelphia and Baltimore became major industrial cities; they reached their height of production during the 1950s, after which industry began to decline.

Manufacturing long played an important role in the life of the region as a significant employer and major source of revenue. In 1900, Megalopolis had almost one in two of all manufacturing workers in the entire country. By 1950, this number had fallen to one in three. The absolute numbers were still significant and in 1954 they were at an all time high of 4.6 million manufacturing workers in Megalopolis, comprising almost one third of all non-farm workers in the region.

The region has lost over 1.5 million manufacturing jobs since 1958 when one in four of all manufacturing production workers in the United States were based in Megalopolis; by 2015, this figure had fallen to just over 1 in 10. The number of production workers in manufacturing has halved while the region's share of national manufacturing employment has shrunk. This region is no longer the manufacturing powerhouse of the US economy as manufacturing jobs across the nation have shrunk due to increased worker productivity, and as a greater proportion of spending is allocated to services rather than goods. There has been also a shift in manufacturing employment shifted to other parts of the national and global economy.

The Tertiary Sector

In Megalopolis, the tertiary sector is the major sector that provides jobs and economic growth. Finance, insurance, real estate, education, medical services, wholesale and retail trade, and information and communication technologies, among others, have replaced manufacturing as key components of the regional economies.

Along with Tokyo and London, New York is one of the three traditional "world cities" that anchor world trade, commerce, banking, and stock transactions. The port of New York/New Jersey, once the main connection between the Atlantic Ocean and the St. Lawrence Seaway (via the Erie Canal), now handles the third-highest tonnage of ship cargo in the United States and is counted among the world's top twenty busiest ports. New York has also gained traction and thrived in the increasingly valuable "creative industries." These sectors are concentrated in different portions of the city, with music and theater in Times Square, fashion in the Garment District, interior design and architecture in Chelsea and SoHo, and advertising on Madison Avenue. These industries not only benefit from city tax incentives for television and film, but also from the talent available at nearby educational institutions, such as Julliard (music), the Pratt Institute (design), and the Fashion Institute of Technology.

The Growth of Services

With the decline in manufacturing, there has been an increase in services, which now accounts for one in every three US workers and almost 30 percent of the gross national product (GNP). The term "services" covers a wide range, from jobs in health care and financial consultancy to computer information companies. The sector includes a range of wildly differing job experiences. At one end are the high-earning Wall Street brokers working in finance and international currency dealing, receiving lucrative annual bonuses that fuel price increases in selected local housing markets. At the other end are contract cleaners of the offices that house these executives. One particularly dynamic sector of services is the knowledge-based industries, the so-called producer services such as banking, financial, business consultancies, and information technology. Together, these sectors constitute the dynamic edge of the US capitalist economy. Financial services continue to be concentrated especially in the global cities such as New York, where the economics of agglomeration and the importance of face-to-face contact continue to make big cities attractive places for business. Manhattan continues to resist de-concentration and loss of population in large part because of the vitality of advanced finance services in its downtown location. High-tech industries have aggregated around a number of innovation centers such as Route 128 in Boston. Here, the pull is other firms, local linkages with universities and government research labs, and the consequent pool of highly skilled labor.

Megalopolis remains a major center of selected producer services. Over one in every two workers in the nation in the important sector of finance and insurance workers are located in Megalopolis. And one in every ten workers are based in the New York metro area. The figures are even higher for the sub-category of securities intermediation, 81 percent of all workers in the US in this category are employed in Megalopolis, with 33 percent located in the New York metro area.

The key sector of professional, scientific, and technical services is also important in Megalopolis. There are almost three million workers employed in this sector, well over a half of all such workers in the entire country. The largest single centers are in Washington, D.C., and New York City.

Tourism

Regional tourism is substantial, both for the residents who spend their vacations within the region and for visitors. Among the largest attractions are New York City, for the city itself and for its many museums and sites (the Empire State Building, the Natural History Museum, Ellis Island Museum, the Tenement Museum, and the Statue of Liberty); Washington, D.C., for its monuments, national museums, and the White House; Philadelphia, the city most identified with independence; and Boston's American Revolution sites.

The coast attracts local residents during the summer, when inland humidity can be stifling and ocean breezes a relief. The wealthy go to Montauk and surrounding communities at the end of Long Island, while gays and lesbians frequent Fire Island and families go to Coney Island. Martha's Vineyard and Nantucket are popular island getaways, as is the Cape Cod coast, led by Provincetown, a former whaling center that now supports a vibrant gay community. Atlantic City, New Jersey, a resort town known for its boardwalk, had declined and then reemerged in the late twentieth century as an East Coast gambling mecca.

BOX 7.10 GLOBAL CONNECTIONS: NEW YORK CITY AS PIVOT OF GLOBAL URBAN NETWORK

The global urban network is connected by flows of goods, people, capital and ideas. Some of the flows have been identified and measured. A substantial body of material has emerged from the Globalization and World Cities (GAWC) research network. In 2000, they collected data on the distribution of one hundred global advanced producers' service firms, which includes accountancy, advertising, banking/finance, insurance, law and management consultancy, across 315 cities. They analyzed the resultant data matrix to identify a global urban hierarchy. In 2012, they extended the analysis to 176 firms in 525 cities.

In all three analyses, New York (NY) and London (LON) dominate. NYLON is an important pivot in this global network and its dominance reflects the historical legacy of London as the center of the British Empire and the continuing importance of New York as the financial center of America's more informal empire.

A Sustainable Future

There are many challenges to a sustainable future in Megalopolis. These include the following:

- air pollution;
- acid rain;
- declining fresh water supply;
- legacy of industrial pollution;
- congestion and overcrowding;
- hypoxia in the Chesapeake;
- suburban sprawl creating more impermeable surfaces, reducing natural habitats, and generating more auto usage; and
- the dense population straining the vital resources of air, water, and land.

Megalopolis is the historic and economic center of the United States and it is embracing sustainable ideals, to endorse a lighter, more efficient environmental impact, and to build green. A new generation of architects and graduates seeks sustainable methods, whether by greening buildings or following the corporate environmental path.

In many ways, Megalopolis is already the future of America. The densely populated multiple urban centers are the ideal for **transit-oriented developments (TODs)**, conservation, and energy efficiency. It already leads the nation in available mass transit, but more rail lines and TODs can add efficiency. The densely populated cities of Megalopolis are well entrenched in reduced carbon footprint mass transit systems and TODs. For example, Boston and New York have reliable rail and bus systems that transport passengers from outlying suburbs and between regional cities. Following the triple bottom line, TODs encourage social, economic, and environmental benefits. Cities such as Boston and nearby Cambridge have adopted public investment policies and guidelines that attract private investment and improve property values. TODs are growing across the nation, but the density of population in Megalopolis has capitalized on them.

In the second half of the twentieth century, New York City experienced several massive blackouts that called attention to infrastructure failure. In 2003, New York, the entire Northeast, and portions of the Midwest had an August blackout that left all residents in darkness for several days and caused a transportation shutdown. These blackouts and several others of shorter duration all show a need for upgrading infrastructure for more efficiency and conservation. Investing in energy-saving appliances can reduce energy demands, cogeneration systems can provide some energy during times of crisis, and experimental hydropower sources such as the East River tide-driven underwater turbines can provide new forms of power.

Megalopolis has been active in sustainable issues, including renewable, sustainable energy and green power. Most state governments have agreed to purchase green power. For example, Connecticut, one of the most progressive states, has ordered state government agencies to purchase 20 percent renewable energy by 2020. In April 2007, New York City followed the carbon reduction standard set by California to reduce carbon emissions 30 percent by 2030. But these reductions are only for state agencies. Residential reduction and incentives are rare, even though residential use is the largest power user in the nation.

Megalopolis, along with fourteen states outside the region, has set standards to provide renewable energy by set dates. State governments have pursued setting renewable and energy standards. A broad regional movement has encouraged clean energy generation.

Companies began purchasing wind offsets, which reduced greenhouse gas emissions—the equivalent of taking cars off the road or planting trees. The interest in renewable energy continues to grow, and wind farms are springing up, such as an offshore farm at Rockaway Beach, Queens. After a decade of opposition, the 130-turbine Cape Wind Project off Cape Cod will make it the first offshore wind farm in America.

Since 2003, New York City has been pursuing green design aggressively. A property tax credit in NYC encourages green roofs. The Leadership in Energy and Environmental Design (**LEED**) certification standards are expensive, as are upfront costs. Several commercial and residential buildings have attained LEED certification, but the high costs of certification, 4–8 percent above normal costs, while absorbed in energy

TABLE 7.2. LEED Buildings in Megalopolis, 2016

State	GSF per capita	National Rank
Washington, D.C.	29.04	1
Massachusetts	3.73	2
New York	2.50	5
Maryland	2.33	8
Virginia	2.31	9

GSF square footage certified by state population
Source: https://www.usgbc.org/articles/infographic-top-10-states-for-leed-in-2016

savings over time, are difficult for many public companies to justify when restricted by quarterly reviews. There remains a need for strong residential incentives. Despite economic limitations, though, green buildings are popular, and they attract more educated and innovative employees (table 7.2).

New York City is a special case for green building. Building costs are high; land is precious. Any institutional building using more than $2 million in city funds must attain LEED certification. This is applauded as a step in the right direction by some, but others, especially those interested in affordable housing, feel that energy costs can be cut without using fancy, expensive gadgets or going through the costly red tape of meeting LEED standards. LEED does not work everywhere equally. Using recycled goods, selling back excess energy, and recycling water to satisfy LEED requirements are difficult in New York City.

The attention to these sustainable issues in the nation's largest city will set some standards for the rest of the nation. Boston and Washington, D.C., have adopted some LEED criteria into their building codes.

Perhaps with time, energy efficiency will become an important part of everyone's lives, as homes and businesses are supported in becoming more energy efficient.

Questions for Discussion

1. What were the early manufacturing industries in New England and how had they evolved by the mid-twentieth century?

2. What natural features have significance in explaining the distribution of cities in Megalopolis? How do New England features differ from the Central Atlantic region?

3. What were determining factors for the growth of Philadelphia and New York City?

4. What has been the historical importance of the Lehigh Valley of Pennsylvania? What has been its industrial history? Why?

5. Why has New York City surpassed all other American cities in population and economic importance?

6. What natural advantages favor New York Harbor over other Atlantic harbors? What human-made advantages favor it?

7. Population pressure and religious intolerance pushed people out of the original Boston settlement area. Where did they migrate?

8. How did Philadelphia's urban planning differ from previous cities, and how did it affect later American urban development?

9. How did Boston's economy evolve from the colonial period to the present?

10. How has immigration impacted the region?

11. In what ways is Megalopolis best suited for a renewable energy future?

12. How have Europeans changed the Atlantic Coast shoreline landscape?

13. What are some of notable sustainability efforts in the region?

14. What forms the basis of the regional economies?

Suggested Readings

Andersen, T. *This Fine Piece of Water: An Environmental History of Long Island Sound*. New Haven, Conn.: Yale University Press, 2002.

Benton-Short, L. *The National Mall: No Ordinary Public Space*. Toronto: University of Toronto, 2016.

Bergman, E. *A Geography of the New York Metropolitan Region*. Dubuque, Iowa: Kendall/, 1975.

Borchert, J. R. *Megalopolis: Washington, D.C., to Boston*. New Brunswick, N.J.: Rutgers University Press, 1992.

Conzen, M. P., and George K. Lewis. *Boston: A Geographical Portrait*. Cambridge, Mass.: Ballinger, 1976.

Cronon, W. *Changes in the Land: Indians, Colonists, and the Ecology of New England*. New York: Hill & Wang, 1983.

Cunningham, J. T. *This Is New Jersey*. New Brunswick, N.J.: Rutgers University Press, 2001.

Ellis, J. J. *His Excellency: George Washington*. New York: Faber & Faber, 2005.

Gottmann, J. "Megalopolis, or the Urbanization of the Northeastern Seaboard." *Economic Geography* 33, no. 3 (July 1957): 189–200.

Harris, C. M. "Washington's Gamble, L'Enfant's Dream: Politics, Design, and the Founding of the National Capital." *William and Mary Quarterly*, 3rd series, 56, no. 3 (July 1999): 527–64.

Harrison, J., and Hoyler, M. (eds) *Megaregions: Globalization's New Urban Form*, London: Routledge, 2015.

Kieran, J. *Natural History of New York City*. New York: Houghton Mifflin, 1959.

Lippson, A., and R. Lippson. *Life in the Chesapeake Bay*. Baltimore, Md.: Johns Hopkins University Press, 2006.

McManis, D. R. *Colonial New England: A Historical Geography*. New York: Oxford University Press, 1975.

McPhee, J. *The Pine Barrens*. New York: Farrar, Straus & Giroux, 1978.

Oldale, Robert N. *Cape Cod, Martha's Vineyard and Nantucket: The Geologic Story*. Rev. ed. Yarmouth Port. Mass.: On Cape, 2001.

Rauber, P. "The Oyster Is Our World." *Sierra* 80, no. 5 (September–October 1995).

Short, J. R. *Liquid City: Megalopolis and the Contemporary Northeast*. Washington D.C.: Resources for the Future, 2007.

Sorkin, M. *After the World Trade Center: Rethinking New York City*. New York: Routledge, 2002.

Teske, P. "Winners and Losers: Politics, Casino Gambling, and Development in Atlantic City." *Review of Policy Research* 10, no. 2–3 (1991): 130–37.

Tuico, E. "The Greenest Building in America?" *Constructor* (May 2002).

Warner, S., Jr. *Greater Boston: Adapting Regional Traditions to the Present*. Philadelphia: University of Pennsylvania Press, 2001.

Wood, J. *The New England Village*. Baltimore, Md.: Johns Hopkins Press, 1997.

Internet Sources

The Quest for a Capital, at http://www.capitolhillhistory.org/lectures/vlach/index.html

Martha's Vineyard Gazette, at http://www.mvgazette.com/

Chesapeake Bay Foundation, at http://www.cbf.org/

Chesapeake Bay and Global Warming, at http://www.cbf.org/issues/climate-change/ and also https://www.conservationfund.org/projects/climate-change-and-the-chesapeake-bay

The Manahattan Project, at http://welikia.org/

Globalization measurements, at http://www.lboro.ac.uk/gawc/

Glaciers in New York City, at http://people.gl.ciw.edu/ecottrell/glaciers/Glaciers_in_NY_Intro.pdf

New York City's Sustainability Plan, at http://www.nyc.gov/html/ia/gprb/downloads/pdf/NYC_Environment_PlaNYC.pdf

Philadelphia's Sustainability Plan, at https://beta.phila.gov/departments/office-of-sustainability/greenworks/vision/

Washington, D.C.'s Sustainability Plan, at http://www.sustainabledc.org/

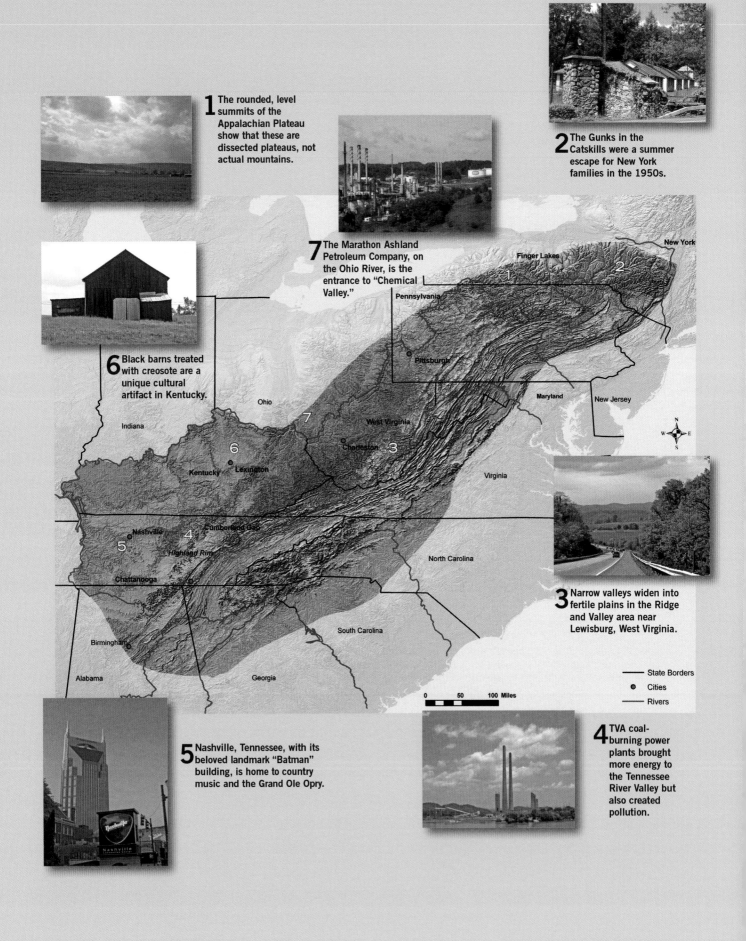

1 The rounded, level summits of the Appalachian Plateau show that these are dissected plateaus, not actual mountains.

2 The Gunks in the Catskills were a summer escape for New York families in the 1950s.

7 The Marathon Ashland Petroleum Company, on the Ohio River, is the entrance to "Chemical Valley."

6 Black barns treated with creosote are a unique cultural artifact in Kentucky.

3 Narrow valleys widen into fertile plains in the Ridge and Valley area near Lewisburg, West Virginia.

5 Nashville, Tennessee, with its beloved landmark "Batman" building, is home to country music and the Grand Ole Opry.

4 TVA coal-burning power plants brought more energy to the Tennessee River Valley but also created pollution.

New York

Finger Lakes

Pennsylvania

Pittsburgh

Maryland

New Jersey

Ohio

West Virginia

Indiana

Charleston

Kentucky   Lexington

Virginia

Cumberland Gap

Nashville

Highland Rim

North Carolina

Chattanooga

South Carolina

Birmingham

Alabama   Georgia

N
W   E
S

0   50   100 Miles

— State Borders
● Cities
— Rivers

8
APPALACHIA
Trying to Love the Mountains

Chapter Highlights

After reading this chapter, you should be able to:

- List and define the five major ranks of coal
- Identify major coal-producing areas
- Describe the major subregions of Appalachia
- Compare and contrast a mountain and a plateau
- Discuss the role of and problems with the Tennessee Valley Authority
- Explain who the Scots-Irish are and where they settled
- Identify Chemical Valley and its importance
- Discuss the challenges to urbanization in the region
- Distinguish between the northern and southern Appalachian plateaus
- Discuss the issues with the Birmingham, Alabama, steel industry
- Describe environmental issues in the Great Smoky Mountains
- Discuss economic challenges in the region

Terms

anthracite
Appalachian Regional
   Commission (ARC)
assimilation
bituminous

canebrake
Clean Water Act (CWA)
cove
eco-industry
headwater stream
lignite
moonshine

mountaintop removal (MTR)
overburden
peat
Pittsburgh Plus
Second Great Awakening
strip-mining
subbituminous

Surface Mining Control and
   Reclamation Act (SMCRA)
Tennessee Valley
   Authority (TVA)
trace
water gap
wind gap

Places

Alleghenies
Appalachian Plateau
Blue Ridge

Catskill Mountains
Cumberland Gap
Cumberland Plateau
Finger Lakes

Great Smoky Mountains
Great Valley
Highland Rim
Interior Plateau

Kanawha Valley
Lexington Basin
Ridge and Valley
Shenandoah Valley

Cities

Birmingham, Alabama
   (2016 MSA 1.1 million)
Charleston, West Virginia
   (2016 MSA 225,000)

Chattanooga, Tennessee
   (2016 MSA 551,000)

Nashville, Tennessee
   (2016 MSA 1.8 million)

Pittsburgh, Pennsylvania
   (2016 MSA 2.3 million)

PHOTO 8.1. Billboard in Beckley, West Virginia. Billboards favoring the coal industry are plastered along all major roadways and in towns. Coal does provide the power for electrical generation, but it has also created a deep divide in West Virginia about the coal industry, especially mountaintop removal.

Introduction

Appalachia is a dissected plateau. Years of water moving through the plateau have cut the mountainous shapes on the outside, but inside, these "mountains" still show their geologic origins. Inside, the layers are horizontal, not folded or uplifted as most mountains are. And inside these mountainous structures is their secret—coal, coal that is easy to access (photo 8.1).

The horizontal geology has shaped the regional economy, and more so as accessing natural resources becomes more expensive. Mining coal from horizontal layers is much easier and cheaper than underground mining, but it is the antithesis of sustainable.

Although not all of Appalachia produces coal, it is the single most important resource within the region. Coal has been a source of wealth for some and steady employment for others. But this has had tremendous consequences for the natural environment. The government has long ignored these problems; if there are regulations, they are seldom enforced. However, many local nongovernmental organizations (NGOs) have formed to attend to the regional issues.

Physical Geography

The Appalachian cultural region follows the spine of the Appalachian Mountains through thirteen states. Only one state, West Virginia, is completely within the region. Portions of Kentucky, Tennessee, Mississippi, Alabama, Georgia, Virginia, Maryland, South Carolina, North Carolina, Ohio, Pennsylvania, and New York that are contiguous to the mountains are also included. The Interior Plateau, the region that connects Appalachia with its Ozark sister region, encompasses western Kentucky and Tennessee.

In higher elevations, spruce and fir share the landscape with oaks. Native Americans used fire to clear fields and open areas for agriculture, while Europeans altered the local vegetation through livestock grazing, agriculture, and logging. Only 1 percent of the pre-European forest remains intact; the remainder has been altered, cut, and replanted.

The local flora and fauna are unique in America. Thousands of years ago during the ice age advances, northern species were forced southward. When the ice retreated, many species remained in Appalachia, making the region one of the most biodiverse in the temperate realm. The many hollows and gorges in the dissected plateau provide microclimates that allow an unusual number of species to survive. But intense farming, logging, and extraction of resources have caused extinction of many species.

There are five types of topography—mountains, valleys, plateaus, flood plains, and limestone prairie—across the subregions:

- The Blue Ridge Province, containing the Great Smoky Mountains
- Ridge and Valley Province, including the Great Valley
- Appalachian Plateaus: Allegheny, Cumberland
- Interior Plateau: Nashville and Lexington Basins

The Blue Ridge Province

The Blue Ridge Mountains, the oldest part of the Appalachians, were created when the dominant Precambrian rocks thrusted over younger rocks. The Blue Ridge, east of the

PHOTO 8.2. The Blue Ridge Mountains near Asheville, North Carolina. TVA coal-burning power plants have created a haze over the Blue Ridge Mountains and seriously impaired visibility.

Piedmont and west of the Ridge and Valley, extends 550 miles. The northern Blue Ridge province extends into southern Pennsylvania, and the southern Blue Ridge includes the Great Smoky Mountains along the Tennessee–North Carolina border. Higher and wider in the south, the Blue Ridge varies from a single northern ridge to complex southern ridges near Asheville, North Carolina. The Blue Ridge Mountains are eighty miles wide at their widest and ascend over six thousand feet (photo 8.2).

The Great Smoky Mountains are named for the "blue" natural mist and contain the nation's most visited National Park and the southeast's only national park (box 8.1). The Great Smoky Mountain **coves** are small, oval-shaped, grass-floor valleys. Precambrian rocks completely surround the exposed and younger limestone and shale coves. Cove microclimates support an array of plant and animal species that differ from the surrounding area.

Cades Cove, Tennessee, is the most famous Appalachian cove. Cades Cove was once a junction of Cherokee pathways, but in 1820 it was settled as a farming community that prospered working the fertile limestone soil. Unfortunately, the community was forced to abandon their homes when they were taken by eminent domain in 1932. Today, Cades Cove is one of the most visited sites within the Great Smoky Mountains National Park (photo 8.4).

More than nine million visit the Great Smoky Mountains Park—and therein lies the problem.

Park boundaries protect and preserve the Smokies' scenery and ecology but cannot stop pollutants, which cause air and land quality to deteriorate. Despite a number of legislative acts to protect the air, the Great Smoky Mountain National Park is being loved to death.

The former one-hundred-mile visibility has now decreased to about twenty miles on an average day. The loss of visibility is a sign of severe point source pollution (from industrial boilers, power plants, manufacturing facilities, and automobiles) and nonpoint source pollution. Coal-burning power plants generate electricity for the region but have the unintended consequence of acid rain caused by sulfur oxides and mercury, which affect the balance between ecosystems, vegetation, soils, and surface water.

Some pollution problems have been addressed. The **Tennessee Valley Authority (TVA)** has begun cleaning up its power plant pollution, and emissions have begun to decline. However, the lack of funding and staffing means that legislation and education to reduce pollution remain a challenge. Furthermore, the area around the National Park is a popular real estate investment area. Although conservation groups work to halt residential development, the surrounding counties' population grew at four times the national rate. Nonprofit environmental groups—Friends of the Smokies, Great Smoky Mountains Association—have contributed millions of dollars and hours of cleanup, but they still cannot solve the root of the problem: the dependence on coal.

Ridge and Valley

West of the Blue Ridge Mountains, the longitudinal Ridge and Valley ecoregion extends more than seven hundred miles from Canada to northern Alabama. The compressed and folded landscape alternates between limestone valleys and resistant sandstone and shale ridges. The regional profile resembles a rug buckling when pushed against a wall.

The easternmost valley, the Great Valley, extends from Canada to Alabama and has been one of the few north–south trending migration paths of American settlers. As settlers confronted the mountains, they followed the Great Valley to the south. Some settled in the valley; others crossed through the Appalachians at the Cumberland Gap. The Great Valley is

BOX 8.1 NATIONAL PARKS: THE BLUE RIDGE PARKWAY

The Blue Ridge Parkway national park is an distinctive national park for two reasons. First, it is deliberately about scenic driving and the celebration of the automobile. The Parkway meanders for 469 miles, providing a diversity of views and scenic overlooks. The Parkway travels through four national forests in Virginia and North Carolina. Many overlooks along the parkway offer spectacular views of the surrounding national forests (photo 8.3).

Second, the Blue Ride Parkway is a planned landscape, planned down to the smallest detail in ways that most visitors do not notice at first glance. Landscape architects and engineers worked to create long-range vistas and close-up views of the rugged mountains and pastoral landscapes of the Appalachian Highlands. They also adopted their own variant of the prevailing "rustic style" of architecture adopted in the national parks. They wanted their own structures to reflect the architecture of the region, and consequently took on the forms of cabins, sheds, and barns in order to create a "backwoods feeling."

The Blue Ridge Parkway is many things:

- It is the longest road planned as a single unit in the US.
- It is an elongated park, protecting significant mountain landscapes far beyond the shoulders of the road itself.

- It is a series of parks providing the visitor access to high mountain passes, a continuous series of panoramic views, the boundaries of its limited right-of-way rarely apparent and miles of the adjacent countryside seemingly a part of the protected scene.
- It is a "museum of the managed American countryside," preserving the roughhewn log cabin of the mountain pioneer, the summer home of a textile magnate, and **traces** of early industries such as logging, railways, and an old canal.
- It is the product of a series of major public works projects that provided a boost to the travel and tourism industry and helped the Appalachian region climb out of the depths of the Great Depression.
- Stretching almost 500 miles along the crest of the Blue Ridge Mountains through North Carolina and Virginia, it encompasses some of the oldest settlements of both prehistoric and early European settlement.

Source: National Park Service Blue Ridge Parkway https://www.nps.gov/blri/learn/historyculture/preservation.htm

PHOTO 8.3. Linn Cove Viaduct in the Blue Ridge Parkway.
Source: iStock/jaredkay

actually a chain of several valleys: from the Champlain Valley in the north, through the Mohawk and Hudson River valleys of New York, the Lehigh of Pennsylvania, Shenandoah and Roanoke valleys of Virginia, the Cumberland and Tennessee River valleys, and Coosa Valley at the southern end.

Appalachian Plateau

The Appalachian Plateau looks mountainous. Streams incise the green, wooded, and rolling landscape, leaving narrow winding valleys among steep-sided but level summits. The plateau extends from Watertown in the Tug Hill section of New York

PHOTO 8.4. Cades Cove, Great Smoky Mountain National Park, Tennessee. The Carter Shields cabin is set against the wooded area. All cove residents were made to believe their community was safe when the park was created, but they were forcibly evicted by eminent domain in 1932.

at the base of the Adirondacks to northeastern Alabama. The elevation rises from about one thousand feet on the western edge to three thousand feet at the Allegheny front. The four-thousand-foot-high Catskills, located about one hundred miles northwest of New York City, are the Appalachian Plateau's highest "mountains."

Allegheny Plateau

Glaciation divided the two Allegheny Plateaus. The glaciated northern plateau of northeastern Ohio, northwestern Pennsylvania, and southern New York is rounded, eroded uplands filled with small lakes and stony fields. Seventy percent of the glaciated plateau is forested, while the remaining area is devoted to dairying. The rugged landscape and higher elevations of the southern, unglaciated plateau is a transition to the Cumberland. European settlement left behind a legacy of irresponsible logging, mining, and waste, but the region still has potential for recreation and resources if managed in alliance with its natural ecology.

Regional rivers formed the rocky gorges of the southern plateau. The Kanawha is a major industrial river, while the New and Gauley rivers are both famous for white water adventures. In the glaciated Alleghenies, streams dissect and separate the Catskill, Shawanagunk, and Pocono ranges. The aptly named Finger Lakes district in upstate New York was formed by glaciation and is a transitional area between the Mohawk Valley and the northern edge of the glaciated Alleghenies.

Cumberland Plateau

The dissected and coal-laden Cumberland Plateau includes western West Virginia, eastern Kentucky and Tennessee, and northern Alabama. The Cumberland Gap cuts through the plateau into the Interior Plateaus of Kentucky and Tennessee.

In the Cumberland, elevation separated the people and the resources. The people live in the forested and rural bottomlands of the narrow, V-shaped valleys (photo 8.5), and coal and logging companies own the higher-elevation resources.

Interior Low Plateaus

The Interior Low Plateau consists of the Highland Rim (Pennyroyal in Kentucky) escarpment surrounding the low-lying Lexington Plain and Nashville Basin. The region begins south of the Ohio River and extends to the Tennessee River. The Interior Plateau vegetation regimes include the hardwoods of the Highland Rim, and in the basins the nearly impenetrable **canebrake** thickets composed of America's native bamboo. By 1799, the canebrakes had yielded to the axe and become grass and pasture lands.

Lexington and the Lexington Plain received their names in 1775 when patriotic hunters camping in the Kentucky clearing heard of the incipient revolutionary battle and commemorated the event by naming the clearing after the Massachusetts town. The Lexington Plain extends north to Cincinnati and west toward Louisville. The undulating limestone plain was transformed from a tangled canebrake to the excellent Kentucky bluegrass—an excellent and palatable turf grass for livestock.

The Nashville Basin in the central Tennessee rolling hills covers about six thousand square miles from Kentucky to the Alabama border. Karst topography underlies the former tobacco-growing region; today, livestock (cattle and poultry) dominate farm production. The southern basin is also home to the Tennessee walking horse farms, although urban sprawl now envelops much of the land.

The karst terrain of underground streams, sinkholes, springs, or caves is the result of chemical weathering when slightly acidic rainwater dissolves limestone. The Interior

PHOTO 8.5. Cumberland Plateau in Raleigh County, West Virginia. The "mountains" are heavily dissected, forested plateaus of roughly equal elevation.

Plateau's limestone layer has created more than a hundred caves, including the largest and best-known Mammoth Cave in Kentucky (photo 8.6).

The subsurface water follows underground paths before reappearing along the valley floors. The water seeps and enlarges porous limestone fissures and develops an interconnected network of subsurface cavities and holes where rainwater replenishes groundwater. Karst has little ability to filter contaminants, so trash, farm waste, microbial contaminants, and septic systems pollute groundwater. Protecting karst waterways means controlling pollution sources and treating water to remove microbial pollution.

Water

Water is plentiful in Appalachia. The rivers, often older than the mountains, cut east–west wind and **water gaps** across the grain of the Appalachians. For example, the Delaware River's water gap carved a gorge through a ridge of the Ridge and Valley. **Wind gaps** were formed by water but are now dry. Gap usage has evolved from native trails, to forts protecting settlers from Indian attacks, to cities, roads, and railways.

Northern rivers in Appalachia—the Delaware, Susquehanna, Potomac, and James—have their headwaters on the Allegheny Plateau and empty into the Atlantic. The earliest European settlement occurred at the river mouths. Most southern rivers—the Nolichucky, Holston—flow to the west and into the Tennessee and Ohio rivers. Settlers followed the river valleys through the Appalachians, and communities developed around salt, coal, and chemical resources.

The Tennessee River headwaters in the Great Smoky Mountains flow more than eight hundred miles through the Cumberland and Interior plateaus to the Ohio River at Paducah, Kentucky. In 1935, President Roosevelt's New Deal program established the TVA, building dams to tame the river, relieve flooding, stop erosion of topsoil, generate power, and provide navigation and recreational uses. The TVA became the nation's largest public power company.

The TVA has successfully improved year-round navigation and offered affordable electricity and economic growth, but the multiple goals of the TVA system are often incompatible. TVA dams control the river and halt floods, but the river no longer free-flows and has effectively become a series of lakes (map 8.2). Dams and flow diversions redirect about two-thirds of southern Appalachian water for industrial use. Providing electricity and recreation and halting floods has also impaired water quality. Dividing water between industrial, agricultural, and urban use has become a serious water management issue.

The TVA supports eleven coal-burning power plants, which supply over 60 percent of TVA electricity. Nuclear, hydropower, wind turbines, and solar installations supply the remainder. The coal-burning plants degrade the regional water and biota.

Chemical and coal-burning power plants have polluted the Kanawha River and the Valley of West Virginia. Fallout, or "snow," from the chemical industry has led to the Kanawha Valley being nicknamed "Chemical Valley."

Since the late 1970s, grassroots organizations have urged cleaning up the waste dumps, dioxin, and other toxins discharged into the rivers, and results have been encouraging, although the work is still incomplete. Enforcing the 1972 **Clean Water Act (CWA)**, which federally governed water pollution, and Environmental Protection Agency (EPA) regulations made 20–30 percent of the polluted waterways suitable for human use.

BOX 8.2   DID YOU KNOW . . . COAL

Coal was created when tropical plants decayed, compressed, and heated over millions of years. In the Appalachian Plateau, the repeated advance and retreat of seas 200–360 million years ago transformed the plants into peat layers, and with time and more pressure added by **overburden** and soil, harder coals formed. The coal ranks are **peat** (the softest and youngest), **lignite**, **subbituminous**, **bituminous**, and **anthracite** (the hardest). In the United States, 90 percent of the coal is subbituminous or bituminous (map 8.1).

Coal in Appalachia is either anthracite (found near Scranton, Pennsylvania) or bituminous (in the Appalachian Plateau and some Ridge and Valley areas). Appalachian coal is much older and more compressed than the other major North American coal deposit, Powder River Basin subbituminous coal. Lignite is located in Texas, Montana, North Dakota, Illinois, and the Gulf Coast.

Anthracite has the fewest impurities and contains 86–98 percent carbon. When the Ridge and Valley folded, the heat and pressure applied to the bituminous coal turned it into the harder anthracite. Anthracite was the most popularly used coal until the 1930s when the Depression, cheaper fuels, and labor costs shifted coal production to the bituminous fields of the Cumberland Plateau.

Bituminous coal was the main source of power during the steel-making era. Its 45–86 percent carbon content produces less heat than anthracite. Most bituminous coal is laden with sulfur, a polluting impurity. Subbituminous coal of the Powder River Basin in Wyoming has a lower sulfur content that makes it the environmentally preferred and less polluting coal in the twenty-first century.

Coal when mined has many impurities. One of the most distinctive is sulfur content. Coal-fired steam plants convert sulfur to sulfur dioxide, a pollutant that causes acid rain. The higher the sulfur content, the more polluting. Appalachian high-sulfur coal must be "cleaned" to meet clean air standards. However, Appalachian bituminous coal is harder and more heat efficient than lower-sulfur subbituminous coal.

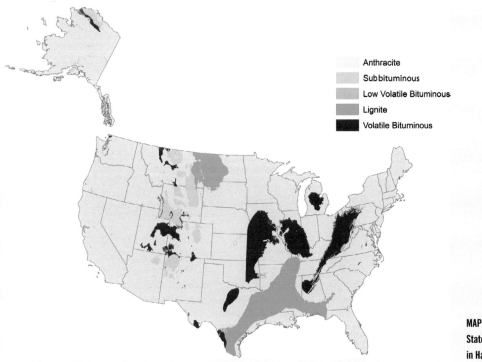

Legend:
- Anthracite
- Subbituminous
- Low Volatile Bituminous
- Lignite
- Volatile Bituminous

MAP 8.1. Coal Bodies in the United States. There are no significant deposits in Hawai`i.

Climate

The temperate-continental Appalachian climate receives the third-highest precipitation, behind the Pacific Northwest and Gulf Coast. The windward western plateau receives between forty and fifty inches of precipitation, while the leeward rain shadow in the Ridge and Valley receives thirty to forty-five inches. About one-quarter of total precipitation falls in the form of snow. The Blue Ridge Mountains bordering the Piedmont receive the most rain in the eastern United States, about eighty inches annually. The growing season varies between 140 days in the north and higher elevations and 205 days in the south and in the lower elevations.

Climate change has a number of implications for Appalachia, most notably higher temperatures, dried-up

PHOTO 8.6. The Rotunda Room at Mammoth Cave, Kentucky.

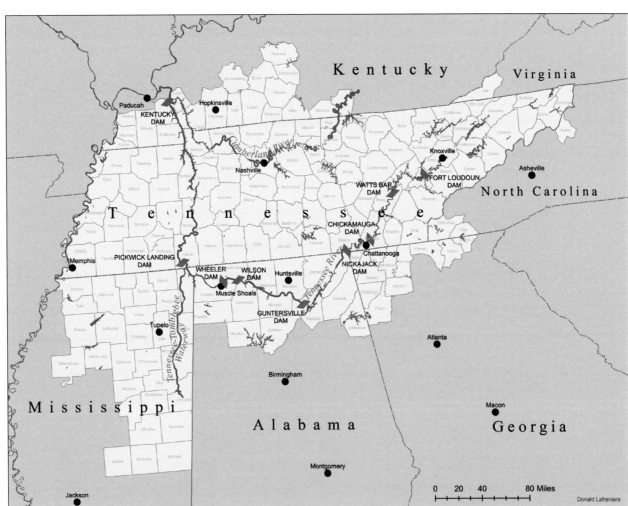

MAP 8.2. Tennessee Valley Authority, Created by Congress in 1933. The TVA was meant to provide flood control, navigation, and electrical generation for the Tennessee Valley, but it has degraded water quality.

BOX 8.3 ENVIRONMENTAL CHALLENGES: WATER POLLUTION

The dependence on coal creates the unintended consequences of acid rain, respiratory disease, soil erosion and landslides, flooding, destruction of native habitats, damage to residents' property, and water pollution. All degraded the quality of life for the entire ecosystem. The burning of coal in power plants creates acid rain downwind over the Midwest, Northeast, and Canadian Corridor. When coal is burned, toxic chemicals from coal waste are spewed onto nearby residents and often inhaled, causing respiratory diseases. The installation of scrubbers to clean sulfur dioxide has decreased the problem, but the use of scrubbers has resulted in an unintended consequence: water pollution.

Coal is not pure carbon but contains toxic by-products that need to be removed to meet clean air and water regulations. Many power plant stacks now have scrubbers installed to collect chemicals. The chemicals—lead, arsenic,

mercury, and many more—are contained in wastewater and the wastewater is either solidified and sent to a landfill or dumped into rivers or lakes that provide drinking water. Some mountaintop removal mining companies build earthen embankments to block valleys, which are then filled with slurry or sludge.

Coal ash impoundments are the slurry from power plant coal waste. The slurry is a toxic watery mixture of impurities in the coal, while sludge is a semisolid ooze of concentrated coal waste material. Coal ash is the leftover toxic material from coal after it has been used in a coal-burning power plant.

The residue, if left alone, can filter into groundwater, but on occasion, the impoundments, holding millions to billions of gallons, break and cause catastrophic floods in the valleys below, killing all life and ruining drinking water for hundreds of square miles.

---

streams, and more forest fires. The stress on the forested areas will lead to a decline in biodiversity as species die out or migrate to cooler climes. As streams become warmer, trout will decline between 50 and 90 percent of present levels. As the climate warms, the Table Mountain pine, red spruce, and striped maple will face extinction in central and southern Appalachia.

Historical Geography and Settlement

Native American

The earliest Appalachian settlement site, Russell Cave in Madison County, Alabama, was first inhabited by Native Americans around 6000 BCE. Several other Alabama and Kentucky cave sites have been dated to this period.

During the Woodland period (500 BCE–1000 CE), settlements in the Mississippi and Ohio Valleys included the Adena and the Hopewell, who were known for their distinctive burial mounds and ornate jewelry. They practiced agriculture, built shelters and earthworks, and made pottery. Their extensive trading network extended through the Midwest and into the Deep South.

The pre-European river bottom landscape of the Interior Plateau basins and southern Appalachia was covered in tangles of native cane species—bamboo and sugarcane. The thick and seemingly impenetrable canebrakes were food for bison during prairie winters; were used variously by Native Americans, especially Cherokee basket weavers; were hiding places for attacking Native Americans; and were hunting grounds for intrepid frontiersmen.

Algonquian tribes occupied the central Appalachians, and southern Appalachia was dominated by the Cherokee, who were linguistically related to the Iroquois. The Iroquoian confederacy—a nation based more on diplomacy than on

warfare—was strong throughout the eastern half of America and overpowered the Algonquian.

European Arrival

Most Appalachian settlers arrived via the Mid-Atlantic hearth, but by the time they arrived, the best land near the eastern seaboard was occupied, or the new settlers conflicted with local inhabitants. The Scots-Irish settled in the plateau valleys, and the Germans settled the more level farmland.

After the French and Indian Wars (1763), the British forbade white settlement west of the Appalachian crest to keep in favor with their Native allies. The colonists objected; they wanted access to Native lands. For a short time, the land south of the Ohio River acted as an unsettled buffer zone between the natives and white settlers.

During the late 1700s, trans-Appalachian pioneers ignored British settlement prohibitions, followed Daniel Boone's Cumberland Gap trail, and settled the grassy Nashville and Lexington Basins. By 1800, the Ohio River Bluegrass south to the Nashville Basin was a continuous zone of settlement.

After European contact, the Cherokee organized the "**Five Civilized Tribes**" and adopted many "white" ways, although it ultimately did not protect their homelands. When gold was discovered on Cherokee soil, settlers encroached on their lands. The Indian Removal Act of 1830 forced abandonment of their Georgia Appalachian home territory so that whites could settle and mine their land. The Cherokee journey to their new home in Oklahoma became the infamous Trail of Tears (see chapter 11).

Appalachian Plateau settlement remained insulated well into the twentieth century. The major influence was World War II, when urban amenities and jobs in the war plants of Pittsburgh, Cleveland, and Detroit caused the "Great Migration." The

BOX 8.4 CLIMATE CHANGE IN APPALACHIA

Scholars studying climate change predict that Appalachia could experience:

- longer growing seasons;
- reduced number and duration of snow pack and ice-over events;
- increasing frequency of days with extreme heat;
- increasing water temperatures; and
- increased evapotranspiration by vegetation and in streams.

According to the Appalachian Landscape Conservation Cooperative, significant changes in precipitation intensity, duration, and timing could have profound effects. The exact changes are also difficult to predict. For example, increased drought could negatively impact water-loving pine trees, but oak forests thrive in drought conditions. Impacts could include changes in species distribution, abundance, and assemblages, or difficult-to-anticipate combinations of these. In addition, changing conditions will likely increase population fragmentation and species extinctions. Competition for sometimes scarce water resources will increase the risk for adversity between urban, agriculture, industry, and natural resource interests.

But the news is not all gloom and doom. Resiliency is related to ecosystem complexity and the Appalachian Mountains are very ecologically complex and still have a good amount of remaining forest cover.

A Nature Conservancy study examined landscapes that are best equipped to handle global climate change. They concluded that the highlight forests of West Virginia may be able to better resist climate change than other areas because Appalachia's varied environments give plants and animals more opportunities to adapt and the hardy ecosystem can endure warmer, drier weather over time.

---

migrants assimilated into the general culture, but they still hark back to Appalachia and often return to visit and later to retire.

Cultural Perspectives

Appalachia derives its name from the Apalache Indians, who lived in northern Florida but whose domain extended into southern Appalachia, and their name was applied to the entire mountain range. Scots-Irish, Celtic, English, and Germans created an Appalachian culture characterized by isolation, individualism, and distrust of government.

Traditional Culture

The largest ethnic group was the Scots-Irish, who often arrived as indentured servants and worked to pay their passage. When their term of service expired, they migrated to find their own land. Often the best land was spoken for or too expensive, so they moved to the less desirable land in the narrow stream-cut valleys of the plateaus. The area was remote, and in many ways remains so today. Although the terrain separated the population from most American progress, it tended to produce close-knit communities sharing common traits.

Over the past two hundred years, many of those traits remain intact including a strong sense of community, settlement patterns, dialects, music, food, and vernacular architecture. The unique regional culture remained separate from the rest of the nation until modern communication and transportation infiltrated. During the Great Depression, the TVA generated hydropower electricity and drew industry to this job-hungry area, connecting portions of Appalachia with mainstream American society. Later, in the 1960s, roads connected Appalachia with the surrounding regions.

The isolated small mountain towns fostered a sense of community that was once common throughout most of America, but was lost as towns grew into anonymous cities. In Appalachia, towns often struggled to survive, but surviving towns are filled with people who have grown and lived their whole life within the confines of the "holler"—the narrow valleys (photo 8.7).

The colorful Southern Mountain dialect heard in Appalachian hollers is a remnant of seventeenth-century Elizabethan English. The Scots-Irish, Celts, and English who brought this dialect to the mountains built upon it in isolated circumstances and, until the twentieth century, had little access to American speech patterns developing in the surrounding area. The use of strange words and grammar ("I done finished," "his'n," "her'n," "I reckon hit don't never . . ."), often denigrated by other Americans, is a wealth of seventeenth-century linguistics, now cherished by those who revel in the origins of language.

Before Appalachian music became commercial, players would congregate at meetings where the main compensation was food. Appalachian food is as traditional and unpretentious as the dialect and the music, and it is influenced by the food ways of the original immigrants.

Appalachian meals center on corn—grits and cornbread—sweetened with honey and sorghum molasses. Meat favors either pork or hunted game. Local foods abound: rhubarb, sassafras, and ramps—the garlicky spinach-like shoots that flourish in the spring. Preserving food is still done by canning, pickling, drying, and salting. Although most residents now have electricity and refrigerators, these conveniences have been common for just over a generation; old traditions die hard in the hollers.

In Appalachia, the quintessential one-room, single-pen log cabin flourished, surrounded by a cluster of rural buildings—corncribs, stock barns, and springhouses. The prototypical pioneer house, the log cabin originated in Delaware but

PHOTO 8.7. Marsh Fork Elementary School, Raleigh County, West Virginia. A coal-processing plant silo was erected directly behind the school. The silo is where railcars are sprayed with chemicals to limit coal dust during travel. The mountain saddle in the background is the location of a billion-gallon earthen dam holding coal waste sludge. NGO groups successfully fought to remove the silo and the plant, and to restore health to students sickened by the nearby toxins.

was popularized in Appalachia and then diffused over the landscape.

Life was hard on the Appalachian backwoods frontier prior to the extraction of coal. Agricultural self-sufficiency ended when struggling farmers, eager to eliminate some of the rigor of life, moved to mine coal and live in the coal company towns.

Moonshine

To fund the military, an excise tax was added to alcoholic beverages in 1790. The tax resulted in the western Pennsylvania distillery revolt called the Whiskey Rebellion. The rebellion collapsed when troops quelled the dissenters, but the indirect result was the illegal **moonshine** industry. Working by the light of the moon, moonshiners evaded tax revenuers. The secluded hollows of Appalachia were a perfect location to practice making moonshine and to add value and longevity to the corn crop. Familiarity with the land was important: moonshiners knew where to hide their stills and how to flavor their potent concoction with plant species from the hills (photo 8.8).

The Scots-Irish brought over their customary drink—corn whiskey, a clear-as-water, 100+ proof drink—described as "swallowing sugar that was on fire." Although Germans, Irish, and English also participated, it was the Scots-Irish who dominated the moonshine-based barter economy.

The heyday of moonshine was during the twentieth-century Prohibition era. Producing or providing alcohol was a path to wealth during Prohibition. The bootleg mafia thrived, and fortunes were made smuggling illegal alcohol into the country, while whiskey moonshiners supplied the local country with their commodity.

Moonshine continues to be made in Appalachia. This region has many dry counties because of religious convictions, but illicit distilling is practiced more in dry than in wet counties.

The Second Great Awakening

The **Second Great Awakening** diffused from Europe to the Americas in the late eighteenth and antebellum nineteenth centuries. Evangelical conversion inspired Welsh, Scottish, Irish, and English immigrants to reinterpret the formal, elite practices of Protestant churches to fit the settlers' real world. For example, Presbyterians required ordained ministers, which were in short supply in the New World, while the new religions bypassed official ordination, so backcountry circuit riders and farmer-preachers who felt the call could preach for less strict denominations.

The Second Great Awakening religion held the Appalachians together, despite their physical isolation from the rest of the country. Long camp meetings—multiple-act preachers or bands, crowds of people of similar background, and dancing and singing—sustained cultural ties. During the revivals, people vowed to change their lives. The first stirrings of the abolition, women's rights, and temperance movements can be traced to the awakening.

Population, Immigration, and Diversity

After the initial European settlement, few others migrated to Appalachia. Throughout the twentieth century, Appalachian population growth lagged behind the nation.

PHOTO 8.8. Old Technology in Making Moonshine.

Source: iStock/artJazz

Coalfield jobs were plentiful during the early twentieth century, and many worked in the mines. But coal fuel energy lost favor to oil, resulting in fewer jobs and stagnated population growth from 1950 to 1960: The number of jobs fell by 15 percent, while the nation's employment expanded by 17 percent. Scarcity of work caused more than two million working-age people to emigrate from Appalachia during the 1950s. Population in many Appalachian counties has declined in every decade since 1950, although the largest drop in the region was between 1950 and 1970. Compounding the job loss problem, in 1960 only 11.6 percent of the population over the age of twenty-five had as much as a fifth-grade education, which was far below the US average.

In the 1960s, the distressed region became a subject of economic development programs. The TVA and **Appalachian Regional Commission (ARC)** were enacted to boost economic growth.

Appalachia's 2010 population of twenty-five million was nearly 7 percent higher than it was in 2000, slightly lower than the nearly 10 percent growth rate for the United States as a whole. And in every Appalachian state except Alabama and Georgia, the part of the state outside the Appalachian region grew at a faster rate. Yet, population change varied greatly within the region. On the one hand, one-third of the region's 420 counties lost population during the decade—mostly in the northern and central counties, as well as in parts of Alabama and Mississippi. However, nearly one in four Appalachian counties grew at or above the national average. Most of the fastest-growing counties were in southern and south central Appalachia, although some counties in Kentucky, Pennsylvania, and West Virginia also experienced rapid growth.

The Appalachian region also has a larger proportion of residents ages sixty-five and older than does the nation as a whole.

Alleghenies

After 1900, population in the Alleghenies expanded and retracted following the movement of manufacturing jobs. In upstate New York, Binghamton, the major Allegheny city in the 1920s, was known for its shoe manufacturing, but the 2016 population of 45,672, less than half its 1920 population of 110,000, and 33.9 percent (2015) were living below the poverty line. The continued loss of manufacturing jobs has crippled this once-thriving area. The city has lost 48 percent of its factory jobs since 1990.

Immigration and Diversity

The Appalachian region is significantly less racially and ethnically diverse than the United States as a whole, and most parts of the region are far below the national average. In two-thirds of Appalachian counties, minorities (defined as anyone who

BOX 8.5 CULTURAL FESTIVALS: TRADITIONAL MUSIC

Traditional Appalachian music combines English ballads and American contexts that maintain an oral tradition of personal historical narratives. Musical influences were American religious gospel and African call and response. The fiddle initiated the music, later augmented by the banjo and then the guitar. Dance revolved around the reel, adapted from the Scottish highlands.

Each area within Appalachia developed its own sound, but they melded as transportation and communication improved in the twentieth century. After the Great Depression and the beginning of commercial bluegrass, the sound evolved into country and western, but the hills and hollers still resound in the folk music played in impromptu gatherings.

PHOTO 8.9. Old-Time Mountain Fiddle Player.
Source: iStock/tsmorton

identifies with a racial or ethnic group other than "white alone, not Hispanic") make up less than 10 percent of the population. There were just twenty-two counties—almost exclusively in southern Appalachia—where minorities' share of the population matched or exceeded the national average. Although Hispanics have become the largest minority group of the United States, they make up only one in twenty-five residents in the Appalachian region.

West Virginia provides an ethnic snapshot of the entire region. The earliest settlers were German or Scots-Irish, followed by a contingent of English and some French Huguenots. In 2004, half the population of West Virginia claimed heritage in these groups, with another 15 percent who call themselves "Americans." Less than 2 percent is foreign born, compared to a national average of 13.2 percent. Seventy-one percent of West Virginia's residents were born in their home state, compared to a US average of 60 percent. The racial makeup of the state was 93.6 percent white (2016); the next largest group was blacks, who comprised 3.6 percent of the population and lived in segregated towns in extreme southern West Virginia. The black population was recruited from the South

during the nineteenth century to construct railroads. Many stayed to work in the coal mines.

Per capita income in West Virginia is $23,450, compared to a US average of $28,930 (2015). Individuals below the poverty line constituted 17.9 percent of the population (2015), higher than the 12.7 percent photo for the United States as a whole.

International immigration has been comparatively low in the Pittsburgh region for the last several decades as low overall job growth and relatively inhospitable economic conditions have dampened the flow of immigrants into the region. Currently, only 8 percent of the city is foreign born and Pittsburgh ranks at the bottom for new migration to major US cities. The city's percentage of net annual international migration—approximately 0.05 percent—is the lowest of any of the forty largest metropolitan areas of the United States.

But that may be changing. According to US Census photos, from 2010 to 2016, the Pittsburgh area gained twenty-two thousand residents from international migration, which offset the fact that the metro area saw more deaths than births during that same time. And during that same time period, twelve thousand residents migrated out of Pittsburgh. Without immigration,

PHOTO 8.10. Steel Production at Birmingham, Alabama. The proximity to raw materials for the steel industry fostered the initial growth of the city, which built a southern steel industry that competed with Pittsburgh. However, Pittsburgh and US Steel passed a "Pittsburgh Plus" pricing policy in 1907 that added fees to eliminate southern shipping advantages. Today the city is home to the University of Alabama and has diversified.

population in Pittsburgh would have declined. Based on these new realities, businesses and government mounted an effort to encourage migration to the city, realizing that to be competitive, the city needs to cultivate the next generation of entrepreneurs and innovators. In a series of community surveys, immigrants reported that the largest hurdles encountered by newcomers included difficulty using public transportation, employment, and connecting and making friends. And many immigrants saw the greatest need for improved services in public transportation, community centers, jobs, and language access. In response, the city launched a program called "A More Welcoming Pittsburgh," outlining numerous strategies to encourage and facilitate immigration.

Urban Trends

There are no large cities in Appalachia; the dissected plateaus and resultant narrow valleys preclude large agglomerations. As a result, Appalachia's urban population is about half the national average. The largest cities, Pittsburgh and Birmingham, are at opposite ends of the region. Both cities are nodes for regional resource convergence and distribution. While both have coal legacies, the cities that grew on coal mining were Scranton and Wilkes-Barre in Pennsylvania, where the first coal rush began.

Birmingham, Alabama
(2016 MSA 1.1 million)

The South had few antebellum cities, but the post-bellum economy fostered the growth of new cities, such as Birmingham, Alabama's largest city. Although Birmingham can be called a southern city, it is geographically situated near Appalachia and its resources.

In 1871, Birmingham, established at the crossing of two railroads, was at the confluence of ore, coking coal, and limestone flux, all important resources for the development of a Southern steel industry. The city flourished as the "Pittsburgh of the South" because of accessible resources and low labor costs. But in 1901, US Steel formed the **Pittsburgh Plus** pricing policy, forcing all steel to be priced based on its distance from Pittsburgh. The policy halted Birmingham's growth and locational advantage in steel production.

In 1907, US Steel purchased the Birmingham Steelworks, but although people rejoiced at the time thinking their jobs were saved, the purchase was made to eliminate competition. The Birmingham Steelworks never grew as people expected. Birmingham's locational advantage was eliminated and the local steel industry was shut down. Government regulators rescinded the Pittsburgh Plus policy in 1924, but the damage to Birmingham's steel industry was complete (photo 8.10). Today, steel is a small part of the local economy.

The population within Birmingham has fallen about one-quarter since its maximum in 1960, but the surrounding suburbs have grown substantially. Birmingham has diversified into banking and to medical biotechnology research at its University of Alabama campus, and it is one of the cosmopolitan "New South" cities.

Pittsburgh, Pennsylvania
(2016 MSA 2.3 million)

Pittsburgh is the largest city near the Appalachian coalfields. Established on the Appalachian Plateau at the headwaters of the Ohio River where the Allegheny and Monongahela ("the Mon") rivers meet, Pittsburgh is an excellent example of

BOX 8.6   NATIONAL PARKS: BIRMINGHAM CIVIL RIGHTS NATIONAL MONUMENT

In 1935, Congress passed the Preservation of Historic Sites Act, which recognized the wealth and diversity of places and people who contributed to American identify. The legislation broadened the Park Services' sphere of influence in historic preservation. National Parks were no longer vast wilderness areas; they were also the time capsules of US culture.

One of the newest national parks in the national park system is a historic site, Birmingham Civil Rights National Monument in Birmingham, Alabama. It was designated in 2017. The National Monument encompasses roughly four city blocks in downtown and includes the A.G. Gaston Motel, which served as the head-quarters for the Birmingham campaign, the 16th Street Baptist Church, and Kelly Ingram Park, a staging ground for civil rights demonstrations.

In 1963, leaders of the civil rights movement, including Reverend Dr. Martin Luther King Jr., took up residence at the A.G. Gaston motel where they strategized and made critical decision about the non-violent campaign that targeted Birmingham's segregation laws and practices. They planned protests and demonstrations in the nearby park.

In 1963, images of snarling police dogs unleashed against nonviolent protesters and of children being sprayed with high-pressure hoses appeared in print and television news across the world (photo 8.11). These dramatic scenes of violent police aggression against civil rights protesters were vivid examples of segregation and racial injustice in America. Public outrage over the events in Birmingham produced political pressure that helped to pass the Civil Rights Act of 1964.

This newest national park highlights the struggle for equality and reminds us that Civil Rights memorials are a litmus test for how far society has progressed towards the goal of racial equality and justice and to what degree society has fulfilled the Civil Rights Movement's goals. This national monument contributes to a broader definition of national history and national identity. The Birmingham National Monument is more than just buildings or statues. It represents the dream for equality, and justice, and a full inclusive democracy.

PHOTO 8.11. Statue in Kelly Park, Part of the Birmingham Civil Rights National Monument.

Source: National Park Service

a site-and-situation city. The site has been so important that it exchanged hands (and forts) between the British and French several times within a century, before it became the jumping-off point for western settlement. The town supplied boats and goods to pioneers heading west on the Ohio River. During the Industrial Revolution, Pittsburgh's steel industry growth was fueled by nearby resources—importing Appalachian coal and Great Lakes ore and limestone.

Pittsburgh's "Mon" became a world-renowned, steel-based industrial complex. For a century, Pittsburgh was the heart of the steel-producing region, until improved productivity, foreign competition, and declining demand reduced the need for labor in the 1970s. By the 1980s, over 150,000 jobs were lost, and the steel-making capacity had declined from 66 percent of the national output to less than 10 percent. Smaller specialty mills have replaced the large steel mills in the local area, as well as in Youngstown, Steubenville-Weirton, and Cleveland, but few jobs have been saved.

Pittsburgh's twenty-first-century renaissance relied on technology and many nonprofit organizations (with a strong arts and culture sector), and it was transformed into a medical center capped by the Carnegie-Mellon Institute.

BOX 8.7 URBAN SUSTAINABILITY BEST PRACTICES: PITTSBURGH

Many cities have developed sustainability plans that are comprehensive and ambitious. A critical path to success is to engage the diversity of businesses and residents in a community. Here we highlight Pittsburgh, which has developed specific programs for different parts of the community. Creating programs for different parts of the community helps to target specific issues, goals, and projects that may help to better advance sustainability and energize efforts.

- **Sustainable Pittsburgh Challenge**: for businesses, nonprofits, colleges/universities, local governments, and K–12 schools. Since 2011, more than 250 organizations completed over seven thousand sustainable actions and in the process saved enough energy to power eleven thousand homes.
- **SWPA Sustainable Business Compact** is a voluntary program for mid-to-large businesses that provides a rigorous, peer-reviewed framework for businesses to advance and publicly demonstrate their corporate sustainability achievements.
- **Sustainable Pennsylvania Community Certification** is a voluntary performance recognition program to help municipalities achieve their sustainability goals to save money, conserve

resources, and encourage innovation. The program focuses on municipal operations, policies, and practices. The certification process also serves as a mechanism for sharing best practices for creating a more sustainable Pennsylvania.

- **Sustainable Pittsburgh Restaurants** is a program that encourages restaurateurs to see the lasting value in operating in socially and environmentally responsible ways, while saving money and increasing business. The program encourages restaurants to select actions from a series of categories directed to making improvements in the areas of energy, water, waste, food sourcing, people, and nutrition.
- **I Am Sustainable Pittsburgh** is for individuals interested in becoming more sustainable at home, at work, and in their communities. Individuals are asked to complete at least six sustainability actions contained in the pledge checklist. The checklist has numerous actions including: not littering, saving money turning off equipment when not in use, donating to a thrift shop, washing clothes in cold water, and treating others with respect and dignity.

To learn more, go to sustainablepittsburgh.org

PHOTO 8.12. Pittsburgh, Pennsylvania. A view of Point State Park, where the Monongahela and Allegheny Rivers conflue to form the Ohio River.
Source: iStock/PhilAugustavo

However, Pittsburgh, an Appalachian and Rust Belt city, made tremendous advances in sustainability. It has adopted strong policies for building Leadership in Energy and Environmental Design (LEED)-certified buildings, as well as offering incentives for retrofitting other buildings, including homes. It has redeveloped its waterfront, has cleaned up brownfields, and is creatively reusing old abandoned factories (photo 8.12).

Kanawha Valley—Ashland (Kentucky); Huntington, Ironton (Ohio) (2016 MSA 359,588); Charleston (West Virginia) (2016 MSA 225,000)

The cities at the nexus of Ohio, Kentucky, and West Virginia lie in the Kanawha and Ohio valleys and share a common manufacturing base in chemical, nickel, oil refining, and steelmaking. The region's economy evolved from salt processing to chemical production.

BOX 8.8   GLOBAL CONNECTIONS: NASHVILLE—MUSIC CITY

Nashville is one of the larges cities in Appalachia. It is also one of the global centers for the making of country music. The roots of this music lie in the cultural geography of Appalachia, where Scots-Irish immigrants brought their music into the isolated valleys of the region where it persisted long after it died out in other parts of the country.

The highly localized music was turned into a global music industry. And one of the centers in this transmission was Nashville. In 1925, the country music radio show Grand Old Opry was first broadcast from the city. The show, still running, provided a sound stage for artists and songwriters to take their music to a national audience. The music was always changing, new style and new subgenres as well as changing names. Country replaced the

hillbilly designation. Varieties include bluegrass, hillbilly boogie, folk, and gospel.

From the mid 1950s, Nashville emerged as major center for this music industry (photo 8.13). The sounds went global. There was a creative clustering of studios, musicians, producers, and financial backers. Bob Dylan recorded most of his 1966 *Blonde on Blonde* album in the city. The city is the second-largest music production center in the country, after New York City. The city hosts the annual Country Music Association Awards. Almost twenty thousand people work in the music industry, and the industry has a total economic impact of over $4 billion. Nashville is a global cultural center that has turned the music of the region into a global musical genre.

PHOTO 8.13. The District Music City Downtown in Vintage Nashville, Tennessee.
Source: iStock/legacy1995

Huntington provided nickel alloys, while Ashland and Ironton have been involved in steel and oil refining. Numerous coal-based, electric power–generating plants and pulp chip mills also lie along the Ohio River and the Kanawha Valley rivers. The industries polluted this area, combining acid rain with air and water pollution. Cleanup has been an ongoing process.

Nashville, Tennessee
(2016 MSA 1.8 million)

Nashville, known today as "music city" for its country music stars and recording companies, was founded in 1779 in the Interior Plateau at the junction of water routes and the buffalo trail that became the Cumberland Trace. Nashville is a major southern city located on the fertile Nashville basin where Native

Americans, French fur trappers, and settlers hunted and grazed cattle. Today, in addition to the music industry, the city is an important meat, cotton, and tobacco-processing area.

Chattanooga, Tennessee
(2016 MSA 551,000)

Located in southeastern Tennessee on the Tennessee River at the transition between the Ridge and Valley and Cumberland Plateau, Chattanooga evolved from a Native American settlement site to a steel-manufacturing dynamo, until its decline from the 1960s through the 1980s. The city's industrial past caused Chattanooga to be named "America's Dirtiest City" in 1969. Industrial pollution, Superfund sites, layoffs, and racial tensions tarnished the city, but decisions to rise again, led by sustainable choices to make the city livable, have reinvigorated Chattanooga. The TVA headquarters and several insurance and banking companies have located there.

Beginning in 1984, city leaders met and established Vision 2000, based on sustainable ideals, and they adopted "economy, ecology, equity," as its slogan. Beginning with a riverwalk along the deteriorated Tennessee River area, the city built shopping areas, inner-city housing, and recreational spaces and walkways to draw people back (photo 8.14). Green spaces, electronic mass transit, urban renewal, affordable housing, and recycling were additional cornerstones of the new and improved "green capitalism" sustainable city—but **eco-industry** was its shining star.

Eco-industry (providing goods and services that are environmentally protective) is more than just companies engaged in environmentally friendly industry. Ideally, eco-industry is a closed-loop, cradle-to-cradle industrial park where waste and the ecological footprint are minimized. Chattanooga has focused on cleanup of contaminated sites and replaced the famed "Chattanooga Choo-choo" with electric buses. The city became one of two American locations that manufacture the buses. In 2011, Volkswagen opened a billion-dollar, environmentally responsible plant in Chattanooga.

Based on the success of Vision 2000, Chattanooga Venture recently completed a Revision 2000 process. Chattanooga Venture challenged people by saying, "Chattanooga looks drastically different, and we are clearly enjoying the city's new image. Now it's time to task ourselves: What does it really mean to us now?" Revision 2000 was also tremendously successful, with twenty-six hundred participants, including 30 percent under the age of twenty-five and 23 percent over the age of fifty-five. Twenty-seven goals were identified and 122 recommendations emerged for further improving the community. Today, Chattanooga has essentially become a "living laboratory" for sustainable projects, and is now implementing its new "take charge" attitude in the areas of education, business development, and community action.

While the city has gained a sustainable reputation, like many cities, equity issues loom. Racial and class biases and the inability to address roots of problems rather than short-term economic fixes remind us that becoming a sustainable city can require addressing systemic and institutional legacies of racism.

The Economy

The Primary Sector

Appalachia is still a resource-based economy with limited secondary industry. While the principal natural resource is coal, there has been and remains an agricultural backbone.

PHOTO 8.14. Fountains and child-friendly activities in Chattanooga help make a vibrant public space and attract residents to the city.

Source: iStock/Shutterstitch

The Shenandoah Valley is a dairying area, rotating corn, alfalfa, and small grains, and continues to produce the country's sixth-largest apple crop.

Most of the rural population lives in plateau areas on small farms. Although the land is forested and mountainous, Appalachia has the most owner-operated farms, although many of the farmers are poor. The farms are undermechanized because the rugged undulating terrain limits farm size, which prevents using expensive, mechanized equipment. The farmers grow pasture crops or livestock, although most augment their income by gathering and selling various roots and herbs from the forested area or by working second jobs.

The Interior Plateau has been known for two distinct agricultural enterprises: tobacco and Kentucky bluegrass horse farms of the wealthy elite.

Kentucky Tobacco   The tobacco farmer averages nineteen acres of tobacco and has depended on the Agricultural Adjustment Act of 1933, which restricted the supply and set a minimum price stabilizing the tobacco earnings. Tobacco became one of the few crops by which a farmer could earn a living on so few acres. An acre of price-supported tobacco can net about $3,000 annually, whereas an acre of wheat nets about $30. Three-quarters of the regional small farmers depended on tobacco as the only profitable crop since the once major crop, hemp, was outlawed in 1937. However, in 2004, tobacco quotas ended and the bottom fell out of the American tobacco-crop market, despite a small buyout. Tobacco production accelerated in China.

About half of Kentucky's tobacco farmers halted tobacco production after the 2004 buyout. In general, tobacco prices have stayed below $2 per pound for the last several decades. The number of tobacco farms that grow tobacco has plummeted as farmers have continued to grapple with the effects of deregulation, lower smoking rates, and foreign competition. In 1997, there were ninety-three thousand tobacco farms. Today, there are forty-two hundred.

Kentucky Bluegrass   The Kentucky bluegrass around Lexington is known for its horse farms and gentleman farmers (photo 8.15). The mineral-rich limestone soil produces grass that builds the bones and muscles of champion horses. This cultural landscape of wealth is rural, with lush, manicured pastures filled with purebred horses; well-maintained, color-schemed fences; antebellum mansions; and matching outbuildings. The culture of the horse set is separate from the rest of the region and revolves around the life cycle of horses and the racing season.

Kentucky bluegrass, a nutritious pasture and lawn grass that is not blue but decidedly green, replaced the native canebrakes. Kentucky bluegrass was the most important source of bluegrass seed in the world in 1939, but growing the seed is no longer economically feasible in the region. The primary region to grow bluegrass seed is in Idaho, Washington, and Oregon, where it helps reduce soil erosion.

The Finger Lakes microclimates favor dairy farms and vineyards. The region contains 85 percent of New York's winery acreage. Over the decades, the quality of the wine, mainly white wine due to the climate, has improved. The larger wineries are now tasting destination sites for tourists taking a wine tour of the lakes.

Logging   Wood is an abundant resource in southern Appalachia; however, a lack of transportation sheltered the forests from harvesting until railroads arrived in the mid-nineteenth century. Once accessible, the hardwood lumber was exploited. During the late nineteenth and early twentieth centuries, lumber companies purchased timber rights and

PHOTO 8.15. Horse Barn in Kentucky.
Source: iStock/JillLang

stripped the lumber, leaving the land bare and prone to erosion and flooding. The hardwood and softwood forests were used for fuel, building homes, and for a variety of household goods.

By 1900, over half of West Virginia's ten-million-acre virgin forest was cut. Some areas were denuded. Hardwood stands had covered the Kanawha Valley, but by 1925 the commercial timber stocks were depleted, leading to the increased dependence on coal production.

Today, second-growth logging is a part of the southern Appalachian economy. Many areas, such as the Great Smoky Mountains, are protected, but others are commercially logged. Logging has changed over the twentieth century from family-run sawmills to chip mills in southern Appalachia.

The controversial chip mills are efficient and satisfy global demand for pulp and paper. Private landowners prefer chip mills because they use poor-quality material, which allows owners to derive the most money from their land. Some local residents welcome logging jobs, while others disdain the clearcut methods and destroyed landscape. Those involved with sustainable practices believe the replanted pine monoculture "managed forests" lack biodiversity, are vulnerable to disease or infestations, and are unsustainable.

Coal   Coal is mined, processed, and shipped from Appalachia to generate electricity and provide heat for homes and industry (photo 8.16). Appalachia's beautiful forested hills conceal layers of coal and have become a battlefield for an energy-hungry nation. Coal production waned in the late twentieth century, but twenty-first-century electricity consumption demands, along with higher costs for imported fuel, resulted in a return to coal.

Coal remains the most polluting, most profitable, and most inexpensive way to generate electricity, but only when environmental and social costs are not calculated. The preferred mining method in the Appalachian Plateau is a massive form of **strip-mining** called mountaintop mining (MTM) by mining companies, or **mountaintop removal (MTR)** by local residents who live with the damage (photo 8.17). The destructive process of MTR involves the following:

1. Raze and burn forest. Do not harvest wood.
2. Scrape land bare (remove topsoil and vegetation).
3. Blast overburden to loosen rock.
4. Dump overburden into adjacent valley.
5. Scoop out the layers of coal.
6. Reclaim land to the minimum allowed by law, or commit to use for a public purpose.

National electricity needs are expanding, and the existing 599 coal-burning power plants are insufficient. However, coal-burning power plant production came under intense scrutiny in 2009, and most states delayed, if not stopped, plans to build more coal-burning plants.

Nonetheless, the national hunger for energy continues to grow along with the population, and alternative energy sources are still expensive and rare.

From the mid-nineteenth century to the 1972 Clean Air Act, West Virginia was the primary source of coal, supplying the Industrial Revolution's economic engine. The Clean Air Act regulated the amount of sulfur in coal, favoring the low-sulfur coal of Wyoming's Powder River Basin. Appalachian coal requires cleaning and processing to meet clean air standards. Wyoming has taken the lead in coal production, but West Virginia and Kentucky, which produce a higher-sulfur coal, still produce 37 percent of US coal, and West Virginian coal still provides over half of Midwestern electricity. In West Virginia, Ohio, Indiana, and Kentucky, coal generates over 90 percent of the electricity.

Coal's legacy is engraved on the land and people of Appalachia's Cumberland Plateau, leaving them poor and the

PHOTO 8.16. West Virginia Coal Company Terminal.

Source: iStock/ScottNodine

BOX 8.9 GEOSPATIAL TECHNOLOGIES: MOUNTAIN MINING

Mountaintop mining involves the removal of the tops of mountains; two studies looked at the spatial distribution. One study, based on 2008 aerial and mining permit data, found that five hundred mountains were impacted.[*] The researchers use aerial imagery from the USDA Agricultural Imagery Program. They found 1.2 million acres had been mined by 2008.

Another study looked at what happened afterwards.[†] They used a geographic information system (GIS) database of five hundred known mountain top mining sites. Using high-resolution true color aerial photography, they found that that few sites were used for economic development. The post-mining lands showed little evidence of productive use.

[*]http://www.ilovemountains.org/reclamation-fail/mining-extent-2009/Assessing_the_Extent_of_Mountaintop_Removal_in_Appalachia.pdf
[†]http://www.ilovemountains.org/reclamation-fail/mining-reclamation-2010/MTR_Economic_Reclamation_Report_for_NRDC_V7.pdf

PHOTO 8.17. Mining in Appalachia.
Source: iStock/Miloslav78

land polluted, while creating wealth for outside corporations. Coal-mining wars over unionization and health concerns such as black lung disease were the issues underwriting laws protecting coal miners and their families. The watershed year for mine safety was 1977, when two acts were passed: the Federal Mine Safety and Health Act (resulting in a decrease of accidental deaths) and the **Surface Mining Control and Reclamation Act (SMCRA)**, requiring mining sites to be reclaimed and restored to their original contours.

SMCRA requirements have not been strongly enforced. Most MTR land is never reclaimed or restored. Reclamation is attempted about 50 percent of the time; 5 percent is restored. By law, land should be restored to its former condition, which requires topsoil. Instead, the topsoil is never returned and the eroded sterile soils are planted with the only plant that will grow in such soil, nonnative *Lespedeza*. The plant limits the return of wildlife or using the land as pasture.

Enforcement of environmental protection laws has been lax. For example, the 1972 Clean Water Act CWA protected water against polluting substances, but the federal government has not enforced the law. Instead, companies sidestep the regulations or outright change them. For example, in 2003, after several lawsuits threatened to enforce the CWA definition of "valley fill," the law was changed. Valley fills became legal by redefining the term. "Waste" was redefined as "fill," thereby legalizing dumping overburden—the layer of rock and soil above a coal seam—into the valleys. In 2009, the EPA reversed the valley fill definition and began to review valley fill permits, aiming to halt this practice.

Surface and underground mining are the most common coal-mining techniques. Surface or underground mining reveal coal seams of varying thickness, from an inch up to one hundred feet. West Virginia continues to be the national leader in underground production, while MTR surface mining now constitutes 33 percent of West Virginia mining.

MTR coal production in the twenty-first century has become the most profitable method of coal recovery, despite devastating environmental effects. The overburden is dynamited and then dumped into adjacent valleys, covering streams and destroying ecosystems, which in turn causes flooding, erosion, and air and water pollution. The artificial "flat" terrain created by MTR is called an advantage by the coal operators, who turn a blind eye to the pollution, destruction of habitats and communities, and the increase in respiratory disease (photo 8.18). The reason for increasing MTR is economic; mechanization requires fewer laborers, increases productivity as it reduces long-term labor costs, and increases the economic bottom line. The environmental and social costs are borne by the local residents and the American taxpayer.

MTR involves destruction of waterways, ecosystems, and local biota. The constant explosions of the mountains to loosen the rock and reveal the coal seams also create problems. After the explosion, the rubble, which was once part of an ecosystem, is bulldozed over the side of the mountain onto the ecosystems below. When the blasting is done and the coal removed, the coal companies deem the artificially flat mountaintop an improvement over nature. They plant useless plants on it (nothing else will grow as there is no topsoil) or "reclaim" it as a prison ground, as in Martin County, Kentucky. Blasting also contaminates wells used for drinking, causes structural damage to homes, and destabilizes the earth and causes mud slides. The deforestation of each cleared area increases erosion and flooding. Lives and homes are lost in floods, and the cost is borne by not only the residents but by the American public, whose taxes support cleanup and restitution.

Local and Ecoregional Impacts The ecoregional impacts of MTR include destruction of streams at their headwaters,

which destroys ecosystems, and periodic floods that rampage through valleys. The coalfield region houses the largest continuous forest in the United States. The trees provide shelter and warmth, and many animals are hunted for food. Over fifty-nine thousand miles of streams provide water and aquatic life for residents and tourists.

Most streams in central Appalachia are primary **headwater streams**—capillary, origin rivulets for larger river systems. Headwater streams are important in the life of a river system, being the transition between water and land, where nutrients are broken down and recycled for other organisms. Burying headwaters destroys a watershed's quality. Some impacts of a poor headwater system are algae growth, floods, water-quality issues, and loss of floral and faunal diversity.

Flash floods created by poor mining techniques threaten Central Appalachian communities annually. Filled areas have no topsoil and little to hold the rocky debris in place. Erosion gullies funnel storm water onto populated valleys below.

In 2000, a sludge dam in Martin County, Kentucky, failed, sending over 250 million tons of toxic sludge into the Big Sandy River. In 2001, three people were killed and parts of twenty-two counties in West Virginia were flooded because of erosion from MTR mining. In 2008, a slurry of coal ash flooded a portion of the Tennessee River Valley, sending 5.4 million cubic yards of sludge across the valley. This was estimated to be the largest environmental disaster of its kind, spewing dangerous chemicals into the river. In 2014, a pipe broke at a coal facility, sending coal slurry into Fields Creek, turning the waters black. Periodic disasters such as these show that there are inherent risks in mining for coal.

PHOTO 8.18. Kayford Mountain, Raleigh County, West Virginia. Mountaintop mining roves the overburden to access the coal. The overburden soil is then dumped into nearby valleys as fill, creating a flat landscape.
Source: Chris Mayda, flight courtesy of Southwings

Hydraulic Fracturing and Appalachia

In the twenty-first century, natural gas was hailed as a solution to reduce reliance on coal. Natural gas is also a nonrenewable fossil fuel, but it burns cleaner than coal. In the 1990s, conventional natural gas resources were limited and the price escalated, which encourged more expensive mining techniques to begin accessing unconventional, harder-to-reach natural gas. The technique known as hydraulic fracturing, or "fracking," has become common across the country but has been highlighted in northern Appalachia's Marcellus shale, located across the Allegheny Plateau and into the Ridge and Valley. The shale lies from four thousand to eighty-five hundred feet below the surface. The location has been of increased interest both because of the gas contained in the pores of the shale and also because of its proximity to Megalopolis.

The gas was formed and dispersed about three hundred million years ago. Horizontal drilling techniques can access more fractures than traditional vertical drilling, but it costs about four times as much. Vertically drilled gas fields that have played out can be reused for horizontal drilling, releasing trillions of cubic feet of gas.

Natural deep-shale gas drilling requires using up to three hundred thousand gallons of fresh water per day per well, and four to eight million gallons per well in total. The extensive water withdrawals deplete the 1 percent of water available as fresh water. The withdrawals come from surface and groundwater and may affect drinking water sources. Essentially, all water used is lost to consumptive use and reuse, due to the multiple chemicals used to fracture the rock. While most of the water remains lost and below the surface, the water returned to the surface is wastewater.

Fracking can impact water quality. Despite potential human health and water-quality threats from the numerous chemicals and contaminants used in fracking, the Safe Drinking Water Act exempted fracking. A number of water-related incidents have raised concerns. For example, failure to seal off the drinking water in one well caused an explosion, and several other environmental hazards have caused damage. The amount of water used for fracking has also damaged ecosystems and caused drinking water impairment. The more water that is used, the more the quality of the remaining water that is threatened (chart 8.1).

The Tiertary Sector

The Appalachian Region's economy, once highly dependent on mining, forestry, agriculture, chemical industries, and heavy industry, has become more diversified and now includes some professional service industries. Many now speak of a "post-coal" economy.

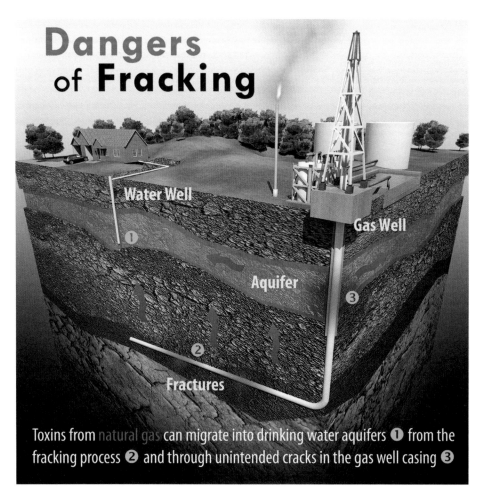

Dangers of Fracking

Water Well ❶

Gas Well

Aquifer ❸

Fractures ❷

Toxins from natural gas can migrate into drinking water aquifers ❶ from the fracking process ❷ and through unintended cracks in the gas well casing ❸

CHART 8.1. The Dangers of Fracking.
Source: iStock/Aunt_Spray

Appalachian coal fueled America's Industrial Revolution, but its resources were exported from the region as raw material, rather than keeping the profits local with regional manufacturing. The reliance on taking resources and profits out of the region is a major cause of the high poverty rates and the devastated Appalachian landscape. In 1965, a federally funded economic development program—the Appalachian Regional Commission (ARC)—aimed to improve the regional quality of life by raising educational levels, building roads in inaccessible areas, and improving the job market.

Over the years, the ARC has built more than 2,100 miles of roads and spent more than $14 billion to industrialize the region and improve the economy. The Appalachia that benefited from the roads and industry were on the region's periphery. The core of Appalachia remains among the poorest in America.

Most small Appalachian towns are still isolated. Thirty-mile drives on narrow winding roads out of valleys and into towns can take an hour and a half. The largest cities are accessible via modern toll roads, but these traverse the Appalachians, connecting the East with the Midwest, not connecting cities and towns within the region. Towns that are only a few miles apart as the crow flies are hours apart because of the dissected terrain.

Tourism

Tourism has become an avenue to economic growth. Thousands of streams and rivers and the distinct rural population captivate tourists seeking natural beauty, folk arts, and crafts. The landscape is beautiful and features fall foliage, folk and artisan centers, and historic towns. From the Catskills of New York to Tennessee's Great Smoky Mountains, the region is now rife with tourist opportunities. The region is becoming a destination for mountain climbing and whitewater rafting, which would mean more service jobs in hotels, restaurants, and shops.

Local tourism began in the nineteenth century when wealthy North Carolina planters left the hot, mosquito-infested, low country for the Blue Ridge near Asheville, North Carolina. Later, regional health centers credited the mountain climate and springs with curing respiratory ailments. Healthy visitors accompanied those seeking a cure and recognized the beauty. Soon more roads were built, accelerating tourism.

The Catskill Mountains were popular with tourists in the late nineteenth century and the first half of the twentieth century. The region has been in the public mind since settlement, for here slept legendary Rip Van Winkle in Sleepy Hollow on the eastern slope of panoramic North Mountain. The Hudson River and the Catskills were nineteenth-century tourist destinations for the New York urban population.

Jewish farmers settled in the Catskills in the late nineteenth century, but limited agricultural possibilities shifted farm production to summer boarders during the anti-Semitism of the 1950s and 1960s. The post–World War II years in the Catskills were a time of great growth, facilitated by automobile travel and the new highways to the "Borscht Belt," perhaps most popularly known through the movie *Dirty Dancing*. Discrimination toward Jewish comedians—Rodney Dangerfield, Lenny Bruce, Milton Berle, Woody Allen—led them to entertain at Borscht Belt hotels and bungalows. They migrated into mainstream comedy as segregation eased. After the 1960s, air travel, **assimilation**, and less anti-Semitism opened up other vacation destinations, and the era of the Catskills' popularity waned. Eventually, many of the wooden bungalows burned down. In the twenty-first century, the remaining bungalows are overgrown or converted to Indian casino establishments.

The Southern Appalachians contain the Great Smoky Mountains, America's premier tourist destination, attracting over nine million tourists annually. Access to the region through the Blue Ridge Parkway, as well as many of the buildings, was courtesy of New Deal agencies: the Civilian Conservation Corps (CCC), the relief program that conserved forests and parks, and the Work Progress Administration (WPA), responsible for many roads and public buildings. Resorts, casinos, and amusement parks catering to the tourist trade are now common throughout the region.

The Great Smoky Mountains Park has become an important part of the economy, but at a cost. Many local people were relocated in order to open the parks and throughways. Crime and air pollution have increased.

Ironically, the abused Appalachian land has also spurred new tourist attractions. Logging has inspired several amusement park rides, including the newest—the lumber camp–themed area of Dollywood outside Pigeon Forge, Tennessee. In "reverse ecotourism," people concerned about environmental destruction are traveling to view MTR sites to learn about union history and to see how MTR is an expression of corporate power.

The Stanley Heirs Park at Kayford Mountain has become a destination. The Park was formed by descendants of nineteenth-century settlers who farmed and worked in the mines. The heirs own both minerals and surface rights to this part of Kayford Mountain, which overlooks an eleven-thousand-acre MTR site on Cabin Creek. Larry Gibson, a Stanley Heir, and his family used to live on the lowest lying part of the mountain, and looked "up" to the mountain peaks that surrounded them. Since 1986, the slow-motion destruction of Kayford Mountain has been continuous. Eighteen years after the "mountain top removal" project began, Larry's land is enveloped in more than seventy-five hundred acres of destruction of what was previously a forested mountain range. He has been prominent in the fight against MTR, and has refused offers from the A. T. Massey Coal Company to sell Kayford Mountain. He regularly hosts public officials, students, journalists, and other interested citizens who have not witnessed an MTR project in person (photo 8.19)

A Sustainable Future

Education, health, and road access have improved, thanks to the WPA, TVA, and ARC public works programs. Appalachian traditional life continues in the hills and valleys, and many

PHOTO 8.19. Larry Gibson Talks about Mountaintop Removal.
Source: Library of Congress

people have remained or returned because they love the familiar friends, neighbors, and communities. The regional traditions maintain many sustainable elements, but substantial work remains, including protecting the landscape from logging and coal resource industries. Major challenges to a sustainable future include the following:

- pollution of the Great Smoky Mountains ;
- environmental and social damage because of invasive coal extraction methods;
- coal sludge, which is susceptible to environmental disasters;
- threats to biodiversity because of logging and mining;
- threat of extinction of many species; and
- a lack of economic diversity that provides safe, decent work.

The Appalachian community lives in the heart of the mining zone and reaching a compromise between King Coal and the local people of Appalachia in terms of both economic security and environmental protection has proved difficult. But the outlook is not hopeless. The region once isolated and considered backward is no longer so. Several organizations are seeking and progressing toward a healthy economy and sustainable life within Appalachia.

The MTR coal situation and other environmental issues are closely followed and fought by several grassroots organizations, including Coal River Mountain Watch, the Ohio Valley Environmental Coalition, and Appalachian Voices. Each of these organizations champions education about their region, informing about MTR, economic and environmental sustainability, and litigation against unsustainable or egregious environmental devastation. These organizations have fought to correct ills in the air, waste disposal, toxic leakage, violations of the Clean Air Act, and MTR.

Appalachia is a region with a high percentage of rural communities and farms that understand the traditional food chain and the importance of sustainable agriculture and local foods. Throughout the region, groups such as Appalachian Sustainable Development in Virginia and Tennessee and the Appalachian Sustainable Agriculture Project in western North Carolina seek to create a nutritious and healthy food system within Appalachia, while enhancing farming communities. In 2010, famed chef Jamie Oliver turned his attention to this region by starting the Food Revolution in Huntington, West Virginia.

Cities such as Nashville, Chattanooga, and Pittsburgh are moving towards sustainability, cleaning up contaminated sites and redeveloping their economies.

Sustainable economic development is important in Appalachia because its industry is headquartered outside the region and often favors unsustainable short-term versus long-term gain. Included within economic development is a burgeoning ecotourism industry, local resources, and self-reliance based on appropriate and green technologies. Other grassroots groups have educated the public about sustainable agriculture, including organic farming, growing gardens, and buying locally.

Appalachia also offers wilderness, something that becomes more precious as the population grows. A growing sense and practice of conservation is helping the region protect its wild areas but requires supporting public education. Appalachians have kept their way of life despite great odds, and hopefully Appalachia will become a source of pride for the country instead of being obliterated without the country ever appreciating its presence.

Questions for Discussion

1. Part of coal industry logic is that flattening the landscape of the Cumberland Plateau is advantageous because it makes the land accessible and usable, unlike the traditional Appalachian hollows. Are there advantages to preserving different physical geographies in different areas?

2. Although the TVA's damming of the river to generate power brought industry to the region and created many recreational sites, could the money have been used for more benefit? Was there a benefit to losing the valleys to flooding?

3. What is the difference between northern Appalachia and the Cumberland Plateau?

4. Who were the Scots-Irish and how did they come to settle Appalachia?

5. Why did cities appear at the north and south ends of the Finger Lakes and not along their sides?

6. How did coal mining affect the development of the Cumberland Plateau?

7. How will Americans get their electricity if not by coal? What does coal production mean for Appalachia?

8. How did Appalachian folk culture develop and what makes it unique? How is it threatened today?

9. What is Chemical Valley and how did it get its name?

10. What geographic factors combined to make Birmingham, Alabama, a center of steel production in the late nineteenth century?

11. In the Great Smoky Mountains, where will the increasing number of people live if development continues to be compromised? Can we afford to shut down power plants, admittedly the largest source of pollution, when the population is growing and more people are demanding more power?

Suggested Readings

Alvey, R. G. *Kentucky Bluegrass Country.* Jackson: University Press of Mississippi, 1992.

"Appalachian Rivers. Lakes and Streams: A Region's Life Reflected in Its Waters." Now and Then: The Appalachian Magazine special issue 18 (Spring 2001): 1–44.

Barney, S. "Coming to Terms with Northern Appalachia." *Now and Then: The Appalachian Magazine* 14 (Winter 1997): 8–10.

Batteau, A. *The Invention of Appalachia.* Tucson: University of Arizona Press, 1990.

Berry, C. "'Upon What Will I Hang My Hat in the Future?' Appalachia and Awaiting Post Postmodernity." *Journal of Appalachian Studies* 6, nos. 1–2 (Spring–Fall 2000): 121–30.

Beth, M. *Appalachia in the Making: The Mountain South in the Nineteenth Century.* Chapel Hill: University of North Carolina Press, 1995.

Campbell, J. C. *The Southern Highlander and His Homeland.* Lexington: University Press of Kentucky, 2004 [1921].

Caudill, H. M. *Night Comes to the Cumberlands.* Ashland, Ky.: Jesse Stuart Foundation, 2001.

Commission on Geosciences, Environment, and Resources. *Coal Waste Impoundments: Risks, Responses, and Alternatives.* Washington, D.C.: National Academies Press, 2002.

Dabney, J. *Mountain Spirits.* New York: Scribner, 1974.

Davis, L. M. "Economic Development of the Great Kanawha Valley." *Economic Geography* 22, no. 4 (October 1946): 255–67.

Drake, R. *A History of Appalachia.* Lexington: University Press of Kentucky, 2003.

Hart, J. F. "Land Rotation in Appalachia." *Geographical Review* 67 (1977): 148–66.

Hofstra, W. R. *The Planting of New Virginia: Settlement and Landscape in the Shenandoah Valley.* Baltimore, Md.: Johns Hopkins University Press, 2004.

Hsiung, D. C. *Two Worlds in the Tennessee Mountains: Exploring the Origins of Appalachian Stereotypes.* Lexington: University Press of Kentucky, 1997.

Isserman, A. M. *Socio-Economic Review of Appalachia.* Washington, D.C.: Appalachian Regional Commission, 1996.

Jones, L. *Appalachian Values.* Ashland, Ky.: Jesse Stuart Foundation, 1994.

MacNeal, D. "How Can You Call Pittsburgh Appalachian?" *Now and Then: The Appalachian Magazine* 14 (Winter 1997): 10–13.

Marsh, B. "Continuity and Decline in the Anthracite Towns of Pennsylvania." *Annals of the Association of American Geographers* 77, no. 3 (September 1987): 337–52.

Meinig, D. W. *The Shaping of America.* New Haven, Conn.: Yale University Press, 1986.

Mitchell, R. "The Shenandoah Valley Frontier." *Annals of the Association of America Geographers* 62, no. 3 (September 1972): 461–86.

Murphy, R. and M.n Murphy. "Anthracite Region of Pennsylvania." *Economic Geography* 14, no. 4 (October 1938): 338–48.

Pollard, K. M. A. *New Diversity: Race and Ethnicity in the Appalachian Region.* Washington, D.C.: Population Reference Bureau, September 2004.

Pollard, K. M. A. , and L. Jacobsen "The Appalachia Region in 2010: a Census Data Overview", *Prepared for the Appalachian Regional Commission,* 2011 at http://auth.prb.org/pdf12/appalachia-census-chartbook-2011.pdfPudup

Raitz, K. B., and Ulack, R. *Appalachia: A Regional Geography.* Boulder, Colo.: Westview Press, 1984.

Rehder, J. B. *Appalachian Folkways*. Baltimore, Md.: Johns Hopkins University Press, 2004.

Shaver, C. L., K. A. Tonnessen, and T. G. Maniero. "Clearing the Air at Great Smoky Mountains National Park." *Ecological Applications* 4, no. 4 (November 1994): 690–701.

Thomas, W. G., III. "The Shenandoah Valley." *Southern Spaces*, at http://southernspaces.org/2004/shenandoah-valley

von Engeln, O. D. "Effects of Continental Glaciation on Agriculture." Part I. *Bulletin of the American Geographical Society* 46, no. 4 (1914): 241–64.

Webb, J. *Born Fighting*. New York: Broadway Books, 2004.

White, W. B., R. A. Watson, E. R. Pohl, and R. Brucker. "The Central Kentucky Karst." *Geographical Review* 60, no. 1 (January 1970): 88–115.

Williams, J. *Appalachia: A History*. Chapel Hill: University of North Carolina Press, 2002.

———. *West Virginia and the Captains of Industry*. Morgantown: West Virginia University Press, 2003.

Wolfram, W., and D. Christian. *Appalachian Speech*. Arlington, Va.: Center for Applied Linguistics, 1976.

Wright, M. "The Antecedents of the Double-Pen House Type." *Annals of the Association of American Geographers* 48, no. 2 (June 1958): 109–17.

Internet Sources

Tennessee Historical Society. *Tennessee Encyclopedia of History and Culture*, Version 2.0, at http://tennesseeencyclopedia.net/

West Virginia Geology: Earth Science Studies. "Geology of the New River Gorge," at http://www.wvgs.wvnet.edu/www/geology/geoles01.htm

National Park Service. "Great Smoky Mountains Air Quality," at http://www.nps.gov/grsm/naturescience/air-quality.htm

Grist. Mountaintop Removal, at http://www.grist.org/article/reece/

U.S. Environmental Protection Agency. *Final Programmatic Environmental Impact Statement on Mountaintop Mining/Valley Fills in Appalachia*, 2005, at http://www.epa.gov/region03/mtntop/eis2005.htm

U.S. Environmental Protection Agency. *Mid-Atlantic Mountaintop Mining*, at http://www.epa.gov/region3/mtntop/

Coal River Mountain Watch, at http://www.crmw.net/

Mountain Justice, at https://www.mountainjustice.org/

Ohio Valley Environmental Coalition, at http://www.ohvec.org/galleries/mountaintop_removal/

Appalachian Voices, at http://appvoices.org/?/site/mtr_overview/.

West Virginia Coal Association. Coal Facts, 2016, at https://www.wvcoal.com/coal-facts/

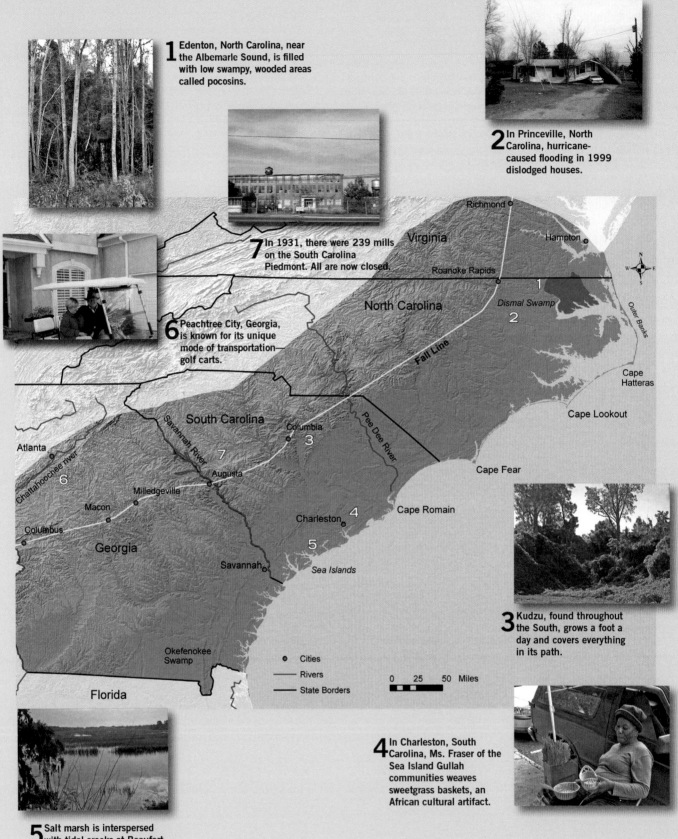

1 Edenton, North Carolina, near the Albemarle Sound, is filled with low swampy, wooded areas called pocosins.

2 In Princeville, North Carolina, hurricane-caused flooding in 1999 dislodged houses.

7 In 1931, there were 239 mills on the South Carolina Piedmont. All are now closed.

6 Peachtree City, Georgia, is known for its unique mode of transportation—golf carts.

3 Kudzu, found throughout the South, grows a foot a day and covers everything in its path.

4 In Charleston, South Carolina, Ms. Fraser of the Sea Island Gullah communities weaves sweetgrass baskets, an African cultural artifact.

5 Salt marsh is interspersed with tidal creeks at Beaufort, South Carolina.

Richmond

Virginia

Hampton

Roanoke Rapids

North Carolina

Dismal Swamp

Outer Banks

Fall Line

Cape Hatteras

Cape Lookout

South Carolina

Columbia

Pee Dee River

Savannah River

Atlanta

Chattahoochee river

Augusta

Milledgeville

Macon

Columbus

Georgia

Charleston

Cape Fear

Cape Romain

Savannah

Sea Islands

Okefenokee Swamp

Florida

Cities
Rivers
State Borders

0   25   50 Miles

9

SOUTH ATLANTIC

Gentry Tidewater, Hardscrabble Piedmont, and the Northern Invasion of Dixie

Chapter Highlights

After reading this chapter, you should be able to:

- Identify the Low Country, Sea Islands, and barrier islands
- Compare the coastal plain and the piedmont
- Discuss the fall line and its importance
- Identify the water war areas of the Atlantic South
- Discuss how the Gullah differed from other slaves
- Give an overview of the development of antebellum and postbellum Southern cities
- Explain textile manufacturing on the piedmont after the Civil War
- Describe tobacco production and how it has changed over the past decades
- Discuss the evolution of hog and chicken production over the past twenty years
- Outline the development of the Southern economy prior to and after the Civil War
- Discuss trends in urbanization and immigration
- List and describe the evolution of plantation crops
- Explain why logging is unsustainable in the South
- Discuss how the economy has changed recently

Terms

antebellum
barrier island
blackwater rivers
boll weevil
cape
Carolina bay
carpetbagger

coastal plain
concentrated animal feeding
   operations (CAFOs)
contract farmer
cotton gin
cracker
Geechee
Gullah

industrial ecology
kudzu
lagoon
maroon
New South
Piedmont
plantation agriculture
Reconstruction

redneck
redwater river
right-to-work state
riparian rights
tidewater
triangular trade
vertical integration
yeoman

Places

Dismal Swamp

Low Country

Outer Banks

Sea Islands

Cities

Atlanta, Georgia
   (2016 MSA 5.7 million)
Charlotte, North Carolina
   (2016 MSA 2.4 million)

Charleston, South Carolina
   (2016 MSA 761,000)
Raleigh–Durham–Chapel
   Hill, North Carolina

(The Research Triangle)
   (2016 MSA 1.8 million)
Richmond, Virginia
   (2016 MSA 1.2 million)

Savannah, Georgia
   (2016 MSA 384,000)

Introduction

The South has changed. The Old South has evolved into a **New South**.

The evolution of the South differed markedly from that of the North. Prior to the Civil War, the self-sufficient plantation economy truncated urban development. After the war, the southern economy slowly evolved from rural to urban, and in the process began mirroring the North. By the late twentieth century, northern urban influences had reshaped the New South. In rural areas, agriculture shifted from time-honored crops (cotton and tobacco) to large-scale livestock production.

While rural areas maximized agricultural production, urban populations grew with northerners who fled the colder climes for the warmer South—once the humidity was controlled by technology. In the past, plantation owners had found ways of dealing with the environment's heat and humidity. Antebellum plantations were located in areas where the air flow limited the high summer heat and humidity. Building materials were local. Foundations were raised and roof styles were shaped to promote air flow and work with the climate. Early design had many sustainable elements, a sense of place that worked with the climate, topography, vegetation, and local materials that was lost during the growth period of the twentieth century, when air conditioning made those designs less relevant.

Physical Geography

The Atlantic **coastal plain** extends from Cape Cod to Mexico's Yucatan Peninsula. Throughout history, the seaward-dipping plain and marshy tracts have alternately emerged from and submerged into the ocean. The inland coastal plain gradually gains elevation, but it seldom rises higher than five hundred feet before it ends abruptly at the fall line where the **Piedmont** commences (photo 9.1). The plain continues as the continental shelf more than one hundred miles out to sea. The gradually descending shelf dissipates wave energy; the mild waves differ from the dramatic waves along the steep descent of the Pacific shore.

Regional ecological systems include forests and marshy coastal grasslands. The soils, moisture, temperature, and geologic variations have created a regional mosaic of small-scale ecologic communities. This region encompasses two major subregions:

- Southeastern Coast and Plain
- Piedmont

The Southeastern Coast and Plain

The coastal plain subregions include the **barrier islands** and the Sea Islands, the southeastern **tidewater** coast, and the rolling upland Southeastern Plain. Ancient geologic rhythms in the tidal areas have periodically submerged and then exposed the coastal bays, inlets, and islands. The plain is widest in the south and narrows to the north. Conversely, the submerged shelf is wider in the north and narrows in the south.

Inland from the marshy coast, the Southeast Plain slopes from the low, rolling sand hills of the fall line to the flat coastal plain. The narrow streams of the inland broaden and meander as they near the coast. The region is two-thirds woodland; the remaining land is farms and pasture.

Appalachian sediment eroded onto the coastal plain and formed alluvial fans on the continental shelf. The alluvium travels a long distance, and along the way it leaves behind the heavier, coarser sand. Seaside sand is therefore white, pure, and much finer than the coarse Pacific sand that travels a shorter distance to the sea.

PHOTO 9.1. Fall Line on the Savannah River, Augusta, Georgia. The fall line is the point where the harder piedmont rock ends and the sandy coastal zone begins; it is delineated by a drop in land level. The power created at the fall line was used to power the piedmont textile mills during the late nineteenth century.

BOX 9.1 ENVIRONMENTAL CHALLENGES: INVASIVE KUDZU

Kudzu (*Pueraria lobata*), a perennial of the legume family, entered the United States as a sample plant during the 1876 Centennial Exposition. The Japanese plant captivated gardeners and became an ornamental and then foraging vine by the 1920s. During the 1930s' drought, the Soil Conservation Service was seeking a plant to halt erosion in deforested areas. They chose kudzu. Farmers were paid by the government to plant kudzu.

By 1953, the government stopped advocating planting kudzu; it was successively named an invasive species, then a weed. The fast-growing vine's only natural enemy is frost, which seldom occurs in the South. The vine overtakes everything and destroys other plants and forests in the process (photo 9.2). The difficult-to-eradicate vine now covers more than seven million southern acres (map 9.1).

The vine does have many uses. In the 1920s, it was a fodder crop and later was used as the raw material for baskets. In China, kudzu is a medicine for dysentery, allergies, and diarrhea. Currently, chemicals in the root are being studied as a cure for alcoholism, and a few researchers are investigating how to convert the vine into a biomass feedstock.

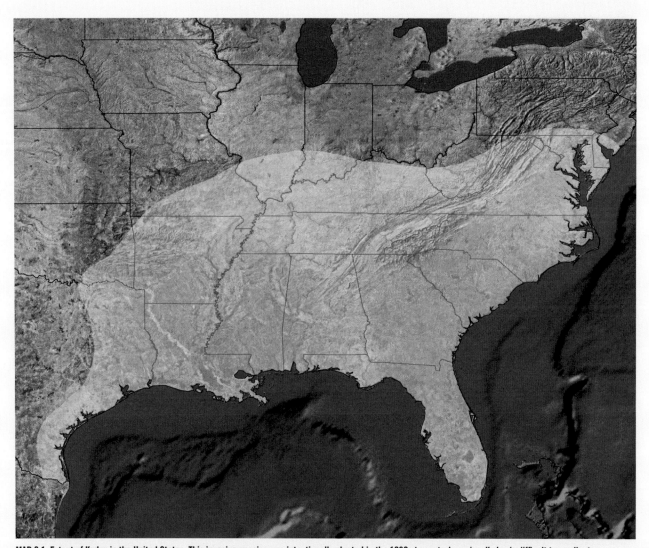

MAP 9.1. Extent of Kudzu in the United States. This invasive species was intentionally planted in the 1930s to control erosion. Kudzu is difficult to eradicate.

PHOTO 9.2. Kudzu Taking Over a Forest.
Source: iStock/LightScribe

TABLE 9.1. Coastal Characteristic along the Atlantic Coastal Plain

	Number of barrier islands	Length of coast
Virginia	9	112 m (180 km)
North Carolina	20	301 m (484 km)
South Carolina	18	187 m (301 km)
Georgia	12	100 m (161 km)

Source: H. Jesse Walker and James M. Coleman, "Atlantic and Gulf Coastal Province," in *Geomorphic Systems of North America*, edited by William L. Graf (Boulder, Colo.: Geological Society of America, 1987)

Barrier Island Coast

Winds, waves, and currents shape the long, narrow barrier islands along the Carolina coastlines. Barrier and Sea Islands together outline and protect about three-quarters of the Atlantic South mainland and continue along the Florida coast (table 9.1). The islands buffer and absorb the shock of the storms and waves. In the process, the sandbar islands are torn apart, then rebuilt in new configurations. The process is endlessly repeated.

The best-known barrier islands are the ever-changing ribbons of North Carolina's Outer Banks. In their natural state, the islands are marshy wetlands, but many have been drained. Today, beaches are renourished with sand so million-dollar homes facing the Atlantic can be built. Understanding the relationship of the barrier island to their new beachfront property is lost in the property value equation. Everywhere there are reminders of the power of the sea. Triangular **capes**—capes Hatteras, Lookout, and Fear in North Carolina, and Romain in South Carolina—jut into the sea, shaped by alternating northeast-southeast storm patterns, and awaiting the next storm that will reshape them (photo 9.3). Storms tear islands into pieces. Cartographers redraw the coastline and construction crews rebuild the houses, and the cycle occurs again.

A reason for rising storm damage is the number of people living along the vulnerable coasts. When the barrier islands are developed, their effectiveness as storm and wetland buffers is reduced. Sea-level rise instigated by climate change now threatens the low-lying islands. The continual rebuilding and renourishment of beaches are expensive and have made insurance premiums rise. When the claims are more than the premiums, everyone pays more. When insurance no longer covers damages, FEMA and state taxes, by way of the American taxpayer, pick up the tab, not only for the houses but also for the infrastructure and the cleanup costs, thereby further subsidizing coastal area inhabitants.

Sea Islands Coast

Marshes separate the mainland from the small, closely knit rectangular Sea Islands that extend from Charleston, South Carolina, to Jacksonville, Florida. Salt-tolerant vegetation covers the miles of tidal creeks, salt marshes, and estuaries that muddle the line between the Low Country Sea Islands and the mainland.

Isolated from mainland activities, the hundreds of islands have harbored both wildlife refuges and the African American **Gullah** culture. The wildlife include deer, tacky horses, and

PHOTO 9.3. Cape Hatteras, North Carolina. The marsh and beach characterize barrier islands in the Outer Banks.
Source: iStock/AG-ChapelHill

aquatics, while the Gullah, once slaves on tobacco and cotton plantations, were the recipients of the "forty acres and a mule" promises for Sea Island freedmen.

Sea Island land was confiscated after the Civil War, during **Reconstruction**, as an experiment to redistribute land from the wealthy white owners to the freemen. Some Gullah maintained possession of small acreages. By the late twentieth century, the Gullah who owned land sold it on Hilton Head and St. Simons to developers who built lavish golf and destination resorts. Many remaining Gullah residents have been forced out of their homes by rising rents and property taxes.

Swamps

Two well-known American swamps lie within the region: the Okefenokee Swamp along the Florida–Georgia border and the Dismal Swamp along the Virginia–North Carolina border.

The Okefenokee, the largest swamp in the United States, covers about seven hundred square miles on the lower coastal plain (photo 9.4). Once part of the sea, the swamp is now inland. An old barrier island, the Trail Ridge, separates the swamp from the surrounding area. The Okefenokee is also the headwaters to the Suwannee River. The forested swamps have been assaulted by drainage, logging, and sawmills. By the late 1920s, a movement urged conservation, and in 1937 it became a wildlife refuge, preserving four hundred species of vertebrates and more than two hundred types of birds.

The Dismal Swamp, straddling the Virginia–North Carolina border, has shrunk to less than half its former size of nine

hundred square miles. The heavily forested swamp was formed during the ice ages, when local climate and vegetation were similar to the current New England climate. As the seas rose and the ice melted, the swamp environment evolved into a hardwood forest in peat sediment. The rich organic sediment has tempted speculative developers of agricultural land since colonial times.

The speculators included the Dismal Swamp Land Company, organized by George Washington and other Virginia planters. Their agricultural goals were unsuccessful because of limited labor and capital, but by 1805 slave labor cleared and dug a twenty-two-mile canal that provided ships safety from the fierce Atlantic swells and treacherous sandbars between the Chesapeake and Albemarle bays. Later, the swamp was an Underground Railroad hideout for runaway slaves called **maroons**.

The Dismal Canal was an important transportation route during the nineteenth century, but it fell upon hard times. In 1929, the canal was sold to the Army Corps of Engineers and refurbished as a pleasure-boat waterway. The swamp became a national wildlife refuge in 1974.

The Piedmont

The Piedmont, "foot of the mountains," stretches almost nine hundred miles from New Jersey into Alabama and is the effective divide between the fall line and the Appalachian Blue Ridge Mountains. One hundred to two hundred miles wide, the Piedmont was once mountainous but now has eroded into rolling hills and narrow stream valleys that end at the fall line as the streams drop to the sandy coastal plain. In the south, the

PHOTO 9.4. The Okefenokee Swamp.
Source: iStock/fowler5338

TABLE 9.2. Middle Atlantic Fall Line Cities and Their Rivers

City	River
Washington, D.C.	Potomac
Fredericksburg, Virginia	Rappahannock
Richmond, Virginia	James
Petersburg, Virginia	Appomattox
Roanoke Rapids, North Carolina	Roanoke
Raleigh, North Carolina	Neuse
Columbia, South Carolina	Congaree
Augusta, Georgia	Savannah
Milledgeville, Georgia	Oconee
Macon, Georgia	Ocmulgee
Columbus, Georgia	Chattahoochee

original major cities were more likely along the fall line than the coast, due to the marshy shallow tidelands between the barrier islands and the mainland (table 9.2). The fall line seldom stops travel upriver today but instead is the path for I-95 into South Carolina, then I-20 through Georgia.

Settlers exploited the characteristic red soil of the Piedmont, the result of iron oxides formed on the warm, moist land. The soil, climate, and rocks supported a native oak and hickory forest, but poorly managed tobacco and cotton plantations replaced the forest and resulted in erosion and the eventual abandonment of the plantations. The disturbed land reverted to pine forests and was never allowed succession to the more evolved hardwood forests because the pine forests were continually logged for paper and chipboard products. The unsustainable practice of growing pine forests exclusively robs the soil of the humus and nutrients that a deciduous forest offers.

Water

The region receives ample precipitation throughout the year. About 70 percent of the rainwater is lost to evapotranspiration, and the remainder replenishes regional aquifers and streams. Groundwater storage is best along the coastal plain, but overpumping has led to saltwater intrusion along several coastal cities—Savannah, Georgia; Hilton Head, South Carolina; and Brunswick, Georgia—which contaminates the freshwater supply. Only by pumping less water can the saltwater intrusion be ended.

The few lakes along the coastal region from Delaware to Florida are called **Carolina bays**, named for the bay tree found near these oval, freshwater depressions. Most Carolina bays are small and shallow swamps that have been degraded or drained.

Pocosins, also called dismal swamps, occur near estuaries. Their impenetrable, vine-laden jungle muck is an excellent filter for water and flood control, but much of it has been lost to agricultural use and rising sea levels.

The fall line affects river flow. Along the Piedmont, **redwater rivers** carrying red Piedmont soil run straight, but along the softer coastal plain, alluvium **blackwater rivers** meander over the lower-relief terrain.

Redwater river elevation loss results in a higher nutrient load that leaches the red clay parent material. Redwater rivers carry a higher concentration of clay-type soils than the sandier blackwater rivers, and therefore they are more fertile. Tidal forests flooded by redwater rivers receive more nutrients than those with blackwater rivers and therefore have more growth potential. The larger redwater rivers are the James, Virginia's Roanoke, and Georgia's Savannah and Altamaha.

Blackwater rivers originate on the coastal plain, have wide floodplains, and flow into estuaries between the mainland and Sea Islands. The darkly stained waters of blackwater rivers are not polluted but obtain their dark color from the rich organic tannins leached from the poorly drained swamps. Blackwater rivers are some of the cleanest natural rivers because they carry little sediment but large amounts of decaying plant material that makes them acidic and oxygen starved. Low levels of dissolved minerals in the almost sterile waters inhibit insect populations and limit the diversity of other animal and tree species. Blackwater rivers include the Blackwater in Virginia, the Edisto in South Carolina, and the Satilla, St. Mary's and Ohoopee in Georgia (photo 9.5).

Water Wars

While we tend to think of "water wars" in the arid west, increased demand for water, even in areas that tend to have high rainfall, can be politically charged issues.

Water rights differ east and west of the Mississippi River. Riparian water rights rooted in English common law govern water east of the river. West of the river, water is governed by prior appropriation rooted in Spanish law. **Riparian rights** have protected South Atlantic waterways in the past, but recent population growth and the increased demand have created a series of water wars. Riparian rights allow all landowners with water frontage to have "reasonable" water use and access. Riparian features include (1) allotments in proportion to water frontage, (2) water cannot be sold separate from the land, and (3) water remains in its watershed.

Despite the protection of riparian right law, political borders rather than natural watersheds divide rivers. The political borders have created conflicts between Georgia, Alabama, and Florida over rights of the Chattahoochee River; Virginia and Maryland over the Potomac; and North Carolina and Virginia over Lake Gaston.

The Chattahoochee River

Originating in the Appalachian foothills, the Chattahoochee River follows a fault line across the Piedmont north of Atlanta and then defines the Georgia–Alabama border before it joins the Apalachicola River and empties into the Gulf of Mexico. Thirteen water storage and hydropower-producing dams that flow through northeast Georgia obstruct the Chattahoochee. The largest dam—storing 65 percent of the water—is Lake Lanier, built in 1960. A favorite recreational lake for Atlantans, it also provides hydropower and drinking water.

During the 1950s and 1960s, poorly monitored urban and industrial growth caused polluted dead zones in the river south of Atlanta. However, pollution solutions since the 1960s—treating municipal sewage and industrial waters, reducing phosphorus and sediment loads, and increasing oxygen concentrations—have resulted in a return of fish to the river.

But Chattahoochee water issues reemerged after 1990. Atlanta was growing rapidly without sufficient planning,

PHOTO 9.5. A Blackwater River near New Ellenton, South Carolina. Blackwater rivers are not polluted but gain their color from tannins leached from decayed vegetation.

resulting in an increased dependence on Lake Lanier water. Fecal coliform (*E. coli*) and bacterial pathogens increased, as did claims for the water from neighboring states—Alabama for its agriculture and Florida for its Apalachicola Bay oyster and sturgeon industry.

Atlanta's wastewater infrastructure—an aging sewer system and a million septic systems—threatens water quality, and multiple uses threaten functionality. Agricultural water uses have increased. The Environmental Protection Agency (EPA) has continually fined the Atlanta wastewater system for spills and overloaded systems. Regional coal- and nuclear-powered plants increased water use as electric power consumption increased.

The region usually receives ample precipitation, but the early twenty-first century registered a multiyear drought. Farmers irrigated from overallocated aquifers, and urban demand strained intrastate allocations and other water uses. Periodic droughts intensify the disputes over water.

Georgia, Alabama, and Florida have battled for two decades over the rights to Chattahoochee River water. No one has enough water; usage is growing but the amount of water is not. In 1990, Atlanta consumed 320 million gallons, but in 2010, it was 510 million gallons daily. Atlanta is expected to outgrow its water sources by 2030. In 2007, 2014, and again in 2015, drought threatened Atlanta's water supply. In response, the city implemented water-use restrictions.

The Potomac River

The Potomac River divides Virginia and Maryland. The water is allocated to Maryland according to the 1632 colonial charter, although Virginia "owns" the mouth of the Chesapeake. A four-hundred-year dispute between the two states over water allocation has been exacerbated by rapid growth in metropolitan Washington, D.C. In 2003, the Supreme Court ruled that Virginia be given equal access to Potomac River water. Maryland held that suburban growth in Virginia was unsustainable and, therefore, water and growth required regulation.

Catawba Water Rights

Water wars have become a constant problem in North Carolina, a region that has plentiful precipitation but also has experienced tremendous population growth since the 1990s. The Catawba River begins in the North Carolina Appalachians and flows through the Piedmont into South Carolina, where it provides water to more than one million people, as well as for agricultural and forested land. Reservoirs impound the river for flood control and hydroelectric power purposes.

Rivers have been deemed economic panaceas to a region's growth and are used to within an inch of their flow. During the drought of the early twenty-first century, water issues mounted between North and South Carolina over use of Catawba River water. South Carolina, fearing economic loss due to lack of water, sued North Carolina over how the river's water was distributed. After millions of dollars spend in legal fees, as the case awaited a Supreme Court judgment, the states negotiated an agreement. The agreement strictly manages water during drought periods.

Drought has exacerbated water wars, and the reasons extend beyond local issues. The abundant regional precipitation from tropical storms and the Atlantic is insufficient to allay the combination of population growth, urban demands, and periodic drought conditions. Millions of gallons are used each day by some thirty cities and seventeen counties for both industry and drinking water. If water use and water demand change significantly for the conditions of the agreement, there could be future lawsuits.

Climate

The Southern Atlantic features hot, humid, rainy summers and mild winters in which temperatures rarely drop below freezing. Rain averages about fifty inches annually in brief thunderstorm torrents or cold winter drizzles. Snow is usually scant and occasional, except in the higher elevations. The coastal plain is generally warmer than the Piedmont, but the humidity is greatest inland, where 100°F summer temperatures are often matched with high humidity.

Between June and November, Southern Atlantic tropical storms and hurricanes can inundate both the shoreline and inland areas. Storm surges may drown and erode sea-level coastal and inland communities, such as in 1999 when Hurricane Floyd penetrated a hundred miles inland and flooded Princeville, North Carolina. The Outer Banks of North Carolina are constantly on the lookout for severe storms. From 1989 to 2003, the Outer Banks were hammered four times, and in 2016, Hurricane Matthew killed twenty-eight people and displaced thousands due to flooding. Hurricane Matthew's impact was felt most strongly in poor towns and low-income neighborhoods.

Hurricane activity waxes and wanes. The current cycle of increased activity began in 1995 and is expected to last into the first decades of the twenty-first century. The relationship of hurricanes and climate change is complex. Warming sea surface temperatures lengthen the hurricane season and make larger storms greater possibility. But at their early stage of development, hurricanes are sensitive to wind shear—the difference in wind speeds at different altitudes—that can destroy a hurricane at this stage. Hurricane activity in the Atlantic is also impacted by sand storm activity in the Sahara. And so while global warming increases sea surface temperatures and hence the possibility of more and larger hurricanes, there are many other factors that come into play. There is no a straight line relationship between warming seas and more hurricane activity. Hurricanes, as well as sea-level rise, will increasingly threaten coastal communities and barrier islands during the twenty-first century.

Historical Geography and Settlement

Mid-Atlantic Native American settlements followed physical and waterway landscape patterns. Generally, the Algonquians lived along the coast to the fall line, the Sioux on the Piedmont,

BOX 9.2 CLIMATE CHANGE IN NORFOLK, VIRGINIA

Norfolk, Virginia, has always dealt with flooding during large storms. The area sits on the Virginia Tidewater, not very high above sea level. Much of the city was built on swamps and streams. The land has been slowly sinking for thousands of years. Natural subsidence combined with low-lying topography and changing ocean circulation patterns contribute to above-average sea-level rise. The Army Corps of Engineers projects sea level could rise as much as six feet in Norfolk by the end of the century.*

Already, flooding is a regular event. In downtown Norfolk, at high tide, the water is just inches from cresting the barrier into the streets. It routinely spills over.

The Norfolk–Hampton Roads area in Virginia is home to the largest naval operation in the world. This area is particularly vulnerable because the land is sinking as sea levels are rising. Planning for that is a national security concern.

The Navy is already implementing adaptation measures. The station has raised some of its piers—at a cost of $60 million each—and is restoring others. The station is also planning a

$250 million restoration project that includes demolishing two of its one-hundred-year-old piers and rebuilding one new pier.

Norfolk city leaders and planners are also considering how to adapt to climate change. They have turned to the world's experts for help: the Dutch.

About two-thirds of the Netherlands sits at or below sea level, and dam-builders and water engineers there have been keeping the ocean at bay for centuries. Their expertise is increasingly in demand as coastal cities begin to plan for rising seas.

In the United States, the Dutch have worked with New Orleans after Katrina and New York City after Sandy.

The Dutch approach is to "live with water." Rather than building only infrastructure or barriers to keep water away, Dutch planners are embracing the water and building sponges—or ways to store water. Building marshes, rain gardens, and pavement that allows water to soak into the ground instead of running off are good examples.

A new Norfolk plan calls for a combination of both barriers and sponges.

*PRI International. "In Norfolk, climate change means dealing with rising water. The Dutch are there to help." June 2016, at https://www.pri.org/stories/2016-06-20/us-city-learning-dutch-living-water-approach

and the Iroquois in the Appalachians. Warfare shaped many cultural traits, such as defensively oriented settlement patterns and tattooed body art signifying spiritual and warrior status. The hunting and agricultural economy featured deer, corn, pumpkin, squash, and tobacco. Early contact with Anglo settlers was positive, but later wars erupted between natives and encroaching settlers.

The first European settlements were along the Virginia and North Carolina coastlines, the drowned valleys, and the heavily indented bays and harbors. Tidewater settlers were less concerned with religious issues than the northern colonials and were often well positioned financially but out of political favor in their homeland. In the Tidewater, settlers had different priorities than colonists to the north.

The settlement of Jamestown represented an early, tenuous step away from feudalism and toward modern capitalism. The English settled this region with the intent to trade with the natives and to seek gold, and only secondarily to establish a settlement. The lack of food crops for the settlers had the indirect result of high death rates, and by 1618, the Virginia Company terminated because of grave management mistakes. Within a generation of establishing Jamestown, the settlers introduced new crops, plants, and processes to the Native American agricultural landscape, forever changing the habitation of the land. Their first major crop was tobacco, and as European demand grew so did **plantation agriculture** and the labor force required for successful cultivation. The tobacco industry in the nascent

plantations highlighted just how dramatically northern and southern economies, racial issues, and land uses diverged early in the settlement process.

The South's intensive agricultural methods harmed the land because Europeans brought with them preconceived agricultural expectations based on the European landscape. Developing agricultural methods appropriate for the American landscape evolved over decades. This new land was very different from the land they left. Europeans found themselves in a strange land and, to survive, at first they changed the land to reflect the world they had left behind rather than adapt themselves. They altered the ecological landscape and thereby hastened the decline of ecosystems and the indigenous population. Ever larger fields of tobacco, indigo, rice, and eventually cotton supplanted the ecological landscape of the natives. The resultant destruction extended beyond the land, ultimately destroying the indigenous way of life. Unable to fight off the encroaching settlers, the natives either fled or died out. When the Native American threat was eliminated, many planters moved to the Piedmont and then, as soil conditions deteriorated again, on to the Gulf Coast and farther west. The former plantation land reverted to wooded acreage.

The settlers envisioned an unlimited, easily exploited land, one that would be profitable, especially as the labor force evolved from indentured servants to procuring thousands of African slaves. But the settlers' nutrient-hungry crops leached and eroded the soil. Since land seemed abundant and endless, the settlers simply abandoned early plots and moved on to new land. The degraded land found today throughout the South began with the short-term, wasteful practices of the early planters, which in many ways have hardly matured to more long-term care.

In the uplands Piedmont, the **yeoman** farmers—including former indentured servants and Scots-Irish—settled and eked out lives at odds with the tidewater whites. In the 1730s and 1740s, Swiss, German, and Scots-Irish settlers immigrated to the Carolinas through the Great Valley, before settling in the upland Piedmont. They became self-sufficient yeoman farmers who had few slaves and had different needs than the Low Country plantation gentry. The social and economic differences created regional antipathies; they were at first ignored by the Low Country aristocrats, but in the 1760s, some yeomen's needs (e.g., roads, courts, protection from Native insurgencies) were addressed.

The last colony established was Georgia (1732), which was settled as a buffer colony between the British and Spanish. Oglethorpe, a utopian idealist, set up alliances with neighboring Native American tribes and then progressed with his army to lay siege to St. Augustine, Florida. His assault was unsuccessful, but he did halt the Spanish at Florida's northern boundary.

The evolution of the antebellum South differed from that of the northern colonies. Transportation infrastructure lagged, as did growth in population. Immigrants entered through northern ports of entry; there was little need for laborers in the slaveholding South. The self-sufficient plantation system traded from private plantation docks, which truncated the need for cities. This system crimped southern urban development. While the North built an Industrial Revolution infrastructure, southern development stagnated within the slaveholding culture and remained agricultural until after the Civil War.

Textile mills began to relocate from the Northeast in the 1840s, accelerating after the Civil War. Northern textile factories urbanized the Piedmont, taking advantage of cheap labor, power, and the location near the cotton fields (photo 9.6). A string of company towns, each with its own textile mill, spread from Augusta, Georgia, to Aiken, South Carolina. Mill jobs lured laborers, and the urban population grew. By 1874, Georgia had the most mills, but by 1900, South Carolina led textile production with 239 mills.

In the 1970s, the textile industry became one of the first US industries to outsource manufacturing jobs. By the early 2000s, the textile mills had shut down and left many small company towns without their main income source. Some mill sites are making a comeback as retail, research facilities, or loft housing, especially if they are near a larger city. Others grow weeds and deteriorate.

Cultural Perspectives

Gullah

The Gullah (called **Geechee** in Georgia) were African slaves who arrived on the Sea Islands to work the rice and indigo fields. In the twentieth century, the development of resort communities threatened Gullah land, culture, and language.

Most New World slaves lost both their rights and their culture, but the Gullah retained some of their African heritage. African language and cultural retention was most pronounced on the isolated and marshy Sea Islands; the malarial conditions kept most whites away, while many of the African slaves had a greater tolerance to the disease. Therefore, the Sea Island plantations were occupied almost exclusively by native Africans and their descendants, and the culture and language that continued bore the marks of their African heritage.

One of the surviving African craft traditions is Gullah basket weaving. The Gullah basket designs are indistinguishable from their Senegalese counterparts. Other Sea Island crafts brought

PHOTO 9.6. Sibley Textile Mill, Augusta, Georgia. The obelisk is the last remainder of the former Confederate powder works on this site, which provided gunpowder for the Confederate Army. The mill decreased production over a decade and was retired in July 2006.

over from Africa are carving, quilting, and grave decoration. Gullah folk tales, such as Brer Rabbit stories, have also found their way into American folk culture. These cultural artifacts confirm that Africans did bring their culture to the New World.

The South Carolina Gullah language is a Creole mixture of African and English dialects. In the late 1990s, about five hundred thousand people were estimated to speak Gullah, although people outside the Gullah community seldom hear the speech because it has been stigmatized. Additionally, as Gullah speakers leave their community, they often adopt the speech patterns of their new home areas. Nonetheless, there has been a resurgence of interest in Gullah language preservation.

A major cultural artifact was Gershwin's "Porgy and Bess," a musical that indirectly questioned the loss of Gullah folkways. Gershwin wrote his folk opera about the Gullah and it was based on his personal experiences on Folly Island, South Carolina.

Until the 1970s, the Gullah population lacked modern conveniences due to isolation and lack of support or recognition from the government. Since most Gullah land was held communally, they also lacked the traditional bundle of rights connected to land ownership. Once infrastructure was modernized, developers exploited the Gullah lack of clear title. Many Gullah were forced off their land and, sensing the end of their culture, sold their Sea Island land to the developers for less than its twentieth-century worth. The remaining Gullah residents were forced to sell and move because escalating prices increased property taxes. The valuable coastal property has been transformed into luxurious resorts. White populations have replaced the Gullah on the Sea Islands, especially commercialized Hilton Head or St. Simon, once Gullah communities, although whites seldom know of the once ubiquitous Gullah heritage on the island.

In October 2006, the Gullah Geechee Cultural Heritage Corridor was officially designated by Congress and given $10 million over the next decade to preserve the culture (box 9.3). The money will help the Gullah maintain their homes, their heritage, and correct at least one environmental problem: sweetgrass, the main ingredient for their finely crafted baskets, has become scarce.

Food Geography: BBQ

Every region has a dominant food that reflects regional resources, culture, and sense of place. Today, many unique regional cuisines are disappearing and being replaced by ubiquitous and unsustainable fast food franchises. Southern regional cuisine, however, survives. Slaves developed soul food cuisine featuring the unwanted or inexpensive food and meats—collard greens, black-eyed peas, corn, sweet potatoes, lesser cuts of pork, wild game, and fish. Fried catfish, pork chops, and chicken were popular. Included within the genre was the development of barbeque.

Many Southern locales claim to have the best barbeque (BBQ, or just "Q"). Barbeque's origins are unclear, but they include Spanish *barbacoa*, Native American roasting techniques, African influences, and various ethnic European origins. BBQ's prevalence in the South and the legacy of slavery ties it with less tender cuts of pork—shoulder and ribs—tenderized and preserved by being barbequed in the days before refrigeration. Often semiwild hogs were let out to root in the forest and then caught when the food supply was low.

However, barbeque varies (map 9.2). Each Atlantic and Gulf South state claims the best Q, which is served in a variety of places, from roadside shacks to church fundraisers. In the South, BBQ means slow-cooked and smoked, not grilled as

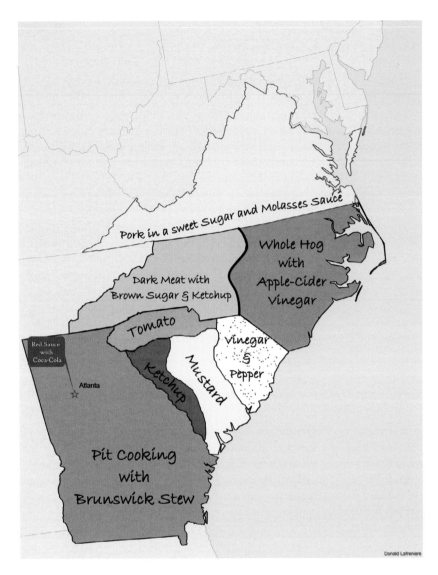

MAP 9.2. Barbeque in the South. States vary in their chosen method and sauce for the best barbeque.

Donald Lafreniere

outside the South. Certain recipes are ubiquitous—chopped, pulled pork, ribs, and sides of cole slaw and beans.

In the Carolinas, a base fire of oak with hickory BBQ is accompanied by sweet tea. Regional South Carolina savory sauces feature tomato, mustard, ketchup, or vinegar and pepper. North Carolina BBQ regions include Eastern North Carolina whole hog and a sharp apple cider vinegar–based sauce; chefs in western North Carolina prefer shoulder (dark meat) and sauce it with brown sugar and ketchup. Georgia cuisine favors pit cooking and often includes Brunswick stew, a combination of lima beans, onions, and potatoes with meat and grain. In Atlanta, a red sauce may include Coca-Cola (whose headquarters is in Atlanta). Virginia barbeque, more prevalent in the southern part of the state, favors pork with a sweet sugar and molasses sauce.

NASCAR

The National Association for Stock Car Auto Racing (NASCAR) has been identified in the public's mind as the quintessential southern sport, one that glorified cars, danger, noise, and alcohol. The sport also has ties to moonshiners and flourished during the Prohibition era, when drivers raced their brew-filled cars to the nearby Piedmont cities. Races between the bootlegging runners were inevitable and evolved after World War II into NASCAR, but its roots reach farther and into a less romanticized history. NASCAR—currently headquartered in Daytona Beach, Florida—was already building its solid and profit-oriented reputation as cars developed and set up races at the turn of the twentieth century. NASCAR did rise in the rural Southeast, but it accepts its mythological past as important for the sport and its fans.

In the 1990s, NASCAR spread across the United States; it became the largest motor sport and the second-largest sporting event on television (behind football). NASCAR has more than seventy-five million fans, and an average of 150,000 fans show up to any one race. The strongest fan base is in the South, but fans are found across the country.

BOX 9.4   ICONIC IMAGES: THE CONFEDERATE LEGACY

On August 12, 2017, the city of Charlottesville saw violence in a clash between white nationalists and Nazi sympathizers on the one hand and counter protestors on the other. The white supremacists and others were in the city to demonstrate against the removal of a statue of Robert E. Lee.

Across the South, there are many memorials and monuments to the Confederacy. While wrapped in the mantle of glorifying the South and the Civil War they, in fact, tell two stories. The first is the commemoration of certain people and events such as the memorials to Jefferson Davis and Stonewall Jackson in Richmond Virginia (photo 9.8). The second relates to the reason why many were built, where they were built, and when they were built. Few memorials were built immediately after the Civil War. In the majority of cases, they were started during Reconstruction as whites regained power in the South and wanted to marginalize blacks. The memorials are a not-so-subtle reminder of institutional racism and black disenfranchisement. Removing confederate statues is not denying history; rather, it is ceasing to celebrate one particular version's history.

Many memorials and monuments fade into the background as long dead generals disappear from our collective memory and often become little more than traffic circles, rarely noticed or observed. But many of the Civil War monuments are less about remembering the past but about influencing the present.

Across the South, names, monuments, and memories are contested sites of historical memory. Where some see a celebration of a romantic past, others see symbols of racial division.

PHOTO 9.8. Monument to Jefferson Davis in Richmond, Virginia. It was erected in 1907 as much a statement about contemporary black civil rights as about honoring the President of the Confederacy.
Source: John R Short

PHOTO 9.7. A NASCAR Event.
Source: iStock/PICSUNV

Crackers and Rednecks

Cracker and **redneck** are two derogatory terms for poor Southern white settlers, usually of Scots-Irish descent; the terms usually referred to a "white trash," uneducated person from the state of Georgia or perhaps northern Florida, although historic references also place them in the Virginia and Carolina backcountry. The term *cracker* has various possible origins: the tendency to crack whips while herding livestock or the practice of cracking rather than milling corn. Both were American adaptations of Scots-Irish culture; the livestock they herded were cattle and pigs, not sheep; and corn grits were the grain of choice, not oat porridge.

The wealthy whites discriminated against poor whites, but in 1932, literary voices began defending their cracker ancestry with Erskine Caldwell's *Tobacco Road* and *God's Little Acre*, continuing in 1999 with Janisse Ray's *Ecology of a Cracker Childhood*. In each, the plain, simple lives are recounted, and reason and context places these people within their milieu and way of life, rather than as caricatures.

Rednecks—salt-of-the-earth "Joe Sixpacks"—can be found anywhere in the United States today, but the term comes from the South and could be derogatory or a source of pride, depending on its source. The **redneck** is the yeoman farmer who may well have arrived as an indentured servant or been dumped on the colonies to rid the mother country of undesirables. Today, in an age of political correctness, the case has been made that the redneck is a scapegoat, the "other." The redneck can be termed the white underclass in the United States and has been pitted against the blacks and despised by wealthier whites. Traits tied to rednecks are loyalty to kin, mistrust of government, and fierce fighting.

The term *redneck* comes from Scotland, where Scot-Irish dissenters remained Protestant rather than join the Church of England. The redneck signed his name in blood and wore a red cloth around his neck to show dissent. When rednecks immigrated to America the name stuck. Some people, though, trace the name to a person from the South who worked in the sun and earned his red neck. Either way, the redneck's ethnic background can be traced to cracker, Scots-Irish, or Celtic roots.

Population, Immigration, and Diversity

Population

There were few Southern antebellum cities. Most people lived on self-sufficient plantations or farms. All of Georgia had but thirty-six towns on the 1860 census; North Carolina had twenty-five and South Carolina only fifteen, whereas northern states had hundreds of towns per state. For example, Vermont alone had more than 360 towns in 1860, although it had less than half the population of South Carolina. After the Civil War, the southern landscape became urbanized. But the South was so far behind northern development that it took a century to develop an urban infrastructure.

Southern population and diversity has a distinct black–white racial profile. The regional black population remains more than double the national percentage. The southern black population is concentrated in the old plantation areas; however, many blacks migrated north during the twentieth century. Until the 1970s, blacks were pushed from the South to escape Jim Crow discrimination and civil rights injustices; they were pulled by employment opportunities in northern manufacturing industries. However, the Civil Rights movement resulted in reform laws against racial discrimination and natural justice; although rights continue to be unequal, conditions are slowly changing for the better.

A major population shift since 1990 is the return of blacks from the Northeast to their southern roots. For example, 70 percent of the blacks leaving New York City since 1990 migrated to the Atlantic South or Florida. They were lured by the lower cost of living and better job opportunities in cities such as Atlanta and Orlando. The South significantly gained black population during the 1990s, while every other US region lost black population.

With few exceptions, both black and white population percentages have declined since 1990 in the Atlantic South. By the time of the 2010 Census, Hispanics replaced blacks as the largest minority in the nation (Hispanics 16.0 percent, blacks 13.6 percent). Blacks are still the largest minority in the southern states.

Immigration and Diversity

Historically, the Atlantic South has limited experience with large-scale immigration. Many states in the region have below national averages for foreign born. For example, Georgia is home to 10 percent foreign born, while South Carolina is home to 4.8 percent (below the national average of 14.2). However, immigration has been increasing in the last two decades. The rise in hog and poultry **concentrated animal feeding operations (CAFOs)** in the South and the inexpensive labor needed to work these jobs has attracted immigrants, particularly Latinos. In addition, the major urban areas of Atlanta and Charlotte have become immigrant gateways with more global appeal.

In 2000, only 10 percent of Atlanta's residents were foreign born. Approximately three hundred thousand new residents who were born abroad moved to metro Atlanta during the 2000s, which represents one of the largest growth rates among the nation's twenty most populous metro areas. There are now more than seven hundred thousand residents of metro Atlanta who were born in a different country, or about 14 percent of the population. More than half of those were born in Latin America, with another 29 percent born in Asia. The vast majority of non-American-born residents of the metro reside on the northern side of the city. The highest concentration of foreign-born residents are found in pockets of Gwinnett, Hall, Forsyth, Cobb, and Clayton counties.

North Carolina has also become a new destination for immigrants. In 1990, immigrants were just 1.7 percent of the state's population; today, it is 7.7 percent. Many immigrants are Latinos. There were very few foreign-born Charlotte residents until the 1990s, when a boom in building, including construction of the towering Bank of America building, attracted Latino construction workers. The strong Charlotte economy, led by banking, has continued to attract immigrants. Between 2000 and 2010, the foreign-born population of Charlotte nearly doubled, and today the city boasts of almost 16 percent foreign born and has become a new immigrant gateway.

Urban Trends

After the Civil War, the Southern economy and population shifted from rural agriculture to urban agriculture and from coastal to Piedmont. The few antebellum cities were on the coast, but currently, the two largest cities in the South are Atlanta and Charlotte, both on the Piedmont. For example, the population in antebellum Atlanta was 9,500 in 1860, but immediately after the Civil War, even after its destruction by General Sherman, the population was 21,780 in 1870 and 37,409 in 1880. By 1900, it grew to almost ninety thousand. Virginia's development differed from the Carolinas and Georgia, because the early cities were already along the fall line, with the exception of Norfolk.

Urban growth followed the development of a manufacturing economy. Textile mills relocated from the Northeast to the Piedmont and created hundreds of company towns and several cities. Low-density non-farming development became common along the Piedmont and remains so today, but the rural population is dependent on urban employment. The Piedmont population, a southern version of sprawl, has more than four million residents spread across the region in what geographers call "Spersopolis."

Cities are prevalent along the fall line (Richmond, Raleigh), on the Piedmont (Atlanta), or along the coastal drowned valley harbors (Norfolk, Wilmington, Charleston, and Savannah). Few significant cities were located within the coastal plain. However, in recent years, tourism-golf-oriented sprawl has developed along the coast around Myrtle Beach, straddling the boundary between North and South Carolina. By 2016, the population of this MSA had increased to 449,295. The area is rich in tourist amenities, especially golf courses, but is vulnerable to storms and rising sea levels.

Richmond, Virginia
(2016 MSA 1.2 million)

Straddling the fall line at the James River, Richmond, the capital of both Virginia and the Confederacy, has been the break-in-bulk center of eastern Virginia's commerce and industry since colonial times. The city developed independent of Washington, D.C., but evolving transportation networks over the past century have drawn Richmond into the national capital's suburban loop. The economy reflects this, as it is primarily driven by law, finance, and government agencies.

In 2012, Richmond created its sustainability plan, *RVAgreen*. In 2017, the city updated this plan to *RVAgreen 2050*, with a special focus on reducing carbon emissions 80 percent by 2050 using 2008 as the baseline year. *RVAgreen 2050* is a comprehensive planning effort to create a healthier, more vibrant, economically competitive and resilient community. It sets targets to increase clean energy resources, enhance the reliability and resiliency of energy systems, and promote more efficient and affordable energy use. Richmond also participates in SolSmart, a national program designed to assist the growth of strong local solar markets by taking key steps to reduce barriers and make it faster, easier, and less expensive to go solar.

Raleigh–Durham–Chapel Hill, North Carolina
(The Research Triangle; 2016: Raleigh pop. 458,880; Chapel Hill 59,246; Durham 236,016; MSA 1,302,946)

These three municipalities are known as the Research Triangle, or locally, simply as the Triangle. Major universities—North Carolina State, Duke, and the University of North Carolina, Chapel Hill—form the basis for this technopole, the largest planned research and development park in the United States. Establishing the technopole in the 1960s helped reverse the North Carolina brain drain. Today, the technopole's success can be measured by the presence of a high per capita rate of PhDs and MDs. The development was not easy.

In the 1960s, Governor Terry Sanford of North Carolina created Research Triangle Park, a partnership between business, government, and higher education. The major industries at the time revolved around tobacco, textiles, and furniture, all of which are still part of the economy. However, the economy has expanded into numerous research facilities, technology companies, and medical centers. In 1965, the first tenants were the National Institute of Environmental Health Sciences and IBM, followed by a number of technological and life science companies. The Triangle is now considered one of the best places to live and work in America.

Raleigh is a certified 4-STAR community and the first community in North Carolina to achieve certification through the national STAR Community Rating System. STAR is a robust sustainability rating system where communities evaluate themselves across seven goal areas: built environment; climate and energy; economy and jobs; education, arts, and community; equity and empowerment; health and safety; and natural systems.

Although the Triangle cities have developed sustainability plans, they remain challenged by car-centered infrastructure and sprawl. More than 88 percent of commuters use their cars and the area is below the national average in commuters' use of public transportation, walking, and biking.

Charlotte, North Carolina
(2016 MSA 2.4 million)

Charlotte is the second-largest city in the Southeast. Situated on the Piedmont, the city began as a cotton-processing center and then a railroad hub after the Civil War. It gained fame as a financial center due to banking acquisitions in the 1970s and

1980s and became home to the Bank of America and other major banks in America.

Perhaps Charlotteans are thinking about climate change more than others, due to some unusual climate events. Although it is two hundred miles from the coast, in 1989 the city was caught unprepared and suffered considerable damage from Hurricane Hugo. In 2002, an ice storm, unusual at its subtropical latitude, knocked out power for weeks. During Hurricane Matthew in 2016, the storm surge from the Atlantic was exacerbated by waters flowing from the Triangle, inundating the low-lying floodplains of eastern North Carolina. The state incurred more than $1.5 billion in damage. Similarly, Hurricane Irma in 2017 did not hit Charlotte directly, but its powerful winds tore down multiple trees and power lines.

Many of the storms that make landfall in North Carolina's coastal communities end up affecting Charlotte both directly and indirectly. In addition to floods and winds that can knock out power, Charlotte also serves as the regional evacuation center for coastal communities during hurricanes. Between 2000 and 2015, seventeen federal disasters and emergencies were declared for floods, hurricanes, and severe storms in North Carolina, yielding $456 million in total assistance from the US government.

Unfortunately, the state has rolled back more proactive measures. One rule that was dropped required natural buffer areas along rivers and streams to limit and filter runoff going into waterways, protecting water quality in rivers and controlling flooding. The legislature determined that the regulation was ineffective and added unnecessary expense for developers. In the same vein, new state policies have made it easier for developers to build projects with impervious surfaces. These setbacks make it more likely that the city will see increased vulnerability to climate change.

Charleston, South Carolina
(2016 MSA 761,000)

English traders established Charleston in 1670, and it became one of the few antebellum southern cities. Charleston's location at the Ashley and Cooper confluence allowed planters to ferry between their plantations and the port. In an era when malaria and yellow fever raged through the coastal swamps, Charleston grew as an ocean breeze refuge and became the social center for southern Low Country planters.

The emphasis on historic preservation is impressive and draws many of the tourists it seeks, but it has become a multimillion-dollar investment that outsiders use for second or third homes and has lost its community and neighborhood charm. Outside the hallowed historic district, the rest of the town and the surrounding area are depressed, except for newly redeveloped but pricey sprawl.

The economy has been uneven, especially when the Navy pulled out in 1996, leaving thousands without jobs and a hole in the city that has since undergone redevelopment, some with a more sustainable footprint. Charleston is also deeply involved in military defense and security centers, which draw a highly educated workforce.

In 2010, the city publicly launched its sustainability plan: *Charlotte 2030: A Sustainable Vision for Our Region*. The plan is the product of countless volunteer hours and the engagement of more than one hundred local citizens and experts from many disciplines using a collaborative and consensus-based process, drawn from government, the nonprofit and private sectors, and academia. The plan is focused around ten key issues: air, energy, food, buildings and homes, economy, parks, trees and green space, recycling and waste reduction, social equity, transportation, and water.

Atlanta, Georgia
(2016 MSA 5.7 million)

Atlanta is Georgia's capital and the largest city in the Atlantic South. In 1837, railroad promoters established Terminus—Atlanta's original name—at the base of the Appalachians, giving it both East Coast and midwestern distribution connections. In 1864, Union troops occupied and burned the city to the ground, with the exception of churches and hospitals. It rebuilt and became the leading southern distribution point for goods up the Atlantic Coast.

The city has become a magnet of opportunities for blacks. Atlanta's inner city black population is middle class, but the city remains racially polarized. Ultimately, Atlanta became a majority black city (54.0 percent black, 38.3 percent white, 5.2 percent Hispanic, 3.1 percent Asian) with a white suburban ring. The power-play tension between the white outlying areas and the black inner core has been palpable.

Atlanta has become the economic center for the South, important in the technology sector, supported by a highly skilled workforce, regulatory incentives, and a political machine that works with research universities and the private sector. Atlanta is also a major tourist and convention destination. Hartsfield-Jackson Airport is the busiest airport in the world and is the Delta Airlines and AirTrans Airways hub.

Metro Atlanta is third to New York and Houston in the number of Fortune 500 company headquarters: Its largest corporation is Coca-Cola, invented for headache relief by a local pharmacist in 1886 as "French Wine Cola." Other major companies and institutions include Home Depot, United Parcel Service (UPS), and the Centers for Disease Control and Prevention (CDC). Turner Broadcasting media headquarters (CNN) is in Atlanta, and the Weather Channel is located in nearby suburban Marietta.

Currently, only 10 percent of Atlanta's metropolitan population live in the city. The remainder sprawl unchecked across twenty counties. The unobstructed geography—flat with no large bodies of water, natural boundaries, or federal land—has created a low-density pattern inconvenient for mass transit (photo 9.10). Atlanta is the least densely populated city in

BOX 9.5 URBAN SUSTAINABILITY BEST PRACTICES: HISTORIC PRESERVATION IN CHARLESTON AND SAVANNAH

There has always been some appreciation of cultural and architectural heritage, but only since the mid-twentieth century have societies become increasingly aware of the significance of our urban historic structures and sites. The most important piece of historic preservation legislation in the United States is the National Historic Preservation Act of 1966. It established new laws, authorized funds for preservation activities, and encouraged locally regulated historic districts. It went beyond merely protecting landmarks to recognizing a variety of historically and architecturally significant buildings, sites, structures, districts, and objects.

Preservation is an important tool of urban revitalization as cities search for a way to celebrate their past while looking to the future. It can be used to preserve neighborhoods and even ecologically important areas within the city. Historic preservation is an important part of urban sustainability. Two of the best examples are found in the South Atlantic in Charleston and Savannah.

Charleston and Savannah are "belles" of the South. About one hundred miles apart, they have long been regional rivals. But these cities have something in common: a strong legacy of preservation.

Charleston has the oldest historic district in the country (dating back to the 1930s). It has carefully preserved the city's grand public buildings, as well as the mansions along the Battery, and the famous Rainbow Row (photo 9.9).

While not as old as Charleston, Savannah's historic district is much larger, stretching from the waterfront to neighborhoods where homes with gas lanterns and intricate iron work sit beneath the Spanish moss.

Both Charleston and Savannah have achieved international reputations for historic preservation and have been able to turn that into a billion-dollar tourist industry.

PHOTO 9.9. Rainbow Row, Charleston, South Carolina, is a beautiful example of the restored Historic District. Eighteenth-century Charleston society was more interested in replicating British society than were the more northern cities. Its buildings were first built with brick but later stuccoed over and still later painted in Caribbean-influenced colors.

America, with 1,370 persons per square mile, compared to 5,400 in Los Angeles. The seemingly endless sprawl has created traffic and environmental problems.

Commute times in the Atlanta region are second only to Los Angeles. Zoning separates residential from office and retail use, so people depend on cars and walkability is low. Commutes of only ten miles can take an hour, and many live up to thirty miles from the city.

Metro city planning lacks consideration of water or air quality. The amount of green space and trees is negligible—the city lost 38 percent of its greenery between 1982 and 1992—creating a heat island effect and more air pollution, especially vexing during an already hot, humid summer.

However, beginning in 1996 with the Olympics and progressing since, several areas in Atlanta have become more sustainable (photo 9.11). Atlanta has supported energy

PHOTO 9.10. Atlanta, Georgia, is considered one of the fastest-growing and most sprawling cities in America. The lack of physical boundaries or nearby federal land allows the city to continue to sprawl in all directions.

Source: John R Short

efficiency and building; it has the most LEED-certified buildings in the Southeast, but it has done little to encourage retrofit incentives or public participation. The transit-oriented developments (TODs) downtown along the MARTA perimeter rail line have created several walkable communities that have escalated in price. But public transport and bicycling serve only 5 percent of the population, so congestion remains near impossible. Connect Atlanta, a new transportation plan, hopes to give more residents access to public transport. Finally, in 2010 Atlanta developed its sustainability plan. Its ambitious targets include the following:

- Transportation: Promote the expansion of public transit, including the continued development of the Atlanta BeltLine and the implementation of the Atlanta Streetcar projects and focusing on improving neighborhood connectivity.
- Climate Change: Reduce greenhouse gas (GHG) emissions within the City of Atlanta's jurisdiction by 25 percent by 2020, 40 percent by 2030, and 80 percent by 2050.
- Water Quality: To restore and maintain water quality standards by enforcing regulations, complying with federal, state, and local laws, and coordinating watershed protection strategies throughout City government.
- Air quality: Improve Atlanta's air quality such that over 60 percent of days qualify as good according to the EPA's Air Quality Index by 2020, 75 percent by 2030, and 100 percent by 2050.
- Waste: Reduce, reuse, and recycle 50 percent by 2015, 90 percent by 2020.

PHOTO 9.11. A New South? Children play in the park built to commemorate the 1996 Olympic Games held in Atlanta.

Source: John R Short

It is worth noting that plans that set specific targets and goals tend to hold a city to better accountability in making timely progress. In this regard, Atlanta's plan is positioned to achieve these specific targets and goals.

Savannah is a city with a reputation; in many ways it is quintessentially southern, personifying the dank, subtropical eccentricities that attract those seeking a real southern experience.

Savannah was founded as a utopian community by James Oglethorpe on the Savannah River in 1733. His idealism led him to create a unique urban plan and to outlaw slavery and drinking—fearing the vices would weaken the colony in the face of the Spanish enemy. Both laws were overturned by mid-century, because settlers believed that the slavery and drinking restrictions weakened the colony. However, the city's original urban plan—with open space and multiple squares—continues to attract those seeking a more convivial atmosphere.

During the Civil War, the city surrendered rather than undergo the ignominy of destruction by Sherman's troops. This allowed the city to maintain its historical buildings, but it took another move in the mid-twentieth century to preserve a fading glory. Historic preservation in Savannah has helped the city become a popular tourist city. In 1994, John Berendt's novel *Midnight in the Garden of Good and Evil* portrayed the eccentric nature of its citizens within the story of a sensational murder. It helped spur even more tourism.

Savannah continues to seek economic isolation and favors maintaining its unique image. But Savannah is an important part of the Georgia economy: It is the main port for Georgia, a main processor of paper pulp from Georgia's vast pine forests, the home to Gulfstream (a leader in corporate jet production), and its dominant industry is historic-preservation-cum-eccentric-oriented tourism.

The Economy

The region's plantation economy discouraged cities, infrastructure, settlers, and manufacturing. Development was retarded until after the Civil War, when northern money and **carpetbaggers** moved south to take advantage of the raw materials and cheap labor. The carpetbaggers invested in railroads, steel, cigarettes, and liquor. The textile industry grew after the Civil War.

After the Civil War, a New South emerged, but the Southern economy remained regional and low wage for blacks and for textile workers (nearly all white). A second "New South" emerged after World War II, when racial tensions and segregation began to ease and southern industrial growth was invigorated. Spurred by the national wage and labor laws of the 1930s, a new ease in transportation, and the advantages of the warmer climate (largely made amenable because of air conditioning), the New

South developed cities that mirrored northern urban plans. The Atlantic South was dependent on agriculture prior to the Civil War and the textile industry into the mid-twentieth century. Today, the New South economy is a blend of all three sectors.

The Primary Sector

Agriculture

South had two types of farmers: the plantation owner and the yeoman farmer. They were separated socioeconomically. The plantation owner was deemed a member of the powerful aristocracy, while the yeoman farmer was relegated to a lesser socioeconomic order, the redneck, cracker, or "trash."

After the Civil War, many plantation owners retained their land by renting to tenant farmers. Freed slaves and poor whites rented and sharecropped the land, with contracts favoring the landowner interests. The owner provided the land, mule, plow, and seed; the sharecropper provided the labor. Often the costs exceeded crop profits. In a way, this kept the "practice" of slavery alive, as often the sharecropper was in perpetual debt to the owner. Thus, the plantation changed from a singly owned and operated economy to multiple producing families living on the land and "sharing" the crop and "wealth." The poor yeoman farmer continued to farm his marginal upcountry soil into the early twentieth century, when most left the farm because competition from mechanization was destroying any hope of profitability.

The South depended on an agricultural economy much longer than the rest of America. The long frost-free periods and soil types were conducive to specific crops: tobacco, indigo, rice, sugar, and cotton. Livestock gained importance when the tobacco crop began to decline in the 1950s. Southern entrepreneurs seeking other agricultural pursuits revolutionized chicken and then hog production and changed the American livestock landscape. Since that time, both tobacco and cotton have undergone transitions as crops. Tobacco quotas have ended, which exacerbated problems for the small tobacco farmer, while cotton has returned to the Atlantic Coastal states after the regional eradication of the **boll weevil** (map 9.3).

Tobacco   Tobacco brought the southern colonies their first economic success. In Jamestown, the English adopted imported West Indies varieties over the local ones because it was a smoother, less biting smoke. Trade began with England within a decade of settlement.

Tobacco brought wealth to the Tidewater landed aristocracy. First grown along the Chesapeake Bay estuaries, tobacco was one leg of the **triangular trade**—tobacco to England, manufactured goods to Africa, slaves to America. Tobacco cultivation spread from the Tidewater to the Piedmont and eventually to Kentucky. Tobacco's labor-intensive workforce evolved from indentured servants to slaves and then, after the Civil War, to tenant farmers who farmed small plots. But labor was not the only problem: tobacco exhausts the soil and requires an intimate knowledge of its physical requirements.

BOX 9.6   GLOBAL CONNECTIONS: COCA-COLA: THE SOUTHERN DRINK GOES GLOBAL

An early variant of what became Coca-Cola was first concocted in a drugstore in Columbus, Georgia, by a confederate colonel, John Pemberton. He was looking for a substitute for morphine, a drug that had him for a while in the clutches of addiction. Coca-Cola was officially launched in 1886 in Atlanta with extravagant claims of its healing properties. The Coca-Cola Company grew from its southern origins into a multinational corporation.

Coca-Cola became associated around the world with the United States.

The ingredients include water, sugar, caffeine, and phosphoric acid, caramel, and natural flavorings. The original drinks included cocaine; coca leaves are still used but in the form of cocaine-free extract.

Coca-Cola is sold and marketed in most countries across the world. And it has a ubiquitous presence in TV advertising. Promotional campaigns flood the mass media.

In recent years, there is mounting criticism of the large dosage of sugar, in the form of sucrose, which is associated with dental decay and obesity, especially in children.

The company is still headquartered in Atlanta although there are manufacturing plants and distribution centers spread across the nation and the world (photo 9.12).

Company website: http://www.coca-cola.com/global/

PHOTO 9.12. Coca-Cola Headquarters in Atlanta, Georgia, is located in Midtown.
Source: J. Glover

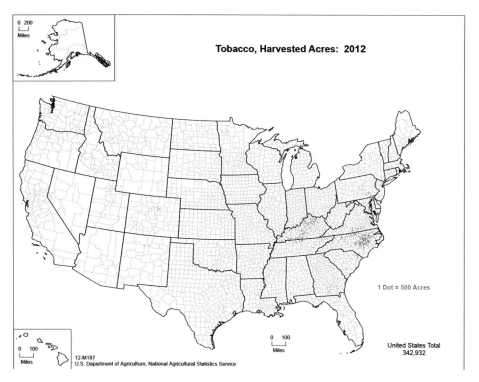

Tobacco, Harvested Acres: 2012

1 Dot = 500 Acres

United States Total
342,932

12-M187
U.S. Department of Agriculture, National Agricultural Statistics Service

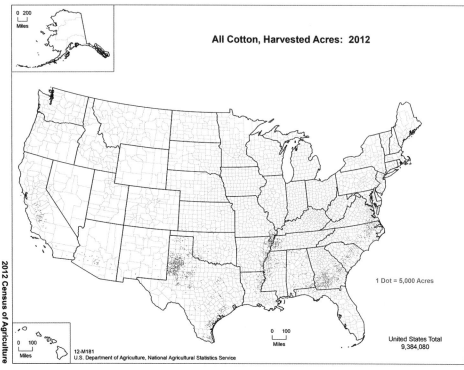

All Cotton, Harvested Acres: 2012

1 Dot = 5,000 Acres

United States Total
9,384,080

2012 Census of Agriculture

12-M181
U.S. Department of Agriculture, National Agricultural Statistics Service

MAP 9.3. Tobacco (A) and Cotton (B), Harvested Acres 2012. Two of the most important crops in South Atlantic history have been tobacco and cotton. Both have undergone changes in the recent past. Tobacco is no longer a quota crop, and cotton has returned to the Atlantic coast after elimination of the boll weevil. *Source:* USDA

The industrialization of tobacco began in the 1880s. For the farmer, mechanization reduced field labor by 80 percent, although tobacco remains more labor intensive than other crops. Cigarette factories were constructed near the crop, because raw tobacco is most profitable when processed locally and then shipped. Until the 1970s, most tobacco products were shipped within the large domestic market where smoking was perceived as "cool." Then the market moved overseas, mostly to China, where US tobacco companies promoted their product a market where nearly three-quarters of all Chinese men smoke. Although the number of smokers in the United States has declined, revenues for US tobacco companies hit $117 billion in 2016, up from $78 billion in 2001.

At the beginning of the twentieth century, the American Tobacco Company controlled 90 percent of the industry, but it was forced to break up the monopoly due to a 1911 antitrust suit. Emerging from the breakup were four companies (in order of market share): a reshaped American Tobacco Company, R. J. Reynolds (Camels), P. Lorillard (Newport), and Liggett and Myers (Chesterfield). R. J. Reynolds and the American Tobacco Company were founded by the Dukes (after whom the university is named) and were centered in Winston-Salem and Durham, North Carolina. Another company, Philip Morris (now Altria Group; makers of Marlboro), would later emerge from the breakup.

Rice, "Carolina Gold" Neither tobacco nor sugar grew well along the swampy, mosquito-infested Sea Islands, but once the land was drained and irrigated, rice became the staple crop of the Low Country. By 1730, the South Carolina coast was a center of rice production. Charleston exported ten thousand pounds in 1698 and more than twenty million pounds by 1730.

Lacking laborers for the burgeoning rice plantations, early-eighteenth-century planters turned to slaves, as had their Virginia tobacco-growing neighbors. The most-sought-after slaves were from the West African Rice Coast, where Africans had grown rice for thousands of years. The arduous work and high mortality rates for whites kept the area almost entirely black for the duration of the rice-growing industry.

Most rice was exported to Northern European countries. But rice was also consumed in the South, and in many Southern cuisines rice remains the staple starch.

Rice growers became very wealthy during the antebellum period and aligned themselves with the Charleston elite. They built grand plantations and gardens, even using Versailles as their model. Their wealth also made them confident that they could break free of colonization and become an independent nation.

After the Civil War, rice production declined in the Atlantic South, while it expanded into the Gulf South. Early in the twentieth century, large-scale rice production ended in the Carolinas. Arkansas is the number one producer of rice in the United States today.

Indigo

Before synthetic dyes were developed, natural dyes were the only way to dye clothes, but most natural colors were muted browns and grays with few colorfast or bright colors. The leaves of the spindly indigo plant created a brilliant blue that was cherished among ancient people and became a favored crop and trade commodity in the subtropics, supplying the "royal" blue that denoted wealth and social standing. The plant grew wild along the South Carolina, Georgia, and northern Florida coasts, but it was war that made indigo a valuable crop.

During the first half of the eighteenth century, England was at war with Spain and France, ending indigo trade with colonial India, Central America, and the East Indies. Britain needed the deep blue dye for its textile industry and paid a bounty for American indigo. The American "indigo bonanza" from 1740 to 1790 doubled investment every three to four years. The

American Revolution ended trade with Britain, and after Britain resumed trade with its other colonies, the market was glutted. Indigo planters in the South shifted to growing cotton, a judicious choice as the **cotton gin** had just been invented and the period of King Cotton began. Cotton exports increased from one million to six million pounds from 1797 to 1800, while indigo went from more than a million pounds exported in 1775 to thirty-four hundred pounds in 1800.

Indigo dye (the color used for denim) is almost completely synthetic today, but wild, perennial indigo plants still bloom in the spring along the roadsides of South Carolina, two hundred years after the industry was abandoned.

Cotton

From the late eighteenth century until World War II, cotton was the single most important crop in the South's agricultural economy. Cotton became the major crop when American and British textile mills demanded more than the plantations could supply, and the labor-intensive process of separating the seed from the boll had been mechanized.

The Atlantic South grew two types of cotton: Sea Island and upland cotton. Sea Island cotton was imported from the West Indies. It had a longer fiber and was easier to clean, but the finicky plant only grew on the small offshore islands and demand exceeded supply. Upland cotton grew inland but was difficult to clean. The cotton gin automated the labor-intensive process in 1793 and was the first of numerous inventions that helped increase cotton production from 1.5 million pounds in 1790 to 673 million pounds in 1840. This period was the slave-dependent era, when nearly 75 percent of the 2.5 million slaves in America worked in cotton fields.

Cotton production was dominant in the Atlantic South but migrated west over time. Production spread into the Piedmont region in the 1830s, when the Indian Removal Program cleared the region of Native Americans.

Continuous cotton production exhausted already poor soils, and the resulting erosion caused the large plantation owners to move their Atlantic South cotton plantations to the Gulf Coast and up the Mississippi River Valley. After the Civil War, large-scale plantation cotton production ended and sharecropping began. Cotton production dropped radically after 1960 due to boll weevil infestations but has rebounded in the twenty-first century. However, cotton has several other environmental and social issues.

Cotton production ranks third behind corn and soybeans for the amount of fossil fuel–based chemicals used, several of which are carcinogenic. Some farmers are now avoiding this problem by growing organic cotton, but the vast majority of cotton is conventionally raised.

The United States is the leading exporter of cotton. There have been several cases of illegal and unfair cotton subsidies brought to the attention of the World Trade Organization (WTO), in which it is claimed that the subsidies given to American farmers undermine developing world farmers' livelihoods and destroy their export markets.

Both poultry and hog production have changed radically in the latter twentieth century, resulting in an increase in meat consumption without a huge increase in price. The cost of plentiful meat, though, came at the expense of ethical and environmental problems.

Poultry "A chicken in every pot" seems strange in the twenty-first century as a saying indicating wealth and prosperity, but before World War II chicken was luxury meat. This dream came to fruition after World War II through the introduction of **vertical integration**—a single large company controlling a commodity, in this case chicken, through the entire highly mechanized process "from semen to cellophane." Prior to vertical integration, each stage of production was owned by a different entity—the farmer, the miller, the processor, the transporter, etc. This method was not providing profit at most levels. Improvement came through vertical integration, which improves supply chain coordination, reduces transportation costs by having all production in geographic proximity, and captures profit margins at all stages of production.

In vertical integration, farmers own the land and the barns where thousands of chickens are raised every six weeks, but the company owns the chickens, the food, and any other part of the production process. The **contract farmer** follows precise instructions for raising the chickens. Contracting for a vertically integrated company has become an attractive alternative for many farmers, but the contracts are not always renewed. The advent of the vertically integrated poultry industry changed the 1910 luxury meat into an inexpensive and readily available meat in the twenty-first century.

Tyson initiated contract chicken production in the 1950s, but several companies in the Atlantic South were also moving toward vertical integration. Georgia emerged as the top producer of chicken and processing chickens is the number one agricultural commodity in Georgia. Turkey and egg production also thrive in the South. North Carolina produces the second-largest amount of turkeys. Egg production in the South is a secondary market, following the Midwest.

Hogs Vertical integration also changed hog production, although integration occurred a few decades after chicken integration. Once again, the dying tobacco industry spurred changes in hog production from dirt-floored pigpens to plastic slats in metal CAFOs. Concentrated vertically integrated hog production added new industry to the Atlantic South. North Carolina became the second largest hog-producing state despite a lack of the dominant feed, locally produced corn.

The person who changed hog production was a tobacco farmer, Wendell Murphy, who was seeking another form of income as the tobacco industry failed around him. He established Murphy Family Farms and brought the traditional southern meat, pork, to the South again, from its hiatus with pork producers in the Midwest. Centered in the Duplin and Samson counties in eastern North Carolina, Murphy began his

rise as the king of CAFO in the 1970s and by the 1990s became the largest individual producer of hogs in the nation.

There were thousands of farmers just like Murphy who lacked a profitable crop but wanted to stay on the land. Murphy provided them a livelihood, the hog—not the few hogs that nearly every farmer raised, but a thousand confined hogs per low-slung metal-roofed holding pen. Murphy's company owned the hogs, but the contract farmers raised them. Contract hogs replaced tobacco as the commodity of choice and provided farmers with a steady income. By 1997, hog production passed tobacco as North Carolina's number one agricultural commodity.

Murphy's method changed hog production across the nation, from thousands of small producers who produced variable-quality hogs to fewer, more regulated hog producers who produced uniform and consistent CAFO hogs of median quality. In 1949, there were 70,496 hog producers in North Carolina who produced about eleven hogs each. By 2007, there were seventeen hundred hog producers, and 75 percent of them had more than five thousand hogs apiece. Nationally, the number of hog producers declined from more than six hundred thousand in 1980 to fewer than one hundred thousand in 2005, although total inventory remained relatively constant.

American pork consumption has remained fairly stable, but to maximize profits the highest-quality meat is exported, most notably to the high-paying Japanese market. Hogs raised in North Carolina are often on the dinner plate in Japan, hardly supporting local production or sustainable practices.

While CAFO hog production has allowed many farmers to stay on their land, it has also had a host of unintended consequences and environmental impacts.

Unintended consequences. CAFO hog farms have polluted groundwater and air, and they are raising human and animal health issues. Fertilizing fields with CAFO waste often results in overfertilization and water table contamination. Waste stored in euphemistically named **lagoons**—often unlined and inadequately constructed—leaks into the groundwater. Air pollution has resulted in respiratory diseases in workers and nearby residents, as well as being infamously malodorous. Additionally, the overuse of antibiotics to stop the spread of disease in pigs has been tied to increased antibiotic-resistant germs in humans. And many define the cheek-to-jowl crowding in CAFO farms as animal cruelty.

Local and ecoregional impacts. Starting in the 1990s, North Carolina hog production exploded from 2.6 million hogs in 1988 to almost 10 million hogs in 2010. The growth has been in large-scale hog production facilities that have had a local and ecoregional impact on water and air.

Hog manure has been stored in open-pit lagoons and disposed of by spraying on fields, a troublesome method that at times is extremely hazardous. North Carolina lagoons are built on sandy soil in areas with high water tables. Because water tables are near the surface, hog lagoons often have to be built with berms to keep the depth out of the water table and protect the groundwater. Nonetheless, the feces-laden water can and

BOX 9.7   SUSTAINABLE CARPET

One of the most renowned American sustainable industrial stories is the conversion of Interface Inc., headquartered in Atlanta, Georgia. Founded in 1973, it is the world's largest designer and maker of carpet tiles with thirty-three manufacturing plants and over three thousand employees. Interface's founder and chairman Ray Anderson read Paul Hawken's *Ecology of Commerce* and had an epiphany on the environmental actions of companies. He vowed to make his company one of the most sustainable in America.

His company has become a leader in **industrial ecology**—a network of industrial processes that interact and live off each other, economically, while eliminating waste. The waste of one company becomes the resource of another company, or it is recycled within the original company. Industrial ecology aims to work as nature works, rather than trying to conquer nature.

Since Mr. Anderson's epiphany, the company has become more sustainable and aims to achieve zero emissions by 2020. In 2003, it was the first carpet company to receive Environmentally Preferable Product certification for its products. In its redefinition of industry, the company has identified seven fronts that define the climb to "Mount Sustainability." In order, they are as follows:

1. Eliminating waste: Reduce and simplify the amount of resources used.
2. Benign emissions: Eliminate toxic substances used.
3. Renewable energy: Operate facilities with solar, wind, geothermal, and other renewable energy sources.
4. Closing the loop: Redesign processes and products to recover materials for reuse and to return organic materials to their natural systems.
5. Resource-efficient transportation: Reduce pollution and GHG emissions to offset CO_2 emissions.
6. Sensitizing stakeholders: Educate all involved in the company about sustainability, and share environmental and social goals.
7. Redesigning commerce: Create a new business model that is sustainably based.

often does leak into the groundwater and contaminate drinking water. During hurricanes, as in 1999 during Hurricane Floyd, flooding cause the lagoons to overflow and dump the hog waste into rivers, causing massive fish kills.

CAFO hog production endangers public health. Widespread administration of antibiotics to confined hogs has contributed to antibiotic resistance in humans. In the United States, 70 percent of antibiotics are fed to healthy livestock to promote growth and relieve health concerns with closely confined animals.

Land located near CAFO facilities decreases in value because of degraded air quality. Most hog farms are located in lower-economic-strata areas; the loss is disproportionately borne by those who can least afford it. The towns that have been saddled with CAFOs are told that the farms will help the economy; in fact they do not, but they help destroy small-scale farmers. Where large hog farms are the standard, it has been unprofitable for local communities, as commodities are often purchased from outside the local area. Rural communities do better socially and economically when there are more farmers rather than having production in the hands of a few. The result is deep-seated rifts between CAFOs and their neighbors.

Sustainability in North Carolina's hog industry would benefit all, and research has begun to maximize profits while introducing some sustainable practices. Capturing the methane produced by the lagoons can create additional fuel that can be sold as a by-products. Manure management systems to capture biogas are expensive (about $250,000 minimum per hog farm), but they have the advantage of helping maintain clean air and water, reduce GHG emissions, and provide biogas to operate the facility. Incentives have helped manure management gain acceptance. However, a lack of government incentives has limited the number of biogas operations to less than 1 percent.

There has been a trend among consumers toward more natural, organic, and locally grown food. Although the amount of meat produced will be less, it will be of a higher quality and sold locally. Reducing the amount of meat produced will also reduce the dependence on corn for livestock production, which in turn will reduce the use of fresh water for growing excess corn crops.

The Secondary Sector

Logging

The presettlement Atlantic South was forested. The land was cleared and used for crop production, mostly cotton, but improper soil use caused erosion and reversion of the land to forest or pasture. The forests of Georgia and North Carolina were stripped in the nineteenth century for use as the nation's naval stores—lumber, rosin, and turpentine to build sailing ships—providing 70 percent of the world supply by the twentieth century. The region was logged during the 1890s, and then the industry left for the more lucrative forests in the Pacific Northwest. A reforestation plan was initiated in the 1940s and has continued, so that the woodland acreage is larger but of less quality today than in the 1930s.

The pulp and paper industry shifted back to the South from the Pacific Northwest in 1982 for two reasons: the spotted owl crisis in the West and the accelerated growth pattern in the warmer southern climate.

Today, Georgia is the number one state for lumber production, and lumber processing has provided 23 percent of manufacturing jobs and 2 percent of all jobs in the state. At $24 billion, lumber is the second-largest industry behind food processing. However, the current lumber industry is unsustainable.

A bright spot in the local economy is the growth in the southern carpet industry, especially in Georgia. From humble beginnings in the 1930s—selling homemade tufted bedspreads—the industry has increased its jobs, from thirty-two thousand to forty thousand since 1997, even as the state lost manufacturing jobs. Part of the reason it has maintained its stability in the face of jobs fleeing elsewhere is the mechanization of the industry and its bulk.

Much of the new growth is in the automobile industry. During the late twentieth century, the industry devolved from the unionized North, and new auto factories opened in the Southern nonunion **right-to-work states** where low land and labor costs beckoned. Spartanburg, Greenville, and Anderson in South Carolina now manufacture automobile parts, tires, or silicon chips. Incentives of $150 million lured BMW to Spartanburg, while North Carolina benefited with lucrative jobs and contracts for auto suppliers. In Virginia, while some manufacturers closed, others received new orders. Roanoke satisfies the demand for railcars as rail traffic escalates. In Greensboro, North Carolina, part of the Carolina Triad (Winston-Salem, High Point, and Greensboro), regional jobs once focused on tobacco and then furniture, but now are shifting to new industries. Honda opened a business-jet-manufacturing facility, while others pursue the biotech industry and research rather than manufacturing.

However, despite the new jobs and manufacturing facilities, the Piedmont economy is frail. Manufacturing jobs are relatively scarce; they pay less than union jobs but still better than the proliferation of poor-paying service jobs. People are employed, but for less money. Median household income dropped 20 percent from 1999 to 2005.

The Tertiary Sector

The region is home to a wide variety of tertiary services—from tourism to banking.

The decline of tobacco production has meant the conversion of tobacco warehouses to condos (photo 9.13). Once known for an economy built on tobacco, furniture, and textiles, North Carolina has evolved into a more diverse economy through growth in the service sector. Biotechnology, energy, finance, and information technology are just a few examples. The Research Triangle has attracted biotechnology and pharmaceuticals and is home to Merck, LabCorp, Biogen, Bayer, and Novartis.

In South Carolina, wholesale trade in automobiles, groceries, and textiles and revenue from tourism are significant parts of the tertiary sector. In addition to tourism, Georgia is home to aerospace, data centers, life sciences, and information technology. Many of these states advertise lower corporate tax rates as a competitive edge.

Banking and Financial Services

North Carolina has become a major player in the national banking field. The banking and finance industry in North Carolina has experienced a skyrocketing growth rate in the last decade, growing by 25 percent since 2002. Today, finance is the third-largest economic sector by gross state product in North Carolina, after manufacturing and government.

Tourism

The Atlantic South has increasingly relied on its heritage and good weather to attract tourists. Tourism is the largest or second-largest industry in each state and accounts for more than 10 percent of all jobs. Civil War battlefields and forts, along with antebellum cities such as Williamsburg, Virginia, or Charleston, South Carolina, are major attractions. Added to these historic sites are the formerly isolated but now developed Sea Islands. Many islands are now connected to major highways, and some islands, such as Hilton Head or St. Simon's in Georgia, are major tourist attractions, while others offer sporting activities such as kayaking and fishing. National Parks, such as the Okefenokee National Wildlife Refuge and the Cape Hatteras and Cape Lookout seashores, also lure visitors. A major tourist-centered metropolitan area had developed around Myrtle Beach along the beach on the border between North and South Carolina.

For example, in 2016, more than fifty million people visited North Carolina, spending a total of $22.9 billion, and helping to support 218,000 jobs. South Carolina saw tourism generate an economic impact of $19 billion. In Virginia, tourism revenue reached $24 billion, and visitor spending supported 230,000 jobs.

A Sustainable Future

The twentieth century changed the South. As cities grow, the rural areas wither, or those close enough to urban areas sprout into extended suburbs. But reducing GHG emissions and CO_2 levels or conserving fossil fuels will only happen as sprawl and the concomitant use of fossil fuels is reduced. Yet, Atlanta is one of the most sprawling and racially polarized cities in America, forcing long commutes and wasted energy. Atlanta's planned perimeter rail line and series of TODs would be a positive step toward density, if the city can overcome its racial tensions.

The agricultural economy has also changed. Large CAFOs have replaced the mom-and-pop livestock farms of the 1900s, and a growing Hispanic community works the low-paying CAFO and processing jobs. While CAFOs have become a prime economic factor in the region, they are destructive to the environment and exploit the wages and health of workers. Rather than eat ever more meat, Americans need to rethink their diet. By eating less meat, they can help preserve the environment and help workers have a healthier workplace.

Even as the New South blossoms, the legacy of the Old South—segregation, racism, and poverty—continues to hold

PHOTO 9.13. Old tobacco warehouses in Richmond, Virginia, are turned into upmarket condos.

Source: John R Short

it back from attaining a sustainable culture for all. The city of Charleston, South Carolina, is aesthetic and soothing—until you step out of the historic district and the pastel single houses fade quickly into rundown tenements.

There remain challenges to a more sustainable South. These include the following:

- poverty of the rural areas;
- environmental and health problems associated with growth of CAFOs;
- air pollution;
- coastal vulnerability to climate change; and
- racial injustice and the contentious legacy of the Confederacy.

Many people of the Atlantic South have become more aware of population's impact on the environment. Atlanta is paying attention to land use and transportation issues. Although the city is one of the most sprawling in the nation, if it achieves its targets in the sustainability plan, it will dramatically improve the quality of the environment.

Some southern states are turning to renewable energy to increase energy availability, while others lag. North Carolina—where 95 percent of the electricity is nuclear

or coal-fired—has begun to overcome the North Carolina Ridge Law, which was passed in 1983 to protect "unsightly developments" for mountaintop homes and has been a barrier to wind generation. Wind turbines have been addressed on a county-by-county basis, with some prohibiting the renewable energy because of the viewshed and others encouraging wind power.

South Carolina is attempting to implement renewable energy policies and offer financial incentives. Additionally, some developments, such as Dewee Island in South Carolina, have adopted sustainable development policies, such as building infrastructure using natural drainage and landscaping instead of traditional lawns, but problems exist. They have not developed into the self-contained communities promised, traffic snarls the outgoing highways, and they are affordable for only the wealthy, with home prices starting at $650,000. This is part of the problem with sustainable housing: it is fashionable and not considered essential; therefore, it is out of the price range for most people.

Industry has also committed to using alternative fuels. In South Carolina, J. W. Aluminum will be heating its new smelter with methane obtained from rotting trash. The forest industry in Georgia is hoping to become the "Silicon Valley of ethanol," converting tree waste to biomass.

Across the region, universities are involved in clean energy initiatives, sustainability, and going green. Both Duke and the University of North Carolina have worked to become more environmentally friendly in construction, landscaping, and water use.

The Atlantic South has developed city and even state sustainability plans showing that there are many who see the future and the possibilities for the region to find jobs, profit, and environmental health in sustainable development.

Questions for Discussion

1. Why did textile manufacturing develop in the southern Piedmont region in the late 1800s?

2. When the southern cotton mills were established, why did the owners choose to build company towns for their workers, rather than rely on private housing markets?

3. How has tobacco production changed since 2004? How has the change affected the tobacco farmer?

4. What has been the impact of poultry and hog production in the southern environment?

5. What is the Gullah language, and where and why did it develop?

6. In what ways will the designation of the Gullah Heritage Corridor preserve this culture?

7. What is the fall line, and how did it influence the development of the Atlantic South?

8. Is the fall line as important for the location of cities today as it was in the eighteenth century? Why or why not?

9. What factors influenced the location of Atlanta?

10. What do Charleston, Savannah, and the Hampton Roads areas share, and how do they differ from the rest of the coastal plain?

11. How are cities in the Atlantic South implementing sustainability?

12. What are the biggest challenges with climate change in this region?

13. What factors led to the demise of cotton in the Atlantic South?

14. Will cotton continue to be an economically viable crop as WTO talks increasingly call for a level playing field?

15. Where was cigarette manufacturing concentrated? Why?

16. Can CAFO production last in the long term?

Suggested Readings

Baird, K. "Guy B. Johnson Revisited: Another Look at Gullah." *Journal of Black Studies* 10, no. 4 (June 1980): 425–35.

Berendt, J. *Midnight in the Garden of Good and Evil: A Savannah Story.* New York: Random House, 1994.

Brown, R. H. *The Greening of Georgia: The Improvement of the Environment in the Twentieth Century.* Macon, Ga.: Mercer University Press, 2002.

Calhoun, D., E. Frick, and G. Buell. "Effects of Urban Development on Nutrient Loads and Streamflow, Upper Chattahoochee River Basin, Georgia, 1976–2001." *Proceedings of the 2003 Georgia Water Resources Conference*, April 23–24, 2003.

Carney, J. *Black Rice: The African Origins of Rice Cultivation in the Americas.* Cambridge, Mass.: Harvard University Press, 2001.

Conner, W., T. W. Doyle, and K. W. Krauss, eds. *Ecology of Tidal Freshwater Forested Wetlands of the Southeastern United States.* New York: Springer, 2007.

Conroy, P. *Prince of Tides.* Boston, Mass.: Houghton Mifflin, 1986.

Egerton, J. *The Americanization of Dixie: The Southernization of America.* New York: Harper's Magazine Press, 1974.

———. *Southern Food: At Home, on the Road, in History.* New York: Knopf, 1987.

Frey, W. H. "Census 2000 Shows Large Black Return to the South, Reinforcing the Region's 'White-Black' Demographic Profile." *PSC Research Report* no. 01-473. Ann Arbor, Mich.: Population Studies Center and Milken Institute, May 2001.

Grantham, De. W. *The Life and Death of the Solid South,* Lexington: University of Kentucky Press, 1992.

Hall, R. L. "Before NASCAR: The Corporate and Civic Promotion of Automobile Racing in the American South, 1903–1927," *Journal of Southern History* 68, no. 3 (August 2002).

Hart, J. F., and J. T. Morgan. "Spersopolis," *Southeastern Geographer* 35, no. 2 (1995): 103–17.

Hart, J. F., and E. L. Chestang. "Turmoil in Tobaccoland." *Geographical Review* 86, no. 4 (October 1996): 550–72.

Hilliard, S. "Antebellum Tidewater Rice Culture in South Carolina and Georgia." In *European Settlement and Development in North America*, edited by James R. Gibson. Toronto: University of Toronto Press, 1978.

Hinderaker, E., and P. C. Mancall. *At the Edge of Empire: The Backcountry in British North America.* Baltimore, Md.: Johns Hopkins University Press, 2003.

Lander, E. M., Jr., and R. Ackerman, eds. *Perspectives in South Carolina History: the First 300 Years.* Columbia: University of South Carolina Press, 1973.

Olwell, R. *Masters, Slaves, and Subjects: The Culture of Power in the South Carolina Low Country, 1740–1790.* Ithaca, N.Y.: Cornell University Press, 1998.

Pendergrast, M. *City on the Verge: Atlanta and the Fight for America's Urban Future.* New York: Basic Books, 2017.

Prunty, M. C., and C. S. Aiken. "The Demise of the Piedmont Cotton Region." *Annals of the Association of American Geographers* 62 (1972).

Ray, J. *Ecology of a Cracker Childhood.* Minneapolis, Minn.: Milkweed Editions, 1999.

Reed, J. S., J. Kohls, and C. Hanchette. "The Dissolution of Dixie and the Changing Shape of the South." *Social Forces* 69, no. 1 (September 1990): 221–33.

Royster, C. *The Fabulous History of the Dismal Swamp Company: A Story of George Washington's Times.* New York: Knopf, 1999.

Smith, C. Wayne, and Robert H. Dilday, eds. *Rice: Origin, History, Technology, and Production.* Hoboken, N.J.: Wiley, 2003.

Walker, H. J., and J. M. Coleman. "Atlantic and Gulf Coastal Province." In *Geomorphic Systems of North America*, edited by William L. Graf. Boulder, Colo.: Geological Society of America, 1987.

Webb, J. *Born Fighting: How the Scots-Irish Shaped America.* New York: Broadway Books, 2004.

Weyeneth, R. *Historic Preservation for a Living City: Historic Charleston Foundation, 1947–1997.* Columbia: University of South Carolina Press, 2000.

Whitehead, D. R. "Developmental and Environmental History of the Dismal Swamp." *Ecological Monographs* 42, no. 3 (1972): 301–15.

Wilkerson, I. *The Warmth of Other Suns,* New York: Random House, 2010.

Wright, G. *Old South, New South.* New York: Basic Books, 1986.

Internet Sources

Atlanta's Sustainability Plan, at https://www.atlantaga.gov/government/mayor-s-office/executive-offices/office-of-resilience/sustainability-initiatives

Charlotte's Sustainability Plan, at http://www.sustaincharlotte.org/vision

Federal Reserve Bank of Atlanta. "Carpeting on a Roll in Georgia," at https://www.frbatlanta.org/regional-economy/econsouth/econsouth-vol_8_no_4-carpeting_on_a_roll_in_georgia.aspx

Richmond's Sustainability Plan, at http://www.richmondgov.com/Sustainability/RVA_Green.aspx

The New Georgia Encyclopedia, at http://www.georgiaencyclopedia.org/nge/home.jsp

U.S. Environmental Protection Agency. Nonpoint Pollution, at https://www.epa.gov/nps

Indigo Development. "Industrial Ecology," at http://www.indigodev.com/IE.html

U.S. Department of Agriculture. *Economic Research Service.* "Types of Tobacco," at https://www.ers.usda.gov/publications/pub-details/?pubid=41167

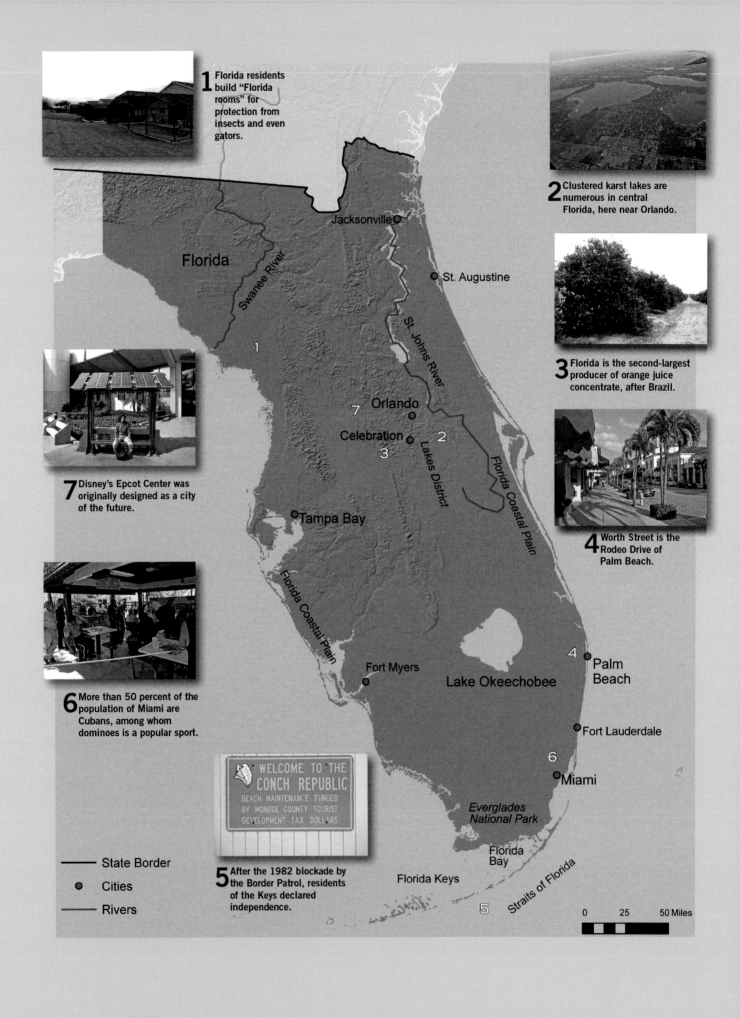

1 Florida residents build "Florida rooms" for protection from insects and even gators.

2 Clustered karst lakes are numerous in central Florida, here near Orlando.

3 Florida is the second-largest producer of orange juice concentrate, after Brazil.

4 Worth Street is the Rodeo Drive of Palm Beach.

7 Disney's Epcot Center was originally designed as a city of the future.

6 More than 50 percent of the population of Miami are Cubans, among whom dominoes is a popular sport.

WELCOME TO THE
CONCH REPUBLIC
BEACH MAINTENANCE FUNDED
BY MONROE COUNTY TOURIST
DEVELOPMENT TAX DOLLARS

5 After the 1982 blockade by the Border Patrol, residents of the Keys declared independence.

Jacksonville

Florida

Swanee River

St. Augustine

St. Johns River

1

7 Orlando

Celebration

3   Lakes District   2

Tampa Bay

Florida Coastal Plain

Florida Coastal Plain

Fort Myers

Lake Okeechobee

4   Palm Beach

Fort Lauderdale

6

Miami

Everglades National Park

Florida Bay

Florida Keys

Straits of Florida

5

—— State Border

● Cities

—— Rivers

0   25   50 Miles

10
FLORIDA
A Victim of Its Own Geography

Chapter Highlights

After reading this chapter, you should be able to:

- Discuss Florida's unique geologic history
- Distinguish the subregions and basic topography, including the shoreline and karst
- Give an overview of the state of the Everglades and list its environmental problems
- Explain Florida's population growth since the beginning of the twentieth century
- Discuss patterns of immigration in Florida
- Describe the agricultural areas of Florida and their environmental impact
- Identify Florida's major agricultural products
- Identify major urban developments in Florida
- Discuss the contributions of the three sectors to Florida's economy

Terms

artesian spring
bioswale

coquina
hammock
imagineer

mangrove
new urbanism
saw-grass

sinkhole
slough

Places

Everglades
Florida Bay

Intracoastal Waterway

The Keys

Lake Okeechobee

Cities

Gainsville
    (2016 MSA 275,000)
Miami
    (2016 MSA 5.9 million)

Jacksonville
    (2016 MSA 1.4 million)
Orlando
    (2016 MSA 2.3 million)

Tallahassee
    (2016 MSA 375,000)
Tampa
    (2016 MSA 2.9 million)

PHOTO 10.1. Everglades Marsh. At the southern tip of Florida, the fragile Everglades ecosystem has been damaged during the past century by channeling the water, by irrigation, and by levees on Lake Okeechobee. These changes have destroyed about 90 percent of the Everglades wetland habitat and endangered a large diversity of species, among them over 350 bird species. The birds pictured are snowy egrets, which were almost hunted into extinction in the late nineteenth century because of the popularity of their plumes. Other factors contributing to dwindling numbers of birds are toxic waste dumping, pesticides, dredging, and urbanization.

Introduction

Peninsular Florida is an immigrant. The Florida platform was once part of Africa, but when Pangaea rifted apart about two hundred million years ago, Florida remained attached to North America. For millions of years the peninsula rose, then returned to the water, only to emerge again.

The population, like the state, has also migrated from other cultures and continents to their new home. One out of six is a foreign-born immigrant, but many others are just seeking warmth in their retirement years. More than 90 percent of Floridians now live in the coastal counties that are vulnerable to hurricanes and sea-level rise.

Florida has been one of the fastest-growing states. Its warmth attracts northerners escaping the winter cold. Tourism has surpassed the state's original agricultural economy. As highways were built, this opened up the coasts for development as the East Coast wealthy established winter homes from Palm Beach to Boca Raton; middle-class retirees soon followed, infilling the remaining coastlines.

Florida has attempted to implement more sustainable programs to reduce carbon emissions and encourage alternative energy, but several issues stand in the way of a sustainable future: continued population growth (more than double the nation's average), the distribution of population along vulnerable coastal counties, agricultural subsidies and quotas on specialty crops, vulnerability to hurricanes, the need for clean water, and the impacts of a changing climate. All of these will be a challenge to achieving a sustainable future.

Physical Geography

The topography and formation of Florida differs from the other southern coastal regions. Florida was once geologically part of North Africa. The entire peninsula is a shallow, sediment-covered limestone shelf. Currently, the eastern edge has emerged (the continental shelf is just off the coast), while the western continental shelf is submerged for miles beyond the current coastline.

Several times during the Pleistocene, the continental shelf of Florida was exposed and the land area was twice the state's current size, but then once again the land submerged, drowning much of the state. The peninsular part of the state may submerge again as sea levels rise caused by climate change. Some computer models predict that southern Florida could be underwater by 2100. Florida's geologic structure increases its vulnerability to various natural hazards that could impact the millions of people settled in the coastal counties.

Florida is an extension of the Atlantic Coastal Plain, but its unique geology, cultures, and physical features set it apart, and it will be examined separately as the Floridian Coastal Plain, Lake District, Everglades, and Keys. Florida's subregion north of Jacksonville is part of the Sea Islands section in the Atlantic Coastal Plain chapter, and the Florida Panhandle is part of the Gulf Coastal Plain.

The Floridian Coastal Plain

Peninsular Florida extends east to west across sand-covered limestone strata. The elevation averages less than one hundred feet above sea level. Water is plentiful, with a profusion of karst topography (map 10.1). A karst landscape is formed when

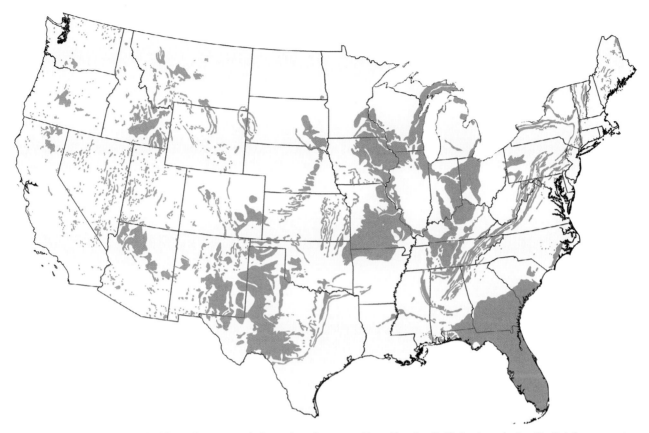

MAP 10.1. Karst Coverage of the United States. Karst topography forms when rainwater combines with carbon dioxide forming carbonic acid, which flows over and through limestone fractures, dissolving the rock and creating caves, springs, and sinkholes.

slightly acidic groundwater dissolves limestone and creates caves, spring, cavities, and **sinkholes**.

Most of the southern Florida residents live along the Gold Coast ridge in Miami, Fort Lauderdale, and Palm Beach. South of Miami at Florida City, the ridge disappears into the Everglades. The Gold Coast ridge is built on a solid rock foundation. The land is a bit higher than the surrounding area and benefits from warmer water and air, because the warm Florida Current sweeps up from the Caribbean, past the Keys, and along the southern coast. Flatwoods, cypress swamps, tidal salt-marshes, and **mangrove** forests dominate the southern landscape. A string of barrier islands and sand bars protects the east coast, while western coast bays and inlets, the largest being Tampa Bay, provide protection from the open sea.

The Lake District

The central region surrounding the Orlando metropolitan area is sandy with undulating dunes and an underlying karst terrain. Water courses through and dissolves the limestone into a system of channels and pockets that allow rainwater to recharge the Floridian Aquifer, the largest aquifer in the southeast, which supplies water to cities from Savannah, Georgia, to Orlando.

The Lake District vegetation of interior grasslands, flatwoods, and coastal pine forest abound with native animals such as the endangered Florida panther and the once endangered but now recovered American alligator. Today, the landscape consists of agriculture, pasture for grazing, and the Orlando Disney complex.

The Everglades

The last of Florida's land to emerge from the sea was the flat Everglades, barely above sea level (photo 10.1) The natural Everglades was not quite land and not quite water, but a soggy amalgamation of the two. At one time, it covered almost one-fifth of Florida. The subtropical Everglades originally extended from Kissimmee south, but during the twentieth century humans drained much of the swamp (map 10.2). The Everglades swamp was a quicksand-like river of sharp, serrated **saw-grass** on a mattress of peat and muddy sediment with little topographic or vegetative relief. Then human activities altered the landscape. For example, cattails have replaced the saw-grass due to the phosphorus-rich pollution near Lake Okeechobee, where toxic chemicals have altered the fisheries and wildlife. A few inland trees grow on isolated **hammocks**—small tree islands rising a few feet above the ridges. Enveloping the coastal areas are saltwater cypress and mangrove swamps. The landscape is distinctive: inhabited by a seemingly infinite variety of insects, reptiles, and rodents, and quiet except for the occasional wildlife screech or howl.

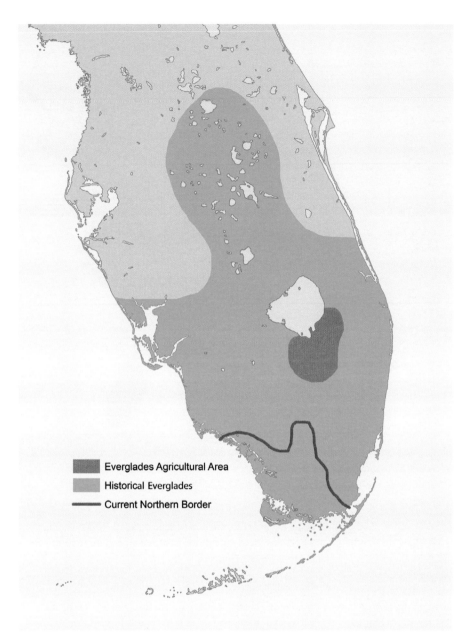

Everglades Agricultural Area
Historical Everglades
Current Northern Border

MAP 10.2. The Everglades Ecosystem. Historically, this ecosystem and water flow originated in the Lakes District near Orlando. Today the system is managed to service the Okeechobee agricultural district (shown in brown). The national park at the southern tip of the state is only a remnant of the once vast Everglades ecosystem.

The Everglades were designated as federal land when Florida achieved statehood in 1845. A few years later, Congress decided there was no economic value in the swamplands and granted the state the Everglades in 1850. The state then began to drain the Everglades swamps near Lake Okeechobee. The draining destroyed ecosystems, but it also created a fertile cropland that reduced US dependence on tropical crops from the West Indies.

Sloughs (stagnant swamps), muck, and hammocks saturate the land between the parallel, low ridges of the Everglades. Historically, Lake Okeechobee, which lies slightly below sea level, regularly overflowed its southern banks and inundated the Everglades. Because the land is flat from Okeechobee to Florida Bay, a shallow sheet of water drained the entire landscape, a natural process that replenished the Everglades waters. But during the 1920s, two hurricanes flooded the land and killed two

thousand people. Protective dikes, levees, and canals were then built around Lake Okeechobee. By the 1950s, extensive levees and canals had drained the land south of Lake Okeechobee, and 65 percent of the Everglades had been converted into sugarcane fields. Converting the land to agriculture nearly destroyed the remaining Everglades biome.

The Ten Thousand Islands southwestern coast is a brackish-water mangrove and cypress swamp. The mangrove grows in salt water and protects shorelines from storm, wave, wind, and flood hazards, and it is valuable as rookeries for crustaceans and fish. Mangroves provide homes for endangered and threatened species, such as the green and loggerhead sea turtles, the American crocodile, and West Indian Manatee.

The islands are part of the Everglades National Park today, but park regulations limiting fire have decreased ecosystem

BOX 10.1   EVERGLADES NATIONAL PARK: THE THREAT OF INVASIVE SPECIES

Everglades National Park was established in 1947 to conserve the natural landscape and prevent further degradation of its land, plants, and animals. The designation of Everglades National Park marked an important shift in the way we designate national parks. The Everglades topography did not suggest drama or splendor or the "scenic views" the way Yosemite, Yellowstone, or the Grand Canyon does. Instead, an emerging field of science, called ecology, led conservationists to argue that the Everglades was worthy of inclusion in the system because of its unique and fragile ecology. The Everglades was the first national park to be based on a conservationist ideology to protect and preserve an ecosystem.

One of the biggest challenges to protecting this distinctive ecosystem is invasive species, plants and animals. In recent years, the nonnative melalueca tree and snakes from around the world have been found in and around the national park. The snakes were most likely either pets that had been accidentally or intentionally released into the wild. The most notorious is the Burmese python which can grow to about 17 feet long and weigh up to 150 pounds. These snakes have no natural predators to control their population and are indiscriminate eaters. There could be thousands of snakes in the park.

Nonnative Burmese pythons now occupy a wide variety of habitats in the park, including uplands, freshwater wetlands, and the saline coastal fringe. These snakes compete directly with other top predators such as the American alligator, and in some instances, very large pythons have been recorded eating alligators. Predation from the python is already changing the delicate balance of the national park's food chain. Twenty-five different bird species, including the endangered wood stork, have been found in the digestive tracts of pythons in Everglades National Park. Scientists report that pythons have hunted the native marsh rabbits to near extinction.

The Nature Conservancy responded by creating "Python Patrol," to train and organize snake spotters and responders. Anyone who sees a python or other nonnative animal should take a photo from a safe distance and report it on the hotline, the free IveGot1 app or at IveGot1.org. Other efforts to control the python population include legalized python-hunting competitions, where hunters are paid for each python they kill. In 2017, for example, ten pythons were captured and killed in less than two weeks in Florida.

PHOTO 10.2. A National Park service ranger holds a captured Burmese python.
Source: National Park Service

productivity. The mangrove swamps and saw-grass marshes along the edges are no longer burned annually to renew nutrients. Today, regulations against burning have created deep and matted saw-grass that has reduced wildlife habitat and feeding grounds.

During the twentieth century, the Everglades were intensely modified and hydrologically and ecologically degraded. Most of southern Florida is now drained, and only the southern tip—a mere 7 percent remnant of the Everglades system—remains a swamp.

One of the major alterations in the Everglades system was the diking of Lake Okeechobee after severe floods in the 1920s. A twenty-foot-high dike surrounds the shallow lake to protect the people, but it has also endangered the complex ecosystem and waterway relations. Pesticide-laced runoff from agriculture settle at the bottom of the lake; arsenic has also been found.

Although the agricultural potential of the Everglades was recognized in 1848, draining did not begin until 1907. By World War II, more than four hundred miles of canals dissected the Everglades, and by the 1960s, over seven hundred thousand acres had been drained.

The Everglades ecosystem is now endangered because Lake Okeechobee levees halt the natural flooding that renourished it. Habitats have been destroyed, invasive species abound, saltwater intrusion inundates freshwater, and polluted runoff contaminates drinking water supplies. The human impact on the land has been immense. Environmental challenges include the following:

- The ridge and slough low-lying relief has become more uniform, and water no longer has a directional flow.
- Fishery and rookery have experienced losses as sloughs fill in with saw-grass and hammocks.
- Construction of canals, highways, and flood-control channels has affected water flow.
- Competition for freshwater has risen, as urban development, tourism, and agriculture deplete the Everglades to less than 50 percent of its previous flow.

- Chemicals from agricultural areas have degraded the ecosystem.
- Lake Okeechobee has experienced eutrophication from dairy and agricultural runoff.
- Invasive species, such as the melaleuca tree and former "pet" Burmese pythons, have proliferated.

The largest ecological restoration project in the history of the United States—the Comprehensive Everglades Restoration Plan (CERP)—began in 2000, incorporating wetland science, ecosystem modeling, and restoration ecology. Goals of the multi-billion-dollar, thirty-year restoration project are to

- increase water flow;
- increase water-storage capacity;
- improve water quality;
- improve water deliveries to maintain estuary health; and
- improve system connectivity by removing some infrastructure, such as canals.

However, the goal is not to restore the Everglades to its former water regime, but to find compromises between the divergent Everglades interests: urban land planners seeking fresh water to support the growing population, environmentalists advocating ecological restoration, and agricultural users wanting to continue growing crops on the drained areas around Lake Okeechobee (map 10.3). To date, only modest progress has

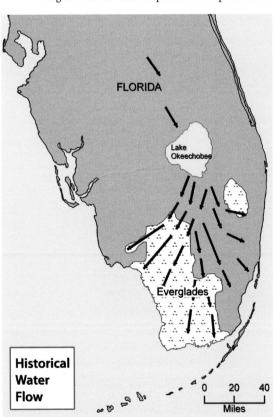

MAP 10.3. Everglades Historical and Current Water Flow.
Source: Remote Sensing Tutor, "The Everglades: America's Most Threatened Ecosystem," at http://rst.gsfc.nasa.gov/Sect3/Sect3_8.html1

been made, notably in the Kissimmee River north of Lake Okeechobee, as well as in restored waterflow in the Picayune Strand area in the southwest corner of the Everglades system.

Florida Bay–Everglades Estuary

Florida Bay, wedged between the southern tip of Florida and the Keys, is the largest estuary in the state. The shallow bay's low tides expose muddy, grassy flats, which act as a rookery and feeding area, as well as a home to dolphins, manatees, American crocodiles, and an array of other aquatic species.

The bay was known for its clear, warm waters until the 1980s, when the ecology changed: The water became turbid, sea grass died, algae blooms proliferated, and aquatic life—shellfish, sponges, pink shrimp—were decimated. The estuary—at the bay and Everglades boundary—is considered extremely sensitive to salinity, nutrients, and freshwater changes. Studies have revealed that the saline content had changed considerably since the 1900s.

Human activity and changes in the natural environment can account for salinity level variances. The interrelations between irrigation canal construction, climate change, and perhaps El Niño events are not entirely understood. Human activities alone are not responsible for environmental change; other causal agents play a role, and researchers are still uncovering the complex science of these processes.

The Keys

The only living coral reef ecosystem in North America is the seventeen-hundred-island Florida Keys archipelago, which curves 150 miles into the Gulf of Mexico. Separating the Gulf from the Atlantic Ocean, the Keys are a series of flat, coral, and limestone islands—the highest point on the Keys is only eighteen feet above sea level. The Keys are represented as a tropical zone; however, the low-lying Keys are too flat to effect airflow rains and are in fact desert islands. Imported water has transformed them to their present, faux-tropical state.

Coral reefs grow slowly, about sixteen feet every thousand years, and are protected from harvesting or even touching, although every year boaters inadvertently damage them, especially when anchoring. Millions of tiny coral polyps form a protective coastal breakwater, which provides shelter and breeding sites for plants, animals, and other organisms. The coral are also important sources of food and reduce wave energy, thereby protecting beaches from erosion. But coral reefs are threatened by habitat destruction, unsustainable fishing, invasive species, and climate change. Coral, which is susceptible to warmer ocean temperatures and pollution, has weakened and become more vulnerable to diseases.

A recent study looked at 240-year-old maps of Florida and its coastline. Between 1773 and 1775, a surveyor with the British Admiralty made maps with the coastline, sea turtle nests, and the corals he saw. The study compared these old maps with present-day satellite imagery and found that half of the reefs recorded in the 1770s are missing from the satellite data, indicating that the coral loss is worse than was thought. A few

possible explanations for the disappearance of the corals involve human activity. Building the causeway through the Keys and dredging the Key West harbor impacted the corals, as did changing the way fresh water flows through the Everglades.

Like a string of pearls, the Overseas Highway connects the islands to the mainland. The islands are, however, vulnerable to hurricanes, which can cut them off from the mainland, disrupt water supply water, and cause coastal erosion.

Water

Florida has plenty of freshwater, but draining the wetlands, lowering water tables, and overconsumption have caused water shortages. In southern Florida, per capita water use is about 50 percent above the national average and unsustainable.

Freshwater supply has become such an issue that the city of Tampa Bay built the nation's largest water desalination plant. Seawater coming into the plant goes through a treatment process that separates freshwater from the seawater using reverse osmosis. Currently, the desal plant supplies 25 million gallons per day of drinking water to the region, about 10 percent of the drinking water supply. Desalinization reduces the stress on Tampa's aquifers and is touted as a "drought proof" water supply. However, the plant requires fossil fuel energy consumption, emitting yet more carbon dioxide. In addition, the plant must constantly monitor the salinity concentration of the discharge of water back to the Bay to prevent harm to fisheries and the aquatic habitat. The plant collects thousands of samples daily near the desalination facility to test for salinity changes in Tampa Bay. So far, reports show there have been no noticeable increases in salinity.

Subsurface Water Features

The karst topography is characterized by subsurface drainage, high water table, **artesian springs**, and many sinkhole depressions—Florida has more sinkholes than any other state. Sinkholes form when the roof of a cavern or cave dissolves and collapses. Sinkholes are both naturally formed and human induced. Natural sinkholes are formed in one of three ways: subsidence, solution, or the most common type in Florida, collapse of a limestone layer above a cavity. Human-induced sinkholes are the result of overpumping groundwater or drilling new water wells.

Artesian springs are formed when pressurized groundwater is released through faults from a confined aquifer. Fully one-quarter of US artesian wells and springs (seven hundred springs) are in Florida. Silver Springs is the largest, discharging about five hundred million gallons daily. The artesian springs are crucial to the freshwater supply, and yet the flow is declining in many and a few have stopped flowing altogether. Reasons for the decline include consumption through drawdown, increased nitrates due to agriculture and urbanization, and the destruction of ecosystems by such modifications as dams. Water conservation, reduced nitrogen fertilizer use, and improved wastewater are needed to protect springs in the future.

Intracoastal Waterway

The Atlantic and Gulf Coasts are connected by the three-thousand-mile Maine to Mexico Intracoastal Waterway, which consists of natural and human-made features. The sandbar barrier islands along the eastern coast separate the mainland from the ocean. Between the barrier islands and the mainland, the Intracoastal Water Project connects a series of lagoons as one long, safe navigation canal between Jacksonville and Miami. Recreational boaters and barges hauling commercial products use the waterway. Along the route, several inlets enter the waterway.

Dredging

Beaches erode and coastlines are dynamic. Migration and recession of sands are part of the natural cycle of coastal environments. Although some question why people would build houses on shifting sands, beaches are popular building sites and the most expensive properties in the state. The dense and growing population along Florida beaches has encouraged dredge and fill operations to create land for development. Maintaining the artificial beaches protects expensive oceanfront properties, but costs taxpayers millions of dollars. It is also a short-term fix: beach renourishment does not stop the natural process of erosion. Experts now report that beach erosion has accelerated due to sea-level rise, caused by climate change.

Many sandy beaches are continually rebuilt from dredged sand (photo 10.3). The dredged sand is discharged through a pipeline and then bulldozed across the beach. However, this process has the unintended consequence of destroying marine habitats and coral reefs. Dredging is an unsustainable practice because the dredged fill is not truly "sand" but strip-mined offshore mud and fossil fragments that destroy the continental shelf fish habitat and biomass. Both the act of dredging and the mud destroy the local habitat.

Siltation and the indirect effects of renourishment have buried reefs along Miami Beach. Continued vacuuming of fill material from twenty to fifty feet deep in the ocean has disturbed many organisms—shrimp, crabs, mollusks, juvenile fish, and sea grasses—along the ocean bottom, which in turn affects game fish habitats. The fill leads to additional and unintentional environmental problems, including the possible collapse of the marine and coastal ecosystems. In addition, sediments stirred up by renourishment are structurally different from fine quartz sand and easily migrate into the surf, turning the water milky, halting photosynthesis, interfering with the feeding process of fish, and obscuring the habitat and reefs, thereby destroying scuba diving and fishing.

In some Florida communities, "beach armor" seawalls were built, especially in places where buildings are too close to the shore. Where sand is insufficient to protect the shoreline, a grid or a seawall is formed and filled in with boulders to protect it from erosion. But seawalls accelerate the natural process of erosion of natural beaches. These negative impacts have led some states including states Oregon, North Carolina, South Carolina, Maine, and Rhode Island to prohibit seawalls.

Every year, the Army Corps of Engineers spends millions of taxpayer dollars to renourish Atlantic beaches. Several other techno fixes such as artificial reefs, jetties, and sand-trapping systems have been used to save beaches, but all are short-term and ultimately cause more erosion. Eventually, artificial measures—dredging, seawalls, and other systems may prove to be too expensive, too environmentally damaging, and too politically problematic.

PHOTO 10.3. Dredging at Palm Beach, Florida. The shoreline is often protected by artificial means. Dredging and placing boulders to protect the shoreline from erosion is a common site. However, dredging costs taxpayers millions each year.

BOX 10.2 GEOSPATIAL TECHNOLOGIES: TRACKING HURRICANES

The National Hurricane Center (NHC), a division of the US National Weather Service, is responsible for tracking and reporting on hurricanes, and is based in Miami, Florida.

Hurricanes that form in the South Atlantic follow a track moving westwards often hitting islands in the Caribbean before causing damage to the coast of the eastern US. A website maintained by the NHC tracks hurricanes in real time and makes predictions about future events. Map 10.4, for example, plots the likely arrival time of tropical storm force winds associated with Hurricane Irma in in Florida and the surrounding region September 2017.

Website: http://www.nws.noaa.gov/gis/

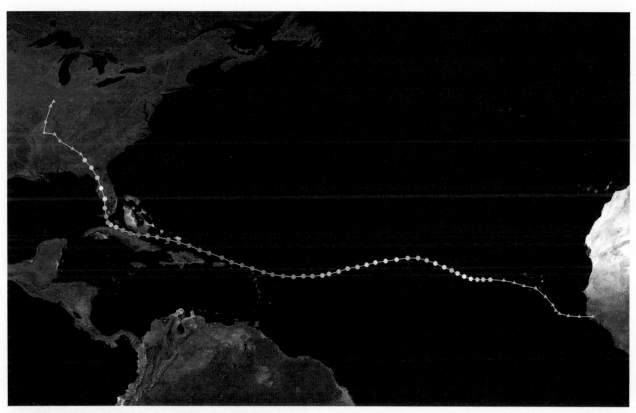

MAP 10.4. Tracking Hurricane Irma's arrival in 2017.
Source: NOAA

Climate

Florida is unique climatically, agriculturally, and geologically. The almost tropical "Caribbean light" peninsula weather is a transition zone between the Caribbean and the temperate mainland. The climate has affected the crops, cities, vegetation, soil, and, of course, the people.

Florida has benefited agriculturally from its subtropical location and accompanying temperatures. The three-hundred-day growing season supports year-round citrus and vegetable production, although occasional frosts threaten crops. Annual rainfall is fifty to sixty inches a year, and along the west coast of Florida, thunderstorms are more frequent than anywhere else in the United States. Rain can fall in any season but favors the hot and humid summer and autumn. Southern Florida has many bright, warm, and dry days during winter and spring, which supports a winter playground with temperatures regularly in the seventies and eighties, while Northern and central Florida winters are cooler and receive more precipitation.

The Gulf Coast atmospheric pressure patterns affect the southern Florida wet season (May through September). The Bermuda high-pressure system shifts annually, sometimes resulting in drought. Decreasing temperatures in winter and spring and the Pacific-based El Niño affect Florida, bringing more wet days but fewer hurricanes, the state's big atmospheric pressure story.

BOX 10.3 CLIMATE CHANGE IN MIAMI

Recent studies have shown that Florida has more residents at risk from climate change any other US state because much of the state is at or near sea level. Climate change impacts may include salt water intrusion into fresh water supply, coastal erosion, and increased frequency of storms and flooding. A recent study by the Army Corps of Engineers found that Miami-Dade County will need roughly twenty million cubic yards of sand (or the equivalent of over ten thousand football fields covered in one foot of sand) over the next fifty years just to maintain its beaches.

Predictions for increased sea levels mean that many of the most affluent neighborhoods may see increased flooding. Florida's drainage systems and seawalls are no longer sufficient to hold back the water and $70 billion worth of property is at risk of flooding over the next fifteen years.

Already, Miami experiences regular episodes of high tides that bring in a foot or more of water inundating streets, parking lots, and basements. Florida State Road A1A runs the entire length of Florida along the ocean, and it too has had increased flooding, even during sunny weather. Flooding also challenges the basic infrastructure that residents depend on every day, from septic tanks to wells.

Although the Florida governor refuses to acknowledge that climate change even exists, a recent poll showed that 80 percent of Maimians want to see the city take action on climate change. Miami Beach mayor Philip Levine filmed a campaign commercial in a kayak on the city streets, betting that being aggressive on climate change would help him get elected. He was right. The city of Miami has begun to implement a multi-pronged Climate Action Plan, placing it at the forefront of climate adaptation efforts. The $400 million Sea-Level Rise Plan consists of a series of storm water pumps, improved drainage systems, elevated roads, and higher seawalls. Currently, the city is raising one hundred miles of roads by two feet, and the new wastewater treatment plant was constructed five feet higher than initial plans (photo 10.4). The city is also installing eighty storm-water pump stations and is actively planting trees and vegetation to absorb flood waters. Along the way, these new roads, bridges, and other infrastructure are not only making Miami more resilient but are also creating jobs.

Still, these are short-term fixes. It is likely that in another twenty years the city will have to rebuild and rethink development. Critics also note that the city's poor—who do not live near the low-lying areas—are paying higher water bills to cover the costs of infrastructure upgrades. As the city spends millions in affluent neighborhoods, some contend that Miami may also experience "climate gentrification," as developers buy up property in areas of higher elevation, pricing out existing lower-income residents.

PHOTO 10.4. The city of Miami Beach has been raising the height of roads to reduce the damage done by periodic flooding.
Source: John R Short

Hurricanes

The northern hemisphere hurricane season extends from June through November, with the prime months being August and September. Hurricanes are violent storms that circulate rain and wind (more than sixty-four knots, or seventy-three miles per hour) and move heat from the tropics to cooler areas.

Florida is annually in the path of at least one hurricane, if not several. In southern Florida, hurricanes have struck on average once every 5.5 years and have caused extensive flooding, loss of property, and loss of beaches (table 10.1). The storm damage losses are a tax burden placed on the entire population of the United States. If Florida were to get a direct hit from a Category 4 or Category 5 hurricane, the damage could be significant and widespread. Today, the cost of homeowners' insurance to live in the hurricane-prone state is the highest in the US. Floridians pay almost twice what other states pay for insurance coverage to cover hurricanes, floods, tornados, and sinkholes.

TABLE 10.1. Hurricanes in Florida since 2005

Year	Hurricane Name	Category	Impacts and Damages
2005	Dennis	3	$1.5 billion
2005	Wilma	3	$20.6 billion; 98% of state without power
2008	Ike	2	Minor damages
2008	Dolly	1	Significant beach erosion at four beaches
2008	Gustav	4	Four drowned
2009	Bill	1	Minor damages
2012	Issac	1	Minor damages
2012	Sandy	2	Minor damages
2014	Arthur	2	Minor damages
2016	Hermine	1	Flooding in several counties
2016	Matthew	2	Twelve killed
2017	Irma	2	Eighty-two people killed in storm-related incidents; heavy damage to the Keys

Historical Geography and Settlement

Native Americans

Indigenous nomads roamed Florida at least since 7500 BCE, although little else is known about them. At the time of European encroachment, the Timucua lived in western Florida, the Apalachee in the Tallahassee Hills, the Calusa in southwestern Florida, and several smaller bands along the eastern coast. The early indigenous preferred the narrow coastal zone for settlement, as the Everglades was a mosquito-infested swamp that appeared uninhabitable.

The tribe most associated with Florida, the Seminoles, did not arrive until the early 1700s. The Seminoles were initially hunters and developed into farmers, but fear of slavery and attacks by whites led them to a half century of Seminole Wars, which resulted in the 1835 removal of many Seminoles to Indian Territory in Oklahoma. About three hundred Seminoles remained in the Everglades; however, they had to fight to maintain land because of settlers' claims. The Seminole descendants now live on reservations, and the tribe is officially recognized, allowing them certain rights. Their former sustainable hunting-and-gathering way of life disappeared with fixed land ownership, so the Seminoles have pursued alternative incomes. Some Seminoles have chosen to use their reservation lands to help preserve their culture; others derive income from gaming, tourism, land leases, and various agricultural pursuits.

Europeans

The Spanish were the first Europeans to establish a permanent settlement in what is now the United States; however, they were more concerned with seeking gold and riches than settling. Their methods of exploration were often brutal and alienated native tribes, making the few settlers uneasy occupants.

The Spanish started exploring the Florida coast in 1513, but by 1561 they were losing interest. A year later, French Huguenots claimed and established a short-lived settlement, but they were routed in 1565 when the Spanish renewed their interest and established St. Augustine.

Settlement remained uneasy, and over time was governed by a succession of three countries. From the end of the French and Indian War (1763) until the first decades of the nineteenth century, Florida was governed by Spain, France, or England. In 1819, Spain ceded Florida to the United States.

Although the peninsula was sparsely populated, the Americans found the French, Spanish, and American land claims difficult to unravel and divisive. Many Spanish settlers chose to abandon and burn their homes rather than leave them to the American settlers. From 1821 to 1845, when Florida gained statehood, political maneuvers among the Americans led to establishing Florida's northern counties as an "Old South," slave-holding, cotton plantation economy. Peninsular Florida was not as lucrative agriculturally, and few settled there.

Americans built forts to protect settlers and to establish their claim to the land. Former fort sites are today's cities—Miami (Fort Dallas), Tampa (Fort Brooke), Fort Lauderdale, and Fort Myers. Natives retreated into the Everglades, but sporadically attacked against invading settlers and American forces. Even after the Seminole threat was removed, Florida remained the least populated state east of the Mississippi. Soon after the Civil War, railroad barons seeking a warm retreat from the cold eastern winters were attracted to the area and the economy and population grew when speculators dredged the peninsula swamplands and imported citrus, agriculture, and cattle.

Florida's popularity began with dreams and speculators, such as Henry Flagler and Henry Plant. Flagler, a Rockefeller partner in Standard Oil, launched Florida tourism by bringing the railroad down the east coast and in 1902 building his house

PHOTO 10.5. Whitehall, Palm Beach, Florida. Built in 1902, Whitehall was Henry Flagler's winter home. Flagler was instrumental in establishing Florida's agricultural and tourist industries. He built the Florida East Coast Railway and hotels to accommodate tourists.

on the barrier island of Palm Beach (photo 10.5). He eventually continued the railroad to Miami, and then over islands and water to Key West. On the west coast, Henry Plant promoted his South Florida Railroad and eight hotels, beginning with the Tampa Bay Hotel in 1891. Both Flagler and Plant were zealous promoters of their vision for Florida, and the coastal populations grew. In the decade from 1900 to 1910, southeast Florida's population quadrupled to seventy thousand.

The rail lines exported the state's agricultural and resource largess—citrus, sugar, cattle, and phosphates—and imported tourists. The swampland was drained, and farmers immigrated, lured by reports of a frost-free, year-round crop. In the 1920s, the Lake Okeechobee area commenced draining, settling, and cultivating winter crops for the northern states.

During the early 1920s, automobiles transported middle-class Americans to the first Florida land boom. Land sales of empty lots and speculative developments prospered, and many chose to move and enjoy the "Florida lifestyle." The Gold Coast—Hollywood, Coral Gables, and Boca Raton—was developed along the southeastern shoreline counties. Since then, there has been a steady increase in population growth and urban development.

Cultural Perspectives

Coquina

Along the barrier islands between Jacksonville and Lake Okeechobee, the coastline has a soft, coastal rock called **coquina,** composed of shells and limestone from marine reefs. The material is soft in the ground, but it hardens when exposed to the open air; it makes an excellent local and common vernacular building material that was used in colonial foundations and chimneys and industrial structures, such as sugar mills.

The Spanish and British used coquina, such as the still-standing Castillo de San Marcos built in 1695 in St. Augustine (photo 10.6); however, many buildings were deserted during the upheavals of the eighteenth and nineteenth centuries, and few were preserved. Those surviving the period were often destroyed intentionally when modern styles were built. During the Depression, the Conservation Construction Corps built a few coquina structures in Daytona Beach.

The Conch Republic (The Florida Keys)

The Conch Republic was proclaimed on April 23, 1982, when a border patrol blockade cut the Keys off from the rest of the United States, while agents searched for locally problematic illegal immigrants and drugs. Many residents now claim to be both Conch Republic and US citizens, and celebrate their annual Independence Day.

Florida Keys residents have been independent and individualistic since they started to populate the *cayos* (*keys* is a corruption of this Spanish term for small island). Some colonial residents prospered by living off the shipwrecks along the treacherous coastline. But this too changed. By the early 1930s, enticed by the Caribbean-like climate, an intellectual crowd led by Ernest Hemingway settled in Key West, then the largest city in Florida. The few natives of the Keys were called Conches, named for the tasty local seafood housed in large seashells found along Caribbean coastlines.

The laid-back culture has attracted many to the Keys. Within the past forty years, the population of the Keys doubled, and more than three million tourists visit the islands annually. An environmental impact of the increased population on the Keys

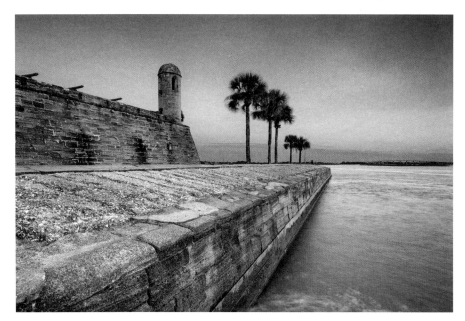

PHOTO 10.6. The Castillo de San Marcos in St. Augustine, Florida.

Source: iStock/SeanPavonePhoto

PHOTO 10.7. Florida Keys. Highway 1 leads to the main street shopping area and attracts tourists who come by ferry boats, cruise ships, and airplanes.

Source: John R Short

identified water pollution due to the reliance on septic systems, which was a poor choice for waste management on porous limestone. Beach closures due to fecal microbe contamination have become a regular part of the Keys' waterways.

As population has grown, and the Keys are a major tourist destination, they have the highest median house price in Florida and are one of the most expensive areas to live in the United States. High living expenses have forced many locals out. The commercial area has also changed from one of individual quirky shops to national chains, and visual pollution along Highway 1 now threatens the once unique cultural landscape (photo 10.7).

Population, Immigration, and Diversity

Florida's population changed dramatically during the twentieth century, from just over a half million residents in 1900 to five million in 1960 to twenty-one million in 2016. Today, Florida is the third most populous state and continues to grow at one of the fastest rates in the United States. Florida is also highly urbanized (over 85 percent) and contains six of twenty fastest-growing cities in the nation including the Villages (a retirement community), Cape Coral, Naples, Orlando, North Port, and Panama City. About 90 percent of Florida's population lives in Florida's coastal counties, which are among the fastest-growing counties in America.

Population

The most recent racial and ethnic breakdown for the entire state of Florida is

- 55 percent white;
- 25 percent Hispanic;
- 17 percent black;
- 2.8 percent Asian; and
- 0.5 percent Native American.

TABLE 10.2. Florida Residents' Background

Residents	Miami-Dade County	Florida
Percentage of foreign-born residents	52	20
Percentage of residents of Hispanic or Latino origin	67	25
Percentage of languages other than English spoken at home	73	28

Source: US Census Bureau, 2016

PHOTO 10.8. A Row of Golf Carts in the Villages. The Villages, located in Sumter County, is a master planned retirement community of approximately 160,000 residents. More than 98 percent of the population is white and it is known as a conservative community that is a popular election stop for conservative candidates. It is also home to two dozen golf courses, and many residents in The Villages use golf carts to travel around the community.
Source: Lisa Benton-Short

The state's minority populations surged, led by an increase in Hispanics and blacks. While the white population has continued to increase, it is at a much slower pace than in the past decade.

Florida is well known for two demographic groups: Cubans and retirees. Cubans have settled throughout the state but are most concentrated in Miami, which has the state's highest percentage (52 percent) of foreign-born residents. Two-thirds of all Cubans living in America live in Florida, and three-quarters of Cubans in Florida live in Miami-Dade County (table 10.2). Thirty-four percent of Miami's population is Cuban immigrants. The median age of Miami's Cuban population is fifty-five, while the median age in Miami is thirty-nine. The Cubans did not assimilate into Miami but acculturated, remaking the city in their own image.

Historically, Cubans arrived en masse after Fidel Castro overthrew the US-backed Cuban government in 1959; an additional flood of immigrants arrived after Cuba lost the support of the defunct Soviet Union in 1992. For decades after, the United States imposed a Cuban travel and trade moratorium, which eased somewhat in 2009 when restrictions were removed for Cuban Americans on family visits and remittances. After more than fifty years of estrangement, the Obama administration renewed relations with Cuba in 2014, allowing travel for business and tourism for any American. In 2015, commercial US flights and cruise ships began crossing the ninety miles separating the two countries.

Gray Florida

While many imagine Florida to be colored "neon pink and turquoise," its real color is gray. A significant demographic group in Florida is retired US citizens. Overall, 20 percent of the Sunshine State's population is sixty-five years and older, the highest percentage in the nation. Many counties have an above-average share of people sixty-five years when compared to the US average of 14 percent; in three counties, this exceeds 30 percent, and in Sumter County, west of Orlando, more than 53 percent of the population is over sixty-five.

The retired population has affected and will continue to affect the south Florida environment because their living pattern needs—housing, transportation, recreation, and health care—differ from those of the rest of the population. Retirees have developed their own style of urban sprawl, both in rings around the major cities and in thousands of hurricane-vulnerable mobile home parks. Developers have also designed numerous master-planned retirement communities such as the Villages, in Sumter County, one of the fastest growing areas in the state (photo 10.8).

BOX 10.4 BEST PRACTICES IN URBAN SUSTAINABILITY: BIOSWALES AND GREEN INFRASTRUCTURE

In many cities, an inch or two of rain will exceed the ability of the city's wastewater treatment plant to process the storm water. Some cities have responded to this problem by building conventional infrastructure such as inflatable dams, underground sewage storage tanks, and storm relief sewers. These are often refereed to as "gray infrastructure," and they can be expensive. However, the best sustainability practices emphasize green infrastructure or low impact development. The objective of low impact development is to capture and treat rainwater where it falls to reduce pollution in urban watersheds. This is particularly important in Tampa, where untreated rainwater ends up in the Bay.

The city of Tampa has incorporated green infrastructure into its sustainability plan as a way to capture stormwater runoff on streets, in parks and around public buildings. Green infrastructure can include **bioswales**, rain barrels, permeable pavement, and green roofs. A bioswale or vegetated swale is a form of bioretention used to absorb water during rains and flooding and

to convey stormwater away from critical infrastructure. Bioswales capture and hold onto a small volume of water, allowing more time for the water to infiltrate soil or recharge groundwater supplies. Plants also filter out debris and pollutants from the water providing initial treatment. They are often used as an alternative to traditional stormwater piping systems. Many bioswales are integrated into parking lot and road medians or integrated into existing ditches.

Bioswales offer multiple benefits. In addition to reducing the total volume of stormwater runoff into the Bay, and allowing groundwater to recharge, bioswales improve biodiversity and increase urban vegetation. So installing green infrastructure can improve issues around water quality and urban forests. Bioswales are also are relatively inexpensive, especially compared to traditional curb and gutter systems. And perhaps best of all, green infrastructure like bioswales keeps rainwater out of the sewer system to begin with, as opposed to implementing more expensive and high tech sewage treatment mechanisms.

Urban Trends

Florida's cities have experienced several growth spurts during the twentieth century. In recent decades, Florida has been home to some of the fastest-growing cities in the United States, spurred in part by retiring baby boomers. Miami-Dade County is expected to double its current population (2.5 million) by 2050, although many current occupants are against further growth.

Since 2000, Florida has promoted smart growth. Smart growth includes neighborhood revitalization, open space preservation, efficient transportation, and matching school density to population density. Smart growth initiatives have since been adopted by many cities and groups within the state. Despite smart growth initiatives, reports still predict a future Florida with massive development, doubled population, and loss of habitat for wildlife.

Tallahassee
(2016 MSA 375,000)

Tallahassee has served as the state capital since 1824 and is the largest city in Northwest Florida. Historically, Tallahassee was in the center of the Cotton Belt and was integral to the slave trade in Florida.

Toady, the city is home to Florida State University and Florida A&M, a historically black university. In addition to education, the city's economy is based on its large number of law firms, lobbying organizations, trade associations, and

professional associations. With its rolling hills and canopied roads of moss-draped oaks, Tallahassee is often considered more "Southern" and is discussed in the Gulf Coastal Plains (chapter 11).

Tampa
(2016 MSA 2.9 million)

In 1824, Tampa was a military trading post. Tampa grew in the 1850s with the Cuban cattle trade and cigar-making. According to scholar Richard Ingalls, during the mid-nineteenth century, Tampa was a Wild West frontier town ruled by a rough breed of gamblers and misfit vigilantes practicing a lynch-happy form of justice. The Wild West attitude continued in Tampa until the 1930s.

Today, Tampa's metropolitan complex, including Clearwater and St. Petersburg, is second in population to the Miami metro area. The economy revolves around tourism, health care, finance, insurance, technology, construction, and resources, such as phosphate and fisheries. An active shipping port serves Central America and the Panama Canal.

Jacksonville
(2016 MSA 1.4 million)

Located at the mouth of the St. Johns River in northeast Florida, Jacksonville is the state's largest city and fourth-largest metro area. It includes within its borders St. Augustine, the oldest permanent settlement in America. Jacksonville was first settled by French Huguenots in 1562, and it changed hands between

BOX 10.5   ICONIC IMAGES: CELEBRATION, FLORIDA

Developed in the 1990s, Celebration is the quintessential Disney-imagineered city—a plastic and vinyl–infused re-creation of Walt Disney's childhood home in Marceline, Missouri. He had long dreamt of building a model town as part of his master plan to create a new magic kingdom in Florida.

Disney envisioned Celebration as a nostalgic ideal "American home town." Features include pastel-colored exteriors, covered front porches so that neighbors can greet each other as they stroll by, white picket fences, garages that are hidden behind houses, and streets lit by "olde worlde" lanterns.

But there is also an element of control and conformism. There are rigid CCRs (conditions, covenants, and restrictions) that limit houses to one of six styles, and there are only certain exterior paint colors from which to choose. Planners even dictate what plants can be grown in front yards. Everything is sanitized and clean, so many who visit the town come away feeling that they just entered a strange time warp (photo 10.9).

Beneath the pastel colors and Mickey Mouse flags is shoddy construction. Little is said about the poor construction publicly, because a main reason that residents moved to the community is the "In Disney we trust" maintenance of high property values.* The estimated median house price is $471,000, about four times the state median house price, so living this dream is beyond the average Floridian income. Another issue is that the town lacks diversity. Of the eleven thousand residents, more than 80 percent of the residents are white, 11 percent are Hispanic (compared to the state average of 55 percent white and 25 percent Hispanic).

And there have been problems. Porches are seldom used because it is often too hot and humid. Alligators have crawled into residents' pools. In 2011, the first murder occurred in the town, shattering the illusion that the community was safely isolated from the real world. And while the town is cited as a landmark for **new urbanism**, it was not built to be sustainably oriented. Although it is designed to be "walkable", there is no full-service market or local services on Main Street, which means residents must drive for basic food needs.

Celebration is an amalgam of fantasy and reality, a tourist attraction, and certainly an atypical master-planned community.

PHOTO 10.9. Downtown in Celebration, Florida. The white picket fences, tree-lined streets, and uniform architecture give it an idyllic quality, but most people seen on the streets are tourists.

*Andrew Ross, *The Celebration Chronicles: Life, Liberty, and the Pursuit of Property Values in Disney's New Town* (New York: Ballantine, 1999).

Spanish, British, and Americans before the city was chartered in 1832. St. Augustine did not become the nexus city for the metropolis because it was hemmed in by a barrier island and lacked the deep-water harbor that made Jacksonville a regional distribution hub. The city diversified into such industries as research, information, and financial and insurance services. It is also the most industrialized city in Florida.

Orlando
(2016 MSA 2.4 million)

Orlando specialized in distribution, high-tech aviation, and citrus before Disneyworld transformed the city in 1965. Disney chose the inland Florida city to avoid the hurricane-threatened coast. Geographer Kevin Archer notes that the Orlando-Tampa conurbation is an "**imagineered** city," and a multi-nuclei city model popular in late-twentieth-century America. Nearby, Celebration epitomizes an imagineered mainstreet (box 10.5). Today, Orlando is the sixth largest city in Florida, the third largest metropolis, and the largest inland city. The Orlando complex of cities stretches across four inland contiguous counties; all have grown in population in the past three decades.

Orlando, a city with a Jim Crow past, remains economically but not legally segregated. Wealthy whites live in the new urban developments, and poorer blacks and a rising number of Hispanics live in the outlying rural areas in the face of the diminishing stock of urban affordable housing.

Orlando and its environs have become a tourist destination. Following Disney, several other amusement parks, including Universal, also opened in the nearby area, as well as the nation's largest convention center. Orlando maintains its original citrus and livestock economy, but it has developed a video gaming industry and capitalizes on its proximity to the coastal Kennedy Space Center. The space center created thousands of well-paid professional jobs, juxtaposed to the low-paying tourism sector. The city's airport was developed in 1970 and is second largest in Florida, handling more than 40 million passengers in 2015.

The Orlando metro area is dependent on cars and has few public transport options, although it is ramping up on charging stations for electric cars. What there is of public transport is converted to cleaner fuels, but still, its CO_2 emissions are only aligned with national standards, instead of the more progressive standards set by many other sustainably aware cities.

Yet, the city does have a sustainability plan, Green Works Orlando. The plan focuses on energy and green buildings, local food systems, solid waste, water, transportation, and livability. For example, the City is working towards a local food system that encompasses the entire cycle of food production and consumption, including growing, transporting, and the use of disposal. To achieve this, Orlando plans to add three hundred more

PHOTO 10.10. Miami Beach, an Iconic Image of Sun, Sand, and Beautiful Beachgoers.

Source: Lisa Benton-Short

community garden plots by 2020, increase farmers markets, and encourage urban farms. They have also set themselves the target of zero waste by 2040. Currently, they are at 27 percent diversion rate; by 2020, they want to achieve 50 percent on the way to getting to zero waste.

PHOTO 10.11. Miami's Art Deco District is home to some eight hundred buildings built between 1920 and 1940. The Art Deco style is marked by neon lights, pastel blues and pinks and greens, porthole windows, fountains and statues, glass blocks and chrome accents that draw visitors from all over to revel in its retro-fabulous style.

Source: John R Short

Miami
(2016 MSA 5.9 million)

The Miami–Fort Lauderdale metropolitan complex is the nation's eight-largest metropolitan area in the United States. It sprawls fifty miles from Miami through Fort Lauderdale to Palm Beach. Miami has been a commercial and tourist destination throughout the twentieth century. It is an immigrant gateway city and has emerged as an important banking center for Central and South America, has a large, busy airport, and the busiest cruise ship port in the world (photo 10.10).

During the middle of the twentieth century, the barrier island across Biscayne Bay was developed as Miami Beach and was bedecked with hotels luring luxury-seeking tourists. But tourism waned due to changing demographics and left a crime-ridden reputation memorialized in such shows as *Miami Vice*, which paradoxically enhanced the island's reputation again. Since the 1980s, the classic Art Deco hotels have been refurbished and have become popular with the wealthy and an icon of retro design (photo 10.11).

The population structure of metro Miami underwent radical change starting in the mid-1950s, when thousands of wealthy Cuban refugees moved to Miami, reinvigorating what was by then a fading resort town and turning it into the Cuban capital of America. A continued stream of refugees from Cuba and other Spanish-speaking countries followed. Today, Miami is a trade entrepôt for the Caribbean and Central and South American countries because of its location and the influx of Cubans.

Miami has little industry outside of tourism, and that has benefited the city; its CO_2 levels are among the lowest in the nation, and it plans to continue reducing CO_2 by supporting public incentives. The city has an ambitious sustainability plan that includes aggressive attempts to adapt to climate change.

The Economy

The Primary Sector

Agriculture

Florida is capable of growing vegetables throughout the winter, making it an agricultural savior for the colder northern states. But the national importance of Florida's agricultural crops has changed since globalization, the World Trade Organization (WTO), and the North American Free Trade Agreement (NAFTA), and many of its crops are no longer competitive with imported goods.

Florida has had a long history of agricultural productivity dominated by open-range cattle, citrus, sugarcane, and warm weather specialty and nursery crops. Between November and February, Florida grows about one-half of the nation's fresh vegetables, despite encroaching urban sprawl and population growth. Florida nursery and greenhouse sales of deciduous flowers, tropical foliage, and evergreen shrubs are second only to California.

Specialty Crops   Florida's southern location gave it a unique agricultural status during the twentieth century. The long growing season and ample precipitation allow out-of-season crops—tomatoes, cucumbers, green beans, and peppers—to grow when most of the Unites States is enduring winter. Florida continues to have a thriving citrus industry in the interior counties.

Citrus   Oranges are native to Asia, but Columbus brought them to the Americas. By 1579, citrus fruits were already well established in St. Augustine, Florida. Orange exports began in 1887, as railcar refrigeration became available.

Until the middle of the twentieth century, most of peninsular Florida land was in cattle or citrus orchards. The north was dedicated to grazing grassland, and south of Orlando, the sandy, well-drained soil, unsuitable for grasses and cattle, was perfect for citrus. Florida became the nation's number one producer of oranges in 1945 for three reasons: (1) Florida grew more Valencia oranges, preferred by the frozen-concentrate industry (whereas California grew navel oranges); (2) Florida focused on the new frozen-concentrate technology; and (3) California's urban growth from 1950 to 1980 replaced orange trees with housing tracts, while Florida expanded its citrus industry in the less populated interior of the state.

The Florida citrus crop produces a majority of the nation's oranges and almost three-quarters of of its grapefruit. Internationally, only Brazil grows more oranges than Florida. Today, the territory between Tampa and Orlando produces about half of the state's citrus, but commercial acreage has declined because of urban and suburban development. The area is also vulnerable to the loss of crops due to hurricanes or winter frost.

Sugarcane   Sugarcane production within the contiguous forty-eight states has been limited to the Gulf Coast states of Florida, Louisiana, and Texas. In Florida, sugarcane is a field crop, the third most important in the agricultural economy, behind nursery and citrus crops. About half of American sugar is produced from cane, the other half from sugar beets. About half of all US cane is grown in Florida. It is subsidized, politically corrupted by lobbyists, and unsustainable. Quotas on sugar have kept the price of sugar above the world market and discouraged imports, which has resulted in higher consumer prices and damages countries that depend on sugar exports.

The best place to grow sugarcane is in the tropics. Florida is subtropical and therefore less than ideal for sugar growth. Prior to the Cuban Embargo of 1962, most Cuban sugarcane was owned by US companies and imported. In the decades after the embargo, Cuban growers migrated to Florida and expanded sugar production by four hundred thousand acres (photo 10.12). The cane grows in one of the wealthiest counties in America, Palm Beach County; however, few people in Palm Beach are aware of it. The cane grows inland in a sparsely populated area near Lake Okeechobee, far from the luxurious

PHOTO 10.12. Sugarcane Fires at Belle Glade, Florida. Fire burns off debris and creates a more efficient sugarcane harvest. Fires are set mechanically and supervised by the Department of Forestry. Each fire last about fifteen minutes, and the smoke and fire can be seen throughout the area. After the fire, the cane is mechanically harvested and then transported to nearby mills.

beachside community. Sugar mills are located near the cane fields, because the cane is too heavy and bulky to ship.

Sugarcane is grown in a climate and on soil that is marginal for sugarcane production. The weather is not quite warm enough for cane, and the land is too wet without drainage, so new varieties that require use of extensive chemicals were developed for Florida. The chemical runoff into the Everglades has created additional damage, such as toxicity and the loss of biodiversity. As noted earlier, the rise in sugarcane production began with the draining of the northern Everglades, yet taxpayers continue to pay billions to subsidize growers. In 2009, a political deal with United States Sugar returned some of the less profitable agricultural land south of Lake Okeechobee to the Everglades.

The American sugar crop is the result of political maneuvering for profit. The polluting and subsidized crop is protected by government controls that limit imports, especially from Caribbean nations. American sugarcane and sugar beet producers, Big Sugar, have been indefatigable lobbyists for price supports and lowered water-quality standards. About one-fifth of the sugar used in America is imported; however, strict quotas and price supports keep the American price for sugar about double the world price.

Livestock: Cattle

Cattle have been an important part of Florida's agricultural production since the mid-1800s. Florida cattle descended from Spanish breeds introduced in the sixteenth century. The mangy, underweight Florida cow, called the "4-H type" (hide, hair, hoofs, and horns), was unacceptable to most Americans' taste; therefore, the market for Florida cattle until the early twentieth century was either local or Cuban, except for supplying Confederate troops during the Civil War. The cattle were immune to Florida diseases and parasites and roamed central Florida's free range until after World War II, when the range was fenced to eradicate a scourge of ticks (blocking Florida cattle from the American market). After World War II, the cattle industry introduced new breeds, changing land ownership techniques, taxation, and fencing laws. Today, Florida is the third-largest cattle producer east of the Mississippi and eleventh in the nation.

The Tertiary Sector

Boom-Bust Florida

Florida real estate speculation—"if you buy that then I have some land for you in Florida"—used its tropic-like location and climate to build dreams.

Florida developers have been hustling swampland and ocean property for almost a century, beginning with the first big boom in 1920. After many years of building cities on bubbles—Miami, Tampa Bay, and St. Petersburg—a collapse in 1925 brought speculation to an abrupt end. Easy credit and rapidly spiraling property values—often quadrupling in a year—reached a fever pitch, as get-rich-quick speculators looked for gullible winter vacationers to buy the undeveloped and often swampy land; the buyers then tried to flip the property before the first overleveraged payment was due. But it could not and did not last.

In the 1920s, railroad congestion caused by transportation of too many construction materials forced an embargo, and prices for transport escalated, beginning a spiral of increased cost of living. Land prices began a downward trend. Hurricanes in

1926 and 1928 caused some development projects to go bankrupt, and the Crash of 1929 ended the first boom. But more cycles of booms-and-bust were to come.

From World War II until the 1960s, Florida developed rapidly. The expansion continued throughout the 1970s through the early 2000s. The recession of 2008 hit Florida hard: Florida led most of the states in mortgage fraud and house foreclosures. Today, the real estate market has recovered in some places, and the "boom" is on again. Miami is emerging as an international and luxury getaway, and foreign investors ranging from Russian oligarchs to Brazilian supermodels have invested cash in residential and commercial properties. But the recovery has been uneven: some Floridians remain underwater in their houses, and the gap between rich and poor has widened.

Space Economy

Florida's fair-weather launching location established a vital role in the space program. The Cape Canaveral "Space Coast" had supported over 180 businesses along the Atlantic coastline and contributed more than $4.5 billion to the state economy. The more than twenty-three thousand jobs generated are considered environmentally clean and are high-paying technical jobs.

However, NASA eliminated the shuttle space program in 2011 and thousands of employees were retired or lost jobs. Since then, Florida's space companies have tried to diversify, offering incentive programs to high-tech space industry companies wishing to relocate in Florida and working with universities to develop further research opportunities. There has been some success. Space Florida signed a deal for a public-private launch pad at Cape Canaveral, but jobs have been slow to return.

Tourism and Port Facilities

Tourism is the number one industry in Florida, bringing in more than sixty billion dollars and eighty million international and domestic visitors annually. Some of these are "Snowbirds," seniors who relocate during the prime winter season. Tourists arrive for its warm winters, Walt Disney World Resort, and natural attractions such as the Everglades and Keys. Although tourism brings in cash and employment, it also has an effect on the local economy, increasing traffic, health care for retirees, public safety (crime), and environmental destruction. An additional burden for Florida residents is the minimum wage jobs in the tourist industry.

Fort Lauderdale, along with Miami, serve as major cruise ports and container ports. Fort Lauderdale ranks number three in cruise ports in the world with almost four million passengers in 2017 and generating some $55 million for the port (photo 10.13). It also has an active containerized cargo port and petroleum terminals. The ports also attract ancillary industries, including security companies, import/export companies, food suppliers, and steamship agents. The port facilities provide about 13,000 direct jobs, some 220,000 indirect jobs, and bring 30 billion dollars worth of economic activity through a diverse combination of cruise, cargo, and petroleum.

PHOTO 10.13. Fort Lauderdale has become a major cruise and cargo port. Almost forty million passengers travel through the port to board cruise ships destined for the Caribbean and beyond. The port is also first in the United States for trade with Latin America, accounting for 15 percent of all US/Latin American trade moves.
Source: Lisa Benton-Short

A Sustainable Future

Critical challenges to a more sustainable future in Florida include the following:

- population growth is expected to double by 2060 (particularly from retirees and baby boomers);
- overpriced real estate/ lack of affordable housing;
- climate change and sea-level rise;
- possible increased frequency and intensity of hurricanes;
- ability of state and local government to fund hurricane damage;
- a high rate of population growth;
- water treatment and discharge, which reduces nitrogen, reduces discharges to rivers, and eliminates failing septic tank systems;
- dependence on natural gas and coal for 86 percent of its energy; and
- weak base of renewable energy.

Along with the threat of natural disasters, energy is likely to be a critical issue. Less than 1 percent of state energy is

BOX 10.6   GLOBAL CONNECTIONS: MIAMI

Miami is not only a major city in the United States; it is the capital of Central America and the Caribbean.

We can look at three of the city's global connections. The first is the banking sector. Miami is an international banking center with the inflow of funds especially from Central and South America. Just south of downtown, the area known as Brickell is now a major financial hub, home to over fifty different banks. The low tax rate, the lack of state or city income tax, and the easy access to cities throughout the Caribbean basin make it an attractive place for people with money to park their funds. The city is 70 percent Latino and so is a comfortable place to do business for Spanish speakers.

Second, much of the luxury-housing sector is dominated by cash sales by foreigners looking for a safe and attractive investment (photo 10.14).

The third connection is the transport links. Miami is a major airport hub with links to the rest of the world and especially to cities in South and Central America. Then there are the maritime links. Miami is the largest passenger port in the world with over four million cruise passengers each year. All the major cruise operators such as Carnival, Royal Caribbean, and Norwegian operate cruise ships from the port. Miami is also a major commercial port with over seven million tons of cargo moving through the port each year (photo 10.15). The cruise and cargo operations support 175,000 jobs in the region.

PHOTO 10.14. High-Rise Luxury Condos in Miami Beach, Florida.
Source: John R Short

PHOTO 10.15. Cargo Moves in and out of the Port of Miami, Florida.
Source: John R Short

renewable. Florida ranks third in the nation for rooftop solar potential, but ranks twenty-seventh in actual installations. The state has no renewable portfolio standards and does not allow power purchase agreements, two policies that have driven investments in solar in other states. A recent report card issued a grade of "C" to tax incentives and a grade of "D" to rebates. So there is much to be improved around energy. Until recently, Florida's reliance on solar power was negligible until the largest solar photovoltaic power plant in the United States was completed in 2010. The plant will generate enough electricity to power eight thousand homes and avoid 2.8 million tons of GHG emissions over a twenty-year period—a drop in the bucket, but a beginning.

Another major challenge will be climate change and sea-level rise, made even more problematic because key Florida's political leaders—including its current governor and US senator—deny climate change science. But that doesn't stop climate change impacts: in 2016, an octopus swam into one of Miami's parking garages during a period of flooding. Fortunately, cities in Florida are at the leading edge of climate mitigation and adaptation because they have no choice. Florida is denying climate change globally, but trying to act locally. Yet, the disconnect between state policy and funding and local responses to climate may impede the best efforts of many cities.

On the other hand, many of Florida's cities have developed comprehensive sustainability plans that focus on many areas of sustainability. Given the urban character of Florida, this represents a very positive step.

The author Carl Hiassen has said that Florida's reputation is one of failures and frauds. Russian oligarchs, climate change denial, hanging chads, security frauds, swamp swindles, poodle-eating gators, and Burmese pythons on the loose—these are common occurrences, past and present, found in a state that has been said to be "a victim of its own geography."

Questions for Discussion

1. Explain why twenty million people is or is not a sustainable carrying capacity for Florida.
2. Is restoring previous ecosystems such as the Everglades really a path toward environmental health? Is nature static?
3. Discuss whether taxpayers should continue to invest in beach restoration and nourishment projects.
4. Explain how the Everglades and Lake Okeechobee have changed since the early twentieth century.
5. The dramatic decline in aquatic life and changes in plants and turbidity have been occurring over the past two hundred years. What do you think is the "natural" ecosystem that needs to be restored? Why?
6. Give an explanation of Florida's coastal disasters and the reasons Florida is prone to them.
7. What was Florida's geologic origin? How is this origin related to the economic development of the region?
8. Where is agriculture most important in Florida? What are the most important crops and why?
9. Discuss urban trends.
10. Discuss the two largest immigrant groups and why they have chosen Florida as their home.
11. What measures has Florida taken to ensure a more sustainable future?
12. How has Miami planned for climate change?
13. What economic changes have occurred in the last two decades?

Suggested Readings

Archer, K. "The Limits to the Imagineered City: Sociospatial Polarization in Orlando." *Economic Geography* 73, no. 3 (July 1997): 322–36.

Barnett, C. *Mirage: Florida and the Vanishing Water of the Eastern US.* Ann Arbor: University of Michigan Press, 2007.

Blake, N. M. *Land into Water—Water into Land: A History of Water Management in Florida.* Tallahassee: University Presses of Florida, 1980.

Brooks, H. K., and J. M. Merritt. *Guide to the Physiographic Divisions of Florida.* Florida Cooperative Extension Service Institute of Food and Agricultural Sciences. Gainesville: University of Florida, 1981.

Culliton, B. "Save the Beaches, Not the Buildings," *Nature* 357, June 18, 1992.

Clark, James. *A Concise History of Florida.* Charleston, S.C.: The History Press, 2014.

Eire, C. *Learning to Die in Miami: Confessions of a Refugee Boy.* New York: Simon & Schuster, 2015.

Hiaasen, C. *Tourist Season.* New York: G.P. Putnam's Sons, 1986.

Ingalls, R. P. "Lynching and Establishment Violence in Tampa, 1858–1935." *Journal of Southern History* 53, no. 4 (November 1987).

Grunwald, M. *The Swamp: The Everglades, Florida, and the Politics of Paradise.* New York: Simon & Schuster, 2006.

Turner, G. *The Florida Land Boom of the 1920s.* Jefferson, N.C.: MacFarland, 2015.

Wilkinson, A. *Big Sugar: Seasons in the Cane Fields of Florida.* New York: Knopf, 1989.

Internet Sources

Everglades Invasive species information, at https://www.nps.gov/ever/learn/nature/nonnativespecies.htm

The Everglades Foundation, at https://www.evergladesfoundation.org/about/

Florida Museum of Natural History. "Mangroves," at http://www.flmnh.ufl.edu/fish/southflorida/mangrove/Introduction.html

Florida State. "Everglades History," http://www.dep.state.fl.us/evergladesforever/about/default.htm

National Park Service "Everglades Facts," at https://www.nps.gov/ever/learn/news/parksignificance.htm

Florida Department of State. "A Brief History of Florida," at http://www.flheritage.com/facts/history/summary/.

Maimi's Sustainability Plan, at http://www.miamidade.gov/GreenPrint/.

Orlando's Sustainability Plan, at: http://www.cityoforlando.net/greenworks/

Tampa Bay's Sustainability Plan, at https://www.tampagov.net/green-tampa

Tampa Bay Seawater Desalination Plant, at http://www.water-technology.net/projects/tampa/

National Oceanic and Atmospheric Administration. "National Hurricane Center," at http://www.nhc.noaa.gov

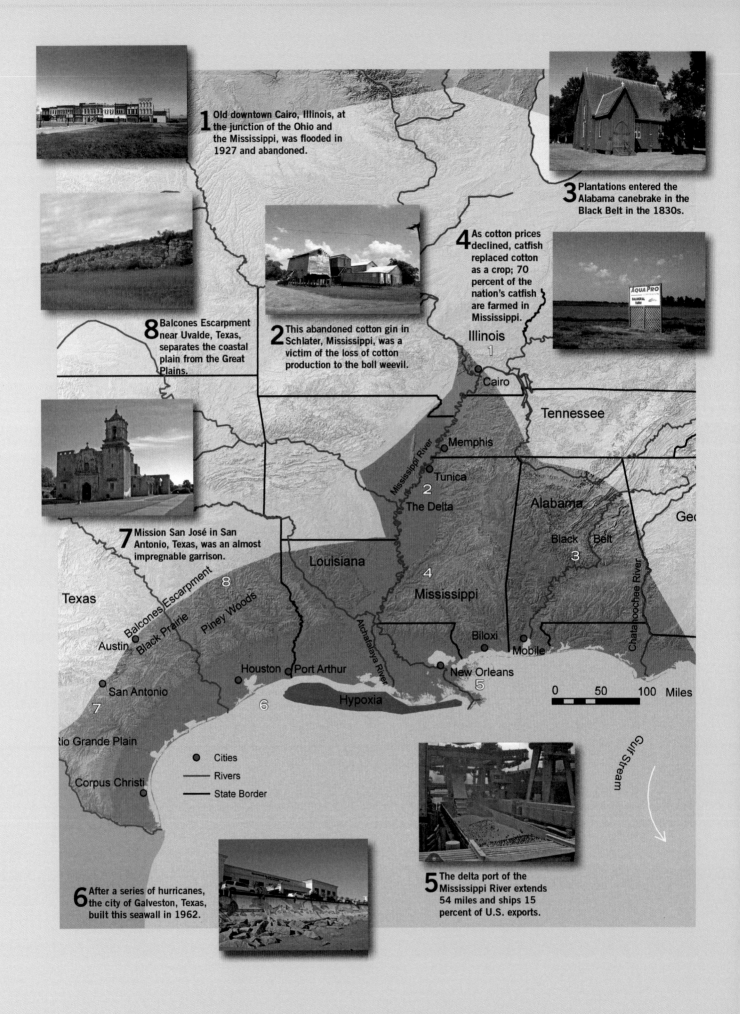

1 Old downtown Cairo, Illinois, at the junction of the Ohio and the Mississippi, was flooded in 1927 and abandoned.

3 Plantations entered the Alabama canebrake in the Black Belt in the 1830s.

4 As cotton prices declined, catfish replaced cotton as a crop; 70 percent of the nation's catfish are farmed in Mississippi.

8 Balcones Escarpment near Uvalde, Texas, separates the coastal plain from the Great Plains.

2 This abandoned cotton gin in Schlater, Mississippi, was a victim of the loss of cotton production to the boll weevil.

7 Mission San José in San Antonio, Texas, was an almost impregnable garrison.

6 After a series of hurricanes, the city of Galveston, Texas, built this seawall in 1962.

5 The delta port of the Mississippi River extends 54 miles and ships 15 percent of U.S. exports.

Illinois

Cairo

Tennessee

Memphis

Mississippi River

Tunica

2

The Delta

Alabama

Black Belt

3

Louisiana

4

Mississippi

Atchafalaya River

Chatahoochee River

Geo

Biloxi

Mobile

New Orleans

5

Texas

Balcones Escarpment

8

Piney Woods

Black Prairie

Austin

Houston Port Arthur

San Antonio

6

Hypoxia

7

Rio Grande Plain

Corpus Christi

0   50   100   Miles

Gulf Stream

● Cities
— Rivers
— State Border

11
GULF COASTAL PLAINS AND MISSISSIPPI VALLEY
Juxtaposition Squared

Chapter Highlights

After reading this chapter, you should be able to:

- Explain the importance of the wetlands along the Gulf Coast
- List the subregions and identify their similarities and differences
- Discuss how landscape change has affected the force of hurricanes
- Discuss how the Mississippi River has been altered and its effect
- Describe the causes and effects of eutrophication and hypoxiai
- Outline the evolution of plantations from the antebellum to Reconstruction periods
- Discuss the reasons for and impact of disease and pestilence in the Gulf region
- Compare and contrast the Old South and the New South
- Identify the Black Belt both topographically and culturally
- Describe urbanization trends in the region
- Explain the strategic importance of New Orleans
- Describe the impact of oil and gas on the Gulf Coast economy and environment
- List the major crops along the Gulf Coast and Mississippi alluvial area
- Discuss economic development in the last twenty years

Terms

Army Corps of Engineers	Creole	hurricane	pulpwood
bayou	cuesta	hypoxia	push and pull factors
bosque	delta	Jim Crow laws	salt dome
Cajun	embayment	levee	sharecropper
chain migration	estuary	Mardi Gras	subsidence
colonia	eutrophication	melting pot	sustainable hazard mitigation
	flatwoods	oxbow lake	sustainable yield
	Great Migration	petroleum	Trail of Tears

Places

Atchafalaya River	Black Belt	Gulf Stream	Rio Grande Plain
		Mississippi River	Riverwalk

Cities

Austin, Texas
(2016 MSA 2 million)

Baton Rouge, Louisiana
(2016 MSA 835,00)

Biloxi, Mississippi
(2016 MSA 390,000)

Corpus Christi, Texas
(2016 MSA 455,000)

Galveston, Texas
(2016 MSA 280,000)

Houston, Texas
(2016 MSA 6.7 million)

Jackson, Mississippi
(2016 MSA 580,000)

Memphis, Tennessee
(2016 MSA 1.3 million)

Mobile, Alabama
(2016 MSA 415,000)

New Orleans, Louisiana
(2016 MSA 1.2 million)

San Antonio, Texas
(2016 MSA 2.4 million)

Tallahassee, Florida
(2016 MSA 375,000)

PHOTO 11.1. The Steamer Natchez in New Orleans, Louisiana.
Source: iStock/EdoTealdi

Introduction

The Mississippi Delta, or the Gulf Coast, is the "quintessential South" (photo 11.1). It is a jumble of juxtapositions: slaves and plantations; black and white; cotton and oil; segregation and integration; Caribbean **Creole** and Canadian **Cajun**; extreme wealth and extreme poverty; thick, black soils and thin, piney sands.

The heavy, dank Gulf Coast has inspired impassioned art and been memorialized in literature, by William Faulkner, Harper Lee, Eudora Welty, and Tennessee Williams, among others. Their stories reflect Gulf Coast life, one of racial conflict, cotton, jazz, gumbo, and the swamps and **bayous**.

The American South includes both the Atlantic and Gulf Coasts, and while they share a subtropical climate, marsh-ridden coastline, and slaveholding past, the two coasts developed very differently. Although the Gulf region remains one of the poorest in America, it is also home to coastal wealth, new industries, and opportunities.

It has been a long road for the Gulf Coast. Recovery from the Civil War took decades. Discrimination and segregation policies encapsulated the "Old South" awaiting the "New South"—a South that blended with the lockstep consumerism and economy of the nation. But the transition was uneven. By the end of the twentieth century, coastal areas transformed into opulent McMansions, while the interior Black Belt remained mired in illiteracy and poverty, emphasizing the wealth and poverty gap. Per capita income in Mississippi's Gulf Coast cities rose more than 50 percent in the past decade; those in the Delta and Black Belt saw no such gain.

The Gulf Coastal Plain has long been a target for **hurricane** destruction because of natural and human events. After Hurricanes Katrina (2005), Harvey (2017), and Irma (2017), and the 2010 Deepwater Horizon oil spill, the Gulf Coast became notorious as the most ecologically devastated region in America. But environmental destruction is not the only change. The Gulf Coast has evolved from seafood and lumber to chemicals, computers, cars, and tourism—especially gaming casinos. Most growth has been along the wealthier coastal area, and its cities continue to experience population increase.

Physical Geography

The Gulf Coast from the Florida Panhandle to the Mexican border shares humidity and rainfall, abundant marshy areas, and a low-lying and once-submerged coastal plain. The Gulf Coastal Plain is an elevated sea bottom that emerges from the seventy-five-mile-wide continental shelf. Varying from 10 to 150 miles wide, the low-lying and swampy coastal plain seldom rises above fifty feet. It is one of the continent's richest ecological regions. The complex ecological communities in the river's brackish wetlands have sustained the local economy. The mixed fresh and saltwater **estuary** habitats shelter species on barrier islands, mangroves, and reefs. More than four hundred species of wildlife and 40 percent of North America's migratory waterfowl live within the Mississippi River basin.

Spanish moss–shrouded oaks, magnolias, and bayou cypress live along the marshes and coastal plain, while inland the swampy **flatwood** forest featured deciduous oak and maple mixed with southern pines, until the forest landscape was removed for crops, urban development, or tree plantations.

What remains are ecologically sterile loblolly tree plantations that are harvested about every thirty years.

The physical landscape of the Gulf Coast contains four subregional plains, all edging the gulf each with their own personalities:

- East Gulf Coastal
- Mississippi Alluvial
- West Gulf Coastal
- Rio Grande

East Gulf Coastal Plain

The eastern coastal plain is characterized by a belted, concentric band of lowlands and **cuesta** ridges, steep on one side, gently sloped on the other. The forested swampy lowland extends over beaches and barrier islands. The northern edge extends to the Alabama **Black Belt,** just south of the Appalachians and west of Montgomery, Alabama (map 11.1). The term was first used to describe the rich, dark soil of the area. Despite the hazards, the

MAP 11.1. Traditional Counties of the Alabama Black Belt. The name was first used to describe the rich, dark soil, but later became synonymous with the large, poor black population living in the area.

demand for oceanfront property has resulted in the construction of second homes or vacation rentals in this area.

Mississippi Alluvial Plain

The Mississippi Alluvial Plain extends five hundred miles from the **delta** northward to Cairo, Illinois, where the Mississippi meets the Ohio River. The fifty-to-one-hundred-mile-wide plains leaves sediment replenishing the soil as it descends to the coast. For thousands of years the river has followed the easiest gradient, changing course multiple times, leaving behind natural **levees**, back swamps, and the large, graceful, curving commas—cutoff or **oxbow lakes**—demarcating old river routes.

An important part of the alluvial plain, "the Delta" lies between the Yazoo and Mississippi Rivers, between Memphis and Natchez. The Delta has its own persona. Alluvial floods laid down the flat pan of the Delta's storied soils, which mutated into slave-run cotton plantations and became the birthplace of the blues, a music form that expresses the longtime tenor of the place.

Just north of the Delta and on the opposite bank is Crowley's Ridge, named after the region's first settler. The ridge is the most prominent topographic feature along the alluvial plain. The loess ridge may have originated as an island within the river, or it may be the result of uplift from earthquakes. Jonesboro and other Arkansas alluvial towns are protected from flooding because of their location on the higher ground of Crowley's Ridge.

West Gulf Coastal Plain

The flat West Gulf Coastal Plain topography contains numerous barrier islands and salt domes. The West Gulf Coast bay-estuary-lagoon complex—the largest is Galveston Bay—separates the mainland and Gulf. **Salt domes**, the buried remnants of a shallow sea, dot the coast and coastal plain. These domes trap reservoirs of **hyrdocarbons—petroleum**—and the discovery of one salt dome, Spindletop, in 1901 ushered in the modern oilfield industry and created companies such as Texaco, Exxon, Gulf Oil, and Sun Oil.

The West Gulf Coastal Plain has two subregions: the eastern Texas Piney Woods and the Coastal Prairie. The Piney Woods are a sandy, agriculturally poor area, whose natural pine-hardwood vegetation has been converted to loblolly pine plantations. The Coastal Prairie grasslands from Houston south to Corpus Christi are all but gone and now grow cotton or graze cattle. The plain spreads inland to the Balcones Escarpment, where the Great Plains begin. At the southernmost edge is the Rio Grande Plain.

Rio Grande Plain

The Rio Grande Plain, occupying the Texas border region south of San Antonio to the Rio Grande River, is a lowland with occasional limestone-capped hills, buttes, or volcanic necks, a transition zone from the coastal plain to the Great Plains. The landscape varies from the intensively farmed flat, fertile flood plain in the south to the drier, semiarid grassy shrub area that sprouts the ubiquitous Texan mesquite.

The cottonwood-mesquite (**bosque**) ecosystem along river bottoms has adapted well to the local arid climate and occasional flood patterns. The natural bosque ecosystem requires no fire suppression, but invasive salt cedar and Russian olive trees have crowded the natural species out, thus expanding flammable debris that is vulnerable to fire. Management programs have reintroduced goats that browse the nonnative tinder as a sustainable conservation measure.

There has been a long history of environmental exploitation in the Rio Grande Valley. First the Spanish grazed too many sheep and caused erosion; Americans followed, overstocking the animal population and building dams and levees to serve urban areas. Land was grazed, cultivated, and, along the Mexican border, urbanized. Water continues to be a major problem, as populations grow and agriculture continues to provide winter season fruits and vegetables.

Water

The Mississippi River

The Mississippi River system is the dominant water source for the continental interior, while the Rio Grande divides a portion of the United States from Mexico. Oxbow lakes are the natural lakes in this part of the country, but dam reservoirs form artificial lakes. Another important water feature is the extensive, poorly drained coastline, much of which has been reclaimed, or developed.

Before human intervention, the sinuous lower Mississippi River meandered in 180-degree turns, losing elevation slowly as it made its way to the coast. The river shifts some of its channels ten to twenty times a century as it courses at four miles per hour, ninety-six miles per day. The river deposits sediment across the broad alluvial valley and delta. As the river approaches the Gulf, sediment shapes the wide "bird's foot" delta below New Orleans, but over millennia, river sediment has also covered about one-fourth of Louisiana's coastline (photo 11.2). The entire basin from Cape Girardeau, Missouri (the geologic head), was once a submerged part of the Gulf **embayment**, but as sea levels dropped it emerged as an alluvial plain.

The middle Mississippi River region between the confluences of the Missouri and Ohio Rivers has been an important settlement area. Native Americans settled in Cahokia, and later the French established the trading and farm towns of Cape Giradeau, Kaskaskia, and St. Genevieve. Along the Missouri confluence was St. Louis (see chapter 12), a city well situated to command trade between the east and west. Along the Ohio confluence was the less successful city of Cairo, Illinois.

Controlling the Mississippi River: Wetlands, Levees, and Flooding

Louisiana's coastline was a water-filtering, storm-buffering wetland providing homes for migratory birds and ducks, and supporting about one-third of the nation's commercial fish and shellfish harvests. Louisiana continues to have more coastal wetlands than other Gulf Coast states, but leads the country in the loss of wetlands.

PHOTO 11.2. The Mississippi Delta's "Bird Foot" from Space.
Source: NOAA

The tidal wetlands along the Louisiana coast have been dissolving into the Gulf despite natural resource management. The wetlands' loss is due to coastal development and because the Mississippi River has been channelized for flood control and to "correct" its path. Human intervention has interfered with the natural cycle of sediment deposition that creates and maintains the wetlands. The wetlands starved, and the result has been the loss of over a million acres of coastlands.

In the 1920s, engineers built a system of canals to connect energy sources for the oil and gas industry. There was little thought to the long-term relationships between the canals, saltwater intrusion, and the loss of land. The canals destroyed ecosystems, eroded wetlands, and infiltrated salt water into freshwater marshes. Under natural conditions, wetlands sediment and nutrients are converted to biologically useful materials and serve as fish and shellfish nurseries. Wetland losses increase inland area susceptibility to salt water and hurricanes. Eroded wetlands allow the water level to rise and expose the coast to flooding, impacting society in an unanticipated way.

By the 1940s, the industry was charged for polluting oyster beds, and some changes reduced the impact. But when the industry moved offshore in the 1950s, the wetland environment was again seriously impacted by miles and miles of pipeline and canal systems to support offshore production. Since that time, many improvements in wetland restoration have been made, but the corrections were too little, too late. The April 2010 Deepwater Horizon oil spill revealed the weakness of protection.

Naturally occurring levees are created by the build up of sediment, protected by wetlands that lie opposite the levees.

During a storm, natural levees will direct some of the water to the wetlands which gradually absorbs the water and then dries; there is an important interchange between natural levees and wetlands. Humans have attempted to protect populated areas by building artificial levees, but these levees do not have wetland buffers. While normal flooding outside natural levees is gradual, artificial levees can cause devastation when the levees are breached.

The Mississippi has always flooded. The historian John Barry tells the tale of the great Mississippi flood of 1927 which inundated twenty-seven thousand square miles and flooded the homes of nearly one million people. The flood was in part caused by steady rains through the entire river basin for months beforehand. The river flooded for one thousand miles from Cairo, Illinois, to New Orleans, Louisiana. What made the river banks so fertile was the steady deposition of alluvium by the river's changing course as it meandered its way to the sea. The flooding become an "urban" hazard as more people settled and moved to the delta regions attracted in part by the rich soils. But attempts to control the river led to the construction of levees that effectively channeled the river that it in turn made the floods that much more devastating.

After numerous commissions and reports in the mid-twentieth century, the **Army Corps of Engineers** proposed to control the Mississippi by a combination of artificial levees, outlets, cutoffs, and dams. They built more than two thousand miles of levees, constructed to prevent the river from flooding. The plan also attempted to control the river's course. In 1963, the Army Corps of Engineers completed the Old River Control Structure to restrain the course of the river and protect the delta infrastructure. Flooding is a regular part of many river ecosystems, but it can be aggravated by land-use changes associated with rapid urbanization and attempts to constrain the river's flow.

The Atchafalaya delta currently receives about 30 percent of the river's flow, and its delta is growing and building new wetlands. But the Mississippi's bird-foot delta no longer builds much wetland area, because it extends so far onto the continental shelf that it now descends into the deep waters of the continental slope rather than building new wetlands and barrier islands. If the river flowed down the Atchafalaya, as its natural course now dictates, the sediment would be deposited on the shallow continental shelf and build additional wetlands and barrier islands.

To protect human habitation and commercial navigation, the river and its silt deposits have been modified and channeled to continue the use of the current infrastructure. But these efforts ultimately have degraded the Louisiana coastline.

Mississippi River Delta Challenges

Louisiana's coastal wetlands, tied to Mississippi River oscillations, absorb the shock of Gulf storms and protect the low-lying areas, but the delta is subsiding and has stopped silting. The coastal delta is disappearing (map 11.2).

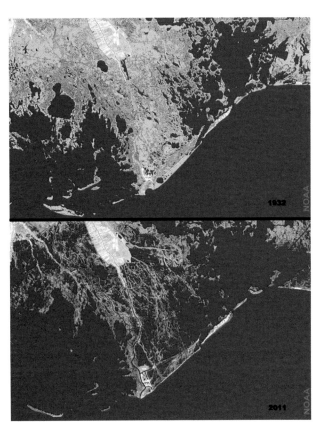

MAP 11.2. The disappearing Coastal Delta is shown in these maps from the National Oceanic and Atmospheric Administration (NOAA). The image on top dates from 1932; the image on the bottom is 2011.
Source: NOAA

The disappearing wetlands expose oil industry infrastructure to open water conditions. The infrastructure—pipelines, roads, ports, and wells—services thousands of Gulf platforms. Wetland loss, infrastructure exposure, and deep drilling in fragile areas lead to more oil spills and have been a factor in inflating oil prices.

Twentieth-century wetland loss accelerated because of human impacts—marsh **subsidence**, levee construction, and grazing by the invasive rodent nutria (introduced by fur ranchers). The Army Corps of Engineers constructed confining levees, altered nutrient distribution to wetlands, and altered sediment accumulation patterns.

If the Mississippi River is allowed to complete the change of its course, the cost will be monumental. Morgan City would be engulfed by the raging Atchafalaya River, and a new port city would have to be built. The offshore oil and gas industry infrastructure would be affected by the saltier water, which would corrode pipes. The delta fisheries could all be altered and oyster beds destroyed. The infrastructure built around the current Atchafalaya would no longer be sufficient to meet the needs of the new and much larger river. New Orleans and all other cities along the Mississippi would still exist but in much different circumstances. Shipping patterns would change, and drinking water would have to come from another source, as the lower level of water in the river would allow more salt water to enter the channel. The cost for our attempt to control nature would be in the many billions of dollars and would interrupt commerce for decades.

Gulf of Mexico

The origin of the Gulf of Mexico is still debated and studied. Geologist Peter Bartok theorizes that the basin was formed during the Triassic period (230 million years ago), as Pangaea broke up and the North American Plate drifted away from the African and South American Plates. Several times, sea water inundated the region and deposited salt, which emerged later as the Gulf region's salt domes.

The warm water Loop Current, a segment of global oceanic patterns, dominates the Gulf of Mexico water flow. The current flows from the Yucatan Peninsula toward the Mississippi delta and then continues out to the Atlantic or returns to the Gulf (hence the phrase "loop current"). The current's only escape funnels through the Straits of Florida between the Florida Keys and Cuba and connects to the Gulf Stream, the warm ocean current that flows northward along the Atlantic coast.

Eutrophication and Hypoxia

Nitrogen is essential for making amino acids, proteins, and DNA; it also boosts crop yields, and when added to fields expands productive land. Natural nitrogen conversion by bacteria is no longer the main source of nitrogen; instead, nitrogen is combined with hydrogen under heat and pressure to create anhydrous ammonia, which can be applied directly as fertilizer to fields. In trying to both have healthy plants and to maximize yields, excess nitrogen runoff has impacted water quality.

In aquatic environments, excess nutrients—nitrogen, sulfur, or phosphorus—causes **eutrophication**, which in turn leads to "dead zones," areas of such low oxygen concentration that animal life suffocates and dies. Signs of eutrophication include algal blooms, fish kills, and eventual ecosystem collapse. Algae feed on excess nutrients and grow exponentially. As the algae die, they allow oxygen-depleting bacteria to grow rapidly as well, and then hypoxia results. **Hypoxia**, a lack of oxygen, kills fish and vegetation, and occurs as the result of a step-by-step process:

1. The polluted freshwater flowing from the Mississippi River is less dense than salty Gulf water, allowing prime algal bloom conditions.
2. Algal blooms are often bright green or even red.
3. Algae die, sink, and are eaten by bacteria.
4. Bacteria population grows exponentially as they feed on the algae.
5. Bacteria deplete the oxygen needed by fish and shellfish.

Dead zones occur annually along the Gulf Coast, the Great Lakes, and along Atlantic inlets, but the largest is west of the Mississippi Delta along the Louisiana coast. The summertime dead zone fluctuates annually, but it averages around eight thousand square miles (about the size of New Jersey) (map 11.3).

Rather than concentrating on the hypoxia zone itself, researchers are studying the entire watershed to better understand its influence on the discharge zone. For example, eutrophication and hypoxia in the Delta is not caused solely by local practices. Midwestern farmers use nitrogen-based fertilizers, which are washed into the river, flow to the Gulf, and contribute to the dead zones. In addition, the use of fertilizers in suburbs also contributes to the problem. By eliminating problems at the source, the discharge zone could be less affected. Some of the proposed changes include modifying farm practices up the entire river so nitrogen will be used more efficiently and diverting Mississippi floodwaters to wetlands where they will be filtered, thus slowing the flow of polluted water to the Gulf.

Rio Grande

The only perennial stream on the Rio Grande Plain is the border-defining Rio Grande, which rises in Colorado and flows through New Mexico to El Paso, Texas, where it begins its journey as the border between the United States and Mexico. Industrialization along the border has increased chemical pollution, and increased population has caused sewage issues in the river. Pesticides from the farms also make their way into the river. By the time the river reaches the Gulf, irrigation withdrawals and overuse relegates the mouth to a mere trickle of water.

Climate

The Gulf Coastal region is influenced by the Gulf of Mexico and the Atlantic Ocean. Moist winds blow onshore, boosting winter and spring precipitation from a high of ninety inches along the Eastern Gulf Coastal Plain tapering to seven inches along the southernmost Rio Grande Plain. During the growing season, thunderstorms and accompanying lightening are almost daily occurrences. The warm, humid region experiences occasional frosts that limit the growing season to 200–240 days. The warm humidity and the ocean mix to bring the most spectacular of its climatic characteristics, the hurricane.

Hurricanes

June through November is hurricane season and a cause for concern along the Gulf Coast. Massive tropical storm systems pound the region with high wind speeds, thunderstorms, and storm surges that can flood the low-lying coast.

On average, about five hurricanes every two years hit somewhere within the Gulf Coast region, but hurricanes vary both in intensity and in periodic activity. During the twentieth century, hurricanes were intense from 1941 to 1965, then calmer until intensifying again about 1990. Cities such as Galveston and New Orleans have been impacted by hurricanes several times and respond by building infrastructure to protect the city and its residents (photo 11.3).

Climate change may play a role in hurricane intensity, frequency, and the increase of temperatures and sea levels. However, the lack of hurricane records over long periods

MAP 11.3. A large dead zone of low oxygen water was detected in the Gulf of Mexico during 2015. The dead zone (shown in red), which forms every summer, was large this year because of heavy rains in June. Heavy rains in the Mississippi River basin flush nutrient-rich water into the Gulf of Mexico where it triggers algae blooms.

Source: NASA

PHOTO 11.3. Coastal areas along the Gulf are low and prone to subsidence and flooding. The city of Galveston, located on a barrier island, has been flooded several times, resulting in the town's building a seawall to stop the relentless ocean, as shown in this historical photo. Despite the seawall, hurricanes continue to cause destruction, as they did in 2003 and again in 2008.

Source: Library of Congress

BOX 11.1 ENVIRONMENTAL CHALLENGES: ARE HURRICANES NATURAL DISASTERS?

Hurricanes cause three main forms of damage: rain, wind, and flood. Hurricanes, especially the large slow-moving ones, can produce downpours of up to twenty-five inches in thirty hours. The high winds tear buildings and other structures away from their moorings. Everything not securely tied down (and even those that are) becomes subject to the vagaries of wind and even secure structures experience wind damage. The high winds also generate waves. Storm surges associated with the high winds can reach over twenty feet above normal sea level, causing massive flooding. For most coastal cities, flooding is a serious problem; for a city below sea level, it is potentially catastrophic. Much of New Orleans is below sea level.

Hurricanes are not unusual events in New Orleans. Since 1887 at least thirty-four hurricanes and twenty-five tropical storms have passed within one hundred miles of the city.

The path of Hurricane Katrina was accurately predicted. As early as Friday, August 26, 2005, people knew it would make landfall close to the city of New Orleans in southern Louisiana.

Hurricane Katrina made landfall just east of the city at 6:10 a.m. on Monday, August 29.

It was not the ferocious winds that damaged the city but the storm surge that breached levees in the city. The city was flooded when parts of levees at 17th Street and Industrial Canal collapsed. Almost 80 percent of the city was flooded, in some cases by water over twenty feet in depth. An estimated one thousand people were killed, most of them drowned by the rapidly rising floodwaters.

When is a disaster a natural disaster? At first glance, Katrina seemed like natural disaster. A hurricane is a force of nature. The flooding of the city was caused by the poorly designed levees that could not withstand a predictable storm surge. It was not Katrina that caused the flooding but shoddy engineering, poor design, and inadequate funding of vital public works. Storms surges are neither unknown nor unpredictable in New Orleans. Yet the levees were poorly constructed with pilings set in unstable soils. They should have been built to withstand fifteen-foot surges but had settled in many places to only twelve to thirteen feet above sea level.

The storm surge itself was particularly severe because of the loss of wetland. For the previous twenty years, wetland was lost in the Gulf Coast at a rate of twenty-four square miles per year. The wetlands have a deadening effect on storms as they absorb much of the energy and water the storm brings. It is estimated that wetlands reduce a storm surge one foot for every three miles of marsh that a surge passes over. The loss of wetlands around New Orleans, something predictable and knowable, added to the potency of the storm surge.

The mayor of the city issued a voluntary evacuation on Saturday, August 27, and a mandatory evacuation the next day. Those with cars were able to get out but there was little provision for the most vulnerable; those with no access to private transport were abandoned. While the more affluent could leave, the very poorest, the most disabled, the elderly, and infirm were trapped. Between fifty thousand and one hundred thousand were left in the city when the hurricane struck and the levees failed. Some

PHOTO 11.4. Post-Katrina Destruction, Ocean Springs, Mississippi. Ocean Springs was an affluent suburb of Biloxi. After Hurricane Katrina, the houses closest to shore were completely demolished. The renewal of the region brought to the fore many issues that were already brewing in America, but Katrina victims had to deal with them first, including the growing gap between the haves and have-nots.

made their way to the Superdome and the Convention Center, which by Wednesday, August 31, housed between thirty thousand and fifty thousand people. They remained for days, a stunning indictment of social and racial inequality in its starkest and bleakest forms.

The effects of Hurricane Katrina on the city were socially and racially determined. Flooding disproportionately affected the poorest neighborhoods of the city. The more affluent, predominantly white sections of the city, such as the French Quarter and the Garden District, were at a higher elevation and escaped flood damage. The flooded areas were 80 percent nonwhite. The hardest-hit neighborhoods were nonwhite and most of the high poverty tracts were flooded. The racial and income disparities in the city were cruelly reflected in the pattern of flood damage. This "natural" disaster appears in closer detail as a social disaster. As a Congressional bipartisan report noted, "Katrina was a national failure, an abdication of the most solemn obligation to provide for the common welfare."*

---

*US Government Printing Office (2006), "A failure of Initiative: Final Repost of the Select Bipartisan Committee to Investigate the Preparation for and response to Hurricane Katrina." Washington, D.C., at http://www.gpoacess.gov/congress/index/html

of time hampers long-term climate change causality or predictions. How climate change will alter the geography of hurricanes is difficult to predict and diminishes scientific confidence about future hurricane predictability. Fewer hurricanes might form (lowering risk) or more will form (heightening risk). They might be stronger (heightening risk) or weaker (lowering it). Fewer might strike land (hazard might be lowered) or more might (heightening hazard). Perhaps the hazard will intensify as larger cities to the northeast (like New York, Philadelphia, Toronto, Montreal, or Boston) or even on the West Coast (San Diego or Los Angeles, for instance) experience more and stronger hurricanes, some maybe for the first time. Despite uncertainty, cities vulnerable to hurricanes have developed hurricane disaster management plans and have building codes these events.

Historical Geography and Settlement

Gulf Coast cultures evolved from four time periods: Native American, plantation, Reconstruction, and New South. Each had a different settlement pattern and impact on the landscape.

Native Americans

Native Americans occupied the Gulf region by 5000 BCE but flourished after 1300 BCE. From 1000 to 1600 CE, the alluvial valley flourished with mound cultures, such as Moundville, Alabama, and Plaquemine and Poverty Point in Louisiana. These less populous cultures lived concurrently with the larger Cahokia Mississippian culture to the north. The mound cultures built flat-topped ceremonial or burial site mounds over one hundred feet wide and ten feet high. These hunter-gatherers also practiced agriculture. The culture declined after contact with European diseases. After the mound builders' demise the "5 tribes" of Cherokee, Chickasaw, Choctaw, Creek, and Seminole migrated into the area.

In the 1830s, land opened to white settlement, Native American treaties were dishonored, Indian wars broke out, and ultimately the native inhabitants were forcibly relocated to Indian Territory in present-day Oklahoma. As part of Andrew Jackson's Indian removal policy, the majority of Native Americans in the Gulf region were removed from their land to make way for cotton plantations and American expansion. The Cherokee people called this journey the "**Trail of Tears**" because of its devastating effects. The migrants faced hunger, disease, and exhaustion on the forced march. Over four thousand out of fifteen thousand of the Cherokees died.

Once the tribes arrived in Oklahoma, they found it difficult to live on land and in climates that differed from their native homelands. As a result, their culture and way of life floundered and struggled to survive. Today, the Trail of Tears is a national park that commemorates a journey of injustice.

European Immigration and Settlement

The Spanish, English, French, and Americans colonized and fought to control the area of the Florida Panhandle to the Mississippi coast, and all influenced the cultural landscape.

The Gulf French

The Spaniard Hernando Desoto was the first European to document the Mississippi River, but he failed to see its value as a potential resource. Meanwhile, the French entered the Mississippi River from the north and settled near the heart of the recently extinct Mississippian culture. The first French settlements in 1699 occurred concurrently along the Gulf Coast and Mississippi River regions, and consisted of Biloxi, Mississippi, built on an ancient Native American site and settlements along both sides of the Mississippi in Illinois and Missouri; their architectural styles remain influential (photo 11.6).

In the eighteenth century, the French colonies in Louisiana, the Great Lakes, and Canada were connected in trading network. Biloxi appears on maps in 1710 and New Orleans in 1718. The first colonists were Roman Catholic French, who were later joined by Huguenots and German-speaking Protestants.

The end of the French and Indian War in 1763 ended the French North American colonies. In the Treaty of Paris, France lost all claims to Canada and gave Louisiana to Spain, while Britain received Spanish Florida, Upper Canada, and various French holdings overseas. Spain returned the Louisiana colonies back to the French in 1801 and in 1803, the French offered Louisiana to Americans, resulting in the Louisiana Purchase. The French and French Creole cultural traits remain

BOX 11.2   GEOSPATIAL TECHNOLOGIES: VISUALIZING HURRICANES

In September 2017, a series of hurricanes struck in quick succession, impacting Houston, Florida, and the Caribbean. Hurricanes Katia, Irma, and Jose are shown in map 11.4. Hurricane Maria followed a few weeks later, destroying large parts of Puerto Rico.

While meteorologists struggled to find the right words to describe the situation of multiple hurricanes threatening land, satellite imagery proved a powerful way to visual the events unfolding.

The visible nfrared imaging radiometer suite (VIIRS) on the Suomi NPP satellite captured the data for a mosaic of

Hurricane Katia, Irma, and Jose as they appeared in the early hours of September 8, 2017. The images were acquired by the VIIRS "day-night band," which detects light signals in a range of wavelengths from green to near-infrared, and uses filtering techniques to observe signals such as city lights, auroras, wildfires, and moonlight.

The ability to track hurricanes during the night is critical to more accurate predictions.

MAP 11.4. Three hurricanes—Katia, Irma, and Jose—threaten the Gulf Coast in 2017.
Source: NASA

pronounced in the region, such as the French Quarter of New Orleans, the exiled Cajuns, and toponyms (Detroit, Michigan; St. Louis, Missouri; and Baton Rouge, Louisiana), along with administrative units of land such as the Mississippi River long lots and Louisiana's parishes (equivalent to counties). The French were said to have given the region its "Dixie" name. There are several theories as to the origin, but a popular one is that the French circulated ten-dollar banknotes that were inscribed with the French word *dix* ("ten") and the South became the land of dixies.

East Texas Settlement

In the seventeenth century, Spanish settlement moved from Mexico into Texas, establishing missions along the Texas Gulf Coast. Catholicism spread to the Native people via a mission system. The first and best-known mission was the Alamo—San Antonio de Valero—built in 1718, followed in 1720 by Mission San José (photo 11.7).

The San Antonio missions received land grants from the king of Spain, and the monks became the first successful Texas cattle ranchers. Despite the small Spanish population, Spanish cultural traits—equipment, dress, saddles, and terminology—influenced the cattle industry.

In 1820, Spain, unable to attract its own colonists, opened settlement of East Texas to Anglo Americans, who were attracted to the inexpensive land (four cents per acre). In 1821, the new Mexican Republic continued the land policy as long as Anglo recruits were Catholic, industrious, and willing to become Mexican citizens. An early Anglo recruit was Moses Austin, father to Stephen Austin. When Moses died in 1821, Stephen fulfilled his father's land grant and established a colony on the Brazos River in what became Austin County, Texas.

In the 1830s and 1840s, Germans and Czechs fled unsettled political situations at home and migrated into the Texas Hill Country. Many town names and architectural styles reflect the region's ethnic origins. German immigrants settled inland

BOX 11.3   NATIONAL PARKS: TRAIL OF TEARS HERITAGE TRAIL

In 1978, Congress approved the National Historic Trails System Act. This act was approved to provide for the ever-increasing outdoor recreation needs of an expanding population and to promote the preservation of and public access to the open-air, outdoor areas and historic resources of the United States. The Act stipulated that trails should be established primarily near urban areas or within scenic areas and along historic travel routes that are often more remotely located. Among the first historic trails is the Lewis and Clark Trail.

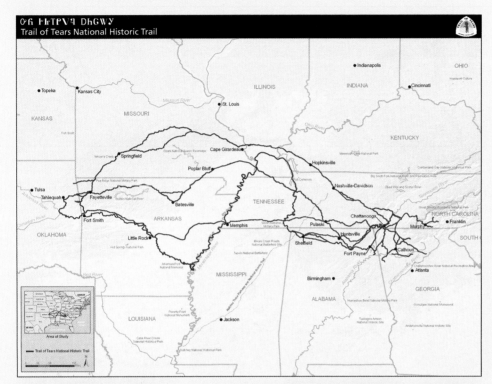

MAP 11.5. The Trail of Tears Heritage Trail Map.
Source: National Park Service

PHOTO 11.5. Cherokees retrace the Trail of Tears at Pea Ridge National Military Park in Garfield, Arkansas.
Source: National Park Service

In 1987, The Trail of Tears National Heritage Trail was added to the park system. The Trail remembers and commemorates the survival of the Cherokee people, forcefully removed from their homelands in Georgia, Alabama, and Tennessee to live in Indian Territory, now Oklahoma. The Heritage Trail is some twenty-two hundred miles and winds through portions of nine states and includes land and water routes (map 11.5). Although some markers had survived along the route, geographers and historians used old maps in combination with modern technology to locate surviving road segments as part of preservation efforts. There are numerous sites to visit along the trail, including museums, interpretive centers, and historic sites (photo 11.5).

The power of the Trail of Tears National Heritage Trail is that it presents a story of racial injustice, intolerance, and suffering, but is also a story of survival.

PHOTO 11.6. French-Creole House, Ste. Genevieve, Missouri. Both the French and Germans settled along this stretch of the Mississippi, bringing with them their cultural architectural models. The architectural style of wraparound porches was adapted to the warmer climate of the Mississippi River Valley. The Bequette-Ribault house is a French-Creole vernacular structure constructed from vertically placed (poteaux en terre) timbers forming the walls. The Bequette-Ribault house is one of five US buildings built in this manner.

from Houston, establishing Hill Country towns such as New Ulm, New Braunfels, Millheim, and Berlin. Moravian Czech immigrants began settlement in 1851 near Corpus Christi, and became the major Slavic population to farm in the United States.

Gulf Plantations

The plantation settlement pattern was established on Delta and Black Belt land. A change in banking practices in 1830 enabled state banks to lend "easy" money on western lands. Many Carolina and Georgia plantation owners abandoned their leached and eroded coastal and piedmont lands for the more promising Gulf Coast.

The Delta was swampy and overgrown, but once cultivated, the land was fertile and grew cotton. Slaves worked the cotton crop and typically outnumbered the whites. In the Black Belt, the population multiplied from 9,000 in 1810 to 310,000 in 1830.

The region's largest cities—New Orleans and Mobile—exported cotton, but they contained a small number of residents as the region was predominately rural. In Alabama, only 2 percent of the population was urban in 1840. The rural plantation ruled the Delta and Black Belt economic and political life for generations.

The Civil War devastated many plantations. With the men at war, women ran the plantations as best they could. Many slaves left to fight or heeded the call of freedom. Some plantation families lost everything and were unable to adapt to postwar circumstances; other families thrived, but often because they smuggled and sold their crop to the northern enemy. After the war, labor was in short supply. Freed slaves left to seek their fortunes, while others stayed on the plantations but in different circumstances.

Blacks who stayed after the war were uninterested in working on a plantation; they wanted to work their own land, become independent, and exercise their political rights. But owning land was seldom an option, and many blacks became **sharecroppers**—tenant farmers who gave a share of the crop to the plantation owners, who lacked both funds and labor to work the land. In the Black Belt, slave cabins were relocated on small plots of land, and former slaves sharecropped cotton and grew subsistence gardens on the plantation owner's land. By 1910,

BOX 11.4   DID YOU KNOW . . . FRENCH ACADIAN "CAJUN"

The Cajuns (a corruption of the word *Acadian*) settled the bayou-ridden coast west of New Orleans. After the end of the French and Indian War in 1853, Acadians living in Canada chose to emigrate to the then Spanish Louisiana. Once in Louisiana, they moved west to the unoccupied swamps and bayous along the coastal parishes from the Texas border to the edges of the Atchafalaya Basin (map 11.6).

The Cajuns adapted to their life in the bayous, fishing, hunting, and trapping in their *pirogues*—canoe-type boats fashioned from native bayou cypress. They trapped muskrat, nutria, or alligator and also farmed on the natural levees and coastal grasslands. The isolated backcountry life forced adaptation to the local topography and resources, and affected their French patois, eventually emerging as culturally distinct Cajuns.

Today, Cajun music and cuisine is popular within the American ethnic mosaic and is widespread outside the Atchafalaya Basin. The music is lively and features the fiddle and accordion. The cuisine has changed significantly from the blander Acadian food of Nova Scotia, adopting local ingredients—crawfish, peppers, and gumbo.

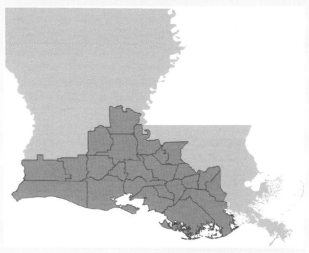

MAP 11.6. Cajun Parishes of Louisiana. The Acadians settled to the west of New Orleans. Vermillion Bay and the Atchafalaya Basin are the heart of Cajun country. The Cajuns adopted and were adopted by many other ethnic groups that settled in the country, including the Native Americans. They evolved as a French-speaking but diverse group of people with a distinctive culture and cuisine.

PHOTO 11.7. The Alamo.
Source: iStock/SeanPavonePhoto

sharecropping constituted 92 percent of the farms, and 95 percent of the sharecroppers were black.

Between 1910 and 1970, more than 1.7 million blacks left the South for jobs in industry in the North. In Mississippi, more than a hundred thousand left between 1915 and 1920. Blacks migrated north following regional rail lines and roads—those from the Mississippi area moved to Chicago, those from Alabama and Kentucky to Detroit, and those from east of the Appalachians to New York or other Megalopolis cities. Once relocated, another pattern of migration, **chain migration,** followed, in which friends or family followed earlier émigrés. The **Great Migration** peaked in the 1950s and 1960s, with **push and pull factors** pushing them away from the South and pulling them toward jobs in northern industry. As a result, black population in the South dropped from 77 percent (1940) to 50 percent (1970).

Blacks who remained in the Gulf South had few opportunities to prosper and little control or profit from the cotton they grew. Few owned land. Even successful towns, such as Mound Bayou, Mississippi, once called the "Jewel of the Delta," was devastated when the local bank was forced to reorganize and farmers had to return to tenancy. Delta planters once again had a firm grip on cotton production.

Despite emancipation, southern blacks were denied the vote and subjected to **Jim Crow laws** that enforced racial segregation in employment and housing, voting discrimination, and violence toward blacks. With more blacks than whites in the South, whites denied the vote to blacks so they could maintain control.

Segregation ended officially with the 1960s' civil rights movement, which focused along the Black Belt Selma-Montgomery Freedom Road. Racism and segregation declined, and living conditions improved for southern blacks. Among the changes was the removal of Jim Crow laws. The results were politically dramatic for southern blacks. Before the Voting Right Act (1965), 72 blacks held elected office in the South; a mere five years later, 711 held elected office. Some migrated blacks, having experienced the underlying racism of the North, returned to the South where they felt they had a better chance of furthering the black cause.

Cultural Perspectives

A wide range of influences formed the Gulf Coast cultural landscape. The oldest and longest-lasting influence is the interaction of the physical landscape with pestilence and pests. In addition, three cultures are each tied to this region's racial divisiveness, the blues of the Delta, Creole, and the Black Belt.

Disease

During the eighteenth and nineteenth centuries, virulent killers—smallpox, malaria, dysentery, cholera, and yellow fever—swept periodically through the region due to regional climate and physiography. The interrelationships between disease, epidemics, contagion, and landscape were not understood, so the causes—viruses (smallpox), unclean water (cholera, dysentery), and mosquitoes (yellow fever, malaria)—were unknown.

Yellow fever epidemics killed thousands during the nineteenth and early twentieth centuries. For example, a wave of yellow fever outbreaks swept through the Mississippi Alluvial Plain in the 1870s. Research by Megan Kate Nelson found that in 1878 alone, Memphis lost half its population of forty thousand to the disease; many fled and thousands died. At the time, diseases were treated by bleeding, quinine, opium, a mixture called calomel (mercury and chloride), and the chief preventative and cure: whiskey. But most treatments were ineffective, and mortality often reached 60 percent during periodic epidemics. Urban density and poor sanitation elevated death rates. Construction of city sewers and drainage canals in the 1860s improved conditions, although periodic epidemics continued to kill thousands in Gulf Coast cities until the twentieth century.

Louisiana and especially New Orleans were subjected to more than their share of disease, because of their numerous swamps, bayous, wetlands, and unsanitary public health conditions, such as open sewage for human waste and lack of a clean water system (photo 11.8). Wealthy residents had better access to sanitation and could go to healthier surroundings during the disease-ridden hot and humid months. Clearing the land and draining the swamps helped rid the towns of mosquitoes, but clearing was irregular until the twentieth century.

PHOTO 11.8. A Lousianna Bayou.

Source: iStock/brucemaloneatx

PHOTO 11.9. Southern Louisiana Cemetery. Tombs in southern Louisiana are often above ground because of high groundwater levels, which cause the graves to fill with water or float to the surface. Modern drainage has allowed graves to be below ground, but the tradition often prevails.

In early New Orleans, graves required special arrangements. The high water table forced the first graves to be shallow. Later, dirt topped the graves to facilitate additional burials. Still later, the indigent were buried below ground, while most others were buried in aboveground tombs, so as not to float to the surface (photo 11.9). The tombs could be elaborate, depending on the wealth of the deceased, and funerals became a regionally distinctive cultural display and even extravaganza. Black cultural influences, such as the jazz funeral, began somber and grew raucous as the body was laid to rest. The funeral procession marches down the street to the cemetery wearing white and returns dancing, singing, and celebrating life.

Pests

The warm and marshy landscape of the Gulf Coast is ideal for the mosquito to lay its eggs and develop. The adult mosquito transmits infectious disease and was the primary insect to affect Gulf Coast residents until the twentieth century, when science made the connection between the mosquito and disease.

The cattle tick and boll weevil also affected animals and crops. The cattle tick was prevalent in Florida and in Texas, where cattle carried the tick but were immune to the effects of the Texas fever ticks carried. In 1868, when thousands of cattle died in the Midwest, the source of the problem was traced to tick-infested Texas cattle driven north. This led to excluding southern cattle from the north, which crippled the southern industry. An eradication program ended the infestation in 1943, when once again the herds could be mixed.

The boll weevil, boring into cotton bolls and eating cotton fibers, caused more than $45 billion in damage before it was controlled. The beetle spread into Texas from Mexico in 1892 and then moved through the cotton-growing areas around sixty miles annually, reaching Virginia in 1922. Eventually the weevil infested the entire Gulf region and then the Carolinas. Some regions have only recently returned to planting cotton. The weevils' influence in infected areas was so pronounced that it entered popular culture through music: Many Delta blues songs feature the weevil.

Pesticide use on cotton is three to five times greater than on corn, but little has been studied about the environmental effects of pesticides on the land and human population. An alternative to direct pesticide application is genetically modified seed; however, many farmers have rejected this seed because of lower yields and poor seed quality.

The Blues

The blues, a music form rising from the Delta's steam and heat, verbalized emancipated black farmers' disillusionment over segregation, Jim Crow discrimination, and endless sharecropping debt. The blues combines African roots (call and response), southern field hollers, and spirituals. It sings of the promises and letdowns blacks found after the Civil War—and has brought respect and fame to many Delta blacks, such as B.B. King and Muddy Waters. Blues was a dominant influence in the evolution of rock and roll, including its most famous white singer from Yazoo County, Mississippi—Elvis Presley. The influence of Blues is present in the Rolling Stones ("Little Red Rooster"), the Animals ("House of the Rising Sun"), and many others.

The blues evolved along Mississippi's Highway 61—from Memphis to Natchez—the birthplace and home of many blues artists. Today, summertime blues festivals enliven the dusty lots and chained-in yards of small towns and villages. But changing times have many people fearing that the blues may be dying, because cotton no longer requires the manual labor that once inspired the songs.

Creole Culture

The Creole arose from the Gulf and West Indies slave sugar plantations where Spanish, French, African, and Anglicans interbred in the seventeenth century. The Creole culture dominated the region until American annexation. Then the Gulf Coast states joined the Confederacy, and with that sealed their fate to keep separate from the mainstream until well into the twentieth century.

Creole is a term that has several definitions: a mixture of several cultures, a free person of color, a mixed-race person. The designations are not clear, and many an argument has erupted over the various definitions of Creole. According to Professor Gerald McNeill,

> Why the argument? Initially, the term meant one who was born in the New World. Now, did that apply to just Europeans or did it include Africans? To some, you had to have French or Spanish ancestry and speak French or Spanish. To others, Creole was not restricted to just Europeans as Creole identified locals of all colors. In the late nineteenth and early twentieth century a totally different Creole designation evolved in Louisiana. Creoles could be White Creole (Europeans descendants), Black Creole (African descendants), or mixed-race Creoles (light-skinned). So, "Who is a Creole?" In today's world, it probably would identify a person of an ancestral mixture living in South Louisiana or having family ties to South Louisiana.

Creole culture has left a significant mark on the gastronomic landscape. Caribbean methods were imported, and pork, barbeque, rice, and the ever-present red-hot chilies were cooked into a hundred varieties of hot sauce. Rum, distilled from native sugar, was the potent alcohol of the region.

The Cultural Black Belt

The Black Belt core is in Alabama, but spreads across the South incorporating the areas that have a high percentage of blacks. Before the Civil War, the Black Belt supported a wealthy, slaveholding plantation economy, and it remained a strong political force and source of wealth into the twentieth century. The Civil War destroyed the Black Belt cotton-growing plantation economy when slavery, the economic lynchpin of the system,

ended and many young, Confederate soldiers were killed. The lack of infrastructure (few roads and no railroads) confined the owners and their freed slaves to the region after the war, and helped isolate the Old South mentality.

Since the turn of the twentieth century, however, the regional economy was devastated by the boll weevil, migration of African Americans, and Jim Crow politics. Today, it is a racially polarized region. While many whites are wealthy, many African Americans are poverty-ridden, poorly educated, and have a higher unemployment rate and less adequate social services than the rest of the region.

Yet it is also home to one of the most powerful political movements of the twentieth century. Alabama's Black Belt was central to the civil rights movement, in which some of its most remembered leaders and battles emerged—Martin Luther King Jr., Rosa Parks, and the Selma March—all of which led to the 1965 Voting Rights Act and the beginning of black political activism.

Today, the former cotton-growing region depends on pine tree plantations, cattle, hunting leases, and continued educational segregation. Private Christian academies are almost exclusively for whites, leaving Black Belt blacks with underfunded public schools. Unfortunately, poverty rates in the Black Belt are higher than the state and US averages, and some counties within the Black Belt suffer poverty rates of 35–40 percent (table 11.1).

Population, Immigration, and Diversity

The Gulf Coast has traditionally not attracted a substantial population. But that has changed in the last several decades, especially along the coastal areas where sea breezes make the humid climate tolerable and the casinos offer other pleasures. Gulf Coast population density has doubled and has grown faster than the national average. For example, in Mississippi, coastal county density is up to 334 per square mile, whereas the Mississippi average is 63 per square mile.

However, the Gulf Coast region has not attracted a large number of foreign born. In Mississippi, only 2.3 percent of its population is foreign born; Alabama has 3.5 percent and Louisiana 4 percent, compared to the US average of 14.2 percent. Even the cosmopolitan New Orleans has only 6 percent foreign born (compare that to Miami with more than 57 percent foreign born).

On the other hand, the Gulf Coast remains home to a significant percentage of African Americans, which make

TABLE 11.1. Comparison of Poverty in the Black Belt Region of Alabama with the State and Country, 2017

	Black Belt	Alabama	United States
Poverty level (%)	32.5	19.2	13.5
Median household income	$27,000	$41,000	$55,700

Source: US Census

BOX 11.5 ICONIC IMAGES: MARDI GRAS

Mardi Gras is a rough translation of the French for Fat Tuesday, and is so named because it is the last hurrah for Roman Catholics before the spare days of Lent prior to Easter. The roots of the end-of-winter-beginning-of-spring season reach back to pagan times, as do many of the holy days celebrated today. Mardi Gras was originally a Christian celebration that in New Orleans turned distinctly more secular and boisterous. Louisiana and especially New Orleans are known for over-the-top Mardi Gras celebrations and numerous parades.

It is a day associate with enjoyment and eating heartily before the ritual fasting of Ash Wednesday and the season of Lent. The name reminds us of the French influence in Louisianan, a state named after a French King. In 1703, French settlers in Mobile held the first Mardi Gras celebrations in the region. The first Mardi Gras celebration in New Orleans took place in 1837. In 1875, it was declared a legal holiday in Louisiana.

On Mardi Gras, floats decorated by local groups, known as krewes, parade through the streets of New Orleans. The parade is a sight to behold as the krewe members in elaborate costumes mingle with marching bands and enthusiastic spectators (photo 11.10). Traditions include the throwing of colored beads, the use of purple, green, and gold color palettes, the eating of King Cake, and the late night revelry as less-than-sober people wander the streets asking for beads from spectators in upper-story balconies. It is more Bacchanalian than Catholic.

The Mardi Gras is now a major event, often seen as the embodiment of a city as much French and Caribbean and North American. The city attracts close to ten million visitors a year, spending in total approximately $7 billion. Mardi Gras provides a powerful marketing image to sell the city for many visitors.

PHOTO 11.10. Mardi Gras in New Orleans.
Source: iStock/Photoservice

up 27 percent of the population in Alabama, 32 percent in Louisiana and 38 percent in Mississippi.

Demographic and settlement patterns are different in coastal Texas, however. Austin, for example, is home to 14 percent foreign born, but with not many African Americans, and Houston is home to 29 percent foreign born (43 percent Hispanic), far above the US averages. The Rio Grande Valley's proximity to Mexico has meant a large Latino population southwest of San Antonio. Although many Latinos in the region are legal, many undocumented workers populate the Texas border regions, living in unincorporated rural communities called **colonias** (Spanish for a settlement of homes, a neighborhood).

Urban Trends

Gulf Coast cities are located along the coastal margins, the rivers, the Balcones Escarpment, and the Rio Grande River. Generally, coastal cities are split between agricultural core ports—Mobile and Biloxi—and the industrialized west—New Orleans and Houston-Galveston. River cities along the Mississippi include Memphis, Baton Rouge, and the geographically curious Cairo, Illinois. Both San Antonio and Austin, Texas, are positioned at the foot of the Balcones Escarpment. Brownsville and Laredo are along the Rio Grande. Most are traditional cities, but Austin and New Orleans have gained special distinctions: Austin as a city working toward sustainability, and New Orleans as a city trying to rebuild sustainably after Hurricane Katrina.

New Orleans, Louisiana
(MSA 1.2 million)

New Orleans has been a multicultural racial and musical **melting pot**. The "Big Easy" is the birthplace of jazz and home to one of the most cultural distinct festivals, the American **Mardi Gras** celebration (box 11.5).

New Orleans' population and demographics changed after Katrina's flooding in 2005. For several years after the levees broke, more than a hundred thousand people remain displaced. Between 2005 and 2010, population estimates in the New Orleans metropolitan area had dropped from over a million to seven hundred thousand and the city was at one-third of its pre-flood population. But in the last five years, the city has repopulated and is above its pre-Katrina population at 1.2 million, although the demographic profile has change. The population today is whiter (33 percent in 2016, up from 28 percent in 2000) and wealthier ($36,000 in 2016, up from $17,000 in 2000) than before the storm.

Ironically, areas destroyed by the hurricane have become the newest attraction, **disaster tourism**. Tour companies, answering popular demand, began to include the devastated sections of the city in their standard tours. The Gray Line advertises its Hurricane Katrina Tour as an opportunity to "drive past an actual levee that 'breached' and see the resulting devastation that displaced hundreds of thousands of US residents" and "to learn the direct connection between America's disappearing coastal wetlands, oil & gas pipelines, levee protection and hurricane destruction."

Rebuilding has been slow and expensive. Katrina's destruction of New Orleans presented the city with a unique opportunity, to rebuild "green." Green buildings are most cost-efficient when constructed from the ground up, using the site to its advantage and using ecologically renewable materials. Several sustainable-oriented companies and organizations—US Green Building Council, Enterprise Foundation, Habitat for Humanity, the Trust for Public Land, and Architecture for Humanity—encouraged rebuilding more sustainably in the Gulf Coast communities (photo 11.11). Such large-scale all-new construction could have been a model for the greening of entire cities across America. However, government incentives and benefits were seldom redirected toward sustainable growth and instead focused on rebuilding as quickly as possible. Many of the new homes re-built below sea level remain vulnerable to floods.

Rebuilding has not been easy for the city, and many poor and middle-class residents cannot afford the more expensive "green" construction and so have not returned. Despite these problems, the process of rebuilding New Orleans, constructing strong levees, building homes on stilts in case of flooding, and following green designs and efficiencies has created a wider discussion about planning for resilience.

Oil Cities

The oil industry spurred the growth of several Gulf cities on the west coast and waterways: Houston, Galveston, Lake Charles, New Orleans, Baton Rouge, Corpus Christi, Beaumont, and Port Arthur. New Orleans and Baton Rouge were established cities prior to the twentieth-century boom. Lake Charles was a mid-nineteenth-century lumber mill town that evolved into petrochemical refining after World War II. Corpus Christi

PHOTO 11.11. Rebuilt Home in the Ninth Ward, New Orleans, Louisiana. Rebuilding in the Ninth Ward is sometimes done with green and sustainable construction, but this type of construction is usually out of the financial reach of the people who live in the ward.

Source: Photo by Warren Hofstra

grew from a small shallow port and resort town into a dredged deepwater port that distributes local agricultural goods and petrochemicals. Beaumont and Port Arthur both grew after the turn-of-the-century Spindletop oil strike.

Houston, Texas
(MSA 6.7 million)

Sprawling across a flat, marshy inland plain, Houston is the largest city in Texas and the South, and the sixth-largest metropolitan area in the United States. A world-famous shipping port and oil, energy, and medical center, Houston is home to such companies as Shell, Conoco, Reliant Energy, Dynegy, and Halliburton.

Houston's earliest trade was in cotton, agriculture, and livestock. The shallow and narrow shipping channel limited access for oceangoing vessels. Houston competed with Galveston for shipping traffic, until the city dredged and widened its waterway in 1914 thereby bypassing Galveston in size and importance. Today the Port of Houston, the second-largest shipping port for America in total tonnage and tenth-largest in the world, is also home to the world's second-largest petrochemical complex. The protected inland channel made Houston a prime shipping port and refinery location. There are more than eighteen hundred oil and gas rigs, many of them belonging to the large energy companies headquartered here. Petrodollars fuel the city's economy, although there have been a series of booms and busts, as oil prices have peaked, then dipped, then peaked again. The current oil bust is impacting the economy, as the number of drilling rigs pumping oil has fallen.

Houston's economy has diversified beyond energy: it is home to the Texas Medical Center, a collection of forty-six hospitals, research centers, and medical schools that together employ more than seventy-five thousand people in an industry that is largely immune to ups and downs of the oil economy.

Houston has confronted numerous environmental problems during the twentieth century, including subsidence, flooding, sewage problems, and air pollution, and has struggled to make significant progress. Public transportation is inefficient and made more so by the city's sprawl and low population density. As a result, long commutes by car have exacerbated air pollution, particularly ozone. Over the last decade, Houston has consistently ranked in the top ten worst cities for air quality. And while the city does coordinate its departments in relation to environmental standards, it has had little success in recycling. It currently recycles 6 percent of its residential waste, lagging far behind the national rate of 34 percent. The poor recycling rate is tied into the city's lack of zoning, which has facilitated urban sprawl. Low density living makes curbside recycling economically more expensive. In 2014, Houston launched a new curbside recycling program called "One Bin For All" allowing residents to mix waste and recyclables together in the same bin to be sorted automatically at a first-of-its-kind facility, built and operated by a private firm. The city also has a mandatory yard waste compostable bag program. But in 2016, the city decided to stop recycling glass, a disappointing setback for recycling.

One of the main sustainability challenges is energy. Given Houston's hot and humid climate, it is also one of the most air-conditioned cities in America, which means high energy use. Houston has been known as the energy capital of the United States and now aims to become the energy conservation capital. Houston has adopted many energy-efficient and retrofit standards to reduce energy consumption, and currently boasts more than one hundred Leadership in Energy and Environmental Design (LEED)-certified buildings. But with nearby oil refineries providing plentiful, cheap energy, the city has a long way to go.

River Cities

The Mississippi River's largest cities were founded when water traffic was the dominant means of transportation. The cities serviced mining and agricultural production. Below Cairo, the eastern bluff cities—Baton Rouge, Natchez, and Memphis—prospered, while the western bank flood plain cities—Cairo, Greensville, and New Madrid—had limited growth and were victims of periodic flooding.

The Rio Grande Valley has several expanding cities along the border region. The largest city, Brownsville, is near the mouth of the Rio Grande. Along the US-Mexican border are several twin cities, such as Laredo/Nuevo Laredo and Eagle Pass/Piedras Negras.

The Balcones Escarpment separates the coastal areas from the Great Plains. Faults create a natural divide, which forced the inland area up while the coastal areas downwarped. Saturated water draining from the uplifted block created springs and artesian wells. The water from the springs and wells determined the locations of San Antonio and Austin.

San Antonio, Texas
(MSA 2.4 million)

San Antonio was established along the escarpment at San Pedro Springs in 1709. The city still depends on the springs and is the largest city in America dependent on groundwater. The Edwards Aquifer is the source of the groundwater, and the city has learned how to use its water wisely.

The battle of the Alamo in 1836, when Mexican general Santa Anna's army massacred a band of Texans, placed San Antonio on the map. The Alamo became the decisive battle for Texan independence a few months later, when Americans angered at the massacre poured into Texas and defeated General Santa Anna.

San Antonio is among the fastest-growing and most Hispanic cities in America, with a 63 percent Latino population and 27 percent white (compared to 37 percent and 45 percent averages for Texas). The city is home to 14 percent foreign born, most of those coming from Mexico and Central America.

San Antonio developed a sustainability plan in 2016, although sustainability efforts predate this. For example, the city has long celebrated it's Riverwalk (photo 11.13). The city identified "a sustainable San Antonio" as a community that has a thriving economy, a healthy environment, and an inclusive and fair community. To meet this definition of sustainability,

BOX 11.6   HOUSTON: HURRICANES AND URBAN PLANNING

In September 2017, Hurricane Harvey became the costliest tropical cyclone on record, causing $200 billion in damages, eclipsing Hurricane Katrina. Most of the damages were due to the wide-spread flooding of the Houston Metropolitan Area. Many areas in the city were deluged with more than thirty inches over a two-day period, which equals fifteen trillion gallons of water. In fact, the National Weather Service added two new colors to the rain index to show the amount of rain accumulated from Harvey,

Throughout Texas, more than three hundred thousand people were left without electricity. More than 48,700 homes were affected by Harvey throughout the state, including over one thousand that were completely destroyed and more than seventeen thousand that sustained major damage (photo 11.12).

One reason for the massive flooding in Houston is the city's relatively flat topography and low elevation.

Another reason for the massive flooding in Houston can be traced back to bad practices in urban planning. To attract businesses, residents, and money, Houston has developed without much planning and practically zero zoning. People have built anything anywhere. One consequence has been the location of oil refineries or chemical plants surrounded by residential neighborhoods, something that would not happen in a city with effective zoning.

In addition, there has been the tremendous increase in Houston's impervious land cover between 2001 and 2015. Native prairies and areas of greenfields were converted to parking lots and roads. Marshes have become malls. Waters that once drained or pooled up in prairies now ruin homes. In the two years before Harvey, sixteen thousand buildings had been flooded, and the city was hit with more than $1 billion in damage.

Flooding is not new to Houston. The devastation from Hurricane Harvey may challenge Houston to rebuild with better zoning measures in place to mitigate the impacts of flooding in the future.

PHOTO 11.12. Hurricane Harvey caused widespread flooding in Houston.
Source: iStock/Karl Spencer

the sustainability plan highlights six focus areas: energy, food, green buildings and infrastructure, land use and transportation, public health, and solid waste. The plan also addresses climate change, which it says is a "cross-cutting" theme because it will affect the way the city plans for changes in temperatures (planning for cooling/heating, ensuring public safety, and protecting public health), changes in precipitation (preparing for droughts, planning for municipal water use, or designing infrastructure to reduce the impacts of flooding), and increases in other extreme weather events (enhancing emergency management and preparedness efforts).

Austin, Texas
(MSA 2 million)

Austin was founded at Barton Springs on the Balcones Escarpment. In 1839, Austin was chosen as the capital of Texas. The city grew slowly until after World War II. In the 1950s and 1960s, the economy expanded into high-technology sectors, when companies such as IBM and Texas Instruments moved in, taking advantage of nearby University of Texas. In the 1990s, Motorola, Dell Computers, and more than eight hundred high-tech companies turned the metro area into a technopole, and Austin evolved into a city with a high quality of life.

PHOTO 11.13. Riverwalk, San Antonio, Texas. In 1921, a deadly flood caused many people to rethink the river. In the 1940s and 1950s, riverside establishments faced the street and the river was a dumping ground. But starting in the late 1960s, more than fifty restaurants, along with major hotels, opened up facing the river, instead of backing to it. The Riverwalk idea has become a redevelopment inspiration for many other cities.

In the 1990s, Austin vowed to become the "Clean Energy Capital of the World" and to grow in a more responsible way. Austin has set renewable energy goals, including the installation of 165 wind turbines that power twenty thousand homes, and has committed to a 20 percent renewable electricity supply by 2020, with the most successful utility-sponsored green building program in the country. So far, the utility has saved enough energy to eliminate the need for additional coal-burning power plants.

In 1991, Austin adopted the nation's first green building program. LEED Silver Certification is required on all city buildings, and residents and contractors are encouraged to build green. To date, Austin Energy Green Building has rated more than ten thousand homes and fifteen million square feet of commercial structures, and as many as one-third of all single-family homes and apartments built in Austin are now green-rated homes. Additionally, most of the new commercial and multi-family buildings downtown and in large-scale developments are Green Building-rated. The program has successfully avoided more than twenty thousand metric tons of greenhouse gas emissions in the last ten years. Recently, the American Planning Association awarded Austin its annual Sustainable Plan Award, recognizing its ambitious and comprehensive sustainability.

The Economy

The Primary Sector

The Gulf Coast natural resources support primary, processing, and shipping industries—from eighteenth-century fur trapping to more current forestry, fish, oil, gas, and agriculture. For many cities in the region, dependence on oil, gas, and fish has been problematic, and there have been attempts to diversify.

Agriculture

European settlement altered the pine forest, the alluvial floodplain, and the semi-desert Rio Grande Valley: Gulf Coast forests were cut, and farms were established on former marshes along the Louisiana Coast or the arid lands of the Rio Grande Valley.

The Port of New Orleans handled the regional crop production, progressing from plantations growing monoculture crops—rice, indigo, and tobacco—in the eighteenth century and sugarcane and "King Cotton" after the 1793 invention of the cotton gin. Today, cotton, rice, and sugarcane dominate current production along with significant corn and soybean crops.

According to geographer John Fraser Hart, most agricultural land in the Rio Grande Valley is pasture, and cultivated "crop islands" utilize ideally suited soils and climate for specific crops. The mild, frost-free winters allow farmers to grow winter specialty fruits and vegetables to supply northern cities.

Cotton   Cotton requires summer precipitation, two hundred frost-free days, and plenty of water during the growing season but little rain in the fall. These requirements have limited the American crop to the South, where cotton was the Gulf Coast economic staple until the boll weevil infestation. **Antebellum** cotton was cultivated on Delta and Black Belt slaveholding plantations, but the labor pool shifted to sharecroppers after the Civil War. After World War II, regional farms consolidated and mechanized.

The Mississippi Alluvial Valley, especially the Delta, still grows cotton, but the cotton market changed when American textile mills shut down in the 1980s. Currently, much of the cotton grown is exported to China, and the ginning techniques have been changed to respond to foreign mill requirements.

BOX 11.7 URBAN SUSTAINABILITY BEST PRACTICES: AFFORDABLE HOUSING IN AUSTIN

Austin, Texas, is a fast-growing city with a population expected to double by 2040. Although the city has been praised for being a green, highly livable city, it acknowledges that it confronts strong patterns of racial, ethnic, and income segregation and endures problems with poverty. While many sustainability plans focus only on environmental challenges, a key element in Austin's 2012 sustainability plan, *ImagineAustin*, is to develop and maintain housing affordability.

Rapid growth has caused median housing prices to rise in many close-in neighborhoods. Affordable apartment rental units have been converted to condominium use, contributing to a shortage of units in the rental housing market, especially for households with incomes less than $20,000. Existing zoning and development codes incentivize low-density sub-urban neighborhoods that has kept housing diversity low.

As a result, many long-time residents of Austin, particularly low-income renters, are finding that they no longer can afford to stay.

In 2017, the city rewrote its land development code and released, CodeNEXT, which not only encourages, but requires more diversity in housing types, such as duplex, multiplex, and rowhouses. By allowing more units and incentivizing a range of unit sizes, the new code could make it easier to develop housing to suite a range of space and economic needs. The city has also pledged to end veteran homelessness and set numerical goals, timelines, and strategies to maintain and create affordable housing for a range of incomes throughout the city.

There is no silver bullet to housing affordability. Yet, Austin's plan is noteworthy for highlighting the importance of addressing issues of equity in sustainability planning.

Recently, nonlocal agribusiness has accrued profits and invested elsewhere, while the remaining farmers rent their land and "retire." At the same time, ethanol, the need for feed grains, and the market for domestic vegetable oils have boosted corn and soy prices. Many farmers have traded growing cotton for corn or soy.

The Delta depends on irrigation for its crops despite more than forty inches of annual precipitation, because summertime drought can reduce crop yields. Although the boll weevil is almost eradicated, the cotton crop is problematic because of unstable market prices and unsustainable groundwater irrigation and soil renewal. The alluvial soil is no longer renewed by periodic flooding of the river. Levees block the river's annual enrichment, and nitrogen-rich fertilizers that are added to the crops wash into streams and rivers, before discharging to the Gulf of Mexico, causing algal blooms and eutrophication.

Rice While rice production in the United States began in South Carolina, cultivation continued in the mid-nineteenth century in the swampy, watertight claypan of the Mississippi Alluvial Valley and southwestern Louisiana. Rice requires constant irrigation and flooding during its growing cycle, in order to alleviate water depletion and soil salinity.

Cajun rice production began during the eighteenth century. By 1900, rice was grown along the western Louisiana and eastern Texas coastlines. These areas continue to grow rice, but by the latter half of the twentieth century, the prime rice-growing region became the Grand Prairie of southeastern Arkansas, where the solid, flat land was perfect for mechanized rice production. Arkansas now cultivates 45 percent of US rice, and the Gulf Coast area, including Arkansas, grows about 75 percent of American rice. Yet, all the rice grown in America is less than 2 percent of global rice production.

Sugarcane Sugarcane is cultivated in only three US regions: the Rio Grande Valley; south of Baton Rouge, Louisiana; and near Lake Okeechobee in Florida (see chapter 10). The Louisiana crop prospered first near New Orleans and then in the South Central Cajun Bayou Teche and Bayou LaFourche country, where it remains cultivated today.

Sugarcane earned its foothold in antebellum Louisiana, and while it was a profitable crop for planters, it imposed the worst conditions for slaves. Slaves faced unending work on the huge sugar plantations and the nearby processing plants. Processing plants were built near the fields, because the sugar juices would sour if not processed immediately. The sugar plantations and local economy were ruined during the Civil War.

Before the Civil War, smaller plantations were the norm, but when railroads arrived in the 1880s, sugar plantations and mills consolidated and created large sugar plantations. The number of plantations diminished from a high of 1,549 in 1849 to 82 in 1969.

Currently, sugar plantations bear little resemblance to the old plantations. New plantations are mechanized, offer few jobs, and run by absentee ownership. New industrial concerns have replaced many old plantations, but problems also exist within sugarcane production.

The dependence on sugar in the American diet offers great opportunities for profit, but the lack of tropical regions to grow sugarcane hampers US production. The US is the ninth-largest producer in the world, far behind the number one producer, Brazil, and other major producers such as Mexico. But as trade restrictions are removed, American production costs cannot compete with Mexico's ideal sugarcane climate, and imported sugar from Mexico has significantly increased, creating heated debates about the politics of subsidies for US producers. Many sugar farmers argue that farmers in Mexico receive subsidies that allows them to dump large amount of sugar on the US market, depressing the price of raw sugar. They claim this is not fair and free trade in sugar and have been pressuring the US government to apply tariffs on Mexican sugar.

Forestry

The Gulf Coast is the largest pine forest in America. The acidic soil complements the native piney woods, but the natural vegetation and species are now rare. The native forests have succumbed to single-crop pine plantations.

In the eighteenth century, Gulf Coast lumber—cypress, cedar, and pine—were exported to the West Indies sugar plantations. In the mid 1800s, forest land was cut and converted to plantations. However, poor management left the land eroded, exhausted, and diseased. The plantations were abandoned, reverted to forest, or were planted as pine plantations. The arrival of railroads after the Civil War allowed Mobile, Alabama, and new ports such as Gulfport, Mississippi, to ship lumber. New Orleans led southern ports in wood exports into the twentieth century.

The Gulf Coast forest industry provided wood for the development of the US market after the Great Lakes forests were cut over, and then again after the 1980s, when Pacific Northwest forest clearance was halted for environmental reasons. Since the mid-1990s, the US Fish and Wildlife Service, the US Forest Service, and several private organizations have promoted diversity in the natural forest. They have worked to restore the longleaf pine forest ecosystem and practiced controlled burns to encourage propagation of pine and the regional vegetation. They have also put pressure on the industry to practice **sustainable yield**, in which trees can be harvested without diminishing the stock.

Early settlers cut over the old growth as they "tamed" the wilderness, so most lumber logged today is second or third growth. Sawed lumber can be attained in forty years, but the ground-up timber called **pulpwood** can be cut in twelve to fifteen years. Today's small-diameter trees, unsuitable for most lumber uses, are pulverized into paper and chipboard, which relies on chemicals that pollute water and cause health problems for industry workers. For example, the most common pollutant is formaldehyde, the source of many common ailments such as asthma and cancer. The reliance on small-diameter logs for chipboard is short-term and unsustainable.

Pulp and paper mills convert lumber to plywood, paper, and chipboard. In fact, lumber is no longer a mill's major product, but instead, an "engineered wood product"—first plywood, then oriented strand board (OSB), and particleboard, small trees glued and pressed into wood chips. The number of mills and board feet magnified as the forests grew. In 1953, there were 60 pulp and paper mills; in 1998 there were 103, each three times as large as a 1950s' mill. But pulp mills are expensive (about two billion dollars or more) and no new mills have been built since the 1990s. Recent competition from international suppliers, and a shrinking demand for paper in an increasingly digital world have meant a declining profits for many pulp mills. Many of the Gulf Coast states have seen paper mills close, including the

largest mill in the region, the Courtland mill in Alabama, which closed in 2014, laying off more than one thousand workers.

Fishery

The marshy coastal water of the Gulf is an excellent fishery for oysters, crab, shrimp, and plankton-eating fish. The multi-billion-dollar Gulf Coast seafood industry employs more than a million people, despite periodic hurricane damage, oil spills, upturned oyster beds, lost docks, and destroyed boats.

The Gulf port shrimp fleets is the nation's largest, and the traditional generational shrimper runs a small family-owned boat. Ironically, while shrimp is the most popular seafood in the United States, American shrimping has been in steep decline (photo 11.14). In the 1990s, 50 percent of the consumed shrimp were from American waters, but today, more than 90 percent of shrimp consumed come from Thailand, India, and Indonesia, where they are farmed in areas of coastal degradation and pollution. Reasons for the decline in American shrimp are multiple—high fuel prices, low shrimp prices as other countries produce massive quantities more cheaply, increased environmental regulation, and overshrimping. Many shrimpers no longer encourage their children to follow in their footsteps.

The Gulf Coast leads oyster production. Half the nation's oyster stock comes from the Gulf Coast, with Louisiana alone supplying 30 percent of the nation's oysters. Louisiana oysters, raised on public property in long-term-leased private beds, have maintained a healthy environment. Privatizing oyster beds in the late nineteenth century allowed the Louisiana industry to thrive, passing Maryland's Chesapeake Bay as the number one producer in 1982. However, in the last several decades, the oyster industry along the Louisiana coast has been impacted by problems with silting, changing salinity, industrial waste, oil production pollution, and biological factors such as predators, bacteria, diseases, and red tides.

Oysters are being asphyxiated, poisoned, and overfished, and people are eating fewer of them because of the fear of bacteria. Hurricanes and storms add to Gulf Coast fishery problems, spreading sediment that covered surfaces that oysters need for adherence and eliminating half of the oyster habitat. Despite efforts to restore the habitat, oystermen have left the industry in droves because of poor oyster harvests.

Aquaculture

Most US fish farming is in fresh water and the aquaculture industry efficiently and profitably converts catfish, tilapia, redfish, eels, and crawfish into seafood. In the wild, the bottom-feeding catfish has been harmed by pollution; however, farmed catfish tend to be healthier. Although there are some environmental issues with catfish farming, it is generally environmentally sustainable.

Several onshore fish farms are located in the Gulf Coast region. Mississippi has the most catfish farms and over a hundred thousand acres of fish farms produce 70 percent of the nation's catfish catch, with the remaining catfish also grown in the South, all farmed and processed in their native region and

PHOTO 11.14. Shrimp Boat, Dauphin Island, Alabama. Most shrimp boats are small, family-operated enterprises. Since the double blow of Katrina and the BP oil spill, shrimping has been in jeopardy.

providing much-needed capital for the local populace. Catfish, long a staple southern fish, became a popular replacement "crop" when cotton prices declined in the 1970s. Cotton acreage was converted to shallow ten- to twenty-acre catfish ponds, although the increased cost of feed has hurt profits and reduced the number of farms.

Once a local commodity, crawfish production in Louisiana is almost year-round with markets across the United States and overseas. Along Louisiana's Atchafalaya River, about twelve hundred crawfish farms and fisheries produced 127 million pounds and 96 percent of the national catch, generating about 172 million dollars. Ninety percent of the catch is farmed but not in the ordinary hatchery and feed of other aquatic farms. Crawfish are grown during the rice or sorghum off-season because the vegetation provides a natural food source for the crawfish.

Many US fish farms employ people who have lost jobs in the traditional fishing industry. Yet, fish farming faces environmental challenges including discharge of waste, pesticides, antibiotics, and chemical use. Lax environmental laws allow other countries to use aquaculture far more cheaply than is possible in the States. For example, antibiotics, now banned in the States, are used to prevent disease in their crowded habitat, and as a growth stimulant.

Mineral Industry

Oil and Gas Gulf Coast states provide about 25 percent of the nation's total crude oil output; the largest source of oil is from offshore platforms near Texas and Louisiana. Stateside production has been dropping while offshore production has expanded. The United States provides 25 percent of its domestic oil supply. Of that, Texas provides 21 percent and Louisiana 3 percent. The US oil supply has been shrinking since 1990. Hurricanes can shut down Gulf oil and natural gas production for months or longer. For example, after Hurricane Katrina, almost half of the Gulf Coast oil and natural gas refineries were closed for several months to a year. As a result of shrinking supply, US consumers saw oil and gas prices increase by as much as 40 cents a gallon within a few weeks, with prices above $3 and even $4 a gallon. Since then, gas prices have averaged more than $3 per gallon for regular fuel multiple times.

Oil and gas have been important revenue sources for Louisiana and Texas. By 1909, Louisiana was home to Standard Oil refineries, and multiple pipelines were built across the state. Between these two states, more than 7 percent of all chemicals and 13 percent of the nation's hazardous waste is produced. Currently, the refineries provide jobs but also harm the health of nearby communities. One example has been the Mississippi River bottomland between Baton Rouge and New Orleans, referred to as "Cancer Alley" by environmentalists, due to disproportionate levels of cancers and birth defects among a poor black populace. After years of environmental and health concerns, the residents of these African American communities fought for environmental justice in the courts; there were a few successes, though much still needs to be done.

Chemical Industry The chemical industry was built on former sugar fields along the Mississippi River and Louisiana coastline. During the boom years, 1978–2000, the lucrative industry ran on cheap natural gas and grew quickly. For example, a Cytec methanol plant built in 1994 for $100 million paid for itself in one year. The lure of profits

TABLE 11.2. Chemicals Produced in Louisiana Plants

Chemical	Uses
Ammonia	Fertilizer, paper manufacturing, refrigerant, household cleaner, pharmaceuticals, fungal control on citrus fruits
Methanol	Plastics, plywoods, paint, explosives, auto gas additive, solvent or antifreeze in paint strippers, aerosol spray paints, carburetor cleaner
Urethane	Refinishing automobiles, refinishing industrial flooring
Melamine	Industrial coatings, paints
Polymers	Aviation and automotive lightweight composites, structural adhesives, water treatment, durable and weather-resistant plastics, safety glass, paper coatings
Specialty resins	Rubber and tire industry, bonding steel-belted tires
Monomers	Coatings, adhesion of latex paints

PHOTO 11.15. Hyundai Plant, Montgomery, Alabama. The Hyundai plant opened in 2004 was the first North American plant built by foreign car manufacturers. Three other companies—Mercedes, Honda, and Toyota—have also chosen to build in the South. All are nonunion shops that pay well for the area but do not have pension plans, thereby reducing money on car costs.

encouraged the rapid growth of hundreds of new chemical plants costing billions of dollars and producing a wide range of chemicals (table 11.2). More recently, pressure by environmental organizations over pollutions and hazards prompted some chemical plants to move offshore where environmental regulations are nonexistent. Rising international competition has also impacted the industry, and the United States, once an exporter of chemicals, is now a net importer.

New chemical plants appeared to be a solution to economic woes, offering jobs and building new towns near the industrial complexes. The industry initially hired many blacks who had worked in the sugar fields, but as computers mechanized the industries, the local skill set was surpassed, leaving many unemployed. Chemical companies were criticized from a variety of angles, from jobs to worker training to neighborhood aesthetics. The companies began training through community colleges, and they improved their community image by becoming more sensitive to historic areas and houses that had been destroyed by the companies in the past.

Additional areas of concern were the sources of pollution. Chemicals dumped into streams and rivers polluted hunting and fishing grounds and emitted caustic pollutants into the air. Chemical companies reduced emissions and complied with environmental laws; however, enforcement is lax and the chemical industry is still not considered a clean source of jobs for a healthy quality of life.

The Secondary Sector

Automobile Industry

Alabama, "Detroit South," is the new automobile capital of America. Beginning in the late 1990s, auto assembly plants opened in various stateside locations. Four companies in separate rural Alabama locations—Mercedes-Benz near Tuscaloosa, Honda near Lincoln, Toyota near Huntsville, and Hyundai near Montgomery—are giving Detroit a run for its money because they are new and flexible, and Alabama has **right-to-work** laws that prohibit compulsory union membership (photo 11.15). The wages, averaging $26 per hour plus benefits including 401(k)s—not pensions—are considerably

BOX 11.8 GLOBAL CONNECTIONS: TRADE THROUGH THE GULF

The old Panama Canal had size restriction. Supertankers from Asia, too big for the canal, unloaded their goods on the West Coast ports of the United States and Canada and then shipped them by road and rail across the continent to the Midwest and Eastern Seaboard. However, the opening of the new Panama Canal in 2016, with greatly enlarged capacity, allows the larger tankers more direct access to the large markets in the eastern United States.

One ripple effect is the opportunity for increased traffic for ports such as Charleston, Savannah, Houston, New York City, and New Orleans. The Port of New Orleans plans to double its capacity by accommodating these new tankers by deepening its port water and building new rail facility to take the goods from the port to areas in the eastern United States. More than $600 million is needed for port enhancement in order to make the port a destination point for the new supertankers coming through an enlarged Panama Canal.

---

higher than the local labor market, and they are meant to keep unions out.

Hundreds of millions of dollars in subsidies have influenced the choice of plant locations, as did inexpensive land, the temperate climate, a nonunion environment, tax abatements, and supportive infrastructure. In addition, the plants are built in rural areas where unemployment rates are higher than in urban locales. For example, the Hyundai plant is built on the edge of the poverty-stricken Black Belt region, and therefore promises new employment opportunities to impoverished local residents. Car assembly plants have also opened in Georgia (Kia), Mississippi (Nissan), Tennessee (Nissan and Volkswagen), and South Carolina (BMW). Foreign car companies have more than forty-five thousand employees, mostly nonunion, and they account for about one-quarter of all US automobile production.

The Tertiary Sector

Tourism

Tourism is a significant portion of the Gulf Coast economy. Mardi Gras, the French Quarter, offshore casinos, ecotours of wetlands, hunting and fishing, and historical plantation tours are a few attractions people enjoy.

Casino gaming has been a moneymaker for struggling Gulf Coast economies. The largest casino area is along the Mississippi River, third only to Las Vegas and Atlantic City. The area has exploded with casinos and plans are in the works for Foxwoods Resort Casino at Biloxi Pointe, a $265 million destination resort to open by 2019. The casino will boast fifty thousand square feet of casino space, more than thirteen hundred slot machines, six restaurants and bars, including a steakhouse, buffet, sports bar and café, a spa, fitness center, pool, and ten-thousand-square-foot bowling and shuffleboard space (photo 11.16).

Tunica, Mississippi, a Delta town an hour south of Memphis, was among the poorest counties in the nation, until 1992, when a group of farmers, Tunica-Biloxi tribal leaders, a Las Vegas gaming company, and the Mississippi gaming commission opened its first casino. Many more casinos followed, and Tunica changed from being a place where 50 percent of the population lived below the poverty line to having an abundance of jobs. The Tunica gambling area became so popular that Highway 61 from Memphis to the casinos had to be widened from two lanes to four—too many people on too small a road.

Since the casinos arrived, Tunica has new public buildings, schools, and an arena. Desoto County, between Tunica and Memphis, is about to convert former cotton fields for an "urban" master-planned community complete with lakes, golf courses, and ninety-five hundred expensive homes.

A Sustainable Future

The Gulf Coast developed much more slowly than the northern areas. The low cost of land and labor has aided Gulf Coast development, but the region still depends on primary industries (logging, fishing, and aquaculture) or the secondary economy (auto production, oil, plastics, and chemical industries) and struggles with poorly developed infrastructure. Only the Balcones Escarpment area is part of the tech-oriented "creative class" profit centers.

There are many challenges to sustainability, including the following:

- endangered delicate ecosystems;
- loss of wetlands;
- overpopulated coastal properties;
- hazards of hurricanes and flooding;
- poverty;
- a legacy of racial discrimination towards African Americans; and
- potentially harmful affects of the chemical and petrochemical industry.

Despite these challenges, the Gulf Coast is also home to exciting opportunities for sustainability. Sustainability planning is the accepted norm and most cities and towns now have sustainability plans. There are more discussions about implementing **sustainable hazard mitigation** that assesses physical vulnerabilities and plans accordingly. Many cities in the region have

PHOTO 11.16. Casinos in Biloxi, Mississippi.
Source: iStock/RobHainer

developed sustainability plans and are beginning to implement their vision. Several green building groups have endorsed and invested in creating a green Gulf Coast, and conferences abound dedicated to green building. Architects, geographers, and geologists call for rebuilding in a sustainable and scientifically based manner so that future storms will not cause the devastation of recent storms. Now all they need are the political will and the government support that the oil companies receive.

Questions for Discussion

1. Explain the evolution of the plantation economy from antebellum to Reconstruction and the New South.

2. How did life change for blacks after the Civil War?

3. How did agricultural systems change in the South after the Civil War?

4. In what ways has environmental justice been and continues to be an important issue in this region?

5. How has the Black Belt of Alabama changed since the antebellum South?

6. Why has the automobile industry moved into the Gulf Coast region?

7. How did the Great Migration change America's demographic distribution?

8. Describe the evolution of agriculture in the Gulf Coast. How did the climate and geography affect the choice of crops?

9. How did the boll weevil affect southern cotton production, human life, and the environment? How did farmers and government agencies deal with the weevil?

10. Why did Houston develop into a major city? What is its geographic association with Galveston?

11. Why has the location of New Orleans been strategic for commercial development?

12. How is the Mississippi River below Baton Rouge threatened?

13. Who are the Cajuns and what is their migration history?

14. What is meant by the phrase "there are no natural disasters"? How does this apply to Hurricane Katrina and New Orleans?

15. After learning about the disease that was prevalent in the New Orleans and coastal areas, and knowing what you do about the hurricanes, why do people choose to live in this region during the warmer months? Should those who do be subject to the motto "Buyer, beware!" and accept the responsibility for their actions?

16. How are some cities planning for a sustainable future?

17. What are key areas of the economy?

Suggested Readings

Austin, D., B. Carriker, T. Mcguire, et al. *History of the Offshore Oil and Gas Industry in Southern Louisiana*. Interim Report. vol. 1, *Papers on the Evolving Offshore Industry*. New Orleans, La.: U.S. Department of the Interior, Minerals Management Service, Gulf of Mexico OCS Region, July 2004.

Baker, O. E. "Agricultural Regions of North America: Part II—The South," *Economic Geography* 3, no. 1 (January 1927): 50–86.

Barry, J. M. *Rising Tide: The Great Mississippi Flood of 1927 and How It Changed America*. New York: Simon & Schuster, 1997.

Bartok, P. "Prebreakup Geology of the Gulf of Mexico–Caribbean: Its Relation to Triassic and Jurassic Rift Systems of the Region," *Tectonics* 12, no. 2 (1993): 441–59.

Brandfon, R. L. "The End of Immigration to the Cotton Fields." *Mississippi Valley Historical Review* 50, no. 4 (1964): 591–611.

Christensen, N. L. "Vegetation of the Southeastern Coastal Plain." In *North American Terrestrial Vegetation*, edited by M. G. Barbour and W. D. Billings, 317–64. Cambridge, UK: Cambridge University Press, 1988.

Colten, C. *An Unnatural Metropolis: Wresting New Orleans from Nature*. Baton Rouge: Louisiana State University Press, 2004.

Cromartie, J., and C. B. Stack. "Black Migration Reversal in the United States." *Geographical Review* 77 no. 2 (April 1987).

Gibson, J. L. *Poverty Point: A Terminal Archaic Culture of the Lower Mississippi Valley*. Baton Rouge, La.: Department of Culture, Recreation, and Tourism, 1996.

Hall, G. *Africans in Colonial Louisiana*. Baton Rouge: Louisiana State University Press, 1995.

Hart, J. F. "Cropland Concentrations in the South," *Annals of the Association of American Geographers* 68, no. 4 (December 1978).

Hartman, C. and Squires, G. (eds.) *There is No Such Thing as a Natural Disaster*. New York: Routledge, 2006.

Marquez, J. *Black-Brown Solidarity: Racial Politics in the New Gulf South*. Austin, Tex.: University of Texas Press, 2013.

McQuaid, J. and Schleifstein, M. *Path of Destruction: The Devastation of New Orleans and The Coming of Age of Superstorms*. New York: Little, Brown, 2006.

Meitrodt, J., and A. Kuriloff. "Thanks to Lease Arrangement, Louisiana Leads Nation in Oyster Production." *The (New Orleans) Times-Picayune*, May 11, 2003.

McCutchan, A. *River Music: An Atachafalaya Story*. College Station: Texas A&M University Press, 2011.

Nelson, M.K., "The Landscape of Disease: Swamps and Medical Discourse in the American Southeast, 1800–1880," *Mississippi Quarterly* 55, no. 4 (October 2002): 535–67.

Ning, Z. H., R. E. Turner, T. Doyle, and K. Abdollahi. *Preparing for a Changing Climate: The Potential Consequences of Climate Variability and Change. Gulf Coast Region*. Baton Rouge, La.: Gulf Coast Regional Climate Change, June 2003.

Penland, S. "Taming the River to Let In the Sea." *Natural History Magazine*, February 2005.

Von Herrmann, D. (ed). *Resorting to Casinos: The Mississippi Gambling Industry*. Jackson: University Press of Mississippi, 2006.

Internet Sources

American Geophysical Union. "Hurricanes and the U.S. Gulf Coast: Science and Sustainable Rebuilding," at http://www.agu.org/report/hurricanes/

Austin Texas Government blog on green buildings, at http://www.austintexas.gov/blog/sustainability-action-agenda-austin-energy-green-building-rating-system-encourages-sustainable-design"

Energy Information Administration. Petroleum and Other Liquids, at http://www.eia.gov/petroleum/

Body Burden. Case Study: Mossville, Louisiana, at http://www.chemicalbodyburden.org/tools.htm#Community%20Case%20Study1:%20Mossvil

Gray Line New Orleans, "Hurricane Katrina Tour" at http://www.graylineneworleans.com/all/tours/hurricane-katrina-tour

U.S. Environmental Protection Agency. "Environmental Justice," at http://www.epa.gov/environmentaljustice/index.html

San Antonio's Sustainability Plan, at http://www.sasustainabilityplan.com/

U.S. Geological Survey. "Nutrients in the Mississippi River Basin," at http://toxics.usgs.gov/hypoxia/mississippi/index.html

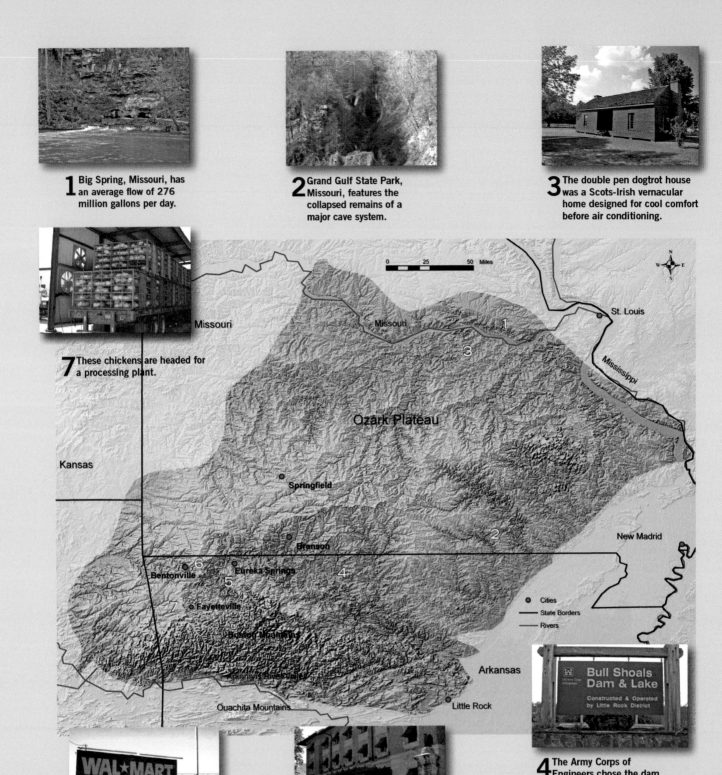

1 Big Spring, Missouri, has an average flow of 276 million gallons per day.

2 Grand Gulf State Park, Missouri, features the collapsed remains of a major cave system.

3 The double pen dogtrot house was a Scots-Irish vernacular home designed for cool comfort before air conditioning.

7 These chickens are headed for a processing plant.

4 The Army Corps of Engineers chose the dam site at Bull Shoals because of the hardness of the rock.

6 Tyson and Wal-Mart, which changed how Americans eat and shop, are headquartered in northwest Arkansas.

5 Natural springs in the Ozarks karst formations appealed to tourists in the 1800s and are still popular today.

Missouri

Missouri

St. Louis

Mississippi

Ozark Plateau

Kansas

Springfield

Branson

New Madrid

6

Eureka Springs

Bentonville

5

4

Cities

State Borders

Rivers

7

Fayetteville

Boston Mountains

Bull Shoals Dam & Lake

Constructed & Operated by Little Rock District

Arkansas

Arkansas River Valley

Ouachita Mountains

Little Rock

0   25   50 Miles

12

THE OZARKS
Unexpected Economic Miracles

Chapter Highlights

After reading this chapter, you should be able to:

- Discuss the advantages and disadvantages of concentrated animal feeding operation (CAFO) chicken production
- Describe the various ethnic groups that have settled in the Ozarks recently and why
- Identify the subregions that have become economically viable in the past fifty years
- Describe the role of religion in the region
- Discuss the cultural quirks found in the Ozarks
- Describe where major urban areas are in relation to the Ozarks and the reasons why
- Explain how logging has changed in the Ozarks and the effect of the changes
- Describe the traditional primary economies in the Ozarks
- Explain why the Ozarks have been sustainable until the late twentieth century

Terms

bald
Bald Knobbers

Bible Belt
broiler chicken
geothermal spring

hillbilly
limestone
losing stream

shut-in
spring

Places

Boston Mountains
Branson, Missouri

Courtois Hills, Missouri
Eureka Springs, Arkansas
McClellan-Kerr Waterway

New Madrid, Missouri
Ouachita Mountains

Ozark Plateau
St. Francois Mountains

Cities

Bentonville, Arkansas
  (2016 Pop. 47,000)

Branson, Missouri
  (2016 pop 26,000)
Eureka Springs, Arkansas
  (2016 pop 2,070)

Fayetteville, Arkansas
  (2016 MSA 525,000)
Little Rock, Arkansas
  (2016 MSA 734,000)

Springfield, Missouri
  (2016 MSA 458,000)
St. Louis, Missouri
  (2016 MSA 2.9 million)

PHOTO 12.1. Ozark Landscape, Van Buren, Missouri. The origin of the term Ozark is possibly an English corruption of the French aux arcs (at the river bend), in relation to the Arkansas River meanders. The Ozark Plateau shares rock types, structure, and landforms with Appalachia.

Introduction

The traditional "down in the Ozarks" life was sparsely populated, laid-back, old-fashioned, and quaint—it was the "**hillbilly**" region, where people were more interested in noodling or hand-grabbin' a catfish than revolutionizing the American lifestyle (photo 12.1). Two definitive Ozark companies, Tyson and Walmart, and one tourist town, Branson, changed this. In 1950, the region was remote, but it is now a well-connected geographic and demographic center.

Appalachian folk migrated to the Ozarks seeking a topographically similar but less populated region where they could continue to live surrounded by family and protected from the outside world. Midwestern and Southern migrants were also attracted by promotional literature from the railroads or dreams of red-apple orchards. The settlers shaped the landscape with their cultural imprint until the mid-twentieth century, when Ozark industry bifurcated. One shed the primary economy and adopted the more uniform cultural landscape of the American dream (tertiary retail, tourism, and religious revivalism); the other seeks out a part of the American dream in one get-rich-quick scheme after another.

Regional religious beliefs remain a basic tenet but have changed since the 1950s. The small, old-timey congregations with roots in the **Second Great Awakening** have been replaced by industrial-sized churches and televised, globalized evangelical religion. The region's homespun ways attract those seeking the nostalgic good old days in vinyl churches based on big-box economies of scale.

The Ozarks lacked an agricultural bounty but provided a sense of security and familiarity for people emigrating from Appalachia. Later, the regional isolation, water, and beauty provided Midwestern urbanites relief from urban ills, but at the cost of turning the countryside into the rural equivalent of urban environmental degradation. The pristine beauty of the Ozarks has given way to polluted waterways, mismanaged forests, industrial chicken farms, and **crank**.

While the region has conquered many stereotypes, there are numerous challenges for a more sustainable future.

Physical Geography

The Ozarks lie in the middle of the continent and form a rough parallelogram over about fifty thousand square miles of southern Missouri and northern Arkansas. To the north, the transitional Missouri River flood plain separates the glacial plains of northern Missouri from the upland Ozarks. The eastern border drifts into the Central Lowlands, but the southern uplifted edge contrasts with the Mississippi embayment. The western border is geologically but not visually differentiated.

The remnant of a five-hundred-million-year-old inland sea left behind a karst landscape pockmarked by caves, sinkholes, and water discharging from rock as **springs**. Karst-formed features are an important part of the tourism economy, but they also cause water pollution problems.

Plains surround the higher-than-hills, lower-than-mountains, dissected-and-uplifted Ozark plateaus. The core is an ancient volcanic rock in the St. Francois Mountains; sedimentary rock overlays the rest of the plateaus.

The Ozark bioregion has three major divisions: the Ozark Plateau, the Arkansas River Valley, and the Ouachita Mountains (map 12.1).

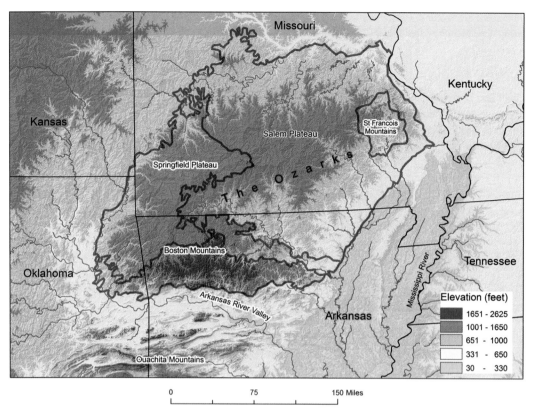

MAP 12.1. Ozark Plateau Subregions.

Ozark Plateau

The Ozark or Central Plateau dominates the southern half of Missouri and extends into northern Arkansas. The plateau blends into Kansas prairie in the west and fades south of the Eureka Springs escarpment in Arkansas. Along the northern edge and bounded by the Missouri River, the small subsistence farms of the Osage-Gasconade Hills are scattered through forested, river-carved ridges and valleys. Farther east is the poorest, most rugged, isolated section of the Ozarks, the Courtois Hills, where timber in the steep-sided **limestone** hills provide the region's principal resource. The hills and hollers kept the plateau culturally insulated until the late-twentieth-century interstate highway system integrated the region with the nation.

The St. Francois Mountains' igneous knobs peek through the forest in southeastern Missouri. These Lead Belt rocks are also infiltrated with iron ores, zinc, and other minerals, all deposited when the region was surrounded by seas 1.5 billion years ago. Mineral deposits have been mined since 1720. The regional landscape is a mixture of unusual topographic features. Unnavigable gorges called **shut-ins** are deep, narrow channels carved into hard rock. Another regional feature is **bald** knobs—hilltop grasslands devoid of trees. Prior to European arrival, the balds were an open refuge from the forests for bison, deer, and other wildlife.

Separating the Ozark Plateau from the Arkansas River Valley, the Ouachita and Boston mountains are two of the few east-to-west ranges in the United States. The hills contain some of the more spectacular sinkholes and springs, the region's highest elevations, and a pleasing forest and glade landscape. The region once grew corn and cotton, but soil erosion and a lack of level land hampered production. The scenic White River Hills have metamorphosed from farmland into a tourist area boasting large human-made lakes, limestone caves, and country music.

Arkansas River Valley

The Arkansas River Valley trough, a transition zone between the Boston and Ouachita mountains, defines the southern extent of the Ozarks. Fort Smith marks the western entrance to the river valley, which extends eastward to Little Rock. The natural east-west valley corridor connects the coastal plain, the Mississippi Valley, and the Great Plains. The fertile bottomlands support a wide range of agricultural crops.

Ouachita Mountains

South of the Arkansas River Valley, the Ouachitas extend westward from Little Rock, Arkansas, into eastern Oklahoma. The rounded features of the low-elevation Ouachita Range were once connected to the Appalachians and as high as the Swiss Alps. Over time, the Mississippi embayment rift separated the Ouachitas from the Appalachians. Tectonic processes have geothermally activated the region and produced areas such as Hot Springs, outside of Little Rock.

Native Americans and Europeans alike have bathed in the **geothermal springs**, but the water's potential energy source has not been capitalized on. However, the water may be a future source of renewable heat for space heating and, when potable, hot water, thereby decreasing dependency on fossil fuels.

Water

Water is plentiful throughout the Ozarks. Water oozes out of karst seeps, peeks out of karst windows, or disappears underground in **losing streams**, which then reappear out of seemingly solid bedrock. Although water is plentiful, the porous limestone increases the possibility of contamination, because of the regional dependence on intensive livestock production, especially chickens and hogs, whose manure compromises water quality and the ecological balance of aquatic species.

Managing Ozark water began after the Depression. The Army Corps of Engineers built dams, and flooded and altered rivers to meet the demands of the increasing human, agricultural, and industrial sectors, but at the cost of environmental degradation. For example, changing the hydrographic profile resulted in wider, shallower stream channels and eliminated deepwater species. For all its forested areas, the Ozark regional ecosystems are fragile and became fragmented when virgin timbers were cut, and then later the remaining forested area was exploited for wood chemicals such as charcoal and methanol, a solvent and chemical feedstock. The result is environmental damage to the soil, game, and timber.

Rivers

The navigable Mississippi and Missouri Rivers define the northeastern periphery of the Ozarks, but smaller rivers—the Arkansas, Gasconade, Meramec, and White—flow through steep-sided river valleys that require dredging and damming to make them navigable. In the second half of the twentieth century, eighteen dams were built along the Ozark rivers. The wilderness morphed into second-home lakeside retreats when dammed rivers created artificial lakes. River water was also reconfigured to improve navigation and agricultural use.

Navigated since 1820, the Arkansas River connects the Great Plains with the Gulf Coast; however, beyond Little Rock, the river was too shallow for navigation by larger and heavier ships. In 1971, the McClellan-Kerr Waterway opened navigation from Little Rock to the Port of Catoosa near Tulsa. The system expanded industrial opportunities through the Arkansas Valley and Oklahoma, but not as much as originally predicted (photo 12.2). Grain is shipped south, whereas petroleum, coal, and chemicals are major northbound commodities.

The Arkansas River is the water source for local agricultural and urban areas. However, groundwater withdrawn for irrigation evaporates, leaving behind mineral salts. The increased salinity has caused declining water quality and lowered crop yields.

Springs

More than twenty million gallons of water from six hundred Ozark springs feed rivers daily, adding up to billions of gallons of water annually. The rainwater-fed springs follow a maze of underground faults before emerging as springs from caves or sinkholes.

Southern Missouri's Big Spring is the largest and once recorded a peak flow of one billion gallons a day. The Arkansas mineral waters include Eureka Springs, but the most popular geothermal springs are in Hot Springs, in the Ouachita Mountains.

Springs were popular with Native Americans and as pioneer settlement sites. Several saline and geothermal springs have

PHOTO 12.2. Offloading Cargo at Tulsa, Oklahoma. Port of Catoosa is the Tulsa port on the McClellan-Kerr waterway. These metal spools came from Japan by way of New Orleans and will be used in refrigeration units.

BOX 12.1   TAKING THE WATERS

The numerous springs and mineralized waters created an Ozark cure, "taking the waters." During the late nineteenth century, local spa towns blossomed, offering a healing cure for a stressful urban life (photo 12.3). The Ozark lifestyle, natural cures, treatments, and baths became and remain attractive. During the late nineteenth century, the main streets of towns like Hot Springs or Eureka Springs were lined with bathhouses, similar to European bathhouses. Both attracted a wealthy clientele.

The Ozarks developed a reputation as a natural region—unspoiled, uncivilized, and clean. The naturalness and the spring-fed land highlighted what was considered a healthy atmosphere, helped bring the Ozarks to the forefront of the Midwestern mind that sought solace from urban ills, and fostered the Ozark tourism industry.

PHOTO 12.3. Sanitarium Ruins, Welch Springs, Missouri. In 1855, homesteader Thomas Welch built a grist mill, which he operated until he sold the property to Dr. Christian Diehl in 1913. Dr. Diehl built this building as a sanitarium and rest camp for asthma sufferers. He claimed the spring and cave air were medicinal and healthful. The sanitarium, never a monetary success, is now part of the Park Service.

been developed commercially for medicinal use. Hot Springs, Arkansas, a popular nineteenth-century spa, was fashioned after the great spas of Europe. The forty-seven springs produce over a million gallons of 143°F geothermally heated water daily.

Geothermal springs are scattered throughout the United States. There are more than 190 therapeutic geothermal spas, including Saratoga Springs, New York; Warm Springs, Georgia; Hot Springs, Virginia; White Sulfur Springs, West Virginia; Hot Springs, Arkansas; Thermopolis, Wyoming; and Calistoga, California. The regional health benefits are not limited to the water, though; the Ozarks have been one of the regions most dependent on natural remedies and cures.

Climate

The Ozarks' four distinct but temperate seasons range from 80°F average, humid and rainy summers (annual mean precipitation is forty to forty-eight inches) to average January temperatures of 34°F. Winter snows are brief because of diurnal temperature variations. The growing season varies between 180 and 200 days. Periodic droughts can be severe and destructive to the economy.

Several climate models estimate how climate change will alter the Ozark environment, ranging from average temperature rising from 1°F to 7°F. But the models do not agree if the climate will be wetter or drier and how carbon dioxide levels will affect the vegetation. While the models vary in their predictions, all agree that changes will reconfigure the forest vegetation. The models indicate that changes could be:

- pines replacing the oak/hickory forest (warmer and wetter);
- forests retreating and being replaced by a grassland (warmer and drier); and
- undergrowth of vines choking out trees by mid-century (rising carbon dioxide levels).

Historical Geography and Settlement

Native Americans have occupied the Ozarks from the Woodland period (100 BCE–900 CE) through the Mississippian period (900–1200 CE). Remnants of these tribes were first encountered by Desoto's 1540 foray into the region, but by 1673

BOX 12.2 NATIONAL PARKS: OZARK NATIONAL SCENIC RIVERWAYS

The Ozark National Scenic Riverways national park is located in southern Missouri. It is the first national park area to protect a river system, and was designated in 1971. The Riverways include 134 miles of the Current and Jacks Fork Rivers and some eighty thousand acres of river, forest, open field, and glade environments. The Park Service considers the Current and Jacks Fork Rivers two of the finest float streams, in part due to the contributions of some of the nation's largest springs. These float streams attract more than two million visitors each year.

Riparian habitats are a major component of the park. Typified by sycamores, maples, cottonwoods, and willows, floodplain forests line the rivers. These provide habitat for Swainson's warblers, wood ducks, great blue herons, and a wide variety of other species. As a significant karst resource, the park contains the world's largest collection of first magnitude springs. It also contains over three hundred known caves, numerous sinkholes, and losing streams.[*]

PHOTO 12.4. Canoers float on the slow-moving Current River.
Source: Kbh3rd

*National Park Service. "Natural Features & Ecosystems in Ozark National Scenic Riverways," at https://www.nps.gov/ozar/learn/nature/naturalfeaturesandecosystems.htm

when French explorers Marquette and Joliet entered the region, the Sioux Nation Osage tribe inhabited the area between the Missouri and Arkansas Rivers.

Most who settled the Ozarks in the nineteenth century were Scots-Irish and Germans. The uplander Scots-Irish often left the "overpopulated" Appalachian region to settle in the hills and hollows of the Ozark Plateau. Into the first decades of the twentieth century, they practiced a self-sufficient lifestyle—hunting; pasturing farm animals; growing corn, sorghum, wheat, and vegetables; and hiring out for lumber

BOX 12.3   CLIMATE CHANGE IN THE OZARKS

The forests of the Ozarks are home to some of the most productive forests of the United States, and a huge logging industry. In much of North America, especially the US West, climate change is proceeding too quickly for tree populations to adapt or migrate, and many forests are declining. For example, in the arid West, long-term increases in heat have been aggravating droughts that starve trees of water—often the main factor controlling growth and survival.

Eastern forests, though, are doing well, particularly those in the south-central United States, where temperatures actually have not changed that much yet.

But the region may soon begin catching up, and the consequences could be immense. Some scientists believe that many common tree species here could be more vulnerable to warming than other trees in the Northern Hemisphere. Some dominant species may die off, while others may do better. Forests may shift composition, changing both economics and ecosystems. In some areas, forests could simply disappear and release large amounts of carbon into the atmosphere, further warming the planet.[*]

Researchers have suggested there may be three possible future scenarios for the Ozarks: first, pines will dominate the Ozarks as the region's deciduous trees die off; second, the forest could become more open country, evolving into savanna or even grasslands; or third, woody vines such as honeysuckle and poison ivy will choke out the trees and the forests will become tangled vines and undergrowth.

The good news is that the Nature Conservancy says that more than anywhere else, the Ozarks have a proven ability to handle weather extremes.[†] The region has a diversity of plants, animals, and habitats that can be sustained as healthy, productive systems, possibly even in the face of a changing climate.

PHOTO 12.5. The Ozarks in Autumn.
Source: iStock/ABDESIGN

---

[*]Kevin Krajick, "How Will Shifting Climate Change U.S. Forests?" *State of the Planet*, Earth Institute at Columbia University, 2016, at http://blogs.ei.columbia.edu/2016/03/15/how-will-shifting-climate-change-u-s-forests/

[†]Nature Conservancy, "The Ozarks: Naturally Resilient," at https://www.nature.org/ourinitiatives/regions/northamerica/unitedstates/missouri/explore/the-ozarks-naturally-resilient.xml

---

work to augment their income. A few farmers owned slaves, but most did not.

During the Civil War, Ozark allegiance was divided: Missouri stayed with the Union, while Arkansas seceded. The result was a war-torn and devastated region, battle-worn and filled with refugees.

After the war, the bald mountaintops acted as signal outlooks for the **Bald Knobbers,** a Reconstruction vigilante group named for the topographic feature. From 1864 to 1885, Bald Knobber ceremonies and patterns became an Ozark stereotype; they were characterized as a group of violent, ignorant hillbillies, who seemed indiscriminant in clearing the land of people whom they deemed criminals.

German farmers immigrated to the United States between 1850 and 1880. Many Germans who had settled in Kentucky continued their westward movement into northern Missouri and the fertile bottomlands along the Missouri and Mississippi River flood plains. In time, they purchased additional land from American farmers. Many Germans maintained ethnic communities, and they

BOX 12.4 NEW MADRID AND THE EARTHQUAKES

Most earthquakes are along tectonic plate boundaries. However, during 1811–1812, more than eighteen hundred earthquakes, many in the 7 to 8 magnitude, occurred far from any plate boundaries, near the small Missouri boot-heel town of New Madrid. A fault line separating the region from the Mississippi Delta passes from New Madrid through Arkansas and then south to the Balcones Escarpment in Texas. The fault line is essentially a scarred weakness from a failed rift formed when Rodinia broke apart 750 million years ago.

The New Madrid earthquakes were strong enough to change the Mississippi River's course, but few humans or their structures were lost in the sparsely settled region. Today, the visible remnant of the quakes is the seventy-mile-long Reelfoot Lake, an oxbow in Western Tennessee, formed when subsurface water and sediment were ejected to the surface, creating subsurface voids that subsided during the violent quakes.

New Madrid has survived as a sleepy town on the Mississippi River, which is still occasionally rocked by earthquakes (map 12.2).*

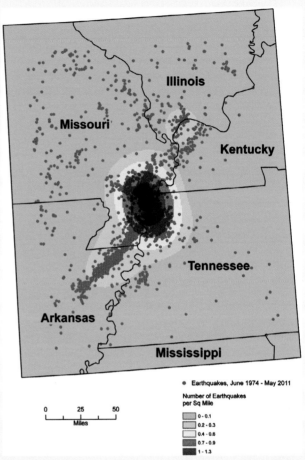

● Earthquakes, June 1974 - May 2011

Number of Earthquakes per Sq Mile

- 0 - 0.1
- 0.2 - 0.3
- 0.4 - 0.6
- 0.7 - 0.9
- 1 - 1.3

0   25   50
Miles

MAP 12.2. New Madrid and Wabash Valley Seismic Zones, showing earthquakes that occurred between June 1974 and May 2011. The intensity of earthquakes centers on the New Madrid Zone, where there were a series of major earthquakes in 1811–1812.

*John W. Reps, "New Madrid on the Mississippi," *Journal of the Society of Architectural Historians* 18, no. 1 (March 1959): 21–26.

---

purchased land from footloose American farmers who moved on.

Cultural Perspectives

The colorful people of the Ozarks are one of America's most recognized rural groups. They share cultural traits such as self-sufficiency, traditional lifestyles, reluctance to accept change, suspicion of outsiders, and political conservatism. The Ozark population pursued hunting, fishing, and home crafts more than in other farming areas.

The Ozark and Appalachian cultural roots differed from the rest of America. Few pursued technological advancement or education. Lacking the tools of industrial progress left them impoverished, but with a strong wealth in kinship and self-sufficiency that set them outside mainstream America. Their independent ways earned them the nickname hillbillies.

Hillbillies

In 1960, the Springfield, Missouri, Court of Appeals ruled on a divorce case involving the use of the term *hillbilly*. Judge Justin Ruark, in the case of *Moore v. Moore* (337 S.W. 2d 781) made the following statement in his decision:

An Ozark hillbilly is an individual who has learned the real luxury of doing without the entangling complications of things that the dependent and over-pressured city dweller is required to consider as necessities. The hillbilly foregoes the hard grandeur of high buildings and canyon streets in exchange for wooded hills and verdant valleys. In place of creeping traffic he accepts the rippling flow of the wandering stream. He does not hear the snarl of exhaust, the raucous braying of horns, and the sharp, strident babble of many tense voices. For him instead is the measured beat of the katydid, the lonesome, far-off complaining of the whip-poorwill, perhaps even the sound of a falling acorn in the infinite peace of the quiet woods. The hillbilly is often not familiar with new models, soirées, and office politics. But he does have the time and surroundings conducive to sober reflection and honest thought, the opportunity to get closer to his God. No, in Southern Missouri the appellation "hillbilly" is not generally an insult or an indignity; it is an expression of envy.

Today, Ozark tourism and music capitalize on the stereotypical hillbilly moniker. Hillbilly music evolved from Celtic and English folk songs into today's country music. However, many people of the Ozarks are not hillbillies. Advancements in communication and transportation increased connections and consumer ideals. Now, those who choose the simpler hillbilly lifestyle do so by choice and not only because of geographic location.

Religion

Many American areas proudly proclaim themselves to be the "Buckle of the **Bible Belt**," because of the dominance of provincial, often fundamentalist or Pentecostal Christian religions that are often evangelical (emphasizing the authority of the Bible). Springfield, Missouri, is home to many individualistic conservative sects.

Several religious denominations are headquartered in the Ozarks. Springfield is home to fundamental Christian colleges and conservative publishing houses. Sharing a basic Christian faith in Jesus and a hope for eternal destiny, the evangelical leaders preach various biblical interpretations and apocalyptic events, sometimes reaching fanatical proportions. For example, some follow white supremacist teachings; others adamantly maintain their bonds and beliefs despite the jailing of their wayward leaders. These marginalized groups are small in number, but their existence highlights the religious fervor of the Ozark region.

Although Christian religions dominate the Ozarks, other pockets of faith exist, from Baha'i to Buddhist, and such imported religions as the animist shamanism of the Hmong, many of whom have migrated to the Ozarks in search of a quality of life similar to their former farming culture.

Population, Immigration, and Diversity

Historically, the Ozarks have been an area of sparse, dispersed population that grew by two means: large families and chain migration. The traditional Ozark family produced a child a year, usually born at home because of a lack of health facilities or state services. Chain migration operated when word was sent back to their former home of a good life, prompting family members to migrate to the Ozarks.

After the 1960s, immigration into the Ozarks expanded to groups without regional ties. By the 1980s, the number of commuters and retirees moving to the Ozarks exceeded national growth averages and continued. Large towns expanded, but the fastest growth was in seasonal homes and retirement communities.

The population in the Ozarks is over 95 percent Caucasian, and approximately 20 percent are age sixty-five or older (the US average over sixty-five is 14 percent). In many small towns, the younger population migrates to well-paying jobs, leaving the elderly behind. Retirement communities such as Bella Vista, Kimberling City, and Branson, Missouri, establish their own programs favoring senior over family interests.

Overall, settlement is sparse in the uplands and dense in the river valleys. The underpopulated areas often have high poverty and unemployment rates. A recent anomaly, though, is the northwest quadrant of Arkansas where Tyson and ConAgra became food processing giants; Walmart reinvented retailing; and trucking dynamo J. B. Hunt took advantage of lenient trucking laws. In this area, the population boomed.

Immigration and Diversity

The Ozarks are far below the national average for immigration and foreign-born population. Missouri currently only has 4 percent of its population foreign born (compared to the 14.2 percent national average). Missouri has a small but growing immigrant community, much of which hails from Mexico. Many immigrants find work in health care and the agricultural sector of the economy. The top countries of origin for immigrants were Mexico (18.6 percent of immigrants), India (9 percent), China (6.8 percent), Vietnam (5.3 percent), and the Philippines (4 percent).

Arkansas is similar, with 5 percent foreign born. The top countries of origin for immigrants were Mexico (38 percent of immigrants), El Salvador (12.8 percent), India (6.7 percent), Guatemala (4 percent), and China (3.6 percent).

Neither Missouri or Arkansas are known for embracing the LBGT community and both states have resisted gay rights by passing discriminatory policies that have been since been declared unconstitutional by either the state or the US Supreme Court. For example, in 2008, Arkansas voters approved a ballot measure to prohibit by statute cohabiting couples who are not in a recognized marriage from adopting and providing foster care; this was declared to be unconstitutional by the Arkansas Supreme Court in 2011. Recently, Arkansas banned same-sex marriage in its state Constitution, although these provisions have also been ruled unconstitutional. Same-sex marriage in Arkansas was briefly legal through a court ruling in 2014, but there have been various appeals that have prevented it from taking effect.

A similar pattern has been true in Missouri. In 2004, 71 percent of Missouri voters passed a law that restricted the validity and recognition of marriage in Missouri to the union of one man and one woman. However more recently, there have been changes to these discriminatory policies. Missouri now recognizes same-sex marriages from other jurisdictions.

BOX 12.5   GLOBAL CONNECTIONS: HMONG POULTRY FARMERS

The Hmong, a small Laotian tribe who sided with American forces during the Vietnam War, were forced to leave their homeland for the United States after the war. Many arrived first in California or Minnesota, and then moved to the Ozarks as their agricultural background led some of them to migrate to chicken concentrated animal feeding operations (CAFOs). But moving to a chicken farm required saving money for twenty years to purchase the farm, and it was not until 2000 when several hundred Hmong took their life savings and bought CAFO chicken farms.

The adults have tried to emulate their former agricultural life. The Ozark landscape felt familiar and the Hmong knew chickens, so the possibility of raising CAFO chickens for Tyson or similar companies was a seeming return to what they knew; it kept their children away from gang influence, and it was a step up from the low-wage and mundane factory jobs that were often the only source of income for their large families.

The Hmong often assumed existing contracts with chicken producers who were selling farms that were unprofitable. The banks and appraisers were supported by the government and therefore may have taken advantage of the refugees and not shown them accurate income projections and expenses.

Hmong farmers began to go bankrupt in the twenty-first century, and they brought their grievances to the courts. A few are beginning to find their way clear of the debt and out of bankruptcy, and they are setting up agencies to warn other farmers with similar dreams.

Urban Trends

The center point of the US population now lies in the Ozarks; however, few urban centers are in the region. Ozark cities lie along the regional perimeter: St. Louis, Little Rock, and Kansas City. The dissected Ozark topography accounts for the lack of cities. Urban growth is often linked to tourist amenities—the natural environment, infrastructure, lakes, health care facilities, and retirement centers. Other cities have grown as gateway cities.

Fort Smith, at the entrance to the Arkansas River Valley, had retarded growth because of its location at the edge of Oklahoma's Indian Territory, but it grew after Oklahoma opened to settlement. Poplar Bluff in southeastern Missouri is billed as the gateway to the Ozarks. America has been impacted by several other Ozarks towns:

- Branson, Missouri: This small town that has a big impact in the country music industry almost tripled between 1990 and 2016, from 3,706 to 11,430.
- Bentonville, Arkansas: Home to Walmart, the world's largest retail chain.
- Springdale, Arkansas: Home to Tyson, the world's largest chicken producer.
- Lowell, Arkansas: Home to J. B. Hunt, the fourth-largest national trucking firm.

The largest and most important regional city, St. Louis, draws a great deal of its commerce from the Ozark hinterland.

St. Louis, Missouri
(2016 MSA 2.9 million)

Strategically located on a bluff near the confluence of the Mississippi and Missouri Rivers, St. Louis has served as a break-in-bulk point, fulcrum of east-west movement, and wholesale outlet for the Ozarks. The city's prosperity and location can be compared to that of another city located at another junction, the low-lying and oft-flooded Cairo, Illinois (pop. 2,359), where the Mississippi meets the Ohio River. The site and situation of St. Louis has everything to do with why it flourished (sitting above flood level) and why the low-lying and often-flooded Cairo stagnated.

In 1764, French traders established St. Louis, a trading post that became the gateway city to the West. When the city lost the gateway raison d'être, growth diminished. Until the Civil War, St. Louis competed with Chicago for midwestern trade, but St. Louis's dependence on river traffic was no match for Chicago's railroad network. It remains, though, the second-largest inland port city. After the Civil War, St. Louis became an important distribution center for the Missouri Iron Belt, but the industry declined as the richer Mesabi mines north of Lake Superior expanded. St. Louis remains a financial and commercial center that encompasses much of the upper Great Plains, Ozarks, and Mississippi Valley.

By 1918, St. Louis was America's fourth-largest city, and it grew to more than 1.3 million by 1930. Today, St. Louis is the nation's twentieth-largest metro area. The city population has declined, and building has stagnated. The growth has been in eight hundred sprawling square miles supporting almost three million residents. This has left the city proper in the familiar pattern of interior America, with an eroding tax base, fewer resources, and aging infrastructure in a time when higher-density cities and personal transportation efficiency have become imperative for American cities.

One of the weaknesses in building a sustainable city is the lack of integration among administration levels. Decisions are scattered among the city, county, and region, making cohesive plans next to impossible. The city suffers from poor air quality and needs to institute a recycling program and education for residents to improve recycling rates (3 percent).

In 2013, St. Louis adopted its first sustainability plan. Developing this plan was not the city's first efforts at sustainability, but the plan sets a series of targets and objectives that prioritize investment. A notable feature of the plan is that it

BOX 12.6   ICONIC IMAGE: THE ST. LOUIS ARCH

The 630-foot-high Gateway Arch gives St. Louis one of the most recognizable skylines in the United States (photo 12.6).

It is also a national park whose formal name is the "Jefferson National Expansion Memorial," named to honor President Thomas Jefferson who championed the Louisiana Purchase and sent Lewis and Clark on their expedition West.

In the 1930s, civic leader Luther Ely Smith conceived the idea of building a memorial to help revive the riverfront and memorialize the story of the nation's westward expansion. Through a nationwide design competition conducted in 1947–1948, Eero Saarinen's stainless steel arch was chosen as the memorial that would celebrate the accomplishments of early pioneers, and celebrate the city of St. Louis as the gateway to the West. Construction started in 1959 and the final section at the top of the Arch was secured in October, 1965. It is the world's tallest arch. Like the Washington Monument, the Gateway Arch is a very modern design, but its simplicity makes it timeless. Architects and architectural historians have written about the Arch's many "moods," as it reflects sunlight, clouds, and rain in different hues.

The Gateway Arch, along with the Statue of Liberty and the Washington Monument are universally recognizable forms and symbols of national identity.

PHOTO 12.6. The Gateway Arch in St. Louis, Missouri. In 2015, the Arch celebrated its fiftieth anniversary.
Source: iStock/f11photo

addresses the triple bottom line in many areas. For example, the plan states, "Air quality is tied to asthma rates in children: if poor air quality exacerbates asthma, a child may have to miss school; his parent may have to miss work to care for him, and perhaps incur medical costs as a result. Consequently, what we emit into the air can impact not just the environment, but health, education, productivity and economy."

Fayetteville, Arkansas
(2016 pop. 838,260; MSA 913,966)

Fayetteville is located near the three largest industries in Arkansas, the Ozarks, and arguably, even the nation—Tyson, Walmart, and J. B. Hunt Trucking. Fayetteville is also home to the University of Arkansas. The location—growing at twice the state rate—has made Fayetteville a magnet for other companies and a retirement center. The metropolitan area has almost doubled since 1990. The growth, while welcome, has also led to sprawl, traffic, and environmental concerns, leading to a controlled growth plan emphasizing infill areas and attainable housing.

The Economy

The Primary Sector

The Ozark economy has been based on primary industry: hog-corn subsistence agriculture, lumber, mining, hunting, and fishing.

While many local residents rely partially on agriculture, crop production in the Ozarks is poor. Most farmers who have depended on crops for their complete income have migrated from the poor soils of the Ozarks to richer land.

Only 10 percent of the Ozarks is good cropland; another 20 percent produces livestock and hay; the remaining 70 percent of the uplands is forested. The good cropland is on the Mississippi and Missouri flood plains, while runoff or thousands of karst pits and sinkholes limit the nutrient-poor plateau soils. Agricultural production and grazing are further deterred by the chert (flint) rock that has broken off from the limestone strata and is now scattered throughout the area.

BOX 12.7 METH

The seemingly hopeless and bleak rural life has created a back-lash culture in places like the Ozark hollers of southern Missouri. These Ozark counties are a region plagued by unemployment and dead-end jobs. Some residents may enter into the excitement of producing "performance-enhancing" methamphetamines (also called meth or crank).

The backwoods are found down rutted roads that lead to the hopeless poverty and hardscrabble lives of the people seeking the only way they see to make ends meet, cooking up the addictive, illegal meth. While taking an additional toll on the local populace, meth leads to desperate measures that further undermine the economy and the future (photo 12.7). High levels of depression also create a demand for measures of escape. Since the millennium, Missouri has been called the meth capital of the US. In 2010, Missouri had 1,917 meth lab seizures out of a national total of 10,247 (map 12.3).*

PHOTO 12.7. Methamphetamine Warning. Rural America has been under the influence of methamphetamine, manufactured in thousands of small labs across the countryside. The ills of meth can be found in some unusual locations, as this sign in a field in eastern Montana indicates.

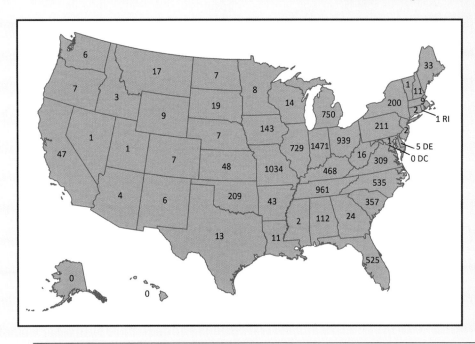

MAP 12.3. Methamphetamine Incidents, 2014. The total number of clandestine laboratory incidents including labs, dumpsites and chemical equipment reported by the Drug Enforcement Agency (DEA) in 2014 was 9,338. The number of incidents in Missouri was 1,034. After a brief lull caused by a crackdown on domestic manufacturing techniques, the highly addictive stimulant is increasing across the country again, particularly in rural areas.
Source: US Drug Enforcement Administation

*US Department of Justice, at http://www.justice.gov/dea/concern/meth_lab_maps/2010.jpg

As agriculture on large and fertile farms prospered in other regions, Ozark farmers were unable to survive economically. Tyson's chicken production methods saved many poor farmers, but at an environmental price. Those who were in the far backwoods areas were left out of a steady economy, and many insulated folk chose what they saw as their only escape and source of income: the quick and easy money of meth.

John Tyson rescued the ailing Ozark agricultural economy. A century of raising cotton and corn or a few chickens or hogs had left farmers poor and dependent on unstable commodity prices. John Tyson mechanized and consolidated chicken production in the 1950s. Under Tyson's intensive production methods, raising chickens became an industrial enterprise entailing contract farming and processing. Instead of raising a few chickens, farmers began to adopt the intensive methods that Tyson perfected. CAFOs house ten thousand chickens in one building and grow them to slaughter weight in six weeks. CAFO chicken farms earn farmers a steady but meager income, but they remove most of the commodity market risk. A $125,000 poultry house provides an income of $4,000 to $6,000 per year, a 4 to 5 percent return on investment. Farmers who signed contracts with Tyson received loans to build two or three CAFO buildings, which provided the necessary income to stay on the land.

Today, **broiler chicken** and turkey production is the Ozarks' major agricultural enterprise. Tyson and a few other CAFO-oriented companies have vertically integrated owning the chicken production process "from semen to cellophane." The chickens, the feed mills, the hatcheries, and transportation are owned and controlled by the corporation, while seven thousand contract farmers provide land and labor. The farmers grow the company's chickens according to exacting instructions from the company. Virtually the entire broiler industry is now contract farmed.

Thousands of CAFO poultry houses were built in the Ozarks during the past half century. Arkansas produces more than 1.2 billion broilers annually, each contributing about 2.5 pounds of manure. Traditionally applied to land as fertilizer, manure has become a significant source of nutrient loading in waterways and raised phosphorus levels in soils. In karst terrain, the limestone formations connecting groundwater with surface water are susceptible to contamination from CAFO lagoon leakage or overflows. In Missouri, one-third to one-half of all streams and creeks test so high for coliform bacteria they are unsafe to touch.

Arkansas is now the second-largest chicken producer in the United States (photo 12.8). Headquartered in Arkansas, Tyson is America's largest processor, with forty-two plants nationwide (photo 12.9). In 2015, Tyson Foods slaughtered 33.41 million chickens each week. While the CAFO industry has grown and profited the economy and saved many Ozark farmers from losing their farms, it has also caused environmental and social equity issues.

CAFO-related environmental issues include the following:

- nonpoint pollution from nutrient load fertilizer on soil and in groundwater;
- litigation over carcinogenic matter in manure dust; and
- antibiotic resistance.

Conservation practices can reduce these problems and keep soils healthy. However, although a number of proposed bills address manure management, protect water quality, and establish renewable energy standards, new rules only apply to new operations. Old operations are grandfathered in.

Mineral Resources

While the Ozarks lack abundant natural resources, mineral resources were a catalyst for some Ozark settlements. Lead and zinc have been mined throughout southeastern Missouri for 250 years and still contribute to the nation's total production of these ores (photo 12.10). The primary ore, galena lead (the state mineral), was originally important for making ammunition and pewter, but it is used today in batteries and as protection from radioactivity and X-rays.

PHOTO 12.8. World Headquarters of Tyson Foods in Springdale, Arkansas.
Source: Brandonrush

PHOTO 12.9. Nineteenth-Century Iron Furnace, Maramec Spring, Southeastern Missouri. Iron production helped St. Louis prosper in the early nineteenth century. In 1826, the site was the first iron furnace west of the Mississippi River. Production continued for fifty years, supplying pig iron and wrought iron.

PHOTO 12.10. Hot Springs, Arkansas. There are forty-seven thermal springs that flow at 147°F. The natural springs and baths were popular health resorts in the late nineteenth century. Their popularity declined after the formation of the Food and Drug Administration.

The New Lead Belt, or Viburnum Trend, located in the Reynolds and Iron counties is the current lead-producing area. These lead, zinc, and copper mines began producing in the 1960s but are close to being played out. The toxicity levels of lead exposure (causing lifelong learning disabilities or behavioral problems in children) have affected local residential yards along the trucking routes to processing plants. In 2005, the Environmental Protection Agency (EPA) began a cleanup of lead-contaminated soils.

Logging

Hardwood forests covered almost three-quarters of the Ozark plateaus, but in the early eighteenth century, the forests were cut over to supply building material for St. Louis and nearby railroads. After the Civil War, the need for timber increased, both for railway ties and for fuel for steam locomotives. After the original forest was cut, second- and third-growth forests were planted. These immature forests were cut as soon as economically feasible and used for pulps. No longer are logs transported to pulp mills, but the mills are brought into the forest so the complete tree can be milled and hauling costs are reduced.

Most forests are no longer grown as natural ecosystems. They are now managed monocultures. The forests that Europeans found when they arrived have long ago been cut and used. In the Ozarks, only about 3 percent of the forested area is intact as it was when Europeans arrived. European arrivals found shortleaf pine forests, but today the region has been converted to loblolly pine plantations—miles and miles of the same species planted row upon row. Pine plantations are economical because they shorten the harvest rotation. The unintended consequences of these short-term profits, though, are multiple: depleted nutrients from the soil, polluted waterways, and destruction of wildlife and fishery habitats. For example, songbirds become more susceptible to predators and parasites when they lack large forested areas or when they are victim to mismanaged forests. And in the twenty-first century, climate change has added to the consequences and affected forest management and practices.

Improperly managed water systems can result in water quality and quantity issues such as increased flooding and an increase in wildfires. An additional unintended consequence is the chemical toxins used to manufacture chip mill wood, which result in polluted water.

Public forested lands are managed to protect wildlife habitat, biodiversity, watersheds, and resource production. However, most of the forested Ozarks are privately held. Many landowners of Ozark forests are poor, and they often make choices based on short-term profit, at the expense of long-term, healthy forested areas. Often regulations, meant to further sustainable forestry practices, are interpreted as bureaucratic. Being educated to the effects of selling wood to mills is the best choice for a timber owner and for the health of the land.

A few private landowners and foundations in the region have begun to conserve the forested natural resources and assure long-term yields supporting sustainable forest management. For example, the Current River and Pioneer Forest area of southeastern Missouri developed a long-term strategy in the 1970s to protect its watershed and timber reserves by practicing uneven-aged management, cutting trees based on quality, over the dominant clear-cutting method of even-aged management.

External Costs: Chip Mills   Using chip mills provides short-term benefits at the cost of long-term health of the forests. For the past 150 years, improperly managed timber harvests have been part of the Ozark economy. Since the 1990s, some owners have sold their forested land to short-term oriented chip mills.

Sawmills had been the standard for wood production until chip mills entered the region. However, with the decline in mature wood, the industry relies on chip mills that use ten times as much wood as a regular sawmill. The chip mills grind entire but immature trees into chips and furnish the pulp and paper industry with low-grade fiber for particleboard or grocery bags.

Achieving sustainable forests requires participation from both public and private landowners to improve and manage growing stock. The demand of chip mills for wood increases clear-cuts, which in turn increase erosion, decrease soil fertility, impair water quality, and accelerate forest fragmentation. Attempts to professionalize and regulate the forestry industry and to develop best management practices have often been stymied due to short-term profit over long-term forest health. The traditional Ozark economy maintained a sustainable landscape of healthy woods, water, and wildlife while practicing within the local economy, but the short-term profit of a globalized economy became the status quo in the forested areas.

The Secondary Sector

Food Processing

With the advent of Tyson Foods and Walmart, northwest Arkansas took on the world. By the late twentieth century, manufacturing was declining in America, although in rural America resource-based manufacturing—from lumber to food processing—retained a local presence. Now Tyson Foods dominates Arkansas industry. Late-twentieth-century food processing enterprises offered dangerous, low-skilled jobs that many local residents shunned. So most workers have been immigrants, usually Hispanics, but in the case of Tyson many workers came from the Marshall Islands, a US territory that allowed legal emigration without visas.

Walmart, the world's largest retail company (with annual sales of more than $300 billion), is headquartered in Bentonville in northwestern Arkansas. In the 1950s, Sam Walton located his first stores in America's underserviced rural areas. Using his marketing techniques, the company grew into a global enterprise. Walmart has adopted many energy-efficient procedures and features in its stores to increase profitability, but it has failed to recognize and act on the social and other environmental responsibilities that accompany a sustainable economy. For example, Walmart has been accused for years of discriminating in paying women less than men.

The Tertiary Sector

Tourism

During the late nineteenth century, Ozark health spas capitalized on natural springs and built health spas, such as Eureka Springs and Hot Springs, Arkansas (photo 12.11). However, the spa health claims diminished when the Food and Drug Administration (FDA) formed in the early twentieth century and enforced truth-in-advertising laws.

By 1950, springs tourism had faded, and Missouri and Arkansas were better known for their rural appeal: more pitching horseshoes than spas. Mineral-spring health spas were no longer fashionable, so the Ozarks reinvented its tourism. When the Army Corps of Engineers constructed Table Rock Dam for flood control and hydroelectric power, it also offered

BOX 12.8 GLOBAL CONNECTIONS: BENTONVILLE, ARKANSAS

Bentonville has strong links with the rest of the world. In fact, it is a vital hub in the global economy. It is the home of Walmart, the world's largest retailers with almost 11,700 stores in twenty-eight different countries that employs 2.3 million people and had revenues in 2016 that amounted to $480 billion.

Walmart relies on global supply chains. Over 80 percent of goods sold in Walmart are made in China. Walmart's relentless push to reduce producer costs forced many manufacturers in the United States to move to cheaper overseas centers such as China.

Producers want to contract with Walmart because while the unit profits are low, the total sales are lucrative. More than eleven hundred different vendors have established sales offices in Bentonville in order to do business with Walmart. This relatively small city in Arkansas is an important cog in the supply chains that link overseas and domestic producers with the global network of Walmart stores.

PHOTO 12.11. The Walmart Home Office in Bentonville, Arkansas. This is the world headquarters of the retail giant.
Source: iStock/wellesenterprises

lakeside lots, enhanced an already thriving fishing and recreational economy, and helped secure Branson, Missouri's entertainment complex. As the rest of America grew more urban, the scenic, laid-back lifestyle made the Ozarks popular as an inexpensive vacationland and retirement community.

A Sustainable Future

The Ozarks are no longer considered backward, but instead they are located at the center of the country's population and the center of food processing, discount retail, retirement communities, and tourism consumer industries. Yet, there are numerous challenges to a more sustainable future that includes the following:

- a weak tertiary sector of the economy;
- urban sprawl;
- point and nonpoint water pollution;

- climate change;
- deforestation;
- environmental impacts from CAFOs; and
- lack of ethnic and racial diversity.

The Ozarks traded their backwoods past for the same environmental problems as the rest of America, namely urban sprawl, point and nonpoint pollution of streams, loss of biodiversity for plant and animal life, and the logging, mining, and hydropower influences on the land and the people. Nonlocal industries, such as chip mills, have exploited the Ozark landscape to the detriment of the local people. Although the karst topography attracts tourism and provides the spring-fed water supply, during the past half century, these features have been degraded because of increased population. Because the water rushes through the karst network, filtration is low. Therefore, industrial or residential waste is more damaging than in less porous areas. Among the many water pollution issues are nitrogen and phosphorus

BOX 12.9   BRANSON, MISSOURI

Early in the twentieth century, author Harold Wright Bell sought refuge from urban ills in the Ozarks. His surroundings so impressed him that he wrote *Shepherd of the Hills,* a thinly veiled fiction about the tribulations of local pioneers. The book, first published in 1907, was instantly successful and attracted thousands to southwestern Missouri. Some locals profited from the ensuing tourism; others bemoaned the loss of their privacy and natural area.

Thus began the Branson tourist complex. Until the novel's publication, Branson was a small logging community. In the 1930s, Branson became more accessible and popular when dams supplied electricity and running water and roads provided access. By the 1960s, Branson began attracting local musical talent that has grown to sixty nighttime venues, concentrated along 76 Country Boulevard. Music and water sports helped the town blossom into a midwestern tourism capital. Unlike the large halls of Nashville, Branson has smaller theaters, which cater to fans seeking more intimate gatherings to see their favorite stars (photo 12.12).

Every year, more than seven million visitors seek traditional and family entertainment values in Branson.

PHOTO 12.12. Branson, Missouri. The entertainment complex of Branson, in the middle of nowhere, is testament to the power of transportation access. Presleys' Country Jubilee was among the first local production groups to locate in Branson. Today, many nationwide music groups have built theaters in the town. Branson can seat up to fifty thousand people at its shows on any day. It rivals Nashville as the capital of country music.

nutrients from chicken and hog manure, chemical spills from the mining industry, and sewage sludge from residential septic systems.

Although population growth was never an issue in the Ozarks before the 1960s and for many is now a blessing (though some regret the loss of their natural homeland), population pressure has indirectly caused pollution and sprawl.

In many ways the traditional Ozark economy, which many urban Americans might describe as "poor," is a self-sufficient and sustainable economy. Perhaps the initial Ozark economy has something to teach the rest of America. Some, of course, realize what has been lost and are working to maintain the quality of life and live within a more sustainable economy.

The Ozark population has become more aware of sustainable ecosystems. Fishers realize that runoff and septic systems affect the water and the fish within them. Chip mills have an impact on erosion and soil fertility and have slowly adopted sustainable forest management systems, and some farmers search for more sustainable methods and local crops.

The land of opportunity has briefly segued into another mode of production, but perhaps the reason that so many chose this natural area is that it unwittingly provided some answers for a sustainable America.

Questions for Discussion

1. Tainted water from chicken waste has been the source of many environmental lawsuits. But chicken farms have enabled many small family farmers to keep their land. If environmental restrictions add to the farmers' cost of chicken production, many may lose their income and farms. What are some options for addressing this problem?

2. Where do the workers in the chicken plants come from, and why are they there?

3. What part of the Ozarks did the Germans settle? What was their chief occupation?

4. Are earthquakes a danger in this region?

5. How have the Ozarks changed economically over the past fifty years?

6. How did the creation of Oklahoma's Federal Indian lands affect growth in Fort Smith and the Arkansas River Valley?

7. How has the White River region of Arkansas changed since the 1980s?

8. What are challenges to urbanization?

9. Why does this region lag behind in attracting new residents and foreign-born immigrants?

10. How did logging change in the twentieth century, and what were the consequences?

Suggested Readings

Burgess, S. "Perspectives on the Sacred: 'Religion in the Ozarks.'" *OzarksWatch* 2, no. 2 (Fall 1988): 4–7.

Embree, D. "The Ozarks: Buckle of the Bible Belt or Haven for Religious Diversity?" *OzarksWatch* 12 (2005): 3–4.

Farley, G. "The Wal-Martization of Rural America and Other Things," *OzarksWatch* 5, no. 3 (Winter 1992), at http://thelibrary.org/lochist/periodicals/ozarkswatch/ow50329.htm

Flanders, R. "Where Is the Ozarks? You Wouldn't Want to Live There—Would You?" *OzarksWatch* 5, no. 3 (Winter 1992).

Gerlach, R. L. *Immigrants in the Ozarks: A Study in Ethnic Geography.* Columbia: University of Missouri Press, 1976.

Gilmore, R. K. *Ozark Baptisms, Hangings, and Other Diversions: Theatrical Folkways of Rural Missouri, 1885–1910.* Norman: University of Oklahoma Press, 1984.

Glassie, H. *Pattern in the Material Field Culture of the Eastern United States.* Philadelphia: University of Pennsylvania Press, 1968.

Hartman, M., and E. Ingenthron. *Baldknobbers: Vigilantes on the Ozark Frontier.* Gretna, La.: Pelican Publishing Company, 1988.

Kersten, E. W. "Changing Economy and Landscape in a Missouri Ozarks Area." *Annals of the Association of American Geographers* 48, no. 4 (1958): 398–418.

Martin, G., and D. Martin. *Ozark Idyll: Life at the Turn of the Century in the Missouri Ozarks.* Point Lookout, Mo.: School of the Ozarks Press, 1972.

Miller, E. J. W. "The Ozark Culture Region as Revealed by Traditional Materials." *Annals of the Association of American Geographers* 58, no. 1 (1968): 51–77.

Otto, J. S., and A. M. Burns III. "Traditional Agricultural Practices in the Arkansas Highlands." *Journal of American Folklore* 94, no. 372 (1981).

Rafferty, M. *Missouri: A Geography.* Boulder, Colo.: Westview Press, 1983.

———. *The Ozarks: Lands and Life.* Fayetteville: University of Arkansas Press, 2001.

———. "The Ozarks as a Region: A Geographer's Description." *OzarksWatch* 1, no. 4 (1988).

Sauer, C. O. *The Geography of the Ozark Highland of Missouri.* Chicago: University of Chicago Press, 1920.

Wright, H. *The Shepherd of the Hills.* Book Supply Company, 1907.

Internet Sources

"Computer Models Estimate Impact of Climate Change on Ozarks," *Missourian*, September 21, 2008, at http://www.columbiamissourian.com/stories/2008/09/21/computer-models-estimate-impact-climate-change-ozarks/

U.S. Department of Agriculture. Rural Development. Contract Farms, at http://www.rurdev.usda.gov/rbs/pub/jul02/farm.html

OzarksWatch, at http://ozarkswatch.missouristate.edu/

Sierra Club. "Chip Mills: Industrial Logging Returns to the Ozarks," at http://missouri.sierraclub.org/SierranOnline/mayjune2000/chipmill.htm

Forest Stewardship Council—U.S. *Forest Stewardship Standard for the Ozark-Ouachita Region*, at http://www.scscertified.com/docs/oo_6.4_NTC.pdf

St. Louis Sustainability Plan, at https://www.stlouis-mo.gov/government/departments/planning/documents/upload/130219%20STL%20Sustainability%20Plan.pdf

1 Dairy Belt farms are growing larger to compete with CAFO dairies.

2 Iowa's economy revolves around agriculture; corn and hogs play an interrelated role.

Lake Agassiz

Red River Valley

Fargo

Lake Superior

U.P.

Lake Huron

Dairy Belt

1

Minneapolis

Great Lakes

Sioux Falls

Lake Michigan

Madison

Driftless

Detroit

6

Dissected Till Plain

2

Chicago

Black Swamp

Cleveland

Des Moines

Corn Belt

Till Plain

Rust Belt

Omaha

3

Indianapolis

5

4

Cincinnati

Mississippi River

St. Louis

Ohio River

N
W   E
S

Osage Plains

NATIVE PRAIRIE

0   75   150 M

Cities

Rivers

State Border

5 Relict wood lots stand out as dark spots in the fertile farmland of Ohio's Till Plains.

3 Native midwestern grasses were long ago plowed up for cropland, but some areas have begun restoration.

Cross Timbers

6 Declining Rust Belt cities such as Detroit have many vacant buildings and homes.

4 This canal in Indianapolis, meant to connect the Wabash River with Lake Erie, was never completed.

13
THE MIDWEST
Corn, Cars, Conundrums, and Hope

Chapter Highlights

After reading this chapter, you should be able to:

- Describe the formation of the midwestern landscape
- Compare and contrast the Driftless and the Till Plain
- Identify the subregions of the Midwest
- Discuss how the Green Revolution and GMO crops have changed agriculture and food
- Describe the evolution of the region's two major economies, agriculture and manufacturing
- Contrast the population dynamics in the Midwest to the rest of the country
- Identify the major cities and discuss their economies
- Discuss critical urban trends including migration
- Identify the location, relationship, and importance of the Dairy, Corn, and Soybean belts
- Explain the impact of deindustrialization
- Discuss strategies to rebuild Midwestern economies
- Explain the importance of the Great Lakes

Terms

agglomeration	deindustrialization	Green Revolution	prairie
brownfield	ethanol	kettle	Redlining
community-supported	family farm	lake effect	till
agriculture (CSA)	genetically modified	Land Ordinance of 1785	township and range system
	organism (GMO)	loess	

Places

Black Swamp	Corn Belt	Erie Canal	Osage Plain
Cayahoga River	Cross Timbers	Great Lakes	Prairie Peninsula
	Dairy Belt	Lake Agassiz	Red River Valley
	The Driftless	Ohio River⊠	Till Plain

Cities

Buffalo, New York (2016 MSA 1.1 million)	Cleveland, Ohio (2016 MSA 2.0 million)	Flint Michigan (2016 MSA 408,000)	Madison, Wisconsin (2016 MSA 560,000)
Ann Arbor, Michigan (2016 MSA 365,000)	Columbus, Ohio (2016 MSA 2.0 million)	Indianapolis, Indiana (2016 MSA 2.0 million)	Omaha, Nebraska (2016 MSA 924,000)
Chicago, Illinois (2016 MSA 2.7 million)	Detroit, Michigan (2016 MSA 4.2 million)	Minneapolis-St. Paul, Minnesota (2016 MSA 3.5 million)	Sioux Falls, South Dakota (2016 MSA 255,000)
Cincinnati, Ohio (2016 MSA 2.1 million)	Fargo North Dakota (2016 MSA 238,000)		

PHOTO 13.1. Ohio Rural Landscape. Agriculture is the most conspicuous human activity in the Midwest and covers most of the land, especially in the Corn Belt.

Introduction

The Midwest became the heartland of America during the nineteenth century, when transportation connected its agricultural bounty to the more populated eastern markets. During the first half of the twentieth century, manufacturing and the automobile restructured the regional industry. Together, the pastoral culture—silos, cornfields, and red barns (photo 13.1)—and steel age factories of the Midwest have created a distinctive place region.

The term "Midwest" conjures up a hard-working blue-collar American image. But this physical-labor economy has nearly disappeared from the region with the loss of small **family farms** and the onset of **deindustrialization**. The rural economy was incorporated into the twenty-first-century agribusiness regime, in which small family farms must identify a niche, contract with a corporation, or be unprofitable. The region, once home to the nation's manufacturing sector, has seen millions of jobs lost as industrial corporations have moved overseas. Many older residents remain tied to their communities, but young residents and college graduates find little opportunity at home and migrate to Sunbelt cities.

Despite these economic changes, this region is rebuilding and rebranding itself. Minnesota, for example, was an early adopter of statewide sustainability principles. Minnesota's economy is healthy, and the Minneapolis metro area receives high marks in technology, innovation, and as a magnet for young, educated, and alternative groups. Chicago has also adopted many green elements into its city structure, energy production, and transportation patterns. Cities that depended on the automotive industry have bled jobs, but other cities—Madison, Indianapolis, and some small cities such as Sioux Falls and Fargo—have begun to find their way onto "best cities to live" lists, attracting residents with their low cost of living and healthy lifestyles.

Physical Geography

The Midwestern Central Lowland landscape can be described as flat but diverse: lakes, rivers, trees, rolling hills, glaciers, grass, dairy, corn, and large factories characterize this region. The physiographic subregions subtly vary, mostly in relation to their glacial history, which in turn affected economic development.

The lake states, one of the major sources of freshwater in the world, rendered their flat and fertile glacial soils into the Corn Belt and the Dairy Belt, two of the most important agricultural regions in the world. The soil, the climate, and the moisture are perfect for corn and dairy, but the pollutants used to grow them endanger the ecosystems. Maintaining this part of the country sustainably, while still maintaining the integrity of the ecological landscape, has challenged the widely divergent interests of industry and sustainable agriculture.

Physical Regions

The Midwestern open grassland **prairie** landscape is the product of glacial weight. The Midwest begins in eastern Ohio and fades into the transition zone between the 98th and 100th parallels, where precipitation falls below twenty inches annually. The Canadian Shield and the Niagara Escarpment denote the northern borders, while the southern border follows the southern extent of glaciation, the Ohio River.

Presettlement vegetation ranged from hardwood forests in Ohio and Indiana to tall grass on the Illinois-Indiana Prairie Peninsula. Ten thousand years ago, during the Pleistocene, no mountains halted the advancing glacial lobes over the Central Lowlands. As the glaciers retreated, wind-blown **loess** accumulated over the prairies, creating a fertile, moisture-retaining

MAP 13.1. The Great Lakes Watershed. With the exception of Michigan, the watershed is narrow around the surrounding states and provinces.

Source: http://www.epa.gov/glnpo/atlas/images/big01.gif

soil. Rolling ridge moraines offer welcome relief to the flat landscape. Commonalities between the subregions include glacial history from the last ice age, an abundance of water, and the lack of mountainous terrain.

The Midwestern Central Lowlands is made up of six physiographic subregions:

- Great Lakes
- Till Plain
- Dissected Till Plain
- The Driftless
- Red River Valley
- Transitional Osage Plain

Great Lakes

The Great Lakes region and watershed includes all of Michigan and portions of Wisconsin, Minnesota, Illinois, Indiana, Pennsylvania, and New York (map 13.1). When glaciers retreated from the Great Lakes region, they left behind thousands of lake and wetland features. For example, **kettle** lakes were formed when a large block of ice calved from a receding glacier, was buried by glacial outwash, and then filled with water as the ice block melted. Smaller kettle lakes, called prairie potholes, are abundant across the northern prairies. Many wetlands on the glacial landscape have been subsequently drained for agricultural production, but at the cost of ecological degradation.

Till Plain

Glaciers deposited Till Plain soil across eastern Ohio west into southern Illinois. Europeans found a hardwood forest landscape, but within a century agriculture replaced the nearly all the forests. The grass fields that had been the result of prairie fires, such as the Prairie Peninsula cutting across Iowa to Ohio, were also replaced by agriculture (map 13.2). Today, agriculture dominates the tall grass prairie.

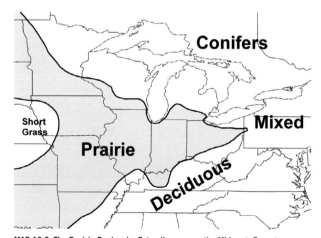

MAP 13.2. The Prairie Peninsula, Extending across the Midwest. Forests surround it on three sides. It has been theorized that the peninsula remained grassy because of prairie fires that retarded forest growth.

BOX 13.1   DID YOU KNOW . . . THE BLACK SWAMP

The Black Swamp was once the lakebed of glacial Lake Maumee, a remnant of the ancestral Great Lakes. When Europeans arrived, the flat, forested Black Swamp surrounded the Maumee River from present-day Toledo west to Fort Wayne, Indiana, and then south to Findlay, Ohio (map 13.3).

The swamp was nearly impassable, so settlement to the north lagged behind surrounding regions. It took six days to cross the oozing, muddy swamp from Cleveland to Detroit, a three-hour drive today.

Settlement hinged on draining the swamps, and once drained the land became fertile agricultural land. By 1930, it was almost entirely farmland. Most large towns are located along the less fertile swamp periphery.

However, the swamp is not entirely gone. The area is dry when there are no extreme precipitation events, but the soil is still wetland soil, and heavy rains periodically flood the region.

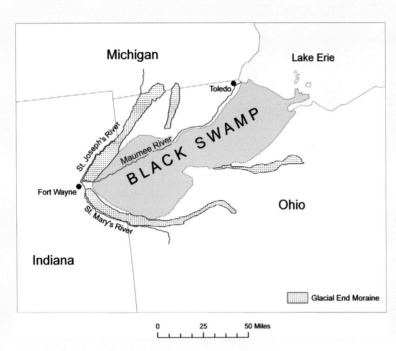

MAP 13.3. The Black Swamp. A remnant of ancestral Lake Maumee, this swamp was drained in the late nineteenth century for agricultural use, but the area is still subject to flooding.

Across the northern edge of the Till Plain, the **Black Swamp** was a remnant of ancient Lake Maumee, a precursor to Lake Erie. Only a few sand ridges allowed sluggish passage through the muddy, insect-infested area to the north, delaying settlement in Michigan until the swamp was drained in the 1840s. Once drained, the land became prime for agriculture. However, when rains come or spring thaws are large, the old Black Swamp area still has wetland soils and is often inundated.

Dissected Till Plain

Four major glacial stages incised the Pleistocene landscape. The first two stages covered Iowa and northern Missouri, but the later glacial advances stopped farther north and the unglaciated Iowa and Missouri **till** eroded and formed the drainage systems of the Dissected Till Plain. Thick loess deposits blanketed the undulating terrain, making it ideal land for growing corn—humid and flat, with hot summers and cold winters. The Missouri River flows through the western plain, and along it are the leading regional hubs, from Sioux City to Kansas City.

The Driftless

The southwestern corner of Wisconsin and sections of adjoining states are together called the Driftless, a landscape that escaped glaciation during the last glacial episode. The Driftless pre–ice age landscape of rough, steep hills, and sandstone or limestone formations is reminiscent of the Southwest, only more verdant (photo 13.2). The Driftless topography, while aesthetically majestic, is less fertile than the surrounding areas and therefore not as agriculturally productive.

Red River Valley

The Red River Valley is a remnant of ancient Lake Agassiz, which was larger than all the Great Lakes combined. Lake Agassiz receded when Hudson Bay became ice-free about seventy-seven hundred years ago, leaving behind Lake Winnipeg, the Red River, and the flat and fertile Red River Valley.

The Red River has the distinction of being the only major north-flowing river in the conterminous United States; it flows into Manitoba and Hudson Bay. However, its northern route

PHOTO 13.2. The Driftless, Southwestern Wisconsin. The Driftless was not glaciated like the surrounding Midwestern area. Its landforms, such as the Three Chimneys, are unlike the rest of the Midwest.

also accounts for the valley's major geographic problem—floods. The northern plains become ice-free later in the spring than the southern areas. As the southern river melts, the frozen north can block runoff. In years of abnormal snowfall when the thaw is rapid, as has happened more frequently, the flooding is monumental. One of the more catastrophic floods occurred in 1997, which submerged communities from Wahpeton-Breckenridge to Fargo-Moorhead to Grand Forks-East Grand Forks and beyond, inflicting billions of dollars in damage across the region. Today, the USGS coordinates the collection and dissemination of geospatial imagery and map products used for flood response and evaluation and maintains a flood forecast website.

Transitional Osage Plain

The Osage Plain on either side of the Kansas–Missouri border is a transition between the eastern tall grass lowlands and the western short grasses. Within the Osage Plain are the Flint Hills, formed two hundred million years ago. The Flint Hill limestone and chert were deposited when inland seas periodically inundated the area. The Flint Hills are a remnant of the native grassy plain that received glacial dust (loess). The Osage Plain agricultural landscape is also transitional, with corn to the east and wheat to the west. The Flint Hills are too rocky for good agricultural crops, and so they are grazed.

The rolling Cross Timbers tract is a remnant of an ancient deciduous forest found cutting across east central Oklahoma and north central Texas. The Cross Timbers occupies a transitional zone between the eastern forests and the western grassland. The stunted post oaks were unsuitable for lumber production, but access to wood was limited across the plains, and few people settled the area until the late nineteenth century.

Water

The continental interior includes two major North American drainage systems, the Great Lakes and the Mississippi River. Both are remnants of the ice ages.

The abundance of freshwater in the Midwest secured agricultural and industrial enterprises, but only after intensive infrastructure—canals, tiling, dams, and locks—controlled the waters. Canals and locks were built when waterways were the main mode of transport. They became secondary after railroads became dominant.

Wetlands

The regions with the highest percentage of total wetlands are those that were glaciated during the most recent ice ages. Wetlands are an integral part of the thousands of midwestern lakes and ephemeral ponds (photo 13.3). Wetlands covered about 20 percent of the midwestern land area prior to European occupation, of which about 85 percent—about 36 million acres—have been drained and converted to agricultural use.

Wetlands filter excess nutrients from agricultural fields. The typical ways to drain midwestern wetlands are to tile fields or dig ditches; the water from both empty into nearby streams. Many fields have become productive because of draining wetlands and dependence on fossil fuel–based pesticides, herbicides, and fertilizers, but this practice has increased the amount of nitrogen and phosphorus flowing into streams and rivers.

PHOTO 13.3. LeFurge Woods Wetland Creation Project, Southeastern Michigan. This restored wetland was formerly in agricultural production. Michigan had eleven million acres of wetland prior to American settlement, but now has about three million acres.

Fertilizers flow into the Mississippi watershed because wetlands have been drained and can no longer buffer between fields and the watershed. Tiles drain wetland fields, but they send nitrogen, phosphorus, and other chemicals directly into the watershed and cause excess vegetative and algal growth, which results in the low-oxygen eutrophic water bodies.

The swampy shorelines of water-laden midwestern cities were filled, stabilized, and polluted.

In Chicago, the Chicago River had been a dumping ground for urban waste. In 1887, the flow of the river was reversed from Lake Michigan into the Mississippi River in order to protect the population from contamination of its drinking water supply. The reversal of the Chicago River was a massive public works effort and was hailed as a monumental engineering achievement. After its completion, waterborne disease rates quickly and dramatically improved, and its water supply system was soon regarded as being one of the safest in the world. With its water source made safe and dependable by the canals, Chicago and the region grew rapidly. Today, however, we can also view this engineering project as an example of human attempts to control the natural processes.

The Great Lakes

The Great Lakes hold nearly 20 percent of the world's freshwater. The five lakes—Superior, Michigan, Huron, Erie, and Ontario—span 750 miles along the US-Canadian border. Lake Superior is the only Great Lake with underlying Canadian Shield rock. It is the largest, deepest, and youngest of the Great Lakes and accounts for 10 percent of global surface freshwater. Sedimentary rocks glacially scoured the remaining lakes, including Lake Michigan, the only Great Lake to reside completely within the United States.

There are several theories on Great Lakes evolution, but all theories agree that glacial movement was involved. A billion years ago, a horseshoe-shaped rift cut across Iowa into the future Great Lakes states, creating the Michigan Basin and intruding copper and silver deposits on the Keweenaw Peninsula. Twenty million years ago, the Great Lakes were formed. Rapids and falls between the interconnected lakes would hinder easy settlement.

During the Industrial Revolution, the Great Lakes region dominated the national economy, but at the expense of water quality. One of the most spectacular pollution accidents occurred in Ohio's **Cuyahoga River** and Lake Erie, where extreme pollution in the late 1960s caused the river to catch fire several times, most spectacularly in 1969. The river became a symbol for the deteriorating environment and was a catalyst for the Clean Water Act and the formation of the Environmental Protection Agency (EPA).

Although many states have pledged to clean up water pollution, progress has lagged. Nearly fifty years after the Clean Water Act, deep lake sediments are still infiltrated with polychlorinated biphenyls (PCBs), which affect hormones and disrupt the endocrine system. The PCBs bioaccumulate as they ascend the food chain; by the time they reach humans the effects are huge. The lakes remain some of the most polluted in North America.

Lake levels have fluctuated throughout history, but recent declines are consistent with climate change forecasts. Other reasons for the drawdown include rising lake temperatures (more than 3°C warmer than the beginning of the twentieth century), higher wind speeds that reduce ice cover, and accelerated evaporation. Human modifications such as dredging and building shoreline structures keep sand on the beaches but

BOX 13.2 ENVIRONMENTAL CHALLENGES: CUYAHOGA FIFTY YEARS AFTER THE FIRE

In June 1969, the Cuyahoga River in the city of Cleveland caught on fire. The river, filled with kerosene and other flammable material was probably ignited by a passing train that provided the spark. Although it burned for only thirty minutes, the incident and the famous photograph of the river on fire became a pivotal part of an emerging environmental movement. *Time Magazine* described the Cuyahoga as the river that "oozes rather than flows" and in which a person "does not drown but decays."[*] The memorable 1969 fire sparked legislation for the Great Lakes Water Quality Agreement and the Clean Water Act of the 1970s. The federal government directed large amounts of money, dealt with industrial polluters, and enforced regulations: the river was on track to get cleaner.

The one-hundred-mile river is composed of the upper half and the lower half (near Cleveland) (Photo 13.4). Today, the lower half of the river is no longer the incendiary sewer of the dark days of 1969. Industrial discharge has been controlled significantly.

However, the river still receives discharges of storm water, combined-sewer overflows, and incompletely disinfected wastewater from urban areas upstream of the park. Nonpoint sources are the result of urbanization, more specifically suburbanization, in metro Cleveland. People are moving into suburbs that were once former open spaces and farmland. And with suburban settlement comes an increase in impervious surfaces such as rooftops, driveways, parking lots, sidewalks, and lawns.

Although much healthier now, some sections of the river remain impaired. Most of the river remains unacceptable for recreational use due to the high concentrations of *Escherichia coli* (*E. coli*), a fecal-indicator bacterium. Contaminant and bacteria levels can still be high, especially after periods of rain. Some of the river's lingering problems include

- trash;
- toxics;
- bacteria;
- fish tumors;
- lack of aquatic diversity; and
- beach closings.

On a more optimistic note, recently a water-quality analyst found a living freshwater mussel in that long-polluted portion of the river—the first reported in more than one hundred years. Somehow the freshwater mussel managed to survive the last century through the worst of the pollution on the Cuyahoga and the mussel population is on the increase.

Learn more about Cuyhoga River history and the many river fires: http://www.pophistorydig.com/topics/cuyahoga-river-fires/

Read the 1969 Time Magazine article: http://content.time.com/time/magazine/article/0,9171,901182,00.html

PHOTO 13.4. The Cuyahoga River runs through the City of Cleveland, Ohio.
Source: iStock/PapaBear

---

[*]J. H. Adler. "Smoking out the Cuyahoga Fire Fable: Smoke and Mirrors surrounding Cleveland," *National Review*, June 22, 2004, at: http://old.nationalreview.com/adler/adler200406220845.asp

Great Lakes Restoration Initiative Projects from FY 2010 – FY 2016

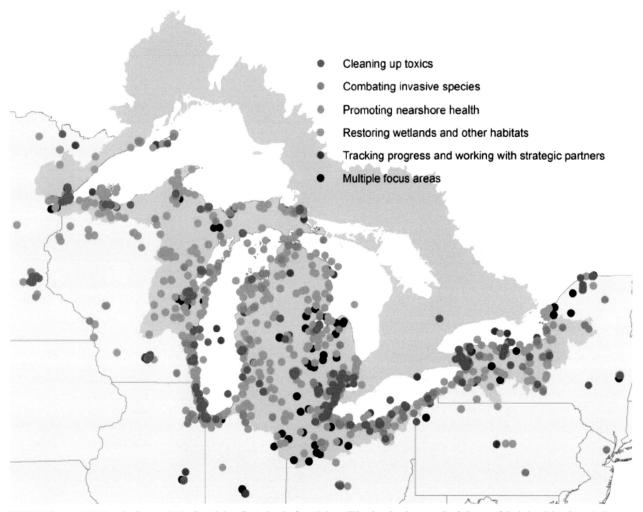

- ● Cleaning up toxics
- ● Combating invasive species
- ● Promoting nearshore health
- ● Restoring wetlands and other habitats
- ● Tracking progress and working with strategic partners
- ● Multiple focus areas

MAP 13.4. Ongoing Initiatives for Clean up in the Great Lakes. Restoring the Great Lakes will involve cleaning up toxics (a legacy of the industrial era), combating invasive species, restoring wetlands and other habitats, and promoting near-shore health.

Source: US EPA, Great Lakes Restoration Initiative Report to Congress and the President, 2016, at: http://glri.us

alter ecosystems and water flows. Other environmental issues include numerous invasive species, beach closings, and the loss of wetlands.

In 2010, the Great Lakes Restoration Initiative was launched to accelerate efforts to protect and restore the Great Lakes (map 13.4).

Smaller Lakes

Each Great Lakes state and province has innumerable glacially formed lakes. Michigan, Minnesota, and Wisconsin have up to ten thousand lakes each; Ontario and Quebec have millions of glacial lakes, wetland marshes, and bogs that pockmark regional drainage patterns. In Michigan, the original land survey viewed the wetlands so negatively it discouraged settlement and farming for years. Today, the wetlands are drained, and most residents are unaware of the former landscape and how it still

affects local landscape patterns. While the land may feel dry, artificially drained landscapes exacerbate flooding and negatively affect water quality.

The Upper Mississippi River Basins and Ohio River

The Upper Mississippi River basin begins at Cairo, Illinois. The rich loess-covered basin was originally part of the tall grass prairie but today is an important corn and soybean producer. The river in the upper basin was inadequate for shipping purposes, until twenty-nine locks, twenty-eight dams, and numerous channelization structures transformed the river and facilitated navigation for agricultural commodities to the south and fossil fuel commodities to the north. The human-built structures have adversely affected riverine ecosystems impacting water quality, which requires managing and regulating restoration projects.

PHOTO 13.5. Bridge Collapse in Minneapolis, Minnesota. This bridge crossing the Mississippi River collapsed in August 2007, killing thirteen people. More than a decade later, the image continues to symbolize the decline in US infrastructure and its maintenance.

The Ohio River drainage basin encompasses fourteen states, including the majority of Ohio, Indiana, and Illinois, and includes 10 percent of the American population (twenty-five million people). Beginning at the confluence of the Allegheny and Monongahela at Pittsburgh, the Ohio flows west to meet the Mississippi at Cairo, Illinois. Along the way, the river receives 95 percent of its runoff from tributary channels, such as the Scioto (Ohio), Wabash (Illinois/Indiana), Tennessee, and Cumberland rivers.

When Europeans arrived, the Ohio River was relatively free of obstacles, excepting the minor falls and rapids at Louisville, Kentucky. But as communities and industry developed along the river, a series of disastrous floods through the area's narrow valleys forced the construction of protective floodwalls. The levees were built to protect human communities, but in the process they destroyed many ecosystems, and now exacerbate flooding.

During the initial period of western expansion, the Pittsburgh–Cincinnati portion of the Ohio River was the nation's most important river and transportation corridor. The river was also an important cultural boundary, separating slave-free Ohio and slaveholding Kentucky, and so became an important crossing for the Underground Railroad.

The river corridor changed. In the early twentieth century, the Army Corps of Engineers constructed locks, dams, and power-generating facilities to control the quantity and quality of flow. A total of twenty dams tame the entire length of the 981-mile-long river. After World War II, industrial and residential traffic on the Ohio River has continued to increase, with each lock averaging ninety million tons annually. But the infrastructure has deteriorated and states have failed to keep up with needed investment (photo 13.5).

Both the Mississippi and Ohio river systems have suffered water-quality issues from pesticide use, artificial levee construction, sediment buildup, and navigation. Pesticide runoff pollutes the watershed and eventually flows into the Mississippi River and Gulf, creating the hypoxic dead zone (see chapter 11).

Climate

The Central Lowlands' humid continental climate fluctuates more than coastal areas, because land both gains and loses warmth more quickly than water. The lack of natural barriers allows winds to blow freely across the prairie. The continentality and winds account for the abrupt diurnal temperature variation, as well as the pronounced four seasons, from the short, dramatic, transitional spring and fall to the long, hot, humid summer and even longer, cold winter.

The lack of topographic barriers means that weather can come from many directions: cold Arctic flows, hot humid Gulf winds, and westward air movement across the continent. However, proximity to large bodies of water, in this case the Great Lakes, has other effects. The Great Lakes stabilize the local climate, allowing fruit production on their leeward side during the spring and summer, and they produce the abundant **lake effect** snow in winter (when evaporating water forms clouds and falls as snow). Although Buffalo and Rochester, New York, are famed for their lake effect snow, New York's Tug Hill Uplands, between the Adirondack Mountains and the leeward (east) side of Lake Ontario, receive the most lake effect snow in the United States, more than two hundred inches annually.

Since 1960, weather stations have noted changing weather patterns, including more extreme event rain and hotter temperatures, which may impact agricultural production.

Historical Geography and Settlement

Mound Builders

Archaeological evidence suggests that prehistoric Adena, Cahokia, Hopewell, and Woodland Period Iroquois and Huron were active in the Midwest for more than twelve thousand years, culminating during the Mississippian period.

The largest prehistoric site was located at Cahokia, near the confluence of the Mississippi and Missouri Rivers. Mound Builders practiced agriculture and traded widely with other Native Americans, as evidenced by the many artifacts found throughout the northern hemisphere. The mounds were large, flat-topped, and often served ceremonial purposes. The largest is Monk's Mound, but more than a hundred have been identified.

Cahokia flourished in the twelfth and thirteenth centuries, but during the fourteenth century residents dispersed for unknown reasons, perhaps because of ecological changes in soil fertility, supply of woodlands, or a decrease in wild game.

Iroquoians

Just prior to European contact, the Great Lakes Iroquoian tribal family was composed of the Hurons (Ontario and Michigan) and the New York area–based League of Five Nations (Seneca, Cayuga, Onondaga, Oneida, and Mohawk). Generally, the sedentary Iroquoian tribes lived in longhouses in semipermanent villages and practiced agriculture, growing corn, beans, squash, and tobacco. The Iroquois became a dominant power in the region, stretching west to the Mississippi and east to the Atlantic. When the British and French came to settle, they had to deal with the fearsome presence and power of this federation.

Native Americans, however, did have an impact on their environment. For example, in the woodlands there was tree clearance for agriculture. Maize, corn, and squash all required cleared land. The use of fire in the woodlands and plains was extensive and served a variety of purposes: suppressing underwood to improve hunting and travel, creating optimal growing conditions for different species, and producing pastures for deer and buffalos and driving game. Many of these tribes routinely set first to the forest and prairie in an attempt to yield greater advantage over their environment.

In the early nineteenth century, settlers spread throughout the region, displacing and ignoring Native American reserves and violating Native American treaties. There was no place for Native Americans; their occupancy of land was seen as a block to progress and their removal justifiable. Many tribes were affected by the 1830 **Indian Removal Act** that forced tribes east of the Mississippi River to relocate to Oklahoma Indian Territory on the Osage Plains. Over sixty thousand Indians were forced westward. The Winnebago of Wisconsin were evicted from their land first in the 1820s, but as the frontier moved towards them they were relocated

again and again. In total, they signed seven land turnover treaties. Eventually they were displaced to the Crow Creek Reservation in South Dakota. Most tribes were left with few economic resources on land that settlers regarded as distant and worthless. They had settled on land that was not connected to their ancestors or their cultural ways. The legacy is that today more than 20 percent of Native Americans live on reservations amid poverty, unemployment, abuse, alcoholism, and disease.

European Settlement

French fur trappers were the first Europeans to traverse the midwestern landscape. Beginning in the late seventeenth century, the French colonized a few places along the main Great Lakes transport routes including Detroit and Mackinaw.

French trading posts and protective forts—Fort Ponchatrain (1701; Detroit), Fort Duquesne (1754; Pittsburgh)—stopped British movement and monopolized the fur trade. The US government also built a series of protective forts at key geographic sites. Many became major cities: Fort Snelling (Minneapolis), Fort Washington (Cincinnati), and Fort Dearborn (Chicago).

The trans-Appalachian territory was French until the Proclamation of 1763 ended the French and Indian War and the territory was ceded to Britain. The British promised the territory to the native tribes and forbade colonists to settle west of the Appalachian Plateaus, but in 1783, they ceded the land to the new American Republic, which encouraged settlement. By 1800, there were one million living west of the Appalachians, 2.5 million by 1820, and 3.5 million by 1830.

The **Land Ordinance of 1785** further divided the land and encouraged frontier settlement (map 13.5). The **township and range system** allowed a quick distribution of land in private sales, group deeds, or homesteading. Rapid settlement meant many areas could petition for statehood once they reached sixty thousand population. Kentucky and Tennessee joined the union in 1790, and Ohio joined in 1803.

The completion of the Erie Canal in 1825 facilitated easier passage through the Great Lakes, enabling Michigan settlement, which had been difficult because of the impassable Black Swamp. The New York canal allowed many New Englanders and upstate New Yorkers to settle in Michigan and points west. Michigan became a state in 1837.

Beyond Ohio's forests, pioneers were confronted with the treeless Prairie Peninsula grassland, a landscape for which they had no cultural precedent. The pioneers initially settled in transition areas near the forest, which gave them access to lumber for houses and heat. Later, when the grasslands proved fertile, the open prairie was also settled, although the rich but heavy soil, very different from the sandier soil of New England, was difficult to plow. An ingenious blacksmith, John Deere, developed a new steel plow for these soils in 1837. Once the plains could be plowed, farms spread throughout the lowlands.

Midwestern railroad trunk lines followed the westward direction of population growth. The major growth cities during the

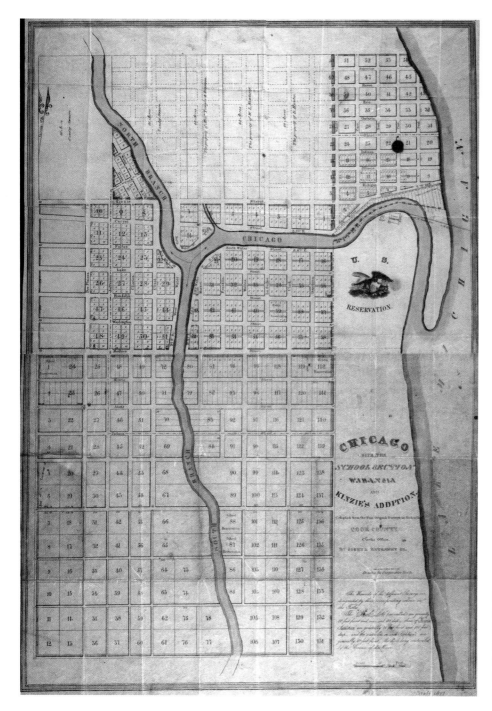

MAP 13.5. The Congressional Land Ordinance of 1785 required land in Western Territories to be laid out in square parcels, which contributed to the rise of the grid system in the Midwest. This Chicago map was created during a real estate boom in the 1830s.

late nineteenth century were along rail lines; Chicago became the preeminent rail center. The railroad transported midwestern agricultural and manufactured products to the nation. Other states expanded and revolutionized national transportation, trade, and the direction of population growth.

European immigration peaked in the 1880s, and by 1920, one out of six Americans was foreign born. As most of the farmland was already settled by 1880, the immigrants settled in urban areas. They tended to follow chain migration patterns and settle in cities with a significant ethnic group: the Polish in Detroit, the Germans in Milwaukee, and the Scandinavians in Minneapolis. The Midwest heartland became the melting pot of the assimilated peoples of the United States.

Cultural Perspectives

Three images form the American perception of the Midwest: red barn farmsteads, steel industries, and main street small towns.

Two-story clapboard farmhouses and red barns are dispersed across the Corn Belt landscape. In the nineteenth

PHOTO 13.6. Round Barn near Muncie, Indiana. Round barns were more economical to build and operate than rectangular barns; however, traditional barn uses are now obsolete agriculturally. Indiana has the most round barns, but only one hundred of the original 225 remain.

century, barns housed draft animals, but now traditional barns are seldom useful, except for nostalgia or for non-farm applications. No longer does every farm have a cow, pig, and a chicken or two along with hay, wheat, and cornfields. Today, in the name of economic efficiency, farmers have large farms where they raise livestock or a single monoculture crop, rather than a mix. The small family farm has been in decline. A recent study found that there has been 4.3 percent decrease in the number of family farms per year. "Old McDonald's farm" is seldom the reality in the twenty-first century. Farms are rarely about agri*culture* anymore, but instead are about agri*business*.

Germans were one of the major ethnic groups to settle across the midwestern farming landscape, and the German barns of Ohio and Indiana represent the region's last remnant of traditional rural architecture (photo 13.6). The white, red, or black wooden barns are being replaced with, if anything, either a uniform-sized pole barn, or a concentrated animal feeding operation (CAFO) hog, dairy, or chicken barn.

The midwestern industrial landscape is also vanishing, and many buildings are abandoned empty shells. Some have been converted into trendy, industrial lofts.

The midwestern small-town landscape with Victorian, tin-ceiling storefronts lingers, but the storefronts are peripheral anomalies in a big-box world. The new reality is: red barns are often near collapse, industrial towns bear rusted factory shells, and Main Street is no longer main. However, historic preservationists find value in respecting and learning from history, retaining the symbolic wooden barns, and reusing and restoring the rusting behemoths that rest on polluted **brownfields**, and the facades of Main Street towns. Many are being adapted for new uses rather than being demolished.

Population, Immigration, and Diversity

Population

Growth in the Midwest has been slow; most states have seen population decline. Between 2010 and 2015, for example, all Midwest states lost population except North and South Dakota (these two states have experienced an economic and population boom due to hydraulic fracturing [hydrofracking]). Overall, the Midwest lost nearly 910,000 people. Five of the ten states with the largest population losses due to movement within the United States were Illinois, Michigan, Ohio, Kansas, and Wisconsin. If the trend continues, it will have political consequences as it is likely that the Midwest may lose as many as four US House Seats and four Electoral College votes after the 2020 Census.

While the outmigration narrative dominates, some states have still been growing (albeit slowly) due to two factors: more births than deaths, and the influx of immigrants.

Between 2010 and 2015, the Midwest population grew at a much lower rate than the national population growth of 4.7 percent. For example, Illinois lost population at 0.2 percent; other states slowly increased: Michigan at 0.4 percent, Ohio at 0.7 percent, and Wisconsin at 1.6 percent. Minnesota fared better, growing at 4 percent. In 1960, midwestern states held 28 percent of the national population: 51.7 million residents. In 2017, this proportion had shrunk to 21 percent of the national population, although population had grown to 67 million people.

The slow growth is attributed to the loss of employment in all sectors and to jobs moving to the more amenities-based southern climates. Increased imports and outsourced jobs caused the United States to lose almost five million

TABLE 13.1. Population and Growth Rates: Midwest, Regional, and US, from 2000 to 2017

	2000 (millions)	2017 (millions)	% Growth
Illinois	12.4	12.8	3.1
Indiana	6.1	6.6	7.5
Iowa	2.9	3.1	6.4
Michigan	9.9	9.9	0
Minnesota	4.9	5.5	10.9
Ohio	11.4	11.6	1.7
Wisconsin	5.4	5.7	5.2
Northeast	53.5	56	4.4
Midwest	64.5	67	3.7
South	100	122	18
West	63	76	17

Source: US Census

manufacturing jobs since 2000, with the heaviest toll in midwestern automobile and associated industries. Industry fled high union wages and environmental regulations, moving to the less unionized South or offshore to developing regions.

As a result of deindustrialization and economic decline outmigration has been pronounced in this region. Many young adults leave seeking better job opportunities and more career choices. When young families leave the Midwest, what remains is an aging population, higher health care costs, and slow economic growth.

The Midwest Has Immigrants?

Although the Midwest has traditionally not been a destination for immigrants this is beginning to change, particularly in the cities. Many demographic experts believe that if the region is to experience any population growth at all by 2030, it will come from immigration. Currently immigration is keeping regional population stable; in some cases it is causing population growth.

In contrast to regional immigration patterns before 1970 when most immigrants to the state came from western Europe—Germany, Norway and Sweden, the region is now home to hundreds of thousands of immigrants from around the world. The Midwest has twice the share of immigrants from Southeast Asia as the United States as a whole, and five times as many immigrants from Africa as the nation as a whole. For example, the sizable Somalian-born community, among others, has meant 21 percent of Minnesota's foreign-born population is from Africa. Many refugees from Sudan, Somalia, and Ethiopia have settled in South Dakota (Ethopians are the largest immigrant group overall there). Africans make up around 15 percent of South Dakota's foreign-born population. In some states, the influx of educated immigrant (and minority) professionals has started to balance out the long-term loss of native-born youth.

Many of the immigrants from Southeast Asia were refugees. Tens of thousands of Hmong refugees living in Thai refugee camps came in the 1990s. The Hmong had historically lived in the mountainous areas of Laos, Vietnam, Thailand, Burma,

Cambodia, and China, but were driven from their traditional lands. Lutheran churches in Wisconsin and Minnesota sponsored Hmong refugees. While the foreign-born Hmong make up less than one-half of one percent of the foreign-born population in the United States, they account for approximately 10 percent of immigrants in Minnesota and Wisconsin.

Similarly, many thousands of Somali refugees settled in the Twin Cities after Somalia's civil war began in 1991. So much so that Minneapolis–St. Paul has become the de facto "capital" of the Somali community in North America. Minnesota has a much larger proportion of Asian and African immigrants than the nation. For example, 22 percent of the states foreign-born residents are from Africa, compared to 5 percent nationally. In part this is due to the welcoming of refugees. Since 2000, more than forty-one thousand refugees have settled in Minnesota.

As with the overall pattern of immigration, most of the foreign-born are settling in Midwest cities, notably Chicago and Minneapolis, although many are now settling in the suburbs and even in rural areas. Immigration is likely to become a critical factor in the region's economic future as well. Michigan is home to the largest Arab-American population in the United States. Nearly half of Wisconsin's dairy workers are Mexican, and a majority of the labor force in the Midwest's food-processing plants are Latino.

Urban Trends

Frontier fur-trading posts and forts developed into national transportation hubs into the interior. Cities were first situated along waterways: the Ohio and Mississippi rivers, the Great Lakes. Cities along the Ohio River include Pittsburgh, Cincinnati, and Louisville, while the Mississippi had Minneapolis and St. Louis. Major cities along the Great Lakes include Cleveland, Toledo, Detroit, and Chicago.

During the twentieth century, industrialization saw the rise of influential cities that became synonymous with economic prosperity in the twentieth century. Many Ohio cities still carry nicknames that remind us of the their industrial prosperity—Akron is the "Rubber Capital of the World," Dayton the "Birthplace of Aviation," Toledo "Glass City," and Youngstown "Steel Valley." But in the wake of deindustrialization and economic decline, most of these cities have struggled to rebuild and rebrand themselves. Today, the industrial shells of the Industrial Belt no longer embellish their output with "Made in America." The unused factories oxidize and rust, hence the moniker the Rust Belt. Many cities continue to experience decentralization: city center population decline, while population grows in the suburbs.

The population decline in many Midwestern cities has led to a new urban term: shrinking cities. Shrinking cities face infrastructure challenges. Some Rust Belt city blocks survive with only one or two remaining houses. The city-size footprint remains, but services are limited and infrastructure decays. The challenge for many cities in the Midwest is how to reorganize and restructure their economies to be attractive and competitive again.

Chicago, Illinois
(2016 MSA 9.5 million)

Chicago's location was favorable, but the soil was not. Buildings and transportation infrastructure sank into the glacial lakebed. Most wastewater was dumped into the Chicago River, and the resulting pollution caused typhoid and cholera epidemics. Chicago solved this problem by taking the unusual step of raising its streets six to ten feet, laying sewer and other utility lines in the intervening space. Building owners were expected to follow suit. However, soon after, in October 1871, a fire destroyed one-third of the city. The cause remains uncertain, but because the city was built primarily of wood buildings the fire spread quickly, killing three hundred lives. The city rebuilt using less combustible Indiana limestone.

Chicago grew because of its location at the south end of Lake Michigan. The city depended on the Great Lakes waterways and the expanding railroad network. As the world's largest railway center, Chicago distributed agricultural and timber commodities. The Chicago Commodities Board of Trade flourished on Corn Belt, cattle, and hog meatpacking products. Chicago became a job mecca for immigrants and the model for Upton Sinclair's The Jungle, a powerful commentary on the horrid conditions of workers in the meatpacking industry.

In 1830, Chicago had one hundred people; by 1890, the population exceeded one million; most of the growth was supplied by European immigration and African American migration from the South. Today, the city is home to 2.7 million. Approximately 33 percent of its population is African American—some 880,000—more than any other city in the United States. Most live on the West or South Side of the city in predominately black ghettos, further fostering isolation and decline. Chicago remains a heavily segregated city (Map 13.6).

Increasingly, Latino immigrants are settling in the city; they now account for 21 percent of the population. These changes are often visible in the landscape: for example, Mexicans have settled in the city's Pilsen area, once home to Czechs.

Chicago was the second-largest city in the country, until Los Angeles surpassed it in the 1970s. Today, the Chicago metro area is one-half the population of metro Los Angeles but still the largest city in the Midwest. Chicago has a vital, walkable central city and good public transit, including a progressive program to encourage bicyclists. The economy is no longer dependent on meatpacking, but has become a regional center for banking and finance, automotive parts, food products, and aerospace technologies, and it continues to function as a center for agricultural trade.

Detroit, Michigan
(2016 MSA 4.2 million)

Detroit was founded in 1701 as a French trading post at the straits of the Detroit River and Lake St. Clair (Detroit was founded as Ville d'etroit, "town at the straits"). The city's growth was slow at first because access from the south was limited due to the Black Swamp. The opening of the Erie Canal in 1825 facilitated easier access, and by 1837, the population had grown to 212,000.

During the Industrial Revolution, Detroit was a steel town. Henry Ford revolutionized the auto assembly line and Detroit became the leading manufacturer of cars, earning it the moniker "Motor City." By 1920, the population exceeded one million, and by 1950, Detroit had almost two million inhabitants. Today, it is home to only 673,000. Detroit remains the largest city in Michigan, but the population has declined 60 percent since its 1950 peak and continues to shrink. This has significant impacts on the landscape. Vast areas of the city are abandoned and in severe urban decay. It is estimated that there are more than forty thousand vacant homes. One-third of the city's enormous land mass is vacant: many parts of central Detroit, overtaken by high grasses, resemble the prairie. One of the areas of economic growth has been demolition and the city has launched a "blight removal program." It estimates it is demolishing and removing about fifteen vacant houses each day, and over the last three years, some twelve thousand vacant buildings have been removed. Demolition is so widespread that the city has a website called the "Detroit Demolition Tracker," so residents can see the status of upcoming demolitions.

City planners have been challenged to "rightsize" Detroit. Rightsizing means cutting services to certain parts of the city and concentrating residents in a central area that could be more efficiently connected to city services like sewer lines and trash collection.

Detroit is the largest African American–majority city in the United States. The city was 83 percent white and 16 percent African American in 1950, but today it is 82 percent African American and 10 percent white. It is also one of the most segregated cities in the US. Whites fled the city for the suburbs after the 1967 riots, a steady increase in crime, and discriminatory **redlining** of building projects. Redlining is an illegal and discriminatory practice of denying credit based on ethnic background or neighborhood.

BOX 13.3 WATER AND ENVIRONMENTAL INJUSTICE: FLINT MICHIGAN

The water crisis in Flint Michigan began in 2015 after residents began to complain about the water. It looked brown. It smelled and tasted bad. State official assured residents the water was safe to drink. But it wasn't. The *Detroit Free Press* reported children were developing rashes and suffering from mysterious illnesses. A few months later, a research team from Virginia Tech tested the water of hundreds of homes and issued a report indicating that 40 percent of Flint homes had elevated lead levels. Thousands of children were affected. In late 2015, residents filed a federal class action lawsuit claiming that fourteen state and city officials, including Michigan governor Rick Synder, knowingly exposed Flint residents to toxic water. The crisis reminded Americans that while we take safe drinking water for granted, there remain a number of threats to our drinking water quality.

The Flint Water Crisis Is the Result of Poor Economic and Political Decisions

After decades of deindustrialization and job losses, the city of Flint was on the brink of financial collapse in 2011. The state took over the city's finances. Officials tried to save money anyway they could, including switching the water supply from Lake Huron which the state had to pay for, to the to the Flint River, which was free. But the Flint River had long been polluted from industrial waste. It had high counts of fecal coliform bacteria, low levels of dissolved oxygen, and numerous oils and toxic substances. It needed to be treated before it could be safely drunk; part of that treatment included adding an anti-corrosive agent to stop the water from corroding the city's lead pipes. Adding the anti-corrosive agent would cost the state about $100 a day. But the state failed to add the anti-corrosive agent to the water. An investigation revealed that the water treatment facility was not capable of adding corrosion control without spending millions of dollars to upgrade old equipment. Without the anti-corrosive agent, lead from aging service lines to homes began leaching into the Flint water supply, putting thousands in danger of lead poisoning.

The National Institutes of Health notes that young children under the age of five are the most vulnerable to the effects of lead because their body, brain, and metabolism are still developing. Two-year-olds tend to have the highest blood level concentration, because they put many things into their mouth, including toys or other products that may contain lead. The health effects of lead in children have a wide range of effects on development and behavior, including increased behavioral effects, delayed puberty, and decreases in hearing, cognitive performance, and postnatal growth or height. Lead also affects adults and cause cause cardiovascular effects, nerve disorders, decreased kidney function, and fertility problems.

The Flint Water Crisis Is Also a Result of Environmental Injustice

Flint, located seventy miles north of Detroit, is a city of ninety-eight thousand, where 41 percent of residents live below the poverty line and nearly 57 percent of residents are African American. Civil rights advocates wondered: if Flint were wealthy and white, would Michigan's state government have responded more quickly and aggressively to complaints about its lead-polluted water? Would it have paid for the needed equipment upgrades?

A report by the Michigan Civil Rights Commission attributed the lead crisis to "systemic racism." They noted that Flint had a history

PHOTO 13.7. Red Cross Workers in Flint, Michigan. Red Cross workers were delivering water and filters to a neighborhood to combat the lead crisis.
Source: iStock/Rick_Thompson

of discriminatory housing and employment policies that resulted in perpetuating high levels of segregation—whites in the suburbs, blacks and poor in the city center. After decades of deindustrialization and population loss, the mostly black and poor population that remained could not support a costly water system designed for a population (and tax base) twice as large.* The report noted that those making decisions related to the crisis were not racists or meant to treat Flint any differently; rather, the disparate response

was the result of a long history of systemic racism that affected the foundation, growth, and decline of the city.

It may be difficult to prove whether or not race and class were factors in the state's slow response, but the result was the same: thousands of Flint's poorest residents, black and white, have been exposed to lead in their drinking water. And the long-term health effects of that poisoning may not be fully understood for years.

*Michigan Civil Rights Commission. 2017. "The Flint Water Crisis: Systemic Racism Through the Lens of Flint," at http://www.michigan.gov/documents/mdcr/VFlintCrisisRep-F-Edited3-13-17_554317_7.pdf

Areas of Chicago over 80% Black or 80% White, 2010

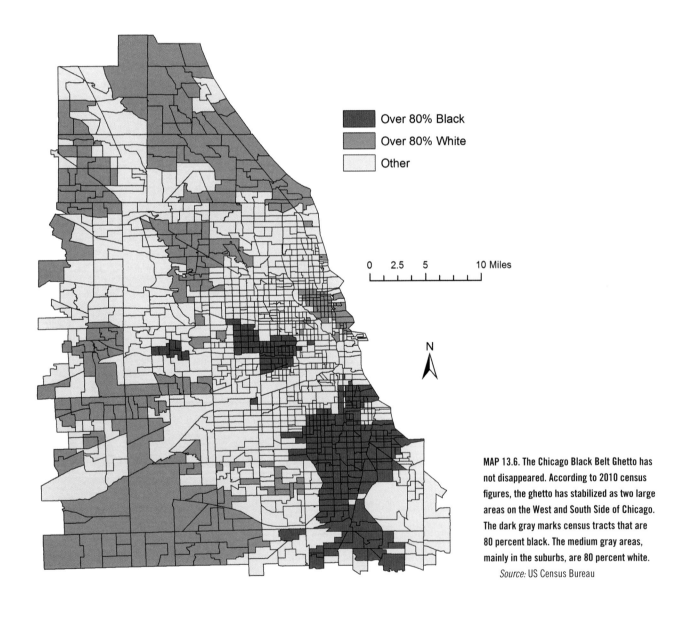

- ■ Over 80% Black
- ■ Over 80% White
- □ Other

0   2.5   5   10 Miles

N

MAP 13.6. The Chicago Black Belt Ghetto has not disappeared. According to 2010 census figures, the ghetto has stabilized as two large areas on the West and South Side of Chicago. The dark gray marks census tracts that are 80 percent black. The medium gray areas, mainly in the suburbs, are 80 percent white.
Source: US Census Bureau

BOX 13.4 URBAN SUSTAINABILITY BEST PRACTICES: CHICAGO'S GREEN ROOFS

Chicago mayor Richard Daley vowed to make Chicago "the greenest city in America." One of his earliest efforts was in 2001 when the city planted a lush garden on the rooftop of City Hall to combat the urban heat island effect and to improve urban air quality (photo 13.8). At the time it was the first municipal rooftop garden in the country. By 2016, Chicago lead the US with more than 350 green roofs covering 5.5 million square feet. The city's plan for the future is even more ambitious: six thousand green roofs by 2020.

The most notable green roofs in Chicago include the following:

- **City Hall:** This was the first green roof in Chicago and the most publicized. It has 150 plant species and covers over twenty thousand square feet. Besides, City Hall has beehives that produce approximately two hundred pounds of honey per year. On energy costs, since the installation, Chicago gas saved about $25,000 on energy costs.
- **Millennium Park:** This covers a rail station, two parking garages, and the Harris Theater. It is arguably the largest green roof in the world covering 24.5 acres.
- **McCormick Place West:** At twenty thousand acres, the McCormick place west was created by the Chicago Botanic Garden. The largest "farm to fork" rooftop garden contains vegetable and herbs that yield over four thousand pounds of fresh produce rising to twelve thousand pounds.
- **Peggy Notebaert Nature Museum:** The teaching and learning center is characterized by five different roofs. It has a twenty-four-hundred-square-foot demonstration roof with various green roof technologies.*

Green roofs are rooftops that are partially or completed covered with vegetation and soil, or a growing medium, planted over a waterproof membrane.

Green roofs are more than just a patch of green on the skyline. They can reduce carbon dioxide, reduce summer air conditioning needs, reduce winter heat demands, reduce stormwater run-off, provide songbird habitat and reduce the heat island effect.

Take the heat island effect. Traditional building materials soak up the sun's radiation and reflect it back as heat, making cities at least 7°F hotter than surrounding areas. By contrast, buildings with green roof can be many degrees color than traditionally roofed buildings. This is critically important in Chicago, where summer heat waves exacerbated by the heat island effect can have disastrous impacts. In 1995, a five-day heat wave in Chicago caused 739 heat-related deaths. Most of the victims of the heat wave were elderly poor residents of the city, who could not afford air conditioning and did not open windows or sleep outside for fear of crime.

PHOTO 13.8. Chicago's City Hall was the first municipal building in the United States with a green roof.
Source: TonyTheTiger

*Victor Bertoni. "The Rise of 'Green Roofs' in Chicago." *U.S. Green Technology*, 2016, at: https://usgreentechnology.com/chicago-green-roofs/

In 1941, a wall built along a section of 8 Mile Road divided black and white settlements (photo 13.9). The name "8 Mile" refers to its distance from the center of the city, but it has greater significance because it marks the end of Detroit and the beginning of the suburbs, and remains a racial divide.

Detroit is still dependent on manufacturing and unionized labor, even as unions weakened in the US economy. Some of the reasons for Detroit's failure to rebuild its economy are geographic isolation (it is a peninsula outside the main interstate highway system), the loss of population, the Big Three automotive companies' struggle to be competitive with Toyota and Honda, a poor mass transportation network, and white flight. The city's inability to attract or keep young professionals with a college education has left it with the lowest percentage of young professionals in the Midwest.

Detroit has remained the third-largest industrial center in the United States, but Michigan continues to fight high unemployment rates, the continued loss of jobs, the loss of its urban tax base, and infrastructure deterioration. Detroit is one of the three poorest cities in America, with a poverty rate of 39 percent living below the poverty line of $24,000 for a family of four (compared to 13.5 percent for the United States). Cleveland was not far behind, with a poverty rate of 38 percent. Unlike Chicago or Cleveland, Detroit has not attracted immigrants; today, the foreign born comprise only 5.4 percent of the population, far below national averages.

PHOTO 13.9. Eight Mile Road, Detroit, Michigan. The Birwood Wall was built in the 1940s near 8 Mile Road. The Federal Housing Administration (FHA) told a white developer that financing was unavailable for a white development in an area where blacks lived, unless his development separated the races. The developer built the six-foot-high, half-mile-long concrete wall and received his financing. The mural was painted in 2006, to help erase the ugly memory of racism.

While Detroit faces multiple challenges, there has been some improvements towards a more sustainable future. Because there is so much vacant land, one response has been to use the land for growing food. Detroit is experiencing a renaissance in urban gardening and urban agriculture. There are as many as fifteen hundred community gardens and farms in the city, and many of these gardens provide produce to local food pantries and directly to low income neighborhoods that lack grocery stores. Some of these farms are large scale covering several acres of once vacant land. For example, the Michigan Urban Farming Initiative has plans for a three-acre "agrihood," an alternative neighborhood growth model that positions agriculture as the centerpiece of a mixed-use development. The agrihood will include a rennovated three-story, thirty-two-hundred-square-foot vacant building, and the planting of a two-hundred-tree orchard in the two acres surrounding it.

Minneapolis–St. Paul, Minnesota
(2016 MSA 3.5 million)

The Twin Cities developed along the only major waterfall on the upper Mississippi River, St. Anthony Falls. They used the waterpower of the falls to saw lumber, process meat, and after the Civil War, mill flour (photo 13.11). Presently, none of these industries remain central to the metro area's economy.

The Twin Cities are known for their youthful population, creativity, and tolerance. The cities have together become the nation's sixteenth-largest metropolitan area and the Midwest's fastest-growing urban center. The cities coexist with their harsh continental weather. They were among the first in the nation to embrace enclosed malls and a series of skyways connecting stores and offices. The largest enclosed space is the five-hundred-store regional tourist attraction, Mall of America, which is now connected to the airport by light rail.

The Twin Cities are also attracting immigrants. Among the ten most populous groups of foreign-born residents are those from Mexico, India, Laos, Somalia, Vietnam, China, Thailand, Ethiopia, Korea, and Canada.

Minneapolis was one of the first cities to integrate sustainability within its city planning programs. Minnesota and the Twin Cities have been leaders in protection and restoration of natural habitats, adopting policies to reduce greenhouse gas emissions, increasing renewable energy use, and establishing incentives for citizens to encourage of energy-saving ideas. The city has devoted 20 percent of its land to green space; it still has fairly good population density but has been lax in building a good public transit system. Bicycling is encouraged, and new bike paths and trails are being built, but still only 8 percent travel by public transit or bike to work.

Cleveland, Ohio
(2016 MSA 2 million)

Founded in 1796 on the southern shore of Lake Erie at the mouth of the Cuyahoga River, Cleveland remained a small town until the Civil War, when industry boomed and many immigrants moved into the city. Cleveland grew due to navigational access to the interior and flat and buildable land near the Erie shore.

The city's mélange of ethnicities included German, Irish, Polish, Italian, and Hungarian immigrants; they settled in separate neighborhoods, but all worked in the industrial city at the foundries, port, or textile mills. Similar to other midwestern cities, Cleveland's manufacturing base suffered an economic collapse in the late twentieth century and lost more than

BOX 13.5 NATIONAL PARKS: MOTORCITIES NATIONAL HERITAGE AREA

The National Park system is not just a celebration of unique and dramatic ecology: it also represents important parts of American history. National Heritage areas are places where natural, cultural, historic, and scenic resources combine to form a cohesive, nationally important landscape arising from patterns of humanity.

One example is the MotorCities National Heritage Area located in metropolitan Detroit. This heritage area is dedicated to preserving the story of Michigan's rich automotive legacy. This includes the history of the automotive industry, as well as the industry's impact on labor, society, and the environment.

Heritage areas are different from many other national parks because they can consist of multiple sites within an area or region. The MotorCities National Heritage Area encompasses over ten thousand square miles in southeast and central Michigan. The park was created in 1998 to tell the story of "how southeast Michigan put the world on wheels."*

The MotorCities Heritage Area includes museums and historic homes, parks and gardens, auto restaurants and inns, and venues for motor sports (photo 13.10). MotorCities destinations include the historic circa-1904 Ford Piquette Plant in Detroit where the Model T was born, to the state-of-the-art Ford F-150 Truck plant in Dearborn, to sites that include the following:

- Automotive Hall of Fame
- Detroit Historical Museum
- Edsel and Eleanor Ford House
- Dearborn Historical Museum

- Ford Piquette Avenue Plant
- Gilmore Car Museum
- Henry Ford Estate—Fair Lane
- Michigan International Speedway
- Packard Proving Grounds
- R. E. Olds Transportation Museum
- The Henry Ford Museum
- Ypsilanti Automotive Heritage Museum

The MotorCities National Heritage area has three purposes: (1) promote educational programs that highlight individuals of the automotive and labor heritage in southeast Michigan; (2) promote automobile tourism that includes car shows, car festivals, automotive cruises, and museums; and (3) provide resources for the preservation and restoration of important sites of automotive history, including homes and factories.

In 2016 and 2017, MotorCities Heritage Area, along with other partners, organized a series of events that explored the rich history of labor including the eightieth anniversary of the Flint Sit-Down Strike and the first UAW-GM contract (1936), the eightieth anniversary of the 1936 Kelsey Hayes Sit-Down Strike and the eighty-fifth anniversary of the 1932 Ford Hunger march. The collective outcomes of these events resulted in big changes in the industrial workplace.

Heritage areas such as these tell the important story of the social and economic transformation of the region, and of the country.

PHOTO 13.10. Lansing's Olds Transportation Museum in Detroit, Michigan. The museum is one of the top-rated automotive museums in the United States and part of the MotorCities Heritage Area.

Source: iStock/smontgom65

*MotorCities Heritage Area. "About Us," at http://www.motorcities.org/About+Us/About+MotorCities-1.html.

PHOTO 13.11. Flour Mill, Minneapolis, Minnesota. Wheat grown in the Midwest and the Dakotas came to Minneapolis for milling after 1860. By the 1930s, three major mills (Pillsbury, General, and Standard) controlled national flour production. In 2003, the last of the flour mills closed. Many have fallen to ruin, but some have been redeveloped as luxury condos.

half its manufacturing jobs. This has resulted in a decline in population.

In 1950, Cleveland was home to more than nine hundred thousand residents; by 2010, there were 396,000, a loss of almost a third of its population. Along with Buffalo, New York, and Detroit, Cleveland has been America's fastest-declining major city not hit by a natural disaster.

Reporting on the extent of population loss in Cleveland, the local newspaper, the *Plain Dealer*, estimated that every day at least forty-two local residents move out. The decline is similar for many major cities in Ohio, including Cincinnati, Columbus, Dayton, Toledo, and Akron. Today, it looks to attract immigrants to make up for its ongoing population loss by focusing on foreign students and immigrant entrepreneurs.

Like many cities impacted by deindustrialization, Cleveland responded by offering tax incentives and other business-friendly spurs to entice local business to stay put and to attract new businesses. Cleveland invested billions of dollars revitalizing its downtown, including public space and tourism attractions such as the Rock and Roll Hall of Fame and the Cleveland Browns Stadium, as a way of making the downtown more inviting. The strategy saw some success and the city was hailed as the "Comeback City." Cleveland has rebuilt its economy to focus on health/medicine, science/engineering, biotechnology, manufacturing, and education. The Cleveland Clinic has become a

driving force in Ohio's economy and is often cited as among the top hospitals in the US. It employs some eighty thousand people and contributes $10 billion yearly to the state and regional economies. While it is too premature to claim that Cleveland is "back," there are some promising signs.

Cleveland has invested in several sustainable projects, including the EcoCity. Ten homes were built as higher-density, state-of-the-art, energy- and resource-efficient townhomes. Since the completion of the first part of the project, plans are to extend it into artist's lofts and cohousing. Shaker Square was one of the first transit-oriented developments (TODs) in the nation and contain a mixed-use and walkable environment centered on public transportation light rail and buses. Other projects include decreasing dependence on cars, more bicycling, and encouraging a healthy economy that includes triple-bottom-line accountability.

The Economy

The Primary Sector

Midwestern agricultural production has been a key component of the national economy. However, increased reliance on fossil fuels and larger monoculture enterprises have created an unsustainable agricultural industry.

BOX 13.6   ICONIC IMAGES: MALL OF AMERICA

In 1982, Minnesota's professional baseball and football teams, the Twins and the Vikings, moved from Metropolitan Stadium in Bloomington to the new H.H.H. Metrodome in downtown Minneapolis. This move created the opportunity to redevelop seventy-eight acres of highly accessible prime real estate.

After considering several options, planners proposed creating the largest indoor shopping mall in the United States, Mall of America. In 1992, the mall opened for business; it housed more than 330 stores, three major department stores (Nordstrom, Macy's, and Sears), and employed ten thousand people.* Several expansions over twenty-five years added more stores, hotels, and parking garages for a total of 4.8 million square feet (with 2.5 million square feet of retail space). Today, there are more than 520 stores and twelve thousand employees. Mall of America just celebrated its twenty-fifth year.

Triple Five Worldwide Group, the development company that built the mall, says Mall of America is more than just a shopping mall. It is a destination, an experience. It was the first mall to mix retail and entertainment. In its early years, the mall's main central space on the ground floor was home to a carousel, wave pool, and the world's only indoor submarine ride attraction (all have since been replaced). It then added an amusement park, Camp Snoopy, which then became Nickelodeon Universe in 2008. Today, Nickelodeon Universe has twenty-seven roller

coasters, rides, and attractions (photo 13.12). The mall also features SeaLife, an indoor aquarium that includes sharks, stingrays, and 350-pound sea turtles, and Moose Mountain Adventure Golf, an eighteen-hole mini golf course. There is also FlyOver America, an aerial tour of the country's most iconic sights via the latest virtual flight technology accompanied by wind, mist, and scents.

In addition to the entertainment complexes, Mall of America features a wedding chapel, where more than eight thousand weddings have been performed since the mall opened. The mall hosts some four hundred events each year, including concerts, job fairs, book signings, circuses, and community fundraising events. At the end of day, tired visitors can stay at the Radisson Blue or JW Marriott hotels, both directly connected to the mall.

Each year there are forty million visitors to Mall of America, eight times the population of the state of Minnesota. The mall generates nearly $2 billion each year in economic impact for the state and has put Minnesota on the map as a tourist destination.

While Mall of America certainly contributes economically to the region, it is not without its negatives. Geographers have critiqued malls for replacing "downtowns," enforcing rules that can keep certain people out (for example, the homeless), and focusing on activities about consumption over community.

PHOTO 13.12. Nickelodeon's Universe in Mall of America features more than twenty-seven roller coasters, rides, and activities, and is a major draw for both tourists and local residents.

Source: Lisa Benton-Short

*Mall of America. "How it Began," at https://www.mallofamerica.com/about/moa/history

The Midwest was large and varied enough to be both the US center of agricultural production and the home to its industrial expansion. While industry concentrated and thrived at river and lake ports, the interior areas were quintessential family farms with a reasonable growing season, ample precipitation, and markets for dairy and agricultural products.

The midwestern agricultural landscape has evolved from forests to late-twentieth-century monoculture. When Europeans settled the forested midwestern Till Plain, farmers felled trees and removed stumps before they could cultivate the land. They transformed the forest into productive cropland. Over the past half century, farms have grown larger, farmers fewer and older, and crops and livestock have shifted geographically. Farming is no longer about country living but rather about big business, razor-thin profit margins, and subsidies. Farming is a lifestyle that many prefer, but the economic circumstances are such now that few young farmers remain, leaving an aging and dwindling farming population.

The Agricultural Past   Traditional agricultural production in the United States has been based on a market cash economy. Midwestern farmers transported their crops to eastern urban markets via muddy roads over the Appalachians, such as the National Road, or down the Mississippi River to New Orleans. Both were expensive and unprofitable modes of transport. The completion of the Erie Canal gave Farmers a more efficient system to transport their goods to market.

Midwestern farms developed in relation to the landscape, precipitation, and growing season and adopted a three-year crop rotation anchored by corn, along with small grain, hay, and livestock. Each rotation completed a nutrient cycle that was healthy for the land, and was therefore sustainable, but rotation is no longer practiced.

Nineteenth-century farmers realized that the Till Plains landscape grew the best corn and that other locations were better suited for dairy or wheat. Dairy replaced grains in sections of Wisconsin, Minnesota, and portions of Ohio and Michigan because weather and growing season limited the corn crop. The shift from grain to dairy proved advantageous, as nearby population centers were a ready market for milk, a perishable commodity. In some areas, notably Wisconsin, much of the milk was converted to inherently less perishable cheese products.

Wheat production was best in areas where precipitation was insufficient for corn production. Minneapolis used its Mississippi River waterpower at St. Anthony Falls to provide energy to operate flour mills.

Mixed farming on a few hundred acres was typical through the early twentieth century. However, in the 1950s, production mechanized, yields increased, crops specialized, and monocultures became the dominant form of agricultural production. Traditional value-added methods of raising and feeding corn to livestock were abandoned. Most farmers now concentrate on either a crop or livestock.

Technologic improvements have increased output but support fewer farmers. In the 1960s, the **Green Revolution** and **genetically modified organism (GMO)** seed modification increased crop production but also created dependence on fossil fuel–based fertilizers and chemicals, which increased water pollution

In the 1980s, grain embargoes, drought, and overproduction depressed crop prices. Many farmers declared bankruptcy; farms were foreclosed. The number of farms in the United States has declined, while their relative size increased, from 213 acres in 1950 to 442 acres in 2016, and 41 percent of all farmland was operated by farms that generate more than $500,000 in sales.

Few Americans are farmers today. The high cost of farming and its low returns have contributed to a rural decline, while unstable weather and changing climatic conditions have increased farming risks.

Another troubling trend is the disinterest in a career in agriculture. Not only are young people avoiding jobs on farms, they are avoiding jobs in the agricultural sector in general. A recent USDA survey found that there are 57,900 jobs available in US agriculture each year, but over twenty-two thousand remain unfilled.

Conventional Agricultural Practices   Traditional agriculture relied on crop rotation that reduced diseases, weeds, and pests while it replenished soil. In the second half of the twentieth century, conventional agriculture transitioned to high-yield corn that depends on petrochemical feedstock and depletes usable water. Using fossil fuels and petrochemical feedstock has been a way to maximize grains and livestock yields. The long-term costs—lower food value, environmental damage, and social inequity—have been excluded in the pricing of food.

As the price of oil increases, however, so do the prices of oil products and, subsequently, food. Yields in organic or traditional crops cannot match petrochemical crop yields. Traditional and organic systems are far more sustainable methods of farming, more nutritious, and use renewable resources. Fossil fuel–dependent methods are less expensive in the short term, but they destroy the soil and therefore decrease crop yields. Sustainable methods are more expensive in the short term, but they create long-term viability for crop production.

Contemporary Agricultural Trends   The family farm has been a staple of American food production. In 1900, about half of Americans were farmers; today, family farmers accounted for less than 2 percent of the population. Yet, the Agricultural Census reports 90 percent of all farms are considered family farms. The story is complex and the dominance of the "family farm" is deceptive for four reasons:

1. The average age of the family farmer is now over sixty. Few farmers want their children to farm, and even fewer children want to farm. As a result, the demographics of the family farm are very likely to change in the future.

BOX 13.7   GEOSPATIAL TECHNOLOGIES: PRECISION AGRICULTURE

You probably know Land O'Lakes as a famous brand of butter. But it is a $13 billion company that includes the Land O'Lakes dairy foods, Purina animal feed, and WinField. WinField provides expertise to farmers to help them plan crop inputs (such as seeds and nutrition) and precision agriculture.

Historically, technology has always played in important role in farm productivity. The mechanized revolution introduced tractors and the biotech revolution introduced pest-resistant seeds. Today, there's another "AgTech" revolution that is using geospatial technology. WinField, for example, has developed the R7® Tool.

The R7® Tool uses satellite imagery to create field maps that display historical weather data, soil variability, and farm-specific data, allowing farmers to see subtle variability across their fields. It can be used to create strategies around genetics, soil type, plant population, cropping systems, and crop protection to help them get the most out of their fields and maximize profitability.

The WinField R7® app can be used to analyze and select the best seeds for their land to maximize yield and profit and what to plant and where, inch by inch. Over the course of the season, it can also be used to react to real-time changes in the field.

One aspect of the R7® app is the "R7® Tool Profitability Map" that connects input costs and yield potential map data to determine the rate on investment. Less profitable areas provide an opportunity to better align input investments with yield potential the following year.

A second application is the Field Response Map that compares yield data to satellite imagery to indicate crop response to the prescription for that field. This provides a way to validate what worked well and what could be improved for future plans.

As a result of this new "AgTech" revolution, Land O'Lakes has become one of the largest purchasers of satellite imagery in the world.

2. While family farms still own the farmland, most crops and livestock are now contract farmed. Corporations own the crop or livestock, and family farmers use their land and labor to meet corporate standards and agreements. The farmer must grow crops to corporate specifications. Livestock must be raised in a uniform and consistent manner to meet mechanized processing guidelines. Consolidation of both buyers and suppliers leaves farmers with few options other than to sell to vertically integrated agribusiness corporations.

3. Increasingly, farmers are "retiring" by leasing their land to other farmers.

4. More than twenty-two thousand jobs in agriculture go unfilled each year in the United States.

A recent trend is a return to traditional practices. Many remaining farmers and a new group of young and sustainably oriented farmers have established niche markets that rejects agribusiness and embrace healthier and sustainable food systems. There are increased profits to be made in so-called "niche markets" such as organic, grass-fed cows and organic and local dairies. Farmers have established **community-supported agriculture (CSA)** featuring local-farm-to-resident produce throughout the growing season. Today, CSAs are popular in many communities around the United States as urban residents see CSA subscriptions as a way to support local farmers and sustainable agricultural practices.

Biofuels

A third trend in agriculture has been the growing demand for biofuels. Rising fossil fuel prices have increased interest in alternative fuels. Sugarcane has been the primary source of fuel in

Brazil, the largest producer of **ethanol** in the world, but corn is currently the dominant crop for bioethanol in the United States.

Biofuels are produced from renewable sources. In theory, ethanol could reduce US dependency on foreign oil and decrease harmful emissions. But the large amount of fossil fuels used in making ethanol has led many researchers to question whether using coal-powered electricity to produce ethanol saves carbon dioxide emissions overall.

In addition, many critics argue that subsidized ethanol production is nothing more than an agribusiness subsidy; Archer Daniels Midland, a heavily subsidized agribusiness giant, produces about 40 percent of US ethanol.

Since 2001, the production of ethanol continues has increased, and the Midwest has taken advantage of this. Nearly 90 percent of all gasoline sold in the US is blended with ethanol. In addition, the introduction of "flexible-fuel" cars, trucks, and minivans that use gasoline/ethanol blends has increased demand somewhat; however, fueling infrastructure has been a major restriction hampering ethanol and "flex fuel" sales.

Agricultural Production and Livestock

Corn   The midwestern physical environment, known as the Corn Belt since 1850, is ideal for corn. Eight of the top ten areas for corn production in the United States were in midwestern states: Iowa, Illinois, Nebraska, Minnesota, Indiana, South Dakota, Wisconsin, and Ohio (map 13.7). The United States alone produces almost half of the world's corn.

The Corn Belt also contributes to livestock production. Livestock consume about 60 percent of cultivated corn. Historically, farmers favored either corn or livestock, depending on which had the better market price. If the market for corn was low, it was fed to the livestock to add value. This value-added

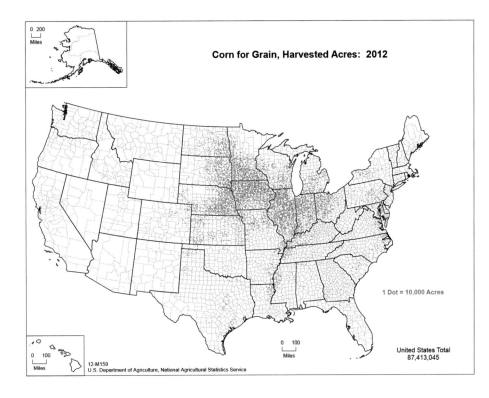

Corn for Grain, Harvested Acres: 2012

0 200 Miles

1 Dot = 10,000 Acres

0 100 Miles

United States Total
87,413,045

0 100 Miles

12-M159
U.S. Department of Agriculture, National Agricultural Statistics Service

MAP 13.7. Corn: Harvested Acres, 2012. Corn is still the most important crop in the Central Lowlands, but it has become increasingly important where the Ogallala Aquifer irrigates the fields. The water table for the Ogallala Aquifer has been dropping, partly because of growing crops, such as corn, that require much more water than the local climate provides.

Source: USDA Census of Agriculture

relationship changed in the late twentieth century, when most farmers chose to specialize in either corn production or livestock, and changed again in the twenty-first century when much of the corn crop went into biofuel production.

Soybeans The Soybean Belt overlaps the Corn Belt. However, corn spread east to west while soybean grow predominantly along the Mississippi and Red River.

In the late twentieth century, soybeans bypassed corn production in volume and were second only to corn in value. The United States now produces half of the world's soybeans and is the leading exporter of soybeans; China imports much of the US soybean crop.

Soybeans, an inexpensive form of protein, contribute to animal diets and are an ingredient in many processed foods. Less than 10 percent is used in the manner many Americans think of soy: as tofu or soy sauce.

Soy is controversial because 92 percent of all soy in the United States is genetically modified and is "Roundup-ready"— able to withstand regular doses of the herbicide Roundup, which kills weeds. Prolonged use of Roundup decreases the effectiveness of glyphosate, the active chemical in Roundup, which is highly toxic to plants and fish. The almost exclusive use of genetically modified soy and its widespread adoption could decrease long-term crop yields and decrease the effectiveness of the herbicide.

However, recently the cost for Monsanto's Roundup Ready GM soybean seeds increased from $35 to $50 per bag while the cost for Roundup herbicide increased from $15 to $50 per gallon. This may lead farmers to consider non-GMO soybeans if they can still capture a good price for their production.

Livestock Traditionally, Corn Belt feed grains fattened midwestern livestock; however, a shift in feed grain production areas has affected livestock production and processing. Livestock production, especially hogs, has also shifted from traditional midwestern bases into the South and Great Plains.

Beef Midwestern cattle production thrives where row crops are less productive. Iowa is the only Midwestern state among the top ten beef producers in the US.

Midwestern feedlots were common during the late nineteenth and early twentieth centuries, when slaughterhouses were located in Chicago and St. Louis. However, as slaughterhouses moved to the High Plains, feedlots moved closer to the slaughterhouses. Cattle are still fattened on a corn mixture prior to slaughter, but instead of cattle being shipped from the plains to the corn-producing states, the grain is now grown or shipped to the High Plains, where cattle are raised, finished, and slaughtered.

Most midwestern areas now have ranchers growing grass-fed beef that service those who support locavore foods. Grass-fed beef is raised without corn finishing, hormones, or antibiotics. Grass-fed beef has less total fat and more omega-3 fatty acids.

Dairy Belt. Dairying is one of the top agricultural commodities in seven midwestern states and is Michigan's and Wisconsin's number one commodity. Dairy provides about half of the agricultural sales in Wisconsin.

Dairy was the center of Wisconsin's family farm until large corporate dairies developed in the late twentieth century. California became the number one milk producer in 1993. Wisconsin remains the nation's leader in cheese production, and nearly all its milk is converted to more than three hundred cheese varieties, many of which are niche market specialty cheeses, such as the artisan cheese market. Most niche diaries belong to cooperatives, which allow them protection in numbers and cut costs. Niche markets focus on the higher-quality milk required by cheese producers. Jersey cows, for example, produce less quantity, but offer higher butterfat and protein content. Most of the popular niche markets are organic, avoid hormones, and graze their cows longer, resulting in a subtle, more natural flavor (photo 13.13).

Hogs. Hogs are the perfect match for Iowa, a corn-producing state. Hogs are an efficient and quick converter of corn to meat. A hog grows from 1 to 250 pounds in six months. Until the 1980s, Iowa and other midwestern states dominated the traditional hog farm industry. Although Iowa remains the number one producer of hogs, the top three counties for hog production are now in the CAFO-reliant states of North Carolina and Oklahoma (map 13.8).

Vertically integrated corporations now own and contract most of the nation's pork. Hogs are raised in CAFOs, where a thousand hogs are raised in each concrete-slatted, metal

PHOTO 13.13. The Comstock Creamery and Cheese Store in Comstock, Wisconsin.
Source: iStock/Wolterk

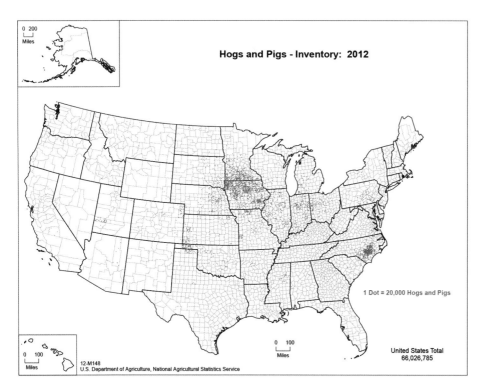

MAP 13.8. Hogs and Pigs, 2012. The relationship of corn and hogs has made Iowa and the Midwest the traditional main hog-producing states, but the Midwest resisted corporate CAFO production methods, and hog production and inventory grew in other regions.
Source: USDA Census of Agriculture

PHOTO 13.14. Hog Confinement in a CAFO. Note the slatted floor.

CAFO barn. In the hog industry, this is succinctly described as "from birth to bacon" or "from conception to consumption" (photo 13.14).

Profitable CAFOs practice economies of scale and rely on hormones, antibiotics, and pesticides. CAFOs cause aquifer depletion, reduction of genetic diversity, air and water pollution, and have augmented human antibiotic resistance despite numerous reports urging a limitation of routine antibiotic use in the United States because of antibiotic-resistant strains developing in humans. The CAFO system currently produces the overwhelming majority of meat, but at a tremendous environmental and social cost.

Chickens. Chicken broiler production is limited in the Midwest; however, layer hens and egg production are important. Iowa, Ohio, and Indiana are the nation's top three egg-producing states.

Egg production has also changed. Chickens roaming and pecking in the yard have been replaced by commercial caged-egg production systems with more than 313 million laying hens producing over eighty-three billion eggs per year. More than 80 percent of all layers are in flocks of more than thirty thousand layers. Iowa capitalizes on its position as number one in soybeans by feeding the soy meal to chickens, thereby directly adding value to their crops.

Mineral Resources

Most minerals discussed in this chapter are actually a part of the Canadian Shield area in location, but their importance and relations are more midwestern. A floristic tension zone runs through central Michigan, Wisconsin, and Minnesota, dividing the agricultural land to the south and where many deciduous trees reach their northern limits, creating a transition to the boreal forest in the north. Most of the midwestern minerals are located within this transitional region.

Copper and iron ore, needed for the Industrial Revolution, were abundant in the north central region that used the Great Lakes corridor to transport resources between its cities including Chicago, Gary, Duluth, Detroit, Toledo, and Cleveland in the United States, and Toronto and Hamilton in Ontario, Canada. The Midwest also has significant and locally important mineral deposits; among the more important of these are limestone and salt.

Iron   Iron ore (hematite) from Lake Superior mines built the industrial core of the United States. From 1840 to 1887, Michigan's western Upper Peninsula was the main source, and from 1887 into the twentieth century, northern Minnesota's Mesabi Range boomed.

Minnesota and Michigan's Upper Peninsula iron ranges expose the iron ore through erosion, although some iron has been mined underground or in open pits.

By the 1950s, the highest-quality iron ore had been removed from the mines, necessitating new mining techniques, such as grinding rock and removing taconite iron to form pellets. Declining mining prices in the mid-1970s slowed production. At one time, six mines operated; today, only Mesabi and Marquette Range open pits are operating. The United States produces about 5 percent of world iron ore and is the seventh-largest producer (China is the largest producer).

Salt   Historically, salt determined many settlement sites. Salt licks provided an important nutritional ingredient for the sequence of buffalo, Native American, and western settlement. Game proliferated near the licks, and the salt was used to preserve beef jerky and salt pork, which was a source of fat for the pioneer diet.

The remains of an evaporated sea lie beneath Michigan and the province of Ontario. Michigan leads the states in salt production. The two forms of salt are brine (water saturated with salt) and rock salt, used for melting snow or refined for table salt. Rock salt mines are located twelve hundred feet below the city of Detroit. The mines continue to operate underground using hundreds of miles of tunnels and rooms. Even after one hundred years of mining, there are billions of tons remaining to be mined. The salt from the Detroit mine is used exclusively as road salt.

The Secondary Sector

During the first half of the twentieth century, Chicago and Detroit were the nation's fastest-growing cities, both in population and industry. The Great Lakes' natural resources fed Chicago's sprawling steel industry along its southern shore, and spread into nearby cities like Gary, Indiana. Iron ore from Minnesota and coal from West Virginia were fashioned into steel and machinery in Chicago. Detroit boasted the economically advantageous assembly line. Many cities, such as Pontiac, Ypsilanti, and Dearborn, Michigan, along with Windsor, Ontario, supplied parts for the auto industry. In Ohio, Toledo and Akron provided glass and tires for the automobiles. Most of these plants are now closed. Foreign automobile manufacturers built plants outside of the midwestern core. Factory shutdowns and layoffs became common midwestern occurrences into the twenty-first century. Low-cost foreign competition, and lack of fuel-efficient American cars diminished domestic demand. This changed the regional employment pattern from well-paid union members to laid-off workers who found it difficult to transition to a postindustrial economy that demanded different skills.

The effects of deindustrialization on traditional industrial cities ain the Midwest have been well documented over the years. It is important to realize that deindustrialization has a deep and lingering impact that continues into the twenty-first century. Many of the cities in the region were ranked at the bottom for a negative percent change in median household income over the last several decades.

Despite deindustrialization, the Midwest remains a stronghold of union authority, especially in manufacturing. This has made recovering from deindustrialization more difficult, as companies prefer regions where unionized labor is weaker or nonexistent (such as the Gulf Coast region).

Auto Industry

The midwestern auto industry grew during the first half of the twentieth century, spurred by Ford's assembly line and vertical integration methods. The industry's large size and broad scope are critical to the continued stability of the manufacturing sector.

The auto industry was geographically concentrated in the early twentieth century; it formed an **agglomeration** in the Midwest. Detroit and Flint, Michigan, and other midwestern areas (Indianapolis: Dusenberg; Toledo: Jeep) built a new industry, and automobile suppliers agglomerated around the factories.

The heart of the old automobile industry was Detroit, "Motor City," the home to the Big Three automobile manufacturers: Ford, General Motors, and Chrysler. Fully one-sixth of the nation's jobs were related to the Detroit-based auto industry. During the first half of the twentieth century, Detroit was home to the largest factories in the world, but deindustrialization was evident long before but was effectively ignored by the Big Three. In the 1960s, overseas auto manufacturers began entering the US market and building foreign-owned, US-based plants outside of the unionized Midwest in such places as Alabama and Tennessee.

Two major reasons the Big Three lost their grip on the automobile industry are the high cost of union contract labor and poor fuel efficiency. For example, union-enforced benefits add an additional $1,500 to the cost of each car sold by the Big Three. Foreign manufacturers have eliminated labor contracts and pensions, replacing them with 401(k) retirement plans. In addition, or perhaps because of, the quality of automobiles from the United States and the continued insistence on manufacturing big cars such as the ubiquitous SUV, the domestic auto companies showed little interest in fuel economy and were late in moving from petroleum-based energy while other auto companies moved toward alternative fuels. By the end of the twentieth century, Detroit was still the Motor City, but more than half of the auto jobs were gone; GM went from 482,000 employees in 1978 to 47,330 in 2009. The city remains economically devastated.

The Tertiary Sector

Although agriculture and industry were dominant in the regions economy, the growth of the service sector is now critical to rebuilding economies in crisis.

The transition to a service-oriented economy has not been a magic fix. In order to compete, many cities provided incentives for high-wage earning workers. Many cities attracted new capital investment, particularly by focusing on certain segments such as high-tech, information-based companies. But along with rebuilding came substantial gentrification. The rebuilding of postindustrial economies in the Midwest has meant prioritizing real-estate development and service-sector capital. Many cities have spent millions of dollars remaking city space oriented to the more affluent—downtown shopping, entertainment districts and upscale condo living.

Some of the new service jobs—highpaying, educationally intensive—has led to the growth of high-income professionals. But the blue-color manufacturing jobs that paid decent wages have been replaced by low-wage service jobs—significantly less unionized. For many displaced by deindustrialization, this has meant a decline in purchasing power and job stability. The result is visible in the landscape: temporary labor agencies, day labor sites, payday lenders, pawnshops, and check-cashing outlets can be found in many low-income areas. Geographer David Wilson calls these the "parasitic economies" because

BOX 13.8 GLOBAL CONNECTIONS: WHAT'S GOOD FOR GM IS GOOD FOR AMERICA?

In 1953, Charles Erwin Wilson, previously the General Motors CEO, was President Eisenhower's nominee for defense secretary, but he was reluctant to sell his GM stockholdings to avoid a conflict of interest. He explained, "What was good for our country was good General Motors, and vice versa." Wilson's famous line has since been frequently misquoted as a boast, "What's good for GM is good for America," to illustrate the presumably patronizing attitudes of wealthy businessmen. But the quote also illustrates GM's relationship to the US market in an era before globalization.

Despite declaring bankruptcy in 2009, GM is still a global carmaker whose vehicles are being bought in large numbers in many parts of the world. GM and its partners produce vehicles in thirty countries. GM, its subsidiaries, and joint venture entities sell vehicles under the Chevrolet, Cadillac, Baojun, Buick, GMC, Holden, Jiefang, Opel, Vauxhall, and Wuling brands (some of these brands are exclusive to the international market).

For GM, the global market is now more important than the domestic market. In 2016, GM sold ten million cars. Three million of those vehicles were sold in the United States. But even more—3.9 million vehicles—were sold in China. Another 311,000 were sold in the United Kingdom, 220,000 in Germany, 263,000 in Canada, and 200,000 in Brazil. GM recorded its fourth straight year of record sales even as US sales fell slightly.

China is now GM's largest market. Sales growth there lifted it to volume it never achieved when it was the world's biggest automaker. Strong sales in China made up for sluggish sales in the United States, leading the largest American automaker to record profit and the rank of third place among world automakers, behind Volkswagen and Toyota.

The US car market may have topped out. US sales are forecast to decline in the next few years and GM has announced three rounds of layoffs at its American plants.

More than ever, GM is a global company, with 72 percent of its sales coming from outside the United States, forcing us to reconsider Wilson's quote in the global age.

these types of services take advantage of the poor or recent immigrants. Payday lenders, for example, provide short-term loans but a very high interest rates.

Technology corridors

The Midwest has attracted new types of service-sector employment. These include jobs in education and health services, niche manufacturing, information and financial services. Many individuals and businesses recognized that the region possesses low housing costs, a relatively good business climate, quality school and available land, and other resources for expansion. Quicken Loans, the country's second largest mortgage-lending company, moved its headquarters and seventeen hundred employees to downtown Detroit in 2010. Today, it employs twelve thousand in its Detroit offices. The Cleveland Clinic began specializing in the late 1990s, beginning with biomedical research, and has become one of the most highly rated health service providers for conditions that require expertise in the latest technology. Even some small-to-medium-size cities such as Des Moines have had success luring high-end business and professional service firms, information service companies, and diversified, innovative small manufacturers.

Many Midwest cities are playing up their advantages. For example, escalating housing costs on both coasts, particularly in metropolitan areas, has hit the working and middle classes particularly hard. In contrast, housing prices in most of the Heartland have remained remarkably reasonable. Lowering housing costs could become magnets for young families.

Tourism

Midwest tourism is largely within state, such as the allegiance of people from southeastern Michigan to travel "up north." One exception to this, however, is the rise of tribal gambling.

Starting with bingo in 1988, the Native American Indian gaming industry has created more than three hundred tribal facilities that cater to ever more sophisticated gambling. In 2004, gaming revenues generated over $19 billion. Several tribal reservations have begun to generate wind power. Gambling enterprises and alternative energy have given many Native Americans hopes for a brighter future and some financial freedom, although often at the cost of cultural integrity.

Today, the Midwest has more than a hundred tribal casinos. It has made many tribes wealthy but has also caused concern, as more tribes, and their financial backers, seek more land to on which to build casinos. Many now believe that the tribes are but pawns to the outside interests that control them. Included in the worries are the possibility of money laundering and a loss of tribal autonomy. And now that other states permit gaming, commercial casinos have proven more profitable in the West Coast (primarily California) or in the Gulf Coast.

A Sustainable Future

There are numerous challenges for the Midwest. Deindustrialization and changes to the structure of traditional family farms have resulted in economic collapse in much of the region. Attempts to rebuild the economy have stalled as global competition has favored other locations in the US or around the world.

Many of the challenges for a sustainable future include the following:

- out-migration of young and college educated who seek opportunities elsewhere;
- a legacy of industrial pollution;
- a need to reduce chemical use;
- disappearing family farms;
- an image of "outdated" economies;
- attracting service sector employment;
- providing social and economic equity to workers; and
- retraining a workforce to meet the skill needs of the postindustrial economy.

A few cities and states have emerged as leaders by overcoming a manufacturing past and entering the technological and progressive economy. Chicago, Minneapolis, Indianapolis, Madison, and Sioux Falls have rebuilt and rebranded themselves and are attracting college-educated residents and many new companies to relocate. In 2009 and again in 2010, a coalition of health advocates presented the Minnesota legislature with a proposal for a universal health care system that would cover all Minnesotans for all their medical needs; unfortunately, almost a decade later, the bill has yet to pass both the state House and Senate.

The bounty of Great Lakes freshwater could attract future populations weary of the continual water wars of the South and West. The abundance of this natural resource could foster an industry based on distributing freshwater, one that brings money and bright minds into the region, not sending them or the water to outside companies or cities. Of course, there will have to be increased attention to water pollution issues, especially in the Great Lakes.

Many midwestern farms and dairies have chosen to be independent from large conglomerates and to pursue smaller, high-quality niche markets. These producers offer organic foods and community-supported agriculture, and they view a more sustainably oriented future.

Finally, there is a sign of hope in one of the most devastated cities, Detroit. Some corporate and educational structures have adopted green roofs and fields as an environmental and aesthetic response to environmental problems. But in energy efficiency, the city stutters. But there is a rising star in Detroit: urban agriculture. The city is a virtual food desert, with few opportunities to purchase fresh goods, yet the surrounding area is filled with empty lots and once occupied houses that are now being converted to urban gardens.

Questions for Discussion

1. Why is the northern Great Lakes region not a cash-grain region?

2. Why has dairying been more profitable than grains in the northern Great Lakes?

3. What are food cooperatives and why are they a model to conventional agribusiness?

4. Is the production of ethanol from corn a feasible answer to the region's economic malaise? Why or why not?

5. How should Midwest cities respond to population and jobs losses?

6. Discuss the tension between preservation of wetlands and the need to rebuild economies by developing land.

7. How did Michigan make the transition from a lumber to an automobile economy?

8. What was the role of the Great Lakes in relation to the development of the steel industry?

9. Why did the iron and steel industry evolve in the Pittsburgh-Cleveland area?

10. How is contemporary immigration impacting the region?

11. What did Chicago do to become the regional center for the Midwest?

12. How do the western and eastern midwestern states differ in economy?

13. How has the city of Chicago and the state of Minnesota distinguished themselves in sustainable actions?

Suggested Readings

Abler, R. *The Twin Cities of Saint Paul and Minneapolis.* Cambridge, Mass: Ballinger, 1976.

Adams, J. S., and B. J. van Drasek. *Minneapolis–St. Paul; People, Place, and Public Life.* Minneapolis: University of Minnesota Press, 1993.

Cayton, A., R. Lee, and S. E. Gray, eds. *The American Midwest.* Indianapolis: Indiana University Press, 2001.

Chappell, S. *Cahokia: Mirror of the Cosmos.* Chicago: University of Chicago Press, 2002.

Cronon, W. *Nature's Metropolis: Chicago and the Great West.* New York: Norton, 1991.

Grady, W. *The Great Lakes: The Natural History of a Changing Region.* Vancouver, B.C.: Greystone Books, 2007.

Hart, J. *The Land That Feeds Us.* New York: Norton, 1993.

Hudson, J. *Making the Corn Belt: A Geographical History of Middle-Western Agriculture*. Bloomington: Indiana University Press, 1994.

Johnson, H. *Up from the Ashes: A Story about Building Community*. Austin, Tex.: Eakin Press, 2000.

Jones, L., and G. Iggers. *Crossing Boundaries: The Exclusion and Inclusion of Minorities in Germany and the United States*. New York: Berghahn Books, 2001.

Kaatz, M. R. "The Black Swamp: A Study in Historical Geography." *Annals of the Association of American Geographers* 45, no. 1 (1955).

Kane, L. *The Falls of St. Anthony: The Waterfall That Built Minneapolis*. St. Paul: Minnesota Historical Society, 1966.

Lampard, E. *The Rise of the Dairy Industry in Wisconsin*. Madison: State Historical Society of Wisconsin, 1963.

Liuzzi, A. "Immigration in Minnesota: a Changing Story." *Minnesota Compass* (May 2016), at http://www.mncompass.org/trends/insights/2016-05-10-immigration chibublib.org/cpl.html

Martin, L. *The Physical Geography of Wisconsin*. Madison: University of Wisconsin Press, 1965.

Misa, T. J. *A Nation of Steel: the Making of Modern America, 1865–1925*. Baltimore, Md.: Johns Hopkins University Press, 1995.

Nelson, D., F. Hu, E. Grimm, et al., "The Influence of Aridity and Fire on Holocene Prairie Communities in the Eastern Prairie Peninsula," *Ecology* 87, no. 10 (2006).

Rubenstein, J. *The Changing U.S. Auto Industry: A Geographical Analysis*. London: Routledge, 2002.

Sauer, C. *The Geography of the Ozark Highland of Missouri*. Chicago, Ill.: University of Chicago Press, 1920.

Schaetzl, R. "Underlying Hard Rock Geology: Geography of Michigan and the Great Lakes Region." *Earthscape* (January 2002).

Shortridge, J. R. *Cities on the Plains: The Evolution of Urban Kansas*. Lawrence: University Press of Kansas, 2004.

———. *The Middle West: Its Meaning in American Culture*. Lawrence: University Press of Kansas, 1989.

Slade, J. W. and J. Lee (eds) *The Midwest*. Westport, Conn.: Greenfield Press, 2004.

Internet Sources

Chicago's Sustainability Plan, at https://www.cityofchicago.org/city/en/progs/env/sustainable_chicago2015.html

Detroit Demolition Tracker: http://www.detroitmi.gov/demolition.

Greenroof Project Database, at http://www.greenroofs.com/projects/plist.php

U.S. Poultry and Egg Association. "Economic Data," at http://www.poultryegg.org/economic_data/

Scorecard: The Pollution Data Site, at http://www.scorecard.org/.

Minneapolis Sustainability Plan, at http://www.ci.minneapolis.mn.us/sustainability/

Minnesota Round Table on Sustainable Development. *Investing in Minnesota's Future*, at http://www.mnplan.state.mn.us/pdf/inv-v3.pdf

U.S. Geological Survey flood maps at https://water.usgs.gov/floods/.

U.S. Census for Agriculture. Washington, D.C.: United States Department of Agriculture. https://www.agcensus.usda.gov/Publications/2012/#full_report

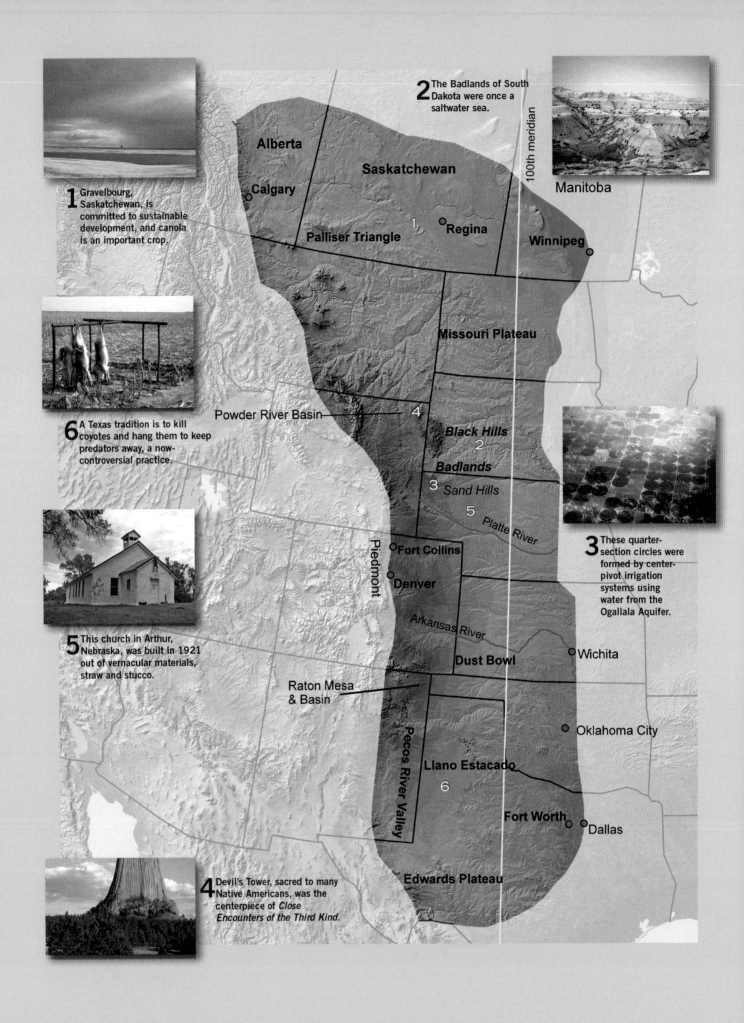

1 Gravelbourg, Saskatchewan, is committed to sustainable development, and canola is an important crop.

2 The Badlands of South Dakota were once a saltwater sea.

6 A Texas tradition is to kill coyotes and hang them to keep predators away, a now-controversial practice.

5 This church in Arthur, Nebraska, was built in 1921 out of vernacular materials, straw and stucco.

3 These quarter-section circles were formed by center-pivot irrigation systems using water from the Ogallala Aquifer.

4 Devil's Tower, sacred to many Native Americans, was the centerpiece of *Close Encounters of the Third Kind*.

Alberta

Saskatchewan

Calgary

Manitoba

100th meridian

Regina

Palliser Triangle

Winnipeg

Missouri Plateau

Powder River Basin

4

Black Hills

2

Badlands

3 Sand Hills

5 Platte River

Piedmont

Fort Collins

Denver

Arkansas River

Wichita

Dust Bowl

Raton Mesa & Basin

Oklahoma City

Pecos River Valley

Llano Estacado

6

Fort Worth

Dallas

Edwards Plateau

14

THE GREAT PLAINS AND CANADIAN PRAIRIE

Land of Opportunity, or Where the Buffalo Roam?

Chapter Highlights

After reading this chapter, you should be able to:

- Identify and label US and Canadian Great Plains and Prairie subregions
- Discuss the importance of the Ogallala Aquifer
- Explain the relationship between corn, hogs, and cattle on the plains
- Describe the settlement process and how it differed from settlement on the West Coast
- Give an overview of the major Plains cities
- Identify the historic range of the buffalo, and explain the theory of the Buffalo Commons
- Distinguish the dividing line between the Great Plains and the Midwest and its connection to climate and agriculture
- Explain how cattle ranching and processing has changed from the late nineteenth century to the present on the Plains
- Contrast farmers and ranchers and discuss the concept of range war
- Describe the place of the Hutterites and the Métis in Canada
- Explain the importance of the Palliser Triangle on the Canadian Prairie
- Discuss important urban trends
- Explain economic changes in the region and the role each sector plays in the regional economy

Terms

aging in place
agribusiness
badlands
caliche
center pivot irrigation (CPI)
chinook
Crow Rate

Dominion Lands Act
dryland farming
Exodusters
Frontier Thesis
frost-freeze cycles
grassland
Homestead Act
Hutterites

meander
Métis
New Homestead Act
open-range ranching
panhandle
prior appropriation
"Rain follows the plow"
range war

sod house
steppe
subsidy
suitcase farmer
tornado
volcanic plug
water table
windmill

Places

100th meridian
Badlands
Black Hills
Edwards Plateau

Great American Desert
High Plains
Llano Estacado
Missouri Plateau
Ogallala Aquifer

Paha Sapa
Palliser Triangle
Peace River Valley
Pecos River Valley
Powder River Basin

Prairie provinces
Raton Mesa and Basin
Rupert's Land
Sand Hills

Cities

Calgary, Alberta	**Oklahoma City, Oklahoma**	**Winnipeg, Manitoba**
(2016 CMA 1.4 million)	(2016 MSA 1.3 million)	(2016 CMA 811,000)
Dallas-Fort Worth, Texas	**Regina Saskatchewan**	**Wichita, Kansas**
(2016 MSA 7.2 million)	(2016 CMA 247,000)	(2016 MSA 644,000)

PHOTO 14.1. Oklahoma Panhandle. The High Plains of Oklahoma are a quintessential regional landscape. The flat, endless expanse of "wide open spaces" is appealing. Windmills pump shallow groundwater for livestock, and winds blow across the open grasses.

Introduction

For many people, driving eighty miles an hour through the Great Plains is too slow, but there is much to see in this ancient landscape. Seas, glaciers, and mountains left their imprints, so that the endless vanishing point ahead is, in fact, diverse and far more complex than it seems.

The Great Plains climate, topography, and vegetation signify a transition zone between the wet and forested Midwest and the dry, scruffy West (photo 14.1). The first explorers and settlers found dry **grassland** filled with millions of buffalo.

But the perception of the plains varied with the weather. The farmers or ranchers who settled there depended on rain to define and grow their crops. Sometimes rain fell in the "proper" proportions, and crops were bountiful. Sometimes there was too much rain; other times, no rain. Both brought despair. Farmers tried to farm the plains in the same manner they farmed the Midwest, but the land and the weather demanded a new regimen, which was not practiced until after the 1930s' Depression and drought.

Today, the Great Plains and Canadian Prairie are major agricultural and livestock regions, but they are also resource hinterlands where the few remaining independent farmers and ranchers struggle to maintain the dream of independent production, land ownership, and profit. Unsustainable production by industrialized agriculture has increased yields for the short term, but at the cost of environmental degradation, diminishing of water resources, and social injustice. Still, despite its challenges, this geologically youthful landscape is among the most valuable agricultural lands in the world.

Physical Geography

About sixty-five million years ago, the Great Plains lay beneath a shallow sea. Thousands of feet of sedimentary rock calcified and accumulated over the Precambrian bedrock. Millions of years later, the Rocky Mountain uplift wrenched the nearby flat topography into the rolling Colorado Piedmont. Stream flows accelerated, washing down alluvial soils from the newly formed mountains and covering the Plains seabed in fertile soils.

Each Great Plains state is part of at least two ecoregions. Some states are partially humid in the east and dry in the west; other states are divided between the Rocky Mountains and Plains climates and topographies. Most of the state or provincial borders are straight lines, ignoring ecoregional patterns. For example, the latitude line that separates Oklahoma and Kansas has nothing to do with the physical landscape (the borders of Oklahoma were what remained after other states claimed their lands). The exceptions along the Texas, Mexico, and Oklahoma borders follow rivers, but not the natural watersheds. Therefore the states are fragmented between watersheds and ecological systems. No Great Plains state is within a single major ecoregion or watershed. For example, Oklahoma includes portions of the Gulf Coast South, the Ozarks, the Central Lowlands, and the High Plains. Colorado is part of the Great Plains, the Rocky Mountains, and the Intermontane. The Missouri River divides North Dakota into the Great Plains to the south and west, and the wetter, glaciated Central Lowlands to the north. The Canadian Prairie provinces share the Canadian Shield to the east, the Rocky Mountains to the west, and the boreal forest to the north.

While the Great Plains' relatively flat terrain is ideal for modern mechanized agriculture, the minimal surface water cannot support massive **agribusiness** without relying on underlying groundwater. But to achieve the yields that are wanted, farmers drill and pump out beyond the recharge rate, so each year the **water table** drops. Furthermore, the native grass structure has changed since the days of the free-roaming buffalo. Today's closed-range cattle ranching system has overgrazed many areas, resulting in erosion and a loss of soil moisture and carbon storage.

The flat, treeless, and dry landscape may seem monotonous and even endless. The High Plains, for example, feel flat but incline toward the Rocky Mountains from twenty-five hundred feet at the 100th meridian to forty-five hundred feet at the Oklahoma–New Mexico border 180 miles away, an increase of about eleven feet per mile. The treeless short-grass prairie relies on less than twenty inches of precipitation annually.

Modern agricultural methods have fragmented the land and its ecosystems and left native species in a discontinuous pattern. Invasive species, such as the deep-rooted Eurasian leafy spurge crowds out native species, reduces crop yields, and is difficult to control. Nonnative seeds can be dispersed through the air or by animals from one ecosystem to another, making for constant instability in ecosystems.

While the Great Plains is generally a semiarid flat expanse, altitude and precipitation patterns define the subregions. The subregions include the following:

- Canadian Prairie and Northern Great Plains
- Dissected Missouri Plateau
- Sand Hills
- High Plains
- Raton Mesa and Basin
- Pecos Valley
- Edwards Plateau and Central Texas Uplift

Canadian Prairie and Northern Great Plains

The Canadian Prairie and Northern Great Plains were glaciated north of the Missouri River, with a few unglaciated areas, such as the rugged Cypress Hills on the Alberta–Saskatchewan border. The rolling Alberta Plains are a mixture of glacial sedimentary deposits and sediment washed from the Rocky Mountains. The Northern Great Plains extends into southern Saskatchewan and contain glacial reminders—thousands of small Prairie pothole lakes and rough **badland** topography (photo 14.2). The northernmost Prairie, the Peace River Valley, straddles the Alberta–British Columbia border just south of the boreal forest. The valley is a former lake bottom, a twenty-five-thousand-square-mile fertile agricultural area, a warm microclimate region of good soils that has been homesteaded since World War II.

Ninety-five percent of the native Canadian Prairie grasslands have been converted to wheat farms or rangelands. In the process, wetlands were drained to create a uniform farming landscape. Only about 20 percent of the original wetlands remain.

PHOTO 14.2. Big Muddy Badlands, Saskatchewan. These compressed clay and eroded sandstone outcrops are just north of the US-Canadian border. Stone circles and effigies mark symbolic and sacred places and perhaps graves of native chiefs. During the late nineteenth century, the Badlands were an outlaw hideout for the Sundance Kid, Sam Kelly, and Dutch Henry. Today, cattle graze the Badlands.

BOX 14.1 NATIONAL PARKS: MOUNT RUSHMORE

Mount Rushmore National Memorial is a sculpture carved into the granite face of Mount Rushmore, a batholith in the Black Hills in South Dakota.

Sixty-foot sculptures of the heads of four presidents—George Washington, Thomas Jefferson, Theodore Roosevelt, and Abraham Lincoln—were carved into the mountain by the sculptor Gutzon Borglum from 1927 to 1941 (photo 14.3).

The idea for the carving originated with South Dakota historian Doane Robinson as a way to promote tourism. Initially Robinson wanted Mount Rushmore to feature American West heroes, like Lewis and Clark or Buffalo Bill Cody, but Borglum decided the the sculpture should have broader appeal and chose the four presidents. The four presidents represent the birth, growth, development, and preservation of the country. Originally, each President was to be sculpted from head to waist, but lack of funding forced the construction to end with just the president's faces completed.

Mount Rushmore has become an iconic symbol of the United States, and it has appeared in works of fiction, as well as being discussed or depicted in other popular works. It attracts over two million visitors annually.

There are two controversies worth mentioning. The first is the site itself. The Black Hills have long been sacred to the Lakota, and an 1868 treaty had granted the Black Hills to Lakota in perpetuity. The United States seized the area around Mount Rushmore from the Lakota tribe after the Great Sioux War of 1876. The federal government opened up the area for mining and settlement to European Americans.

In 1971, the American Indian Movement led an occupation of the monument to protest the history of broken federal treaties and promises.

Another controversy relates to the destruction of the mountain face in the age of sustainability. In order to create his "shrine" to democracy, some argue Borglum destroyed the mountain face, highlighting a value system that promotes humans attempting to control or conquer the natural environment. Others counter that he "improved" the mountain face with the remarkable carvings. What do you think?

PHOTO 14.3. Mount Rushmore.
Source: iStock/Kjsmith47

Dissected Missouri Plateau

West of the Missouri River, the Central Lowlands open into the big-sky West. The Missouri Plateau, a transitional landmass north of the High Plains, begins at the Pine Ridge Escarpment along the Nebraska–South Dakota border. In southern South Dakota, the Badlands and Black Hills punctuate this semiarid, eroded, and rolling plain. The underpopulated plain is dryland farmed (not irrigated) or grazed.

Near the meeting place of South Dakota, Wyoming, and Nebraska, the contorted Badlands plateau offers a visual break from the High Plains. The **badland** gullies, towers, canyons, and mesas are the result of seasonal downpours and **frost-freeze cycles** that loosened and cracked rocks into fantastic shapes.

The scenic Black Hills are named for the forests that darken the slopes. The hills are sacred to the native Lakota, who call them Paha Sapa ("the hills that are black"). The Black Hills boom-bust region of gold, tin, and lead-mining camps currently depends on tourism, featuring Mount Rushmore and the Crazy Horse monument honoring the chief who fought to preserve the Lakota way of life. The area is too rough for farming but acceptable grazing land.

Also sacred to Native Americans is the nearby columnar **volcanic plug** called Devil's Tower. Its igneous core was exposed after its sedimentary rock covering eroded over millions of years.

Sand Hills, Nebraska

North America's largest sand dunes—the Sand Hills—are composed of sand left behind after the finer silt and clay loess were blown and deposited eastward (photo 14.4). Wind and rain shaped the maze of sand dunes into their irregular, grass-covered shapes covering almost twenty thousand square miles north of the Platte River in west central Nebraska. Lakes in the basins of the dunes replenish the Ogallala Aquifer below.

Buffalo once grazed the land but were hunted to near extinction by the time of the Civil War. Afterwards ranchers invested in cattle and grazing remained the prevalent use of the land until the 1960s. Since the 1960s, some of the native Sand Hills grassland was altered by center-pivot-irrigation farming supplied by the Ogallala Aquifer.

High Plains

The quintessential Great Plains is the treeless, flat landscape, more often traversed than settled. It was marked on early maps as the Great American Desert because the lack of trees and the lack of surface water appeared to be a land unfit for farming.

The slight elevation gradient and high evaporation rates created a semiarid landscape with few streams or rivers. The uplifted limestone plateau, as wide as the Oklahoma and Texas

panhandles, extends almost featureless from the South Dakota–Nebraska border south to Texas's Edwards Plateau. Only the colorful buttes and mesas of the Gypsum Hills of southwestern Kansas (photo 14.5) punctuate the transition to the drier West.

The southern High Plains plateau begins south of the Canadian River in western Texas. Explorers named these treeless plains the Llano Estacado ("Staked Plains") for the buffalo-bone stakes that served as rudimentary milestones. The Ogallala formation—limestone rock debris washed down from the southern Rocky Mountains—once extended to the foot of the mountains, but rains, streams, and the Pecos River have eroded it into the Pecos River Valley.

Pecos River Valley

Nestled between the Llano Estacado and the Guadalupe Mountains, the sluggish Pecos River runs almost parallel to the Rio Grande until they meet near Del Rio, Texas. The river may be sluggish, but the need for water has caused water wars between Texas and New Mexico throughout most of the twentieth century. The river valley is a transitional landscape between the Great Plains to the east, the Basin and Range to the west, and the Rocky Mountains to the north.

At the eastern edge of the valley is Carlsbad Caverns, the largest cavern system in the world and one of many local limestone sinks and caves. The formation was a reef in an inland tropical sea 250 million years ago. Over time, the sea evaporated and the remaining reef was buried under salt deposits. A few million years ago, the area was uplifted and water seeped into cracks, dissolving the limestone and creating spectacular stalagmite and stalactite formations.

PHOTO 14.4. The Sand Hills of Nebraska.

PHOTO 14.5. Gypsum Hills, Kansas. The hills near Medicine Lodge are red from iron oxide and are capped by gypsum.

Raton Mesa and Basin

Named for local rock rats, the Raton Mesa in southeastern Colorado and northeastern New Mexico is one of the few forested areas within the Plains. Capped by lava flows and riddled with dissected mesas, the transitional landscape lies between the Great Plains and the Rocky Mountains. At eight thousand feet, the steep and narrow Raton Pass cuts below volcanic peaks and above grassy valleys. Raton Pass was one of the Santa Fe Trail's most difficult traverses, but that was overcome in 1879 by the Atchison, Topeka, and Santa Fe Railroad.

Edwards Plateau and Central Texas Uplift

The limestone Balcones Escarpment separates the Gulf Coastal and Great Plains regions and is the defining feature of south central Texas's Edwards Plateau. The Edwards Aquifer—recharged from local rivers and lakes—supplies water for more than two million San Antonio and Austin residents, although overdevelopment has caused pollution that threatens the supply.

West of the escarpment is a deeply dissected canyon land commonly known as the Hill Country, a favored recreational getaway for Texas residents. Shrubs, oaks, and junipers populate the grazed land.

Water

The lack of surface water has compelled humans to modify the Great Plains water systems by building reservoirs, wells, **windmills**, pipelines, and ditches to use the limited surface water and to access deep groundwater.

Great Plains waterways are usually small and often ephemeral. The gentle slope of the land allows even the largest of the perennial rivers—the Missouri, Platte, and Arkansas—a sluggish **meander** across the Plains toward the Mississippi Basin and into the Gulf of Mexico. Another waterway into the Gulf is the Rio Grande, which has been a victim of drought and poor water management. Mexicans, Americans, and Native Americans all seek court approval to obtain water rights to the drought-stricken river.

Missouri River

Prior to the last ice age, Northern Plains rivers drained into Hudson Bay. But glaciation blocked the northern routes; with each glacial advance the rivers were routed south, until the edge of glacial advance formed the Missouri River, which drained into the Mississippi River and eventually into the Gulf of Mexico.

Navigating the "Big Muddy" Missouri was difficult for traders, because frost cut the season short and sand bars, snags, and logs impeded the flow. Over time, the Army Corps of Engineers constructed controlling dams, which improved navigation and protected against flooding. However, the Corps is to multiple, often competing, agendas: farmers, towns, tourists, wildlife, and environmentalists. For example, environmental groups seek to repair imbalances and restore the river, while economic pressure continues to seek profitable solutions.

North Platte River

The "mile-wide, inch-deep" North Platte River, named after an Omaha tribal word for "flat water," is a major tributary of the Missouri River. Westward-moving pioneers and their prairie schooners depended on the Platte for water and direction. Near Ash Hollow, Nebraska, the Platte splits into a southern and a northern branch. Oregon Trail pioneers followed the northern branch into Wyoming along the Middle Rockies to South Pass.

To utilize the snowmelt water of the Platte for irrigation and electric generation, Kingsley Dam was built in 1941 in western Nebraska's North Platte Valley. The earthen dam forms Lake McConaughy, "Big Mac." Water levels have been inconsistent, however. Recent droughts have reduced lake levels, but normal rainfall years help to refill the lake. The lake, sometimes called Nebraska's ocean, has been an economic boon attracting a million visitors annually, but the lower water levels have threatened the recreational economy (photo 14.6).

Arkansas River

The Arkansas River begins in the Colorado Rockies, and flows east over fourteen hundred miles to the Mississippi River southeast of Little Rock. From 1820 to 1846, the Arkansas River marked the boundary between the United States and Mexico.

The river flow varies from major whitewater near its Colorado headwaters to the wide, meandering Arkansas River Valley following the Santa Fe Trail through Kansas. The Kerr–McClellan commercial waterway altered navigation from Tulsa to the river's confluence with the Mississippi.

The Arkansas River Valley near Pueblo, Colorado, has traditionally supported agriculture, but increased urban demand, power generation, and salinity have cut agricultural water in half over twenty-five years.

Ogallala Aquifer

The Ogallala was laid down about ten million years ago by fluvial deposition from streams that flowed eastward from the Rocky Mountains during the Plicoene epoch. The Rocky Mountain uplift both created the aquifer and then cut it off from its original water source. Only scant regional precipitation recharges the aquifer's fossil water from the last glacial period. This means the Ogallala is an unconfined aquifer, and virtually all recharge comes from rainwater and snowmelt. As the Great Plains has a semiarid climate, recharge is minimal. Recharge varies by amount of precipitation, soil type, and vegetation cover and averages less than one inch annually for the region as a whole.

The aquifer underground reservoir lies one hundred to four hundred feet below eight High Plains states (map 14.1). It is estimated that the aquifer stores as much water as Lake Huron (almost three billion acre-feet). The aquifer provides water to nearly one-fifth of the wheat, corn, cotton and cattle produced in the United States, and is the main water supply for people throughout the region. More than 95 percent of the aquifer water is used for irrigation.

Two challenges confront the Ogallala aquifer: depletion and pollution. Ogallala water is overdrafted, and the inability to replenish is a source of concern for the agricultural community. Irrigation withdraws much groundwater, yet little of it is replaced by recharge. Since large-scale irrigation began in the 1940s, water levels have declined more than one hundred feet in parts of Kansas, New Mexico, Oklahoma, and Texas. In the 1980s and 1990s, the rate of groundwater mining, or overdraft, lessened, but still averaged approximately 2.7 feet per year. A recent study reports that with current rates of use, farming in that Kansas is likely to peak by 2040 or so due to water depletion (photo 14.7).

Groundwater contamination is also a problem. Surveys of groundwater samples have detected traces of pesticides and nitrates. Sources include irrigated agriculture and confined livestock feeding operations.

PHOTO 14.6. Declining Lake McConaughy, Nebraska. The lake is a source of irrigation and power generation for the state. The lake has declined more than 80 percent during the twenty-first century, affecting irrigation, the Nebraska corn crop, and the tourist industry. The shore has retracted hundreds of feet, and launching boats in what is left of the lake has become increasingly difficult.

MAP 14.1. Ogallala Aquifer. The High Plains aquifer, of which the Ogallala is the largest part, underlies portions of eight Great Plains states. Since the 1960s, fossil fuel–pumped irrigation water has been pumped onto the fields at a rate at least four times faster than recharge.

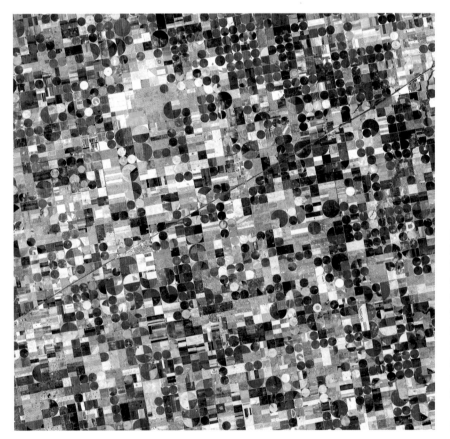

PHOTO 14.7. Center Pivot Irrigation in Finney County in Southwestern Kansas. Commonly irrigated crops are corn, wheat, and sorghum. Green areas in the image are healthy vegetation. Light colored cultivated fields are fallow or recently harvested. The image shows center-pivot irrigation systems that are 800 and 1,600 meters in diameter (0.5 and 1 mile). This area utilizes irrigation water from the Ogallala aquifer, that underlies an area from Wyoming to Texas.

Source: NASA/METI/AIST/Japan Space Systems, and U.S./Japan ASTER Science Team

BOX 14.2   GEOSPATIAL TECHNOLOGIES: MEASURING WATER IN THE OGALLALA

One of the biggest questions about the long-term future of the Ogallala aquifer is: How much water is left?

Many groundwater basins, like the Ogallala, are being depleted, but scientists do not have accurate data about how much water remains in them, which in turn means we do not have a good estimate of how long the remaining water will last.

Unfortunately, groundwater use is difficult to monitor, but this may be improving. NASA's Gravity Recovery and Climate Experiment (GRACE) mission provides the first opportunity to directly measure groundwater changes from space. By observing changes in the Earth's gravity field, scientists can estimate changes in the amount of water stored in a region, which cause changes in gravity. GRACE provides a more than ten-year-long data record for scientific analysis. This makes a huge difference for scientists and water managers who want to understand trends in how our resources are being consumed over the long term.[*]

Researchers are using the satellite-derived groundwater loss rates to what little data exist on groundwater availability to better understand how largest groundwater basins are being rapidly depleted by human consumption.[†]

[*]NASA. "GRACE Tellus," at https://grace.jpl.nasa.gov/applications/groundwater/
[†]NASA. "Study: Third of Big Groundwater Basins in Distress." NASA Jet Propulsion Lab, at https://www.jpl.nasa.gov/news/news.php?feature=4626

Climate

The Great Plains climate is extreme, dramatic, and decidedly western in its aridity. Four physical factors differentiate the Great Plains from the eastern United States:

- **Climate**. The Pacific air mass moves eastward, losing moisture as it passes over mountain ranges. The Great Plains are in the rain shadow of the Rocky Mountains. The western Plains lack precipitation because of the rain shadow, while the eastern Plains are more affected by the Gulf Coast air mass and consequently more humid.
- **Precipitation**. A dry climate regime beginning around the 100th meridian has less than twenty inches of precipitation.
- **Soil**. The scant precipitation cannot leach carbonates from the soil, often leaving a calcium carbonate soil horizon locally called **caliche**. The topsoil is fertile, but precipitation limits its production.
- **Vegetation**. Only scruffy grasses with long, moisture-seeking roots can survive the climate, soil, and precipitation limits in the west; farther east the grasses grow taller due to increased precipitation. The few trees in most Plains areas are limited to riverbed areas.

The Great Plains have a continental climate—a lack of large water bodies that moderate land temperatures. Because land loses heat faster than water, land far from water bodies tends to have more extreme weather: very cold winters or hot, windy summers, along with the periodic and opposing extremes of drought or flood.

The rain shadow limits precipitation along the Rocky Mountain front. The precipitation increases near the 100th meridian, affected by the Gulf of Mexico. East of the 100th meridian, the increased precipitation augments agricultural production. To the west of the 100th meridian is the wheat-growing Great Plains; to the east, the corn-growing Midwest.

Precipitation and temperature averages have the greatest seasonal variation of any region, and they become more pronounced farther north (table 14.1). Precipitation can fall in one thunderous storm that produces flash floods or not fall for years on end. The Northern Plains are affected by winter's frigid Arctic air masses, causing blowing snowstorms.

Extreme weather on the Great Plains includes thunderstorms and hail that can precede the violent rotating **tornadoes** (map 14.2). The extreme weather occurs during the spring and early summer, when Arctic and Gulf fronts meet over the Great Plains. Oklahoma and southern Kansas receive the most tornadoes, although tornadoes also batter the midwestern states.

Hail, a spectacular form of precipitation, forms in unstable air during severe spring or summer thunderstorms. Damaging hailstorms are most frequent in the Great Plains. Hail consists of ice and water in alternate layers that adhere and grow in size and collide with supercooled water in a cumulonimbus cloud. Hail usually falls for about fifteen intense minutes, damaging crops, buildings, and livestock. Cars pockmarked by hail are common sights in storm areas.

On the Canadian Prairies immediately east of the Rockies, dry winds called **chinooks** or "snow eaters" descend the mountains in winter bringing warm Pacific air, capable of melting two feet of snow and raising temperatures to 40°F in fifteen minutes. For many people, the chinooks are a welcome relief to the normal snow cover and Arctic cold. But the winds remove soil moisture (causing "chinook burn"), increase the risk of forest fires, and remove winter snow insulation from plants.

TABLE 14.1. Average Temperatures in the Great Plains and Prairies

	July high	January high	Yearly average
Lemmon, South Dakota	85°F	26°F	42.9°F
Guymon, Oklahoma	93°F	43°F	57°F
Gravelbourg, Saskatchewan	80°F	−2°F	37°F

Source: CLRSearch, at http://www.clrsearch.com

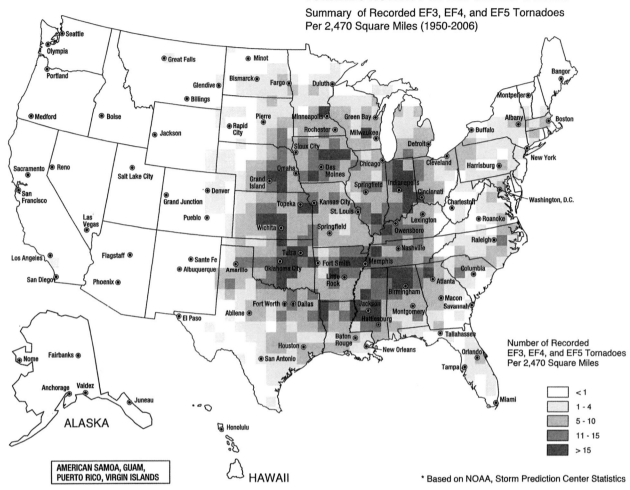

TORNADO ACTIVITY IN THE UNITED STATES*

Summary of Recorded EF3, EF4, and EF5 Tornadoes
Per 2,470 Square Miles (1950-2006)

Number of Recorded
EF3, EF4, and EF5 Tornadoes
Per 2,470 Square Miles

	< 1
	1 - 4
	5 - 10
	11 - 15
	> 15

AMERICAN SAMOA, GUAM,
PUERTO RICO, VIRGIN ISLANDS

ALASKA

HAWAII

* Based on NOAA, Storm Prediction Center Statistics

MAP 14.2. A Map of the Frequency of F3 and Greater Intensity Tornadoes by Area. The darker colors highlight the areas typically known as Tornado Alley. Tornadoes occur where there are no obstacles stopping cold Canadian air meeting moist Gulf air, usually in thunderstorms. Wind speeds up to three hundred miles per hour can result, destroying everything in the tornado's path.

Source: NOAA

Historical Geography and Settlement

The physical landscape and climate of the Plains have always limited settlement. Because the Plains lacked surface water, permanent Native American settlements were unusual; most Plains tribes lived a nomadic lifestyle following the buffalo. The semiarid lands were unappealing to American settlers while lucrative lands elsewhere were available. Later economic and political incentives, such as the **Homestead Act**, and propaganda, such as "**Rain follows the plow**," aroused interest.

Plains Indigenous Peoples

Twelve thousand years ago, as the last ice-age glaciers retreated, the Plains indigenous tribes led a seminomadic life revolving around where they could walk in a day to gather berries and seeds, practice elemental agriculture, and hunt wooly

mammoths and buffalo. In the sixteenth century, the Spanish arrived, introducing horses and firearms to the Natives. The Native culture was changed forever. By the early eighteenth century, horses and firearms had expanded Native mobility and warfare. Tribal groups repositioned across the Midwest and Plains: the Sioux Lakota from Minnesota to the Plains, Shoshones into the Intermontane. The Lakota and the Crow became powerful horsemen, secure in hunting, trading, and waging war, although at the cost of cultural loss; the dependence on the horse shifted their social structure, degraded the Plains ecology, and intensified warfare.

The United States acquired most of the Great Plains from France in the 1803 Louisiana Purchase. By 1851, a series of treaties redefined Lakota territories and allowed westward wagon train passage. However, few pioneers settled on the Plains until the passage of the Homestead Act (1862) and the end of the Civil War (1865).

BOX 14.3   CLIMATE CHANGE AND THE OGALLALA AQUIFER

Climate change will alter the temperature, precipitation, and distribution of crops, and it is therefore monitored in fields across America. Climate change will impose additional expenses to already slim agricultural profits. Scientists are working to understand how climate change will impact the Ogallala aquifer, and the consequences for agricultural production.

Two parameters studied on the Plains are atmospheric warming, which produces the greenhouse effect, and the introduction of Ogallala water. The greenhouse effect changes the location of crops and the choice of seed. For example, North America's growing season (the time of plant growth from the last frost to the first) has been increasing over the past twenty years, and is now about twelve days longer than twenty years ago.

Seed is specific to several variables, such as temperature range and growing seasons. As global warming progresses,

regional seed preferences will shift with the temperature and require ongoing research to find the most viable alternatives.

Large-scale irrigation modifies climate, although the long-term impact is still unknown.* The ability to forecast realistic and sustainable models is an important element of a long-term sustainable food supply. Despite advances in water-saving technology, the aquifer still loses more water than it gains through precipitation. Additional environmental consequences of irrigation dependence are increased soil salinity, water pollution, and destruction of ecosystems. If the Ogallala continues to be pumped at an unsustainable rate, **dryland farming** will be the only alternative, which will decrease the food supply as the population continues to grow.

Several options have been discussed to improve water availability, such as increased aquifer management, increased storage, reduced consumption, and conservation.

---

*Rezaul Mahmood, Kenneth G. Hubbard, and Christy Carlson, "Modification of Growing-Season Surface Temperature Records in the Northern Great Plains due to Land-use Transformation: Verification of Modeling Results and Implication for Global Climate Change," *International Journal of Climatology* 24 (2004): 311–27.

As settlers encroached on tribal hunting grounds, Native American tribes fought to save their nomadic lifestyle. Uprisings and massacres continued as late as the 1870s, when most tribal groups were assigned to reservations.

Surveying the Great American Desert

Lewis and Clark traveled along the Missouri River through the "Great American Desert," reporting of dry creek beds in a "desert and barren" region. Lieutenant Pike in 1806 visited and wrote of a vast interior American desert. He and others attributed the treeless area to soil sterility and lack of moisture, fuel, and vegetation.

In 1820, Major Long concurred with Pike, claiming the entire region "wholly unfit for cultivation, and of course, uninhabitable by a people depending upon agriculture for their subsistence." Timothy Flint's *The History and Geography of the Mississippi Valley* (1833) likened it to "the great Sahara of the African deserts." In the 1870s, general settlement began because no other lands were affordable or available. Then the Great Plains began to be farmed in the fashion of the wetter East.

The Cowboy and Cattle

Four cultures—Spanish, Anglo, Gulf Coast, and subcontinental India—created the American cattle industry. The cattle drive diffused the Spanish-Anglo cattle-raising traditions across the West. Spanish words— *ranch, lasso,* and *corral*—were adopted into English. In the mid-nineteenth century, Brahman cattle from India—capable of withstanding heat, grazing large areas, and immune to insects and diseases—were introduced into the Gulf Coast. Brahman were then crossbred with European cattle to create the climatically suited Texas longhorn and then bred

with other varieties to accommodate the western landscape and the Anglo palate.

The legendary cattle drive and horseback cowboy originated in Texas. The cattle drive delivered millions of longhorn cattle to rail yard cow towns such as Abilene or Dodge City, Kansas, where they were shipped sequentially to the corn-rich midwestern feedlots, the slaughterhouses of Chicago or St. Louis, and finally to East Coast markets. A cattle boom ensued across the Plains and was the favored "get rich quick" investment of the 1870s. In 1867, thirty-five thousand cattle were shipped at $4 to $5 a head; in the East they were worth $50. By 1871, Abilene alone shipped more than seven hundred thousand cattle to Chicago.

During the 1870s, the cattle-grazing industry boomed on the open plains, displacing the millions of native buffalo that were relegated to near extinction. The boom-bust-cycle cattle ranches had undisputed possession of the Plains, and everyone was either a cattle rancher or wanted to be one. When the market collapsed in the 1880s from drought, blizzards, and overinvestment, the western cowboy and the cattle drive crashed. Meanwhile, Great Plains ecosystems were profoundly altered by killing the buffalo for sport and replacing them with cattle.

Fourteen million buffalo had roamed freely, following the perennial grasses and the seasons. They did not overgraze areas because they moved on when the grass was sparse. Buffalo were a sustainable biotic system for the Plains, but the buffalo's nomadic grazing was unfit for the rigid and permanent European agricultural and ranching system, where fenced-in cattle eat introduced species of annual grass, often to the point of destroying the root. Many perennial grasses became scarce.

Canada's cowboy heritage is sometimes difficult to disentangle from the American version, but it lives on, especially in

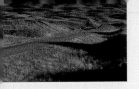

BOX 14.4 JOHN WESLEY POWELL AND HIS VISION FOR THE WEST

John Wesley Powell, the second director of the US Geological Survey, led several expeditions west of the 100th meridian, the dividing line between the drier West and the moister East. His experiences led him to devise theories of the West that differed from those of his contemporaries. He believed that a lack of water and insufficient rainfall made the West unsuitable for eastern land uses. His policies have not been followed to this day.

Powell's 1878 study of the region, *Report on the Lands of the Arid Region*, described a realistic but ultimately politically unacceptable settlement pattern, one where watersheds were respected, conservation enforced, and cooperative self-reliance was practiced, rather than depending on government-subsidized water projects. Powell also stated that western state boundaries should follow watersheds instead of politics. He spoke to Congress,

Now, what I wish to make clear to you is this. There is not water enough, runoff water enough to irrigate all the lands. When all the rivers are used, when all the creeks and ravines, when all the springs are used, when all the reservoirs along the streams are used, when all the canyon waters are taken up, when all the artesian waters are taken up, when all the wells that are sunk or dug that can be dug in all this arid region, there is still not sufficient water to irrigate all this arid region. There is still not sufficient water to irrigate all the land.

During Powell's tenure in government posts, he consistently spoke and wrote for developing the West based on judicious water rights that went with land titles, but his vision, though prescient, was not followed. Powell understood then what many still do not see: water must be treated in a different manner in the West than in the East. Water is a scarce commodity and requires adjusting the water policy to correspond to western realities.[*]

*William deBuys, ed., *Seeing Things Whole: The Essential John Wesley Powell*. Washington, D.C.: Island Press, 2001.

Alberta. The late-nineteenth-century cattle-ranching industry began with large ranches granted to an elite few. Cattle ranching and its perceptual aura continue, although in muted form. By 1906, frontier settlement replaced the open range, and today "cowboys" are more likely to be working in Alberta's oil fields than on the ranch. Nonetheless, Alberta, and especially Calgary, where the cattle industry was the initial economic stimulus, is replete with cowboy culture—roundups, stampedes, blizzards, barbed wire, songs, and rodeos. Calgary is home to the largest cowboy rodeo anywhere, the Calgary Stampede.

With the exception of dude ranches and artificial cattle drives in both countries, the cattle-drive cowboy has disappeared, although the heroic legend remains. Throughout the Great Plains, indeed throughout America, people still dream of having a "home on the range"—although today the "ranch" is five acres in suburbia.

Farming and Ranching

Farming and ranching on the Great Plains required farmers to adjust and dryland farm (without irrigation). Wet years brought bounty, dry years despair. Nonetheless, propaganda transformed the image of the "Great American Desert" and attracted settlers who believed they could tame the plains. Congress passed the Homestead Act in 1862, offering quarter sections for almost nothing if the land was settled. Although it has been perceived by later generations that as a great giveaway, the act was a last-ditch effort by Congress to produce income while ridding the government of excess poor land. The 1870s, the period of greatest settlement of the US Plains, proved wetter than the norm and "rain follows the plow" seemed plausible.

After the Civil War, a new group of farmers were seeking land for the first time. Freed black families, the **Exodusters**, were pulled to the Plains after the Klu Klux Klan and Jim Crow racial oppression pushed them out of the South. Twenty thousand freed blacks migrated seeking their fortunes. They formed more than thirty independent farm communities in Kansas, and about three-quarters of the migrants eventually owned their own farms. Some towns still exist but are dying, such as Nicodemus in north central Kansas. Seeking respect and opportunity, other freed African Americans joined the military; they were dubbed "buffalo soldiers" by their Cheyenne and Comanche opponents.

"Free" land, though, was not an easy answer. On the surface, the lack of water, wood, and tools to work this dry land often exhausted settlers' resources. For example, fencing land often cost more than purchasing land in the East. Eventually, fencing the Plains became a major component of the **range wars**.

Range Wars

Friction between ranchers and farmers caused the range wars in the late nineteenth century. Cattlemen, sheepherders, and farmers clashed in how they used the fragile landscape. Cattlemen with large spreads inhibited the small farm operators and often cut through fences to access free range. Farmers wanted cattle fenced out of their fields. Ranchers wanted unwelcome farmers to bear the fencing cost, since the farmers arrived after the ranchers. Shepherds allowed the grazing sheep to crop grass close to the ground, preventing regrowth and therefore ruining the grass for cattle grazing.

The 1874 invention of barbed wire offered a far less expensive way to fence. Billed as "cheaper than dirt and stronger than steel," barbed wire was strung on a minimum of wooden posts. But although it solved one dilemma it caused another: the cost of labor.

Ranchers were upset at the high labor costs for fencing and the loss of open waterways for their cattle. Eventually, states adopted fencing laws that shifted the burden of fencing to one party or another. At first, most western states allowed livestock to roam at will. **Open-range ranching** allowed cattle to graze on unfenced range. The farmer was expected to fence the cattle out. Eventually, states adopted a closed-range fencing policy, which effectively ended the cattle drives. The cost and time of "riding fence" has continued to be a large expense and a source of irritation and litigation. Some old-time ranchers still complain about the loss of the open range.

Northern Plains

The Northern Plains settlement pattern differed from the High Plains since the Northern Plains were far from the cattle trails, and the Europeans who settled the Dakotas were more culturally preadapted to the regional landscape. Settlers from Sweden and Finland understood the long, cold winters and the agricultural conditions. They brought with them four valuable tools for the Northern Plains: (1) a Protestant work ethic, (2) seed adapted to the northern latitude, (3) a winterproof mentality, and (4) cold-weather traditions that included festivals and saunas that broke the monotony of long winters.

The Canadian Prairie

Métis and Louis Riel

The **Métis** (a French term meaning "mixed," akin to the Spanish *mestizo*) are a people of mixed Aboriginal and European descent, the descendants of Native women and French trappers. Métis hunted, trapped, and traded in the Great Lakes wilderness of Canada and the northern US, and they were fundamental in the settling of Manitoba's Red River Valley. The ten thousand Métis of the late nineteenth century formed their own culture; they lived more like a Native nation than European, adopted Catholicism, and spoke French or their mixed language, Michif. They depended on the buffalo and traded animal pelts with Hudson Bay posts. Their sense of nationhood developed under the leadership of Louis Riel.

In 1870, Canada purchased Rupert's Land (renamed the Northwest Territories) and European settlers began to arrive in Manitoba's Red River Valley where many Métis were settled. The new settlers disputed the earlier Métis claims. The Métis were starved by loss of their land claims, drought, and the loss of the buffalo herds.

The Métis appealed to Louis Riel, who had been instrumental in obtaining the Manitoba Métis Indian Treaty land. But mistreatment by the Canadian government led him to retreat to a quiet life in Montana. After entreaties to return and lead his people, Riel reluctantly returned and fought for their treaty-promised land. Canadian forces quashed the uprising and forced the Métis to surrender. Riel was tempted to return to Montana but chose instead to surrender and stand trial. He was executed in what can only be called a death of political expediency. He died a martyr for his cause and remains a hero in Canadian lore.

His death was more than a loss to the Métis; his French-Canadian roots represented a loss for Quebec as well, and his death widened the gap between French-speaking and English-speaking Canadians. Today, Métis and First Nations peoples live on reservations and experience the same social and economic problems as American tribes.

The Métis have become the fastest-growing ethnic group, although some of the growth can be attributed to awareness of Métis issues and rights. In 1982, the Métis were granted legal status as Native people. About 32 percent of all Aboriginals (451,000) were reported in the 2011 Canadian census to be Métis. Most in the Prairie provinces and make their living by fishing, guiding tourists who hunt, procuring seasonal jobs, and a bit of subsistence farming.

Canadian Prairie Settlement

John Palliser explored Canada's prairie in 1857 to assess settlement possibilities and concluded that the grassy, dry "Palliser Triangle" extending from southwestern Manitoba to southern Alberta was unsuitable for agriculture. Nonetheless, Canada purchased Rupert's Land in 1870. Settlement began after (map 14.3).

Canadians asserted their sovereignty over the newly acquired land with the **Dominion Lands Act** (1872), which closely resembled the 1862 US Homestead Act. Although the Dominion Lands Act was meant to encourage settlement, relatively few settlers were attracted. Success increased when the government offered additional incentives: loans, larger acreage, reserves of land, and military exemptions. For example, several thousand pacifist Mennonites and Icelanders fleeing Icelandic volcanic eruptions settled Manitoba and the upper Midwest beginning in the 1870s. But still the expansive West had too few settlers, many of whom migrated from Canada into the States.

The Canadian Shield was a barrier to transcontinental transportation. Traveling to the Canadian Prairie could only be accomplished by crossing the American Great Lakes states. The Canadian transcontinental railroad (1885) provided a direct route through Canada's Shield from northwestern Ontario into Manitoba and tied British Columbia to the rest of the fledgling country.

With the railroad complete, populating the Prairie region became the mission of Canadian Prime Minister Sir Wilfred Laurier, who came into office at the dawn of the twentieth century and launched what was known as the "Laurier boom" (1896–1911) in migration.

A push-and-pull migration followed. The push was from political, religious, and economic repression. Eastern Europeans and landless American and Canadian immigrants were pulled by free land on the Canadian Prairies. Another pull factor was a shift in economic well-being; both the United States and Canada emerged from the 1890 depression amid rising wheat prices that brought settlers to the last frontier on the Canadian Prairies.

Under Laurier, the administration eased immigration restrictions and land acquisition, and developed a publicity/propaganda campaign to encourage settlement. These publicity tours became the most successful immigration device

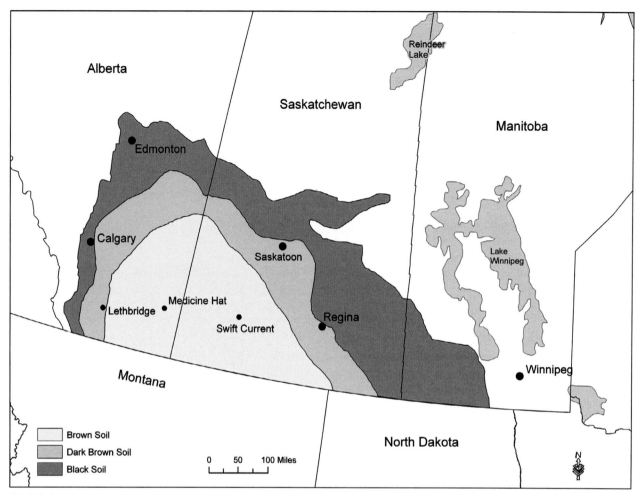

MAP 14.3. Canadian Prairie. The Palliser Triangle is the northern extension of the Great Plains. These fertile prairies produce the most grain in Canada.

in Canadian history. Between 1896 and 1911, more than two million land-seeking Canadians, Americans, and exiled **Hutterites** and Ukrainians settled the Prairie region. Among them were six hundred thousand midwestern tenant farmers seeking their own land; they reversed the previous trend of immigration to America. Many of the immigrants did not stay; the climate was far harsher, the land more marginal than advertised. But many did stay, and in time, improved technology, such as quickly maturing strains of wheat that fit the short growing season, made life bearable.

In 1897, the **Crow Rate** subsidized the transportation of crops to market by reducing the cost of transporting grain over Crow's Nest Pass to Vancouver in the West and to the Great Lakes in the East. The **subsidy** was a benefit for prairie farmers and supported the development of the railroad in Western Canada, but it hindered the development of western industry because the Crow Rate distorted production costs. The Crow Rate was abolished in 1995, and thereafter prairie farmers' exposure to unstable economic conditions increased as environmental conditions degraded. Severe droughts affected crops. Wheat price instability left farmers with erratic incomes, at a time when transportation costs escalated by as much as 40 percent.

Cultural Perspectives

Dwellings: Vernacular Architecture

The lack of transportation and the scarcity of wood on the Plains and Canadian Prairie forced settlers to build their initial homes with local materials—sod and hay. Because of superior insulation qualities, both hay and sod buildings have made a comeback since 1970, mostly by environmentalists who see the advantages of building with well-insulating local materials.

Sod Buildings

Sod houses were well adjusted for the semiarid climate. The short, tufted grasses were supported by a deep root system that improved the soil, prevented erosion, and served as a building material because the grass roots held the sod blocks together. Sod house construction varied in relation to the culture adapting the building material. Some houses were cut directly from the sod, built brick upon brick; others dug into the ground; while others were built from rammed earth or wattle and daub, a construction technique intertwining branches and twigs and then smearing them with mud.

Although cramped and uncomfortable, the sod houses were well insulated, a necessity for the continental climate extremes. Among the many inconveniences of living in a sod house were insects and snakes living in the walls and the inevitable washing away of the walls with each rain. Few of the original sod houses remain today, due to the temporary nature of their unbaked soil construction (photo 14.8).

Straw Bale Buildings

For hundreds of years, Europeans built straw-bale homes and many still stand. They are inexpensive to build, use local material, and their insulating qualities make them energy efficient. The bales are stacked like bricks and then held in place with rods driven through the bales. The Sand Hills of Nebraska in the Great Plains were the birthplace for American straw-bale homes during the late nineteenth century, driven by the invention of the steam-powered baler.

Today, straw bale buildings are considered a sustainable building material. People who build these homes aim to be off the grid as much as possible, so solar heating, rainwater collection, and solar hot water are part of the straw-bale package. The US Department of Energy has also endorsed this energy efficient and renewable house form.

The 49th Parallel

The goal of the Convention of 1818 was to establish a permanent border to end Great Plains border disputes. The ideal was to have waters flowing into the Gulf of Mexico (Mississippi-Missouri Rivers) for the United States and waters flowing into Hudson Bay for Britain. Up to that time, the land had been divided along watersheds: Hudson Bay in Canada and the Mississippi-Missouri in the United States. However, the watersheds were difficult to survey in 1818, so a compromise was chosen: the 49th parallel.

The physical region continues beyond the 49th parallel into the Canadian Prairie region with little to physically divide them other than the International Boundary Commission's 20-foot-wide (6 m) swath marking the border. Yet, on either side of the border the crops usually differ, matching each country's agricultural policies. The Montanan farmer may plant wheat, while his Albertan neighbor directly north is a rancher; yet, they share common climate and soil. Government policies and tariffs often determine whether a farmer will grow canola or wheat or be a rancher. Generally, Canadian beef and hogs flow south as exports.

Population, Immigration, and Diversity

Population

Historically, the Great Plains Native American population was sparse and nomadic. The Native American followed the buffalo herd, the cowboy followed the cattle, and the settler followed (in historic sequence) trails, rails, and highways. European Americans were slow to settle the Plains, until the 1870s when the population in Nebraska more than tripled to almost half a million and in the 1880s when the population in Kansas reached a million. Every Great Plains state grew during the late nineteenth century.

In 1893, the Wisconsin historian Frederick Jackson Turner in his **Frontier Thesis** declared the frontier and a chapter of American history closed. The thesis identified powerful American psyche images, among them the cowboy and the pioneer's rugged individualism. Using statistical data from the 1890 Census, a first in modern social science, Turner analyzed the data and told a politically charged story, identifying a shift in demography from rural agricultural settlement to urban. By 1900, half of all Americans were living in urban settings, and the percentage of farmers was in a continual decline.

PHOTO 14.8. Sod House in Texas County, Oklahoma. The last sod house in the county is protected from cattle by a fence, has a metal roof, and is whitewashed to maintain its structural integrity. This sod house was a semidugout, with a front door and excavated walls.

While the Dakotas reached Turner's critical population of two people per square mile in the 1890 census, the population density has declined since. In North Dakota, for example, only six of its fifty-three counties gained population between 1990 and 2000; most counties in the western part of the state were below two people per square mile, despite a boom economy beginning in 2007 when oil field work in the Bakken formation brought a flood of RVs and campers filled with temporary workers into the small towns.

Current Population Issues

The rural population of the Great Plains and Canadian Prairies has the highest percentage of Americans and Canadians over the age of sixty-five. **Aging in place** creates demographic and economic dynamics that place strains on social services. The constrained budget of an elderly population does not support the consumer economy as much as a fully employed youthful population. An economic structure based on the gross domestic product (GDP) and consumer spending ill-fits an older population and may signal a new economic order. Older populations also require additional health care facilities that further restrain limited budgets, especially when health care is not universal.

In the Great Plains, many elderly are isolated in low-amenity rural settings, a situation very different from higher-income areas such as Florida and Arizona. Aging in place hinders population growth on the Plains, because while the older population remains, the younger population often chooses to migrate outside the area and further alters the population balance

Living on large, dispersed farms made sense in the nineteenth century when transportation was limited; however, fewer people live on their farms now that transportation allows more freedom. "**Suitcase farmers**" plant and harvest the farm but live in the city. They farm their land using capital-intensive, technology-dependent mechanization, and new technologies frees farmers from the fields and from labor-intensive chores.

Prairie settlers included Canadians and Americans. Eastern and northern Europeans were the largest ethnic groups immigrating during the Laurier boom period at the turn of the twentieth century. Pacifist German Mennonites and Hutterites fled religious persecution first into the Russian Ukraine and then, when threatened with conscription, onto the Canadian Prairie. Immigrating to the harsh climatic conditions of the Canadian Prairie was not quite as onerous for the Hutterites as for other groups, because the climate resembles the Ukrainian **steppes**

and the Hutterites understood that landscape. Hutterites continue to live in isolated, agricultural, communal settlements, while many Mennonites have assimilated into Canadian society.

The Canadian Prairie and the Great Plains share rural changes: Farms are growing larger, the workforce is growing smaller, and small towns are disappearing. Fewer people equates to a loss of political influence for the remaining farmers and ranchers.

Immigration and Diversity

While farmers may be leaving the Canadian Prairie, others are settling in the provinces. Alberta is currently the province with the fastest-growing population in Canada. The largest factor in Alberta's population growth came from immigrants arriving from outside the country. In 2011, the foreign-born population was 18 per cent; it could increase to 24 percent within twenty years. While many foreign born come from the Americas and Europe, the largest source of immigrants is Asia and this will continue to increase; it is estimated that by 2036, more than 60 percent of immigrants in Alberta will arrive from Asia, particularly China, India, and the Philippines.

Saskatchewan joins Alberta as one of the fastest-growing provinces in the nation because of crude petroleum production. Saskatchewan is seen as a more affordable location, with cheaper housing prices than in other areas. Manitoba, too, has not only seen increased immigration but is also actively engaged in attracting immigration. Manitoba launched the Provincial Nominee Program which targets prospective immigrants with skills and experience in demand to receive a Manitoba Provincial Nomination Certificate, which speeds up the overall immigration process. Skills include those who have farm business experience and sufficient capital to operate a farm, and entrepreneurs wishing to do business in the province. Another recruitment tool is the website www.immigratemanitoba.com, which lists numerous reasons for choosing Manitoba, including affordability and size, noting that "some choose Manitoba to be closer to family, some for employment opportunities, and for others it is an attraction to a part of Canada that is not too big and not too small."

While many of the Prairie provinces are growing through immigration, this is not the trend in the US Great Plains. Outside of Texas, most of the US states in the Great Plains have diversity and foreign-born populations under the national average (table 14.2).

TABLE 14.2. Diversity in Selected Great Plains States, by Percentage

US National Average	Kansas	Nebraska	North Dakota	Oklahoma	South Dakota	Texas	Wyoming
White 76.9	86	89	88	74.6	85	79.4	92.8
African American 13.3	6.2	5	2.9	7.8	2	12.6	1.3
Hispanic 17.8	11.6	10.7	3.6	10.3	3.7	39.1	10
Foreign Born 14.3	6.9	6.6	3.2	5.8	3	16.6	3.6

Source: US Census Bureau, 2016

Urban Trends

The Great Plains is not known for its urban centers but for its dispersed farms and ranches. Large urban centers located on the region's periphery are juxtaposed to hundreds of small towns, which reflect the changed economy and transportation patterns.

Small Towns

The Great Plains was settled in a dispersed pattern. The region's agricultural and manufacturing economy cannot support large populations. Towns have been small and served the local farming population, but the economic, social, and political viability of these towns is waning. Historically, US and Canadian speculators planned Great Plains towns every fifteen miles—a day's round-trip journey—along the railroad lines. The centerpiece of each town was the grain elevator (photo 14.9). As long as the grain elevator was operating, the town remained viable. Local farmers brought their grain to the elevator and their business to the town. When a town lost its grain elevator, the town's reason for existence went with it.

Reliance on local community was further weakened when rural electrification became a priority and reality in rural America and Canada. Although over 90 percent of urban dwellers had electricity in 1930, only 10 percent of rural residents did. By 1939, 35 percent of the rural populace had electricity and by 2000, over 90 percent did. Electricity changed the way farming was done, allowing more mechanization and extending working hours. But electricity did not halt the migration of rural families into cities or stop the growth of corporate farming.

Numerous Great Plains towns have tried economic development ideas in order to save their small and aging towns. For example, Guymon in the Oklahoma panhandle has continually run after the most popular economic panacea of the times. In the 1990s, Guymon courted a pork-processing plant. After its success, the newcomers increased crime levels and caused new problems. As with many towns and cities, there have been redevelopment efforts that include the designation of a Cultural Arts District, and the establishment of a Certified Industrial Park and Enterprise Zone.

There has been proposed legislation to reverse declines in rural population declines. Starting in 2003 and each year since, Senators Byron Dorgan (D-N.D.) and Chuck Hagel (R-Neb) have introduced (and reintroduced) the **New Homestead Act**. The act would offer incentives to move into small Plains towns and would counter out-migration by offering tax credits and capital for starting businesses in these towns. It would also forgive college loans and offer home-buying assistance. To date, the bill has not passed.

Major Cities

The Great Plains metropolitan areas are on the periphery of the region. Denver and the Front Range complex (see chapter 15) and the Calgary–Edmonton corridor in Alberta are gateway cities. Dallas–Fort Worth, the largest metropolitan complex, is located along the eastern margin of the Plains, while on the Osage Plain, Oklahoma City and Kansas City are both transitional cities between the Central Lowlands and the Great Plains.

Cities on the Eastern Margin

Great Plains agricultural and resource wealth has supplied eastern markets. Transitional cities—Minneapolis–St. Paul, Kansas City, Omaha (see chapter 13), and Dallas–Fort Worth—developed along the eastern margins, distributing Plains commodities and livestock to eastern markets.

PHOTO 14.9. Grain Elevators, Southern Saskatchewan. Grain elevators, originally designed for nineteenth-century operations, stood in each town about fifteen miles apart, a day's travel. Newer elevators are much larger and more widely spaced, accommodating modern travel. Towns bypassed by the newer elevators lose their identity when the local elevator closes.

Dallas–Fort Worth (2016 MSA 7.2 million)

Dallas–Fort Worth was founded at a transportation junction in the 1860s. Dallas and Fort Worth began as separate cites with separate hinterlands, but they coalesced over time into the sprawling metropolis (called the Metroplex locally) it is today.

Dallas's hinterland is to the east in the Texas Blacklands, where 40 percent of US cotton was grown in the nineteenth century. Dallas was the distribution city for cotton, hence the naming of the Cotton Bowl football classic. In the 1930s, the discovery of oilfields near Dallas provided a future beyond cotton. Today, Dallas is a regional center for transportation and finance and a gateway for wholesale trade (photo 14.10).

Fort Worth's history is tied to western cattle, oil, and railroads. The Chisholm Trail was Texas's major cattle trail through Fort Worth and on to Abilene, Kansas. Fort Worth remains tied to cattle and agricultural production and its distribution. Today, the combined "twin" cities are the second-largest population in Texas after Houston.

Dallas–Fort Worth is considerably more diverse than most of the cities in the Great Plains. Fifty percent of the population is white and 42 percent Hispanic. The city is also home to 24 percent foreign born, with the top countries of origin being Mexico, India, Vietnam, El Salvador, and South Korea.

While Dallas is not known as being especially aware of its sustainable options, like many US cities, it launched its sustainability plan *Green Dallas* in 2012. Prior to this, environmental initiatives were dispersed throughout the city bureaucracy. The plan focuses on pragmatic, near-term goals rather than a broad vision, but some of the highlights of the plan include improving air and water quality, zero waste by 2040 and to reduce nonrenewable energy consumption—certainly a major step forward in this oil-rich city.

Oklahoma City, Oklahoma (2016 MSA 1.3 million)

Oklahoma City is the capital of the US state of Oklahoma. It is known for its cowboy culture and capitol complex, surrounded by working oil derricks (photo 14.11). Oklahoma City has the largest municipal population of any city in the Great Plains region of the central US as well as all neighboring states excluding Texas.

The economy of Oklahoma City, once just a regional power center of government and energy exploration, has diversified. Oil and natural gas related industries remain important, but key service sector employers now include: the state government, US Federal Aviation Administration, Integris Health, University of Oklahoma Health Sciences Center, Hobby Lobby (headquarters), and Boeing.

The city experienced a domestic terrorist truck bombing in 1995. The truck bombing of the Alfred P. Murrah Federal Building killed 168 people, injured 680 others, and destroyed one-third of the building. As a result of the bombing, Congress mandated that all federal buildings in the United States increase security by restricting access, installing cameras, and requiring a perimeter (or safety zone) around the buildings. The proliferation of bollards, barriers, and screening devices at federal buildings are a direct result (box 14.5).

Canadian Prairie Cities

The capitals of each prairie province are located in the more populated southern part of the provinces. Winnipeg is a wheat distribution center, while Regina is a center for natural resources. But the major urban centers in the Canadian Prairie are in Alberta. Both Calgary and Edmonton are gateway cities to other regions, Calgary to the Rocky Mountains, and Edmonton to the boreal north and its booming oil sand economy. The energy sector supports their booming economies.

PHOTO 14.10. The Dallas Skyline.
Source: iStock/f11photo

PHOTO 14.11. Oil Derricks in Downtown Oklahoma City, Oklahoma. It is not uncommon to see working oil derricks in the city.
Source: iStock/benkrut

Calgary (2016 CMA 1.4 million)

Calgary is the fourth-largest and the fastest-growing city in Canada. Immigrants and Canadians from outside the province fuel the growth to the oil-rich province (photo 14.13). Calgary is one of the four most religiously diverse cities in Canada (Vancouver, Toronto, and Edmonton are the other three). Calgary's population is skilled and educated; 60 percent have a postsecondary education, the highest in the province. They seek local quality-of-life amenities and low tax rates, and they have the highest employment rate in North America.

Calgary started as a cattle-ranching center and evolved into the Prairie's financial, natural resource, and transportation center. In 1883, the Canadian Pacific Railroad chose the southern route through Calgary over Edmonton, thereby assuring Calgary's growth. The 240-mile urban corridor between Calgary and Edmonton contains 2.2 million people (about 72 percent of the provincial population). Calgary is Canada's second-largest center of corporate headquarters (behind Toronto).

However, Calgary's fortunes tend to rise and fall with oil prices. Relatively low oil prices over the past several years have curtailed the robust growth the city enjoyed for much of the early twenty-first century. The city has been trying to diversify its economy by attracting research and companies around renewable energy (especially wind generation), film and TV, and financial services.

Calgary has been recognized as a city working toward sustainability, especially in water efficiency. Calgary sits in the rain shadow of the Canadian Rockies and receives only about 16 inches (41 cm) of precipitation annually. Recognizing the city's growth and its high water consumption, the city adopted "30-in-30 by 2033." The goal of the plan is to keep water consumption at the same level in 2033 as it was in 2003, despite the expected population growth of about eighteen thousand people annually. The population is being asked to reduce water consumption by 30 percent over thirty years.

In 2010, the Office of Sustainability developed a ten-year strategic direction toward sustainability, called *2020 Sustainability Direction*, and a long-range one-hundred-year plan, called *ImagineCalgary*. The plan recognizes the metro area has an increasingly aging population and increased immigration and is vulnerable to the boom/bust energy cycles. Some of the goals for 2020 include the following:

- one hundred percent of eligible low-income Calgarians have improved access to low-income programs and services;
- no adoptable animal is euthanized;
- to be an age-friendly city;
- to support six hundred festival and event days per year; and
- reduce greenhouse gas emissions by 20% from 2005.

The Economy

The Great Plains economy revolves around agricultural production and traditionally, crops and livestock were distributed to the eastern US population centers. By the late twentieth century, however, another "East" emerged as the main market for Great Plains crop production. Successful Asian economies invested in Great Plains crops and livestock. Technology and shifting transportation patterns augmented this change. The transportation patterns are dependent on fossil fuel use and may require reconsideration as new transportation patterns emerge in a more sustainable economy.

BOX 14.5   ICONIC IMAGE: OKLAHOMA BOMBING MEMORIAL

Not all iconic images celebrate. Some are about grief and loss.

On April 19, 1995, at 9:02 a.m., Timothy McVeigh detonated a two-ton fertilizer bomb packed in a rental truck in front of the Alfred P. Murrah Federal Building in Oklahoma City. The explosion, which destroyed the entire front of the building, killed 168 people, including 15 children who were in the daycare center.

Within a few months, Oklahoma City Mayor Ron Norick appointed a 350-member Memorial Task Force charged with developing an appropriate memorial to honor those affected by the event. Members of the Memorial Task Force gathered input from families, survivors, and the general public about what visitors to the bombing Memorial should feel and experience. According to the architects, the design process was heavily influenced by family members and survivors who insisted that the names of each individual who died be incorporated into the memorial. They also noted that the process involved a great deal of compromise on their part with family members.

Within five years, the Memorial had been designed and dedicated. Today, the site of the Murrah building is occupied by a large memorial. This memorial, designed by Oklahoma City architects Hans and Torrey Butzer and Sven Berg, includes a reflecting pool bookended by two large "doorways", one inscribed with the time 9:01, the opposite with 9:03, the pool between representing the moment of the blast. On the south end of the memorial is a field full of symbolic bronze and stone chairs—one for each person lost, arranged based on what floor they were on (photo 14.12). The seats of the children killed are smaller than those of the adults lost. On the opposite side is the "survivor tree", part of the building's original landscaping that somehow survived the blast and the fires that followed it. The memorial left part of the foundation of the building intact, so that visitors can see the scale of the destruction. Around the western edge of the memorial is a portion of the chain link fence erected after the blast on which thousands of people spontaneously left flowers, ribbons, teddy bears, and other mementos on in the weeks following the bombing.

The Oklahoma memorial also raises issues around commodification of grief. Many monuments and memorials are often accompanied by visitor centers, gift shops or kiosks, selling an assortment of "souvenirs": books, videos, refrigerator magnets, and t-shirts, none of which interpret or enhance the memorial experience. Sociologist John Urry has commented upon the emergence of a "tourist gaze" which seeks to consume "visually"—to take pictures and buy postcards and souvenirs—without necessarily thinking through the complexities of the experience.* In other words, society prefers to see, not think.

Off to the side of the Oklahoma City Bombing Memorial, which more than anything reflects sadness and loss, the Memorial Store sells jewelry, t-shirts, and stuffed animals. However, when visitors spend more time shopping for souvenirs of the memorial than they did thinking about the memorial, and contemplating its significance, then the memorial has become commodified—something to be consumed. This may ultimately trivialize the message of the memorial.

PHOTO 14.12. Oklahoma Bombing Memorial, Oklahoma City, Oklahoma.
Source: iStock/AwakenedEye

---

*John Urry. *The Tourist Gaze*, 2nd ed. London: Sage Publishers, 2002.

BOX 14.6   URBAN SUSTAINABILITY BEST PRACTICES: UNIVERSITY OF OKLAHOMA

Many universities are small cities. University of Oklahoma (OU), located in Norman, Oklahoma, just south of Oklahoma City, has thirty thousand students and employs just under three thousand faculty and staff. Universities with the most progressive efforts around sustainability typically have an office of Sustainability (that focuses on campus facilities) and academic and research initiatives (such as degrees and institutes in sustainability). It is also important that the university leadership embrace sustainability.

In April 2007, OU president Boren signed the *American College and University Presidents' Climate Commitment*, becoming the first institution's president in Oklahoma to sign the commitment and one of 152 college and university presidents and chancellors who have become charter signatories of the commitment at that time and pledged to eliminate greenhouse gas emissions over time. The commitment provides a framework

and support for colleges and universities to become climate neutral. The framework includes completing an emissions inventory, establishing a framework and interim milestones for becoming climate neutral, taking immediate steps to reduce greenhouse gas emissions, integrating sustainability into the curriculum and making it part of the educational experience, and making the action plan, inventory, and progress reports publicly available. By signing the charter, OU leadership recognized the responsibility that institutions of higher education have as role models for their communities and in training the people who will develop the social, economic, and technological solutions to reverse global climate change.

One example of this is that since 2013, 100 percent of the OU's purchased power comes from wind energy. OU has shown that Crimson is the new green.

The Primary Sector

The Great Plains and Canadian Prairie are major resource hinterlands for their respective countries.

Agricultural Landscape

The United States and Canada have supported a family farm agricultural economy that remains a standard in name, although most farmers are no longer independent family

operations. The family farm is tied to corporate inputs (feed, mechanical, and technological) and unless they have identified a niche market, it is also tied to corporate buyers. In order to remain in business, the family farm must produce according to corporate demands. Little is left to chance or the open market. Eighty percent of farmers now operate on negative income and would go out of business providing food for America if not for agricultural **subsidies** and off-farm jobs.

PHOTO 14.13. Calgary, Canada. Calgary's skyline at night with the Scotiabank Saddledome in the foreground. The dome with its unique saddle shape is home to the Calgary Flames NHL club, and is one of the oldest of the professional hockey arenas in North America.
Source: iStock/jewhyte

The average age of a US farmer today is over sixty years, and less than 8 percent are under the age of thirty-five. Every year there are larger farms and fewer farmers; less than 1 percent of the total population now claim farming as their major occupation.

Without government subsidies and corporate contracts, Canadian and American family farmers may disappear in the next generation. Farms are getting bigger and more expensive to operate; technological improvements are capital intensive and often require government-subsidized megafarms.

Although both the United States and Canada have prided themselves in maintaining a cheap food policy, subsidies are hidden costs that consumers pay with tax dollars. Subsidies have become a controversial subject both within the United States and within the globalized economy. Opponents argue that if farmers were any good they would not need subsidies. Farmers in less developed countries feel subsidies interfere with their right to compete. Yet without subsidies, American farmers would be unable to compete with the lower prices from abroad and food security would be weakened.

Irrigation

Irrigation artificially waters fields from sources other than precipitation. It is usually used in dry areas, or in areas with insufficient precipitation during the growing season. In the United States, irrigation is common in the major agricultural areas of the Mississippi River Valley of Arkansas, the High Plains, the Snake River Valley, the Columbia Plateau, and the Central Valley and Coachella and Imperial valleys of California.

On the Great Plains, unreliable natural precipitation has forced farmers to try several methods to stabilize water access. The lack of surface water has turned attention to larger water projects including unsuccessful diversion projects, such as the Trans-Texas Canal, and the successful Rocky Mountain trans-mountain diversion (see chapter 15). Dams built on the upper Missouri River and in Nebraska controlled flooding, provided irrigation, and generated power. West of the 100th meridian, 55 percent of all harvested cropland has been irrigated since the 1980s. Accessing the Ogallala Aquifer water has been the single most important resource for Great Plains agricultural production.

Water remains the single largest determining factor for crop yields. Technology-driven irrigation systems such as **center pivot irrigation (CPI)** support the High Plains corn, cow, and hog production. Irrigation systems have increased efficiency and conservation of water over the years, but the growth has exceeded the savings. Irrigation farming is most efficient and economical in flat country, such as the High Plains, so more than two hundred thousand wells were installed since Ogallala irrigation became viable in the 1960s, and water-efficient CPI circles now dot the otherwise dry landscape. Irrigated fields yield two to three times what dryland fields produce, but the challenge to maintain agricultural production for future generations requires analyzing current irrigation practices to determine sustainability.

The availability of irrigation water has also changed the choice of crops. While wheat and sorghum require little water, they are marginally profitable. More profitable crops such as corn require consistent water.

In the United States, water rights differ in the East and West. East of the Mississippi, riparian rights allocate water rights to all owners of water frontage land. Western water law revolves around "first in time, first in right" principle of **prior appropriation**, which allows "usage for any useful or beneficial purpose." In the West, water right law relegates water as a commodity that can be sold separate from the land. Senior rights holders may use or sell what they want, without regard to junior rights. Western water rights encourage those with first rights to waste water so they do not lose their rights. Current water rights laws are not national or regional, but statewide, and they often contradict the laws of surrounding states, which is adverse to sharing and water conservation.

Crops

Great Plains crops range from intensively grown cotton and sugar beets to extensive monocultures of grains, wheat, corn, and soy. The region produces over 60 percent of the wheat, 87 percent of the sorghum, and a third of the cotton, and it also raises over 60 percent of the nation's livestock. Crops are grown with capital-intensive tilling methods promoted by the Green Revolution, genetically modified crop (GMO) production, and fossil fuels (table 14.3).

Wheat   The United States grows about one-eighth of the world's wheat, and two-thirds of wheat production is on the Great Plains. At 50 percent, the American wheat crop is the most exported crop. Two types are grown, winter and spring wheat (map 14.4). Winter wheat is grown in the southern Great Plains and spring wheat north of the Nebraska Sand Hills. Wheat has been a dryland crop grown where precipitation was inadequate for thirstier corn.

Corn   The United States produces more corn than any other country in the world (map 14.5). Corn requires thirty inches of growing season precipitation, which was impossible on the Plains until fossil-fuel pumping of Ogallala groundwater was introduced in the 1960s. Great Plains corn production damages the landscape because growing corn in a region with more evaporation than precipitation upsets the water balance equilibrium. The fossil fuels used to grow corn and process it into food and other products far outstrip what it supplies in calories and energy.

Traditionally, about 70 percent of all corn is for livestock consumption, although in the twenty-first century, increasing amounts have been converted to ethanol. The remainder is used for human consumption in processed foods or as sweeteners

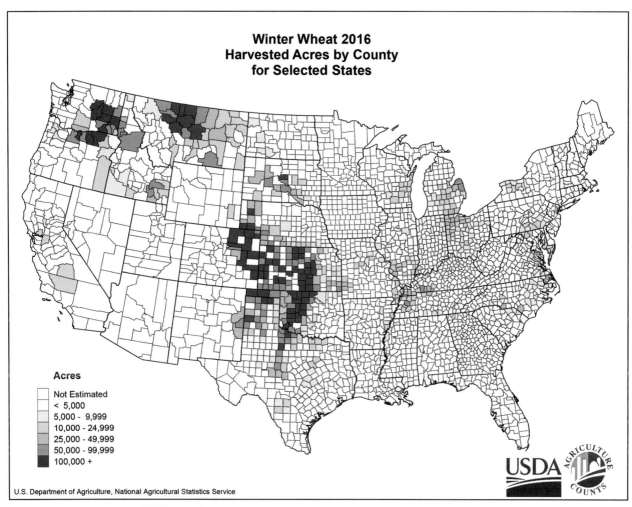

Winter Wheat 2016
Harvested Acres by County
for Selected States

Acres

- ☐ Not Estimated
- ☐ < 5,000
- ☐ 5,000 - 9,999
- ☐ 10,000 - 24,999
- ☐ 25,000 - 49,999
- ☐ 50,000 - 99,999
- ■ 100,000 +

U.S. Department of Agriculture, National Agricultural Statistics Service

USDA · AGRICULTURE COUNTS

MAP 14.4. Wheat, Harvested Acres, 2013. Wheat is the main crop grown in the Great Plains, because wheat is naturally suited to the semiarid climate and precipitation. Winter wheat is prevalent in the southern plains and spring wheat to the north.

Source: USDA

(high fructose corn syrup). Most corn grown is feed corn, not the sweet corn that is eaten on the cob.

Canola   In 1974, Canada satisfied a shortage of mono-unsaturated domestic oil by engineering a new crop, canola, from rapeseed. Used for industrial purposes, rapeseed oil is toxic to humans because of erucic acid. Canola was created and later genetically modified to substantially reduce the toxic acid. Canola is a cooking oil, a margarine, and a feed grain for sheep and cattle when there is a shortage of other feed grains. Fields of bright yellow canola grace the Northern Plains and the Canadian Prairie, where it is a major cash crop on a par with wheat production.

Livestock and the Meat-Processing Industry

Grazing land is usually unsuitable cropland because it lacks either fertility or water. The US and Canadian Plains have been long-time livestock producers. Today, the Plains supply 60 percent of grain-fed cattle and have over half of all

US and Canadian beef-processing plants. The cattle, dairy, and hog industries have grown apace with access to the Ogallala.

Cattle   Cattle have been an important industry on the Plains. However, the patterns have changed. Shipping beef to slaughterhouses in Chicago is no longer necessary. Refrigeration and transportation allows meat to be grown, fattened, and processed within miles of each other and then shipped globally. All three segments of beef production are now located on the High Plains. In Canada, 40 percent of beef cattle production is in Alberta, where feed and processing are combined.

Turning cattle into beef is a three-step process. Cows are grass-fed for six months, finishing in feedlots for eight months; then they are taken to the slaughterhouse. Feedlots are used for two reasons: feedlot cattle gain weight rapidly, and Americans have been told they like the taste of corn-fed meat over grass-fed. However, cattle are not genetically disposed to eating corn,

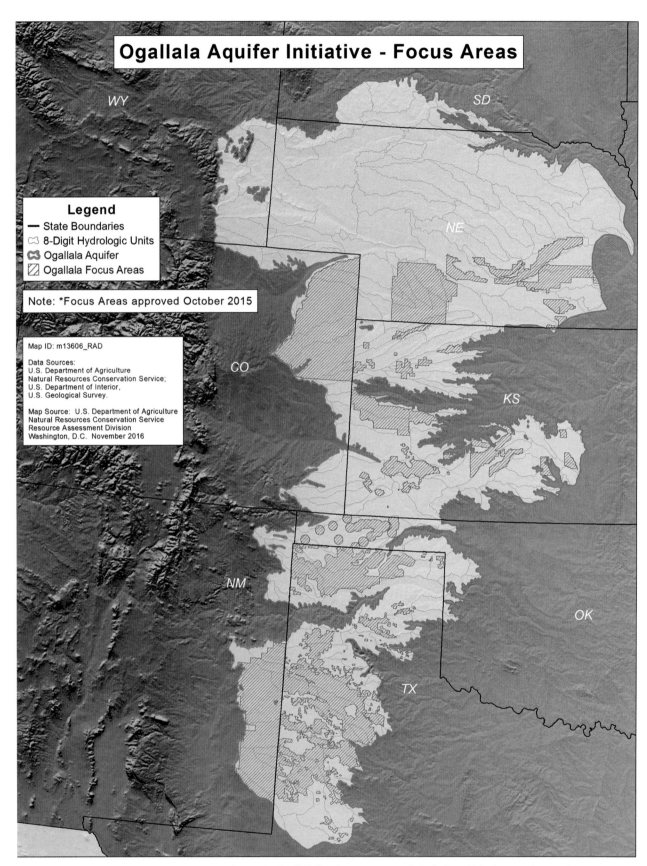

Ogallala Aquifer Initiative - Focus Areas

Legend
— State Boundaries
⌇ 8-Digit Hydrologic Units
🌀 Ogallala Aquifer
▨ Ogallala Focus Areas

Note: *Focus Areas approved October 2015

Map ID: m13606_RAD

Data Sources:
U.S. Department of Agriculture
Natural Resources Conservation Service;
U.S. Department of Interior,
U.S. Geological Survey.

Map Source: U.S. Department of Agriculture
Natural Resources Conservation Service
Resource Assessment Division
Washington, D.C. November 2016

WY   *SD*   *NE*   *CO*   *KS*   *NM*   *OK*   *TX*

MAP 14.5. Corn Harvested and Water Dependency on the Ogallala Aquifer, 2013. Corn is not grown naturally in the Great Plains because of a lack of moisture. After tapping the Ogallala Aquifer, corn crop production increased using aquifer water, but unsustainably.

Source: USDA

BOX 14.7 GLOBAL CONNECTIONS: US AGRICULTURAL EXPORTS

Agricultural exports have historically been a large part of US trade. Since 2000, developing countries—led by China—had been the main drivers of US export gains. Over the past ten years, US agricultural exports to China have grown over 13 percent annually on average. The top five markets for all agricultural exports are: Canada, China, Mexico, the European Union (EU), and Japan. US agricultural exports account for about $140 billion. Main exports include cotton, tree nuts, wheat, soybeans, fresh fruits, and pork.

China, one of the largest export markets for the US, purchases about $21 billion worth of soybeans, grains, hides and skins, pork, and cotton. China also receives much of the US-grown GM canola, corn, cotton, and soy products. Half of China's soy consumption is with US-grown GM soy, although the market may have peaked due to more US farmland raising corn for biofuel production.

US agricultural exports to Mexico account for approximately $18 billion and include corn, soybeans, pork, dairy products, and prepared food. Since the 1990s, the highest quality concentrated

animal feeding operation (CAFO) pork has been exported to the Japanese, who pay up to eight times more than Americans for fresh pork. US agricultural exports to japan totaled $11 billion in 2017. Along with pork, the Japanese import corn, beef, soybeans, and wheat.

Agricultural exports to the EU have been waning. The EU has restricted acceptance of GM products. As a result, US agricultural exports to the EU have vastly underperformed compared to the overall growth in US agricultural exports to the rest of the world. Since 2000, global US agricultural exports have increased 176 percent while exports to the EU have increased only 54 percent.* The ability of US agricultural and food exporters to penetrate the EU market is also constrained by tariff and nontariff trade barriers in combination with increased global competition. For example, over the past decade, Brazil has overtaken the United States as the top supplier to the EU notably in soybean and soybean meal shipments, which have grown much faster than US shipments.

*US Department of Agriculture, Foreign Agricultural Service. "Agricultural Exports to the European Union: Opportunities and Challenges," at https://www.fas.usda.gov/data/agricultural-exports-european-union-opportunities-and-challenges

---

as they are ruminants, but the fast weight gain for corn-fed meat has made this method almost ubiquitous.

A grass-fed beef niche market has evolved for those who prefer the health benefits and more direct transfer of solar energy to humans. Grass-fed beef are far less reliant on fossil fuels and are high in saturated fats and low in omega-3 fatty acids; corn-fed beef is responsible for increased heart disease. And cattle raised on grass and moved so as not to overgraze are similar to buffalo in relation to environmental health.

Livestock use only about 3 percent of regional water. However, livestock are fed corn. When water for corn is factored into livestock production, over 90 percent of water withdrawal from the aquifer is for livestock production. Additional environmental questions concern the intensive cattle-processing industry, manure disposal methods, and air and water pollution. The consequences of CAFOs can include the following:

- odors caused by gases created when manure decomposes;
- animal waste runoff (high in phosphorus and nitrogen) causes hypoxia and fish kills, degradation of water quality, and contamination of drinking water;
- low-wage and dangerous jobs, often taken by undocumented immigrants;
- health costs to CAFO farmers that include heart disease, stroke, diabetes, cancer, and respiratory illness; and

- antibiotic resistance in human population caused by overuse of antibiotics for growth promotion in cattle and hogs.

Hogs In 1995, CAFO hog production began in the Oklahoma and Texas panhandles and then diffused across the Plains states. The pork industry rationalized its move to the Plains by saying it would create jobs, stimulate a moribund rural economy, increase the tax base, and create a more efficient method of pork production. Other unstated reasons included the economic benefits, the availability of Ogallala water, the access to feed, a sparsely populated space, and lax environmental regulations. CAFO hog production in vertically integrated companies has prospered economically but has had dire environmental and social consequences (photo 14.14).

Mineral Resources

The quest for gold and other extractive minerals and possible riches is part of North America's legacy, and it has created numerous boom-bust stories. Coal and gold created boom-bust cycles that had geopolitical and environmental impacts in the Plains.

Oil and Gas Oil has shaped the economies of Texas and Oklahoma since the 1920s, when natural gas and oil fields across the Oklahoma panhandle and Texas's Permian basin provided about one-sixth of US petroleum production. Oil-well

PHOTO 14.14. Texas County, Oklahoma. Hog barns and lagoons are a common site on the Panhandle fields. Each hog barn holds a thousand hogs, whose waste is flushed into the lagoon. Lagoon wastewater fertilizes nearby fields, sometimes resulting in overfertilization and water pollution.

production boomed again in the early twenty-first century, when gasoline prices rose.

Two areas have increased oil and gas production: the northern Alberta oil sand fields (see chapter 18) and North Dakota's Williston Basin Bakken formation. North Dakota became the fourth major oil production site in the United States. Three to four billion barrels are estimated in the formation, and drilling has accelerated in the North Dakota–Saskatchewan region (map 14.6, photo 14.15).

A Sustainable Future

John Wesley Powell understood in the nineteenth century what the West still struggles with today: regional water is insufficient for a large population or for large-scale irrigation. Across the western states from the 100th meridian west, water conservation should be a priority, but few, Calgary excepted, have practical plans to institute conservation. In addition to water, there are numerous challenges to sustainability in the region, including the following:

- water access and quality and the long-term sustainability of the Ogallala Aquifer;
- climate change impacts on agricultural production;
- the decline of family farms;
- the recent expansion of hydraulic fracking in North Dakota and Saskatchewan;
- an economy based on the primary sector;
- a lack of diversity in population in many areas; and
- an aging population.

Despite these challenges, there are promising developments.

The Great Plains remains a primary producer of agricultural and livestock goods and maintaining this production has forced farms to seek more sustainable answers. Sustainable agriculture has been an important subject on the Plains for the past quarter century. Groups supporting Great Plains sustainability include the Grassland Foundation, Powering the Plains, the International Institute for Sustainable Development (IISD) in Winnipeg, Manitoba, and the venerable Land Institute in Kansas. The Land Institute has been working on developing sustainable agriculture, especially perennial over annual grains. A primary aim of the institute is to redesign agricultural methods to follow natural ecosystems while maintaining high yields.

The Grassland Foundation seeks to regenerate devastated grassland ecosystems that have converted to agriculture. Another project is to develop arrangements with cattle ranchers to improve and create sustainable grazing grasslands.

Powering the Plains is a regional effort by Manitoba and the northern Great Plains and Prairie states to address climate change while promoting economic development. The regional scale allows the states to work cooperatively in economic activities, including renewable and carbon-neutral energy sources. They seek to reduce carbon dioxide emissions to 80 percent of 1990 levels by 2050 and thereby create a more sustainable environment.

In addition, there has been advances in renewable energy, particularly wind power. Traditional Great Plains windmills are used to pump water for cattle and homes. In the past, several

PHOTO 14.15. Drilling the Bakken Formation in the Williston Basin.
Source: Joshua Doubek

decades more powerful wind turbines generate electricity. Texas, Iowa, and California remain the leaders in wind energy production, but northern Great Plains states and the Alberta Prairie are investing heavily in this abundant and sustainable resource. North Dakota alone has the potential to generate 36 percent of the nation's electricity.

Rural towns and farmsteads have found wind farms beneficial. A single tower producing a megawatt of electricity costs more than $1 million; however, towers also increase property taxes, farm incomes, tourism, and construction jobs. Wind farms provide jobs in aging farm communities that are losing young families. At first, companies built turbines on leased land that provided farmers with royalty payments, but farmers are now forming cooperatives to build and own turbines outright. Native Americans have also taken advantage of wind power.

The Standing Rock and Spirit Lake Sioux and the Turtle Mountain Chippewa are generating wind turbine electricity. In 1996, the Spirit Lake Sioux installed a wind turbine at Fort Totten, North Dakota, to power the Spirit Lake Casino. The purpose was to evaluate and establish the feasibility of wind power. In an area of high unemployment, wind farms also provide about 66 percent more jobs than either gas- or coal-fired power plants.

Alberta has been at the forefront of Canadian wind generation. Since 1996, windy Pincher Creek, just outside of

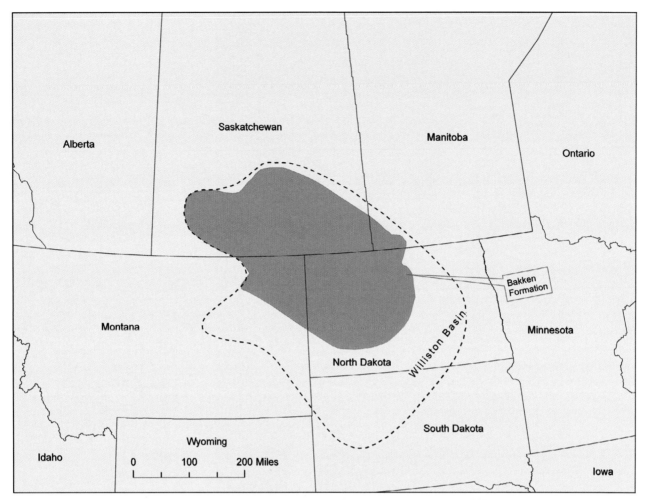

MAP 14.6. The Bakken Formation, North Dakota. Oil production dependent on hydraulic fracking has been booming since 2007, making North Dakota the fourth-biggest oil producer with more than four billion barrels of recoverable oil.

Lethbridge, Alberta, and at the junction of the prairie and the Rocky Mountains, has supported several large wind farms using the typical wind turbines along with the Canadian egg-beater turbines (photo 14.16). The wind farms provide some of southern Alberta's energy and give residents the option of buying green energy. Alberta now ranks third in Canada with an installed wind energy capacity of 1,479 MW. The province's wind farms produce enough electricity each year to power 625,000 homes, equivalent to about 6 percent of Alberta's electricity demand. The provincial government's new climate change plan promises to phase out the province's 6,300 MW of coal-fired electricity generation by 2030, and replace two-thirds of it with renewable energy. The percentage of demand met by renewable sources is expected to triple from 9 percent today to as much as 30 percent within fifteen years.

And in the heart of oil- and gas-rich Texas, wind power has been on the rise, so much so that Texas now produces the most wind power of any state. In fact, if it were its own country, Texas would be the fourth-largest largest wind-producing country in the world. Wind power accounted for about 12.5 percent of the electricity generated in Texas in 2017, avoiding the generation about 28 million tons of CO_2 emissions and saving nearly fifteen billions gallons of water—in a very thirsty region. Farmers may lease their land to wind developers, creating a new revenue stream for the farm. For many in the political conservative state, this is less about "sustainability" and more about green bucks—farmers and ranchers getting rich on windmills. Annual land lease payments in 2016, which went mostly to farmers and ranchers, were in excess of $60 million.

Wind's rise in Texas has been aided by the expansion of transmission capacity and market reforms. Strong state government incentives have played an important role. A 2005 law required every Texas citizen to pay for the building of transmissions line connecting the windy plains to population centers like Houston, Austin, Dallas, and San Antonio. It is a hopeful sign that a red state such as Texas, a state that depends heavily on oil and gas and therefore could see renewable energy as an economic threat, is taking the lead in wind power.

PHOTO 14.16. "Egg Beater" Wind Turbines, Pincher Creek, Alberta. Vertical-access, "egg beater" wind turbines generate power and tax money for the small town. Seventeen percent of Pincher Creek's 2006 revenue came from its wind farms. The federal and Alberta governments offer incentives to boost wind power production.

Questions for Discussion

1. How is the Great Plains a land of opportunity and a region of tragedy in America?

2. What was the original vegetation on the Plains and how does it differ from its current use? Is the current use sustainable? Why or why not?

3. Discuss the unique physical and ecological features of Great Plains topography, climate, water, and grasses. What features made European settlement of the Great Plains different from settlement of the eastern seaboard region?

4. Discuss urban trends and why this region is not highly urbanized.

5. Discuss the differences between immigration in the Great Plains versus the Canadian Prairie.

6. Describe the cattle industry in the past and in the present. How has irrigation affected the location of cattle feeding?

7. Where is the land irrigated on the Plains? What is grown on these areas? Is it sustainable?

8. How did railroad access affect regional production?

9. How has the Missouri River changed since European settlement?

10. What are the advantages and disadvantages of altering the course of rivers?

11. Why are subsidies offered to American farmers?

12. Discuss the types of water conservation efforts that would benefit this region.

Suggested Readings

Abbott, C., S. J. Leonard, and D. G. McComb. *Colorado: A History of the Centennial State*. Niwot: University Press of Colorado, 1994.

Beatty, C. B., and G. S. Young. *The Landscapes of Southern Alberta: A Regional Geomorphology*. Lethbridge: Alberta University at Lethbridge, 1975.

Bonanno, A., and D. H. Constance. *Stories of Globalization: Transnational Corporations, Resistance, and the State*. University Park: Pennsylvania State University Press, 2008.

Bowden, M. "The Great American Desert and the American Frontier, 1800–1882: Popular Images of the Plains." In *Anonymous Americans: Explorations in Nineteenth-Century*

Social History, edited by T. K. Hareven. Englewood Cliffs, N.J.: Prentice-Hall, 1971.

Brooks, E., and J. Emel. *The Llano Estacado of the U.S. Southern High Plains*. Tokyo: United Nations University Press, 2000.

Callenbach, E. *Bring Back the Buffalo! A Sustainable Future for America's Great Plains*. Berkeley: University of California Press, 2000.

Francis, R. D., and C. Kitzan, eds., *The Prairie West as Promised Land*. Calgary, Alberta: University of Calgary Press, 2007.

Hamalainen, P. "The Rise and Fall of Plains Indian Horse Cultures." *Journal of American History* 90, no. 3 (2004).

Hamilton, M., and Z. Macaulay. *These Are the Prairies*. Regina, Saskatchewan: School Aids and Text Book Publishing Co., n.d. (approximately 1950).

Hart, J. F., and C. Mayda. "Pork Palaces in the Panhandle." *Geographic Review* 87 (1997).

Hewes, L. *The Suitcase-Farming Frontier: A Study in the Historical Geography of the Central Great Plains*. Lincoln: University of Nebraska Press, 1973.

Hudson, J. C. *Crossing the Heartland: Chicago to Denver*. New Brunswick, N.J.: Rutgers University Press, 1992.

James, E. *Account of an expedition from Pittsburgh to the Rocky Mountains*. Philadelphia, Pa.: H. C. Carrey, 1823.

Jordan, T., J. L. Bean Jr., and W. M. Holmes. *Texas: A Geography*. Boulder, Colo.: Westview Press, 1984.

Leonard, S. J., and T. J. Noel. *Denver: Mining Camp to Metropolis*. Boulder: University Press of Colorado, 1990.

McIntosh, C. B. *The Nebraska Sand Hills: The Human Landscape*. Lincoln: University of Nebraska Press, 1996.

Meinig, D. W. *Southwest: Three Peoples in Geographical Change, 1600–1970*. New York: Oxford University Press, 1971.

Merchant, C. *American Environmental History*. New York: Columbia University Press, 2007.

Mutel, C. F., and J. C. Emerick. *From Grassland to Glacier: The Natural History of Colorado*. Boulder, Colo.: Johnson Books, 1984.

Norris, K. *Dakota: A Spiritual Geography*. Boston, Mass.: Houghton Mifflin, 1993.

Opie, J. *Ogallala: Water for a Dry Land*. Lincoln: University of Nebraska Press, 1993.

Pollan, M. *Omnivore's Dilemma: A Natural History of Four Meals*, New York: Penguin Press, 2006

Potyondi, B. *In Palliser's Triangle: Living in the Grasslands*. Saskatoon, Saskatchewan: Purich Press, 1995.

Spry, I. M. *The Palliser Expedition*. Toronto: Macmillan, 1963.

Starrs, P. *Let the Cowboy Ride: Cattle Ranching in the American West*. Baltimore: Johns Hopkins University Press, 1998.

Steward, D. "Tapping Unsustainable Groundwater Stores for Agricultural Production in the High Plains Aquifer of Kansas, Projections to 2110." In *Proceedings of the National Academy of Sciences* 110, no. 37 (2013), at http://www.pnas.org/content/110/37/E3477.abstract

Webb, W. P. *The Great Plains*. Lincoln: University of Nebraska Press, 1931

Welsted, J. E., C. Stadel, and J. C. Everitt, eds. *The Geography of Manitoba*. Winnipeg: University of Manitoba Press, 1997.

Worster, D. *Dust Bowl: The Southern Plains in the 1930s*. New York: Oxford University Press, 1979.

Internet Sources

Calgary's Sustainability Plan, at http://www.calgary.ca/PDA/pd/Pages/Office-of-Sustainability/Office-of-Sustainability.aspx

Dallas's Sustainability Plan, at http://greendallas.net/sustainability-plan/.

Great Plains Nature Center, at http://www.gpnc.org/

Statistics Canada. Browse Alberta, Saskatchewan and Manitoba at http://www12.statcan.gc.ca/census-recensement/2016/dp-pd/prof/index.cfm?Lang=E

Kansas Department of Agriculture. Ogallala–High Plains Aquifer, at http://agriculture.ks.gov/divisions-programs/dwr/managing-kansas-water-resources/information-about-kansas-water-resources/ogallala-high-plains-aquifer

Kansas University/Kansas Geological Survey High Plains Aquifer Atlas, at http://www.kgs.ku.edu/HighPlains/HPA_Atlas/index.html

Manitoba's Visa Provincial Nominee Program, at http://www.canadavisa.com/manitoba-provincial-nominee-program.html

NASA's "GRACE Tellus," at https://grace.jpl.nasa.gov/applications/groundwater/Northern Prairie Wildlife Research Center, at http://www.npwrc.usgs.gov/

Oklahoma University's Sustainability Report and Updates, at http://www.ou.edu/content/sustainability/currentpractices.html

U.S. Geological Survey. "America's Volcanic Past: South Dakota," at http://vulcan.wr.usgs.gov/LivingWith/VolcanicPast/Places/volcanic_past_south_dakota.html

U.S. Department of Agriculture. Natural Resources Conservation Service, the Ogallala Aquifer Initiative, at https://www.nrcs.usda.gov/wps/portal/nrcs/detailfull/national/programs/initiatives/?cid=stelprdb1048809

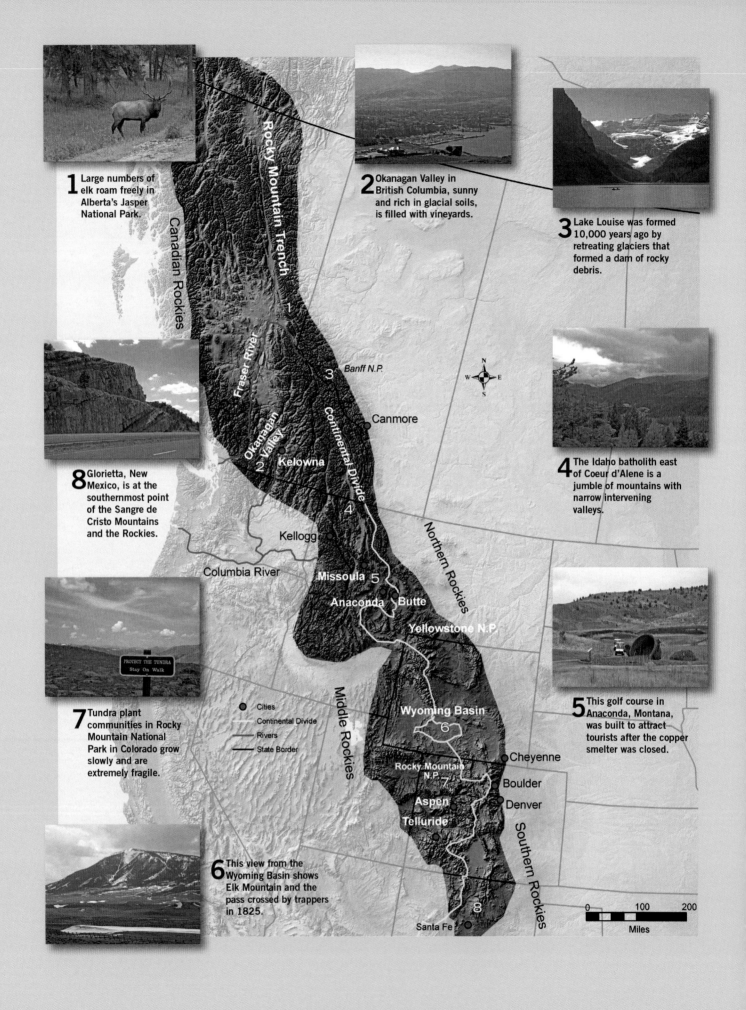

1 Large numbers of elk roam freely in Alberta's Jasper National Park.

2 Okanagan Valley in British Columbia, sunny and rich in glacial soils, is filled with vineyards.

3 Lake Louise was formed 10,000 years ago by retreating glaciers that formed a dam of rocky debris.

4 The Idaho batholith east of Coeur d'Alene is a jumble of mountains with narrow intervening valleys.

5 This golf course in Anaconda, Montana, was built to attract tourists after the copper smelter was closed.

6 This view from the Wyoming Basin shows Elk Mountain and the pass crossed by trappers in 1825.

7 Tundra plant communities in Rocky Mountain National Park in Colorado grow slowly and are extremely fragile.

8 Glorietta, New Mexico, is at the southernmost point of the Sangre de Cristo Mountains and the Rockies.

Canadian Rockies

Rocky Mountain Trench

Fraser River

Okanagan Valley

Continental Divide

Banff N.P.

Canmore

Kelowna

Kellogg

Columbia River

Missoula 5

Anaconda Butte

Yellowstone N.P.

Northern Rockies

Middle Rockies

Wyoming Basin

6

Rocky Mountain N.P. 7

Aspen

Telluride

Cheyenne

Boulder

Denver

Southern Rockies

8

Santa Fe

Cities
Continental Divide
Rivers
State Border

N
W   E
S

0   100   200
Miles

15
THE ROCKY MOUNTAINS
High in Elevations, Aspirations, and Appreciation

Chapter Highlights

After reading this chapter, you should be able to:

- Identify the major subregions of the Rockies in the United States and Canada
- Explain the Mining Law of 1872 and the environmental issues with abandoned mines
- Describe the location and importance of South and Crowsnest passes
- Define a boom and bust town and discuss the consequences
- Identify and discuss the importance of Okanagan Valley
- Compare and contrast Canmore and Banff
- Discuss the impact of recent population growth in the Rockies
- Identify and describe the importance of the Canadian Rockies areas and major ice fields
- Describe the significance and location of the Rocky Mountain continental divide
- Discuss the historic and current settlement patterns within the Rockies
- Discuss the ways natural resources remain a key part of the regional economy
- Discuss the importance of the tertiary sector of the economy

Terms

batholith
boom and bust town
Bureau of Land
   Management (BLM)

carbon neutral
continental divide
cordillera
ghost town
hogback

land trust
Law of the Indies
Mining Law of 1872
park
transhumance

transmountain diversion
tree line
trophic cascade
vertical zonation

Places

Banff National Park
Canadian Rockies

Colorado Mineral Belt
Columbia Icefield
Front Range
Middle Rockies

Northern Rockies
Okanagan Valley
Rocky Mountain Trench
Southern Rockies

Wyoming Basin
Yellowstone National Park

Cities

Anaconda, Montana
   (2016 MSA 9,000)
Boulder, Colorado
   (2016 MSA 322,000)
Butte, Montana
   (2016 MSA 33,900)

Cheyenne, Wyoming
   (2016 MSA MSA 98,000)
Denver, Colorado
   (2016 MSA 2.8 million)

Fort Collins, Colorado
   (2016 MSA 164,000)
Kelowna, British Columbia
   (2016 CMA 125,000)

Missoula, Montana
   (2016 MSA 116,000)
Santa Fe, New Mexico
   (2016 MSA 148,000)

PHOTO 15.1. Bighorn River, Alberta, Canadian Rockies. The river is named for the bighorn sheep in the area.

Introduction

The sight of the Rocky Mountains exhilarates almost everyone who has driven the hours and miles of the flat Great Plains (photo 15.1). Here is where the West begins.

The physical barrier of the Rockies governs the weather, precipitation, and—most importantly for the West—the flow of water. Before World War II, water was not as much an issue because few people had settled in the region, but that has changed; water has become a critical commodity to a growing population.

The booms and busts are cyclic: property is worth nothing one day, a fortune the next, and nothing again the day after. Same too for population growth. The current population boom has been where the water is not. The Great Plains lie in the rain shadow of the Rocky Mountains, and the largest cities of both the Plains and the Rockies (Denver and Boulder) lie in that rain shadow, along the Front Range (photo 15.2). Providing water for the growing Front Range population has required major diversions that have impacted entire watersheds and their ecosystems.

The Native Americans used the Rocky Mountains as a hunting ground. The first Europeans arrived as fur trappers and mined beavers almost to extinction when, luckily for the beaver, these fur hats went out of fashion. Next, miners exploited the resources, resulting in toxic pollution from the mining methods. When mining was played out, the region reinvented itself as a recreational frontier.

For much of the nineteenth and twentieth centuries, mining and logging extraction dominated the economies and politics. Since the 1970s, however, federal policies encourage development of extraction industries; while environmentalists push back for preservation; the recreational public wants the mythic West; the affluent have made the Rockies home to two of America's wealthiest counties. Ranchers have grazed their livestock on federal land for a century, but urban development brings new residents with different agendas. The result has been clashes between ranchers, environmentalists, industry, the recreationally oriented public, and new residents. It's the new Wild West out there.

BOX 15.1 DID YOU KNOW . . . THE ROCKIES

- The Rocky Mountains extend about 3,000 miles (5,000 km) from New Mexico to the Yukon Territory.
- They are composed of many ranges. For example, Wyoming alone has twenty ranges.
- They range in elevation from 4,500 feet (1,500 m) to 14,000+ feet (4,267+ m).

- Most 14,000-foot peaks are in the Southern Rockies.
- Range width is between 70 and 400 miles (120 and 650 km).
- Climate change is altering vegetation and wildlife.

PHOTO 15.2. Front Range, Rising behind Denver, Colorado. The contrast of the elevated Rockies after miles of the flat Plains is a dramatic sight.

Physical Geography

The many ranges of the Rocky Mountain **cordillera** stretch from Alaska to New Mexico, rising above the Plains to the east and melding into the western plateaus. The narrow mountain system in the south widens in Colorado (300 miles), tapers in the Northern Rockies of Montana (150 miles), and widens again into the multiple ranges of the Canadian Rockies. The **continental divide** separates the Atlantic and Pacific watersheds along the crest of the Rocky Mountain system, dividing ecoregions. In the Canadian Rockies, the divide separates British Columbia and Alberta for a considerable distance, as does the border between the Yukon and the Northwest territories.

The multiple ranges and rock types of the Rockies were formed in stages over millions of years. Uplift, deposition, and erosion along with tectonic activity shaped the mountains and the distribution of surface water and groundwater. During the most recent uplift, deposits eroded, tilted, and exposed ancient core rocks, such as the steeply tilted **hogbacks** along the Piedmont of the Front Range.

For example, Rocky Mountain runoff discharge once fed the Ogallala Aquifer, but uplift cut the aquifer off from its water source, and today the recharge is limited to the scant precipitation that falls. Aquifers underlying the Denver Basin are also cut off from rivers and are difficult to recharge, making water conservation ever more critical in a region that has been one of the fastest growing in America. While Denver relies on surface water, growth areas outside of Denver depend on aquifers and are withdrawing water far more quickly than the aquifers are being recharged. This has forced the transport of water and affected environmental areas far beyond the immediate area.

Rocky Mountains

The Rocky Mountains are divided into five latitudinal subregions:

- Southern Rockies (New Mexico and Colorado)
- Middle Rockies (Utah and Wyoming)
- Northern Rockies (Montana and Idaho)
- Canadian Rockies (Alberta/British Columbia)
- Brooks Range (part of the Alaska/North; chapter 18)

BOX 15.2 NATIONAL PARKS: RETURNING WOLVES TO YELLOWSTONE

Yellowstone National Park is much beloved. It is America's first national park, known for scenic views, dramatic canyons, alpine rivers, gushing geysers including Old Faithful and hundreds of animal species including bears, bison, elk and antelope.

It is also known as an example of a **trophic cascade.** A trophic cascade is an ecological process that starts at the top of a food chain and trickles down to the bottom. A classic example of this is the reintroduction of wolves in Yellowstone.

The gray wolf was present in Yellowstone when the park was established in 1872. Westward expansion in the late nineteenth and early twentieth centuries brought settlers and their livestock into direct contact with the parks native predator and prey species, and park managers instituted a policy of "predator control." At the time, park managers believed the wolves destroyed "more desirable" wildlife species such as deer and elk, and hunted livestock. Between 1914 and 1926, at least 136 wolves were killed in the park; by the 1940s, wolf packs were rarely reported.[*] This policy occurred in a era before geographers, biologists, and ecologists fully understood the concepts of ecosystem and interconnectedness of species.

In 1973, a better understanding of ecosystem dynamics led to the passage of the Endangered Species Act. Under this law the US Fish and Wildlife Service is required to restore endangered species that have been eliminated, if possible. Because all wolf subspecies were on the federal list of endangered species, Yellowstone park management began to study the possible reintroduction of the gray wolf. In 1995, thirty-one gray wolves from western Canada were relocated to Yellowstone (photo 15.3).

Scientists have been studying the impact of this reintroduction. Studies have documented the dramatic changes to the park ecosystem, concluding that the presence of a small number of gray wolves triggered a still-unfolding cascade effect among animals and plants.

Although bears and cougars still preyed on deer, the absence of the wolves removed a significant predatory pressure off the elk and deer. As a result, elk populations pushed the limits of the park's carrying capacity. The elk also did not move around as much in the winter since there were no wolves to keep them on the move. In turn, the elk overgrazed young willow aspen and cottonwood plants. That limited the beaver population, who need willows to survive in winter.

When wolves were reintroduced they began to hunt and kill elk, but that was not the most significant change. They radically changed

PHOTO 15.3. The gray wolf has been reintroduced to Yellowstone Park.
Source: iStock/NathanHobbs

the *behavior* of the elk, who began avoiding areas where they could be trapped easily by wolves, such as the valleys sides and gorges. And those places began to change. Trees began to grow higher—aspen and willow returned and then the number of songbirds started to increase. The wolves killed coyotes, which in turn lead to an increase in rabbits and mice, which in turn attracted more birds of prey such as hawks, weasels and foxes. Scavengers such as ravens and magpies have also benefited. Beaver populations began to increase, and since they are "ecosystem engineers," the dams they built in the rivers provided habitats for other animals such as otters, muskrats, and ducks. Beaver dams have multiple effects on stream hydrology. They even out the seasonal pulses of runoff; store water for recharging the water table; and provide cold, shaded water for fish. Studies showed that rivers experienced less erosion, because regenerating forests helped to stabilize the banks of the rivers.

Although small in number, wolves transformed not just the ecosystem of Yellowstone but also its physical geography.

It may be too soon to declare that the reintroduction of wolves "saved" Yellowstone. Some scientists disagree about the impact of the wolves. Ecosystems are so complex we still do not fully understand (or agree on) their dynamics.

Regardless, the reintroduction of the wolf and the ensuing debate about ecosystem change have given scientists the rare opportunity to document what happens when a key species is added back into the ecosystem equation.

---

*National Park Service. "Yellowstone Wolf Restoration," at: https://www.nps.gov/yell/learn/nature/wolf-restoration.htm

Southern Rockies

The Southern Rocky Mountains extend from New Mexico into Wyoming, but the core and highest peaks are in Colorado, "the Rocky Mountain State." The glaciated peaks range from six thousand feet to more than fifty peaks over fourteen thousand feet. The high-elevation Southern Rocky Mountains make travel difficult, so most trails are to the north or south. There are the undulating rhythm of ranges and **parks**, the treeless, broad, grassy plateaus between the ranges. The mountains surround the high elevation parks, and although the surrounding ranges have deep snowpack, the rain shadow protects the parks from heavy snowfalls, allowing ranchers to graze their livestock and grow a few crops.

The fifty-mile-wide swath of the Colorado Mineral Belt (pyrite, gold, silver, and copper) stretches between the Four Corners area (Arizona, New Mexico, Utah, and Colorado) and Boulder, Colorado. Most of the boom-bust towns in the Southern Rockies are within this belt.

Dividing the Southern Rocky Mountains from the High Plains is the transitional Colorado Piedmont basin. The gateway cities to the Rockies—Denver and Colorado Springs—lie along the Piedmont's South Platte and Arkansas rivers and their tributaries.

Middle Rockies

The Middle Rockies occupy most of Wyoming, northern Utah, and edge into eastern Idaho. The Middle Rockies are not as impressive or as tall as the southern ranges, but they contain the majestic Tetons and the transition to the Northern Rockies, home to Yellowstone National Park. Other distinctive features are the Wyoming Basin, South Pass, and the Great Divide. The gradually ascending Wyoming Basin (six thousand to eight thousand feet) connects the Great Plains and the Colorado Plateau through the gap between the Laramie and Bighorn mountains. The basin divides the Middle and Southern Rockies and can be approached from the east at the headwaters of the North Platte and Green rivers. The Wyoming Basin provides entry to the Intermontane without ever crossing a mountain range.

The Great Divide Basin splits the Wyoming Basin near Rawlins, and it contains numerous sand dunes and alkali flats. Water from the Great Divide Basin stays within the divide, as it loses more water by evaporation than it gains in precipitation. The basin has been a primary mining site for oil and gas deposits and uranium.

Northern Rockies

The isolated Northern Rockies span western Montana, the Idaho Panhandle, and the northeastern corner of Washington to the Canadian border. Twenty-one percent of Idaho and Montana land is national forest, most of it within the Northern Rocky Mountain system. The national forest has multiple uses, including lumber, oil, mountain biking, hiking, and preservation of species. In some cases, these various uses are not compatible with each other and the "right" use of a forest has become both contested and political.

The Idaho **batholith** (intrusive igneous rock) lies north of the Snake River Valley. Rivers have cut and eroded multiple uneven and narrow valleys (photo 15.4). The only linear range, the Sawtooth Range, is located just north of the Snake River Valley. Across the northern panhandle, only one major road traverses the jumble of granitic mountains.

PHOTO 15.4. The Idaho Batholith, East of Coeur d'Alene along Highway I-90, the Only Major Highway across the Panhandle. The mountains are characterized by narrow intervening valleys was taken. Notice the clear-cuts on the mountainsides.

Montana's Bitterroot Mountains frame the eastern edge of the batholith. The downfaulted Bitterroot Valley once held a lake, but it drained through a river-cut gorge. The lake alluvium, temperate climate, and abundant water supplies were well suited to agriculture, making the valley the "bread basket" for mining campus throughout southwestern Montana in the late nineteenth and early twentieth centuries. Later, the lumber industry began its development.

The Bitterroots were the site of a controversial logging of burned-over forest, pitting environmentalists against the local job-seeking population. Wilderness resources have become lucrative areas for exploitation, particularly as resource availability in other areas becomes stressed, and as prices rise, more people extract resources from the wilderness.

Canadian Rockies

The Canadian Rockies extend across the interior ranges and plateaus of British Columbia. Along the Yukon border, the mountains are interspersed with plateaus, lowlands, and valleys. The Liard Plateau at the Yukon border breaks the Rocky Mountain continuity and, some believe, terminates the Rocky Mountain system, although others contend that the system ends in Alaska's Brooks Range. Two major passes—Crowsnest and Yellowhead—along the Alberta–British Columbia border provide rail and highway access between the coast and the Plains. Crowsnest, near the US border, is the lowest-elevation pass across the Canadian Rockies.

Between the 49th parallel and the 54th parallel, more than thirty of the ruggedly handsome mountains surpass ten thousand feet, the tallest being Mount Robson (12,989 feet) near Yellowhead Pass. The narrow, folded, and faulted ranges tower above long, flat-floored valleys. The Alberta valleys contain the tourist towns of Banff, Jasper, and Canmore, while British Columbia contains several valleys, including the Okanagan and the Rocky Mountain Trench.

The westernmost valley in the cordillera is the long, narrow Rocky Mountain Trench (one thousand miles by fifteen miles), which stretches north from Flathead Lake in Montana. The trench is of uncertain origin, although both glaciers and faulting played a part in its formation. Numerous rivers—the Kootenay, Columbia, and Fraser—have their headwaters in the trench.

To the west of the trench, the Columbia Mountains are composed of the Purcell, Selkirk, Monashee, and Cariboo ranges. The glacially derived Kootenay, Arrow, and Okanagan lakes lie in valleys between the ranges.

The United States and Canada share the slender, mountain-ringed Okanagan Valley (Canada spells it Okanagan, the United States Okanogan) along the Okanagan Lake and River. The sunny Okanagan Valley interior plateau separates the coastal mountains from the Rockies; it extends hundreds of miles north and also south into Central Washington. At the border in Osoyoos is Canada's celebrated and only desert, a northern outlier of the Sonoran Desert.

Seventeen icefields crown the Canadian Rockies. The largest, the Columbia Icefield, lies between Banff and Jasper, feeds six glaciers, and is the largest glacial agglomeration south of the Arctic Circle. The snow dome atop the icefield straddles three continental divides, so water from the dome may flow into the Pacific, Atlantic, or Arctic oceans. The Athabascan glacier is the largest glacier in the icefield, but it has retreated more than a mile over the past hundred years and continues to retreat about six feet annually (photo 15.5).

PHOTO 15.5. Athabasca Glacier, Columbia Icefield, Jasper National Park, Alberta, Canada. The glacier has retreated more than a mile since 1890 and continues to retreat about six feet per year. The drift between the glacier and the sign are moraines.

TABLE 15.1. Major Rivers Whose Headwaters Are in the Rockies

River	Length(miles)	Watershed basin (square miles)	Subregion	Headwater near
Columbia River	1,243	260,000	Canadian Rockies	Columbia Valley, Rocky Mountain Trench, British Columbia
Fraser River	850	89,962 (233,000 km²)	Canadian Rockies	Yellowhead Pass, Mount Robson, British Columbia
North Saskatchewan River	800	15,830 (41,000 km²) Branch of Saskatchewan River, confluence near Prince Albert Sas.	Canadian Rockies	Saskatchewan Glacier, Columbia Icefield, Alberta
Snake River	1,038	72,000 Tributary of Columbia River	Middle Rockies	Jackson Hole, Wyoming
Missouri River	2,315	500,000	Middle Rockies	Yellowstone National Park, confluence of three rivers (Madison, Gallatin, Jefferson)
Green River	730	30,000 Part of Colorado	Middle Rockies	Wind River Range, Sublette County, Wyoming
Colorado River	1,450	246,000	Southern Rockies	Rocky Mountain National Park
Arkansas River	1,459	247,000	Southern Rockies	Leadville, Lake County, Colorado
Platte River	990	90,000	Southern Rockies	Routt National Forest, Park Range, Colorado
Rio Grande	1,900	185,000	Southern Rockies	San Juan Mountains, San Juan County, Colorado

Water

The Rocky Mountain river watershed drains about two-thirds of the continent into three continental drainage basins (table 15.1); the Southern Rockies drain two-thirds of its runoff to the Atlantic, whereas 80 percent of the Northern Rockies and southern Canada drain to the Pacific (with the remainder draining to the Arctic).

Rivers

The Rocky Mountains serve as the wellspring for the major western rivers. The Missouri, Platte, and Arkansas rivers all have their headwaters in the Rockies and drain into the Mississippi watershed. The Colorado River begins in Colorado and is the main water source for the driest part of the United States; it drains into the Gulf of California. The Columbia, Snake, and Fraser Rivers all begin on the Pacific slope of the continental divide.

Lakes

Faulting, glacial deposits, and structural depressions form Rocky Mountain lakes. For example, faulting, glacial deposits, and volcanic action formed Yellowstone Lake, the largest lake in the Middle Rockies. It once drained southward into the Snake River, but faulting blocked the outlet; it now drains into the Yellowstone River, eroding the Grand Canyon of the Yellowstone in the process.

Many of the lakes on the western slope of the Rocky Mountains are artificial, formed by damming waters for water storage and diversion. These reservoirs, such as Shadow Mountain, Willow Creek, and Granby lakes on the western slope and Carter Lake and Boulder Reservoir on the eastern slope, are part of the Colorado Transmountain River Project (see below).

Water Transfers

The Great Plains and the West lack their own water sources and depend on Rocky Mountain water, most of which flows to the sparsely populated West, not the more populated and drier Front Range cities (map 15.1). Supporting the growing Front Range population requires controlling the water for irrigation projects using dams and interbasin water transfers.

Water transfers were also attempted in Canada, with disastrous results. In 1966, British Columbia built the Peace River Valley W. A. C. Bennett Dam, which transmits its power six hundred miles to Vancouver. The adverse environmental impact and social damage to the local West Moberly First Nation peoples was unrecognized for decades.

Colorado Transmountain Water Projects

Colorado has a water problem. Most of the water is west of the continental divide (the windward side of the mountains) but most of the people live along the drier Front Range to the east. Colorado's Front Range cities contain about 80 percent of the state's population; however, they are in the rain shadow and receive little precipitation and only 15 percent of stream runoff. Agriculture claims most Front Range water, leaving little for the urban population. Since water rights can be sold in the West, entrepreneurs in the Front Range created water markets to transfer western water to their homes. Claims for water rights in urban developments often require a water broker and must go through water court. It gets expensive.

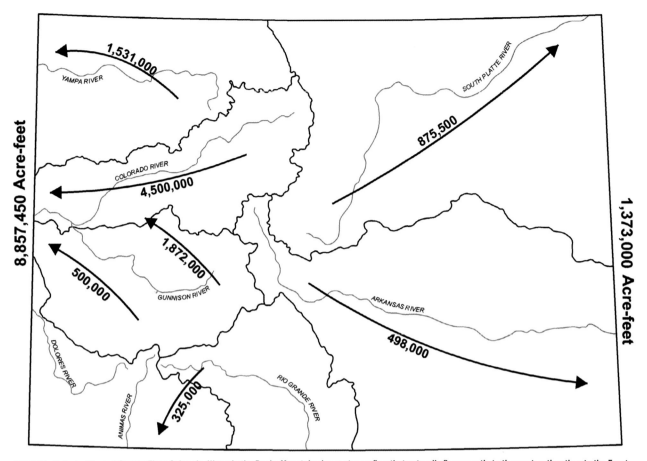

MAP 15.1. Historical Annual Stream Flow, Colorado. Water in the Rocky Mountains has a stream flow that naturally flows mostly to the west, rather than to the Front Range where most of the population lives. Large water diversion projects like the Big Thompson have changed this flow to the Front Range, at great economic and environmental cost.

Deals for urban water are made privately, without government involvement. In Colorado, the Front Range Piedmont residents must pay a tap fee to receive water. While Idaho residents may pay $325 per acre-foot of water (326,000 gallons = 1 acre-foot), Colorado residents pay as much as $20,000 per acre-foot. The water deals are made with the private right holders, and prices have escalated as demand grows. The major water source to the Front Range cities has been western slope water. More than twenty **transmountain diversions** ship water over the mountains.

The Colorado River Basin, located along the western edge of the Southern Rockies, has 97 percent of its water diverted for agricultural use and yet it also provides 35 percent of Denver's and 65 percent of Colorado Springs' water supply via transmountain diversion.

The Colorado–Big Thompson Project (the Big T) serves thirty cities and includes twelve reservoirs and thirty-five miles of tunnels that provide water for some 925,000 residents. It also irrigates some 640,000 acres of farmland in northeastern Colorado. Tunnels transport water from the western slope of Colorado River Basin under the continental divide to eastern slope reservoirs. Water then generates electricity and is allotted for agricultural and urban uses.

The transmountain diversions have impacted the environment and generated controversy. While the project was originally built for agricultural purposes, it serves multiple demands including municipal and industrial supply, hydro-power generation, recreation, and fish and wildlife. In recent years, however, water supply demands have shifted, making municipal and industrial supply the main water beneficiary, rather than irrigation. Recent droughts, in combination with climate change (and shrinking snowpack), could mean limited supplies will force Coloradans to make difficult choices among the state's municipal, agricultural, energy, recreation, and environmental needs.

Climate

The temperature differential between the Rocky Mountain peaks and the adjacent Great Plains is 35°F, about the same as between the Great Plains and Alaska. Although the Rockies adjoin the Plains, the difference can be accounted for by the air temperature decrease when elevation increases—**vertical zonation.**

Vertical zonation and latitude characterize Rocky Mountain climate patterns and the distribution of plants and wildlife. In the southern ranges, plants and animals are desertlike at the

BOX 15.3   CLIMATE CHANGE IN THE ROCKIES

The planet's temperature has risen 1.4°F, and while 1.4 degrees is barely perceptible to human skin, it is warm enough to melt snow.

A million square miles of spring snow-cover in the Northern Hemisphere has disappeared in the last forty-five years—including 20 percent of the spring snowpack in the Rockies and 35 percent in the Cascades. According to data from the National Oceanic and Atmospheric Administration (NOAA), the National Aeronautics and Space Administration (NASA), and the United Nations, spring snowpack in many parts of Western Washington, Oregon, and Northern California has dropped 50–70 percent since the early 1900s. Spring arrives in California's Tahoe ski resort two and a half weeks earlier now than in 1961.

Studies suggest that by 2050, winter temperatures in the Northwest could warm by 5.4 degrees, and the Cascades could lose another 40–70 percent of their snowpack. One study speculates that the Rocky Mountains will warm an additional seven degrees in the next eighty-five years, leaving Park City with no snow and Aspen with only the upper quarter of its current terrain snow-covered.

This will have a big impact on ski resort towns in the Rockies whose economies are dependent on snowfall. Colorado state is home to twenty-five ski resorts that draw over 12.5 million skiers each winter. The ski business generates $4.8 billion in annual economic impacts and supports over forty-six thousand jobs. It may sound obvious but if it does not snow, no one comes to town to ski, buy apres cocktails, or stay in hotels. A study by the University of Maryland estimated that Colorado could lose $375 million in revenue and forty-five hundred jobs by 2020 due to skier attrition from lack of snow.[*]

In response to growing concerns, more than 190 resorts around the United States and Canada have adopted the "Sustainable Slopes Charter" launched in 2000. The Charter contains voluntary environmental principles that affect ski areas, including resort operation, planning and design, water and energy use, habitat and forest management, and waste management.

Ski resorts like Aspen and Telluride are also part of the Charter's "Climate Challenge Program." These resorts inventory and report on their carbon footprints, set goals for carbon reduction, implement at least one on-site carbon reduction strategy per year, and engage in climate change advocacy efforts. Aspen, for example, is implementing projects that include lighting retrofits and high efficiency snowmaking as a way to reduce carbon emissions. Copper Mountain in Colorado Copper Mountain Ski Resort installed occupancy sensors, a wind turbine, a solar furnace, and timers on various electrical devices.

*Sean Williamson, Ruth Matthais, Kim Ross, and Daraius Irani. *Economic Impacts of Climate Change on Colorado*, for the Center for Integrative Environmental Research, University of Maryland (2008), at http://cier.umd.edu/climateadaptation/Colorado%20Economic%20Impacts%20of%20Climate%20Change.pdf

---

lower elevations and tundra at the highest elevations, whereas in the high-latitude ranges, especially in the Brooks Range of Alaska, even the lowest-elevation vegetation is limited to matlike tundra. In the Southern and Middle Rockies, ponderosa pine populates low-elevation forested areas, and as elevation increases, Douglas fir, pines, and aspen grow sequentially up the slopes to timberline (9,000–9,500 feet), afterwhich tundra, consisting of bare rock, fragile lichens, and mosses, ekes out a harsh existence.

The Rocky Mountain climate is generally warm and dry in summer, and cold and wet in winter. Considerable summer showers are mediated by winds, low humidity, and evaporation. The winter snowpack provides most of the measurable precipitation. The westerly winds influence precipitation, sending the western ranges ample summer rain. The accompanying valleys and parks are in the rain shadow, receiving only six or seven inches of precipitation annually. During the winter, the weather is both cold and dry, so snow is powdery and may lie until spring thaw.

Climate Change

While much of the talk about climate change has focused on low-lying urban centers and coastal areas, climate change in the Rocky Mountain peaks has already affected plants, fire, and water flow. At the **tree line**, where forest gives way to tundra, increased nitrogen levels subject the spruce—like Ingleman spruce—to insect infestation and disease. Throughout the Rockies the tiny mountain pine beetle has infested pines, killed trees, and threatens the boreal forest—all a legacy of long-term fire suppression. In addition, erratic winter temperatures mean a lack of sustained cold weather necessary to keep the beetles in check. Periodic outbreaks of native bark beetles have occurred throughout the history of the park. However, none have been as severe as the recent outbreak. Though bark beetles cause a substantial loss of trees, they are recognized as part of "natural conditions." Currently, the National Park Service has been spraying carbaryl to protect some of the trees near campgrounds, historic landscapes, picnic areas, park buildings and infrastructure, and visitor centers. However, spraying is only effective when it is applied directly to trunks, and each tree must be sprayed every year until the outbreak has subsided. However, there is no effective means of controlling the large beetle outbreak. The issue of beetles reminds us of nature's ability to change beyond human control.

Similarly, the whitebark pine is valued for its seeds (pine nuts), which are a source of fats for grizzly bears preparing for winter hibernation. Fire suppression has caused the number of whitebark pine to diminish, and now firs and spruce grow in

BOX 15.4   GEOSPATIAL TECHNOLOGIES AND WILDFIRES

Increased wildfires in the Rocky Mountain region have cost billions in damages. The USGS has responded by offering real-time data on wildfires. GEOMAC (https://www.geomac.gov/) provides fire managers near real-time information. This can be critical information since wind, temperature, and precipitation change hourly and can affect the spread of fire. Fire perimeter data is updated daily based upon input from incident intelligence sources, GPS data, and infrared (IR) imagery from fixed wing and satellite platforms. Map 15.2 shows the fire perimeter for the fire in Montana's Adair Peak, near Glacier National park, in September 2017.

The GEOMAC website allows users in remote locations to manipulate map information displays, zoom in and out to display fire information at various scales and detail, and print hard copy maps for use in fire information and media briefings, dispatch offices, and coordination centers. The fire maps also have relational databases in which the user can display information on individual fires such as name of the fire, current acreage and other fire status information.

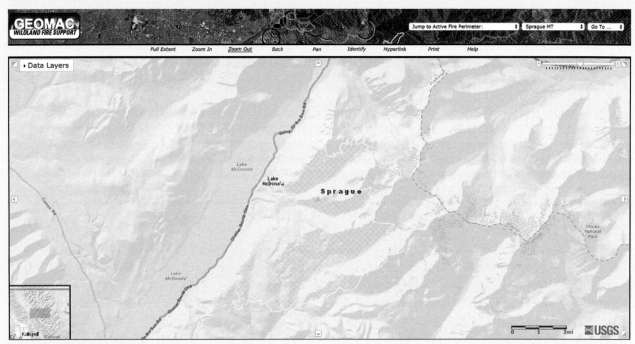

MAP 15.2. The GEOMAC map shows real-time data on the 2017 Sprague fire in Glacier National Park in Montana. In August and September 2017, numerous wildfires raged across Montana, including the Sprague Fire in Glacier National park. Collectively, hundreds of thousands of acres burned, and air quality was code red for several weeks. But these wildfires occurred at the same time as Hurricane Harvey flooded Houston Texas and Hurricane Irma devastated the Caribbean and Florida and did not get as much attention in the news.

Source: USGS at https://www.geomac.gov/viewer/viewer.shtml

former whitebark habitats. The loss of the pines affects grizzly populations, which in turn affect others in the ecosystem. Wildlife has also been affected because of human intrusion into the mountains. Grizzlies, aquatic species, and wolves have all suffered losses or are near extinction.

Other plants react to warmer temperatures with erratic growth and diebacks, or in the tundra, more grasses and fewer wildflowers. The erratic nature of these changes makes predictions uncertain.

More recently, warmer temperatures have been melting glaciers, some of which may disappear within the next twenty-five years. Climate change may also reduce snow and water,

increase drought, and bring higher temperatures at lower elevations. For example, if climate change continues, Aspen may be as warm as Flagstaff is today and Missoula as warm as Denver.

Climate change can cause intense and fast-spreading fires. In addition, these changes may be amplified by El Niño, an interaction between ocean and atmosphere that occurs over the Pacific Ocean periodically and alters global weather patterns. In the Rockies, El Niño brings more rain, which influences the brush-tinder ratio in subsequent drier years. As temperatures rise, river headwaters gorge early in the season and upset ordinary water flow; the result is drought, floods, or moisture robbed from the soil. When combined with continued sub-urban sprawl, wildfires in the suburban fringe have become far more commonplace. Significant fires in 2012, 2013, and again in 2017 burned hundreds of thousands of acres and destroyed hundreds of homes. There were three large fires in 2013; one of the fires, the Black Forest fire destroyed five hundred homes. Yet, few have questioned the wisdom of allowing more urban development. In a sign of the changing times, the Denver Post has an interactive map that tracks wildfires in Colorado.

Historical Geography and Settlement

The Rocky Mountain region has always had few people but many resources. Native Americans hunted but seldom lived in the region; whites exploited furs followed by minerals and water. Each came and went, taking what was important to them. Even today, many high-country inhabitants are part-timers, using regional amenities during the favored season and then departing. Today, winter sports and tourism dominate how the Rockies are used.

Native Americans

Since the last ice age, the Rocky Mountains were home first to Paleo-Indians and then to the Native American tribes of the Crow, Cheyenne, Arapahoe, Sioux, Ute, Kiowa, Comanche, Apache, Caddo, Wichita, Navajo, Hopi, Nez Pierce, Shoshoni, Shebits, Kaibab, Utah, Ouray, and Paiute.

The Ute people are among the oldest residents of the region, inhabiting the mountains and vast areas of Colorado, Utah, Wyoming, Eastern Nevada, Northern New Mexico, and Arizona. In early spring and into the late fall, men would hunt for elk, deer, and antelope; the women would trap smaller game animals in addition to gathering wild plants such as berries and fruits.

As expert hunters they used all parts of the animal. Elk and deer hides were used for shelter covers, clothing, and moccasins. The hides the Utes tanned were prized and a sought after trade item. The Ute women became known for their beautiful quill work, which decorated their buckskin dresses, leggings, moccasins, and cradleboards.

During the sixteenth century, Spaniards began to push west-ward into the region they introduced horses, livestock, and tools, but they also brought small pox, cholera, and other diseases that would decimate many of the Native American tribes.

Mountain Men

By the beginning of the nineteenth century, Americans and French Canadians trapped the Rocky Mountains to satisfy the need for hats made from felted beaver fur. They engendered the legendary mountain men.

Four countries—Spain, Russia, Britain, and the United States—claimed territory from the Rockies to the Pacific, but only Britain and the United States seriously explored the high country. Britain, under the auspices of the Hudson's Bay Company claimed the Columbia River drainage basin and dominated trapping during the second decade of the nineteenth century. The era of American mountain men began around 1825 and lasted until 1840.

British trapping was an enterprise meant to profit the stockholders, control trapping, and occupy the West. Between 1823 and 1841, Hudson's Bay Company employees trapped entire watersheds with the intent of exhausting the resource supply to keep American trappers out of the lucrative Northern Rockies and British Columbia hunting grounds. Across the Plains to the Rockies, the 49th parallel had been defined as the border during the Convention of 1818, but west of the Rockies remained disputed territory between the British and Americans until 1846.

The first American trappers were French Canadians who responded to newspaper ads for employment or explorers who left expeditions to join fur companies. John Colter, a member of the Lewis and Clark expedition, left in 1806 to join two fur trappers in one of the first American fur-trapping companies. American trappers were seldom independent; most joined a company for security.

Trappers explored the unknown territories and discov-ered geographical features (holes, rivers, springs, and passes), establishing a knowledge base for the Rocky Mountains and points west. Later, after the decline of the fur trade, some trappers remained as guides; one of the better known was Kit Carson. Other trappers, such as David Thompson and Jedediah Smith, were well known as both trappers and geographers.

The British relied on a permanent fort system to claim and ship the annual fur bounty. Forts were difficult to defend on the fron-tier, so beginning in 1825 Americans traded at the annual rendez-vous. The trading and social function revolved around trapping near the South Pass trail at a series of "holes"—Cache Valley, Utah; Jackson Hole, Wyoming; and Pierre's Hole, Idaho. The rendezvous system continued until 1840, at which time the demand for beaver fur declined as silk hats became the fashion. By this time, though, the beaver was almost extinct due to overtrapping.

Exploration

In 1793, Alexander Mackenzie first crossed the Canadian Rockies through the Peace River Valley of northern Alberta–British Columbia. Shortly after, David Thompson surveyed the Canadian and Northern Rocky Mountains, becoming the first European to explore and map the Columbia River from source to mouth. In 1858, the Palliser Expedition explored, analyzed, and mapped western Canada. Three explorers from the expedi-tion entered the Rockies, searching for suitable railroad passes.

American exploration of the Rockies began after the Louisiana Purchase, when President Jefferson sent the Lewis and Clark Expedition (1803–1806) across the continent to explore its potential. During the mid-nineteenth century the US government commissioned surveys of the Rocky Mountains. One of these surveys was John C. Fremont's 1845 *The Report of the Exploring Expedition to the Rocky Mountains*, which discusses a possible railroad route through the Southern Rockies. In the 1870s, geologists Hayden, King, and Powell documented landforms, glaciers, flora, and fauna in the West, including the Rocky Mountain area, and published their findings in geological reports.

With the exception of the Front Range and a few small, wealthy enclaves of part-time residents, the Rocky Mountains remained a sparsely settled region. Nineteenth-century mining or logging camps inhabited the region for resource exploitation, but most towns were abandoned after their boom period.

Cultural Perspectives

Geography of Wealth: Aspenization

Aspen, Steamboat Springs, Breckenridge, and Crested Butte all began as remote mining towns cut off by annual snows. Before railroads reached the small towns, "Norwegian snowshoes" were used to traverse the deep snows. In the early twentieth century, rails reached the towns, and by the 1950s highways became the prevalent Rockies transportation routes, and the "Norwegian snowshoes" were renamed skis.

Skiing grew in popularity during the 1970s and many wealthy began to invest in homes in the quaint "ski villages." Today, the isolated mining towns with worthy ski slopes have become secluded world-class second hometowns for the wealthy. Pitkin County, Colorado (Aspen), and Teton County, Wyoming (Jackson Hole), are two of the wealthiest counties in America. The infusion of wealth, combined with social tension and environmental impacts led to what Michael Naimark termed "Aspenization."

Wealthy newcomers build and move into their "dream home" but often ignore or do not understand their impact on the local traditional economy or their own impact on the wilderness. The wealthy will often close off or place in "land conservation" fishing and hunting areas that the less wealthy locals have used for generations.

The shift from extraction to aesthetic amenities has altered regional economies. Towns like Aspen are small, private landholdings surrounded by large swaths of protected wilderness—public land that cannot be developed and hence becomes an investment amenity. The limited available land skyrockets in price, and full-time locals who service the economy are unable to afford homes in the community. For example, the current median housing price in Aspen is $4.8 million and there are numerous listings of houses priced above $10 million.

In some of these communities, wealthy homeowners try to control growth and preserve open space. Attempts to control growth include placing caps on building permits or creating land lotteries. Controlling growth has had the side effect of eliminating affordable housing. The same can be said of open space programs, in which large amounts of land are taken off the market, thereby driving up the price of the remaining land and increasing property taxes.

Other costs to an Aspenized economy are overcommercialization, in which everything is for the tourist, and a weak job market, either because most of the homeowners have no need of jobs or because the jobs that exist do not pay nearly enough to support living in the area. The consequence is one of a growing gap between rich and poor and the elimination of the middle.

Apsenization has spread to other regions in the United States, affecting Nantukcet, Massachusetts, and the San Juan Islands in Washington State.

Boom and Bust Towns

Boom and bust towns in the West have relied on natural resource extraction. Most Rocky Mountain mining towns prospered and then withered in relation to the price and quality of their ores. Many towns faded into history, visited only by those who seek out the past in the remains of **ghost towns**; others boom-bust and then boom again.

Telluride, Colorado
(2016 pop. 2,450)

Telluride is an example of a boom-bust and boom again success. Telluride was a hard-drinking 1880s southwestern Colorado mining town set in an avalanche-prone box canyon. The area's numerous silver- and gold-mining towns are mostly ghost towns today. Telluride was a bust in the 1920s, became a hippie hangout in the 1960s, and then was reborn in the 1970s with a new gold—snow.

Victorian homes that went for $300 in 1960 were $30,000 in 1970 and are just under a $1 million today. Now an annual skiing crowd of 190,000 shop and après-ski along the Victorian Main Street, and the tourism continues throughout the year, highlighted by the thirty-year-old Telluride Labor Day film festival. Arts, entertainment, and recreation employ 42 percent of the local workforce.

In Telluride, housing development is limited by the town's isolated geography—forty miles of steep, windy roads to the next town. In addition, the town is surrounded by Forest Service and **Bureau of Land Management (BLM)**. For years, town employees opted to camp out in the surrounding woods, until it was made illegal. Now most town workers must navigate the treacherous road down the mountain where there is more affordable housing. In town, the smaller, old, and somewhat affordable homes are purchased, torn down, and replaced with megasized second homes.

Kellogg, Idaho
(2016 pop. 2,100)

Kellogg was a silver boomtown founded in 1885. Over the decades, Silver Valley mining employed many families, but the environmental cost left the town with polluted water, smokestack emissions, and lead buildup. In 1981, the price of silver fell, the mines shut, and the town went bust. Population fell 28 percent to three thousand during the 1980s. In 1983, the Environmental Protection Agency (EPA) Superfund helped to start clean up of the lead and zinc in the water and chemically denuded hills.

Along with clean up, the town sought to rebrand themselves by constructing "the world's longest gondola" on the recently cleaned Superfund ski hill, trying to make light of its polluted

PHOTO 15.6. Gondola in Kellogg, Idaho. Developers saw it as the next Vail, while residents hoped tourism would replace the closed mines. The town voted to raise taxes to build the world's longest gondola as an attraction. But the town has struggled to overcome high lead pollution and high unemployment.

PHOTO 15.7. Ghost Town: Garnet, Montana. This late-nineteenth-century boom town was completely abandoned by 1950. Today it is a well-maintained ghost town, where students study the relics of the past.

past calling it "superfun." They sold the ski hill in 1996 to an investment company that started building condos, and median home prices have continued to increase (photo 15.6).

Some of the closed mines such as Crystal Gold Mine and the Sierra Silver Mine have been reopened as a tourist attractions. Both tourism and the silver mines are ongoing. New mines continue to operate when the price of silver remains high enough to make them profitable. Given the cyclic nature of mining, the town may be impacted if prices plummet; similarly, the tourist economy is both fickle and aging in the valley.

Ghost Towns

Unlike the success of Telluride and Kellog, there are hundreds of Rocky Mountains ghost towns spread throughout the Southern Rockies Mineral Belt. Outside the Mineral Belt are other ghost towns, such as the Alberta coal-mining towns of Nordegg and Bankhead, or Garnet, a well-preserved gold-mining town high in the Northern Rockies near Missoula, Montana.

Garnet was established in 1895 after the discovery of gold in the granite veins of the nearby mountains in this steep-sided mountain valley, attracting more than a thousand in just a few years. But Garnet was not built to last. The wooden buildings provided the temporary shelters needed while working the twenty mines. By 1905, gold extraction became more elusive or expensive, and the town population dwindled to only 150 residents. A commercial-district fire and World War I halted population growth, and by the 1950s the last inhabitants abandoned the town. Today, only those who appreciate ghost towns and historic preservation travel the rough gravel road to Garnet (photo 15.7).

BOX 15.5 ICONIC IMAGES: MARLBORO MAN

Starting in the 1950s, Phillips Morris launched a new advertising campaign for its Marlboro cigarettes. The campaign was conceived by Leo Burnett as a way to popularize filtered cigarettes, which at the time were considered "sissy or effeminate" and lacking in flavor. Burnett's "Marlboro Man" character was exceedingly masculine, a rugged cowboy portrayed in a natural setting with only a cigarette. And Marlboro Country might have been Montana, Wyoming, or Colorado.

"Some might remember the moving image of a man on horseback, cloaked in a duster, charging across the snow-dusted prairie to that woodstove-heated shed, scenes that ended with the optimistic uptick of a violin. The print ads featured groups of chisel-faced wranglers sitting around a campfire, or a solo cowboy astride a horse, cupping his smoke against the bitter winds somewhere in the red rock deserts and high plains of an ambiguous American West."*

The Marlboro Man campaign had very significant and immediate effects on sales. In 1955, when the Marlboro Man campaign was started, sales were at $5 billion. By 1957, sales were at $20 billion, representing a 300 percent increase within two years.[†]

The *Los Angeles Times* reported that the reality of the Marlboro Man was far darker than the image of the tough, self-sufficient, hardworking cowboy. At least four actors who have played him in ads have died of smoking-related diseases.[‡] Eric Lawson died of respiratory failure in 2014, and in 2015, one of the original Marlboro Men, Darrell Winfield, passed away from an unspecified "lengthy illness" at his ranch in Riverton, Wyoming, while in hospice care.[§]

Although tobacco telvision ads haven't aired since the 1970s, this iconic image remains instantly evocative of a mythical Marlboro country and of a mythical American cowboy.

Die EG-Gesundheitsminister:

Rauchen kann
tödlich sein

PHOTO 15.8. The Malboro Man has become a global icon. This advertising statue is located in Germany's Hamburg airport. The caption below the ad in German says "Smoking can cause death."
Source: iStock/aldorado10

*Adrian Shirk. "The Real Marlboro Man." *The Atlantic*. February 17, 2015, at https://www.theatlantic.com/business/archive/2015/02/the-real-marlboro-man/385447/

†Advertising Age. "The Marlboro Man." March 29, 1999, at: http://adage.com/article/special-report-the-advertising-century/marlboro-man/140170/

‡Matt Pearce. "At least four Marlboro Men have died from smoking-related diseases." *Los Angeles Times*. January 27, 2014, at http://www.latimes.com/nation/nationnow/la-na-nn-marlboro-men-20140127-story.html.

§Shirk, "The Real Marlboro Man."

Population, Immigration, and Diversity

Population

The Front Range population has been booming since the 1960s. Since the 1990s, rural and resort developments have grown rapidly in northern New Mexico, western Montana, and the province of Alberta. The entire region has grown, but urban and exurban sprawl has been a distinctive feature of growth in this region, especially along the panoramic Front Range.

Such growth means the conversion of land from agricultural to residential. In Colorado alone, more than 250,000 acres of agricultural land is lost each year. In Denver, population growth and increased population density has resulted in access to open space (acres per person) below the national average. The open space symbolizes a better quality of life to suburban residents, but at the expense of wildlife and longtime ranchers who populated the Front Range prior to the current suburban sprawl.

Most relocating residents are nonranching retirees, telecommuters, and second homeowners who live on miniranches, while long-term owners are traditional livestock ranchers. Most residents of both groups prefer the open space landscape and have an interest in the abutting federal- or state-protected forests. The ranchers, though, use the protected lands as grazing grounds, whereas the new residents see the public lands as providing them anonymity, privacy, and higher property values. Conflict has ensued.

The continued decline in beef prices has made it difficult for any but the largest ranchers to be viable and has resulted in consolidation; 10 percent of the ranchers control 50 percent of the inventory. Consolidation has benefits: lower production costs for the rancher and lower food prices for the consumer; this makes the United States more competitive globally, but it also destroys rural communities and local businesses, favoring large scale corporate concerns and outside control.

Economies of scale have forced many of the remaining small ranchers to turn to alternative income, such as dude ranches or hunting preserves; others have sold their land to developers or to preservation **land trusts**. On the positive side, land trusts help preserve open space. On the negative side, by preserving open space, available land is limited, which effectively escalates prices so only the wealthy can afford land.

Immigration and Diversity

Immigration has been increasing in the Rockies, but many areas in the region remain below the national average of 14.3 percent. As with other regions, immigration tends to be higher in the cities than in rural areas. In Santa Fe, New Mexico, 17 percent of the population is foreign born; in Denver, 16 percent of the population is foreign born. In Boulder, more than 10 percent of the population is foreign born, many of Hispanic origin. But in other cities such as Missoula, Montana, and Cheyenne, Wyoming, only 3 percent of the population is foreign born.

On the other hand, these states have a higher-than-average percentage of Native Americans and many choose to live on reservations. There are numerous reservations on the Colorado Plateau, including the Southern Ute Indian Reservation, the Ute Mountain Reservation (in Colorado) and the Unitah and Ouray Reservation in Utah. Many others are in New Mexico and Arizona (see chapter 16). There are also reservation lands in Wyoming (the Shoshone and Cheyenne), Montana (Crow), and Idaho (the Nez Pearce).

American Indian reservations are some of the poorest communities in the United States. According to a study by Maura Grogan, 39 percent live in poverty; unemployment is four times higher than the US average, and incomes are less than half those of other US citizens.

Indian poverty persists despite the fact that many Native American reservations contain considerable energy wealth. The Department of the Interior recently estimated that Indian lands have the potential to produce five billion barrels of oil, thirty-seven trillion cubic feet of natural gas, and fifty-three billion tons of coal. Indian energy resources amount to 30 percent of the nation's coal reserves west of the Mississippi, 50 percent of potential uranium reserves, and 20 percent of known oil and gas reserves. All of these energy resources could be worth nearly $1.5 trillion.

But federal control of Indian lands largely deprives tribes of the opportunity to benefit from such wealth. Any attempt to explore or develop resources on tribal lands must endure a costly rigmarole of bureaucracy and regulations.

Urban Trends

No major cities lie within the Rocky Mountains but gateway cities border the mountains: Santa Fe, Denver, and Salt Lake in the Southern Rockies; Spokane and Boise in the Northern Rockies; and Calgary and Edmonton in Canada.

In the United States, Pueblo, Colorado Springs, Denver, and Fort Collins are the largest cities between Chicago and the West Coast; Provo, Salt Lake City, and Ogden are positioned along the western side of the mountains (see chapter 16). Nearly all of these cities depend on water from the Rockies.

The Wyoming Basin has a different population pattern. Laramie, Rawlins, Rock Springs, and Cheyenne were developed as Union Pacific Railroad "hell on wheels" towns, known for their loose morality and ethics when they were established. A few other towns were built along river valleys: Casper on the North Platte and Cody on the Shoshone River.

In British Columbia, the Rocky Mountains have been protected from development because most mountain areas are within national park boundaries. However, development has increased outside park boundaries.

Denver, Colorado
(2016 MSA 2.8 million)

Situated along the South Platte River on the Colorado Piedmont, Denver was founded as a supply town for the mountain mining camps and has evolved into the major gateway to both the Plains and the Rockies, serving the agricultural and meat industries of the Plains, the mining interests of the Rockies, and also employing a major federal workforce. But it had to fight to earn these titles.

The transcontinental railroad bypassed Denver, which might have doomed it to second-class status. In 1870, the Denver boosters built the Denver Pacific line to the main transcontinental rail trunk and so secured its place as the gateway to Colorado mining areas. Population tripled over the next four years.

When extractive industry crashed in the 1980s, it brought Denver down along with them, but the city diversified its economy with a university research focus on IT and health care services. Denver grew beyond a regional hub based on these industries, augmented by a highly educated population and local amenities—hiking, skiing, climate, and scenery. Denver continued its growth into the biotech and renewable energy sectors. Yet, growth has not been without consequences.

Like Los Angeles, Denver is particularly susceptible to the production of smog due to its geography. Because of Denver's high altitude the city experiences frequent temperature inversions when warm air is trapped under cold air and cannot rise to disperse the pollutants to wider areas. As a result, smog may hover in place for days at a time, generating a "smog soup"

that envelopes the city. Most of the smog is produced by transportation sources—cars, trucks, and trains. The city has been aggressive at trying to reduce smog and it has had some success, but currently remains in nonattainment for ozone pollutants.

Denver has also been committed to sustainability and has been recognized for many of its efforts. In 2006, the mayor announced sustainable plans for "Greenprint Denver," a coordinated effort across city agencies that includes more energy-efficient city vehicles and by 2012 a 10 percent reduction in greenhouse gases relative to 1990 levels. A revised sustainability plan called *Denver 2020* focuses on twelve areas: air quality, climate change (reduce citywide emissions below the 1990s' level) energy, food, health (increase access to primary care), housing (increase affordable housing units), land use, workforce, materials, mobility (increase walkability), and water quantity and quality (photo 15.9).

Boulder, Colorado
(2016 MSA 322,000)

Boulder attracts people for its beauty and its progressive, sustainable outlook. Its beautiful setting, flanked by the Rocky Mountains, bohemian air augmented by its university, and forward-thinking residential ideals have set it apart from most of

PHOTO 15.9. Denver Chalk Art Festival on Larimer Square is a two-day street-painting festival where more than two hundred artists turn the Square into a museum of chalk art. Many cities have encouraged these types of events for the vitality they bring to the downtown.

Source: istock/JRLPhotographer

America. In the 1960s, the city implemented antisprawl policies and began to purchase open space for greenbelts, and allocated 20 percent of its transportation budget away from automobiles and toward alternative transport methods.

Boulder has a diverse economy supported by the university, federal labs, and a diverse mix of small and large businesses in a range of industries. These factors lure many to the city that continues to grow. Housing prices continue to increase with population growth and demand, although the city has prioritized adding a majority of the new units as multifamily housing units.

Increased parking rates and doubled fines in the downtown area encourage more than half of the residents to use alternate transit; there is an active bike program, such as "Bike to Work" weeks and free bike use in the central business district. Boulder's 1987 Greenways program was designed to encourage bicycle and pedestrian trails along Boulder Creek while enhancing fish and wildlife habitat. Boulder's initiatives establish it as a multi-modal city. Today, residents walk, bike, and use transit for a higher percentage of trips than their counterparts in the region. Boulder's daily vehicle miles traveled hit a peak in the mid-2000s and haven't grown appreciably since then, despite continued increases in both population and jobs.

There are many positive health and social trends in Boulder, including better-than-average personal health among residents, a high-quality educational system, and high levels of community satisfaction with key amenities such as parks and open spaces. But challenges remain. In the last ten years, Boulder has emerged from two wildfires, a major flood, and an economic downturn. Social issues, such as homelessness, remain a primary area of concern for the community. And although

Boulder stopped sprawling into its mountains and established a greenbelt, it could not stop Denver from sprawling toward the town and contributing its smog.

Santa Fe, New Mexico
(2016 MSA 148,000)

The Pueblo Indians lived on the Santa Fe site as early as 1000 CE. By 1608, the site, now a ruin, was chosen as the Spanish Nueva Mexico capital, and Santa Fe became the oldest continuously settled city in Spanish America. The city was a natural site for settlement and a gateway—lying on the boundary between the Basin and Range, the Great Plains, and the Southern Rockies. Santa Fe functioned as the trading post for the Plains and Pueblo Indians; it was the end of the eponymous trail and a terminus for the first southern railroad route.

The town of Santa Fe was centered around a plaza in the traditional Spanish **Law of the Indies** style that regulated architectural, social, political, and economic life. But in the ensuing years, Santa Fe developed looking like other American cities, until citizens realized in the early twentieth century that the city's popularity was declining. To maintain the city's heritage and attract tourism, the Spanish Pueblo or Territorial architectural styles were enforced (photo 15.10). Today, the city and surrounding area are an artists' colony, tourist center, and wealthy enclave.

Fort Collins, Colorado
(2016 MSA 164,000)

Fort Collins has been a leader in habitat protection, affordable housing, growth management, and green energy investment. More than 50 percent of Fort Collins adults have at least a

PHOTO 15.10. San Miguel Mission, Santa Fe, New Mexico. This mission was constructed in 1610 and is the oldest church in America. Santa Fe architectural styles were based on antecedent structures like this, reflecting Spanish and Pueblo influence.

BOX 15.6 URBAN SUSTAINABILITY BEST PRACTICES: SANTA FE

In 2008, Santa Fe adopted the Sustainable Santa Fe Plan and has since pursued a variety of sustainability programs and projects. But the most notable step towards sustainability happened in November 2014, when the City Council passed Resolution 2014-85 declaring the City's goal of becoming **carbon neutral** by 2040.

The concept "carbon neutral" or having a net zero carbon footprint refers to achieving net zero carbon emissions by offsetting any carbon released with an equivalent amount of sequestered or offset carbon. There are three main ways to achieve carbon zero.

The first is *reducing* or limiting energy usage and emissions from transportation (by walking, using bicycles or public transport, avoiding flying, using low-energy vehicles), as well as from buildings, equipment, animals, and processes.

A second way is to obtain electricity and other energy from a *renewable energy* source, either directly by generating it (installing solar panels on the roof for example) or by selecting an approved green energy provider, and by using low-carbon alternative fuels such as sustainable biofuels.

A third way involves sequestering carbon or buying carbon offsets. Sequestered carbon can include planting trees, or funding carbon projects that would prevent future greenhouse gas emissions. It can also mean buying carbon credits. Carbon offsets enable organizations to reduce their environmental impact by supporting projects that reduce, absorb, or prevent carbon and other emissions from entering the atmosphere. A carbon offset is created when one ton of greenhouse gas is captured, avoided, or destroyed in order to compensate for an equivalent emission made. An example of a carbon credit could be investing in a sustainable forestry project in the Pacific Northwest or a biogas project from farms in the region.

Being carbon neutral is increasingly seen as good social responsibility. Companies such as Google, Dell, and PepsiCo have pledged to achieve carbon neutrality; countries such as Iceland, Sweden, Scotland, and Costa Rica have as well. The city of Santa Fe joins an impressive list of companies and countries with ambitious sustainability targets.

Individuals can also buy carbon credits—to learn more about how to offset your individual carbon emissions, go to carbonfund.org.

---

college degree. They have invested their time and energy in inventing sustainable and renewable businesses and ideas.

The city grew rapidly since 1970 and began to purchase open spaces after passing a one-cent capital improvement sales tax. Fort Collins has a long established green wind program. It has been active in reducing greenhouse gas emissions and increasing renewable energy use. To encourage energy efficiency, the city provides zero-interest loans for energy improvements and offers rebates on several energy-saving devices.

New city-owned buildings are LEED Silver, and homeowners are guided toward interest-free, energy-efficient building. City, developers, and Colorado State University work together to create sustainable services and green practices. Students at the college work on sustainable entrepreneurship, and Fort Collins tourism packages feature bike tours, local foods, and wines.

Missoula, Montana
(2016 MSA 116,000)

The first inhabitants of the Missoula area were American Indians from the Salish tribe. They called the area "Nemissoolatakoo," from which "Missoula" is derived. The word translates roughly to "river of ambush/surprise," a reflection of the inter-tribal fighting common to the area. The Indians' first encounter with whites came in 1805, when the Lewis and Clark expedition passed through the Missoula Valley. With the arrival of the Northern Pacific Railroad in 1883, Missoula became a trading center in earnest, distributing produce and grain grown in Missoula and in the agriculturally prosperous Bitterroot Valley.

Like many frontier towns, logging was a mainstay industry until the 1970s, when it began to disappear. Today, education and healthcare are the basis for the economy; the University of Montana and the city's two hospitals are critical to job growth.

The city has over four hundred acres of parkland, twenty-two miles of trails, and nearly five thousand acres of conserved open space. Nearby rivers are popular for white-water rafting, kayaking, and fly-fishing.

The Economy

The Primary Sector

The Rocky Mountain economy has been based on primary sector industries—mining, timber, and livestock ranching—but has shifted to a tertiary service economy of tourism. As profits and employment in primary industry decline, the tourism economy accelerates. However, much of the labor in the tourist economy is low-wage.

Agriculture and Livestock

Rocky Mountain agriculture flourished during the boom and bust nineteenth century when food costs to miners were high, which allowed local farmers to profit from growing and selling their fruits and vegetables. Today, few farmers grow fruit and vegetable crops; they are replaced by irrigated hay or niche markets, such as chiles in New Mexico and ginseng in British Columbia.

Livestock Grazing   The basin and park bottomlands grow irrigated hay and graze cattle and sheep. **Transhumance** grazing, where livestock are moved to high pasture during the summer and low during winter, is on private and BLM land. Valley land produces supplementary hay in summer and supplies low-elevation pastures during the winter.

Okanagan Valley Agriculture   The Okanagan Valley of British Columbia is a 125-mile-long semiarid valley in the rain shadow of the Coast Mountains. Early settlers were cattle ranchers, because it was the most economically viable. The valley was dry until after World War I, when irrigation turned the brown soil to green apple orchards. Fruit, especially apple orchards, became profitable after irrigation and rail access, but orchards are being razed in the twenty-first century because of high production costs and low market value. In the 1970s, there were more than twenty-four thousand acres of apples, but by 2001, apple orchards had declined to eighteen hundred acres. One reason for this decline has been fewer young people going into the orchard business. A second reason is that many of the fruit trees in the region are old and may not be replaced if the site is in poor condition. Experts believe that orcharding will become less export-oriented and move towards an industry which is primarily a supplier for the local, provincial, and western Canadian markets.

The winery industry has replaced apple orchards, Winery tours have boosted the local economy. The Okanagan Valley is the second largest wine region in Canada with approximately four thousand hectares of vineyards; it also produces 90 percent of wine in British Columbia.

The Okanagan Valley has excellent vineyard conditions: sunshine is abundant, glacial benches rich in till line the valley walls, and the lake in the valley floor moderates temperatures and nearby climatic extremes, creating microclimates that benefit the vineyards, which are at the same latitude as the wineries of north Germany and France.

Ginseng, a perennial herbaceous plant that looks like parsnip, grows in arid areas such as the Okanagan. The root is grown on small acreages (often under five acres), with occasional farms in the hundreds of acres. Maturing in four years, the crop is then dried and sold to ginseng brokers at about $25 per pound. Ninety percent is shipped to Asian markets, where it is used in tea, soups, candies, drinks, and capsules.

Today, the valley is changing again, as retired Canadians are attracted to Canada's sunniest and longest growing season (175 days) (photo 15.11). The Okanagan faces several sustainable challenges in the future, but the biggest challenge may be the heavy demands on the limited water supply.

PHOTO 15.11. Kelowna, Okanagan Valley, British Columbia. A housing boom and rising prices have been a hallmark of the Okanagan Valley in recent years. The region has been known for its apple orchards historically, but it now supports a retirement community and a growing wine industry.

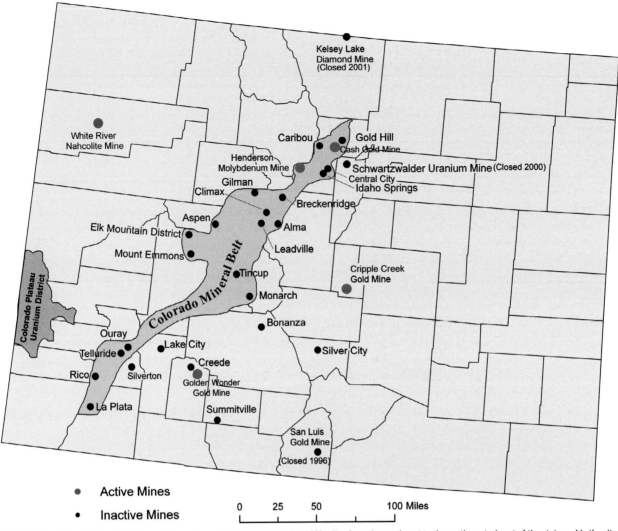

MAP 15.3. The Colorado Mineral Belt lies within a system of faults that trend about 250 miles from the southwest to the north central part of the state and is the site of most of Colorado's major mining areas. Ores found in this zone include gold, silver, lead, zinc, uranium, and molybdenum.

Mineral Resources

Both the Canadian and American Rocky Mountains have rich mineral deposits. Rocky Mountain mining reached its pinnacle in the nineteenth century.

Mining is easiest in mountainous areas because the rock veins are closer to the surface, but not all mountains share in the mineral wealth. Most of the mining in the Southern Rockies has been in the Colorado Mineral Belt (map 15.3). The Northern Rockies also had significant mining districts, as did the Cariboo and Kootenay districts of British Columbia.

Miners heading for the California gold fields did some preliminary panning in the Rockies, then returned after the California rush had subsided. The first metal to be mined in both the Southern and Northern Rockies was gold. By 1859, gold was found near Pikes Peak in Colorado, the Idaho batholith near the Salmon River, and in Virginia City, Montana.

Private companies have free access to metallic minerals on public land because of the **Mining Law of 1872**. Before this

law, it was technically illegal to mine on public lands. The law codified the informal system and practice of mining claims on public land. The law gave all citizens of the US the right to locate a mining claim on any federal land (for example, platinum, gold, silver, copper, zinc, etc.). The legacy of mining has left behind abandoned mines, released chemicals into watersheds, cut roads through wilderness, displaced wildlife, and damaged ecosystems. Mining damage lasts for decades after the activity has ended, and it necessitates governmental cleanup.

Cleanup began in 1993 and involves groundwater contamination remediation, identifying other sources of drinking water, capping tailings piles to minimize leaching, and purging waste piles. But the complexity of the watershed means that cleanup is difficult. More than twenty-five years later, clean up is not complete and remediation efforts continue. But there are some signs that the ecosystem is recovering and water quality improving, such as the return of trout to formerly contaminated streams.

BOX 15.7   ENVIRONMENTAL CHALLENGES: ABANDONED MINES

The long legacy of mining has left the Rockies with abandoned mines containing physical and environmental hazards, such as acid mine drainage, metal leaching, destroyed aquatic habitats, contamination, open shafts, and steep pit walls. Cleanup of these sites has been ongoing, involving the EPA, Superfund, and various state agencies. There are some seventeen thousand mines throughout the Colorado Mineral Belt, the copper mines of Montana, and radioactive uranium mines. In Canada, ten thousand mines have been abandoned. Some sites have been cleaned or are in the process, but many others still require remediation. In some areas, environmental rules are being rolled back or are not fully implemented.

Clear Creek, Colorado. About thirty miles west of Denver is the Clear Creek drainage basin, containing more than thirteen hundred abandoned mines, tailings, waste rock piles, and more than a hundred abandoned mine tunnels that drain into the watershed (map 15.4). The region was an important mining area from 1860 to 1890, when Leadville mines dominated. Clear Creek mining continued at a lesser level until about 1950. In 1983, the area was declared a Superfund site.

The most significant impact has been from acid mine drainage. About 250,000 people in Denver depend on Clear Creek water, which is contaminated from water flowing through the waste piles and mining tunnels. Other contributing factors

are heavy metals (cadmium, arsenic, lead, zinc, and copper) and mine wastes (photo 15.12). The drainage has also degraded fishery and aquatic habitats.

PHOTO 15.12. Old Stanley Mine, Idaho Springs, Colorado. The Stanley Mine was mined for gold, silver, copper, and lead, bringing in more than $3.6 million in 1910. Today the mine is a probable source of mine waste, low pH groundwater, and mine tailing contamination in the Clear Creek watershed, which provides water for part of the Denver metro area.

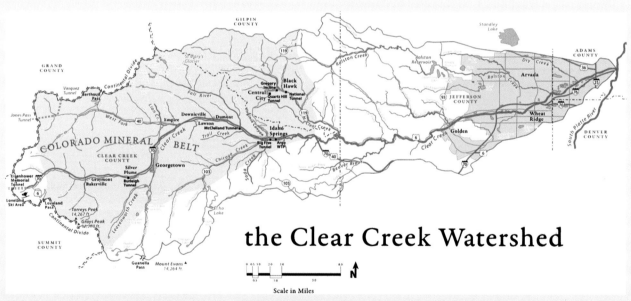

the Clear Creek Watershed

Scale in Miles

MAP 15.4. Clear Creek Watershed, Colorado. The 575-square-mile Clear Creek Watershed spans from fourteen-thousand-foot mountain peaks at its western edge on the Continental Divide down to the urbanized plains at its confluence with the South Platte River just north of the mile-high city of Denver.

Source: http://clearcreekwater.org/watershed-map/

Colorado. Denver, Pueblo, Golden, and Colorado City vied to be the gateway city into Colorado's Mineral Belt country, but Denver prevailed because of proximity to the Cherry Creek and Central City mines. The mines evolved slowly and lacked technology, but access improved with the railroad in the late 1860s. The initial mining boom, which was dependent on easily accessed shallow mines, ended during the 1920s.

Northern Rockies. In 1876, the Butte, Montana, mining boom began, first in silver, then in gold, and finally in copper. The copper-mining process required power to refine the ore. Dams built along the Missouri River provided cheap electricity, but a smelter was necessary to process the ore. In 1884, the town of Anaconda built up around a copper smelter.

Copper is an excellent conductor of electricity and was immensely important for the development of American energy, but processing is toxic. The toxins used during the mining operation may have affected Butte residents' health.

Canada. Eighty-nine percent of all Canadian land is Crown Land, which is managed and protected by the federal or provincial governments. In British Columbia, 92 percent of the land is provincial Crown Land, 1 percent federal, and the remaining private land. Much like BLM land in the states, Crown Land is leased to mining and logging companies for resource extraction or sold to interested parties at fair market value.

The 1860s' gold rush in the Cariboo Mountains of British Columbia created several boom and bust towns, such as Barkerville and Quesnel. Other towns, such as Wells, mined gold from the 1930s until the 1960s. In the Kootenays, the Sullivan mine in Kimberley was mined for lead, zinc, and silver until 2001.

Mining continues in British Columbia. The world's largest zinc- and lead-smelting complex is located in southeastern British Columbia at Trail, originally a silver-mining town established in the nineteenth century. Other mines include copper and molybdenum, the largest located in Highland Valley, southwest of Kamloops in the interior plateau.

Oil and Gas   The Rocky Mountains contain vast oil shale deposits, estimated as high as eight hundred billion barrels. During the 1970 oil crisis, the deposits seemed an energy find, and domestic oil and gas drilling proliferated. As oil prices fell in the 1990s, so did interest in shale. Interest has picked up again once oil exceeded $50 per barrel.

Drilling in the Rocky Mountains boosts domestic oil supplies but also generates controversy. The extraction of oil and gas damages environmentally sensitive areas, generates air pollution, and generates tons of mining waste. Oil shale mining uses vast amounts of water that leach into the groundwater supply. Many of the oil and gas recovery sites are located in wilderness areas used by hunting and fishing guides, who argue they will lose their livelihood should drilling proceed.

Logging   American Rocky Mountains. The US Rocky Mountains have approximately two hundred million acres of fir, pine, and spruce alpine forests, mostly protected from logging. The Northern Rockies harbor 58 percent of the American Rocky Mountain growing stock, and they provide about 10 percent of US timber cut.

By the early twentieth century, huge tracts of Idaho white pine supplied sawmills, but the land was stripped of old-growth forests. Logging continues, but the small-diameter trees lack the high-quality wood of old-growth forests, and therefore much of the wood is now produced into lesser wood products, such as plywood and oriented strand board (OSB).

Canadian Rockies. Both British Columbia and Alberta operate significant pulp and sawed lumber mills for global markets. British Columbia coniferous forests provide about half of Canada's total softwood inventory. Rocky Mountain lodgepole pine and spruce is used throughout the world for lumber, pulp, paper, shingles, and plywood. Poplar and aspen wood from northwestern Alberta Rocky Mountain foothills contribute to the growing OSB market.

The Tertiary Sector

While the primary and secondary sector remain important to the regional economy, the tertiary sector is increasingly contributing to growth. For example, service industries now make up the largest portion of Colorado's gross state product. The Colorado Office of Economic Development and International Trade recognizes the following service industries as critical growth areas:

- Aerospace
- Bioscience
- Creative Industries
- Defense and Homeland Security
- Electronics
- Financial Services
- Health and Wellness
- Infrastructure Engineering
- Technology and Information,
- Tourism and Outdoor Recreation
- Transportation and Logistics

Service industries make up the largest portion of Colorado's gross state product. Community, business, and personal services (private health care; hotels and ski resorts; and engineering, legal services, and software development) rank first. Second is finance, insurance, and the real-estate industry. Denver is an important regional bank and finance hub. Wholesale and retail trade services rank third and include automobile dealerships, groceries, and restaurants. Denver serves as the distribution center for the Rocky Mountain region. Retail outlets include automobile dealerships, food stores, and restaurants.

In Idaho, health care and tourism have been growing rapidly; in Montana, financial activities including insurance companies, banks, financial firms, real estate, and rental agencies have been the largest contributor to the state's gross domestic product (GDP). In Wyoming, the "Cowboy State," mining remains the biggest economic contributor, but government services and real estate are now more important than ranching.

BOX 15.8 GLOBAL CONNECTIONS: WHO OWNS THE SKI SLOPES?

Many avid skiers may not realize that the new form of mountain economics means that the entire mountain—from the ski lifts to equipment rentals, food, beverage, and even hotels—are owned by one company. The mountain is now like a cruise ship or amusement park, where vertical integration has become the norm. To make this type of integration possible requires capital, which in turn means ski resorts are increasingly owned by a larger company. Vail Resorts, for example, is not only the the proud owner of America's most popular mountain, Vail, but it is also the largest ski resort company in the United States and owns or operates eleven ski areas in North America that include

- Vail, Colorado
- Beaver Creek, Colorado
- Breckenridge, Colorado
- Keystone, Colorado
- Park City Mountain Resort, Utah
- Heavenly, California
- Northstar, California
- Kirkwood, California
- Afton Alps, Minnesota
- Mount Brighton, Michigan
- Wilmont Mountain, Wisconsin

Vail Resorts has international holdings. In 2015, the company acquired Australia's Perisher Resort for a reported $136 million. The company is looking to expand in Japan and other parts of Asia and Europe.

This is just the latest in the "globalization" of ski resorts. Back in the 1990s, for example, Japanese Kamori Kanko Co. bought Heavenly Valley, in South Lake Tahoe, California. At the time, Japanese investors already owned such premier ski resorts as Breckenridge and Steamboat in the Colorado Rockies and Stratton in Vermont. They have since sold some of these properties to Vail Resorts.

PHOTO 15.13. Skier in Vail, Colorado.
Source: iStock/TB1353

Today, a key part of the Rocky Mountain economy is tourism and recreation, ranging from scenic viewing to hiking and climbing in the warm months and winter sports in the cold months. Major Rocky Mountain travel destinations include national parks, towns dependent on ski resorts, and the Front Range cities such as Boulder. The challenge to these complexes is to maintain their "sense of place" character while promoting sustainable tourism and recreational use.

The ski industry is famous throughout the Rockies, from Taos, New Mexico, to Banff and Jasper in Canada, but Colorado is the most influential ski tourism state. Many skiers favor the dry, powdery, Rocky Mountain snow, the result of a continental climate and high elevation. The major ski resorts occupy a path along the Colorado Mineral Belt such as Vail and Aspen. Many ski resorts are large complexes with more than twenty-five miles of ski trails and can command daily ski passes that average more than $150. Both became known as high-priced developments, where wealthy "owner's clubs" offer first-class amenities—no ski lines, coveted parking, and gourmet restaurants—that the average skier cannot afford.

Many ski resorts promote themselves as "green." On the one hand, they advocate "green" renewable energy, but on the other, they artificially make snow. Snowmaking is dependent on fossil fuels and exerts pressure on water resources. Making artificial snow withdraws water from streams, stressing aquatic life.

The terrain in the Southern Rockies is perfect for ski runs for all levels of expertise at ski resorts. During the summer months, peaks can be reached by strenuous hikes, but the less energetic may reach the tops of Pikes Peak and Mount Evans by road. Fishing and hunting have long been a reason many of the local residents came to the communities, but as large developments purchase more land, local hunting and fishing grounds are often closed and wealthy newcomers, who destroy or remove the natural amenities with preserves or development, are resented by the local populace.

Tourism has both of positive and negative influences. It can bring people to areas where local extractive economies have failed, but it can also damage the environment. Tourism is usually not as environmentally damaging as the extractive industry, although it too can wreak havoc on fragile rural landscapes. Golf and ski industries, for example, can fragment ecosystems and wildlife habitats, as well as pollute water and land.

The Rocky Mountain allure varies with the visitors and the time of year. Each visitor profile has different needs: the hunter seeks open space; the skier, après-ski amenities; the hiker, rustic infrastructure and a trail system. Towns seeking to satisfy all or one of these groups may damage the environment for the others, or may harm the landscape by trying to satisfy all groups. Locals and affluent newcomers may have different perceptions about local development and industry. Newcomers often want to save the environment after they have arrived, stop what they see as overdevelopment. In so doing, this can take away job opportunities of longtime residents who are not as affluent as their new neighbors. Many newcomers may not understand or value the fact that extractive and tourist industries provide income for the local residents, who may find that newcomers overdevelop hunting and fishing grounds, or ruin the authenticity of the town and its attraction to other tourists.

Tourism is encouraged not only for the local economy but also because it places part of the local tax burden on nonresidents. Colorado, well aware that its many tourist towns face economic hurdles, partially because of a poorly paid tourism workforce, finds that higher taxes for lodging, rentals, and airport fees help reduce the residents' tax base—but higher taxes also discourage tourism.

A Sustainable Future

The future of the Rocky Mountains certainly faces numerous challenges for a sustainable future. These include the following:

- water supply and water distribution;
- a legacy of environmental contamination from extractive industries such as mining and logging;
- the resource needs of an increasing urban population;
- increase in hazards, such as wildfires, as urban sprawl continues;
- the lack of affordable housing;
- tension between "preservation" of the natural landscape and its use for economic growth;
- tension between long-term residents and newcomers;
- land trust and reserves that protect open space, but also increase land prices; and
- air pollution issues in some Front Range cities such as Denver.

And yet there are many examples of how this region has begun to move towards sustainability.

Alliances such as the Coalition to Protect the Rocky Mountain Front in Montana work to protect the landscape. The coalition consists of ranchers, hunters, business owners, conservationists, and weed experts (to inform on invasive species). Conventional wisdom would suggest that such a coalition would be doomed to disaster. But they have worked effectively together. In 2006, the coalition worked to pass legislation halting new oil and gas leasing on the Front. The coalition is now working to create a four-hundred-thousand-acre Rocky Mountain Front Heritage Area; such a designation may ensure various uses remain protected.

Environmental groups, such as the Nature Conservancy and the Freshwater Initiative, along with provincial and statewide groups, join forces to provide annual ecoregional assessments analyzing all aspects of the ecological subdivisions and their interactions, and to lay out plans for the future.

Communities, companies, institutes, and universities advocate for sustainability. Throughout the region, cities and towns are seeking economic development while integrating holistic thinking. For example, Alamosa, Colorado, an agricultural community located in the San Juan interbasin near the Sangre de Cristo Range, has reinvented itself by building one of the largest high concentrating solar photovoltaic power generation facility in the world in 2012. Among the positive attributes of the location are its high elevation (seventy-eight hundred feet above sea level), which means there is less atmosphere for the rays to pass through and, hence, greater insolation. The plant eliminates the generation of approximately 43,250 tons per year of carbon dioxide emissions.

Companies committed to the triple bottom line are investing in recycling and biofuels, while institutes, such as the Rocky Mountain Institute, are engaging in renewable energy research, resource planning, and green buildings. Universities, led by the University of Colorado, Boulder, and at Fort Collins, have embraced sustainable goals and sustainable education to prepare students for their future.

Many communities are engaged in promoting renewable energy, being proactive around climate change, and working to reduce water consumption. However, sustainable practices need to extend to the second-home complexes and the extraction industries, and they need to ensure social equity for local residents so that all can benefit now and in the future.

Questions for Discussion

1. Why were the endangered or threatened wolves reintroduced into the Rocky Mountains? What have been the impacts?

2. Should oil and gas drilling be allowed in environmentally sensitive areas? Why or why not?

3. Is tourism the right industry for the Rocky Mountains? If so, why; if not, why not? What would be alternatives?

4. Should a burned-over forest such as the Bitterroots be logged, or is it healthier to allow it to evolve with the ecosystem in place?

5. Is it better to let wildlife roam free, killing what they need, including cattle or sheep, or should wildlife who roam onto cattle ranges be shot by ranchers?

6. Tax laws currently allow full mortgage interest deductions on second homes, which generates towns with more empty second homes than full-time residents. Is this type of tax deduction sustainable for the entire community?

7. Do you think this region will attract more migrants (domestic and foreign born)? Why or why not?

8. Land preservation and trusts have become big business, but what are the advantages and disadvantages socioeconomically? At what point do the rights of one animal or human begin and end?

9. How are Rocky Mountain cities leading in sustainability?

10. The debate over what should be kept as wilderness areas is not simple. Explain the reasoning for both sides and what some of the related issues are.

11. How has the Mining Law of 1872 been controversial and affected current mining operations?

12. Explain how tourism and recreational use are both boon and bane to a sustainable economy.

Suggested Readings

Baron, J. S., ed. *Rocky Mountain Futures.* Washington, D.C.: Island Press, 2002.

Diamond, J. *Collapse: How Societies Choose to Fail or Succeed.* New York: Viking Press, 2005.

Ferguson, G. *Land on Fire: the New Reality of Wildfire in the West.* Portland, Ore.: Timber Press, 2017.

Grogan, M. *Native American Lands and Natural Resource Development.* New York: Revenue Watch Institute, 2011.

Mathews, D. *Rocky Mountain Natural History.* Portland, Ore.: Raven Editions, 2003.

Mercier, L. *Anaconda: Labor, Community, and Culture in Montana's Smelter City.* Urbana: University of Illinois, 2001.

Morgan, D. L. *Jedediah Smith and the Opening of the West.* Indianapolis, Ind.: Bobbs-Merrill, 1953.

Naimark, M. "Aspen the Verb: Musings on Heritage and Virtuality." *Presence Journal* 15, no. 3 (June 2006), at http://www.naimark.net/writing/aspen.html

Sprague, M. *The Great Gates: The Story of the Rocky Mountain Passes.* Boston, Mass.: Little, Brown, 1964.

Stowkowski, P. A. *Riches and Regrets: Betting on Gambling in Two Colorado Mountain Towns.* Niwot: University Press of Colorado, 1996.

Utley, R. M. *A Life Wild and Perilous: Mountain Men and the Paths to the Pacific.* New York: Holt, 1997.

Veblen, T. T., W. L. Baker, G. Montenegro, and T. W. Swetnam, eds. *Fire and Climatic Change in Temperate Ecosystems of the Western Americas.* New York: Springer, 2003.

West, E. *The Contested Plains: Indians, Goldseekers and the Rush to Colorado.* Lawrence: University of Kansas Press, 1998.

Wyckoff, W. *Creating Colorado: The Making of a Western American Landscape, 1860–1940.* New Haven, Conn.: Yale University Press, 1999.

Yorath, C. *How Old Is That Mountain? A Visitor's Guide to the Geology of Banff and Yoho National Parks.* Rev. ed. Madeira Park, B.C., Canada: Harbour, 2006.

Internet Sources

Aspen's Sustainability Report, at https://www.cityofaspen.com/390/ Sustainability-Report

Boulder Sustainability Plan, at https://bouldercolorado.gov/planning/ regional-sustainability

Colorado Office of Economic Development and International Trade. *Annual Report*, at https://choosecolorado.com/wp-content/ uploads/2016/07/2016-OEDITAnnualReport.pdf

The Denver Post's Interactive Map for Wildfires, at http://www. denverpost.com/2017/07/07/colorado-wildfires-map/

Denver Office of Sustainability, at https://www.denvergov.org/content/ denvergov/en/office-of-sustainability.html.

National Park Service. "Rocky Mountains System," at https://www.nps. gov/articles/rockies.htm

National Ski Areas Association, *2016 Climate Challenge Annual Report* (2016), at: http://www.nsaa.org/media/274957/2016_Climate_ Challenge_Annual_Report.pdf

Rocky Mountain Climate Organization, at http://www. rockymountainclimate.org/

Rocky Mountain Institute, at http://www.rmi.org/

1 Dry Falls in eastern Washington, formed during the Missoula floods, were once the world's highest falls.

2 Potatoes thrive in the soil, climate, and irrigation of Idaho's Snake River Plain.

3 The Mormon Temple is the center of Salt Lake City and the initial node for the state's baseline and meridian.

4 The Anasazi may have abandoned Colorado's Mesa Verde in the thirteenth century for environmental reasons.

7 This central Arizona aqueduct was built to supply water from the Colorado River to the state's cities.

Central Arizona Project
● Cities
— Rivers
— State Borders

Washington
Spokane
Channeled Scablands
Palouse
Columbia River
Montana

Bend
Boise
Oregon
Idaho
Snake River Plain
Wyoming

Nevada
Great Basin
Salt Lake City
Colorado
Reno
Basin & Range
Utah
Canyon Lands

Death Valley
St. George
Colorado River
Four Corners
Santa Fe
Las Vegas
Arizona
Grand Canyon
Albuquerque
New Mexico
California
Coachella Valley
Mogollon Rim
Imperial Valley
Sonoran Desert
Phoenix
Mexican Highland
Tucson
Central Arizona Project
Texas
Rio Grande River
Pacos River

N W E S

6 The Anza-Borrego Desert in southeastern California gets less than 2 inches of rain a year.

5 The Great Basin conceals many possible secrets, such as those in the movie *Independence Day*.

16
INTERMONTANE
Baked, Beguiling, and Booming

Chapter Highlights

After reading this chapter, you should be able to:

- Discuss how the region has changed since 1960 and why
- Identify the major water sources and explain their relationship to the region
- Compare and contrast western versus eastern water rights
- Discuss ranching and its relationship to the Bureau of Land Management
- Explain the influences of Hispanic, Basque, and Mormon culture within the region
- Discuss the major environmental issues
- Describe what makes the Great Basin unique
- Identify major cities and explain critical urban trends
- Discuss immigration patterns and how these impact the region
- Explain the role of the service sector and the economic structure of the region

Terms

acculturation	butte	flash flood	mesa
alluvial fan	canyon	Gadsden Purchase	Mexican Cession of 1848
arroyo	Colorado River Compact	glacial erratic	open pit mine
basin	Columbia Basin Project	grass banking	playa
Basque	coulee	haboob	scabland
	ecological balance	*la raza*	
	exotic stream	Manifest Destiny	

Places

Anza Borrego	Central Arizona Project	Columbia River	Imperial Valley, California
Basin and Range	Channeled Scablands	Death Valley	Mogollon Rim
Bonneville Salt Flats	Coachella Valley, California	Four Corners	Palouse
Canyonlands	Colorado Plateau	Grand Canyon	Snake River Plain
	Colorado River	Great Basin	Sun Belt
	Columbia Plateau		

Cities

Albuquerque, New Mexico
   (2016 MSA 909,000)
Bend, Oregon
   (2016 MSA 181,000)
Boise, Idaho
   (2016 MSA 691,000)

Las Vegas, Nevada
   (2016 MSA 2.1 million)
Tucson, Arizona
   (2016 MSA 1.05 million)
Reno, Nevada
   (2016 MSA 458,000)

Phoenix-Mesa-Scottsdale,
   Arizona
   (2016 MSA 4.6 million)

Salt Lake City, Utah
   (2016 MSA 1.1 million)
Spokane, Washington
   (2016 MSA 556,000)

PHOTO 16.1. The Basin and Range. This subregion contains a series of dry, north-south-trending faulted mountains and valleys between the western ranges and the Rocky Mountains.

Introduction

Between the Sierra Nevada and the Rocky Mountains lies the driest and most beguiling region in the United States (photo 16.1). The physical and climatic geography of the region have interrelated over time to create a baked and dramatic landscape. For years this "empty quarter" was dry, rough-hewn, unproductive, and sparsely populated. But by the 1960s, Americans began to move to desert areas when air-conditioning became common in the 1960 and housing was affordable. Many Intermontane residents abandoned the harsher climates and gritty cities of the Midwest for **Sun Belt** swimming pools and golf courses. The few remaining farmers and ranchers profited more from selling their land to developers than working the land.

By 1990, the hot, arid metropolitan areas of Phoenix and Las Vegas boomed, and each surpassed one million residents. But as with other regions, this lifestyle depends on seemingly plentiful water resources in a dry region. The spectacular population growth in a region with too little water makes the Intermontane a modern miracle—but can it last?

Physical Geography

The Intermontane is hot and dry. Life requires water, so the harsh, dry desert is more vulnerable than its tough-looking exterior might suggest.

Tectonic and volcanic forces deranged and contorted the Intermontane into a combination of arid plateaus, deep-gorged **canyons**, and a series of dramatic ridges and valleys that continue to reconfigure this restless landscape.

The Intermontane region is composed of three major subregions. They are

- the Columbia Plateau;
- the Basin and Range; and
- the Colorado Plateau.

The Columbia Plateau is divided into two provinces: the Palouse and the Snake River Plain. The Basin and Range is divided into three provinces—the Great Basin, the Sonoran Desert, and the Mexican Highlands—and the Colorado Plateau is a jumble of mesas and canyons, highlighted by the Grand Canyon.

Columbia Plateau

Mountains surround three sides of the two-hundred-thousand-square-mile Colombia Plateau. Intense and repeated lava flows over a ten-million-year period (ending about six million years ago) left behind a six-thousand-foot-thick blanket of alternating basalt and soil. While basalt defines the foundational plateau, it was only the canvas for a more dramatic progression of events.

Roughly fifteen thousand years ago, toward the end of the last ice age, an ice dam plugged Idaho's Clark River, creating Lake Missoula, which was as large as Lakes Ontario and Erie combined. Over time, the ice dam cracked. The cracks grew until a cataclysm of water—estimated at ten times the combined flow of all of Earth's rivers—burst through the dam and thundered across the Columbia Plateau. The wall of water gouged lava beds, scoured huge pothole lakes, eroded the soil to its basalt base, and formed the Columbia Gorge as it rushed toward the Pacific Ocean. The process was repeated from eighty to one hundred times over the next three thousand years, and so the descriptively named Channeled Scablands were shaped.

The combined lava flows and the repeated floods sculpted the broken landscape and carved deep canyons, creating a **scabland** of exposed lava rock. The Missoula floodwaters scraped the Columbia Gorge walls bare. The gorge wall dropped hundreds of feet, and streams that once flowed peacefully into the Columbia became dramatic waterfalls into the gorge. The floodwaters settled in the Willamette Valley as far south as Eugene, exposing sand and debris bars that molded the northern bend of the Columbia River where Portland, Oregon, is located. Floods laid down fertile soils through the Scablands, the Palouse, and the Willamette Valley and also deposited huge **glacial erratics**, which settled near places like Lake Oswego. Today, the floodwaters are long gone. Left behind are dry gulch **coulees** and the Columbia River, the only perennial river through the bare Scablands.

The Palouse

Floods, lava flows, and deposition of hundreds of feet of wind-blown loess (finely ground glacial sediment) formed the now peaceful, undulating hills of the Palouse subregion—south of Spokane, Washington, and west into Idaho. The Palouse was once open grassland, but over 90 percent is now cultivated. To the east are the rippled Camas Prairies.

Snake River Plain

Idaho is a mountainous state, with the exception of southern Idaho's flat crescent Snake River Plain, which was shaped as the North American Plate migrated over a stationary hot spot of lava flowing from the earth (map 16.1). The Snake River rises in the Wyoming Tetons and flows through the eponymous plain, joining the Columbia River at Pasco, Washington. The hot spot

MAP 16.1. Snake River Plain, Idaho. The distinctive crescent-shaped swath was created by the hot spot moving beneath the plain.

now underlies Yellowstone, but as the continental plate journeyed across the Snake River Plain, the hot spot caused basalts and other volcanic rock to be deposited on the surface. Fresh lava flows are sterile and barren, and it can take thousands of years before the soil can support vegetation. Once vegetation colonizes the rock, it breaks down into a rich soil. The Snake River Plain is Idaho's best agricultural land, and it contains most of the state's population.

Basin and Range

Averaging less than ten inches of precipitation annually, the nation's most arid region is exactly what it is called, a basin and range, with topography composed of more than 150 short, north-south-trending ranges interspersed with broad, flat desert **basins**. The five-hundred-mile-wide expanse, hemmed in from Utah's Wasatch Range to the Sierra Nevada, widens to nearly seven hundred miles along the southwestern border of California, east into Texas near El Paso. In the north, the indefinite boundaries blend into the Columbia Plateau, and in the south they continue into Mexico.

The major subregions in the Basin and Range are

- the Great Basin;
- the Sonoran Desert; and
- the Mexican Highlands.

The Great Basin

The Great Basin consists of most of Nevada, the western half of Utah, and surrounding areas. Named for its closed internal drainage system, the Great Basin is confined east and west by mountain systems that keep the water from ocean outlets. It is one of the driest areas because evaporation exceeds precipitation. What water there is sinks into the ground to the water table, emits from groundwater springs along fault lines, or evaporates, leaving high-mineral-content water in saline lakes. Water is regionally important, not because of its prevalence but because of its scarcity. The lack of water leaves the land stark, parched, and capable of providing for few humans, although many other species abound.

The land has not always been so dry. The wetter and cooler Pleistocene climate supported over a hundred lakes, but today, most are **playas** (dry lakebeds). The two largest Pleistocene lakes were Bonneville and Lahontan. The Great Salt Lake and Pyramid Lake are remnants of those former lakes. Some lakes accumulate water during the spring runoff, evaporate and leave behind salts, and then repeat the cycle annually; other lakes are more ephemeral, appearing irregularly in relation to precipitation.

This region was earmarked in the 1940s as a nuclear test site. It is also home to Area 51—the loneliest road in America—and Yucca Mountain, a designated storage area for nuclear waste. In 2002, Yucca Mountain was officially designated as the site to store the nation's spent fuel and high-level radioactive waste. The Department of Energy spent an estimated $8 billion studying the site and constructing the exploratory tunnel

PHOTO 16.2. Death Valley, California. The lowest elevation in the United States, Death Valley is part of the Mojave Desert and lies within the Basin and Range subregion. In the background are the Sierra Nevada, with the highest elevation in the conterminous United States.

beneath the mountain. But the site has been controversial: many worry it is not a suitable site; opponents were concerned about radiation standards and there were numerous lawsuits. In 2011, funding for the construction of Yucca Mountain was stopped. Today, the site is abandoned and the US remains without a permanent repository for nuclear waste.

Mojave Desert The southern Great Basin consists of a maze of uplifted mountains and downfaulting basins. When it does rain, streams deposit sediment, shaping **alluvial fans** at the base of the ranges. Regional vegetation varies from low desert xerophytic plants (resistant to drought) (photo 16.2), including creosote bush, ocotillo tree, and the cholla cactus, and high desert plant life, featuring the distinctive Joshua tree.

Owens Valley, in the rain shadow of the Sierra Nevada, receives scant precipitation, but the abundant runoff from the mountains allowed valley residents to raise cattle and orchards. The growth of Los Angeles and its demand for water changed the local economy in the early twentieth century, robbing the Owens Valley of its water and thus its agricultural livelihood. The valley remains dry and depends on outdoor tourism to support the local economy. Owens Valley and Los Angeles water rights remain controversial (photo 16.3).

The Sonoran Desert

The Sonoran Desert extends from southeastern California, across southern Arizona, and south into Mexico. Subregions include the Salton Trough, Anza Borrego Desert, California's Coachella and Imperial Valleys, and Arizona's Gila Desert. Intense summer heat limited habitation to the desert edges or the few water oases, until air-conditioning enabled regional growth.

Lower-elevation native plants in the Sonoran Desert are xerophytic; the saguaro cacti are the indicator species. Higher elevations support chaparral and evergreen trees (photo 16.4).

The Mexican Highlands

The Mexican Highlands lay between the Sonoran Desert and the Colorado Plateau and spread from Arizona to Big Bend, Texas. Volcanic activity faulted and deformed mountains between the higher-elevation plateaus and the desert. Torrential **flash floods** cut **arroyos** (Spanish, "dry creek") into the plains, creating a physiographic anomaly: people can drown in the desert.

The Mogollon Rim, a series of high escarpments that run from Sedona, Arizona, to the New Mexico border, separates the Colorado Plateau from the Sonoran Desert. The rim was home to western storyteller Zane Grey, who featured this "Tonto Rim" in his books. Forests dominate the mountains, while grasslands, creosote bushes, mesquite trees, and sagebrush inhabit the basin.

The easternmost Basin and Range province is a transition zone holding the tension between the Intermontane, Great Plains, and Rocky Mountains. The thin, fractured crust of the Rio Grande rift zone may eventually widen into a gulf or ocean basin, but it currently separates the Great Plains and the Intermontane; to the north, distinctive hogback formations introduce the southern extent of the Rocky Mountains Sangre de Cristo range.

Colorado Plateau

A maze of uplifted, eroded mesas and canyons shapes the mile-high, 150,000-square-mile Colorado Plateau, leaving a rocky, difficult-to-traverse region of colorful sedimentary layers.

PHOTO 16.3. Mono Lake, Southeast California. Lake water levels began to decline after 1941, when Los Angeles began diverting its streams. The lake water levels dropped and the salinity doubled, causing the ecosystem to collapse. The Mono Lake Committee, an organization started in 1978 by concerned citizens, has filed lawsuits, helped pass legislation, and led restoration efforts. Today, water levels are rising, minimizing the salt flats (white areas at lake margin). Yet much remains to be done to get water levels back to levels that better sustain the ecosystem.

PHOTO 16.4. Saguaro Cactus in the Sonoran Desert.
Source: iStock/tonda

The Colorado River cuts through the layers, creating the Grand Canyon and draining 90 percent of the plateau. To the north and east rise the Rocky Mountains, and to the west and south, bold escarpments overlook the Basin and Range. Within the plateau are the Canyonlands, a maze of colorful slickrock-sandstone arches, and the flat-topped **mesas** and **buttes** that are home to four national parks, monuments, and several national forests.

The lower-elevation mesas are wooded with piñon and juniper cedar, and spruce, pine, and fir at higher elevations. However, the attractive grasslands of the lower plateau have been overgrazed and reduced to desert scrub due to poor range management.

Water

Intermontane rivers—the Columbia, Colorado, and Rio Grande—are **exotic streams** (originating in a humid area but flowing through an arid area) and have been a battleground for water rights. In 1878, John Wesley Powell wrote his *Report on the Lands of the Arid Region of the United States.* He concluded

BOX 16.1   NATIONAL PARKS: GRAND CANYON

Grand Canyon National Park is one of the Crown Jewels of the National Park system. The canyon is immense in size: up to 18 miles wide and 1 mile deep and features 227 miles of river. In addition to its natural features, it has many sites of archeological significance and historic structures. Grand Canyon was designated a National Park in 1919, three years after the creation of the National Park Service.

Today, Grand Canyon National Park receives close to five million visitors each year. Most of these visitors expect clean air and clear views. But Grand Canyon suffers from air pollution. The park lies downwind of polluted air from coal-fired power plants in the Four Corners region, nearby mining, and urban and industrial pollutants from Mexico and California.

The impacts of air pollution on the park are many and include the following:

- Fine particles of air pollution cause haze in the park, affecting how well and how far visitors can see vistas and landmarks.
- Nitrogen and sulfur in air pollution are carried into the park through rain, snow, and "dry deposition" (dust). Nitrogen and sulfur compounds deposited from air pollution can harm surface waters, soils, and vegetation. In some ecosystems, nutrient effects from nitrogen deposition cause changes to soil nutrient cycling and the species composition of plant communities.

- Ground-level ozone in the park sometimes reaches levels known to harm plants. Ozone enters and leaves through pores (stomata), where it can kill plant tissues, causing visible injury and reduced photosynthesis, growth, and reproduction.
- Toxic contaminants including mercury accumulate in the park's Colorado River. Concentrations of mercury and other metals in the Colorado River have exceeded Environmental Protection Agency (EPA) drinking water criteria at times. Airborne toxic contaminants, including heavy metals like mercury, can deposit to soils, lakes, and streams, then enter the food chain and accumulate in the tissues of wildlife and humans.*

In response to these problems, the National Park Service Air Resources Division administers an extensive Air Monitoring Program that measures air pollution levels in national parks. The purpose of the Program is to establish current air quality conditions and to assess long-term trends of air pollutants that affect park resources.

One change the Park Service has implemented is using an environmentally friendly alternative fuel vehicle fleet and a shuttle bus system for park visitors, reducing the number of vehicles on some of the busiest roads and reducing air pollutant emissions in the park.

PHOTO 16.5. View of the Grand Canyon from the Colorado Plateau.
Source: National Park Service

PHOTO 16.6. Haze from Air Pollution Impedes the Same View.
Source: National Park Service

*National Park Service. "Air Quality at Grand Canyon National Park" (2017), at https://www.nature.nps.gov/air/Permits/aris/grca/

that there was not enough water to support large populations or large-scale agriculture. His prophecies went unheeded in the late nineteenth century, but have proven to be prescient.

The Intermontane West was divvied up by speculators and a Congress that wanted to populate the West quickly. The results

are evident today in river water policies. For example, dams along the Columbia and Colorado rivers supply irrigation water for agriculture and provide half of the nation's waterpower resources, but at a cost of overallocation and destruction of natural habitats.

BOX 16.2   DID YOU KNOW . . . THE SALTON SEA

The Salton Sea was created in a 1904 irrigation accident that caused the Colorado River to overflow into the Imperial Valley Trough. Thousands of years previously, the trough had been covered with Lake Cahuilla, whose wave-cut shoreline can still be seen along the hillsides. The mud left from the lakebed is the fertile soil now farmed in the Imperial and Coachella valleys. The trough was formed by the earthquake-prone rifting system that stretches from the Gulf of California to north of San Francisco.

The Salton Sea—a closed hydrologic basin where evaporation exceeds precipitation, resulting in salty water—has gone through a number of transformations, from accident to seaside resort in the 1950s to ecological wasteland since the 1970s.

Today, the sea is forty-five miles long and fifteen miles wide and has three uses: a drainage basin for southeastern California irrigation, a wildlife refuge, and a settlement site. For years, the sea has been receding through evaporation and reduced agricultural drainage from irrigation. It has been kept alive by water from the Colorado River. But as the Colorado River continues to be diverted to thirsty cities, some experts say the sea may shrink by 60 percent by 2030. Salinity might increase threefold, killing off the remaining fish and leaving millions of birds without food or nesting habitat.[*]

The good news is that there has been momentum to restore the Salton Sea, and in 2016, California budgeted $80 million to build canals and artificial wetlands.

---

*Tyler Hayden. "How Do We Save the Salton Sea?" *Audubon Magazine* online (summer 2016), at: http://www.audubon.org/magazine/summer-2016/how-do-we-save-salton-sea

PHOTO 16.7. Lake Mead as Seen from the Hoover Dam. The white "bathtub rings" are calcium markings on the rock formations that show how drought has significantly lowered water levels.

Columbia River

The Columbia River, second in size only to the Mississippi River system, is the largest North American river to enter the Pacific Ocean. Mountain snowpack supplies the water for the thirty dams that provide irrigation and generate power. Beginning in the 1930s, the **Columbia Basin Project** converted dryland crop areas into higher-yielding irrigated land. The project centerpiece, Grand Coulee Dam, irrigates more than six hundred thousand acres of land and is the largest producer of hydroelectric power in the United States. The Snake River flows from near Jackson Hole, Wyoming, across Idaho's Snake River Plain into Oregon, passing through deep, dark canyons, the Palouse, and then joining the Columbia. The Yakima River flows from the Cascades to eastern Washington. Both irrigate the surrounding dry but fertile agricultural land.

Colorado River

The Colorado River is the most important river in the arid southwestern United States. The Colorado flows fourteen hundred miles from the Rocky Mountains through the Colorado Plateau and the southern Basin and Range. Seven western states depend on the river's water for their agricultural and urban needs. Beginning in 1935, Hoover Dam transferred the river's water to irrigate Los Angeles, the Coachella and Imperial Valleys, and later Las Vegas. Other dams and the Colorado River Aqueduct followed, continuing to irrigate more than five hundred thousand acres of land.

From Glen Canyon to Lake Mead, dams divert and control river waters and diminish flow into the Mexico borderlands. In the last decade, a series of serious droughts depleted the flow and reduced the amount of water in Glen Canyon and Lake Mead (photo 16.7). In 2016, the water levels marked the lowest the lake had since it was filled in 1930. Today, the lake is about 38 percent full. Low water levels have now become the norm for Lake Mead, and it will take decades of good snow fall in the Rockies to restore the Lake's water levels.

In the early twentieth century, a growing Los Angeles diverted Colorado River water at the expense of other states. In order to secure future rights to the river's water, the seven western states agreed in the 1922 **Colorado River Compact** to divide the waters between them. California received one-quarter of the water and any unused surpluses. But increased population growth and drought in the southwestern states has meant reducing the amount of water destined for California. There have been numerous and ongoing renegotiations about specific state allocations. Compounding the problem is the fact that the Compact was based on an average flow of water in the 1920s; continued drought and lower water flow has meant new regulations about how to allocate the river water in the event of water shortages.

Rio Grande

The Rio Grande originates in the San Juan Mountains of southern Colorado and flows for almost two thousand miles before it becomes navigable near the Gulf of Mexico. Gorges and mountain slopes flank the torrential river from its source to the Albuquerque, New Mexico, plain, where the river enters a desert environment and the Rio Grande rift trough. For approximately two-thirds of its course, the river serves as the boundary between the United States and Mexico.

Salt Lakes

Salt lakes are the termini of inland drainage basins, where evaporation exceeds precipitation, leaving behind concentrated salts and minerals. The interior basin remnant lakes are three to five times saltier than ocean water.

The Great Basin has several dry lakes. Historically, the largest of these was Lake Bonneville, which was thousands of feet deep and ten times larger than its fluctuating remnant, the shallow Great Salt Lake. Today, Lake Bonneville is a dry, flat salt bed, where alkaline minerals are mined industrially. Bonneville Salt Flats is the largest salt flats west of Salt Lake. The flats have long been used for motor racing. In the months of August "Speed Week" and September "World of Speed," cars trucks and motorcycles attempt to set land speed records.

The Great Salt Lake, located in the northern part of the state of Utah, is the largest salt water lake in the Western Hemisphere. The Great Salt Lake is salty because it does not have an outlet. The lake is too saline to support fish and most other aquatic species, although brine shrimp and brine flies can tolerate the level of salinity and feed on lake algae. Water levels in the lake have been erratic thwarting attempts to develop its shoreline. As a result, much of the lake is ringed by extensive wetlands, making Great Salt Lake one of the most important resources for migrating and nesting birds.

Sinks

Many Great Basin streams are ephemeral or disappear into sinkholes, where they leach into groundwater or evaporate, leaving behind salts and minerals. Within the Great Basin are two major sinks: the Humboldt River, which disappears into the Humboldt Sink near Lovelock, Nevada; and the Carson Sink, once the deepest part of ancient Lake Lohantan. The saline sinks are the only source of local water and are a stopover for migratory wildlife. The sinks were the last source of water for pioneer wagons until the Sierra Nevada.

Water, Drought, and Conservation

Population growth and land use change over the past three decades have exacerbated long-term water problems. Drought has made these problems even more challenging. The Intermontane continues to rely on irrigated agriculture. Arizona, the Imperial Valley, and the Columbia Basin continue to grow water-hungry, irrigated cotton and corn, where dryland cropping or less water-thirsty crops may be a wiser water choice. Western water rights—the law of prior appropriation and the law of beneficial use—contort water usage for both agricultural and urban use. Historically, prior appropriation was adopted due to the initial amount of time and work necessary to irrigate the dry land. While at one point it made sense to reward the initial irrigators, the system has since become unbalanced.

Delivering water to thirsty residents has been another challenge. The Central Arizona Project (CAP) was formed in 1946, when Arizona became the final signatory to the Colorado River Compact. The federally funded CAP aqueduct was completed in 1993. The project was allocated to Arizona's portion of the Colorado River, 336 miles from Lake Havasu to Tucson (photo 16.8). The $4 billion aqueduct system was initially design to supplement agricultural water, but a serious groundwater overdraft due to increased population shifted the use from agriculture alone to municipal and industrial use. The CAP aqueduct serves residents in both Phoenix and Tucson.

Despite the past decade of prolonged drought and continued population growth, water conservation has been uneven. The dry Phoenix area sports vast greenbelts, and nearby affluent Scottsdale sports noontime sprinklers despite temperatures over 90°F through October. The Phoenix area, where residents are often complacent and in denial, accesses an overdrafted underground aquifer that has dropped the water table and caused subsidence. While the city touts that it is conserving water, its efforts are not always visible.

Climate

The lack of precipitation is the defining climatic attribute of the Intermontane. The rain shadow of the Cascade Mountains and the Sierra Nevada halts most coastal moisture from the west, and the Rocky Mountains block any connection to eastern humidity. The result is a dry region, from the barren Anza Borrego Desert, receiving less than two inches of precipitation annually, to the loess-covered Palouse, with its beneficent six to sixteen inches annually. Even that scant precipitation often evaporates, leaving the region even drier.

Cloudbursts rain on the thinly vegetated land and then run off, eroding and transporting soil. The continental climate oscillates between hot summers and cold winters, although diurnal summer patterns result in hot days and cold nights.

The Colorado Plateau averages fifteen inches of precipitation annually, mostly through summer thunderstorms that produce runoff and a little groundwater recharge. During the winter, the high plateau receives some snow, which nourishes the plant life.

PHOTO 16.8. Aerial View of the Central Arizona Project.
Source: Dicklyon

The Sonoran Desert temperatures, winds, and moisture govern a sporadic summer monsoon season of higher humidity. Large and sometimes dangerous dust storms called **haboobs** may precede short, intense monsoon rains (photo 16.9).

Historical Geography and Settlement

The first inhabitants of this rugged region moved into the region around 200 AD. Later, Europeans battled against the desert landscape.

Native American

Major indigenous tribes included the Nez Perce in the Columbia Basin; the Paiute in California, Nevada, and Arizona; and the Navajo, Hopi, Hohokam, and Mogollon across Arizona and New Mexico and the Anazasi who lived in the Four Corners area. Each had a distinct culture that adapted to their natural habitat.

The Anasazi (The Ancient Ones) thought to be the modern Pueblo Indians, lived in the Four Corners country of Utah, Colorado, New Mexico, and Arizona from about 200 AD to 1300. The Anasazi lived in elaborate cliff dwelling, some of them reaching five stories in height and containing dozens of rooms (photo 16.10). They farmed corn and squash. Their artistry weaving intricate baskets earned them the name "basketmakers." By 750 AD, they were making red clay pottery and gray or black/white painted wares. By 1400, almost all the Anasazi left and moved into larger pueblos around the drainages of the Little Colorado and Rio Grande rivers in Arizona and New Mexico. One theory is that a

BOX 16.3 CLIMATE CHANGE: IT'S GETTING HOT IN HERE

When it comes to extreme heat, Arizona is one of the many states at risk. In June 2017, temperatures in Phoenix reached 120 degrees for several days. The National Weather Service issued an excessive heat warning for the city noting that "heat of this magnitude is rare, dangerous and very possibly deadly."

American Airlines cancelled more than fifty flights from Phoenix's Sky Harbor Airport, citing concerns about flying in temperatures exceeding 118 degrees. The airline was concerned about how the heat might affect the electronic systems, and how heat can affect aerodynamic performance making it more difficult for planes to take off in thinner, hotter air.*

Canceled flights were an inconvenience, but set off yet another round of discussion about potential impacts of climate change in desert cities. The 2014 National Climate Assessment Report notes that Phoenix is the second-fastest warming city in the United States over the past fifty years, while Las Vegas comes in at third and Tucson at seventh. Climate change is largely responsible for boosting those background temperatures, increasing the odds of setting record highs like those in June 2017.

According to the report, climate models suggest that the already parched region is expected to get hotter and significantly drier. Arizona, Nevada, and parts of New Mexico have heated up markedly in recent decades, and the period since 1950 has been hotter than any comparably long period in at least six hundred years. The decade 2001–2010 was the warmest in the 110-year instrumental record, with temperatures almost 2°F higher than historic averages, with fewer cold air outbreaks and more heat waves.

The impacts of climate change could be numerous. Some predictions are that Phoenix and most of Arizona will suffer more deaths and economic losses than most of the country under current climate change projections. Projected temperature increases, combined with the urban heat island effect, will pose increased threats and costs to public health in southwestern cities, which are home to more than 90 percent of the region's population. Disruptions to urban electricity and water supplies could exacerbate these health problems. In addition, Phoenix has long struggled to supply its growing population with enough water. It and other cities like Los Angeles, Las Vegas, and San Diego are preparing for dwindling water supplies due to climate change.

*Brian Kahn. "It's So Hot in Phoenix Planes Can't Take Off." *Climate Connection* (June 20, 2017), at: http://www.climatecentral.org/news/phoenix-heat-wave-planes-takeoff-21558

PHOTO 16.9. Intense dust storms, called haboobs, occur regularly in arid regions in Arizona and Nevada.
Source: iStock/BigRedCurlyGuy

prolonged drought that began in 1276 may have forced them to relocate.

The Nez Perce arrived in the northern Intermontane around twelve thousand years ago. They lived in scattered villages and developed a salmon-harvesting culture along the rivers. They hunted wildlife, harvested the local camas bulbs to make bread,

and traded goods with Natives from both the coastal and interior areas. After contact with Europeans in the late eighteenth century, smallpox and other deadly epidemics decimated the Nez Perce.

The Northern and Southern Paiute were only related linguistically. The Northern Paiute lived in the Great Basin, where they

PHOTO 16.10. An Anasazi Cliff Village in Mesa Verde National Park. These villages were usually multistoried and multipurpose and included apartments, and cultural and civic spaces.
Source: iStock/YinYang

fished and gathered roots and seeds. The Southern Paiute lived along the Colorado River and Mojave Desert. Wars, slavery, and smallpox eventually devastated both Paiute groups.

In the Basin and Range, ancestral Native groups had attained a high stage of civilization, but these tribes had disappeared prior to European contact. When the first Europeans arrived, the Navajo, Hopi, Pueblo, Apache, and Utes were living on the landscape, growing maize and creating pottery and weavings.

European Incursion

The Spanish arrived in New Mexico in 1598 and quickly forced rule over the local tribes. During the seventeenth century, Pueblo revolts about religion, the destruction of their culture, and abusive labor practices disrupted Spanish occupancy, but ultimately the Spanish prevailed. American dominance began in the mid-nineteenth century.

Initial geographic information about the Basin and Range came from Spanish exploration, followed years later by information from American fur trappers. In the northern Intermontane, the British fur trappers dominated the regional landscape. However, despite these nineteenth-century incursions, the Intermontane was settled slowly; it was bypassed during the mania for continent-wide **Manifest Destiny** (divinely ordained expansion) (map 16.2). Only later would it be settled.

The Intermontane region entered the Union as territories in the 1840s. In 1846, the Oregon Country was defined along the 49th parallel. The Treaty of Guadalupe-Hidalgo ended the Mexican American War, and the **Mexican Cession of 1848** ceded 525,000 square miles of New Mexico, Arizona, California, Colorado, Utah, and Nevada to the United States for the bargain price of $15 million. Following annexation, the California Gold Rush and the Silver Lode in Nevada drew settlers into these areas and speeded their statehood. Despite the gold and silver rushes, most of the Intermontane remained a sometimes traversed but sparsely settled area into the mid-twentieth century.

Opening Up the Intermontane

Trails marked the dry and difficult passages through the Intermontane (map 16.3). The Oregon Trail crossed the Wyoming Basin and Utah, and then followed the trickling Humboldt River to the Sierra Nevada. The Santa Fe Trail traversed desert terrain south of the Rocky Mountains. On the Columbia Plateau, traveling down the Columbia Gorge to the Willamette Valley was treacherous.

When a transcontinental railroad was first considered, the most feasible Pacific-bound route was not through the higher elevations of the Wyoming Basin but through the more easily traversed Southwest a route along the 32nd parallel.

The most obvious southern route followed the tributaries of the Gila River—an area south of the Mexican Cession. In 1853, James Gadsden negotiated the purchase of thirty thousand square miles from Mexico for $10 million. The **Gadsden Purchase** was a strategic political move. It also proved a coup for the southern railroad route.

But building a transcontinental railroad proved contentious. A congressional battle ensued between the northern and southern route, which remained unresolved until the secession of the southern states. The first transcontinental railroad line was completed in 1869, across the more northerly Wyoming Basin route. The route reflected the bias against the South after the Civil War. The Southern Pacific line, through the Gadsden Purchase land, was completed in 1881, long after the end of the war.

The progression of transportation and technology transformed Native American trails into rail lines and later, in the twentieth century, highways. The railroads opened up the Intermontane to settlement.

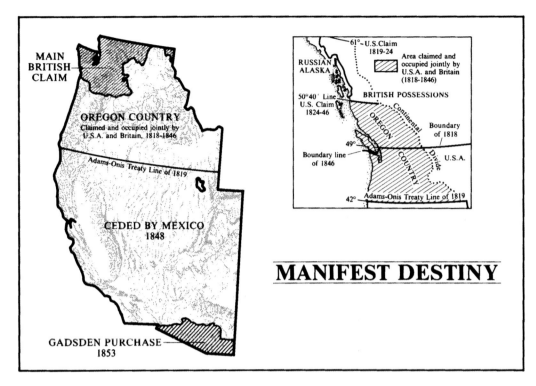

MAP 16.2. Manifest Destiny Territorial Acquisitions in the Far West.

Source: Thomas F. McIlwraith and Edward K. Muller, eds., *North America: The Historical Geography of a Changing Continent,* 2nd ed. (Lanham, MD: Rowman & Littlefield, 2001)

Cultural Perspective

Over time, five distinctive cultures have populated the region: Native Americans, Hispanics, Mormons, Basques, and retirees. Native Americans settled first, and for the most part remained after European settlement. The Hispanic culture arrived in the seventeenth century and strongly influenced the southern Intermontane. The Mormons escaped persecution by relocating to culturally disparate Utah, whereas the Basques were culturally preadapted to their new mountainous home-land. Retirees comprise a twentieth century cultural phenom-enon of pensioned seniors who relocate for climate, lifestyle, and amenities.

Native American Culture

About 23 percent of the three million Native Americans living in the United States continue to live on reservations. Although scattered throughout the region, the largest concentration is in the Four Corners region of the southwest Basin and Range.

Thirteen percent of the national Native American pop-ulation, Ute, Hopi, Jicarilla Apache, and Navajo, occupy reservations in the Four Corner states (map 16.4). The Navajo Nation occupies the largest reservation, consisting of sixteen million acres of land spread throughout Arizona, New Mexico, and Utah. The Navajo (*Diné Bikeyah*, meaning "Land of the People") are also the largest recognized Native American tribe, with more than 286,000 people claiming ethnicity; more than 85 percent of them live on the reservation.

The Apache and Navajo are related to the Athabascan family of Native Americans. They migrated to the Southwest from the Athabascan territories in Canada about a thousand years

ago. The Navajo have maintained their more sedentary lifestyle living in their homeland after European settlement. The Jicarilla Apache were seminomadic, living in southern Colorado and into New Mexico. Their reservation land is rich with oil and gas, which, along with casinos and ranching, support the people—although they continue to be known for their intricate basketry.

At present, 40 percent of the Navajo live below the poverty level, with a per capita income of $7,200. About one-third of Navajo homes homes lack electricity and plumbing, 38 percent lack water services, 86 percent lack natural gas, and 60 percent lack telephone services.

Navajo income sources include pastoral herding, Black Mesa mineral rights, and tourism.

The agricultural Hopi reservation is surrounded by the Navajo reservation (map 16.4). Hopi and Navajo lands have been adjacent, but contentious land disputes between the tribes predate European contact. Since the 1950s, differences in tra-ditional land use systems and the Black Mesa coal deposit within the reservation area exacerbated the disputes, until an agreement was reached in 1996.

The Mountain Utes occupy southwestern Colorado and have progressed from hunters and gatherers to livestock raiders. Currently, the Utes are known for their beading work and have entered the casino industry.

For many Native Americans in this region, there have been ongoing issues with the Department of the Interior's Bureau of Indian Affairs (BIA). Despite spending some $19 billion yearly, the BIA has been criticized for the woeful state of schools on tribal lands, continued poverty, and a failure to invest in technology and infrastructure. A 2016 Government Accountability Office report said the Bureau has not used best

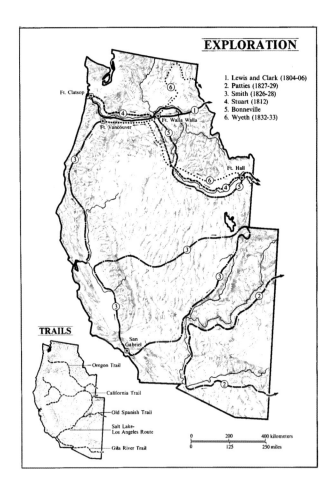

Ft. Clatsop

Ft. Vancouver

Ft. Walla Walla

Ft. Hall

San Gabriel

TRAILS

Oregon Trail

California Trail

Old Spanish Trail

Salt Lake–
Los Angeles Route

Gila River Trail

0   200   400 kilometers
0   125   250 miles

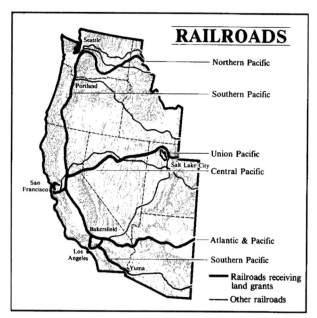

RAILROADS

Seattle

Portland

San Francisco

Bakersfield

Los Angeles

Yuma

Salt Lake City

Northern Pacific

Southern Pacific

Union Pacific

Central Pacific

Atlantic & Pacific

Southern Pacific

Railroads receiving
land grants

Other railroads

MAP 16.3. Intermontane Exploration. The Intermontane was explored by Lewis and Clark and several others before settlers began to arrive via the various wagon train trails. Many settlers traveled beyond the Intermontane on trails that led to the far West. As transportation for crops and livestock via the railroad became available in the 1870s, farmers and ranchers began to settle the dry area.

Source: Thomas F. McIlwraith, and Edward K. Muller, eds. *North America: The Historical Geography of a Changing Continent.* 2nd ed. Lanham, MD: Rowman & Littlefield, 2001

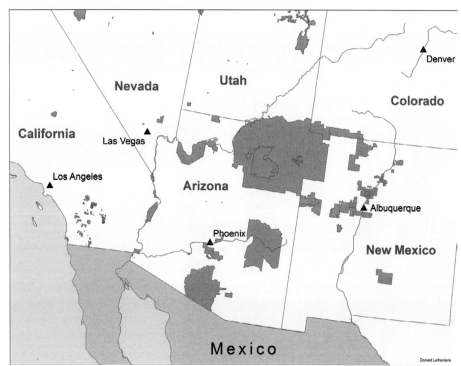

Nevada

Utah

Denver

Colorado

California

Las Vegas

Los Angeles

Arizona

Phoenix

Albuquerque

New Mexico

Mexico

Donald Lafreniere

MAP 16.4. Four Corners Reservations. Native American reservations in the Four Corners region of the United States. The Navajo have the largest reservation in the States, 27,635 square miles. The Hopi reservation is completely surrounded by the Navajo reservation, which is the largest brown area near Four Corners.

practices in carrying outs its mission and called for an overhaul of the agency, noting fraud, waste, and mismanagement were widespread.

Hispanic Culture

For four hundred years, Spanish culture has influenced the southwestern landscape, creating the following cultural artifacts:

- The Law of the Indies plaza-style city pattern, built to work in harmony with the sun's rays;
- Hispanic livestock-raising methods that became the basis for cowboy culture;
- The southwestern architectural style, using adobe and tiles made from local sources, which is ubiquitous in Arizona and New Mexico;
- The Western water policy of "first in time, first in right," based on Spanish law;
- The introduction of horses to the Native Americans, which changed their cultures permanently;
- The influence of the Spanish language in speech and toponyms; and
- Mexican cuisine, which is based on local ingredients.

The National Council of La Raza (from the Spanish *la raza*, "the race") is a Hispanic American ethnocentrist organization. La Raza is characterized by its exclusive use of Spanish. It is both a separatist movement and as a means to reduce poverty, discrimination, and to improve the Hispanic American quality of life. The La Raza philosophy emphasizes family unity. This cultural difference slows **acculturation** between the Anglo and Hispanic cultures, while calling attention to the successes and failures of both cultures and what can be learned from each.

Mormon Culture

In the mid-nineteenth century, Mormon settlers fled religious persecution and migrated from New York sequentially to Ohio, Illinois, and Missouri, searching for their promised land. John C. Fremont's writings on Great Salt Basin influenced their leader, Brigham Young, to settle in Deseret (the state of Utah) in 1847, and establish Mormon outposts throughout the Intermontane. Their towns are modeled upon their primary city, Salt Lake City, which was planned as the biblical Zion, with a rigid settlement pattern that enforced social interaction among the settlers.

Utah was settled as a religious theocracy, the New Zion. Under the leadership of Brigham Young, the Mormons systematically colonized Utah and a constellation of regional oases by establishing community-based but hierarchically formalized irrigated farms. Utah statehood was delayed until 1896, when the Mormon practice of polygamy was banned. Despite the ban, some fundamentalists in Utah's hinterland areas still practice polygamy today, although officially the Mormon Church disowns them for continuing this practice. Today, Utah remains a Mormon stronghold (photo 16.11).

The Basques

The **Basque** homeland in the Pyrenees of Northern Spain was near both the mountains and the ocean, a fishing and sheep-raising economy. Basques migrated to California's Gold Rush originally, but after the Gold Rush decline, many Basques settled in the Intermontane, which physically resembled their mountain homeland and allowed them to continue their sheep-based livelihood. They settled in northern California, Nevada, eastern Oregon, and southwestern Idaho.

As latecomers to these areas, the Basques contributed few visible cultural landmarks in the Intermontane. However, a Basque influence can be found in regional restaurants that

PHOTO 16.11. The Salt Lake Temple, Salt Lake City, Utah. The temple is located on Temple Square in Salt Lake City. It is considered sacred by the Church of Jesus Christ of Latter-day Saints and its members, so there are no public tours inside the temple.

Source: iStock/AndreyKrav

feature communal-style meals that specialize in cuisine featuring lamb and seafood.

Retirement Culture

Americans have gravitated toward more nuclear rather than multigenerational homes and families. The breakup of multigenerational families has been accompanied by the rise in financially and physically able retirees moving to amenity-rich areas. Since 1960, the preferred destination for retirees has been the Sun Belt. Arizona is second to Florida in having the largest percentage of those over the age of sixty (17 percent), a number which is expected to only increase.

Retirees move either to planned retirement communities, where entry is limited to those over age fifty-five, or to Sun Belt cities that have become retirement meccas with a far higher-than-US-average senior population. Lake Havasu and Oro Valley in Arizona and St. George in Utah have more than 25 percent of their population over sixty-five years. And growth is predicted for Phoenix and Las Vegas. Retirees affect the cultural landscape because their social requirements and decisions are based on different criteria than that of the younger population. For example, their needs tend to include more health care facilities, specialized housing, transportation, and social services.

One of the biggest impacts they have had is on the creation of retirement communities for those over age fifty-five. There are retirement communities in Tucson, Phoenix, Prescott, and Flagstaff. Perhaps the most famous is Sun City, home to forty thousand residents all over fifty-five years of age. Sun City pioneered the "active adult" concept with the notion that residents should be able to live in an entirely self-contained community with access to numerous amenities. The community boasts the largest golf holes per capita, and golf-cart-legal streets provide a mode of transportation to the recreation and shopping centers within the community.

Population, Immigration, and Diversity

The Intermontane rate of growth since the 1990s has been much higher than in the United States as a whole. In 1950, five states within the region (Arizona, Idaho, Nevada, New Mexico, and Utah) contained 1.9 percent of America's population. In 2010, those same states held 5.1 percent of the total population. Today, Utah is the fastest growing state, followed by Nevada, although all the states in the Intermontane are above the national average. Growth occurs as a result of internal migration to warmer climes by retirees, and by young midwestern Americans seeking more job opportunities, better weather, and more active cities.

Reasons for internal migration vary. For example, increased housing costs is fueling emigration from California. At present, more than a third of Nevada's population growth is the result of Californian emigration. In fact, Nevada, Arizona, and Oregon can all claim domestic migration as their main source

of growth, while other states, such as Idaho, New Mexico, Washington, and Utah (with the highest fertility rate in the nation at 2.6 children per woman), owe much of their population rise to natural increase.

Utah's population has grown, but it is no longer only Mormon. In 2004, 62 percent of the population in Utah was Mormon; this percentage continues to decline. Some experts predict that by 2030, Mormons may no longer be a majority of the state population. The Mormon majority in Utah declined for two reasons: the non-Mormon birthrate and the influx of non-Mormon aerospace and defense workers who come to the region for such amenities as ski resorts and mountain recreation.

Population statistics indicate that white non-Hispanics have been the largest contingent of recent legal migrants, although ethnic group representations are growing disproportionately. For example, the black population was at 3 percent in Arizona in 1990 and rose to 5 percent in 2017, whereas the Hispanic population grew from 18.7 percent to 31 percent during that same time. In the Columbia Plateau, population is mostly white, but 10 percent are diverse population groups, mostly residing within the cities. For example, the population of Spokane, Washington, the largest city in the Columbia Plateau, is 90 percent white and the remainder of the populace is a mix of other ethnic groups.

Forty-two percent of the Basin and Range population are of Hispanic descent, with the highest percentage living in the Albuquerque–Santa Fe region, which historically was 90 percent Hispanic, but after 1900, the percentage declined as Anglos migrated to the region. Other states in the Southwest (including southwestern Texas and southern California) also have a large legal and undocumented Hispanic population. The Hispanic population increased in all of the Intermontane states, with the largest number settling along the border states and counties.

Some of the states and cities in the Intermontane attract significant numbers of foreign born. Arizona is home to 13.5 percent foreign born (just below the national average), and Phoenix's population is 20 percent foreign born. More than 60 percent of the foreign born in Arizona are from Central or South America, with most of those from Mexico, which is not surprising since the state borders Mexico. But two hundred thousand residents, 20 percent of the foreign born, come from Asia. Nevada is also home to 19 percent of foreign born. It is interesting to note, however, that the composition of foreign born does vary within the region—for example, there are few foreign born from El Salvador in Arizona, but in Nevada they account for almost 5 percent (table 16.1).

Not all of the Intermontane is a destination for foreign-born immigrants. Only 5.5 percent of Spokane's population is foreign born and less than 5 percent are in Bend, Oregon.

Much of the Intermontane is still "frontier" with a population below two people per square mile, including 80 percent of Nevada, 44 percent of Idaho, 41 percent of Utah, 27 percent of New Mexico, and 27 percent of Oregon. This is the land of the

BOX 16.4   GLOBAL CONNECTIONS: SURVEILLANCE ON THE BORDER

Boundary lines are one of the most visually defining landscape elements of the border and highlight a divided sense of transborder relationships in North America. Increased investments in border infrastructure, such as border markers, fences, "point of entry" facilities, and bridge crossings, limit the movements of transborder flows, assert national sovereignty, and promote unilateral policy making. Post-9/11 policies have tightened border security particularly between the United States and Mexico.

At the national level, the US Border Patrol (USBP) and the *Patrulla Fronteriza Mexicana*, Mexican Border Patrol, enforce national security policies on the ground by apprehending unauthorized crossers, monitoring flows through the point of entries, and using surveillance techniques to secure border areas. Starting in 2008, USBP began storing data collected about border crossers as part of a database of information used to identify suspicious activity and provide probable cause for conducting more extensive searches of border crossers. Other

surveillance techniques include USBP checkpoints, the use of tethered aerostat radar systems, and unmanned aerial systems (UASs—often called "drones"). Agents at USBP checkpoints along US Interstate 10 and state highways near border communities stop, monitor, and inspect vehicles, asking passengers to state their citizenship. Six aerostats located along the US–Mexico border provide radar support for drug interdiction efforts and six UASs deploy in the US–Mexico border region to provide visual support for interdiction efforts in remote areas (photo 16.12). Yet, these UASs are expensive, costing some $3,000 per flight hour. Critics argue that the high cost and low numbers of apprehensions using UASs make them impractical, but Border Patrol argues that UASs help in many other surveillance capacities beyond simple apprehension. In remote areas near places like Naco, Arizona, a town of only one thousand residents, UASs provide support to on-the-ground USBP agents that drive along the border fence and stand watch in mobile towers to spot border crossers (photo 16.13).

PHOTO 16.12. Aerostats such as this are located on the US–Mexico border.

Source: iStock/CochiseVista

PHOTO 16.13. Border Fence Dividing the United States and Mexico in Nogales, Arizona.

Source: iStock/mdurson

TABLE 16.1. Immigration Profiles for Arizona and Nevada, 2015

Arizona Foreign Born: Top Countries of Origin		Nevada Foreign Born: Top Countries of Origin	
Country	Percentage	Country	Percentage
Mexico	57	Mexico	40
Canada	4.3	Philippines	14.3
India	4.1	El Salvador	4.8
China	3.1	China	4.1
Philippines	3	India	2.1
Vietnam	2.3	South Korea	2.1
All other countries (less than 2% each)	26.2	All other countries (less than 2% each)	32.6

Source: Migration Policy Institute Database, at: http://www.migrationpolicy.org/data/state-profiles/state/demographics/AZ/NV/

rancher and the cowboy, where concerns center on whether cattle are grazing on public or private land, although concerns are changing as cities seek water rights from rural areas.

Urban Trends

Urban development patterns have varied within the Intermontane. Although the Southwest expanded, federally owned land has hampered Great Basin growth. The Columbia Plateau remains a farming region, although the Spokane metropolitan area has grown faster than national averages.

Southwest settlement patterns feature sprawl and lower population densities than east of the Mississippi River. Las Vegas, hemmed in by public lands, has expanded faster than available land and has adopted a high-rise profile. Phoenix's sprawl has resulted in air pollution and gridlocked streets and miles and miles of strip malls.

PHOTO 16.14. Aerial View of Las Vegas, Nevada. One of the fastest growing cities in America, Las Vegas has sprawled despite a severe lack of water, high summer temperatures, and its desert location.

Las Vegas, Nevada
(2016 MSA 2.1 million)

Las Vegas (in Spanish, "the meadows") began as a desert oasis watered by springs that seeped from a groundwater aquifer. The city has grown from five thousand people in 1930, to more than two million in the metro area in 2015.

The first settlers in 1855 were Mormons, but they were recalled to Salt Lake City, and the official city began in 1911 as a desert railroad stop. When the railroad pulled out of Las Vegas in 1925, the town seemed doomed, but in 1931, the city's location near the Hoover Dam construction site and the legalization of gambling caused significant expansion. In the late twentieth century, Las Vegas grew quickly with an estimated seven thousand to eight thousand new households being added each month in a city that lacks both land and water (photo 16.14).

The city of Las Vegas has reached the limits of its available land. The federal government controls 80 percent of Nevada land—more than in any other state. On occasion, the government sells land to developers, but the cost is extreme because so little land is privately held in Nevada. The result has been a high-rise "Manhattanization" of Las Vegas hotels and condominiums. The cost of housing also increased from $150,000 in 2000 to $274,000 today.

Water is a critical issue. Lake Mead provides Las Vegas with 90 percent of its water. Water plays a prominent role in the fantasy of the city, including extravagant displays of water in swimming pools, fountains and water jets, and the lush green fairways of well-watered golf courses. For many years, the city defiantly negated its desert setting in a fantasy of urban spectacularization. By 2005, the city had grown to over half a million and water consumption was just over four hundred gallons per person.

But in the last ten years, the city has implemented water conservation. Although the Bellagio's fountain is iconic for its lavish water use, in fact casinos account for only 8 percent of water use. Most of the water consumed is by residents and their landscapes. Grass is difficult to keep alive in the desert, yet a lush lawn was part of the Vegas lifestyle. In 2003, the city banned new sod in the front yards of residential development; it also outlawed watering in the heat of the day. Today, water consumption is down to 219 gallons per person (compared to

BOX 16.5   ICONIC IMAGES: THE VEGAS STRIP

There is not a more iconic image in the region than the Vegas Strip. It is lined with upscale casinos and hotels, and when the sun goes down, the city shines brightly with hundreds of thousands of neon lights—the Strip is quintessential Las Vegas (photo 16.15).

In 1931, Clark County, Nevada, issued a gaming license to a downtown Las Vegas club. A three-mile dusty desert road reinvented itself as the Strip. One of the earliest strip resorts was the Flamingo Hotel built by gangsters "Bugsy" Siegel and Meyer Lansky. By the 1950s, Elvis, the Rat Pack, and Liberace made Las Vegas a vacation destination and dubbed it "Sin City."

The Strip is always in a state of change: building, expanding, and remodeling. In the 1990s, new high-end luxury hotels like the Mirage and MGM Grand were built and Las Vegas shifted its emphasis from gambling to being an upscale resort destination. Today, there are still casinos but there are also foodie tours, Club Crawls, magic shows, Cirque du Soleil shows, and Miley Cyrus in concert. You can ride a gondola at the Venetian, or enjoy the fountain shows at the Bellagio. And more than thirty-eight million visitors do just that each year.

The city has been branded and rebranded. In 2003, marketers felt Las Vegas needed to rebranded as more than gambling and launched the city's "What Happens Here, Stays Here" slogan. It is one of the more famous taglines in modern tourism marketing and one of the most quoted, talked about, and recognized ad campaigns in any industry.

PHOTO 16.15. Neon Lights Up the Las Vegas Strip. If all the neon lights along the three-mile strip were lined up, it would create a train of neon lights fifteen thousand miles long. However, the introduction of LED lights may mean neon signs will become a fading relic.

Source: iStock/lewkmiller

San Francisco at 46 gallons per person). The city aims to get to 199 gallons per person by 2035. There is still a long way to go.

Water shortages have become a part of everyday Las Vegas life. A progressive conservation program instituted by the Las Vegas water manager has forced the city to face its water denial and enforce conservation measures. Cutbacks on the water allotted for personal domestic use have been augmented with a moratorium on green lawn plantings. Lawn watering is illegal between 11 a.m. and 7 p.m., and water recycling and conservation measures have been instituted for casinos. Xeriscaping (a way of landscaping that negates the need for extra irrigation) has become de rigueur. The inability of some people to accept the "monotonous" desert landscape has resulted in a blossoming of artificial turf cropping up on former lawns, but in general, Las Vegas is accepting some of its prior desert denial.

Phoenix, Arizona
(2016 MSA 4.6 million)

Arizona's capital city of Phoenix's has seen rapid and continued growth since 1950. More than 90 percent of the city's population has moved to the city since 1950. Today, it is the fifth-largest city in the United States and is projected to grow by 30 percent by 2050.

Prior to the invention of air-conditioning, Phoenix was just a small desert town based on Salt River Valley–irrigated agriculture. Since the 1960s, the city has been one of the fastest growing in the nation, increasing 35 percent in each of the past two decades. Three of the major migration groups to the Phoenix area are Hispanics (many of whom are undocumented), retirees, and blue-collar midwesterners, all searching for better climate, jobs, and lifestyle.

The US National Science Foundation funds long-term ecological research projects at twenty-four sites in a long-term ecological research network (LTER). Only two of them specifically study the ecology of urban areas. The two sites, one in Baltimore, Maryland, and the other in Phoenix, Arizona, provide information on urban ecological process and trends.

The goal of the Central Arizona–Phoenix LTER based at Arizona State is to foster social-ecological urban research aimed at understanding these complex systems. There are numerous ongoing research projects.[*]

One research project examined lead in soils.[†] Lead is a toxin that affects cognitive abilities in children. Children can be exposed to lead through contaminated soil. Researchers examined lead in Phoenix metropolitan area soils, using an archive of two hundred soil samples from around the area.

They found elevated lead concentrations in the central core of the Phoenix metropolitan area as well as in southeastern parts of the region (map 16.5). They then compared lead concentrations with the building year of houses, and found that areas with housing built before 1978 had soil samples with high lead concentrations. Samples from areas of housing built before the 1940s had the highest concentrations.

Their next challenge was to understand who in the Phoenix metropolitan area was most likely to be exposed to lead. Using US Census data, they focused on wealth, race, and vulnerability to lead exposure (children under the age of five). Statistical techniques of regression analysis and spatial autocorrelation revealed that areas with relatively high soil lead concentrations are more likely to be Hispanic neighborhoods with a large percentage of renters.

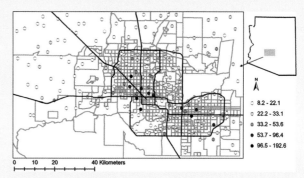

MAP 16.5. Map of Lead Levels in Phoenix, Arizona. Researchers examined lead in Phoenix metropolitan area soils, using an archive of two hundred soil samples from around the area. When they mapped the results, they found elevated lead concentrations in the central core of the Phoenix metropolitan area as well as in southeastern parts of the region.

Source: Xiaoding Zhuo, Chris Boone, and Everett Shock. "Soil lead distribution and environmental justice in the Phoenix metropolitan region." *Environmental Justice* 5, no. 4 (2012): 206–13

These results reveal an environmental justice issue in the Phoenix area where there is an inequitable distribution of risk associated with lead exposure. The Hispanic population at risk includes many immigrants, some of whom have limited English skills and immigrated illegally to the United States. Landlords do not always maintain properties in low-income neighborhoods, allowing paint to peel on properties, and low-income renters seldom have much leverage over their housing conditions. Hispanic renter households, those in the population with limited ability to mitigate lead exposure and the least social and political power, are the most exposed to this toxin.

---

[*]To learn more, go to https://sustainability.asu.edu/caplter/research/

[†]Xiaoding Zhuo, Chris Boone, and Everett Shock. "Soil lead distribution and environmental justice in the Phoenix metropolitan region," *Environmental Justice* 5, no. 4 (2012): 206–13.

Phoenix has been ranked among the top ten cities in the nation in employment growth. The capital city and its surrounding area are home to government, education, and high-tech jobs that have relocated to Arizona because of its highly educated workforce and desirable quality of life.

The economy also depends on a strong tourist and retirement population. More than ten million people visit the region annually, including snowbirds—northerners escaping winter. Arizona had more than three hundred thousand snowbird visitors in 2008.

Like most cities, Phoenix has created a sustainability plan. Phoenix achieved its goal of a 15 percent reduction in greenhouse gas emissions in 2016 and proposed a new goal of a 40 percent reduction by the year 2025. It is also recycling 84 percent of the city's wastewater, and it leads the nation in

the use of alternative fuels for city vehicles. And, capitalizing on its locational advantage, Phoenix has installed 32 MW of solar power on city property. In 2016, the City Council adopted the *2050 Environmental Sustainability Goals* that includes targets around water use, waste, food, transportation, air quality, and buildings. These ambitious goals include the following:

- Provide a clean and reliable 100-year supply of water;
- Reduce carbon pollution from vehicles, buildings, and waste by 80–90 percent;
- Triple the number of light rail miles in Phoenix;
- Achieve zero waste;
- Double the tree canopy to 25 percent; and
- Become carbon neutral by 2060.

BOX 16.7 URBAN SUSTAINABILITY BEST PRACTICES: BEND, OREGON

The state of Oregon has been a leader in sustainability efforts, sustainable energy technology, and sustainable tourism. Bend Oregon is home to a large-scale photovoltaic solar panel manufacturer, Advanced Energy, and a locally owned coffee roaster, Strictly Organic. Downtown, the Oxford Hotel made national headlines as an "Eco-Chic" boutique. The city has numerous recreational amenities including mountains and lakes. It is also one of the fastest growing cities in Oregon, which presents a challenge: how to grow sustainably.

Some cities have tried to control and guide growth and development by establishing an Urban Growth Boundary (UGB). UGBs identify what land is urbanizable—meaning able to be used for housing, transportation, and employment. UGBs are considered one of the effective tools to limit urban sprawl and unplanned development because they direct growth into the core through redevelopment and infill and relieve pressure to develop open space. Growth occurs inside the UGB; areas outside the UBG are preserved in its natural state or used for agriculture.

The state of Oregon was a pioneer in UGB, passing legislation in 1973 that required cities to develop a long-range plan for managing growth. The city of Portland was the first US city to establish a growth boundary in 1979; Bend adopted one shortly after in 1981.

As a city that is attracting new residents, Bend recognized to plan for growth and development. In 2016, the city voted to approve an amended UGB. The UBG is Bend's plan for growth for the next twelve years. Rather than a sprawling, eight-thousand-acre expansion, it focuses the majority of new growth inside the existing growth boundary, along transit corridors and the urban core, and keeps the growth boundary expansion to twenty-three hundred acres. To avoid urban sprawl, the completed UGB plan is a blend of expansion as well as infill. With redevelopment directed in the core, about 70 percent of the projected growth in jobs and housing can be accommodated inside Bend's current growth boundary. The rest will happen gradually over time.

The UGB also seeks to create complete neighborhoods, which means more people will have a full range of services and amenities near their home. Over time, this will encourage families to rely less on their cars and will reduce congestion and the need for costly new transportation infrastructure that comes with sprawl. The plan also focuses on increasing the diversity of housing types to ensure affordable housing for people of all ages and income levels. Finally, the adopted UBG protects the natural areas and habitats that support Bend's outdoor lifestyle and recreation-dependent economy.*

*The Environmental Center of Bend. "2016 Sustainability Award Winners Recognized," at: https://envirocenter.org/wp-content/uploads/merged.pdf

Salt Lake City, Utah
(2016 MSA 1.1 million)

Salt Lake City is the capital of Utah and the Latter Day Saints' (Mormons') core city. The city is just west of the Great Salt Lake, which is located on the lakebed of Pleistocene Lake Bonneville. Prior to Mormon settlement, local Shoshone, Paiute, and Ute tribes used the area for temporary gatherings.

Salt Lake City lost population to the suburban front from 1980 to 2000, but it has since begun to grow again. The population is about 75 percent white, 22 percent Hispanic, 4 percent Asian, and 3 percent black.

The broad-based economy's strong service sector contains high-tech jobs. Also important is mining in the nearby mountains, an example of which is the Kennecott Copper Mine, one of the largest **open pit mines** in the world. Other employment markets include government, church, and tourism. Many move to Utah for amenities such as the mountains, which provide world-class skiing, summertime hiking, and camping opportunities. Pollution is a big concern, as some of the worst smog in the nation is trapped in atmospheric inversions, especially in the winter.

Salt Lake City is dependent on the Rocky Mountain snowpack for its water, and the unevenness of the snowpack each year, a result of climate change, has made the city adopt some sustainable goals. The city now uses compact fluorescent light bulbs and LED lights at traffic signals; has purchased smaller, more fuel-efficient cars for the city's fleet; and converted commercial vehicles to run on natural gas. All future state buildings will be energy-efficient designs incorporating recycled materials. The savings from these initiatives have been invested in wind power. It is notable that in the reliably "red" state of Utah, Salt Lake City's *SustainableSaltLake Plan 2015* sets ambitious goals to reduce greenhouse gases and to create a climate adaptation plan.

Spokane, Washington
(2016 MSA 556,000)

The natural resources of Eastern Washington—fertile soil, timber, and mineral wealth—attracted settlers to the area in the 1870s. Spokane was transformed by the Northern Pacific Railroad and linked into the transcontinetntial system in 1883. In that same year, Spokane experienced its first boom when the discovery of gold in the Coeur d'Alene mining area established Spokane as the service center for the Idaho mines. Spokane became the center of regional commerce and the main gate to the Pacific Northwest. Within a few years, its population increased to twenty thousand.

The expansion and growth of Spokane began to slow as coroporations took control of regional mines and resources and diverted the capital outside of the city.

Throughout the second half of the twentieth century, the city boosters marketed the city as a good place for raising a family rather than a dynamic growth area. In 1974, Spokane hosted the World's Fair and Expo bringing with it a modest increase in the city's notoriety and population. Spokane still holds the record as the smallest city ever to host a World's Fair and was the first city to ever host a fair with an environmental theme.

But by the 1970s, falling silver, timber, and farm prices started an economic decline that would last into the 1990s. Spokane is still trying to make the transition away from a primary economy to the service-oriented economy. There have been efforts at urban revitalization with some success, although the city still has a scarcity of high-paying jobs. Spokane boasts twenty-seven microbreweries and more than two dozen wine-tasting rooms and wineries. The good news is that housing remains affordable—the median house price is $180,000.

The Economy

The Intermontane has led the nation in both population growth and job creation. The Columbia Plateau and Basin and Range continue to support primary industries; however, the more populated southwestern region has diversified and contains significant tertiary and quaternary economies.

The Primary Sector

The Columbia Plateau and portions of the Basin and Range are important agriculturally. The Basin and Range remains an important mining region. Early settlers mined gold and silver, but trends have changed, and at present, copper is the main ore mined in the Intermontane. The Colorado Plateau is rich with strip-mined coal deposits.

Agriculture

Historically, Intermontane agriculture has been devoted to ranching, with only a fraction of the land growing crops because of the rugged terrain, lack of water, and remoteness of the area from population centers. However, the Desert Land Act and Mormon immigration spurred irrigation projects and more farming. Ranching is still a major enterprise, but the region now boasts some of the nation's most productive farmland. Both ranching and irrigated farming have implemented some sustainable methods of crop rotation, such as planting no-till crops over conventional tillage areas, preventing the eroding of topsoil.

The southeastern Californian Coachella and Imperial Valleys enjoy a year-round growing season, while the higher-latitude or higher-elevation Columbia and Colorado plateaus are frost-free for less than 120 days per year. However, both of these fertile subregions depend on irrigation to produce profitable yields.

Currently, more than forty-three million acres of western cropland are irrigated, which accounts for 90 percent of regional freshwater consumption. (table 16.2; map 16.6.). Only grasses and wheat can be grown as dryland crops, and irrigation increases their yields.

Subregions and Crops

Snake River Plain. Southern Idaho's lava-covered Snake River Plain is dependent on irrigated agriculture for its survival. The plain's long summer days and cool nights are ideal for growing root crops, such as sugar beets, and the nation's largest potato crop, which includes the potatoes used for McDonald's french fries.

Columbia Plateau. Once dismissed as a wasteland, the Columbia Plateau, thanks to the Columbia Basin Project, is now

TABLE 16.2. Intermontane Irrigated Areas and Their Crops

Area	Location	Specifics	Crops
Columbia Plateau	Rain shadow of Cascades, Yakima, Washington	Columbia Basin Irrigation Project Water diverted from Columbia River	Apples, hay, field corn, hops, potatoes, vineyards, cherries, onions
Snake River Plain	Southern Idaho above Snake River	Irrigation projects and well irrigation Large farms, corporate, capital intensive	Hay, potatoes, sugar beets
Palouse (subunit of Columbia Plateau)	Southeastern Washington, southwestern Idaho	More rain than rest of Columbia Basin, thick layer of fertile loess	Cereal grain, field crops
Salt Lake Oasis	Great Salt Lake, Wasatch Mountain valley	Established by Mormons	Hay, grains, wheat, sugar beets, fruits, apples, peaches, cherries. Livestock, chickens
Salton Trough	Imperial and Coachella Valleys	Depend on migratory labor Water from the Colorado River	Alfalfa, lettuce, carrots, vineyards, citrus, dates
Salt River Valley	Central Arizona	First major federal irrigation project Highest cost of irrigation	Cotton, hay, wheat, barley, citrus
Rio Grande	Near El Paso, Texas, southern New Mexico	Oldest irrigation on continent, pre-Columbian	Cotton, poultry, pecans, grapes Feed grains, dairy
Colorado Grand Valley	West central Colorado	Rocky Mountain water, Colorado and Gunnison rivers	Corn, small grains, alfalfa, fruit crops, peaches

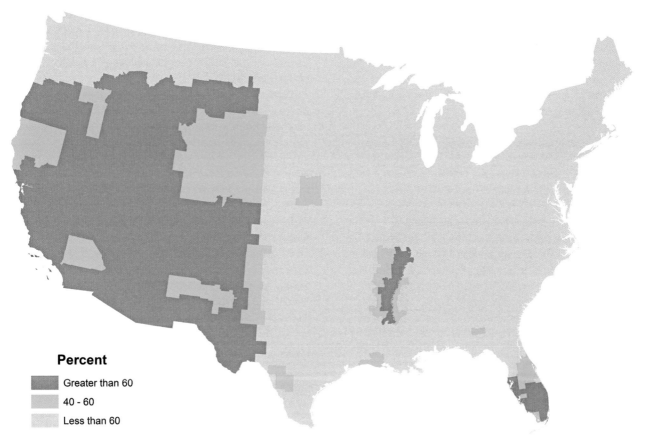

Percent

Greater than 60

40 - 60

Less than 60

MAP 16.6. Acres of Irrigated Harvested Cropland as Percentage of All Harvested Cropland Acreage. Most cropland in the Intermontane is irrigated.

a fertile agricultural area that grows wheat, hay, corn, potatoes, and wine grapes.

The physical geography of the land has created an ideal foundation for wine grapes. The Lake Missoula floods left behind loess-covered benches, which augment the good air circulation and warm days with natural drainage for the vineyards.

Palouse. The fertile Palouse receives the most rain in the region, but it is still dependent on irrigation to grow crops. The loess soils produce the highest-yielding winter wheat on the continent. Three-quarters of this wheat is exported to Japan and India, where it is made into noodles. Other crops cultivated in the Palouse include peas, lentils, barley, and clover alfalfa.

Coachella and Imperial Valleys. The southern locale, sunny weather, and fertile soil of southeastern California's Imperial and Coachella Valleys support year-round farming on over six hundred thousand irrigated acres. Because the region receives only three inches of precipitation annually, it must rely on Colorado River irrigation to provide the commercial crops with up to thirty-six inches of water annually. The desert valleys produce the nation's specialty crops, including lemons, table grapes, nursery stock, and dates.

Arizona. Cotton requires irrigation when grown in dry western regions like the Salt River Valley of Arizona, and yet cotton production in Arizona is the eleventh highest in the nation. Cheap water, subsidies, and cotton prices on the world market make cotton farming profitable. While cotton is still

grown, urban development has taken over more than half the cotton acreage.

Rangelands

Prior to nonnative settlement, the natural vegetation was perennial grasses in wetter areas and sagebrush in the drier areas. There were few hoofed animals. As settlers and their domesticated animals arrived, the grasses switched from perennial to annuals, which are less efficient at using water and maintaining soil fertility.

Ranching techniques evolved when Spanish herdsman unfamiliar with the drier Intermontane climate increased the number of cattle and sheep and overgrazed the land. The loss of grasses encouraged invasive species such as cheatgrass and leafy spurge. Cheatgrass is partly edible to cattle but has lower protein content, is a fire hazard, and affects biological diversity. Cheatgrass seems to thrive where cattle have disturbed ecological systems by overgrazing and may have been intentionally introduced to stabilize damaged grazing lands. Climate change may increase the spread of cheatgrass because it creates more favorable fire season conditions.

The noxious leafy spurge spreads by an extensive underground root system and, if left uncontrolled, will outcompete the native grasses. Some ranchers have supported multiple grazing techniques (cattle and sheep), so if the cattle do not eat the plant, the sheep will. Since leafy spurge comes from Europe and has a host of natural predators there, many researchers have argued for biological controls in the United States.

Both cheatgrass and leafy spurge can be controlled, but they require extensive and long-term range management, including fossil fuel–based pesticides. By far the best vegetation for the region is the native perennial grasses that existed prior to western ranching techniques.

Overgrazing and Range Management The US government controls about 70 percent of all western land (map 16.7). For example, more than 80 percent of Nevada's land and 72 percent of Arizona's land is federally owned; other government agencies control additional land, which is usually hot, dry, rocky, or steep land that is undesirable for farming.

Much of this land is under the Bureau of Land Management (BLM) which administers the multiple uses of federal land and mineral rights. The BLM leases land to mining and ranching enterprises, and it is responsible for more than 250 million acres, more land than any other agency in the United States.

Yet, the BLM has been challenged by chronic underfunding and controversy. Some claim the BLM caves in to industry demand for oil and gas leases; others have been highly critical of what they see as a trend towards overzealous confrontation between ranchers over BLM land.

Charging fees for grazing private livestock on federal lands is a long-standing but contentious practice. Generally, livestock producers who use federal lands want to keep fees low, while conservation groups believe fees should be increased.

Government grazing fees are charged per animal unit per month (AUM). The formulaic fees are less than private grazing fees and do not cover the costs for maintaining the land in a healthy condition. The consequences have been overgrazed, eroded land depleted of the natural vegetation, beginning a domino effect of deterioration in the entire ecosystem.

Grazing fees on BLM land have never aligned with actual costs and have actually decreased over time. In 1980, the grazing fee AUM was $2.31; in 2014, it had decreased to $1.35. Ranchers effectively pay grazing fees equivalent to a tenth of

MAP 16.7. Federal Land as a Percentage of Total Land Area. Federal land ownership is overwhelmingly in the drier western region, with 55.5 percent of land federally owned, compared to, for example, 0.2 percent of the Northeast.

Source: Bureau of Land Management, Public Land Statistics, at http://www.blm.gov/public_land_statistics/pls10/pls10_combined.pdf

private land costs and the grazing fees are divided among the treasury, states, and federal agencies. As a result, the BLM spends more money to protect against overgrazing than it receives in income.

The BLM contends that raising grazing fees will allow better land management and protection from overgrazing. Cattle ranchers counter that grazing fees should not be raised because of low cattle prices and razor-slim profits. Environmental opponents believe that public land is poorly protected, and that raising grazing fees to fair market value will end the subsidizing of the largest owners, who benefit from the current policy at taxpayer expense. Taxpayer subsidies of large ranching operations are a continued debate.

Some cattle ranchers practice a form of cooperative conservation called **grass banking**, in which ranchers pool their herds and move them from ranch to ranch. Grass banking allows land to rest for long periods, which provides relief from stresses on grazing land such as in times of drought. Large herds of cattle are grazed on grass-banked land but are moved often to allow the land to rest and recover. Benefits include forming conservation easements to halt development and prevent land fragmentation, an increased awareness of perennial native grasses, and strength in numbers for the traditionally individualistic ranchers who now must market their cattle together in order to receive better prices. A unified ranching voice has been influential politically in conservation and ranching.

Grass banking has been successful from New Mexico to Oregon into the Great Plains of Montana. But it is not a panacea. Its use on public lands can still result in overgrazing; however, grass banking encourages ecological restoration and is a more sustainable use of private and public grazing lands.

Mineral Resources

Boom and bust mining operations have been an important part of the Intermontane economy from the mid-nineteenth century to the present.

Copper   Copper is currently the most mined resource in the Intermontane. The US is the second-largest producer of copper in the world (Chile is the largest); however, it also consumes more copper than any other country. The major copper-producing states are located in the southern Basin and Range region. The largest single copper producer in the world, the open pit mine in Bingham, Utah (near Salt Lake City), produces about 25 percent of the nation's copper, while Arizona and New Mexico account for the remaining copper ore. Arizona had several copper districts, but only Morenci continues to mine copper. The few copper boomtowns that remain, such as Jerome, survive on tourism.

Copper mining requires enormous capital investments for machinery and the processing of low-grade ore. Most copper mines are open pit, some are underground, and a growing number leach under weak acid conditions to dissolve copper. Methods of removing metal from rock are environmentally dangerous, and they require rethinking in order to maintain environmental health. Costs for mined resources have been erratic in the twenty-first century. From 2000 to 2005, copper prices doubled, but then fell dramatically from 2006 to 2009, only to soar again in 2010. Since 2011, copper prices have declined.

The hard rock–mining industry is America's largest source of toxic pollutants. More than 90 percent of open pit mining rock removed is broken and crushed to extract the copper, and then stored in a toxic-laden lake.

The extraction of copper from the Kennecott Copper Mine west of Salt Lake City (Bingham) produces toxic leachate solutions and tailings, which are disposed into streams and contaminate groundwater aquifers for many miles around. These actions, among many more, have created problems for local flora and fauna, and they have produced high rates of cancer in copper-mining communities. The Bingham mines have worked to minimize their waste, and they have met government standards for contaminated soils in most of their exposure sites. Over the years, Kennecott purchased surplus mining land, some of which was contaminated, and cleaned these areas up. They have also remediated former mine sites by building sustainable development projects.

Uranium   Mining companies continue to seek sources of uranium, oil, oil shale, and natural gas on the Colorado Plateau. Uranium, used in nuclear reactors, generates electricity, but there is a perpetual danger of radioactivity. A *Salt Lake Tribune* article noted that the uranium mill waste equals six times the debris taken from the collapsed World Trade Center. Along with the mildly radioactive uranium, it contains ammonia and other pollutants—threats to several endangered species and the Colorado River water supply used by twenty-five million people downstream.

Uranium was originally considered a nuisance mineral found with gold. Once Madame Curie discovered the uses of radiation—X-rays and irradiation of foods—old gold mines were reworked to recover uranium. The need for nuclear reactor fuel and the US government's purchase of all mined uranium sparked a 1952 uranium boom. Boomtowns like Moab, Utah, burst upon the Colorado Plateau and provided the labor force for the more than eight hundred mines.

The boom fizzled out in 1962 when accidents deflated interest, and the government had already acquired ample reserves of the mineral. Toxic tailings from uranium mines are located throughout the area, and some exist on the Colorado River flood plain, which will require remediation. People throughout the Moab area still suffer radiation poisoning from the mines, and lawsuits have been filed and await settlement. After the Fukushima nuclear plant disaster in Japan and the growing concern about the hazards of nuclear reactors, uranium prices began to fall further. In 2012, President Obama banned uranium mining around the Grand Canyon for twenty years. The move enraged mining companies but was praised by environmental groups.

Although the region now depends on nonrenewable sources of energy, the region is geographically well situated to foster renewable energy sources such as geothermal, wind, and solar power. Natural gas is the primary fuel for power generation in Nevada, but the state gets almost half of its renewable power generation from geothermal resources and has wind power potential along the state's mountain ridges. Arizona, a state awash in sunshine but also awash in a traditional conservative culture, has been slower to adopt solar power. However, this is changing. Arizona was one of the top five states in the installation of new solar facilities in 2015 and ranked second in the nation after California in total installed solar electric capacity. Today, solar energy contributes about 4 percent to Arizona's net electricity generation, but the state's overall renewable goal for regulated electric utilities is 15 percent by 2025. New Mexico requires at least 5 percent to be renewable, and Nevada has the highest solar generation per capita in the nation. There is high potential for renewable energy is this region and more aggressive plans for solar, wind, and geothermal power development could transform the region's energy profile.

The Tertiary Sector

Since the 1970s, Arizona and Utah have invested in and profited from a growing tertiary sector.

Because Arizona boasts more than three hundred days of sunshine; ideal for stargazing, testing, and flying, it has become home to more than twelve hundred small- and large-scale aerospace and defense companies. Raytheon, Honeywell, Boeing, Lockheed Martin, and General Dynamics are located there, boosted by lower taxes, less burdensome government regulations, and competitive incentives packages. A 2015 study by the International Trade Administration, WorldTradeStatistics.com, showed that Arizona's aerospace and defense total exports rose by more than 21 percent from 2011 to 2014, reaching a $3.47 billion in total. The increase was primarily due to a near $400 million increase in aircraft, engines, and parts exports. Currently, Arizona ranks fourth nationwide in aerospace industry payroll and fourth in aerospace revenue at $15 billion, making this state America's third-largest supply chain contributor for aerospace and defense.

Arizona has also attracted other tertiary sector businesses including biosciences and health care, which now contribute approximately $21 billion in annual earnings and employ about 320,000. And Arizona has attracted data centers and data-processing companies including American Express, eBay, and PayPal, and some 360 others that employ approximately 9,200 people. Arizona ranks eleventh for employment in data processing. Arizona also benefits from from Arizona State University and the University of Arizona whose research expertise and graduates have helped to build the postindustrial economy in information technology, optics/photonics, biotechnology, aerospace, environmental technologies, and advanced composite materials.

Utah has also seen economic growth and development in the tertiary sector. And like Arizona, aerospace and defense and software and financial services have helped Utah's economy grow among the fastest in the country. Aerospace companies located in Utah include Boeing, ATK, Northrop Grumman, Lockheed Martin, and General Atomics. Utah's aerospace industry accounts for nearly one thousand companies and more than thirty thousand jobs in the state.

Another growth area for Utah has been in product distribution, advertizing the Salt Lake City International Airport as "located within two-and-a-half hours of half of the country's population." Companies with distribution facilities in Utah include Cabela's, Family Dollar, United States Cold Storage, and Petzl America.

Finally, Utah has seen investment from digital media. Utah is home to the Sundance Film Festival, the largest independent film festival in the country. Digital media companies that call Utah home include Chair Entertainment, Disney Interactive Studios, Electronic Arts, Move Networks, Sandman Studios, and Tandem Motion Picture Studios.

Tourism

Tourism has become an important part of the Intermontane economy. The Colorado Plateau is a major American tourist destination, offering a colorful landscape that awes and inspires visitors. In the Basin and Range state of Nevada, the gambling meccas of Las Vegas and Reno form the major industry. Arizona reported some forty-three million visitors to the state in 2016 who collectively spent $21 billion.

The Colorado Plateau has the nation's greatest concentration of national parks, which are mostly located along the Colorado River. The most popular parks are the Grand Canyon and Saguaro in Arizona, and Zion, Bryce, and Arches in Utah (photo 16.16). These treasures are located in sparsely populated areas. The National Park Service says Grand Canyon National Park's five million annual visitors provide nearly $470 million in economic benefits.

Las Vegas attracts some forty million visitors annually to its casinos and resorts. Laughlin, Nevada, along the Colorado River, is also casino-laden, strategically located to take advantage of the river's recreational crowd. Gaming revenue contributes about $11 billion annually in Nevada, with most of that coming from Las Vegas.

A Sustainable Future

The Intermontane has undergone an extreme makeover since the mid-twentieth century when it was a hot, dry, and relatively empty section of the United States. Now hot, dry, air-conditioned, and populated, it confronts some significant challenges to sustainability. These include the following:

- dependency on irrigation and dams;
- prolonged drought;

PHOTO 16.16. Arches National Park, Moab, Utah. The park is one of eight national parks within the Colorado Plateau. Arches is famous for its more than one thousand red sandstone arches and natural bridges.

- possibility of water wars;
- climate change that may bring hotter, dryer conditions;
- public land that is controlled by powerful ranching lobbies;
- continued urban growth; and
- a reliance on fossil fuels, despite tremendous potential for renewables.

There are, however, examples of change. Although sustainability within the ranching world has a long road ahead, some ranchers now see the worth of healthy ranching practices and have introduced grass banking and other conservation practices.

The Southwest has also inspired architects and designers to work with nature. Frank Lloyd Wright built his signature-style winter home, Taliesin West, in Scottsdale, Arizona, during the 1930s. The home respects nature, and it is built to withstand fire and use sunlight efficiently. A school of architecture continues at Taliesin West, spawning ideas among new generations of architects following in Wright's footsteps.

Perhaps the most exciting signal that this region is moving towards sustainability is found in the example of Arizona State University. Under the leadership of a forward-thinking university president, ASU established the first comprehensive School of Sustainability in the US in 2006. The School of Sustainability is an interdisciplinary program consisting of faculty from various disciplines and schools and offers undergraduate and graduate degrees and minors, as well as doctoral and professional leadership programs.

Questions for Discussion

1. As this region continues to grow, it will require more water. Where should this water come from?

2. Should the region divert water from other less populated areas to cities such as Las Vegas?

3. Is a desert-like region sustainable when water is artificially introduced?

4. Can the lopsided growth in the driest part of the United States continue and be sustainable within the nation?

5. A highly civilized grouping of peoples (Anasazi, Mogollon, and Hohokam) lived and farmed in the extended Four Corners region until 1300, at which time they dispersed, and possibly became the Pueblo tribe. However, the Pueblo way of life is radically changed from their historical antecedents. What are some of the reasons this dispersion happened? If the reasons are environmental, what can be learned today, if anything, from their travails?

6. What is the Great Basin, and what is significant about it?

7. Where did the Mormons settle, and how did they affect the region?

8. What are the site and situation of Reno and Las Vegas? Why are these factors not enough to explain the growth of these cities?

9. What historically has been the transportation problem on the Colorado Plateau?

10. What are the reasons for using Yucca Mountain for the storage of nuclear waste? What are the problems?

11. How has the region approached alternative energy sources? What is the impediment to more robust renewable energy?

12. Technological inventions such as air-conditioning have changed the landscape and population of the Intermontane. Do geography and natural obstacles matter any longer?

13. What are some of the challenges of diversity and immigration in this region?

14. What are desert cities such as Las Vegas and Phoneix doing about sustainability?

15. How will climate change impact the economy and cities of the Itermontane?

Suggested Readings

Abbey, E. *Desert Solitaire*. New York: Simon & Schuster, 1968.

Acrey, B. P. *Navajo History: The Land and the People*. Shiprock, N.M.: Department of Curriculum Materials Development, 1994.

Arrington, L. J. *Great Basin Kingdom: An Economic History of the Latter-Day Saints, 1830–1900*. Cambridge, Mass.: Harvard University Press, 1958.

———. *History of Idaho*. 2 vols. Moscow: University of Idaho Press, 1994.

Branch, M. *Raising Wild: Dispatches from a Home in the Wilderness*. Boulder, CO: Roost Books, 2016.

Deitch, L. *The Arizona Story: a Geography and History of the Grand Canyon State*. Independently published, 2017.

Espeland, W. *The Struggle for Water: Politics, Rationality, and Identity in the American Southwest*, Chicago, IL: University of Chicago Press, 1998.

Fradkin, P. L. *A River No More: The Colorado River and the West*. Berkeley: University of California Press, 1996.

Garreau, J. *The Nine Nations of North America*. Boston: Houghton Mifflin, 1981.

Gibbs, J. *Planning Development in the Desert Southwest*. Independently Published, 2017.

Griffiths, M., and L. Rubright. *Colorado: A Geography*. Boulder, Colo.: Westview Press, 1983.

Meinig D. W. *The Great Columbia Plain*. Seattle: University of Washington Press, 1995.

Moehring, E. P., and M. S. Green. *Las Vegas: A Centennial History*. Reno: University of Nevada Press, 2005.

Morrissey, K. *Mental Territories: Environment and the Creation of the Inland Empire, 1870–1920*. New Haven, Conn.: Yale University Press, 1990.

Rothman, H. *Neon Metropolis*. New York: Routledge, 2003.

Schumacher, G. *Sun, Sin & Suburbia: the History of Modern Las Vegas*. 2nd ed. Reno Nevada: University of Nevada Press, 2015.

Starrs, P. *Let the Cowboy Ride*. Baltimore, Md.: Johns Hopkins University Press, 1998.

Stegner, W. *Beyond the Hundredth Meridian*. New York: Penguin Books, 1992.

Wauer, R. *Naturalist's Big Bend*. Austin: Texas A&M University Press, 1980.

Williams, F., L. Chronic, and H. Chronic. *Roadside Geology of Utah*. Missoula, Mont.: Mountain Press, 2014.

Internet Sources

Arizona State University School of Sustainability, at https://schoolofsustainability.asu.edu

Arizona Department of Water Resources, at http://www.azwater.gov/azdwr/default.aspx

Arizona Office of Tourism "Economic Impact" at: https://tourism.az.gov/research-statistics/economic-impact

Bend, Oregon's sustainability plan, at https://www.bendoregon.gov/city-projects/sustainability

Landry, A. "Not Alone in the Dark: Navajo Nation's Lack of Electricity Problem," *Indian Country Today*, February 11, 2015, at: https://indiancountrymedianetwork.com/news/native-news/not-alone-in-the-dark-navajo-nations-lack-of-electricity-problem/

Las Vegas Office of Sustainability, at https://www.lasvegasnevada.gov/portal/faces/wcnav_externalId/ci-sustainability?_afrLoop=8708263526882345&_afrWindowMode=0&_afrWindowId=null#%40%3F_afrWindowId%3Dnull%26_afrLoop%3D8708263526882345%26_afrWindowMode%3D0%26_adf.ctrl-state%3D1acdp5lb8c_4

Navajo Nation, at http://www.nnwo.org/

National Climate Assessment Report 2014, at http://nca2014.globalchange.gov/report

Phoenix's sustainability plan, at https://www.phoenix.gov/sustainability

Podnar, P. "Top 5 Industries in Utah," *Newsmax*, April 2015, at: http://www.newsmax.com/FastFeatures/industries-in-utah-economy/2015/04/09/id/637492/

U.S. Geological Survey. "Water Quality in the Central Columbia Plateau, Washington and Idaho, 1992–95," at https://wa.water.usgs.gov/pubs/ofr/fs-91-164.htm

U.S. Department of Energy. "Energy Efficiency and Renewable Energy," at http://www.eere.energy.gov/

U.S. Geological Survey. "Changing Water Use and Demand in the Southwest," at https://geochange.er.usgs.gov/sw/impacts/society/water_demand/

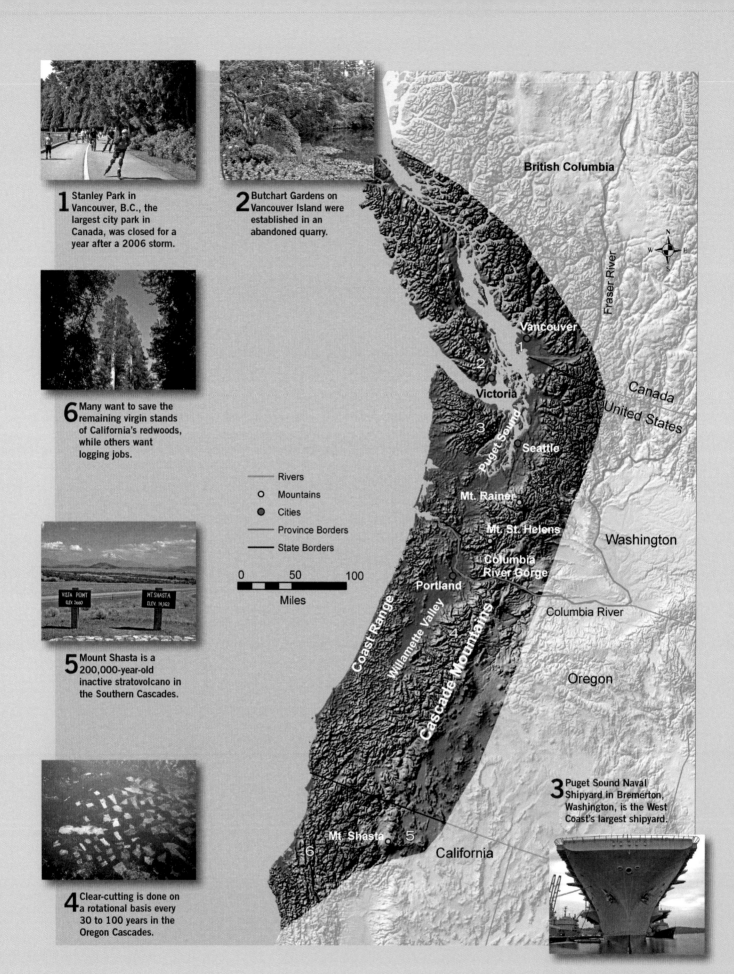

1 Stanley Park in Vancouver, B.C., the largest city park in Canada, was closed for a year after a 2006 storm.

2 Butchart Gardens on Vancouver Island were established in an abandoned quarry.

6 Many want to save the remaining virgin stands of California's redwoods, while others want logging jobs.

5 Mount Shasta is a 200,000-year-old inactive stratovolcano in the Southern Cascades.

4 Clear-cutting is done on a rotational basis every 30 to 100 years in the Oregon Cascades.

3 Puget Sound Naval Shipyard in Bremerton, Washington, is the West Coast's largest shipyard.

Rivers
○ Mountains
● Cities
Province Borders
State Borders

0   50   100
Miles

British Columbia

Fraser River

Vancouver
1
2
Victoria
3
Puget Sound
Seattle
Mt. Rainer
Mt. St. Helens
Columbia River Gorge
Portland
Columbia River

Coast Range
Willamette Valley
Cascade Mountains

Canada
United States

Washington

Oregon

Mt. Shasta   5
6
California

VISTA POINT ELEV 2660   MT. SHASTA ELEV. 14,162

17
PACIFIC NORTHWEST
Environment as Lifestyle

Chapter Highlights

After reading this chapter, you should be able to:

- Identify the subregions within the Pacific Northwest
- Compare and contrast the eastern and western parts of Washington and Oregon in relation to climate and precipitation
- Describe the major mountains in the region and their impact on the climate
- Discuss the importance of the Inside Passage
- Explain how the Ring of Fire impacts the region
- Compare and contrast farmed salmon with wild salmon
- Discuss the important cultural traditions of the Pacific Northwest Native Americans
- Describe population growth in the region
- Describe critical urban trends
- Describe the past and present economies in the subregions
- Discuss ways the region is moving towards sustainability

Terms

bioaccumulation
clear-cut

fish farm
fish ladder
hatchery
keystone species

lahar
managed use
marine climate
old growth

potlatch
stratovolcano

Places

Cascade Mountains
Coast Mountains
Coast Range

Columbia Gorge
Columbia River
Fraser River
Inside Passage

Mount Rainier
Mount Shasta
Mount St. Helens
Olympic Mountains

Puget Sound
Ring of Fire
Willamette Valley

Cities

Portland, Oregon
(2016 MSA 2.4 million)

Seattle, Washington
(2016 MSA 3.7 million)

Vancouver, British Columbia
(CMA 2.4 million)

Victoria, British Columbia
(2016 CMA 367,000)

PHOTO 17.1. Mount Rainier, Washington. Located in the Seattle–Tacoma metro area, Mount Rainier rises more than a mile above the surrounding Cascades and dominates the skyline. It is one of two dozen towering volcanoes in the Pacific Northwest Cascade Range. Pollution often mars viewing Mount Rainier from the metro area.

Introduction

The mountains dominating the Pacific Northwest (photo 17.1) form a barrier separating the region from the rest of the country to create a distinct geography and culture. The physical landscape evokes dreams of an ecological utopia. The region was used as a prototype in Ernest Callenbach's book *Ecotopia*, a region that favors ecological land-use policies versus overdevelopment and industrialization, a sensible decision in this verdant region of dramatic coastlines and volcanically punctuated timberland slopes.

The three major cities of the region—Portland, Seattle, and Vancouver, British Columbia—have been growing at a rate well beyond the national level. Outbound migration is almost nil, even as spiraling land costs impact Portland, as traffic, pollution, lumber, and economic imbalances affect Seattle, and as gridlocked Vancouver reflects its lack of a highway system. Logging, fishing, and water pollution top the Pacific Northwest list of environmental concerns. The three ills are interrelated and together create a plethora of environmental problems, including diseases, pests, habitat loss, land fragmentation, invasive species, agricultural grazing, coastal pollution, fishery destruction, water quantity and quality issues, and forest management practices. There is also the outbreaks of forest fire and occasional droughts.

Yet, regional residents lead the nation in controlling urban sprawl and securing a quality of life that features local foods and a healthy, green, environmental attitude. The Pacific Northwest may not be the fabled Ecotopia, but environmentalism and sustainability are almost synonymous with the Pacific Northwest lifestyle. Residents revel in outdoor living, hiking, biking, and horticulture. But it has not come easily or evenly. Despite its Ecotopia reputation, the Pacific Northwest has severe environmental problems just like the rest of America. Only the specifics differ.

Physical Geography

Nestled between the Intermontane and the Pacific Ocean, the Pacific Northwest spans two thousand miles from the Alaska Panhandle to northern California. The region is usually wet in the west, moist in the trough, and divided from the dry Intermontane by rugged, snow-covered mountains. The region, part of the Pacific Basin Ring of Fire, is volcanically active and delineated by a north-south line of steep-sided and occasionally explosive **stratovolcanoes.**

The moderate climate and visually stunning landscape have attracted those seeking a healthy lifestyle, but the increased population and the volatile nature of the volcanoes causes ecological issues.

The Pacific Northwest topography defines the three subregions:

- the Coast Ranges and Mountains;
- the Puget Sound Trough, Willamette Valley, and the Inside Passage; and
- the Cascade Mountains.

Coast Ranges and Mountains

The Pacific coastline is dramatic: Mountains rise abruptly from the ocean, and the continental shelf plunges into the abyss just a few miles offshore. British Columbia's Queen Charlotte

Island Basin descends more than three thousand feet only four miles from the shore. The evenly crested Oregon and northern California Coast Ranges hover over the narrow coastline (photo 17.2). The action of waves and tectonics through the ages has eroded and then lifted the stepped terraces sixteen hundred feet above the sea.

The coastal mountain systems include British Columbia's Coast Mountains, Olympics, Klamath, and Coast Ranges. These coastal ranges form a spectacular backdrop to the ocean. The region is much younger than the East Coast and still tectonically active.

In British Columbia, the rugged and fjorded Coast Mountains rise precipitously ten thousand feet above the ocean, blocking interior access while offsetting the modest elevations of Vancouver Island and other Inside Passage islands. But they also set the stage for the numerous alternating mountain ranges and trenched valleys between the Cascades and the Rocky Mountains (chapter 15).

Washington's glacier-clad Olympic Mountains dominate the steep glacial cuts of the Coastal Range. Mount Olympus surmounts the four-thousand-square-mile rainforest wilderness. The Olympic Peninsula coastline contains numerous sea cliffs and offshore rock pillars.

The Olympic Peninsula and Vancouver Island receive the most rain in their respective countries, although the moisture is fickle, drowning some areas (in the west) in moisture and leaving others relatively dry.

The Oregon Cascades and Coast Ranges converge at the Klamath Mountains, and then diverge at California's Central Plateau into the California Coast Range and the Sierra Nevada.

The California Coast Ranges rise from the coast in a complex mélange of faulted valleys and bold escarpments. A jumbled mountain-valley rhythm continues inland, restricting transportation between valley troughs.

Puget Sound

Nestled between the Coast Range and the Cascades, the Puget Sound waterway extends from the Inside Passage south to Olympia, Washington. Puget Sound is an estuary fed by freshwater coming from the Cascades and the Olympics. Washington's largest cities—Seattle, Tacoma, and Olympia—occupy the trough (photo 17.3).

Inside Passage

North of Puget Sound, the Inside Passage is protected from the turbulent Pacific Ocean by Vancouver Island's Insular Mountain Range. The eight-hundred-mile-long Inside Passage has been the preferred shipping route since the 1897 Klondike Gold Rush. Today, thousands of cruise ships annually bring tourism and the accompanying pollution to the delicate passage environment.

The Puget Trough

The Pleistocene ice sheet depressed Puget Sound under a mile of ice. About ten thousand years ago, the glacier retreated and left glacial drift, thousands of islands, the deeply gouged Puget Trough, and the Inside Passage channel. Seattle and Tacoma edge the dramatic Puget Trough landscape.

The Puget Trough extends into Oregon, where the Willamette River drains the broad Willamette alluvial valley.

PHOTO 17.2. Arch Cape, Oregon. The Pacific coastline is much younger and more rugged than the Atlantic coastline. Flat land along the coast is at a premium.

PHOTO 17.3. Puget Sound with Mount Baker in the Background.
Source: iStock/philotera

The Columbia Gorge connects the trough with the interior. The trough encompasses only 5 percent of Washington and Oregon land, but half their population resides there.

Cascade Range

Seven hundred miles long and fifty miles wide, the Cascade Range extends from northern California to southwestern Canada. The Cascades' elevation varies from three thousand to nine thousand feet, but the volcanic peaks within the range are much higher, the most massive being the majestic 14,415-foot Mount Rainier (map 17.1). The Columbia River divides the rugged volcanic crustal mass of the northern Cascades from the gentler but still volcanic southern Cascades. The volcanic action is created by the subduction of the Juan de Fuca tectonic plate beneath the North American plate. The subduction increases temperatures and pressure, which melts rock and forms magma that rises to the surface, erupts, and creates the Cascade volcanoes.

The northern Cascades are a granitic mass thrusted amid lava flows and volcanic debris and then carved by streams and glaciers. The range holds hundreds of small glaciers, including twenty-eight on Mount Rainier.

Over 120 volcanoes and numerous cinder cones, lava flows, hot springs, and mud pools blanket the southern Cascades from Lassen Peak to Mount Hood. Rising abruptly from the Cascades, the volcanoes, including Oregon's Mount Hood, Crater Lake (the remains of Mount Mazama), and California's Mount Shasta, are locally spectacular sights.

Mount Hood, a still active snow-covered stratovolcano, is located along the Columbia River between Portland and The Dalles (photo 17.4). The last major eruption occurred in 1782, but since then several smaller eruptions sent muddy **lahars** down the mountain.

The remains of Mount Mazama form the intensely blue Crater Lake (photo 17.5). The original nine-thousand-foot peak collapsed about 5700 BC, in an eruption forty times as powerful as the 1980 Mount St. Helens explosion. Continued lava flows sealed the opening of Mazama and sired the lake within the caldera.

Located about two hundred miles north of Sacramento, fourteen-thousand-foot-high Mount Shasta soars more than ten thousand feet directly from the base. Its old-growth, incense cedar forest was **cut over**, cleared of timber, and ingloriously made into pencils.

Water

Although water is usually abundant in the Pacific Northwest, the region has become more mindful of water use because of extended drought, population growth, and the concomitant growth in energy and water consumption. Important rivers in the Pacific Northwest include the Columbia, the Willamette in Oregon, and the Fraser River in British Columbia.

Snowmelt provides about 70 percent of the western water supply. The abundant rain and snow delineate Pacific Northwest waterways through the Coastal Ranges, although only the Columbia River dissects both the Coastal Range and the Cascade Mountains. The two major cities in Puget Sound—Seattle and Vancouver, British Columbia—depend on Cascades snowmelt for their water. Because no rivers transverse California's coastal ranges, northern California's coastal towns remain isolated from the interior, which has slowed regional population growth.

Columbia River

The Columbia River is the major regional source of water and power. The river originates in the Selkirk Mountains of British Columbia and flows through the Rocky Mountains, the

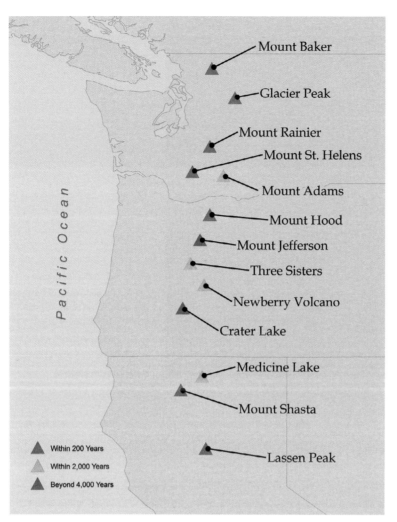

Within 200 Years

Within 2,000 Years

Beyond 4,000 Years

MAP 17.1. Volcanoes in the Cascade Mountains. The Cascades are punctuated with many volcanoes, some of which are still active.

PHOTO 17.4. Mount Hood, Oregon. The Mount Hood volcanic peak rises abruptly above the Cascade Range. Seen here from The Dalles, it occasionally is still visible through the Portland haze. The Dalles has been and remains a busy railroad route connecting the Northwest with the interior.

PHOTO 17.5. Crater Lake, Oregon. The Crater Lake caldera, the deepest lake in the United States at 1,932 feet, is about six miles in diameter. The Wisdom Island cinder cone emerged later from explosive eruptions in the caldera.

Intermontane, and the Pacific Northwest to the Pacific Ocean. The Columbia has the third-largest flow in America, and the steep gradient provides hydropower to the region.

In the United States, the Columbia is dammed for all but 50 miles of its 632-mile course, and in Canada, only the 140 miles nearest the headwaters are not dammed. Thirty dams generate hydropower, stimulating industrial growth and irrigating land, but they also disturb the salmon runs.

Astoria, at the mouth of the Columbia, was bypassed as the major Oregon port because of the hazardous, ship-sinking waters that earned it the name "Graveyard of the Pacific." The shipping channels are dredged regularly so ever-larger ships can enter the river on their way to Portland. But dredging upset the crab fishery, and the earlier loss of the salmon fishery and the canneries added to Astoria's woes (photo 17.6). Today, Astoria is a quaint tourist town. Portland thrives on the dredging that helped kill Astoria's economy.

Portland's port is entangled with its own water woes. Despite extensive cleanup work on the Willamette River in the 1960s, inspiring the rest of America to wake up to environmental issues, the river had become a toxin-filled sump again by 2000, the result of wood creosote factories, shipyards, and coal and oil storage facilities. The Willamette became a Superfund site. Toxins in the river have harmed fish (people are warned not to eat the fish) and cause cancers. Actions to decrease pollution since the Superfund designation include the port's commitment to clean up contaminated sediment. Portland's century-old sewer lines carried both waste and storm runoff, but they have recently been augmented by Big Pipe, which treats 96 percent of sewage formerly dumped directly into the river. In November 2011, Portland completed a twenty-year combined sewer overflow (CSO) control program that greatly reduced untreated waste to the Willamette River. Before CSO control, combined sewers overflowed to the river an average of fifty times a year. This led to high levels of bacteria in the river (exposure to bacteria is the greatest health concern for people swimming or enjoying other sports on the river). Since 2012, however, data collected show that bacteria are almost always at healthy levels in Portland. Still, in 2015, the Oregon Department of Environmental Quality gave the river a grade of "B−" because indicators showed a worsening trend from upstream to downstream in water quality and in habitat.

Fraser River

Southwestern British Columbia's Fraser is the largest and longest river in the province (850 miles), flowing from Mount Robson to Vancouver. The river drains about 25 percent of the province and is a major salmon producer, containing five types of salmon and other fish species. Environmental pressures include urbanization and agriculture development, punctuated by Vancouver's population growth.

Water Pollution

Increased Pacific Northwest population, logging, and tourism have polluted water and decreased wildlife habitat. Although protection has been implemented to stop pulp mills from polluting Puget Sound, much work remains to be done.

PHOTO 17.6. Cannery Remains at Astoria, Oregon. Located at the mouth of the Columbia River, Astoria was once a major salmon cannery, but the canneries are now gone. All that remains in the place of one of the old canneries is the pilings, the old boiler, and an office building.

Puget Sound

Aquatic life in the Sound is dying due to toxic chemicals and climate change. Polychorinated biphenyls (PCBs), polybrominated diphenyl ethers (PDBEs) (flame retardants), lead, mercury, and dioxins discharged into Puget Sound threaten residents and plant, animal, and aquatic ecosystems. The **bioaccumulation** (a process where toxic levels become more concentrated as they move up the food chain) has been linked to developmental effects in children. The marine bird population has halved since the 1970s, and 20 percent of shellfish beds have closed since 1980. The loss of fish has resulted in a dramatic decline in fish-feeding marine birds. Thousands of fish species and aquatic mammals are on the Sound's endangered list. A 2005 study blamed warmer water for a two-hundred-thousand-salmon kill in Puget Sound. Average summer surface water temperatures have risen about 4°F in the past thirty-five years. The Hood Canal has been plagued with hypoxia, killing crabs, shrimp, and finfish, and along the Pacific coast of Washington a summertime low-oxygen zone extends down the entire length of the state.

Reasons for the hypoxic conditions are both natural and human induced. A sill blocks the narrow entrance, slowing deepwater flushing and circulation in the sixty-mile waterway. Increased sunlight, along with nitrogen and phosphorus, and warmer temperatures stimulate algal growth, which increases the phytoplankton in the system.

Adding to the hypoxic conditions are human activities, including nitrogen loads from septic systems, animal waste, storm water, and agricultural and residential runoff. The continual population growth along the canal has exacerbated problems. The southern portion is now hypoxic year-round, and the northern end is now oxygen starved about half the year. In 2015, warm marine water that lingered in the Pacific Northwest—known as "The Blob"—prevented a normal flushing of Hood Canal with oxygen-rich water; die-offs were common throughout that summer. Several studies and groups are working to restore health to the canal, but progress is slow.

The busy Tacoma and Seattle shipping lanes transport more than fifteen billion gallons of oil, and sometimes there are oil spills. Even small oil spills require millions of dollars to clean up.

Several governmental and nongovernmental groups in the Puget Sound Basin address pollutant issues, including a partnership formed by the governor of Washington to clean up the Sound by 2020, making it one of the most environmentally ambitious cleanups in the nation. Cleanup groups focus on studies alleviating population and health issues for fish and humans, studying storm intensity models, flood areas, and levees to minimize losses in the future. Wastewater systems and reclaimed water are now built into the planning process.

Inside Passage

The Inside Passage has been a vital seaway and home to the many tribal groups dependent on the forest and salmon for their livelihood. But beginning with the Klondike Gold Rush in 1897, the passage sequenced through salmon canneries, logging, tourism, **fish farms**, and oil. Along the way the passage took a beating.

BOX 17.1 ENVIRONMENTAL CHALLENGES: HYPOXIA IN HOOD CANAL

The Hood Canal, on the western side of Puget Sound Basin, was formed millions of years ago, but only fifteen thousand years ago, glaciers carved its elongated shape (map 17.2). The Hood Canal fjord has traditionally been a spawning ground for finfish and an excellent breeding ground for shrimp, clams, oysters, and crab. However, since the 1930s the canal has been hypoxic (oxygen starved), which resulted in sporadic fish kills that became severe in the twenty-first century.

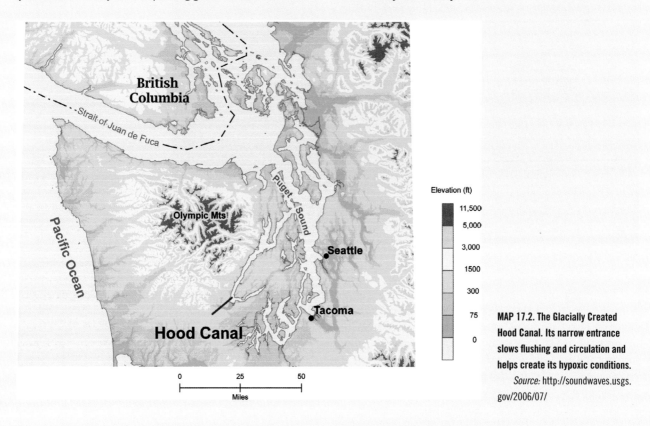

MAP 17.2. The Glacially Created Hood Canal. Its narrow entrance slows flushing and circulation and helps create its hypoxic conditions.
Source: http://soundwaves.usgs.gov/2006/07/

In high season, cruise ships carry more than a million passengers through the waterway. Many ships ignore pollution regulations and dump their waste, bilge water, and untreated sewage into the water. US environmental laws that prohibit waste dumps and require onboard treatment have been unenforceable; few ships are checked. Canada, however, has no laws stopping ships from dumping into its water. The polluting chemicals and oil-laden bilge water threaten several Inside Passage whale species.

Jobs along the Inside Passage—forestry, fishery, and cruise ships—pay low wages. Hopes for a better economy hang on more ecotourism or mining oil from the Queen Charlotte Basin. The basin, estimated to hold almost ten billion barrels of oil and twenty-six trillion cubic feet of gas, is within the continental shelf and therefore fairly shallow and accessible. If oil production is pursued, a future challenge will be protection of the Passage from the mining, while maintaining the ecotourism economy. Separating the Sound from the ocean is a group of islands, the Queen Charlotte Islands (Haida Gwaii). They are renowned for their flora and fauna, as well as for harboring a traditional Haida village.

Climate

The moist, gray climate is not as ubiquitous as its reputation. For three seasons, the temperate **marine climate** receives plentiful precipitation. The northwest corner of Vancouver Island is inundated with 250 inches annually, and Mount Olympus on the Olympic Peninsula receives more than 200 inches annually.

In the Cascades, westerly winds cause abundant orographic precipitation on the windward side and much less on the leeward rain shadow side (map 17.3). But regional precipitation varies widely. From the Olympics to the eastern Cascades town of Wenatchee, a distance of about a hundred miles, the annual rainfall diminishes from more than one hundred inches to less than ten inches.

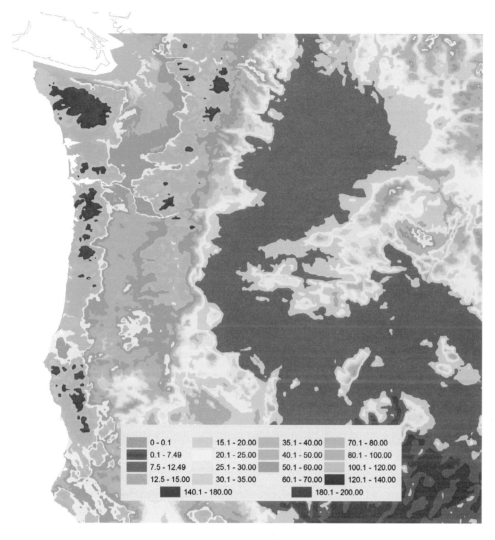

MAP 17.3. Precipitation in the US Pacific Northwest. Although precipitation is heaviest along the Olympic Peninsula, Seattle and Portland receive around forty inches of rain annually and have many drizzly days. The eastern side of the states is in the rain shadow, and the precipitation drops off rapidly.

0 - 0.1	15.1 - 20.00	35.1 - 40.00	70.1 - 80.00
0.1 - 7.49	20.1 - 25.00	40.1 - 50.00	80.1 - 100.00
7.5 - 12.49	25.1 - 30.00	50.1 - 60.00	100.1 - 120.00
12.5 - 15.00	30.1 - 35.00	60.1 - 70.00	120.1 - 140.00
	140.1 - 180.00		180.1 - 200.00

Cold ocean air decreases air pressure, and storms move up the mountains and release the moisture as rain or snow, depending on elevation. The Puget Trough receives less rain than the coast because the Coast Range acts as a moisture barrier. The Seattle area receives about forty inches of rain, three-quarters of it from October through March. However, less than a hundred days a year are clear, and jokes abound when the overcast days extend well past May into "Junuary."

Nestled between the Coast and Cascade Ranges, the Willamette Valley is sunnier and drier than the coast, but is wetter and cooler than eastern Oregon.

Climate Change

In April 2005, residents of Seattle were asked to conserve drinking water. The 1998–2005 drought in the Pacific Northwest halved the average snowpack, which provides more than half its water. The reduced snow may be a result of long-term climate change, but it also may be an anomaly; tree rings show alternating wet and dry periods in the past. Average snowpack returned during the winter of 2006, and conservation worries ended, for the time being. There was snowpack drought in 2015, but since 2011, no drought warnings were issued in Oregon and Washington. Forecasts for the future, though, include higher temperatures (about 1.8°F [1°C] every twenty-five years), an increase in precipitation, and more rain than snow. Climate change, along with steady increases in population and consumption, will continue to stress local water sources. Inland from the coast, the drier-than-normal conditions have led to significant wildfires in the past three years.

Historical Geography and Settlement

Native Americans

Humans migrated into the region about ten thousand years ago, some three thousand years after the last glacial retreat. The inhabitants lived in fishing villages and depended on abundant natural resources including shellfish and salmon.

Prior to European arrival, the region was the most densely populated Native American region. Coastal tribes—Algonquian in northern California; Chinook in Washington and Oregon; and Haida, Tlingit, and Tsimshian in British Columbia—lived in permanent villages.

BOX 17.2 CLIMATE CHANGE IN PUGET SOUND

From the peaks of the Cascades and Olympics to the saltwater of the Sound, climate has shaped the physical landscape of the Puget Sound region. While natural variability has always been (and always will be) part of the regional story, climate change is becoming a significant factor.

In Puget Sound, the ten warmest years on record have all occurred since 1998, and 2015 was the warmest year on record for Washington State since 1895. In 2015, an interdisciplinary team of researchers at University of Washington published a report on climate change in Puget Sound.* They listed the following projected changes due to climate change:

- Average air temperatures in Puget Sound will rise by between 2.9°F and 5.4°F by the 2050s.
- Ocean levels will rise by 6 inches by 2050.
- Winter flooding will increase due to rising oceans, more winter precipitation falling as rain rather than snow, and more frequent and intense heavy rains.
- Rivers are projected to carry more sediment downstream, as glaciers recede and expose loose material, and higher river

flows and more intense rainfall will likely act to increase erosion.

- Warmer air, less meltwater, and lower summer flows will combine to raise river temperatures in the summer, making many waterways less hospitable for salmon.
- Heat waves are expected to become more frequent.
- Warmer oceans will likely favor more frequent toxic algae blooms.
- Increasing acidity of seawater will affect the shellfish industry, and may increase the toxicity of some algal blooms. Impacts on other marine life are not yet fully known.

The report concludes that the ultimate impact of climate change in Puget Sound depends not only on greenhouse gas emissions, but also on the choices leaders make in dealing with the effects of climate change. This is not work that can be done in disconnected silos. It requires collaboration across sectors; government, businesses and communities must all work together, as water, land use, public health, economic development, transportation, and supply chains will all be affected.

*G. S. Mauger, J. H. Casola, H. A. Morgan, R. L. Strauch, B. Jones, B. Curry, T. M. Busch Isaken, L. Whitely Binder, M. B. Krosby, and A. K. Snover. *State of Knowledge: Climate Change in Puget Sound.* Report Prepared for the Puget Sound partnership and the National Oceanic and Atmospheric Administration. University of Washington, Seattle, 2015. doi:10.7915/CIG93777D, at https://cig.uw.edu/resources/special-reports/ps-sok/

After mid-eighteenth-century European discovery, smallpox, and other European diseases devastated the indigenous population. Today, despite environmental problems, the remaining cultural traditions continue including a salmon-based lifestyle, **potlatch**, and totem poles.

The Coming of the Whites

Lewis and Clark were the first white explorers in search of a transcontinental water route. Their published works influenced John Jacob Astor to extend fur trapping into the territory.

Astor's fur-trading company established the western trading post of Fort Astoria (1811). The trading post languished until the Oregon Trail was established and immigrants settled the area. The British Hudson's Bay Company (1824) erected the competing Fort Vancouver, Washington, across from present-day Portland. The trading companies competed, and both claimed land to the mouth of the Columbia River.

The Oregon Trail symbolized America's credo of **Manifest Destiny** and the expanding power over the British. In the early 1840s, settlers followed the trail to its end at The Dalles in Oregon. The way to the fertile Willamette Valley was treacherous, requiring either traversing the Cascades or portaging past the waterfalls on the Columbia. Thousands of settlers left the East to seek a more promising life two thousand miles to the west.

American settlers in the Willamette Valley soon outnumbered the Canadian Métis settlers. Both American and British claims on the valley remained unresolved until the 1846 Oregon Treaty extended the 49th parallel boundary to the Pacific Coast, establishing the border for the United States and the British.

Settling the Pacific Northwest Cities

The Pacific Northwest supplied commodities to California during the gold rush. California outgrew its own natural resources, so businesses eyed the resources of Oregon and Washington, especially timber. Several small company towns along Puget Sound, such as Port Townsend, Port Gamble, and Seattle, all competed and prospered, cutting timber for the California market.

Portland also benefited from gold rush demands and distributed Willamette River and Columbia River crops. Steamboats navigating the Columbia to the Willamette River established a market-based lumber and agricultural economy. Portland grew from a handful of houses in 1850 to a population of 2,874 in 1860. Rail access in 1883 sealed Portland's position as the regional trading center.

Seattle was founded on a deep harbor in 1851. When tiny Tacoma was chosen as the most profitable choice for the terminus of the Northern Pacific Railroad (1883), Seattle built its

BOX 17.3   CULTURAL FESTIVALS: POTLATCH CERMONY, ABORIGINAL RIGHTS, AND LAND TITLE

Potlatch was a important ceremony of the Pacific Northwest gift-giver cultures.

Historically, many Pacific Northwest tribal groups distributed lavish gifts in potlatch feasts and ceremonies. But potlatch was more than gifts; it also conveyed oral histories among non-literate societies and marked a rite of passage for tribal members. Potlatch displayed wealth and power that held the expectation of future reciprocation. The potlatch created alliances, and was closely tied to the rights for salmon streams, and was a method of avoiding war. Potlatch maintained peace.

In British Columbia, Aboriginal claims were treated differently than in the rest of Canada, and Native groups lost most rights, so that the maximum land could be opened for settlement and resource development. Natives were allotted individual claims of ten or twenty acres, rather than the larger communal claims that allowed the continuation of hunting and fishing as a way of life.

In 1884, the Canadian and American misunderstanding of the potlatch's cultural importance for sharing culture and peace led the two countries to outlaw the practice. But the essential ceremony was practiced covertly until the ban was lifted in 1951.

Aboriginal groups sustained a long-term battle to secure several rights—potlatch, legal counsel on land claims, land claims, the vote—even as their traditional lands were being subsumed by the rights given to large resource development projects. The inconclusive state of Aboriginal rights left First Nations groups in British Columbia economically impoverished and with numerous social ills. Following a series of court cases in the 1970s, the federal government realized they needed to recognize Aboriginal title as first recognized in the Royal Proclamation of 1763, and the tide slowly began to turn in favor of the Aboriginals.

In the 1997 Delgamuukw Case, the Canadian Supreme Court firmly established Aboriginal title and reestablished the Royal Proclamation as the precedent to Aboriginal title in the province. The case was a watershed for Native groups, who rapidly sought to negotiate treaties to hold their land communally in accordance with Aboriginal title.

---

own railroad into the interior and became the gateway to the 1897 Klondike gold rush.

Vancouver was founded as a sawmill settlement in 1886. The fortunate timing of the Klondike gold strike positioned Vancouver as Canada's Klondike gateway.

Cultural Perspectives

Salmon Culture

The Pacific Northwest indigenous cultures continue to depend on two natural resources: salmon for their diet and lumber for their structures. Salmon need cold water to survive. The cold, oxygenated Pacific Northwest water has been an ideal habitat.

A visual survey of Pacific Northwest airport concession stands reveals salmon's local iconic status (photo 17.7). Every shop sells boxes of smoked or dried salmon. Salmon is seemingly everywhere, but perhaps not. The salmon may be farmed instead of wild. Most First Nation people believe farmed salmon destroy their way of life and their relationship with the Pacific Northwest environment.

Europeans overwhelmed the region while Natives continued their traditional salmon hunts until 1866, when whites opened the first salmon cannery. Soon, the tribal groups worked for and in the canneries. In the 1930s, the canneries became obsolete when refrigeration enhanced the market for fresh fish. After 1950, salmon migration routes were disrupted due to overfishing, habitat degradation, and dammed rivers. Tribal fishing grounds were eliminated.

Treaties guaranteeing Native American fishing rights were repeatedly ignored, and fishing was outlawed in "usual and accustomed" waters after 1900. A pivotal 1974 court decision finally restored Northwestern tribal rights.

The salmon culture continues today, though greatly modified. Tribal groups continue to rely on salmon as their chief food source and have tried to maintain a culturally consistent salmon fishery. The number of fishing boats has decreased because of quotas on salmon and other fish stock. Salmon hatcheries and fish farms—commercially bred fish in sequestered areas—have all but replaced wild salmon. Maintaining a sustainable commercial and tribal salmon fishery is the ideal, but so far has been unachievable.

Population, Immigration, and Diversity

Population

As the region connected to the rest of the nation and the Pacific Basin became economically important during the latter third of the twentieth century, the regional population grew. Washington's rate of growth was highest surrounding Seattle's King County. In Oregon, the greatest surge was in counties west of Portland and in the Willamette Valley.

An anomalous growth pattern includes Willamette-area retirees east of the Cascades in Bend, Oregon. Bend is located in Deschutes County, the state's fastest-growing county. From 1990 to 2000, Bend more than doubled in size, reaching 52,000 in

BOX 17.4   THE LEWIS AND CLARK ROUTE AND THE OREGON TRAIL

Lewis and Clark opened Oregon Territory trade for both the United States and the British. Heading west past the Missouri River, the continental divide, and the Columbia River, the presidentially appointed expedition explored to the Pacific Ocean. The following year, 1805, the Lewis and Clark expedition followed the Columbia to the Snake River along a well-traveled Native American buffalo trail. This was the shortest route, but skirmishes between the Lewis and Clark party and the Blackfoot tribe halted most future passage. Instead, settlers tracked another route west over what became the Oregon Trail, through the Green River Basin, the North Platte, and the Wyoming Basin.

Continued use refined the Oregon Trail. The first small parties of settlers arrived in 1839. Nine hundred settlers arrived in 1843, and 11,500 settlers braved the Oregon Trail in 1849. The Oregon Trail became the standard route for quick access to the Pacific.

PHOTO 17.7. Salmon Portrayed in American Native Art. Salmon are often used to as a symbol of determination, renewal, and prosperity. Salmon are also clan animals in some Native American cultures. Tribes with Salmon Clans include the Tlingit and Kwakwaka'wakw (Kwakiutl) tribes.
Source: iStock/LeshaBu

2000 and 91,122 in 2016; it is expected to continue growing as the national population ages.

Southwestern British Columbia has 60 percent of the provincial population. Other population centers in the province are Vancouver Island, the Okanagan Valley (chapter 15), and the northern towns of Prince Rupert and Prince George along the Canadian National Rail line.

Two population groups, immigrating Chinese and retirees, have elevated Vancouver's population density. Vancouver's 1,905 people per square mile far outweigh the British Columbia average of twelve people per square mile.

Many Canadian retirees migrated west to sunny British Columbia, which has caused concern over senior health care issues for the provincial system. Between 1980 and 2004, over twenty-four thousand moved to the province, and more are expected as baby boomers retire. In 2002, British Columbia seniors accounted for 13 percent of the population but accounted for 50 percent of prescriptions and 55 percent of hospitalizations. Twenty-five percent of British Columbia's population will be over sixty-five by 2031, increasing prescription and hospitalization costs.

Immigration and Diversity

In Oregon, foreign-born residents make up 10 percent of residents. The state is home to a sizeable community of immigrants, many of whom hail from Mexico. More than a third of Oregon's farmers, fishers, and foresters are immigrants, as are nearly 23 percent of all production employees. The top countries of origin for immigrants were Mexico (37 percent), China (6 percent), Vietnam (5 percent), India (4 percent), and Canada (3.6 percent).

Oregon is a "Sanctuary State" and the law Oregon law prohibiting the use of state and local resources to enforce federal immigration law if a person's only crime is being in the country illegally has been in place for more than thirty years.

In Washington, one in seven Washington residents is foreign born, and over half of the state's farmers, fishers, and foresters are immigrants. Immigrants comprise about 13.7 percent of the state's population in 2015. The top countries of origin for immigrants were Mexico (24 percent), the Philippines (7.4 percent), India (6.7 percent), China (6 percent), and Vietnam

(5 percent). While Oregon and Washington are similar in terms of percentage of foreign born, there is different immigrant stock in these two states: more Mexicans in Oregon, while Washington has more Filipinos and Indians.

In 2017, President Donald Trump sought to restrict the flow of immigrants and refugees into the United States, particularly those from certain predominantly Muslim nations. There have been recent reports of immigrants from these countries using Washington as "steppingstone" to get into Canada, where they feel more welcomed.

British Columbia is the Canadian province with the second largest foreign-born population and a very diverse ethnic population, with immigrants coming from about 170 countries around the world (chart 17.1). The province is also home to a large number of immigrants that have lived in the province for thirty years or less. The top ten source countries are China (23 percent), India (14.7 percent), the Philippines (12 percent), South Korea (5.7 percent), UK (5.5 percent), the United States (4.3 percent), Iran (4 percent), Taiwan (3.8 percent), Japan (1.3 percent), and Pakistan (1.3 percent).

Also present in large numbers relative to other cities in Canada (except Toronto), and also present in British Columbia ever since the province was first settled (unlike Toronto), are

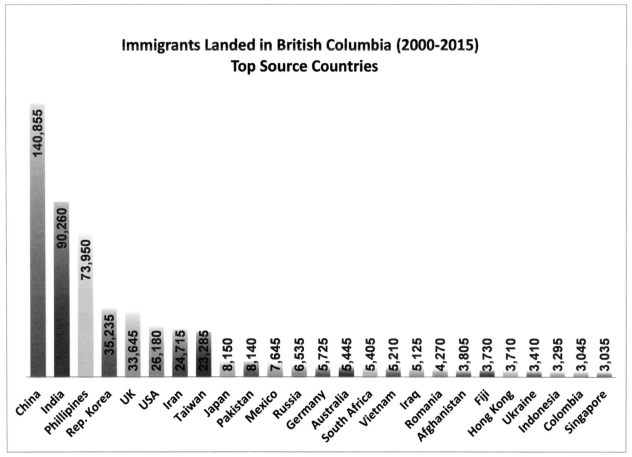

CHART 17.1. Chart of Top Sending Countries to British Columbia.
Source: Statistics Canada

PHOTO 17.8. Downtown Seattle on the Puget Sound was originally interspersed with marshes and hills. In the early twentieth century, the hills were sluiced and the marshes drained, developing a more amenable cityscape for the growing metropolitan area.

many European ethnicities of the first and second generation, notably Germans, Ukrainians, Scandinavians, Yugoslavs, and Italians; third-generation Europeans are generally of mixed lineage, and traditionally intermarried with other ethnic groups more than in any other Canadian province. The percentages add to more than 100 percent because of dual responses (e.g., "French-Canadian" generates an entry in both the category "French" and the category "Canadian"). In addition, the province is also home to almost 6 percent Aboriginal population: 3.8 percent First Nations, 2.8 percent Metis and a small number of Inuit.

In recent decades, the proportion of those of Chinese ethnicity has risen sharply, though still outnumbered by the historically strong population of those of German ancestry. The Chinese are British Columbia's largest visible minority. They compose 10 percent of the population. Most live in Vancouver and nearby Richmond. Chinese originally arrived in the late nineteenth century and worked in sawmills. The most recent Chinese immigration was prior to the 1997 transfer of Hong Kong to China. Unsure of their future in the People's Republic of China, many left Hong Kong and moved to the Vancouver area, capitalizing on a shared British Commonwealth status that eased immigration requirements.

Comparing foreign-born residents in Oregon and Washington to British Columbia, there are several notable differences. First, the overall percentage of foreign born is much higher in British Columbia than in Oregon and Washington. And the composition of the foreign born is also quite different. In British Columbia, there is not a large number of immigrants

from Mexico or Central America; only 1 percent of the foreign born hail from this area. There are far more Chinese, Indians, Pakistanis and Iranians—found in much smaller numbers in Oregon and Washington. Some of this difference is due to the Canadian connection with the British Commonwealth countries.

Urban Trends

Polls cite Seattle and Portland as favorite places to live in the United States because of their reputations for a healthy quality of life. They are typically listed within the top US cities in sustainability. Vancouver is consistently rated one of the world's best-quality-of-life cities. Each of these cities has a stronger sustainable community practice than is found in most US and Canadian locales, including a commitment to compact neighborhoods and strongly developed sustainability plans.

Seattle, Washington
(2016 MSA 3.7 million)

Seattle, the Emerald City, is green both in its thinking and its foliage. The thinking stems from the love of the aesthetics of this place, while the foliage flourishes because of ample precipitation (photo 17.8).

But green does not mean natural. The flat portions of the downtown Seattle landscape are artificial. Located on a narrow isthmus between Puget Sound and Lake Washington, Seattle's hills blocked growth, travel, and ease of construction. The city quickly outgrew its original purpose as a timber resource hinterland and evolved into the Alaskan gateway. As the hilly city grew during the late nineteenth century, it was regularly flooded and in need of reclamation. The Great Fire of 1889 provided the impetus the city needed to rebuild by improving nature. It began hydro-sluicing hills and filling in lowlands to improve the landscape.

Seattle developed its port and large industrial areas by filling in the tidal flats during the early twentieth century. The city continued to grow and become more important for the national welfare during World War I, providing Puget Sound lumber, fish, and shipbuilding. During World War II, a small local aircraft company, Boeing, took off, along with the aviation industry, and Seattle boomed. Today, Boeing is still important, supporting 3 percent of the economy and supplying eighty thousand jobs, but the Pacific Northwest economy is now more diversified and no longer dependent on Boeing.

During the 1990s, the Puget Sound economy grew at twice the national rate, and per capita income was 20 percent above the national average. But Seattle has not been immune to millennial issues. The city that spawned Starbucks, Microsoft, and Amazon entered the new millennium with a staggering Asian economy, a dot-com bust, a Microsoft antitrust suit, WTO riots, and a downturn in the airline industry, especially after 9/11. However, the Pacific Coast location has helped the port economy.

Two days closer to Asia than Los Angeles, the Seattle and Tacoma harbors are deepwater ports capable of handling large container ships. The overflow of Asian imports has stressed local ports and traffic infrastructure.

Constructed in the 1950s, US port infrastructure is not as modern as that of Chinese and Indian ports. The lack of modern infrastructure in America has hindered the flow of goods and added to shipping costs. Ships have grown larger than American ports can handle. Although deepening channels is an option, the environmental consequences are negative and require a global agreement regarding shipping practices. Additionally, port congestion affects the environment by releasing more harmful diesel emissions into the air and water, and truck traffic is hard on local roads and increases congestion. Despite the environmentally sensitive problems, the Puget Sound allure and belief in its continued success remains, partially because of its commitment to sustainability.

Seattle is grounded in the nonprofit "Sustainable Seattle" organization formed in preparation for the 1992 Earth Summit in Rio. Through an active program of grants and community participation, city administrators have developed sustainable goals more successfully than in any other US city. In 2004, Seattle adopted its first comprehensive sustainability plan.

The Office of Sustainability has focused on climate, buildings and energy, transportation and land use, waste, food, water, and trees and green space. And to a great deal of success: the American Council for an Energy Efficient Economy ranks Seattle third in the nation for policies and programs advancing energy efficiency. The city has many Leadership in Energy and Environmental Design (LEED)-certified buildings and has implemented a retrofit program that has created thousands of jobs. Seattle has worked to decrease automobile use by revamping its transit system, using buses, a new light rail, an extensive ferry system, and bicycle lanes. Seattle has joined an elite group of cities where less than 50 percent of workers commute by single occupancy vehicle. The city has also made strong commitments to improve access to affordable, local, healthy, sustainable, culturally appropriate food. Over the last ten years, Seattle has doubled the amount of publically accessible land for growing food, saw a $1 million increase in farmers market sales, and used a federal grant to launch "Fresh Bucks," a program that makes healthy food more affordable to low-income families by doubling federal food assistance benefits (SNAP, or food stamps) at Seattle farmers markets.

Seattle has been among the leaders in sustainability, and perhaps the most influential of progressive sustainability policy has been the Mayors Agreement on Climate Change (box 17.5).

Portland, Oregon
(2016 MSA 2.4 million)

Built at the confluence of the Columbia and Willamette Rivers, Portland's location benefited from access to the Pacific and to Willamette Valley agriculture. Later, an intercontinental rail connection established Portland as a main distribution point for the Northwest. But today, Portland is best known as the "greenest city in America," because of its dedication to renewable energy, commuting patterns, and healthy buildings.

Portland has addressed climate change for nearly twenty-five years and has steadily cut carbon emissions for more than a decade. In 1993, Portland was among the first to adopt a plan to reduce carbon dioxide emissions. In 2005, the city had achieved its goal of cutting carbon emissions below 1990 levels. By 2014, the metro area was 21 percent below 1990 levels, and Portland led the country in emissions reductions. In 2016, the city was recognized by the international community of cities (C40) for its updated climate action plan of 2015.

It is an ambitious plan that targets a 40 percent reduction in carbon emissions by 2030 and an 80 percent reduction by 2050 (compared to 1990 levels).

The strategy for this achievement included adopting long-term sustainability principles, which are fully integrated within city administration operations, including an incentive program for using public transport or building green. Portland's successful light rail and bus systems have a ridership level of seventy-six million annually and is considered a model for other cities (photo 17.10). Free downtown public transport, the venerable Powell's Bookstore, numerous public gardens, and the perfect climate for blooming plants, added to an outspoken civic stance and strong laws against sprawl, make the "City of Roses" many people's favorite city.

Portland's urban growth control has attracted large companies, such as Hewlett-Packard, Intel, and Hyundai, and educated workers who seek a high quality of life. The riverside location has substantial geographic and economic advantages for freight

BOX 17.5   URBAN SUSTAINABILITY BEST PRACTICES: SEATTLE

In March 2005, Seattle mayor Greg Nickles and nine other US mayors, representing more than three million Americans, joined together to invite cities from across the United States to take additional actions to significantly reduce global warming pollution. Three months later, in June, the Mayors Climate Protection Agreement was passed unanimously by the US Conference of Mayors. This climate agreement is remarkable in that it occurred primarily because the Bush Administration refused to ratify the Kyoto Protocol. In the absence of national leadership, cities have committed themselves to the achieveing the agreement's goals on greenhouse gas emission reduction.

Mayors that signed the agreement were encouraged to develop a Climate Action Plan, which many cities did. This Agreement also helped to create the Energy Efficiency and Conservation Block Grant (EECBG) Program making it possible for the first time in US history for cities to receive grants specifically to fund energy-efficiency projects. This funding was used to accelerate city energy and climate initiatives to cut greenhouse gases.

By 2017, the Mayors Climate Protection Agreement included 1,060 mayors from the fifty states, the District of Columbia and Puerto Rico, representing a total population of over eighty-eight million citizens. Many US cities have initiated local climate goals and targets that go beyond the Kyoto Protocol to embrace the targets of the 2015 Paris Agreement on Climate Change. In 2017, after the Trump administration pulled out of the Paris Agreement, more than 380 mayors who were signatories to the Climate Protection Agreement publically committed to upholding the Paris Agreement (although the cities cannot technically join the agreement, they can informally agree to its guidelines).

The legacy of Seattle's leadership on Climate is far reaching wide. The 2005 Mayors Climate Protection Agreement has continued to encourage cities to plan for climate mitigation and adaptation. Maybe even more importantly, in the process of creating climate plans, many cities realized the importance of developing more comprehensive sustainability plans. The fact that many US cities now have sustainability offices and sustainability plans can be traced back to the 2005 meeting in Seattle.

---

shipment. Portland is ranked as the third-largest-volume port on the West Coast, the nation's largest wheat exporter, seventh-largest export gateway, and fourteenth-largest container port.

Portland has been at the forefront of sustainable issues, but there has been a price, including price differentials between undeveloped land and land that is allowed to be developed and the widening gap in jobs. Portland continues to attract residents. Jobs in manufacturing are down, and so is the median income. Yet, more people continue to move to the city to enjoy the quality of life and sense of place. Many are wealthy and work outside the city, commuting weekly by air, returning on weekends to play in their private utopias. They move to Portland because they can afford to, and in so doing they economically squeeze many locals out.

But there is reason for optimism. Between 1990 and 2016, Portland has seen 33 percent more people residents and 24 percent more jobs while carbon emissions have declined 21 percent. This trajectory demonstrates that it is possible to achieve significant carbon emission reductions while growing the economy and population.

Victoria, British Columbia
(2016 CMA 367,000)

Victoria began its existence in 1843 as a Hudson's Bay outpost to protect British interests on Vancouver Island and in 1848 developed sawmills for timber bound for San Francisco. When gold was discovered along the Fraser River, Victoria (Vancouver did not yet exist) was the dominant city in the Canadian Cordillera and the transshipment point for miners. Vancouver eventually competed with Victoria for economic and political power. Despite being overshadowed by Vancouver, the older and more established Victoria became the capital when British Columbia joined the Confederation in 1871.

Situated at the southern end of Vancouver Island, regular ferries from Washington State or Vancouver provide access. Once in the town, the genteel atmosphere of hanging flower baskets, Butchart Gardens, and the fairy-lit domed capitol is a world away from the high-tech power of Vancouver (photo 17.11). As the capital, the city economy is largely governmental, augmented by tourism and services.

Vancouver, British Columbia
(2016 CMA 2.4 million)

Vancouver, the economic core of British Columbia, is one of the most livable and green cities in both the United States and Canada; it has spawned the buzzword *Vancouverism*, such is its appeal to numerous cities imitating its sustainable resolve. The fast-growing Canadian city was intentionally founded as a terminus to the Canadian Pacific Railroad, which received and shipped goods from Canada's interior. Although it was founded thirty years after Victoria, a mere fifteen years after its founding, Vancouver in 1901 became the largest city on Canada's West Coast, with a population of thirty thousand.

Sitting at the mouth of the Fraser River, the city is the largest port in Canada, shipping lumber, western Canadian crops, and minerals, such as potash from Saskatchewan and coal from the Rocky Mountains. Biodiesel and ethanol plants have increased the need for oilseeds, so canola exports have been on

BOX 17.6   NATIONAL PARKS: A NUCLEAR WASTE SITE?

In 2015, the Hanford Engineer Works was designated as part of the Manhattan Project National Historical Park and one of the newest national parks in the system. The Manhattan Project Historical Park preserves portions of the World War II-era sites where the United States first developed atomic weapons in a secret program called The Manhattan Project. It includes three specific locations: Hanford; Los Alamos, New Mexico; and Oak Ridge, Tennessee. Each site performed a unique and critical role in the success of the project.

Hanford Engineering Works was built to create large quantities of plutonium at a six-hundred-square-mile site along the Columbia River in Washington State. Among its many structures is the famous B Reactor National Historic Landmark, which produced the material for the Trinity test and the plutonium bomb.

At Hanford, all of the production reactors and most associated facilities have been shut down, and each is in some stage of cleanup, decommissioning, or rehabilitation. As cleanup efforts continue at Hanford, the B Reactor has been deactivated; however, the Manhattan Project–era equipment and setting are still intact. The B Reactor now tells a story about the people, events, science, and engineering that led to the creation of the atomic bomb (Photo 17.9). It is a story about the condemnation of private property and the eviction of homeowners and American Indian Tribes to make way for the massive facility.

But more importantly, it represents a "new type" of national park: a former nuclear site stands in stark challenge to the concept of national park as a pristine natural landscape. Is it appropriate to preserve this contaminated site or is this part of our history that the national parks can not afford to ignore?

PHOTO 17.9. The Hanford B Reactor.
Source: Billatq

the rise. The city is also a major port for cruise lines. The Port of Vancouver is a destination for many Asian goods, and Asian developers fund many buildings.

The city thrived economically until a downturn in the 1950s and 1960s, when suburbanization sapped energy and the rail and port manufacturing economy flagged. During this time, the city considered standard renewal programs, building freeways through the city and into the suburban sprawl, but instead arrived at a more locally based, participatory land-use and planning policy. The policy separated Vancouver's growth from the rest of Canada and the United States. Vancouver's

postindustrial knowledge-based economy replaced the resource and manufacturing economy. Today, central Vancouver is a densely populated compact city—the only large North American city without freeways bisecting the core.

The lack of freeways leaves the city with traffic congestion, but neighborhoods remain whole. Vancouver modeled a new paradigm, one based on density, public transport, walking, and bicycle paths. The city developed into an innovation storehouse for Canada and the world. It adopted a Livable Region Strategic Plan in 1996 and a one-hundred-year plan that anticipates climate change, pollution, sprawl, disease, and terrorism, all the

PHOTO 17.10. Portland's electric transportation train is considered innovative among US cities.
Source: iStock/neicebird

PHOTO 17.11. The Capitol, Victoria, British Columbia. Victoria won the provincial capital, but Vancouver is the larger and more economically important city.

while conserving energy and water and aiming to become a thoroughly sustainable city.

The appeal of Vancouver and its lifestyle is marred by becoming one of the least affordable cities in the world, especially in housing. Although the city has increased affordable housing for low-paid service economy employees, the amount does not nearly meet the needs.

Debates about affordability and gentrification emerged with regards to the 2010 Winter Olympics. In the lead-up to the 2010 Olympics, questions of how the city should be shaped,

and in whose interests, came to the fore. Vancouver is the least affordable global city, with a then 2010 median house price of $540,900 but a median household income of only $58,200. The city's Downtown Eastside neighborhood, which has long been known as the poorest postal code in Canada, was adjacent to the official 2010 Olympic Village. Between 2008 and 2010, over fifteen hundred market-rate units of housing—mostly condominiums—were built in Downtown Eastside; during the same period, over sixteen hundred affordable units of housing were lost in the area. The housing churn, activists believed, was the result of Olympics-fueled speculation. In response, housing activists set up what they dubbed an Olympic Tent Village in the heart of Downtown Eastside. They took over a parking lot owned by a major developer, set up about 150 tents, and created a twenty-four-hour community space, complete with free meals, a conflict resolution system, and even recycling. Pressure brought by the encampment resulted in over forty homeless residents of the tent village securing long-term housing; the village itself served as a reminder that urban space is highly political, and that urban dwellers working together can determine how spaces in their city are used.

The Olympics were a catalyst for urban redevelopment, environmental remediation, and improvements to infrastructure. The city spent hundreds of millions to upgrade facilities, build new venues, and create the Olympic Village. The positive benefits included the construction of new roads and sewer systems, and the creation of improvement of parks, plazas, and streets. Perhaps the largest infrastructural legacy is the upgrade of airports, telecommunications, mass transit schemes, and road networks that now connect the city even more effectively to global flows of people, ideas, and commerce.

The city of Vancouver has a long history of environmental activism. In 1971, Greenpeace was founded there; in 1990, the city became the first city in North America to attempt to address climate change when it published its report *Clouds of Change*. The plan was ambitious, but nothing materialized. In 2011, the city revamped its climate plan and integrated it into its *Greenest City Action Plan*. This plan established ten goals to be achieved by 2020, including increasing green jobs and the number of companies actively engaged in greening their operations; reducing community-based greenhouse gas emissions; and increasing the number of green buildings. In 2015, Vancouver announced that it had achieved 80 percent of the "high priority actions" identified as most necessary to achieve the *Greenest City* targets. For example, the city cut greenhouse gas emissions by 7 percent, an 18 percent decrease per capita since 2007, and it also announced that it had achieved its goal of having 50 percent of all trips being made by sustainable transportation—walking, biking, and mass transit—five years early.

Vancouver is now a recognized leader in green building and sustainable planning and in 2017 was rated second in the United States and Canada in the Green City Index (photo 17.12).

The Economy

Lumber, hydropower, and fish have anchored the Pacific Northwest economy. While the Washington and Oregon economies have moved from reliance on primary industries, British Columbia still depends on them, although it too is developing the quaternary economy. But the regional economy is at a crossroads: The lumber industry has an environmental and political crisis; hydropower is no longer competitive; wild salmon is expensive, while farmed and **hatchery** fish—with their environmental issues—are cheap, plentiful, and short-term oriented.

During the 1990s, the economy flourished, led by a flurry of dot-com companies, Seattle-built airplanes, and the Columbia River dams that provided cheap power for ancillary industries. The dot-com and 9/11 crashes ended the economic euphoria but not the livability. The computer industry has rebounded, but outsourced, although both countries still have profit centers. Microsoft remains near Seattle but hires from a global human resource pool. No longer economically isolated, the Pacific Northwest reaches outside its boundaries and into the global market.

PHOTO 17.12. The Vancouver Skyline.
Source: iStock/jamesvancouver

PHOTO 17.13. Clear-Cuts in Oregon as Seen from the Air. Clear-cuts are difficult to see from the ground because the lumber companies usually leave a line of trees along highways.

The Primary Sector

Farmland in Oregon and lumber in Puget Sound attracted the first settlers. Both of these activities are still influential, but they have evolved into one of the most sustainable and innovative in either country, although still largely dependent on fossil fuels and, therefore, unsustainable in the long run.

Agriculture

The coniferous forested hillsides of the Pacific Northwest are unfit for farming. The Willamette Valley became the regional agricultural heartland because of the plentiful rain, fertile soil, and temperate climate. Dominant farming activities are dairying, truck farming, vineyard culture, and forage crops.

Oregon grows more than 225 crops, the third most diverse in the nation (after California and Florida). Two million acres of crops dominate Willamette Valley agriculture. The location and climate enhance its specialized crops, including fruits and berries grown for local consumption. Specialized farms in Willamette Valley also provide grass seed and such nursery products as roses, irises, and grafted fruit trees for the national market. A recent trend has replaced old orchards with vineyards. Oregon has about 350 wineries, and the Puget Sound area of Washington has 50 wineries.

The Western Washington Bellingham Plain and Cowlitz Valley specialize in dairying, and the Puyallup area specializes in daffodil and tulip production, followed by berry and truck gardening for local markets. As growth continues in the Seattle Plain, farms and concentrated animal feeding operation (CAFO) dairies are moving farther afield, such as Skagit Valley north of Everett. However, the bulk of Washington agricultural production remains east of the Cascades.

The British Columbia coast produces crops for local urban markets and has a thriving marijuana industry, taking advantage of laxer Canadian laws.

Northern California also has a thriving but illegal marijuana industry, especially in the northern areas near Humboldt University.

Logging

Throughout the windward side of the Pacific Northwest, mountain conifers, such as the Douglas fir, dominate the ecosystem; they are the primary habitat for many species. The Douglas fir, a large tree capable of living five hundred years, has always been part of the ecosystem, naturally complemented by western hemlock and western red cedar. The logging industry favors Douglas fir, because it grows quickly, yields the most timber per tree, and regenerates readily in **clear-cuts** because they thrive in full sunlight.

The **old growth** forest stands and natural and unplanned, but commercial stands result in even-aged managed forests. Cutting old-growth forests on public land in the United States is virtually eliminated. **Managed use** is a contentious phrase, whose definition varies between anthropocentric and environmental points of view. To a lumber company, managed use rationalizes clear-cutting (removing all trees in an area at one time) as beneficial to the forest and their logging interests; however, environmental activists endorse preserving the entire ecosystem as is (photo 17.13). Environmentalists' efforts have saved

BOX 17.7   GEOSPATIAL TECHNIQUES: FIRE IN FORESTS

Wildfires and cause significant economic, social and environmental damage that can exceed $350 million each year around the world. For this reason, many geographers are working to figure how to use GIS to apply risk science to analyze wildfires.

Oregon and Washington have more than sixteen national forests that cover more than 10.5 million hectares. In an interesting study[*], scientists at the US Forest Service, based in the Pacific Northwest using a range of GIS databases, examined the fire history in national forests in Oregon and Washington; they identified areas with greater burn probability. Identifying areas more liable to catch fires is a useful data source to base fuel management and for preparedness priorities.

[*]A. A. Ager, M. Buonopane, A. Reger, and M. A. Finney. "Wildfire exposure analysis on the national forests in the Pacific Northwest, USA." *Risk Analysis* 33 (2013): 1000–20.

many acres of forest but perhaps at the cost of an unhealthy ecologic stagnation. A sustainable point of view would allow wood to be cut, but only at a rate that will ensure long-term productivity. The best forest to maintain ecosystems is a mixture of old growth and younger varieties that would allow the complex ecological communities to evolve. A mixed-forest ecosystem is also healthier for biodiversity and fire protection.

While environmental concerns "saved" US forests, America's unabated consumption of wood continued—about 718 pounds per person annually, the highest in the world by a factor of three. American forests had reduced their logging, but Canadian logging increased, with most wood exported to the United States.

In northern California, timber production has dropped 80 percent since 1990, and many mills have closed because of pressure from imports and from environmental groups. The surviving companies must wade through environmental regulations and lawsuits regarding sustained yield, clean water, and habitat-sensitive cuts while maneuvering around issues like the spotted owl, old growth, and pollutants.

The Pacific Northwest was 90 percent forested and an important resource when the first nonnatives arrived. Native Americans built wooden houses and dugout canoes from readily available wood. European explorers found cedar logs made excellent masts for their ships. Most cities and many smaller company towns were founded on the timber trade. Only recently has the warmer Southeast, where trees grow twice as fast, bypassed Washington and Oregon in lumber volume.

Since the 1980s, lumbering jobs have declined, but the timing was perhaps fortuitous for the region, if not the lumbermen. The economy was diversifying, and the net loss of jobs in lumbering was made up for in other parts of the economy.

Big corporations and huge sawmills operate vertically integrated production facilities based on efficiency and economies of scale. A typical vertically integrated company owns the land, mills, and all production from raw material to the finished product: "from primeval to paper." The US government subsidizes these globalized producers.

The commercial logging industry considers clear-cutting to be a long-established, sound, silvicultural practice. The advantages are its efficiency and the ease of replanting, but its disadvantages are a scarred landscape, erosion, and a monoculture "forest" that is ecologically unstable. Natural forests are complete ecosystems with multiple interactive species, but lumber companies plant trees as forest crops chosen for their genetic disposition to quick growth and return on investment.

Several issues have environmentalists concerned, including the following:

- taxpayer subsidies used for short-term profit in the commercial logging industry;
- dismantling of protected wild forests;
- opening up old-growth forests to logging; and
- loss of diversity.

British Columbia has half of all Canadian spruce, pine, and fir forests. The lumber industry has been important and the leading employer in the early twentieth century.

In Canada, softwood lumber—used to frame buildings—is the fifth-largest export to the United States and had been a long-standing source of trade disputes. When American logging was virtually halted during the 1980s, lumber was imported from Canadian forests, especially those of British Columbia. The bulk of the old-growth forest remained in British Columbia, where logging interests, First Nations, and environmentalists fought over regulating logging in Calyquot Sound on Vancouver Island. A 1999 agreement limited the cut and preserved the forest, which was soon declared a UNESCO biosphere site.

Lumber disputes between the United States and Canada revolve around the US claim that the federal and provincial governments of Canada unfairly subsidize the lumber industry. US timber interests claim that Canadian imports unfairly undercut the real cost of softwood lumber, used extensively in housbuilding.

British Columbia forest policies have been severely criticized both for damaging rural economies and for not providing sustainable forest systems. People seeking rural economic improvement depended on local answers over provincial or national policies. The argument has been made and continues that economy alone is not the answer to a thriving community, and that stability is dependent on sustainability.

BOX 17.8 GLOBAL CONNECTIONS: STARBUCKS

Starbucks is a global coffee chain that began in Seattle. The very first Starbucks opened in the city on 1971. By the late 1980s, more stores were opened on Midwest and Canada. By the 1990s, stores were opened across the US, and in 1996, the fist overseas store opened in Tokyo. During a twenty-year period between 1987 and 2007, the company was opening two new stores a day across the globe. Today, there are more than twenty-seven thousand Starbucks stores—only half (13,930) of these are in the United States. The country with the second-largest number of Starbucks stores is China.

Starbucks is now so big that it can afford to pay for premium sites, run at a loss, and ease out competitors. While it is known for its progressive policies and relatively high wages, it is also involved in complex tax payments in countries across the world. In 2015, the European Commission ordered the company to pay around $30 million in overdue taxes.

From its simple beginning close to Pike's Place Market in Seattle, the company is now a major global corporation and a significant element in the urban landscape and coffee-drinking culture of cities around the world.

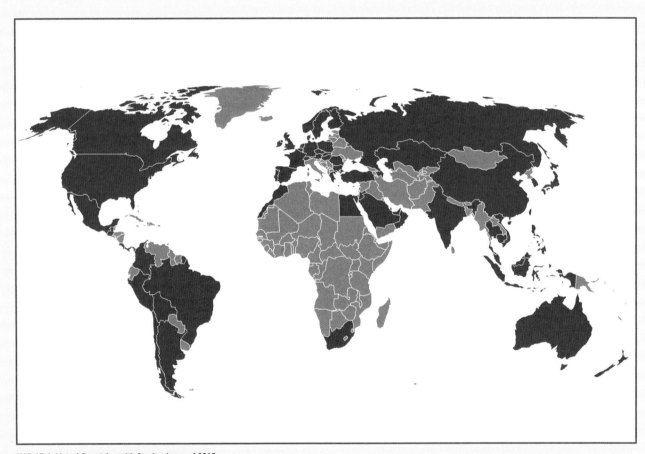

MAP 17.4. List of Countries with Starbucks as of 2015.

Source: Using data from Starbucks Corporation

Fishing

Regulations to commercially fish salmon, tuna, shrimp, and crab on the North Pacific Coast have tightened, resulting in a 90 percent drop in fishing incomes. Commercial fishing fleets are as endangered as the fish. Commercial, sport, and Native American fishers have endured quotas and other limitations resulting in drastic reductions. The salmon fishing season has shortened each year, and it was completely shut down in California and Oregon in 2008. The revenue loss devastated the commercial fleet and the charter-fishing industry. Ocean-dependent areas have gradually turned to tourism, such as whale watching and cruise ships.

Pacific salmon disappeared from about 40 percent of their breeding grounds and run sizes declined up to 90 percent. Columbia River salmon stock is down 80–90 percent.

Salmon play an important role in complex Pacific Northwest ecosystems. Flora and fauna depend on the salmon, a cornerstone or **keystone species**. A keystone species is important because it acts like a keystone in an arch: if it is taken out, the arch fails. Salmon affect the entire food chain, and they, in turn, are also affected. Polluted and overfished ocean habitats upset a healthy food chain, and climate change, now an accepted reality, disrupts habitats more.

Forty wildlife predators, such as gulls, eagles, and bears, feed on salmon. Diminished salmon stocks upset the ecosystem balances

Many salmon species have been listed as either endangered or threatened, because damming of rivers made their freshwater habitat inaccessible. For example, **fish ladders**, a series of shallow pools built around dams to facilitate fish migrations, sometimes are ineffective or absent altogether, resulting in dramatically reduced salmon fisheries. Other degradations are a result of logging activities, farming, and urbanization.

Hundreds of Pacific Northwest dams have restricted returning and spawning salmon in their home ground, which in turn limits ocean-bound juvenile salmon. Spill water from the dams simulates the necessary currents directing salmon to the ocean as juveniles and to their breeding ground as adults. Regulating the currents leaves salmon open to predators, but allowing more spills decreases hydropower potential.

Salmon habitats are disproportionately disturbed. Coastal salmon are generally healthier than inland, and the Pacific Northwest American salmon fishery suffers more than in British Columbia or Alaska. Warmer weather in the twenty-first century stresses the vulnerable fish. Salmon thrive best in water that is below 68°F. Washington's Puget Sound water temperatures regularly exceeded 70°F in 2004. At 77°F, the salmon die.

There have been several examples of fish kills. Warmer water may have caused more than 1.3 million sockeye salmon to not return to their Fraser River spawning grounds. Maintaining a healthy ecosystem will become increasingly complex as climate change progresses.

The Tertiary Sector

Although the primary sector remains an important part of the economy, the tertiary sector is where the real economic growth has been recently. High-technology, aerospace, film, and tourism have become important in this region.

As with many regions examined in this book, the rise of a high-technology sector, including software development, and information communications and technology have become increasingly important to economic growth. Numerous high-tech companies have located to the Pacific Northwest for the high quality of life. Many jobs in the high-technology and communications industry are highly paid. In Washington State, some two hundred thousand are employed in high-technology and communications. It is difficult to ignore the economic strength that the Seattle metropolitan region brings to the state. Companies like Amazon and Microsoft continue to hire by the thousands each year, and most of the jobs are high-paying.

Aerospace, life sciences/global health, and the military/defense sector are also major employers in the state. Washington has been a leader in seeking out "Clean Tech." Clean Tech spans many industrial sectors and represents a wide range of manufacturing processes, services and products. For example, clean tech in the electric utility industry can include a technology that allows utilities to purchase or re-sell more electrical power from renewable sources. The clean tech industry in the state of Washington employs nearly ninety thousand workers and is backed by more than a billion dollars in venture capital. These companies are supported by world-class research institutions including the Pacific Northwest National Laboratory, the University of Washington, and Washington State University.

During the past three decades, Oregon has made the transition from a resource-based economy to a more mixed manufacturing and marketing economy, with an emphasis on high technology. However, the state's growing high-tech sector has centered around Portland and rural Oregon counties were generally left out of the shift to a new economy. In the last ten years, professional and business services added 55,100 jobs to the state, the most of any sector.

British Columbia has also seen growth in the tertiary sector. Tourism is key in Victoria, as are government jobs. In addition to the high-technology jobs, Vancouver has been called "Hollywood North" and is home to ten percent of Hollywood movies. Many US television films series are shot exclusively in Vancouver. This is due to several factors, including tax credits provided by the government of British Columbia, and that Vancouver's diverse architecture and natural features can make it appear like many different locations around the world. Today, Vancouver is North America's third-largest producer of movies after Los Angeles and New York, and North America's second-largest producer of television shows.

A Sustainable Future

The Pacific Northwest tries to live up to its Ecotopia nickname. The Pacific Northwest takes sustainability seriously. Sense of place is meaningful to residents, and lifestyle choices indicate that people are thinking about their impact on the land and how to deal with economic and population issues while maintaining a high quality of life. Portland, Seattle, Vancouver, and Victoria are all leaders in sustainability and climate action. For some, the region has performed poorly by its own standards, largely because of continued growth, its inability to keep sprawl in check, and a growing income gap.

The regional economy was blessed with a wealth of old-growth timber and a healthy, robust, wild-salmon fishery. The economy, though, has changed. It has stabilized since the challenges of the millennial dot-com bust, but the stability of the salmon and timber industries is of questionable duration. Old-growth wood and wild salmon have become precious commodities.

The Pacific Rim position and the growing Chinese and Indian economies enable regional port growth. Seattle remains Washington's largest port, while Portland continues to increase its share of containerized shipments. Vancouver is Canada's largest port and second-largest (behind Los Angeles) on the West Coast. Continued trade with the Pacific Rim will benefit all these ports, but only if pollution problems, shipping bottlenecks, and infrastructure renewal are addressed and if long-distance shipping is sustainable.

There are still critical challenges to sustainability in the region that include the following:

- logging of old growth forests;
- fishing;
- water pollution;
- affordability; and
- urban growth and sprawl.

Cities have attempted different solutions to control sprawl and population growth. Vancouver, British Columbia, has become known for its walkable neighborhoods. Vancouver and Seattle work to improve their transportation network by encouraging better public transport, including using hybrid bus engines, cycling networks of greenways, and developing transit-oriented developments (TODs) aiming to improve transportation networks, all of which have the goal of reducing greenhouse gas emissions, congestion, air emissions, and transportation costs.

As a leader in sustainable living and conservation, the Pacific Northwest continues to espouse lofty goals of a healthy economy, a healthy ecosystem, and a quality of life that other regions strive to attain. It continues to seek innovative methods of sustaining a large population, a good employment record, and a high quality of life. Although its overall sustainability still has room to grow, it is far beyond what most US and Canadian regions have attained.

Questions for Discussion

1. What is the general attitude toward sustainability in the Pacific Northwest? How does it differ from the rest of America?

2. What did Portland, Oregon, do to change the sprawl of the city? What was the result?

3. How did Seattle establish itself as the leading city in Puget Sound?

4. How does a wild salmon differ from a fish farm salmon? Where are most salmon aquaculture farms located (geographically)?

5. How has immigration and diversity impacted the region and its economy?

6. How have the cities of Portland, Seattle, and Vancouver become leaders in sustainability?

7. What role has timber played in the Pacific Northwest's development? What have been some turning points in the timber industry?

8. What is the role of the tertiary sector in the region?

Suggested Readings

Ambrose, S. *Undaunted Courage: Meriwether Lewis, Thomas Jefferson, and the Opening of the American West.* New York: Simon & Schuster, 1996.

Ashbaugh, J. G., ed. *The Pacific Northwest: Geographical Perspectives.* Dubuque, Iowa: Kendall/Hunt, 1994.

Barnes, T., and R. R. Hayter, eds. *Trouble in the Rainforest: British Columbia's Forest Economy in Transition.* Victoria, B.C.: Western Geographical Press, 1997.

Beckey, F. *Range of Glaciers: The Exploration and Survey of the Northern Cascade Range.* Portland: Oregon Historical Society Press, 2003.

Berelowitz, L. *Dream City: Vancouver and the Global Imagination.* Vancouver, B.C.: Douglas & McIntyre, 2005.

Berg, L., ed. *The First Oregonians.* 2nd ed. Portland: Oregon Council for the Humanities, 2007.

Callenbach, E. *Ecotopia.* New York: Bantam, 1990. First published in 1975 by Banyan Tree Books, Berkeley, Calif.

Cooley, R. A. *Politics and Conservation: The Decline of the Alaska Salmon.* New York: Harper & Row, 1963.

Egan, T. P. *The Good Rain: Across Time and Terrain in the Pacific Northwest.* New York: Vintage Books, 1991.

Freedman, B. *Environmental Science: A Canadian Perspective.* Scarborough: Prentice Hall Canada, 1998, Chapter 12.

Garreau, J. *The Nine Nations of North America.* Boston: Houghton Mifflin, 1981.

Goble, D. D., and P. W. Hirt, eds. *Northwest Lands, Northwest Peoples: Readings in Environmental History.* Seattle: University of Washington Press, 1999.

Hammond, P. E. *Guide to Geology of the Cascade Range: Portland, Oregon, to Seattle, Washington.* Washington, D.C.: American Geophysical Union, 1989.

Harris, C. *The Resettlement of British Columbia: Essays on Colonialism and Geographical Change.* Vancouver: University of British Columbia Press, 1997.

Hume, S., A. Morton, B. Keller, et al. *A Stain upon the Sea: West Coast Salmon Farming.* Madeira Park, B.C.: Harbour, 2004.

Jackson, P., and J. Kimerling, eds. *Atlas of the Pacific Northwest.* 9th ed, Corvallis: Oregon State University Press, 2003.

Johannessen, C. L., W. A. Davenport, A. Millet, and S. McWilliams. "The Vegetation of the Williamette Valley." *Annals of the Association of American Geographers* 61, no. 2 (June 1971): 286–302.

Mackie, R. *Trading beyond the Mountains: The British Fur Trade on the Pacific, 1793–1843.* Vancouver: University of British Columbia Press, 1997.

Manning, R. *Inside Passage: A Journey beyond Borders*. Washington, D.C.: Island Press, 2001.

Markey, S., J. T. Pierce, K. Vodden, and M. Roseland, *Second Growth: Community Economic Development in Rural British Columbia*. Vancouver: University of British Columbia Press, 2005.

McKee, B. *Cascadia: The Geologic Evolution of the Pacific Northwest*. New York: McGraw Hill, 1972.

Montgomery, C. "Futureville." *Canadian Geographic* 126, no. 3 (May–June 2006): 44–60.

Robb, J., ed. *Atlas of the New West*. New York: Norton, 1997.

Robbins, W. G. *Landscapes of Promise: The Oregon Story, 1800–1940*. Seattle: University of Washington Press, 1997.

Weisheit, R. A. *Domestic Marijuana: A Neglected Industry*. New York: Greenwood Press, 1992.

Williams, H. *The Restless Northwest: A Geological Story*. Pullman: Washington State University, 2002.

Wood, Colin J. B., ed. *British Columbia, The Pacific Province: Geographical Essays*. Victoria, B.C.: Western Geographical Press, 2001.

Internet Sources

David Suzuki Foundation, at http://www.davidsuzuki.org/

Ecotopia, at http://www.ecotopia.com/

Bureau of Planning and Sustainability, Portland, Oregon, at http://www.portlandonline.com/bps/index.cfm?

Portland's Climate Plan, at https://www.portlandoregon.gov/bps/49989.

Seattle's Office of Sustainability, at https://www.seattle.gov/environment/about-ose

Sightline Institute, at http://www.sightline.org/

Metro Vancouver, at http://www.metrovancouver.org/Pages/default.aspx

Vancouver's sustainability plan, at http://vancouver.ca/green-vancouver.aspx

1 About 1,200 seasonal employees live and work at the Unisea fish processing plant in Dutch Harbor.

2 Kotzebue is an indigenous trading post located 30 miles north of the Arctic Circle.

3 Spruce bark beetles have killed millions of trees in Alaska and the Yukon.

7 Many caribou are killed for their antlers alone; 500,000 of them migrate between Canada and Alaska.

5 The Inside Passage between Seattle and Alaska was once used by gold seekers, now by cruise ships.

6 Turnagain has the second-highest tidal fluctuation in the world.

4 Skagway, Alaska, entrance to Klondike Gold Rush National Historical Park, is almost entirely dependent on cruise ship tourism.

Beringia

Bering Sea

Pribolof Islands

Dutch Harbor

Aleutian Islands

Shishmaref

Nome

Seward Peninsula

Yukon River

Brooks Range

Arctic Slope

Prudhoe Bay

Arctic National Wildlife Refuge

Fairbanks

Mt. McKinley

Alaska Range

Anchorage

Alaska Pipeline

Yukon

Kenai Peninsula

Chugach Mts

Prince William Sound

Klondike

Whitehorse

Tongass National Forest

Alexander Archipelago

Juneau

18
ARCTIC SLOPE, PACIFIC BORDERLANDS, AND BOREAL FOREST

Feeling the Heat

Chapter Highlights

After reading this chapter, you should be able to:

- Label on a map the Alaskan subregions and Canadian territories and subregions
- Identify the location of the Pacific panhandle, boreal forest, and Arctic Slope
- Identify and discuss the Aleutian Islands
- Explain why Alaska and the North are called the bellwethers of global warming
- Explain the relationship of Inuit to the land and how westernization has changed it
- Describe population trends in Alaska and the Canadian territories since 1960
- Discuss the importance of the primary economy in the North
- Describe the mining industry in the Arctic regions
- Explain the importance of the various fishing industries in Alaska

Terms

Aboriginal
archipelago
biomimicry
bush
cache

caribou
Dene
ice road
Inuit
island arc
isostatic rebound

lichen
Mackenzie Valley Pipeline
muskeg
oil sands
permafrost
seismic line

subsistence economy
syncretism
territory (Canadian)
thaw lake

Places

Aleutian Islands
Alexander Archipelago
Arctic Circle
Arctic National Wildlife
    Refuge (ANWR)
Bering Sea

Brooks Range
Canadian Shield
Dutch Harbor
Fort McMurray
James Bay Project
Kenai Peninsula
Klondike
La Grande River

Mackenzie River
Mount McKinley
North Slope
Northwest Passage
Northwest Territory
Nunavik
Nunavut
Prince William Sound

Prudhoe Bay
Ring of Fire
Seward Peninsula
Shishmaref
Tongass National Forest
Yukon
Yukon River

Cities and Towns

Anchorage
  (2016 MSA 401,635)
Dutch Harbor
  (2016 Pop 4,437)

Fairbanks
  (2016 MSA 100,605)
Iqaluit
  (2016 Pop 7,082)

Yellowknife
  (2016 Pop 19,569)
Yukon
  (2016 Pop 23,276)

Whitehorse
  (2016 pop 25,085)

PHOTO 18.1. Tormented Valley, Northern British Columbia. This glacially scraped landscape along the Klondike Highway to the Yukon is pockmarked with lakes and wetlands. The twenty-eight hundred-foot elevation is just above tree line, so the only trees that grow are stunted.

Introduction

Alaska and Northern Canada's territories—Yukon, Northwest Territory, and Nunavut—were home to **Aboriginal** peoples who adapted to the harsh environment for thousands of years before the late-eighteenth-century arrival of Europeans. The indigenous Arctic population used local resources to establish a healthy way of life. The Europeans arrived seeking to exploit the natural resources. Resource extraction began with animal resources and escalated to mineral and energy resources. The industrial expansion left the finely honed Aboriginal culturally devastated.

The first European interlopers arrived to exploit beaver and sea otters. The Russians (otters) and Hudson's Bay Company (beaver) annihilated these resources and then sold off the "worthless" land to the United States and Canada, respectively. However, in the twentieth century, abundant natural resources—lumber, fish, oil, and diamonds—vindicated the American and Canadian purchases. The exploitation continued. The resources have enriched both countries for the short term.

Climate change presents a new shared experience for the two countries, one which has the potential to be the largest Canadian-American disaster in history. Rising sea levels, **permafrost** melt, and receding glaciers have impacted the northern latitudes, making them a bellwether region.

The indigenous peoples' traditions, already weakened by Western intrusion, are now further endangered, as the effects of climate change may destroy villages and undermine traditional hunting practices. Yet the governments have been slow to recognize and act upon these new threats, leaving indigenous groups in peril.

This cold land is now feeling the heat.

Alaska

Aleutian Natives, the Unangan, named Alaska the "great land," referring to the large mainland in relation to the much smaller Aleutian Islands. Alaska is one-fifth the size of the entire contiguous United States. Resource exploitation progressed from furs to gold to oil; today oil provides 80 percent of Alaska's revenue. And the exploitation of resources without any care for the environmental damage has been a strong feature in Alaska's economic development.

Canadian Territories

In the northern wilderness of Canadian territories the sparse population is largely Aboriginal, and the economy revolves around resources. The Aboriginal population and settlement have historically been sustainable. However, during the second half of the twentieth century, the federal government contorted Aboriginal lives to simulate southern Canadian lives. The semi-nomadic Aboriginal life, developed over millennia and fitting the environment, was forced into permanent communities, compulsory education, social programs, and an economy that disregarded the fragile landscape and subsistence cultures.

Modern conveniences—rifles, metal knives, and snowmobiles—have entered Aboriginal cultures. Few Natives could refuse the temptations, but modernity is an uneasy fit for replacing the Aboriginal economy, lifestyle, or cultures honed in this harsh climate. By the late 1970s, the devastation of the Aboriginal lifestyle was recognized by the Ottawa-based federal government, and in an attempt to retain some semblance of a healthy culture, treaties and agreements granted Native groups more sovereignty and created several autonomous regions.

Physical Geography

The northern regions may be divided into four broad landscapes:

- the Pacific borderlands of British Columbia, Alaska, and the Aleutians;
- the boreal forest, or taiga, forming a large swath across the continent from Labrador to the Bering Sea;
- the Arctic Slope tundra in the northernmost region; and
- the Canadian Shield (that covers territory of the other three categories).

From the Alaskan Panhandle to the western end of the Aleutians, coastal mountains hem in the Pacific Borderland region. Two physical forces—tectonics and glaciers—molded this region: The faulting thrust of colliding tectonic plates built mountains, and glaciers eroded them, leaving behind dramatic fjords and islands. Between the coastline and the turbulent open sea are mountaintop islands of the Alexander Archipelago and the protected Inside Passage. The region is part of the tectonically active Ring of Fire that partially encircles the Pacific Ocean. Some of the largest earthquakes ever recorded have been along the Alaskan coastline.

The northern part of the Ring of Fire consists of the Aleutian Islands, one of the most tectonically active margins in the world and the scene of powerful earthquakes. Extending a thousand miles west beyond mainland Alaska, the Aleutian **archipelago** (large group of islands) separates the Bering Sea from the Northern Pacific Ocean. The volcanic **island arc** delineates the boundary between the North American and Pacific plates (map 18.1). The dense Pacific plate subducts beneath the floating North American plate along the deep Aleutian Trench south of

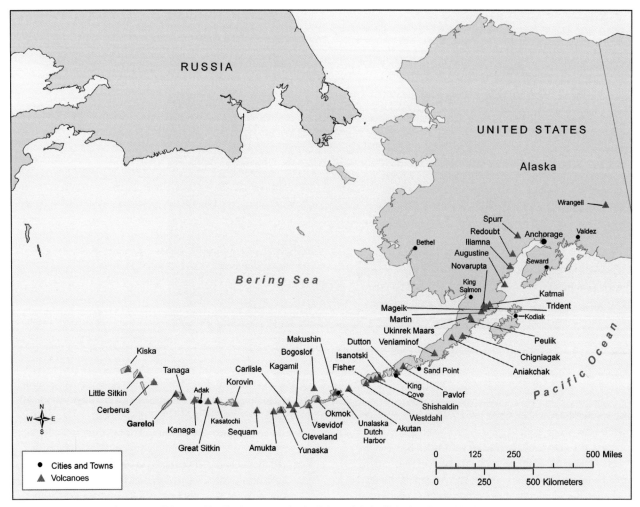

MAP 18.1. The Aleutian Archipelago and Volcanoes. The Aleutians are a volcanically formed chain of islands called an island arc.

BOX 18.1 DID YOU KNOW . . . CARIBOU, REINDEER OF THE AMERICAS

The ungulate caribou roam throughout the Yukon, Northwest Territories, and eastern Alaska (photo 18.2). Similar to Eurasian reindeer, caribou are larger, and both males and females have antlers. Caribou have genetically adapted to the Arctic environment. Their hooves are shaped to walk on the tundra and act as shovels digging out their diet of edible grasses. Caribou skin has air cells insulating them from the cold; their fur is structured to repel blizzards, making them waterproof and buoyant for Arctic Ocean migrations between islands and the mainland. Textile and clothing companies are learning through **biomimicry** about caribou genetic adaptations so they can incorporate the knowledge into their products.

Subsistence indigenous and western hunters hunt caribou as a source of food. In the early twentieth century, twenty to fifty million caribou roamed the Arctic, but in 2016, herd size was estimated at 365,000; despite strict controls, the herd continues to diminish. Environmental issues limiting caribou herds include reduction in grazing land, large-scale oil exploration, and global warming. For example, global warming can upset island caribou migration patterns; they swim each year from islands to the mainland when ice melts; climate change means freezing times change, thus making the passage treacherous.

There are three distinct herds in Alaska, named after the main birthing grounds: the Western Arctic Herd, the Central Arctic Herd, and the Porcupine Herd, which has the longest annual migration of fifteen hundred miles.

The caribou presence on the Arctic Slope has been contested in an ongoing debate between environmentalists, oil companies, and the local population. The Porcupine caribou herd uses the coastal plains of the Arctic National Wildlife Refuge (ANWR) for spring migration calving because of the nutritious moss and lichens. It is possible that oil-company drilling will upset the coastal plain, and thereby disturb or destroy the caribou calving area. The debate is answered by widely varying responses, and further complicated by the herd migrating each year to the best location for forage and snow cover, regardless of politics.

PHOTO 18.2. Alaskan Caribou.
Source: iStock/Viperry

the islands. In the process the oceanic plate, exposed to great pressure and heat, will melt and form magma, which erupts as the Aleutian volcanoes.

The numerous mountain ranges are divided between the Pacific Borderland mountains, the Alaskan interior, and the Canadian Arctic Cordillera. The Pacific Borderland mountains stretch from the Aleutian archipelago through the Gulf of Alaska, and then south four hundred miles through the Alaskan Panhandle and into the Pacific Northwest.

Most North American glaciers are located along the Pacific Coastal Mountains from Anchorage to Seattle. Alaska's one hundred thousandglaciers cover 5 percent of the state. Most glaciers form along the relatively warm coastal zone, influenced by ocean currents. Glaciers form when winter snow exceeds

BOX 18.2 GEOSPATIAL TECHNIQUES: MEASURING ICE THICKNESS IN THE NORTHWEST PASSAGE

The Northwest Passage is a system of gulfs, straits, sounds, and channels in the Canadian Arctic Archipelago connecting the Beaufort Sea in the west with Baffin Bay in the east. Usually, even in summer, there is enough ice to prevent shipping transport. If climate change melts enough ice, as it has in recent summers, it could present a potential Arctic shipping route between markets in the northern Pacific and Atlantic regions that is much shorter than routes through the Panama or Suez Canals.

But there is great uncertainty as to how thick the ice is, and how and when it might break up.

A 2015 study[*] used geospatial technology to better estimate the thickness of sea ice in the Northwest Passage. Prior to this research, there was little information about the thickness of sea ice in the Northwest Passage. Yet, next to ice coverage and type, sea ice thickness plays the most important role in assessing shipping hazards and predicting ice breakup.

The research team measured ice thickness in 2011 and again in 2015 using an airplane equipped with an

electromagnetic induction sounder or "EM bird." The Bird's height above the ice/water interface was determined by means of electromagnetic induction in the conductive sea water, using a set of transmitting and receiving coils to generate and sense an alternating electromagnetic field. The Bird's altitude above the snow or ice surface was measured with a laser altimeter. Ice-plus-snow thickness results from the difference between the electromagnetically determined altitude above the ice/water interface and the laser-measured altitude above the snow or ice surface.

The researchers were surprised to find a good deal of thick ice in the region in late winter, despite the fact that there has been more and more open water in recent years during late summer.

How climate change will affect the summer ice in the Northwest Passage in the future is difficult to predict. Further melting could cause more multiyear ice from the Arctic Ocean to drift into the passage, making it less, not more passable.

*C. Haas, and S. Howell. "Ice thickness in the Northwest Passage," *Geophysical Research Letters*, September 2015, doi: 10.1002/2015GL065704.

summer melting. The Alaskan glacial mass has been shrinking, a telltale sign of global climate change.

Boreal Forest—Taiga

The Canadian boreal forest, the largest contiguous forest remaining on Earth, covers 35 percent of Canada and constitutes about 30 percent of the global boreal forest. The boreal forest makes oxygen, distills water, fixes nitrogen, makes complex sugars and food, is habitat for hundreds of species, and is a carbon sink that stores some ninety billion tons of carbon. Forests are more than just wood and trees.

The boreal forest has been called the lungs of the planet, because it offsets the carbon dioxide (CO_2) made by humans and their interventions. The boreal forest is also one of the largest filters of freshwater; peatlands filter water through the area's estimated 1.5 million lakes. Clean, fresh water, breathing forests, and the sequestration of carbon maintain stable atmospheric carbon levels and global temperatures.

The forest extends from Alaska across Canada to Labrador, passing through the western cordillera, the Mackenzie River Valley, across the shield, and dipping south into the Superior Uplands of Michigan, Minnesota, and Wisconsin. Low plateaus and river valleys composed of meadows, peatlands, and barrens form the boreal interior. The Brooks Range (blocking polar weather) and the Alaska Range (blocking Pacific precipitation) shape the taiga climate. The taiga has more snowfall than the Arctic, but less than the Pacific Borderlands.

The eastern boreal forest lies over the exposed Canadian Shield craton. The western forested area continues into the

prairie along the Manitoba-Ontario border, follows the northern prairie line into the cordillera of British Columbia and the Yukon Plateau, and then follows the Yukon River drainage basin through interior Alaska (photo 18.1).

The exploitation of lumber, oil, gas, and minerals supports taiga cities—Fairbanks, Alaska; Dawson and Whitehorse, Yukon; Yellowknife, Northwest Territory; Fort McMurray, Alberta; and Sudbury, Ontario.

Arctic Slope—Tundra

The Arctic Plain is a paradox. Literally a desert, this inhospitable land receives less than six inches of precipitation annually, yet it is also classified as a permafrost wetland because of its low evaporation rate. The region extends from northern Quebec's Canadian Shield (Ungava Peninsula) to the Arctic Slope of Alaska, interrupted only by the Hudson Bay and the Mackenzie Delta.

Limited plants, sluggish drainage, lakes, marshes, and resources define the fragile permafrost environment above the Arctic tree line. Fragile vegetation hugs the relatively warm ground, avoiding the colder air temperatures. The plants have adapted to the Arctic environment by retaining leaves through winter so that in spring they may photosynthesize sunlight as soon as possible. The moss, fungal **lichen**, and grass vegetation in the active layer of permafrost can support small herbivores and large, migratory animal populations, such as **caribou**, although the extreme climate and vegetation variety limit the ecosystem. Beyond the 70th parallel, even tundra vegetation becomes scarce, and the land is barren.

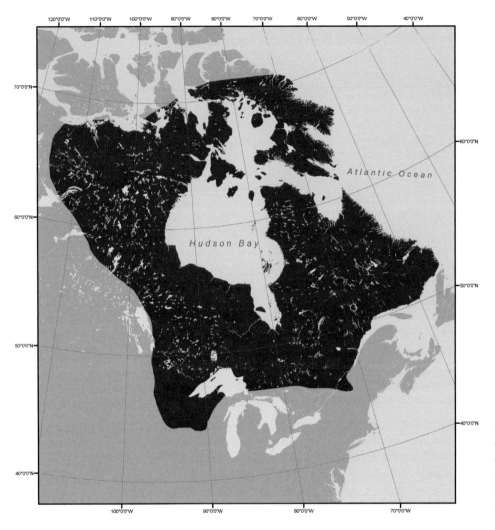

MAP 18.2. The Canadian Shield has the oldest rocks in the world, and they have remained permanently above sea level. The last ice ages created more than a million lakes and removed much of the soil.

Across the tundra landscape, ice-cored *pingos* (an **Inuit** word for small hill) appear to be small volcanoes, but they are frost-heaved mounds caused by frozen water expanding and pushing up the soil. They are most prevalent along the Mackenzie River delta.

The northernmost Arctic includes a sea ice cap and the Arctic Archipelago on the continental shelf. Farther north, the Arctic cordillera includes the remote Innuitian Mountains, hovering over the extreme northern islands. The Arctic ice cap encased the polar region during the modern era, but its melting has become a harbinger of climate change. Since the 1970s, the Arctic ice cap has shrunk approximately 30 percent. Ice thickness in the Northwest Passage has declined between 4 and 10 percent per decade; the ice is melting at the rate of 9 percent per decade. Although the ice is too thick for shipping routes to be opened up on a regular basis. However, it is not out of the question to soon have an ice-free Arctic prompting neighboring countries to seek oil and mineral rights.

Canadian Shield

The Canadian Shield, whose core is 80 percent igneous granite, spreads across six provinces and territories (Newfoundland, Quebec, Ontario, Manitoba, Nunavut, and the Northwest Territory), composing over 40 percent of Canada's total land area (map 18.2). The horseshoe-shaped landmass around Hudson Bay, extends across the taiga of the eastern provinces, and ends near the eastern Manitoba border. It also stretches north through the Arctic Archipelago and south into the Adirondacks of New York.

The ancient shield was once a mountain range, but numerous glaciations removed soil; reduced the mountains to a rough, rolling landscape; and left millions of pothole depressions that became lakes and wetlands. Glacial movement formed hills and mounds of till, sand, and gravel, which are sometimes capable of agricultural production but are usually just cold marshes.

The Hudson Bay and its lowlands extend along the southwestern edge of Ontario and into Manitoba near Churchill. The bay is experiencing **isostatic rebound** since last glaciated and is calculated to resurge another three hundred feet, causing most of the shallow bay to be aboveground in the next ten thousand years or so. The lowland surrounding the bay is a **muskeg** (a permafrost region dominated by an undrained, spongy sphagnum moss and a few stunted trees) with only a few small settlements,

PHOTO 18.3. Canadian Shield, Ontario. Shield rock is some of the oldest rock in the world. This part of the craton was heavily glaciated and is covered by a thin soil layer.

the largest being Churchill, Manitoba (pop. 1,000), an old Hudson Bay trading post. Recently, Churchill has become a conservation site for that harbinger of climate change—polar bears. As the temperature warms it reduces snow and ice cover and limits access to the bear's preferred diet, ringed seal.

The rugged shield landscape obstructed travel and exploration from Ontario to the western provinces, until the granitic rock was blasted out while building the transcontinental railroad in the 1880s (photo 18.3). In the twenty-first century the shield has been exploited for resources.

Water

Water is plentiful in the north. Shifting glacial drainage patterns have left a landscape with seemingly more water than land. Permafrost prevents water from percolating downward, and therefore it lies on the surface and creates impassable muskegs during the brief summer period. During the winter, the frozen landscape becomes more accessible. In the past, Natives used dog sleds, but today's transportation options range from riding snowmobiles to driving ice roads.

Freshwater covers about 9 percent of Canada's landmass, making it one of the world's largest freshwater reservoirs. Canadian rivers discharge 7 percent of the world's renewable water supply. Twenty-five percent of the world's wetlands cover about 14 percent of Canada's land area.

Rivers

The Arctic North has two major rivers—the Yukon and the Mackenzie —and many smaller rivers, as well as millions of lakes. Additionally, the Anchorage complex depends on the Susitna River, which rises from the Susitna glacier in the Alaska Range and flows into Cook Inlet west of Anchorage. Alaska's populated area near Anchorage depends on local agriculture from the glacially derived silt deposited by the Susitna, Matanuska, and Knik rivers in the Matanuska-Susitna Valley (photo 18.4).

The two-thousand-mile-long Yukon River, the third longest in America, has headwaters in northern British Columbia and flows through Whitehorse and Dawson City, Yukon Territory, before turning west through Alaska's interior into the Bering Sea. Many of Alaska's rivers are tributaries to the Yukon.

During the gold rush era and until the Alaska Highway opened in the 1940s, the Yukon served as a transport link between Whitehorse and the Bering Sea. More recently, the Yukon is a popular sporting river for canoeing, kayaking, and fishing.

The river has served as a transport artery between interior villages and a crazy-quilt ice highway during the winter. Extreme winter temperatures freeze the river. The river's course is altered each time the ice breaks at a weak point; the water spreads across the flat river plain until it too freezes, causing huge ice buildups.

The Mackenzie River, also called Deh Cho by the local Athabascans (who call themselves the **Dene**), is the longest river in Canada and the world's tenth largest (map 18.3). It channels one-fifth of Canada's water supply and is almost unique among the world's largest rivers because it has no major dams or diversions along its course.

The Mackenzie flows north through various ecoregions from the glacial meltwater–fed Great Slave Lake in the Northwest Territories into the Arctic Ocean. The southern headwaters are

PHOTO 18.4. The Braided Susitna River, North of Anchorage, Alaska. Glacial braided rivers deposit gravel from one side to the other, creating new channels; thus the river continually changes its flow pattern. The Susitna's fluctuating discharge and variable sediment loads braid the glacially carved river and have formed broad floodplains.

within temperate coniferous forests but flow north through the boreal forest/taiga to the tundra at its mouth. The taiga extends farther north as the river flows through the protected river valley. But permafrost and Arctic climatic extremes leave the trees skinny; their branches reach only a foot or so beyond their trunks and the trees are heaved in odd directions; they are known locally as the "drunken forest."

The Mackenzie basin was the Dene homeland for ten thousand years before fur trappers arrived in the nineteenth century. Since the 1920s, the Mackenzie has been an oil-producing region, but in the twenty-first century the much larger Mackenzie Project will produce both energy and a new Aboriginal rights policy (see below).

Hydropower

Hydro-Québec generates two-thirds of Canada's electricity and produces 13 percent of the world's hydropower. The drop in elevation from the Canadian Shield into the Hudson Bay and its drainage basin has more potential for hydropower than anywhere else in the country. The La Grande River hydropower project, part of the James Bay Project (see below), lies in the remote Quebec side of James Bay.

Lakes

Alaska has thousands of lakes that range from uncultivated, sparsely settled **bush** lakes used for fishing expeditions to **thaw lakes** along the Arctic coastal plain. Thaw lakes are the major surface feature on the coastal plain and may be a help (sequestering carbon) or hindrance (releasing CO_2 into the atmosphere) as they are affected by climate change. What happens to the lakes will also affect the vegetation, fauna, and human habitats of the region.

The largest of Alaska's many lakes is Iliamna Lake (1,033 square miles), southwest of the Cook Inlet. Accessible only by air or water, the bush lake is known for its scenery, incredible fishing, and possibly a nearby large and controversial gold and copper mine. Studies are being done to see if a sustainable fishery can exist with a large-scale mining operation. For example, the mine would require roads, which would interfere with salmon spawning sites and with a caribou herd's territory and calving site.

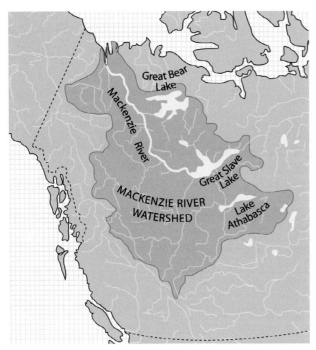

MAP 18.3. The Mackenzie River is the longest in Canada and the tenth largest in the world.

The lake has also been a site for scientific research that aims to understand the systems dynamics of the remote lake, polluted by industrial polychlorinated biphenyls (PCBs).

Canada has more than two million glacial meltwater lakes, especially in the glacially scoured, poorly drained north, where water acreage may exceed land. The Northwest Territory has both the largest (Great Bear at 12,095 square miles) and deepest (Great Slave) lakes in the country. Quebec's shield contains a million lakes and also has more waterways than any other region in Canada.

Climate

Arctic and subarctic climates dominate. The dividing line between Arctic and subarctic conditions is defined as

1. the region where the average July temperature is 50°F (10°C);
2. the area where the vegetation taiga gives way to tundra; and
3. the place where cold and short growing seasons no longer support the growth of trees.

This climatic dividing line follows the northeastern edge of the Great Bear and Great Slave lakes and continues upward to the Arctic coastal slope. The Arctic begins more or less where the annual mean air temperature is 14°F (−10°C), which is close to the northern limits of trees.

The Arctic and interior regions are colder than the Pacific Borderlands, which are warmed by the Kuroshio/Alaska Current. The Pacific Borderlands temperatures and precipitation patterns keep the weather mild in winter and cool in summer (table 18.1). The warm Kuroshio Current flows to southeastern Alaska, where it splits (map 18.4). The northern arm, renamed the Alaska Current, flows toward the Gulf of Alaska. Winds pick up the warm air, carry it to the mountains, and condense the water vapor, which results in heavy precipitation and the creation of Alaska's snowiest region. The Aleutian Low, where the Kuroshio Current meets the cold Bering Sea water, is the birthplace of Pacific storms, which follow prevailing winds tracking from west to east along the Aleutian archipelago.

The Arctic interior has a continental climate with extreme seasonal temperatures, because the Alaska and Brooks mountain ranges block the interior of Alaska from moderating maritime influences. Long, dark, cold winters and rainy Pacific air masses dominate most of the year. Summers are short and warm. The mosquito-filled summer temperatures can rise to 100°F (38°C) north of the Arctic Circle (latitude 66°32' N), where the sun never sets from May until August and never rises during winter. Across Canada, the boreal forest interior experiences similar weather conditions and poor drainage, resulting in an expansive area of marshes and bogs.

The Arctic Slope has cold, dry air with scant annual precipitation, making it a polar desert; snowfall stays on the ground most of the year, broken only in the heart of summer when continuous daylight melts the snow and stimulates vegetation. The Arctic Ocean keeps the coastal areas colder during the summer, but during the long, dark winter the frozen-over ocean provides heat, because it is warmer than the ground.

Climate Change

The North is the harbinger of climate change. Over the past forty years, the average Arctic atmospheric temperature has warmed 3.5°F to 5°F (1.5°C to 3°C) versus the 1°F (0.6°C) worldwide average. Scientific evidence of warming has left few doubting the changing climate, although the US and Canadian governments have reacted to these changes differently. Despite

TABLE 18.1. Average Weather Conditions in Alaska and Canadian Territories

	January (°F)	July (°F)
Anchorage, Alaska	14.9	58.4
Barrow, Alaska	−13.4	45
Fairbanks, Alaska	−10.1	62.5
Juneau, Alaska	24.2	56
Iqaluit, Nunavut	−13	46
Resolute, Nunavut	−23	39
Whitehorse, Yukon	0	57
Yellowknife, Northwest Territory	−17	62
Unalaska, Aleutian Islands (Alaska)	36	54

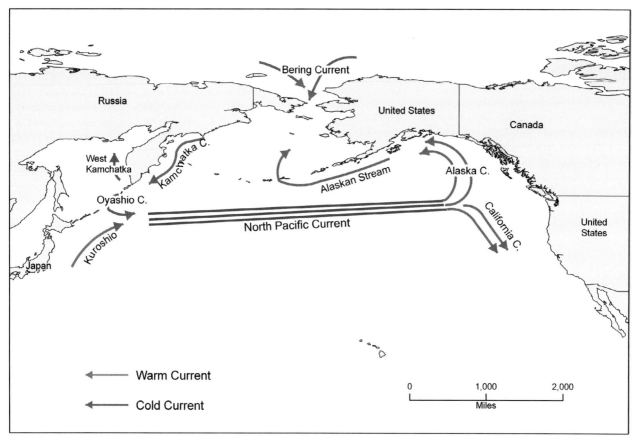

Warm Current

Cold Current

MAP 18.4. Northern Pacific Ocean Currents. Currents that flow along the western edges of oceans are warm, along eastern edges, cold. The Kuroshio Current flows along the western edge of the Pacific and then splits into two currents at the eastern edge. The Alaska Current is warm and moderates the Pacific Borderlands climate.

Source: http://www.pmel.noaa.gov/np/pages/seas/npmap4.html

intense research confirming climate change, the United States has been in denial for many years, while Canadian public policy has been more accepting.

The effects of climate change in Alaska and the Canadian Arctic include shrinking glaciers, melting permafrost that turns into a miasma of mud, buckling roads and structures, and erosion and flooding in more than 180 Native Arctic villages. Other effects of climate change range from insect infestations to forest fires and loss of sea life. Forest fires have almost tripled, destroying as many as 2.5 to 7 million acres since 1970. Warmer temperatures have allowed spruce bark beetles on the Kenai Peninsula to reproduce at twice their normal rate. The beetle infestation killed nearly four million acres of trees. The infestation has now spread south into Colorado.

Populations of whales, sharks, salmon, and marlins have plummeted 90 percent. The diminishing Arctic sea life and ice cover disrupt Inuit subsistence hunting. Hunters now have to literally tread on thin ice when hunting for seals. Some have

changed their mode of transportation from snowmobiles to boats, after unsuspecting snowmobilers have fallen through the fragile ice to their deaths.

Climate change has caused terrestrial vegetation to shift from tundra to taiga. Climate change was expected to extend the range of the boreal forest north, but also to extend the season of the existing boreal forest. Instead of growing healthier, the forest has been browning, suffering disease infestations and more fires and slowing growth. One result of these disturbances is decreased CO_2 absorption that reinforces a feedback loop: The more the forest does not absorb CO_2, the faster it warms.

Climate change has disproportionately affected Alaskan Native villages, perched along river and ocean shores. Thawing permafrost has affected numerous Arctic and Bering Sea villages. The ice pack has decreased 2–3 percent each decade since the 1970s, handicapping subsistence hunting. Alaska's interior weather has less snow and more rain, affecting hunting habits and age-old cultures.

BOX 18.3 CLIMATE CHANGE AND PERMAFROST

Permafrost (ground that is continually frozen for at least two years) underlies more than two-thirds of Alaska and all Canadian territories (map 18.5). Permafrost is up to half a mile thick in the north, but the thickness decreases to the south. Low-lying and very fragile vegetation protect and insulate the permafrost. Most permafrost is overlain by an active layer of soil, which freezes in winter but thaws each summer. The low-lying bogs and ponds called **thaw lakes** are formed when the top layer of the permafrost melts, because the water cannot seep into the frozen ground below. The lakes are a water source for vegetation and fauna in a region with little precipitation.

A sign of climate change in the bellwether northern latitudes is the discharge of greenhouse gas (GHG) as permafrost melts (photo 18.5). For example, as permafrost thaws due to climate change, carbon sinks release potent GHG into the atmosphere, creating a positive (amplifying) feedback loop that in turn further increases global warming, as well as increasing wildfires and insect outbreaks. The permafrost thaws because of increased CO_2 in the atmosphere, releasing methane, which in turn causes more warming, which releases more methane—and the cycle, the positive feedback loop, goes on and on.

The melting permafrost has several disadvantages, including shorter development seasons for oil and gas exploration and drilling; changing ecosystems; and the loss of biodiversity, Native villages, and traditional lifestyles.

The permafrost thaw comes earlier each year and wreaks havoc on infrastructure. As the climate warms, damage becomes

MAP 18.5. North American Permafrost. The dotted line is the current Arctic tree line, the northernmost latitude capable of supporting tree growth. Farther north is too cold for the sap lifeline to continue flowing, and permafrost can halt root growth.

more widespread and expensive to prevent or repair. Unless specialized building techniques are used, most structures built on permafrost conduct heat into the ground, causing the permafrost to melt. Buildings in permafrost areas should be constructed on pilings or insulated from the frozen ground below the active layer. Elevating buildings on pilings allows air to circulate below them so that the ground remains frozen. Piling construction is more expensive than construction in more temperate regions. But if structures are not properly constructed, the thawed ground buckles and destroys buildings, roads, and rail lines.

PHOTO 18.5. Permafrost Melt. Permafrost is named because it is permanently frozen. But climate change has been impacting areas where permafrost is found. Each summer researchers at George Washington University have been measuring how much permafrost has melted. Here, one of the project leaders stands on an area of permafrost that has melted, and separated from surrounding soils.
Source: Dr. Dmitry Streletskiy

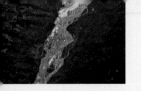

BOX 18.4   CLIMATE CHANGE AND INUIT VILLAGES

Two Inuit groups affected by global warming are the Yup'ik and the Inupiaq. Both groups live along the Bering Sea and have been competing for funding to move their villages to safer grounds.

The Yup'ik live along the Bering Sea coastline near the mouth and up the Yukon River. There are about twenty-two thousand living in Alaska, spread among seventy small communities. Prior to Western incursion, the Yup'ik were seminomadic, although regional goods allowed them to be more self-sufficient and permanently settled than the Inupiaq or similar groups.

Newtok, a village of 340 on the Ninglick River near the Bering Sea, is one of the many Native villages where a seasonal camp of the Yup'ik became the permanent settlement in the 1950s because of compulsory education. Permafrost is defrosting and can no longer protect the village from storm surge thaws. Newtok is falling into the river; most buildings are sinking into the ground as the permafrost melts.

In November 2008, the US Marines, Navy Seabees, and other branches of the military agreed to provide assistance to moving the village to higher ground over the succeeding four years. By 2010, the first of the infrastructure for a new village located nine

miles away was built, with plans to relocate other buildings on barges.

The Inupiaq settled along the Seward Peninsula and the Bering Sea coastline. The group's practice of harpoon hunting brought them in contact with Europeans, whose diseases eventually devastated the Inupiaq. Today's Inupiaq continue to partially subsist on their traditional food sources, but most now live in Western-style permanent villages instead of traditional summer camps and winter semi-subterranean earthen structures.

Shishmaref, located along the northern edge of the Seward Peninsula, has six hundred people hoping to move from their permanent settlement. They, like the Yup'ik, were once seminomadic and chose their island location when compulsory schooling became mandatory. Over the past twenty years, storm surges and warmer temperatures have eroded up to three hundred feet of coastline, damaging the village's land and buildings. The natural ice **caches** where their food is stored have melted, and lives have been lost due to the thinning ice. The Native Inupiaq pleaded for relocation money but have been denied. Estimated costs are over $100 million to move this village.

In the United States, climate change has been most evident in Alaska. Many of the Native villages are experiencing infrastructure damage. About 183 of 213 Native villages will require funds for flooding and erosion problems.

Estimates for the cost of replacing public infrastructure alone are between $3 billion and $6 billion by 2030. Moving the villagers will add to the cost. Many people want the villagers to move into public housing in Fairbanks or Anchorage, but the destruction of indigenous cultural life has already taken a large toll in alcoholism, violence, and suicide; villagers want to maintain what they can of their communities and identities.

More than half of Canada lies north of the Arctic Circle, where climate change has been most extreme. The Canadian government encourages energy efficiency and conserving fossil fuel resources, even while it mines the profitable **oil sands** in northern Alberta. The foci of Canada's concerns are the past decade's extreme weather (Prairie drought, British Columbia forest fires, the 1998 ice storm, and Hurricane Juan in 2003); an imperiled Aboriginal way of life; and economic costs, particularly to the primary sector industries.

Historical Geography and Settlement

Native Peoples and Initial European Contact

Alaskan and Canadian **Inuit** occupy the Bering Sea and Arctic Ocean coastline. They are linguistically and culturally related to the Inuit of Russia. Arctic Circle natives have lived seminomadic subsistence lives as hunters, fishers, and gatherers

and have successfully adapted to the harsh surroundings with innovations that include the kayak, the dog sled, and the igloo. Today, Inuit retain many traditions; however, Western appliances such as cable television, cell phones, and snowmobiles have entered everyday Inuit life. There has been a trading of cultural information—the Western cultures learn to respect traditional knowledge; the natives learn from the West—but finding a balance of the old and new has caused tumult in the Native cultures.

The Aboriginals of Alaska's Aleutian Islands are called Unangan; they are distant linguistic relatives of the Inuit, from whom they separated roughly ten thousand years ago. Like the Inuit, the Unangan were village-sized tribal groupings of similar cultures, each adapting to their homeland. Historically, Unangan were a sea-hunting culture dependent on the whale, seal, and walrus, which provided them with food, shelter, and clothing. Life on the Aleutian Islands was stressful, dependent on a marine-based diet, and punctuated by regular volcanic eruptions, earthquakes, and long bouts of isolation.

The Dene are composed of many subgroups living in the Alaskan and Canadian boreal forest. The Navajo and Apache, who are linguistically related, moved south from the subarctic into their current homelands, while others dispersed into more local sub-Arctic regions, such as the Slavey near the Great Slave, and the Tli Cho or Dogrib, who live between the Great Bear and Great Slave lakes.

The Dene nomadic hunters and gatherers became dependent on French fur traders. The fur trade and religious missionaries disrupted the Dene lifestyle, and various epidemics and toxins decimated the population. Today, most Dene live in cities or in permanent homes near the trading posts.

The Haida, Tsimshian, and the dominant Tlingit populated the Pacific Borderlands. Salmon dominated the rich natural resources in this temperate environment and supported a more sophisticated and advanced culture than farther north. The culture expressed itself in the practice of artistic crafts, in which they excelled. The Tlingit and Haida, known for their carvings, such as totem poles, were among the first to trade with the Russians and Europeans. Most Tlingit and Haida still live along the Alexander Archipelago, especially near Prince of Wales Island, and continue to fish, work in fish-processing plants, or practice traditional crafts.

Aboriginals of the Algonquin (east), Athabascan (west), and Inuit (north) tribal groups populate the shield area of Quebec and the territories. The Athabascans arrived first; Algonquin arrived about eight thousand years ago; and the Inuit, who settled along the northern shore and Hudson Bay, arrived about three thousand years ago. Most Aboriginals still practice traditional activities such as hunting, trapping, and fishing.

Evolution of the Alaskan State

In 1867, the United States purchased Alaska from the Russians for $7.2 million, a purchase that was derided as "Seward's Folly." The economics of the sale are no longer derided.

From 1867 until statehood in 1959, Alaska was an American territory that was owned and exploited like a colony. The "Alaska Syndicate," a consortium supported by J. P. Morgan, the Guggenheims, and various Seattle enterprises, invested in mining, salmon canning, and steam and rail transportation. Seattle companies still control most of Alaska's salmon and fishing industry.

Alaskan statehood was a controversial subject for years, because outside interests insisted the territory was poor and unable to support itself. Upon gaining statehood in 1959, the state, which was required to provide an economic base and financial security, claimed 104 million acres of land along with its mineral rights from the federal public domain.

Following Alaska's annexation, Native land claims remained in limbo. In 1968, the discovery of Prudhoe Bay oil prompted a quick resolution to Native land claims because many Native claims crossed the pipeline route. Passage of the Alaska Native Claims Settlement Act (ANCSA) in 1971 was the largest land claim settlement in US history.

ANCSA settled longtime land claims and helped Native areas develop economically. It gave Alaskan indigenous groups a special identity as shareholders in regional corporations, managing community land and resources while revitalizing their cultures, languages, and identities. Claims stipulated rights to land near the villages, and both hunting and subsurface mineral rights.

The formation of ANCSA was and still remains controversial. All Native claims were extinguished, and in return, thirteen ANCSA regional corporations were allocated $962 million and forty-four million acres of state land to develop their resources

and become self-sufficient. The formation of these corporations was done without a general vote of tribal groups. Many felt that the regional corporations leaned toward supporting corporate more than tribal interests, and that the timing of ANCSA was forced because of oil development speculations. The political nature of the formation and the continued politics have created varied rates of success in the corporations.

Evolution of the Canadian Territories

The original Northwest Territory once included the Yukon, Nunavut, and much of Alberta, Saskatchewan, and Manitoba. The Northwest Territory was part of the Hudson's Bay Company fur-trapping empire, until Canada purchased the company in 1869 and subsequently annexed the land. No landform divides the northern territories from the rest of the country, so the boundary was established at the 60th parallel.

In 1897, the Klondike Gold Rush began along the Yukon River near Dawson. Within a year, forty thousand would-be miners trudged up the highest coastal mountains in the world enroute to the goldfields. The Yukon's Dawson and Alaska's Skagway and Dyea became boomtowns during the gold rush period, only to shrivel or die after the rush. More recently they have been revived by late-twentieth-century cruise ships.

As Westerners moved into the region, the northern Aboriginal and Métis lifestyles changed. Westerners wanted the Native children to attend schools and learn English or French rather than their native languages. The Aboriginals understood that their children's future required a Western education, but attending a permanent school interfered with their traditional hunting activities and seasonal migrations. Parents were forbidden to abandon their children to go hunting. The loss of their traditional hunting patterns dealt a severe blow to Native cultures. Parents were deprived of their livelihood and their children never learned how to hunt. The northern way of life changed forever when World War II arrived. Economic development for oil, gas, and minerals to carry out war-related production brought more Westerners and their influences to the indigenous land.

By the late 1950s, the Inuit were starving because of a lack of game to support their subsistence diet. The Canadian government's response to this crisis was to move the Inuit into trading posts and villages, essentially ending their previous lifestyle. Children living in the trading post villages assimilated into the Western culture and lost the close relationship that their parents had with the land. The disruption of Native life contributed to the Natives' hard-fought battle to establish Native territories, which focused on reorganizing the lost lifestyle of the Aboriginal people and creating a livable economy.

A Canadian **territory** operates under the legislative authority of the federal government and has fewer rights than a province. A territory receives a lesser share of natural resource income than a province. However, power has begun to shift away from Ottawa and toward the territories in an attempt to right the Aboriginal cultural devastation.

During the end of the twentieth century, the Canadian government agreed to varying levels of independence for several

Native cultures; however, neither country volunteered to right the wrongs of Native land claims. The Natives had to fight for them. From Nunavut to the Ungava Peninsula to Alaska, various tribal groups began to patch together some hope to renew their cultures.

Nunavut and Other Native Enclaves

Carved from the eastern Northwest Territory and established in 1999, Nunavut (Inuktitut for "our land") had been a twenty-year-long dream and battle for the eastern Inuit.

Nunavut consists of three regions and twenty-eight communities run by local people. The Inuit were granted self-rule and a territorial settlement grant of $1.2 billion, allowing them control over 18 percent of the territory, which included some subsurface and mineral rights. The Canadian government granted one-tenth of their total mining area rights, which has encouraged Inuit-based mining, including the development of a diamond mine.

Nunavut is somewhat different from other Canadian territories because the Native heritage and culture in Nunavut have been incorporated into the government. The federal government transferred many powers to the territory, although about 90 percent of the budget is provided by the federal government. The indigenous people speak their native languages and utilize English as their second language. The economy is still based on trapping, mining, and natural resources, although a noteworthy crafts industry featuring Aboriginal carvings has augmented local financial welfare.

Alcoholism, drug abuse, and suicide are common, and still only 25 percent graduate from high school. Nunavut has consistently had the highest birthrate in the country, which has resulted in 38 percent of the population being under fourteen.

The lack of basic skills has left the Inuit unable to fill available government jobs. Only 45 percent of public jobs are filled by Inuit, although 85 percent of the population is Inuit. There are persistent reports of widespread financial mismanagement.

Cultural Perspectives

Habitat Destruction: The Inuit

The Canadian and American indigenous populations have not fared well. The Inuit seminomadic life relied on hunting, fishing, and following game throughout the year. But in the late twentieth and early twenty-first centuries, the Inuit were caught between their traditional culture and a Western consumer economy.

In the 1990s, those who continued to hunt and fish as their forefathers found that climate change had thinned and depleted the sea ice, leading to the decline of Arctic prey such as seals, walruses, and polar bears. These hunters lost their "living off the land" **subsistence economy** and their connection to the environment. The current Inuit food supply is deficient in game, nutritionally poor, and considered out of balance—yet another reason for the endemic cultural decline of the Inuit people.

Homes

Traditional Inuit housing, the igloo, has become an icon (photo 18.6). Some people still think that all Canadians live in snowhouse igloos, but the Inuit igloo was one of several types of shelters, including the temporary shelter that used the icy local resources. The Inuit also built sod igloos and igloos that combined snow with other materials. During the hunt, temporary igloos were built by Inuit hunters, who cut and shaped

PHOTO 18.6. This isolated igloo in the Yukon is just one type of shelter built by the Inuit.
Source: iStock/Thomas Camp

the ice into blocks. The more permanent Arctic and boreal forest sod igloos of the Inuit provided warmth in a cold climate. Aboriginals built a variety of different "pit" houses, using whalebone or driftwood for the structure and sod for insulation (photo 18.7). The houses were one-room affairs, built into the ground for further protection against the elements. A hole covered by semitransparent animal intestine provided light to the shelter.

Today, the average house in a northern Native village is similar to US and Canadian homes; however, they differ because of climate (more insulation) and landscape. Modern homes in permafrost locations are built on pilings for air circulation and to stabilize home foundations (photo 18.8).

In Alaska, some Native groups are returning to more traditional local materials and energy-efficient building methods, because the high costs of Western-type homes and heating with imported energy are making Natives appraise more sustainable and culturally appropriate options. For example, Anaktuvuk Pass in the Brooks Range has had a long-term housing shortage, and existing houses inefficiently use air and energy. Several projects of the Cold Climate Housing Research Center were completed in 2009, using traditional earth-berming techniques combined with solar power, green roofs, and passive ventilation to build an energy-efficient home. Another was designed in Quinhagak on the Yukon delta in 2010.

Language

When cultures assimilate, two traditional features—food and language—are the last to go. Many Alaskan Native groups have maintained fluency in one of the twenty recognized indigenous languages. The Tlingit and Haida languages and dialects still survive along the Alaskan Panhandle, but others such as Eyak

PHOTO 18.7. Indigenous Sod "Pit" House in Alaska. This house was built with whalebone structure and sod covering. Seldom seen today on the landscape, this one is at a museum site.

have all but disappeared. In the Aleutians, Native languages were discouraged fifty years ago, and few elders speak the languages today, although the current generation has been learning their native tongue in school. One-half of the more isolated Yup'ik along the southwestern coast of Alaska still speak one of several Native dialects at home. Native languages reflect the adaptations of the culture, and specifics cannot be easily replaced with a Western language that does not share the same environment.

Nunavut native languages have been encouraged since the region became a territory. The mother tongue for 75 percent of the northern population is not the official English or French language, but an indigenous language, especially Inuktitut and Inuinnaqtun, dialects of the Inuit language of Inukut. Nearly

PHOTO 18.8. Building on Permafrost in Nome, Alaska. This house was built on pilings, but the garage was not. Permafrost melting has caused movement. Notice the board holding up the door and keeping the roof from further buckling.

PHOTO 18.9. "Spirit Houses" at Eklutna, Alaska. The colorful spirit houses (graves) occupy the cemetery of the local Russian Orthodox church. The spirit houses meld Athabascan and Russian Orthodox beliefs. Colors identify clans, and crosses represent the Church.

BOX 18.5   CULTURAL FESTIVALS: THE IDITAROD

The Iditarod Trail runs almost one thousand miles form Seward to Nome. It is based on the trails and paths made by numerous indigenous peoples including the Athabascans and Inuit. The trail was used by thousands of people immediately after the discovery of gold in the region in 1910. It is designated as a National Historic Trail to commemorate its role in the development of Alaska.

The Iditarod Sled Dog Race was established in 1973. It runs along the National Historic Trail for roughly one thousand miles. It takes place in March of each year and runs from Settler Bay to Nome (photo 18.10). In odd years it takes a southern route through the ghost town of Iditarod that gives its name to the trail and the race. In even years it takes a more northern route. The alternating routes are used to minimize the impact of the race on small villages along the route. In 2015 and 2017, the race was rerouted due to lack of snow. Around fifty teams of sixteen dogs pull a sled along the trail. The race lasts between eight and fifteen days. The fastest time is a little over eight days and three hours. It is a popular event in Alaska but is also known worldwide.

PHOTO 18.10. The Iditarod.
Source: iStock/mdcooper

70 percent of the population of Nunavut speak a variant of Inukut.

Religion

The Alaskan and Canadian Native American bands worshipped animistic deities, whose spirits were imbued within animals and landscape features. Closely tied to Native religion, but separate, were the shamans, who these bands believed worked with dangerous and mysterious powers beyond the human realm. They divined hunting rituals, were central sources of wisdom, and diagnosed and treated diseases.

Many Natives had little reason to adopt the religion of their oppressors, but devoted Russian missionaries often won the Natives' faith. For example, the Tlingit of Southeastern Alaska were wary of the Russians until a smallpox epidemic swept through the area in 1830, killing 40 to 50 percent of the Tlingit; the Russians suffered considerably less because they were vaccinated. The power of the Russian "medicine" swayed many Tlingit toward the Russian church, especially in light of the shamans' inability to combat the disease. Another example of missionary religious conversion was the development of written languages and translation of the Bible into the Native languages.

The Church was a lasting cultural influence of Alaska's Russian occupation. The American and Russian Orthodox missionaries Christianized the Alaskan Natives by the early 1920s. Today, the Orthodox Church has forty Alaskan parishes and over fifty thousand indigenous followers. The onion-domed churches are visible in many communities.

While Arctic Aboriginals converted to Christianity, **syncretism** imbued their Christian vision with their past religious expressions, such as in the Athabascan spirit houses in Eklutna and on occasion along roadsides (photo 18.9). The spirit houses are shrines to the deceased, where the living can bring offerings to the spirits and the spirits can visit the living.

Population, Immigration, and Diversity

The vast and sparsely populated North is the Inuit, Athabascan, and Algonquin homeland, along with the Métis of Canada and a sprinkling of whites. Many Native groups have retained cultural integrity despite grievous losses in the past and have increased their population in the twenty-first century.

Alaska

Alaska, one of the least populous American states, has been growing faster than the national average. The population was 741,000 in 2016, a 14.5 percent increase over its 2000 population. The sources of this growth are natural increase and petroleum industry in-migrations during the 1970s and 1980s.

The Anchorage metropolitan area has the largest population in the state. Anchorage is also the most ethnically diverse area, with 66 percent white, 5.4 percent black, 6.4 percent Asian, 7.5 percent Hispanic, and 7.9 percent Native American or Alaskan Native. The ethnic breakdown of all Alaskan inhabitants is about 66.7 percent white, 3.3 percent black, 5.4 percent Asian, and 14.8 percent Native. This has changed radically since the 1930s, when the Native population was the majority at just over 50 percent

Ontario and British Columbia have the most First Nations people numerically, 301,425 and 232,290, respectively, but they only represent a small portion of the total population: less than 2.4 percent of Ontario's population and 5.4 percent of the population of British Columbia. In the territories, the Native groups have the highest population concentrations. Eighty-six percent of the 27,360 Nunavut population (2006) are Aboriginal; they make up about one-half of all Canadian Inuit. In the Northwest Territories, First Nations people are 51 percent, composed of Dene, Métis, and Inuvialuit, and about 11 percent are Inuit. In the Yukon, 23 percent are Aboriginal.

The Inuit birthrate is about twice Canada's national birthrate, making the Inuit the fastest-growing group relatively. The Inuit are also the youngest compared with other First Nations peoples, and with a median age of 23, much younger than the median age of the Canadian population at 39.5.

The overall populations in the Northwest Territories and the Yukon have been declining, as are the populations in the largest cities and capitals, Yellowknife and Whitehorse. Driven by a high birthrate, Nunavut and its capital, Iqaluit, are gaining population.

Immigration and Diversity

This region is diverse in that there are significant numbers of Native Alaskan and First Nations people. However, the numbers of foreign born are small. The state of Alaska is home to 7.4 percent foreign born, almost half the national average. Juneau is close to that with only 7.8 percent, but Anchorage fares somewhat better at 10 percent. The top five countries of birth for immigrants in Anchorage are: Philippines (26.5 percent), Korea (12 percent), Mexico (7 percent), Thailand (5.5 percent), and the Dominican Republic (3.5 percent). Filipino seamen are

recorded as having contact with Alaskan Natives as early as 1788, and Filipino immigrants continued to arrive as workers in Alaska's developing natural resource industries: as sailors on American whaling ships; as ore sorters for gold mines; and as salmon cannery workers. Alaska's Filipino community has a long history of interaction and intermarriage with Alaska Native communities, and many Filipinos in Alaska also claim Alaska Native heritage. Filipino migration to Alaska has continued, due to existing family ties and the history of the migration pathway. Today, many Filipinos work in the health care sector, retail trade, and food services.

Urban Trends

Urban centers in Alaska and the Canadian territories are small in comparison to temperate-climate cities. There are, however, seven communities of significant size in Alaska, and each Canadian territory has a regional center, populated by about half the territory's residents. In Alaska, the largest city by far is Anchorage, followed by Fairbanks (pop. 32,751) in the interior, and in the Panhandle region Juneau, the capital (30,388), Sitka (8,830), and Ketchikan (8,208). The three Panhandle cities have no road connections outside the Panhandle, yet all are crowded with automobiles (all of which have to be transported in by water or air). Although in the past the Panhandle economy has been forestry and fishing, increasingly it is tied to the cruise ship trade. The population varies growing during the tourist and summer seasons, declining as the days shorten. Several other communities—Barrow, Nome, Valdez, and Seward—are regional centers.

The Canadian North has few people, but nonetheless the urban structure is discrete, divided between three types of communities: the government-service communities, such as the capitals; resource communities, such as the oil sands town of Fort McMurray in northern Alberta; and the small Native communities:

- Iqaluit (2016 Pop 7,082)
- Yellowknife (2016 Pop 19,569)
- Yukon (2016 Pop 23,276)
- Whitehorse (2016 Pop 25,085)

Anchorage, Alaska
(2016 MSA 401,600)

Anchorage in south central Alaska is set against the scenic Chugach Mountains (photo 18.11). Situated in a protected area of the Cook Inlet, the city sits on glacial silt and rock between the Knik and Turnagain arms. Anchorage and Stockholm, Sweden, sit at about the same latitude and share similar weather moderated by water. In Anchorage, average summer temperatures range from 55°F to 80°F (13°C to 27°C), and winter temperatures from 5°F to 20°F (−15°C to −7°C).

Founded in 1915, the railroad construction camp consisted of plank sidewalks and rows of tents. Anchorage grew during World War II, when Alaska became a strategic location in

PHOTO 18.11. Downtown Anchorage, Alaska. During the spring and summer, Anchorage looks like many other American cities, except for the dramatic backdrop of the Chugach Mountains. Half of Alaska's population lives in the Anchorage area.

response to the Japanese threat. Military installations and infrastructure shaped the city for its future development, as the city grew from eight thousand before the war to forty-three thousand after. Today, half of Alaska's population lives within twenty-five miles of Anchorage.

Anchorage's transportation links helped it to become the region's most important city and oil production business center. After World War II, suburban developments in the Matanuska River Valley, Wasilla, and down the Kenai Peninsula alleviated housing shortages. Anchorage is a gateway into the interior, serviced by a railroad, two highways, and Alaska's largest airport. It is also the service and distribution center for farming, oil production, and military and governmental activities, and it is the dominant tourist stopover. Anchorage also provides a local shopping area for many Alaskans, including a mall filled with familiar American stores.

Anchorage has adopted a number of sustainable features, although it does not yet have an official sustainability plan. It developed a climate action plan in 2009, but it has not yet been adopted. The city has yet to develop a comprehensive analysis of its emissions or outlined formal targets for reductions, steps taken by dozens of other major cities around the country and world. Still, there are a handful of Leadership in Energy and Environmental Design (LEED)-certified buildings and street lighting. The city has changed a quarter of the streetlights to energy-saving light-emitting diodes (LEDs), which is expected to save the city about 30 percent on street lighting costs. Since Anchorage has very long periods of darkness during the winter, the savings are welcomed. In 2016, the municipal utility opened a new natural gas power plant

that emits 30 percent less CO_2 to generate the same amount of electricity as legacy plants.

Ironically, while climate change may disproportionately impact this region and urban area it has ceased to be a priority for the state government, and the last several governors have done very little to advance either climate action or sustainability. Because Alaska has far fewer GHGs emissions than most other states, they have argued that climate mitigation will have little impact but will chase away business. As a result, Alaska lags behind many other regions in being more aggressive around climate and sustainability. Many Alaskans are frustrated with the pace of change.

Canadian North

The combined Canadian territorial population is less than the population of Anchorage. The largest city in each territory (Whitehorse, Yellowknife, and Iqaluit) is also the capital.

Whitehorse (25,085 pop. [2016]) has been the Yukon capital since it replaced Dawson City in 1952. Whitehorse was founded in 1900 upon completion of the White Pass and Yukon Railway. Whitehorse accounts for three-quarters of the territorial population, and it is the territory's tourism, transportation, and freight hub.

Yellowknife, Northwest Territories (19,659 pop. [2016]), was founded as a gold-mining town in the 1930s and is now a center for diamond-mining operations. The town, accessed via the Mackenzie Highway, is located about nine hundred miles north of Edmonton (photo 18.13).

Iqaluit, Nunavut, located on Baffin Island (7,082 pop. [2016]), was formerly called Frobisher Bay after the

BOX 18.6 URBAN SUSTAINABILITY BEST PRACTICES: JUNEAU

Every summer, Juneau's downtown cruise ship dock welcomes hundreds of thousands of happy tourists eager to visit (photo 18.12). But this type of tourist economy has environmental costs. Cruise ship engines burn diesel fuel, spewing not only GHG emissions, but also sulphur oxides, nitrogen oxides, and particulate matter. When ships are at dock they must leave their engines running to provide power to the ship. A mid-size cruise ship's diesel engine can use 150 tons of fuel each day and some estimate that one cruise ship can emit as much particulate matter as a million cars in a day.

Juneau, in partnership with Princess Cruise Lines, has taken the lead in an innovation that allows ships to "plug in" to shoreside power—rather than run their polluting diesel engines—when they are sitting at the dock. Using power from the city's grid instead of the engines to power the ship's onboard services reduces emissions while docked, which means less GHG emissions and improved local air quality.

Cruise ships were not previously built with the capability of plugging into shoreside power, so older vessels must be retrofitted to access the new systems. Princess Cruise Lines has converted most of their ships with this infrastructure. Other cruise lines are considering this investment.

The groundbreaking technology has now grown to include systems in Seattle, Vancouver, Los Angeles, San Diego, San Francisco, and Halifax, and is planned to roll out in other ports that have made commitments to shore power programs, including New York. It may not be the ultimate pollution control system, but in a state that has avoided aggressive climate mitigation, it is a start.

PHOTO 18.12 The Cruise Ship *Sea Princess* Departing Juneau, Alaska, by Way of the Gastineau Channel. More than 1.7 million tourists visited Alaska in 2016, more than half come by cruise ship.

Source: iStock/deebrowning

sixteenth-century Northwest Passage explorer Sir Martin Frobisher. Frobisher Bay was a US Air Force base linking North America and Europe during World War II; it became Nunavut's capital, reverting to its Inuit name (meaning "many fish") in 1987. This least-populated Canadian capital is more than three times the size of the next largest Nunavut town, and the only territorial capital currently gaining population. It is the transportation and service focus for the territory. Only local roads service the town. Outside access is by air.

Fort McMurray, Alberta, is an oil sands boomtown that has averaged six new people daily, growing from 20,000 in 1977 to 66,500 in 2016. Fort McMurray is expected to grow drawing from eastern and less prosperous Canadian provinces.

Since the collapse of the Atlantic cod fishery, many from Newfoundland migrated to work in the Fort McMurray oil sand industry, giving it the colloquial title of the "second-largest city in Newfoundland." This may be changing, though, as the Newfoundland economy picks up with its own oil industry and the demand for labor falls in the oil sand industry.

The Economy

The Primary Sector

Alaska and territorial Canadian economies are resource based. Agriculture is unimportant economically, although both crops and livestock are grown in southern areas.

PHOTO 18.13. Yellowknife, Northwest Territories, Canada.

Source: iStock/JosefHanus

Mining became a primary source of income in the North in the twenty-first century, when commodity prices escalated, making northern investments lucrative. Mineral and fossil fuel production has become substantial; however, the friction of distance functions as a deterrent.

Mineral Resources

Mining, fishing, and lumber overshadow the northern agricultural economy. The lowland slope and forest areas are accessible and rich in hydrocarbons. Many of the world's largest producing mines are located in the Arctic and boreal regions.

The taiga economy depends on mining, which is the basis for most of the settlements. However, mines and their towns are usually boom-or-bust propositions that follow world market prices and demand.

Diamonds are the lead mining story in the Canadian North. Other significant minerals include gold, zinc, copper, and coal. Historically, mineral production has been limited because of the distance; however, decreased resources, increased prices in temperate climatic zones, and technological advances have caused boreal and Arctic resources to become economically viable.

Gold   Alaska has had several significant gold rushes including:

- Gastineau Channel in the 1880s, which established the capital, Juneau, named after a prospector in the region;
- Nome in 1899 and 1900, at which time Nome was the largest city in Alaska; and
- Ester, near Fairbanks, in 1902.

Nome's gold rush was known as the "poor man's gold rush," because small-time prospectors could find gold on the town's beaches. In other areas, the cost of extraction limited gold production to large operations.

In 2006, the price of gold surpassed $600 per ounce and rose in 2011 to more than $1,800 per ounce. The price jump has rekindled interest in gold mining. The beaches of Nome were once again filled with placer prospectors and dredgers mining gold. Gold mining has also begun again north of Fairbanks at the Fort Knox open-pit mine.

Gas and Oil   Parts of the Arctic Slope contain major deposits of petroleum and natural gas, which were formed about two hundred million years ago when the area was submerged in a shallow sea and the organisms (which are the source material for oil) died and were pressurized and heated until they were transformed into hydrocarbons.

In 1967, Alaska sold leases in the Prudhoe Bay area to oil companies, and in 1973 the oil crisis accelerated investment in Alaskan oil production. The Trans-Alaskan Pipeline System (TAPS) began commercial production in 1977. It was built to transport crude oil from the North Slope to Valdez, where tankers were loaded and the oil shipped to Washington and California refineries.

Oil company profits have been taxed numerous times, the most recent being a 22.5 percent tax. Over the years, the state economy has yo-yoed in relation to the collected taxes. Low oil prices and reduced production kept the state near bankruptcy in the 1990s, but a rise in oil prices in 2003 created a boom that brought more money into Alaska despite the continued decline

BOX 18.7 NATIONAL PARKS: ARCTIC NATIONAL WILDLIFE REFUGE

If national parks are America's best idea, then national wildlife refuges are America's best kept secret. The 19-million-acre Arctic National Wildlife Refuge (ANWR) was created in 1960 and is America's largest wildlife preserve, supporting 169 species of birds, 28 species of fish, 44 species of mammals, and an unknown number of plants and lichens (photo 18.14).

Wildlife refuges are not in the national park system, but are run as federal lands through the US Fish and Wildlife Service, whose mission is to conserve America's fish, wildlife, and plants. However, because these are not national parks, they are not as strongly protected from development pressures such as logging, mining, or oil and gas extraction. Some have called on Congress to designate ANWR as a wilderness area or national park to provide better protection.

In 1980, oil and gas development were prohibited unless specifically authorized by an act of Congress. However, in the early twenty-first century, debate grew about whether to open the reserve to oil and gas exploration along the 1.5 million coastal plain acres, 8 percent of the refuge. It is both the most likely place to find oil and the most fragile area for habitat preservation. The alleged benefits would decrease dependence on foreign oil and would augment American oil and gas production in a time of escalating prices.

Environmental groups criticize the possible destruction of the fragile tundra ecosystem. The ANWR coast is the last part of Alaska's North Slope closed to drilling. Environmentalists believe that the amount of oil is nowhere near the stated claims of those favoring development. Comparative oil industry test drilling results are unavailable to the public.

The effects of drilling are controversial and wide ranging. Those who favor ANWR oil production believe that as little as 0.1 percent of the preserve would yield more than one million barrels of oil a day for thirty years. Drilling the preserve would bring in more jobs, but environmentalists have fought these initiatives, citing destruction of the Alaskan coastal plain, caribou migration routes, and calving patterns. They also point out that drilling within ANWR is a short-term answer that will not free America of oil dependence. In 2006, a crisis of escalated oil and gas prices brought the issue to the forefront again, and US and Canadian companies agreed to develop the Beaufort Sea area.

Some oil companies continue to invest in Alaskan oil production and found new reserves in the Cook Outlet, Kenai Peninsula, Chukchi Sea, and along the North Slope. The government and oil companies focus on efficient production and development of new oil fields. Oil has been explored in the Beaufort Sea along a disputed international boundary between the United States and Canada.

There is also an increased interest in North Slope and Cook Inlet natural gas field development, which provides heating and electricity for Alaskan communities. The Alaskan government and many residents favor developing a pipeline to the lower forty-eight. The proposed pipeline would run about thirty-six hundred miles from Prudhoe Bay to Calgary and then to Chicago, delivering about four billion cubic feet of natural gas daily.

PHOTO 18.14. Coastal Plain in the Arctic National Wildlife Refuge, Looking South toward the Brooks Range Mountains.
Source: iStock/mtnmichelle

BOX 18.8   ENVIRONMENTAL CHALLENGES: OIL SANDS

A sea once covered the plains of Alberta. Over time the plants and animals from that sea were heated, pressurized, and converted into the extensive oil and gas fields that account for 85 percent of Canada's oil and gas. Alberta has reaped profits from these deposits in the last half of the twentieth century. In the process, the balance of political power shifted toward the Outer Canada Prairies for the first time since Canadian Confederation.

As conventional oil production declines, the biggest news and fastest-growing industry is oil sands, whose largest reserves are north of Edmonton at three sites: Peace River, Athabasca, and Cold Lake (map 18.6). The largest and most accessible reserve is the Athabascan oil sands, along the Athabasca River near Fort McMurray. Only Saudi Arabia has larger oil reserves than Canada.

Almost one-quarter of all oil imported into the United States is from Canada.

Alberta oil sand deposits contain 1.7 to 2.5 trillion barrels of oil. The oil sands produce more than one million barrels daily, which is expected to grow to three million barrels daily by 2020. Technologies to extract the oil from the sands are more expensive than conventional methods and are only profitable when the price of oil is high. Saudi oil costs about $2 to $3 per barrel to pump, whereas Alberta bitumen (the molasses-like crude extracted) costs from $8.50 to $12 per barrel. The crude oil leaves Fort McMurray by underground pipeline to Edmonton or to the United States, where it is refined into gasoline, home heating oil, and jet fuel. The Keystone Pipeline and Keystone XL extension is a proposed system of transporting the thick oil through the United States to the Gulf Coast. The proposed pipeline has been controversial due to potential environmental impacts, including passing over the Sand Hills of Nebraska and the Ogallala Aquifer and the potential harm of a pipeline leak.

The extreme environmental impact of oil sands mining has affected land, air, water, and health. The oil is mixed with sand and clay; separating the oil takes heat, pressure, and chemicals, all of which cause additional problems for the climate and environment. The oil removal process, the number one source of GHGs in Canada, is two to three times more polluting than conventional oil development. Two tons of oil sands produce one barrel of crude oil.

The current pit surface mining methods have displaced more than 150,000 acres that must be reclaimed, including resurfacing and planting trees and greenbelts for wildlife habitat. The disruption to the land and the cost to reclaim it are immense, and reclamation has yet to be satisfactorily fulfilled, although the companies have invested millions to attempt reclamation with little success. The adjacent rivers, which run north to the Arctic Ocean, are heavily polluted. Few dare to eat the fish, though not that long ago they were a source for subsistence food.

Oil sands extraction uses Athabascan River water, causing water quantity and quality problems. The water is seldom recycled but dumped in unrecoverable toxic ponds. Residents downriver from the oil sands have reported high incidences of asthma and respiratory illness, but even more disturbing is the high incidence of cancer, as reported in Alberta's oldest settlement, Fort Chipewyan. The fort sits on the shore of Lake Athabasca—the Athabasca River drains into the lake. Among the carcinogenic chemicals in the water are benzene and arsenic, while fish have high mercury levels.

The oil sands have brought an economic boom and political power to Alberta, but pollution remains a significant environmental challenge.

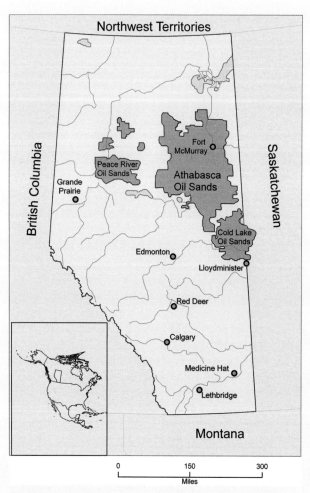

MAP 18.6. Canada's Oil Sands Deposits. These deposits are found mostly at three sites. The Peach River and Athabasca sites are in Alberta, and the Cold Lake site is within Alberta and Saskatchewan.

in production. The more recent fall in oil prices since 2008 has negatively impacted the state economy and revenues.

Since nearly all mineral rights are on public land, the state set up a Permanent Fund Dividend (PFD, as it is called in Alaska) derived from oil production revenues. The PFD gives every state resident an annual check derived from the amount of oil produced. In 2001 the PFD check was $1,500, but it has varied in the intervening years. In 2010 the PFD was $1,281; in 2015 the PFD was $2,072.

In the Canadian North, oil and gas production mostly depends on Alberta oil sands production, located in three major oil sands deposits: Peace River, Cold Lake, and the largest near Fort McMurray.

Logging

Forests are carbon sinks, so cutting them decreases the ability to store CO_2, increases the level in the atmosphere, and contributes to climate change.

One of the collective oil and gas exploration and forestry issues in northeastern Alberta's boreal forest has been **seismic lines**, thirty-foot-wide strips bulldozed across the taiga landscape to facilitate drilling and dynamiting. Almost as much land is cleared for seismic lines as for logging, but seismic lines remain deforested, which affects natural habitats and fragments the forests. These disturbance corridors aggravate soils, vegetation, and aquatic systems and give hunters and poachers forest access.

Pulp mills harvest Alberta and British Columbia forests. The wood is then exported: 60 percent to the United States, a growing market in China, and much of the remainder to Japan. The mills, built on the Athabascan and Peace rivers, dump mill effluent, cause pollution, and contain carcinogens, such as dioxin. However, some companies are addressing ecosystem pollution. Abitibi Consolidated, a large paper mill supplying newsprint to the United States, is working with the Aboriginal Kaska Dena to establish an environmentally sensitive logging operation.

In Alaska, the Tongass National Forest spreads across almost seventeen million acres of southeastern Alaska and the Inside Passage. As the largest temperate rain forest in the world, the Tongass contains about 29 percent of the planet's total unlogged temperate rain forest. The near-perfect conditions for the conifer forests are the result of air masses coming off the Pacific and rising against the mountains.

The Alaskan forests were not cut over like Great Lakes forests, because of the distance from lumber markets and the time period of possible development. By the 1950s, many lower-forty-eight forests were logged, and Forest Service and state territory campaigns were focused on building an Alaskan logging industry to ensure economic development and local employment. In the late nineteenth century, Tongass wood was cut and used for local production and cannery needs, but building the necessary infrastructure for an international market required substantial capital and was never achieved.

The rise of environmental consciousness in the 1970s and 1980s changed how people viewed the Tongass. Some Alaskan

areas were set aside as wilderness areas, while logging peaked in other areas. By 1997, the government imposed cut restrictions that left nearly 80 percent of the forests protected. Increased global competition (the opening of the Russian-Siberian market) affected the remaining forest's profitability, and by 1997 the pulp mills were closed.

The logging industry plays a minor role in the Alaskan economy. But increased pressure to reopen Tongass logging has been a popular sentiment, although the industry now faces increased global competition. The region still has an abundant forest, but its location and high American labor costs are unfavorable. However, conservation and logging interests continue to battle their interests in court.

Fishing

Upon statehood, Alaska's primary industry was fishery. After oil production grew in the 1970s, fishing became Alaska's second- and then third-largest industry (after tourism), but it continued to provide nearly six billion pounds of seafood annually. Most attention has been on the lucrative salmon fishery, but low salmon prices and dwindling fish stock, along with quotas, have curbed the wild-fish commercial fishery. The largest-volume fishery, dominated by species other than salmon, remains in the Bering Sea.

Salmon has remained important in the Native diet, but it is also an American delicacy. However, for years little attention was paid to salmon sustainability; instead, the anadromous salmon's homing instinct was exploited. Presently, Pacific Northwest fishing resources are down by 90 percent, due to overfishing and dam construction. To combat this shortage, fish farms proliferate and threaten the viability of the Alaskan wild fishery.

The per-pound price for salmon waned in the 1990s as a result of increased competition from Norwegian, Chilean, and Scottish farm-raised salmon. A small rebound in wild fish occurred in the twenty-first century but remained lower than in the past. Fishery experts believe the rebound is the result of increased environmental awareness of antibiotic, insecticide, and colorant use in farmed fish.

Ninety-eight percent of the world salmon supply was wild in 1980. By 1997, farm-raised salmon exceeded the wild salmon catch in value. Salmon continue to account for the largest share of Alaskan fishing receipts, but king crab, snow crab, halibut, cod, pollock, and several other fish are also valuable. Strict quotas control and restrict fishing. The principal fishing grounds are in the panhandle area, the Gulf of Alaska, Kodiak, Bristol Bay, and the Bering Sea. The Bering Sea alone accounts for one half of the US catch, but it is overfished. Dutch Harbor in the Aleutian Islands has become the number one port in the nation for seafood volume (photo 18.15).

Local fish-processing plants employ thousands of nonresidents, who live in dorms near the plant during the processing seasons. The two main seasons are during the winter (crab, halibut, and pollock) and summer through fall (halibut, cod, turbot, and pollock). The processed seafood is converted

PHOTO 18.15. Unalaska, Alaska, on the Aleutian Islands. Unalaska has become the primary fishing port by volume for the . Its history goes back to Unangan Natives, who were followed by Russian fur traders. Today Unalaska remains influenced by its Russian past and the port town of Dutch Harbor.

to surimi (restructured fish flesh or fish paste, colored and reshaped to resemble more expensive seafood, such as crab) and shipped to Japan. Other fish are processed into bone-free blocks and cut into patty shapes to be used by fast-food chains. All fish parts are processed. Fishmeal is made from by-products. Fish oil was once an unprofitable by-product until experiments in the late 1990s perfected another use: green energy. Biodiesel fuel is used approximately fifty-fifty with fossil fuel in the plant generators and in the powerhouse. The fish oil is biodegradable and less polluting than diesel.

The Alaskan fishery, the largest in the United States, struggles with continued out-of-state ownership, decreasing fishery profits, and the annual closure of canneries. Many towns along the Alaskan Peninsula and the Aleutians depend on the fishery, and they have been protected by quotas implemented in 1992.

The Tertiary Sector

The government sector employs eighty thousand Alaskans. In Juneau, the state capital, the pay structure is lopsided; well-paid jobs within the government provide two-thirds of the employment, but reduced oil revenues have curtailed the abundance of government jobs. The remainder is made up of low-paying tourism-related jobs. Government jobs are also important in the Canadian territories, where jobs are scarce outside the mining industry.

In addition to government jobs, there has been growth in education and health care. However, the biggest tertiary growth has been in tourism.

Tourism

Alaska tourism emphasizes a Disneyland-like romanticized and simplified Alaska that contrasts with the reality; however, tourism is one of the largest sources of income in Alaska. Cruises along the Inside Passage began during the late nineteenth century but intensified during the late twentieth century. Most Alaskan towns profit from tourism. In 2016, some 1.7 million tourists visited the state of Alaska, spending almost $950 each there. Almost half of the tourists arrived on cruise ships.

Keeping tourist dollars within the local economies and not exporting profits to outside corporations is a continuing challenge. Profits leave the locale and leave locals with low-paying jobs and reduced community services. However, Seattle has been the headquarters for many Alaskan companies for the past century. For example, Princess Cruises and Tours are headquartered in Washington, as are the large fishing companies. Princess Tours controls nearly all the tourist dollars it generates with its own ships, hotels, bus lines, and tour packages.

Alaska has many scenic and outdoor sites with over fifty-one million acres of national park land, including Denali (Mount McKinley) and Glacier Bay. Towns on cruise-ship lines rely on tourism for their sustenance. Skagway, for example, was a ghost town until cruise ships reinvigorated the town of eight hundred. Over four hundred cruise ships visit annually, up to five per day visit during the May to September tourism season. During the off-season, the town shuts down.

BOX 18.9   GLOBAL CONNECTIONS: WITHIN AND BEYOND ALASKA

While much of the continental United States is smoothly connected to the rest of the country and the world, Alaska poses special difficulties. Permafrost and rough terrain force most Alaskan transportation to be on water or in the air. Vast distances, difficult terrain, and smothering regulations all add to the difficulty.

Air

Seventy-five percent of Alaska is inaccessible by road. Bush pilots have achieved legendary status flying small, light planes anywhere within the region, from fishing enclaves to mining operations (photo 18.16). They land on almost any surface, such as gravel bars, water, and glaciers. Hundreds of Alaskan bush flights take off daily. Lake Hood, near Anchorage, has the most, with five hundred flights a day.

PHOTO 18.16. Bush Plane. Bush planes are a vital part of the transportation network in the bush wilderness areas of Alaska and the Canadian Territories.

Shipping

The 1920 US Maritime Act, commonly called the Jones Act, stipulated that all commercial ships traveling between two American ports needed to be American-built, staffed, and owned. Alaska, at the time only a territory and underrepresented in Congress, was singled out as the only place in America where foreign ships were forbidden. The act was political. Alaska became the vassal of the state of Washington. All ships had to be routed through Seattle.

The act is still in force today and affects Alaskans on a daily basis. Most goods are not driven into the state, which is far more expensive than shipping, but the limitations of the Jones Act disallow inexpensive shipping practices. Most shipping and fishing companies today remain based out of Seattle rather than in Alaska, which takes away from the local economy. The major port for Alaska cruises is now in Vancouver, which has been a boon to their tourism business but has hurt American ports. Additionally, oil tankers shipping Trans-Alaskan Pipeline System (TAPS) crude

must all be built in America and of American components. The shipping industry remains one of the major uses of American steel. The Jones Act has made it nearly impossible to compete with overseas shipbuilding techniques and costs.

Oil Pipeline

The TAPS was started in 1973. It runs eight hundred miles fro Prudhoe Bay to Valdez. It was built during the time of growing environmental awareness, and the pipeline taught engineers several geographical and environmental lessons (photo 18.17). Some of the lessons learned were

PHOTO 18.17. The Trans-Alaska Pipeline System (TAPS). The pipeline runs eight hundred miles from Prudhoe Bay to Valdez. This section is between Glenallen and Valdez.

- Warm crude oil flowing through the pipeline would harm the fragile permafrost.
- The pipeline was originally conceived to be underground, but as permafrost and its ecosystem relation were understood, the pipeline became about fifty-fifty under and above ground.
- Construction costs in permafrost areas are double those in non-permafrost areas.
- Seismic and vehicle trails over tundra destroy vegetation. Winter snow cover and ice roads are usually the least damaging methods to move over the tundra.
- Road construction has been both a positive and negative influence for the pipeline route.

The pipeline had both positive and negative consequences:

Positive: It increased communication within the region and among its residents; it brought jobs and also brings tourism.
Negative: It alters animal habitats, increases competition for subsistence resources, and brings tourists, who damage fragile tundra. It has endorsed relying on nonrenewable natural resources over conservation of resources.

Transportation difficulties limit the economic growth of this region. Transportation across the tundra has always been difficult. Natives and early Western inhabitants traveled the Mackenzie River by canoe or barge in the summer, but mosquito-infested bogs and marshes limited the ability to carry the heavy equipment needed by extractive industries. Winter travel by dog sleds and snowshoes was in many ways easier than summer travel. In the late nineteenth century, the railway came into Dawson City, Yukon, but the costs of infrastructure to maintain a permafrost railway were enormous. Roads have slowly developed in the North, but few penetrate the Arctic. The Northwest Territory and the Yukon have a combined total of thirty-six hundred highway miles. Nunavut has no long-distance highways.

Permafrost roads are built with a thick insulating gravel layer built atop the tundra mat, because cutting into the tundra results in muck. An elevated gravel road can withstand the changing active layer better than a permanent roadbed. The two major Arctic highways, built to support mineral and petroleum extraction, are the Alaska Dalton Highway from Fairbanks to Prudhoe Bay, which services the oil pipeline, and the Dempster Highway, which provides the required road to reach petroleum deposits in Canada's territorial North.

Travel through the Arctic to resource sites, such as the diamond mines, is best done in the winter trucking over **ice roads** made of compacted snow, because in the summer the muskeg makes the route impassable. Although the ice roads have been rebuilt each winter since the 1980s, they may soon become impractical. Climate change is shortening the ice-road season.

A Sustainable Future

The "pristine North" is an illusion. Many environmental ills originating in the industrialized South have found their way into the Arctic, and many are now generated in the North and wreak bioaccumulation havoc on the region. The reality of Arctic climate change has resulted in ecosystem and habitat destruction. The Arctic role in global resources is recent; as temperate-climate resources reach their economic limits, Arctic resources are being tapped. Additionally, a significant discovery of diamonds in the Northwest Territory has realigned the worldwide diamond cartel; this discovery ensures the region's economic viability at least temporarily, but it also requires mitigation to reduce environmental damage.

Arctic oil is a contentious issue. Local residents want the resource to be developed because they want the jobs provided by the industry. However, mounting evidence in environmentalists' reports indicates that oil development in the ANWR would damage local flora and fauna, including the declining Porcupine caribou herd that supplies local residents with food. Ultimately, the question of Arctic oil development and the short-term benefit it offers the US oil supply (possibly a year's worth of oil) becomes a less important issue than the question of when and how the United States will evolve beyond its fossil fuel dependence.

Challenges for a sustainable future include the following:

- climate change;
- permafrost thaw;
- risks due to oil production and pipeline transport;
- an economy still dependent on the primary sector; and
- lack of support for comprehensive sustainability and climate planning.

There has been progress, however. Sustainability studies are more common in Alaska and territorial Canada, because of the "canary in the coal mine" role the region plays regarding climate change. The area is now being studied by climate researchers who are advancing an understanding of this complex issue. And some small actions have taken place. Environmental issues have been addressed with the Alaskan Pipeline, the Keystone Pipeline and Extension, and the possible construction of a natural gas pipeline.

Inuit and First Nations bands have pursued sustainable research to support the continuation of their culture and to document environmental changes. At the University of Alaska, Fairbanks, the Alaska Native Knowledge Network and the Cold Climate Housing Research Center are studying cultural resources and investigating renewable energy options and local housing materials. Geothermal power has been pursued on Unalaska in the Aleutians. First discovered in 1982 on the flank of Matushin Volcano, the hot-water source has yet to be tapped for use. Geothermal opportunities are rare in Alaska, except along the volcanic subduction zones.

In Canada, several organizations favor seeking sustainable methods and management. The work involved in protecting the Stellar sea lion is among the projects, as is monitoring the Porcupine caribou herd; this work is being led by the Arctic Borderlands Ecological Knowledge Co-op.

Because this is a region that may experience climate change sooner than most, it is imperative to take more aggressive action on sustainability.

Questions for Discussion

1. Why is Alaska called the bellwether state in regard to climate change? Give an example.

2. What are the issues for drilling in the ANWR?

3. What are the advantages of mining in the North and the Canadian Shield? What are the disadvantages?

4. Who is in charge of Alaska's fishery, and how does it affect the state?

5. What are the political, economic, and cultural implications that have made the James Bay Project controversial?

6. What is permafrost, and how is it an impediment to construction? How does the construction industry get around the impediment?

7. Why is permafrost thaw a concern?

8. How have Inuit lifestyles changed in recent decades, and what problems do they face today?

9. Why was the Trans-Alaska Pipeline considered environmentally sensitive? How did the oil companies work to protect the environment? What are ANCSA Corporations (Alaska Native Corporations) and what has been their impact?

10. How is climate change a social equity issue in this region?

Suggested Readings

Abel, K. *Drum Songs: Glimpses of Dene History*. Buffalo, N.Y.: McGill-Queen's University Press, 1993

Alaska Energy Authority. "Alaska Energy: A First Step toward Energy Independence." January 2009, at http://chpcenternw.org/NwChpDocs/AlaskaEnergy_AFirstStepTowardEnergyIndependence.pdf.

Bone, R. M. *The Geography of the Canadian North: Issues and Challenges*. Toronto: Oxford University Press, 2003.

———. *The Regional Geography of Canada*. Toronto: Oxford University Press, 2000.

Bourassa, R. *Power from the North*. Scarborough, Ontario: Prentice Hall of Canada, 1985.

Canadian Arctic Resources Committee. "On Thinning Ice." *Northern Perspectives* 27, no. 2 (Spring 2002).

Charndonnet, A. *On the Trail of Eklutna*. Chicago: Adams Press, 1991.

Collier, R. "Fueling America: Canadian Oil Showdown." *San Francisco Chronicle*, 2005.

Committee on the Alaska Groundfish Fishery and Stellar Sea Lions, National Research Council. *The Decline of the Stellar Sea Lion in Alaskan Waters: Untangling Food Webs and Fishing Nets*. Washington, D.C.: National Academies Press, 2003.

Davis, N. *Permafrost: A Guide to Frozen Ground in Transition*. Fairbanks: University of Alaska Press, 2001.

French, H. M., and O. Slaymaker, eds. "Canada's Cold Environments." *Canadian Association of Geographers Series in Canadian Geography*. Montreal and Kingston: McGill-Queen's University Press, 1997.

Gibson, J. R. "Russian Expansion in Siberia and America." *Geographical Review* 70, no. 2 (1980): 127–36.

Gruening, E. *The Battle for Alaska Statehood*. Fairbanks: University of Alaska Press.

Huberman, I. *The Place We Call Home: A History of Fort McMurray as Its People Remember 1778–1980*. Fort McMurray, Alberta: Fort McMurray Historical Book Society, 2001.

Jablonski, N. G., ed. *The First Americans: The Pleistocene Colonization of the New World*. San Francisco: University of California Press, 2002.

Kolbert, E. "Disappearing Islands, Thawing Permafrost, Melting Polar Ice. How the Earth is Changing." *The New Yorker*, 2005, at http://www.wesjones.com/climate1.htm

Krümmel, E. M., R. W. Macdonald, L. E. Kimpe, et al. "Aquatic Ecology: Delivery of Pollutants by Spawning Salmon." *Nature*, 2003, 255–56.

Lischke, U., and D. T. McNab, eds. *The Long Journey of a Forgotten People: Métis Identities and Family Histories*. Waterloo, Ontario: Wilfrid Laurier University Press, 2007.

Lucier, C. V., and J. W. Vanstone. *Traditional Beluga Drives of the Inupiaq of Kotzebue Sound, Alaska*. Fieldiana, new series, no. 25. Chicago, Ill.: Field Museum of Natural History, 1995.

Naske, C. M., and H. E. Slotnick. *Alaska: A History of the Forty-Ninth State*. Norman: University of Oklahoma Press, 1987.

Stager, J. K., and H. Swain. *Canada North: Journey to the High Arctic*. New Brunswick, NJ.: Rutgers University Press, 1992.

Tarr, R. "Glaciers and Glaciation of Alaska." *Annals of the Association of American Geographers* 2 (1912): 3–24.

Welsted, J. E., C. Stadel, and J. C. Everitt, eds. *The Geography of Manitoba: Its Land and Its People*. Winnipeg: University of Manitoba Press, 1996.

Wynn, G., and M. Stoll, eds. *Canada and Arctic North America: An Environmental History*. Santa Barbara, Calif.: ABC-CLIO, 2006.

Internet Sources

Alaska Department of Natural Resources. Division of Oil and Gas, at http://dog.dnr.alaska.gov/

Carbon Dioxide Information Analysis Center. Global, Regional, and National Fossil Fuel CO_2 Emissions, at http://cdiac.ornl.gov/trends/emis/em_cont.html

North Country Public Radio. Hydro Power in Cree Country, at http://www.northcountrypublicradio.org/news/hydrocree.html

U.S. Geological Survey. Sea Level and Climate. http://pubs.usgs.gov/fs/fs2-00/

Statistics Canada. Family Income, at www.statcan.gc.ca/tables-tableaux/sum-som/l01/cst01/famil108a-eng.htm

The Wilderness Society, "Greater Than Zero: Toward the Total Economic Value of Alaska's National Forest Wildlands," at http://wilderness.org/content/greater-than-zero

Statistics Canada, at http://www.statcan.gc.ca

1 Mission San Francisco Solano in Sonoma, now a parish church, was the only mission built under Mexican rule.

3 Income from this closed Monterey cannery has been replaced with tourism.

2 The hills and cable cars of San Francisco are a continuing tourist attraction.

4 The eastern side of the Sierra Nevadas is a classic fault-block range with a steep escarpment.

7 The main entrances of these upscale homes in Marina Del Rey, California, consist of garages and no windows.

6 Orange trees were planted near Bakersfield to replace those in Los Angeles lost to urban sprawl.

5 Yosemite Valley, on the western Sierra slope, is a magnificent glacially carved valley.

Klamath River

California

Sacramento

Napa

San Francisco

San José

Monterey

Sacramento River

Sierra Nevada

Hetch Hetchy Aqueduct

San Joaquin Valley

Mt. Whitney

Fresno

Bakersfield

Los Angeles Aqueduct

Santa Barbara

Los Angeles

San Diego

Pacific Plate

North American Plate

San Andreas Fault

California Border
Rivers
California Aqueducts
Cities
Mountains
San Andreas Fault

0   50   100
Miles

19

CALIFORNIA

Having It All, and Then Some

Chapter Highlights

After reading this chapter, you should be able to:

- Label and identify on a map the California subregions
- Describe the southern California climate and how this relates to agricultural production
- Describe some of the critical environmental issues in California
- Explain how plate tectonics affects California's physical landscape
- Explain the history and impact of the Spanish on the California landscape
- Compare and contrast the culture and physical characteristics of Southern and Northern California
- Identify the largest cities in California and the bases of their economies
- Discuss major urban trends in Californian cities
- Explain the impact of the informal economy
- Describe how statewide demographics have changed since 1960
- Explain the impact of international migration
- Describe the importance of the three economic sectors in the region
- Discuss ways that California is moving toward sustainability

Terms

alternative lifestyle
chaparral ecosystem
Chinese Exclusion Act
containerization
desalination

fortress living
Gold Rush
Hispanic
homeless
informal economy
Latino

liquefaction
mission
polynucleated city
presidio
pueblo
rancho

smog
specialty crop
thermal inversion
Treaty of Guadalupe Hidalgo

Places

Central Valley
Coastal Range
Hetch Hetchy

Inland Empire
Los Angeles Aqueduct
Monterey Bay
Mount Whitney

North American Plate
Pacific Plate
Salinas Valley
San Andreas Fault

San Joaquin Valley
Sierra Nevada
Silicon Valley

Cities

Bakersfield
   (2016 MSA 888,000)
Fresno
   (2016 MSA 979,000)

Los Angeles
   (2016 MSA 13.3 million)
Riverside
   (2016 MSA 4.6 million)

Sacramento
   (2016 MSA 2.3 million)
San Francisco
   (2016 MSA 4.6 million)

San Diego
   (2016 MSA 3.3 million)
San José
   (2016 MSA 1.9 million)

PHOTO 19.1. Huntington Beach, California, is also known as "Surf City." An iconic image of California is one of sand, sun, and surf.
Source: Lisa Benton-Short

Introduction

California is complex, diverse, and extreme. The state has a complex topography, diversified demography and economy, and extremes in elevation, climate, and vegetation. The highest and lowest elevations, Mount Whitney and Death Valley, are within view of each other and experience glacial cold and extreme heat, respectively. Climate ranges from always-sunny Southern California to the colder, foggy interior and north; rainfall ranges from less than three inches in the desert to one hundred inches in the northern Coastal Ranges. The state's vegetation varies from xerophytic cacti and shrubs to giant redwoods. The extremes do not end there. California, the most populous state, has water problems exacerbated by periodic droughts. In recent years, California faced mounting foreclosures and continued budget crisis.

Despite its extremes, California's effect on the nation and the world is significant. Nearly everyone knows where California is located and what it signifies—sun, sand, money, and stars—but it also home to tremendous diversity (photo 19.1). California's diverse demographics embody large populations of every major ethnic group and are representative of the future of the United States.

Physical Geography

The topography and almost everything else about California's geology are equally complex and diverse. California spans more than 770 miles from Mexico to Oregon and 250 miles from the West Coast to its eastern boundary. California's topography is mountains–valley–mountains: Coastal Range–Central Valley–Sierra Nevada and Basin and Range. Parts of the state are included in three major regions: Pacific Northwest,

Intermontane, and this chapter's concentration, the core where more than 95 percent of the people live (map 19.1). The core contains the following three subregions:

- Sierra Nevada and Coastal Range;
- South Coast and Los Angeles Basin; and
- Central Valley.

Sierra Nevada and Coastal Range

The steep, rugged Coastal Range parallels and edges the Pacific Ocean. Structural depressions, such as Salinas Valley and San Francisco Bay, separate the series of linear northwest-to-southeast-oriented coastal mountains. The local physiography is a jumble of igneous-infused sedimentary rock, liquefaction soils, and microclimates such as the hot and dry **chaparral ecosystems** with their moisture-retaining shrubs that are fire and drought resistant.

Farther south, near the intersection of the San Andreas and Garlock earthquake faults, are the east-west-trending Transverse and Tehachapi ranges. The San Gabriel and San Bernardino mountains encompass that part of the populous Los Angeles Basin that does not face the sea. San Gorgonio (11, 490 feet) towers over its pass, which connects the Inland Empire extension of the Los Angeles Basin with the Basin and Range city of Palm Springs. To the south of the Los Angeles Basin, the Peninsular Range separates the San Diego watershed basin from the much drier Anza Borrego Desert within the Colorado River watershed. The coastal mountains separate the coast from the Central Valley, which is separated from the Basin and Range by the Sierra Nevada.

South of the Cascades, the Sierra Nevada, 350 miles long and 60 miles wide, divide the Intermontane Basin and Range

MAP 19.1. California Regions. The state of California is included in three major regions: the Pacific Northwest; Intermontane Basin and Range; and California. The northern coast is part of the Pacific Northwest. The eastern sections are part of the Basin and Range (Modoc Plateau, Owens Valley, Mojave Desert, Sonora Desert), and the area with the most population, agriculture, and largest economy is the core of California: the San Francisco Bay, Central Coast, Central Valley, Sierra Nevada, and South Coast.

from California's core region (photo 19.2). The pine-forested Sierras rise some nine thousand feet above the five-thousand-foot valley floor, culminating in 14,494-foot Mount Whitney. California's major rivers originate in the Sierras. The fault-block granitic escarpment tilts sharply upward in the east and gradually descends west under Central Valley sediments. The abrupt rise of the eastern face of the mountains is related to the underlying geology and the number of earthquakes that uplifted the mountains and continue to shake California.

South Coast and Los Angeles Basin

The South Coast encompasses the skinny coastal plain to the Mexican border. Coastal ranges separate Los Angeles from the Inland Empire counties of San Bernardino and Riverside (part of the Intermontane), which are included in the greater metropolitan area (including Los Angeles, Orange, and Ventura counties), known as the Southland.

Tectonics shaped the Los Angeles Basin fifteen million years ago. The resulting crust collapsed into a sediment-filled bowl,

until another tectonic event uplifted the basin about five million years ago. The bowl contains thirty thousand feet of gravel, sand, and clay sediments over the bedrock. The lack of bedrock close to the surface explains the gelatin-like **liquefaction** of soil during seismic events, and it leaves Los Angeles Basin prone to earthquake damage.

Central Valley

The four-hundred-mile by fifty-mile Central Valley, wedged between the Coast Ranges and the Sierra Nevada, is flat, fertile alluvium converted from grassland and marsh to the richest agricultural plain in America. Today the native grasslands are less than 6 percent of their original extent. The valley has two significant rivers (but small when compared to the mighty rivers of America): the Sacramento in the north and the San Joaquin in the south. Both empty into the San Francisco Bay. Water is a major issue in the valley and in California. Rainfall diminishes from north to south, from twenty inches to less than ten. The rainfall was sufficient for ranching operations as

PHOTO 19.2. California's Sierra Nevada Mountain Range.
Source: iStock/Ron_Thomas

the Spanish practiced them, but irrigation became the norm as Anglos assumed control.

West of the Central Valley, the Salinas Valley is hemmed in by the coastal mountains east of the Monterey Peninsula. The valley emerged from an ancient inland sea. The Salinas River drained the valley and deposited the sandy, well-drained alluvium soil that now grows bountiful **specialty crops**.

Water

Water is a major environmental challenge in California. The state is drought prone, and the water is unevenly distributed. The northern third of the state has 70 percent of the water, while the southern two-thirds have 80 percent of the demand. California's three major drainage basins, the Sacramento, San Joaquin, and Tulare, all drain into the San Francisco Bay, but their flow is modest in relation to the state's current needs. The state water system is complex and political, with constant battles between agricultural and urban uses.

Southern California has grown into the second-largest conurbation in America. It has more than one-half of the state's population, but only 2 percent of its natural runoff. Southern California's lack of water has been a long-standing and expensive problem; billions of dollars have been spent on water systems and studies continue to seek water access.

Southern California receives two-thirds of its water from various nonlocal water aqueducts and reservoirs. The balance is met with groundwater and runoff. In 1922, the Colorado River Compact apportioned the river's water among the western states, but California claimed more than its share of water with little competition from the less-populated contiguous states. However, the Basin and Range Intermontane states have grown

considerably since 1990 and have now claimed their legal share of water.

The water-starved south has also diverted Northern California water, something very unpopular among Northern Californians. Many dams were built for Southern Californian use, but in the twenty-first century, dams have fallen out of favor. Rather than build more, the current trend is to remove established dams, such as the Hetch-Hetchy.

Some possible solutions to the lack of water include conservation, recycling, mandatory restrictions, desalination, and building more storage facilities. While conservation, recycling, and restrictions are now commonplace, they are insufficient to satisfy the water needs; so California has pursued desalination possibilities.

Desalination (desal) has become a popular consideration for many cities. Desal removes the salts from ocean water, but the process is at least four times the cost of urban water and ten to twenty times the cost of California's agricultural water. One reason for the expense is that oil or alternative energy sources are required to desalinate water. Still, the increased pressure to find freshwater has driven technology in the desalination industry. In the early 2000s, there were more than twenty proposed desal plants, up and down the coast.

In energy- and conservation-conscious California, desal plant proposals have met with some resistance in local communities. Desal plants have raised concerns about the impact on aquatic ecosystems disturbed by the pumping process and return of concentrated salt brine to the ocean. As a result, many of the desal plants that were proposed in have been delayed in construction. Only two have been constructed. It took more than fourteen years to build a desalination plant in Carlsbad, a town north of San Diego. The Carlsbad desal

BOX 19.1 DID YOU KNOW . . . WATER USAGE

Did you know how many gallons of water it takes to produce

a serving of lettuce? **Six**
a serving of steak? **Twenty-six hundred**
an eight-ounce glass of milk? **Forty-nine**
a day's food for a family of four? **Sixty-eight hundred**
an average American's food for a year? **1.5 million***

US water usage remains the highest in the world, despite a 2 percent drop in water usage since 1990. An American uses between eighty and hundred gallons a day, whereas their French or German counterparts use fifty-five to sixty gallons per day. Most of the water use goes to flushing toilets, taking showers and baths, and doing laundry. Showers that do not have low-flow showerheads use about five gallons per minute; washing machines use about twenty-five gallons per load of laundry. It starts to add up.

After implementing water conservation efforts, Californians have reduced their consumption from about 140 gallons to 85 gallons of water per person daily. Water conservation measures have included the installation of water saving devices inside the homes such as low-flow showerheads. Recent years of extreme drought have led to temporary emergency water conservation

measures that include: no outdoor watering during or within two days after a rain, and no hosing down of sidewalks. Residents have also been encouraged to shower for only five minutes, install high-efficiency toilets, and turn off the water while brushing their teeth. Many residents have filled their pools and replaced their grass with drought-resistance plantings (xeriscaping) or artificial turf.

Tackling residential water use is only part of the solution. In California, 80 percent of the water goes to agriculture. At $8 per acre-foot versus $200 per acre-foot for urban use, agricultural water is sold much cheaper to farmers. Drought has been of concern given that the state is the largest producer of many fruits and vegetables. Some crops are "thirsty" crops—rice, alfalfa, and cotton—that consume 40 percent of the water but produce less than 1 percent of the income. Most recently, almonds have become the villain. It takes a gallon to grow a single almond and California produces 80 percent of the world's supply. Almonds use up as much water each year as the city of Los Angeles does in three. And nearly two-thirds of almonds are exported, generating about $5 billion. Enticed by these lucrative numbers many famers have ripped out crops like tomatoes and melons in favor of almonds. Production for export has dramatically increased, and so has water consumption. That's nuts.

*http://www.nwf.org/nationalwildlife/article.cfm?issueID=68&articleID=928

---

plant became operational in 2015. The plant provides fifty million gallons of water per day, as fresh water from the plant is sent by a ten-mile-long, 4.5-foot-diameter pipeline, utilizing six pumps, to connect to the San Diego's water distribution system. Initially the cost for the desal plant was estimated at $320 million but the final project ended up costing $1billion. A similar desal plan has been in the works for Huntington Beach for many years. This desal plant will operate in a former power station and proponents hope it will be operational by 2019. However, like many other plants, this too has been delayed by requirements for further study before permits are issued and construction begins. Scientists are concerned about the possible impacts concentrated salt water (discharged from the desal plant) could have on aquatic ecosystems.

Water access allowed the Southland to grow in the twentieth century. The lack of access may either halt growth or require even more conservation.

Climate

California's mild weather and Mediterranean precipitation pattern have been prime attractors. Annual coastal temperatures average between 50°F and 80°F (10°C and 27°C), so neither heating nor air-conditioning is usually required.

Inland valleys have more temperature variation; they often climb over 100°F in the summer and on occasion freeze in the winter.

The Mediterranean semiarid wet winter–dry summer climate seldom experiences more than twenty inches of precipitation annually, except in the Sierras, where snow packs of ten feet or more are common.

San Francisco Bay

The San Francisco Bay estuary cools the surrounding area and keeps the temperature mild. A well-known saying (wrongly attributed to Mark Twain) captures the experience of many in the city: "The coldest winter I ever spent was a summer in San Francisco."

The city does have an unusual weather pattern, which is caused by the currents and pressure zones. During the summer, the Aleutian Low accompanies the south-flowing California Current. Cold water upwells along the coast and mixes with the warmer summer air, producing fog and keeping the weather cool and gray. During the winter months, the ocean current flows to the north, bringing warmer water and air to the bay. The city's weather is also part of a much larger and more complex pattern of microclimates formed by the interaction of the hill and valley features and the bay's oceanic winds and currents.

BOX 19.2   SAN FRANCISCO BAY

A series of valleys are tucked between California's coastal ranges. San Francisco Bay was once one of the valleys, but the estuary has been inundated with saltwater multiple times in the past fifteen million years, until the present shallow bay was created about ten thousand years ago. The elongated bay is also a major West Coast estuary, receiving freshwater from the Central Valley and saltwater from the gap spanned by the Golden Gate Bridge.

During the twentieth century the Bay Area became a densely populated metro area of some seven million people and land costs have skyrocketed. To satisfy the need for more land, many wetland areas have been filled in. When Europeans first arrived, the bay was about 680 square miles, but today it is less than four hundred square miles (map 19.2). Airports, freeways, and development have reclaimed land and shrunk and polluted the bay, while killing many endemic organisms. Urban and agricultural runoff, along with industrial sewage, has contaminated

the estuary. Within the remaining Bay Area, the Army Corps of Engineers began dredging the bay to keep the ports viable, but the disposal of the dredged material has had an effect on the fishing and environmental communities.

The effects of fill and dredging have destroyed biologically productive estuarine zones and altered weather patterns. In the nineteenth century, 90 percent of West Coast wetlands were in the bay. Tidal marshes covered an area nearly twice the size of the bay itself. Today, over 95 percent of the tidal marshes have levees or are filled in. The bay was also a natural air conditioner for the Bay Area; with less water, inland towns have warmer weather.

Since the 1960s, numerous federal programs and local conservation networks work to acquire, restore, and study the bay. For example, the Coastal Conservancy projects underway include restoration of one hundred thousand acres of wetlands, and building hundreds of miles of new trails.

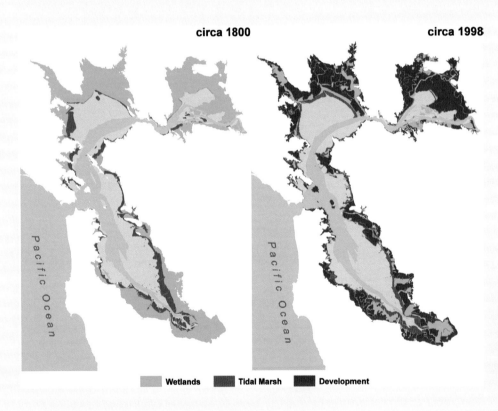

circa 1800   **circa 1998**

Wetlands   Tidal Marsh   Development

MAP 19.2. San Francisco Bay, Filled-In Lands. Dikes, levees, and land reclamation reduced the bay in size from 680 square miles in 1850 to less than 400 square miles today. Over 95 percent of the tidal marshes have been drained.

Central Valley

Central California's multiple valleys are increasingly drier and more continental as one moves eastward. The Central Valley proper has blistering hot days and nights during the summer, and cooler "tule fog" days during the winter, named after the tule reeds that grow in the Central Valley marshes. The regular

winter fog rolls in on clear, windless nights, limits visibility, and often causes multiple car accidents. The semiarid climate and precipitation pattern reflects its Coastal Range rain shadow position. Only five to twenty inches of rain falls on the valley floor. Crops require irrigation because of the scant Mediterranean precipitation patterns during the summer growing season.

The plentiful Sierra precipitation follows the Mediterranean weather pattern. Air masses bring the wet winter season over the lower-elevation Coastal Range and over the valleys, and then the air is forced upward on the western slopes of the Sierras causing precipitation, usually in the form of snow. Precipitation is more episodic and of higher intensity than in the Cascades. The erratic Sierra weather patterns depend on elevation and on hill and valley wind patterns. The eastern leeward flank of the mountains is in the rain shadow, where the dry Basin and Range environment commences.

Environmental Challenges

Photochemical Smog

Smog occurs when volatile organic compounds (VOCs) react with nitrogen oxides and oxygen in the presence of heat and sunlight. Pollutants undergo reactions that form ground-level ozone, or smog. Smog is not emitted directly into the air, but is created through a series of chemical reactions. It is produced by the combination of pollutants from many sources including smokestacks, cars, paints, and solvents. The US Environmental Protection Agency (EPA) estimates that almost 60 percent of smog is produced by transportation sources—cars, trucks, and trains. Smog is found primarily in urban areas and is often worse in the summer months when heat and sunshine are more plentiful.

Geography, wind patterns, and the local weather compose the toxic chemical stew sitting over the basin and cooking in the sun. The confined **thermal inversion** airflow in Los Angeles is nothing new (photo 19.3). The Native Americans called the region the "Land of Smoke" for the same entrapment reasons.

The flow layers the air in the mountain-enclosed basin. Warm air hovers over the cooler marine air. The usual light winds are unable to clear out pollutants. The coastal winds blow the pollutants from the coast inland and against the mountain barrier. The San Gabriel Mountains trap the smog in Pasadena and the San Gabriel Valley. Only the coast is pollution free, because of onshore and offshore winds.

The most recent American Lung Association's State of the Air report once again found California has the dubious distinction of being home to the majority of the top ten cities with ozone and particle pollution in the United States. Los Angeles topped the national list, followed by Bakersfield, Fresno and Vasila. Modesto, San Diego, and Sacramento were also in the top ten. Unfortunately, these cities have been in the top 10 since 2000.

Short-term exposure can cause eye irritation, wheezing, coughing, headaches, chest pain, and shortness of breath. Long-term exposure scars the lungs, making them less elastic and efficient, often worsening asthma and increasing respiratory tract infections. Because ozone penetrates deeply into the respiratory system, many urban residents are at risk including the weak and elderly, but also those who engage in strenuous activity. For those who were born and have lived in smoggy cities such as Los Angeles, long-term exposure may be breaking down the bodys' immune system, increasing the chances of suffering respiratory illness and harming the lungs in later life.

More than 90 percent of Californians live in areas with unhealthy air at some point during the year, but perhaps the most alarming is that Los Angeles received an "F" for 2017, with more than 202 days of the year designated "Code Red" defined as unhealthy for everyone. Estimates are that 1.2 million Los Angelenos suffer asthma due to air pollution. Minorities and children suffer disproportionately. African Americans are at

PHOTO 19.3. Los Angeles Smog.
Source: iStock/MattGush

higher risk for asthma. Children also suffer from respiratory problems, burning eyes, and asthma due to the ozone levels on hot, smoggy days and face long-term health problems. Los Angeles schools regularly have numerous "Code Red" smog days, when no one is allowed outside to play.

Because of the long history with smog, California was the first state to tighten vehicle emissions standards back in 1965. The state has continued to pursue clean air by tighter and more progressive standards than any other state. The good news is that many cities have made progress; the bad news is that increased population growth, combined with sprawl and an automobile-centric culture means that clean air is still a challenge to a sustainable future.

Natural Hazards: Earthquakes, Fire, and Landslides

For all its beauty, California's apocalyptic side includes erratic but devastating natural hazards such as earthquakes, fire, and landslides, making it essential to understand the relationship between geography and urban land use. Most of California's major cities are built near or on earthquake faults. Fire is an indirect hazard of the Mediterranean climate, and landslides often are the result of exposing the bare, fire-scarred soils to the winter rains.

Most of America occupies the North American Plate, but Southern California lies on the Pacific Plate west of the world-famous San Andreas Fault (map 19.3). Faults riddle the meeting place of the North American and Pacific plates. The San Andreas extends on land seven hundred miles from the Gulf of California to Mendocino. The Pacific Plate moves two inches per year in a northwest direction. This movement creates the stresses and friction that trigger earthquakes, especially in the mountains near the San Andreas.

California is always waiting for the "big one." Each year the southern California area has about ten thousand earthquakes (photo 19.4). Most of them are so small that they are not felt. Only several hundred are greater than magnitude 3.0, and only about fifteen to twenty are greater than magnitude 4.0. Earthquakes are so normal that residents greet them casually with comments like "That felt like a 4.0. What do you think?" But the state has also experienced large or very large earthquakes that have caused death and destruction (table 19.1).

Fire and the Mediterranean climate are related in California. Fires rage during the dry months when the hills are golden and the dry Santa Ana winds blow from the desert to the coast. The winds desiccate vegetation and raise the possibility of wildfires. Each year some part of California has a wildfire, usually in October at the end of the dry season when the vegetation is driest. Extreme drought and years of fire suppression makes

TABLE 19.1. Selected California Earthquakes and the Magnitude on the Richter Scale

Year	City	Magnitude
1906	San Francisco	7.8
1980	Eureka	7.3
1999	Hector Mine	7.1
2010	Baja California	7.2
1989	Loma Prieta	6.9
1994	Northridge	6.7
1971	San Fernando	6.7
2003	San Simeon	6.6
2014	South Napa	6.0

PHOTO 19.4. Northridge Earthquake Damage. Apartments built over garages fell on cars in the magnitude 6.7 Northridge earthquake of 1994. The earthquake caused over $44 billion in damage.

BOX 19.3   GEOSPATIAL TECHNIQUES: VIEWING PLATE TECTONICS

Tomales Bay lies about 30 miles (50 km) northwest of San Francisco, along the edges of two tectonic plates that are grinding past each other. The boundary between them is the San Andreas Fault that partitions California for hundreds of miles. To the west of the bay is the Pacific plate; to the east is the North American plate. The rock on the western shore of the bay is granite, an igneous rock that formed underground when molten material slowly cooled over time. On the opposite shore, the land is a mix of several types of marine sedimentary rocks.

The Operational Land Imager (OLI) on Landsat 8 captured this natural-color image of part of the Tomales Bay. The image shows an obvious difference between dark green coniferous forests that dominate the western shore of Tomales Bay and the lighter green grasslands on the east side. Of course, the differences between these two areas run much deeper than the vegetation.

MAP 19.3. This view shows the San Andreas Fault, which runs in the middle of the Tamales Bay in Northern California. The western shore is on the Pacific Plate, where dark green coniferous forests dominate. On the opposite shore to the east, lighter green grasslands dominate.

Source: earthobservatory.nasa.gov

the likelihood of wildfires even more pronounced, and it is not uncommon for thousands of acres of hillsides to burn each year, somewhere in the state.

The common practice of forest fire suppression in California allows understory brush to proliferate and fuel fires. Americans have treated fire as an enemy that must be halted, but fire is a natural pattern that regenerates forest health. The anthropocentric view of fire excludes the overall ecology of natural vegetation and wildlife. Combined with continued sprawl and suburban development, many residential areas are in fire-sensitive, mountainous viewsheds. The expensive homes in these areas can be burned out, rebuild, and burned out again. Directly or indirectly, taxpayers support this unsustainable practice.

In California, hillside view lots are premier home locations—but there is a hidden cost. Half of the region's scant precipitation may fall in a single rainstorm and cause landslides. If the previous winter is wet, the threat of landslides multiplies. Landslides occur in two situations: when massive

BOX 19.4 ENVIRONMENTAL CHALLENGES: WILDFIRES

Although earthquakes are prominent in the California imagination—and on film—wildfires are equally problematic.

Grass fires and forest fires have long been a feature of ecosystems. Fires caused by lightning are an environmental fact of many arid and semiarid and dry ecosystems. These fires are natural in the sense that they may occur naturally, but they are social in that their effects are exacerbated by urban growth that has pushed settlement into fire hazard areas. Cities in California are so affected.

Much of coastal California is semiarid and susceptible to fire. These areas become urban hazards as suburban growth snakes its way into the less urbanized, more vegetated and hence more at risk, environments. At the end of summer with dry vegetation and high, dry winds, California is particularly vulnerable. In the last five years, fires have burned millions of acres and destroying thousands of homes mostly during July, August, and September, when the hills are the driest.

Wildfires are the new normal. There were as many as sixty-nine hundred wildfires in the state in 2016, burning more than a half million acres, killing six, and damaging hundreds of homes and buildings.

The most recent fire occurred in October 2017, ravaging the North Bay in one of the most destructive fire emergencies in the state's history. The firestorm was actually a series of ten to fifteen fires that included cities in Napa, Sonoma, Lake and Mendocino Counties (map 19.4). More than 245,000 acres burned, destroying thousands of structures and forcing the evacuation of more than twenty thousand people. In Santa Rosa, the largest city in Sonoma County, hundreds of homes and businesses were destroyed.

The fires also impacted air quality in the entire Bay Area. For ten days the EPA reported the air quality was nearly five times what is considered safe. Residents were advised to stay indoors and, if available, to use breathing masks.

The environmental historian Steven J. Pyne has written about fires and the spectacle of burning houses—which occur at the "wild land-urban interface fire." He notes "these fires occur in lands whose use has become scrambled into an ecological omelet, involving abandoned agricultural land as well as public preserves. Their existence and the hazards they pose are simply the result of unmanaged growth: the untrammeled growth of natural vegetation and the uncontained growth of our increasingly far-flung suburbs. The wild and the urban have become the matter and antimatter of the American landscape. When they collide, we should not be surprised by the occasional explosion."[*]

As suburbs spread into drier environments the risk of fire increases. In the longer term, controlled burning may provide prevention. Perhaps there is a need to reconsider the siting of residential areas in fire risk areas. However, this poses a more problematic political conundrum with long-term fire safety considerations often outweighed by development interests and the forces of housing development and urban growth.

MAP 19.4. Fires in the San Francisco Bay Area, in October 2017. The smoke visible in this satellite image shows more than a dozen fires burning in the North Bay.
Source: NASA's Earth Observing System Data and Information System (EOSDIS)

---

*Source: Pyne, S. J. "The Fires This Time and Next." *Science* 294, no. 5544 (2001): p1005

amounts of rainfall and rock separate from steep cliffs, or along California's many fault zones. As a result, hillside home foundations become unstable, and homes may slide down the mountain. Autumn fires can accelerate erosion, while winter rainfall destabilizes already weak foundations and may trigger additional landslides.

Historical Geography and Settlement

Effectively, there have been two Californias, divided approximately by Monterey Bay. The separate demography and culture of each half evolved in relation to the physiography, vegetation, and climatic patterns.

Native Americans

Northern and southern California Native cultures were distinctly different, each aligned culturally and linguistically more with their tribal neighbors than each other. The northern tribes were similar to the Klamath and Modoc, while the southern were similar to southwestern tribes. The tribal cultures evolved in relation to the mild weather and temperate vegetation.

The approximately 310,000 Natives in California at the beginning of the Spanish mission period (1769) were reduced

to less than 10,000 by the end of the period (1848), the result of disease and forced tenure at the Spanish missions.

The Spanish Period

The Spanish built twenty-one **missions** along the California coastal region to secure possession of the territory. The Spanish were aware of the Russians progressing southward from Alaska in search of otter fur. The Russians came as far south as Mendocino County, where they established Fort Ross on the Russian River.

The Spanish established four **presidios** (military fortifications) to protect the missions and establish their political claim to California. The presidios were in geographically strategic locations and would become population centers for California (San Diego, Monterey, San Francisco, and Santa Barbara). The Spanish also established agricultural towns called **pueblos**, two of which were San José and Los Angeles. The main connecting road became known as El Camino Real, and in places is called Highway 1 today (map 19.5).

Spanish rule in California ended with the establishment of Mexico in 1822 but the legacy has continued imprinted in the landscape with its land tenure system, urban plans, architecture, and toponyms (photo 19.5). Far from the center of Spain's

MAP 19.5. The Missions of California.

Source: Shruti Mukhtyar

PHOTO 19.5. Mission San Juan Capistrano, California. This is one of twenty-one missions built by the Spanish beginning in 1769. Spanish-style architecture remains popular in California.

New World holdings, California's residents were retired presidio soldiers who were granted land grants for their service. The Spanish and later the Mexican governments granted more than ten million acres as **ranchos**. Each grant ranged over several square miles and established the soldiers as *dons,* landowners in the under-populated territory. California ranchos raised cattle only for their hides and tallow, as the isolated region was far from populated markets until the 1848 **Gold Rush**.

California's Sierra Gold Rush began in 1848 and lasted into the early 1860s. It made San Francisco the dominant California city. In the Central Valley, Sacramento was the largest city to service the Gold Rush region, whicle other towns, such as Placerville, and Sonora were established in the Mother Lode hills and valleys. Over $2 billion of gold were found in the Mother Lode veins and hastened the entry of the state into the Union.

In 1848, the Mexican Cession granted California and much of the Southwest to the Americans. The **Treaty of Guadalupe Hidalgo** promised to respect the property rights of Mexican landowners. Over time, the new State ignored Mexican rights and the land-tenure system; most rancheros eventually lost their land to the Americans.

The Anglo Period

By the 1880s, Anglos controlled California. The growth began in the north near the Gold Rush areas, where San Francisco became the largest city and economic hub. Later, the Mediterranean climate, dry heat, and sunshine made Southern California attractive to Americans seeking an escape from the ague and fevers of the humid East. The completion of the Southern Pacific Railway line in 1876 and the Santa Fe line in 1887 encouraged transcontinental travel and connected California to the nation, furthering immigration, trade, and the agricultural industry. Los Angeles County became one of America's most productive agricultural centers.

During the first half of the twentieth century, California-dreaming became a national obsession, and many relocated to the land of orange groves and sunshine. During the Dust Bowl, farmers from Oklahoma and Arkansas sought refuge picking orchard fruit in the Central Valley. Later, the motion picture industry accentuated and enhanced the unreal realities of the Golden State. The New Years Day broadcast of the Rose Parade in Pasadena, in sun and warmth, contrasted with the frigid midwestern January morning enticed a cascade of migrations to California.

The Multicultural Period

California has been a multicultural and discriminatory land from the beginning of European settlement but the Gold Rush opened up California to immigration. Chinese arrived to work on the transcontinental railroad in 1864 and continued to arrive until the **Chinese Exclusion Act** of 1882 limited their employment and few Chinese immigrated between 1882 and 1965. The 1965 Civil Rights Act reformed immigration policy and since then many Chinese have immigrated to America, usually through the gateways of San Francisco and Los Angeles.

The Japanese arrived in America a few years after the Chinese. Most were either railroad workers or domestics, but soon they moved into agricultural work and settled in Southern California or the Central Valley. Japanese were discriminated against, especially during World War II when more than 110,000 Pacific Coast Japanese were forced into ten internment camps in remote areas despite the fact that over half of them were US citizens.

Large-scale black immigration began during World War II, when President Roosevelt ordered defense industries to hire blacks. About eight thousand blacks lived in California between 1900 and the beginning of World War II. By 1943, more than ten thousand per month arrived in Los Angeles, eager to earn more than ten times their southern wages. By the end of the war, California's black population had increased 272 percent, while Mississippi's black population had dropped by 8 percent.

However, California has a problematic legacy of civil rights discrimination. In the 1920s, Los Angeles enacted exclusionary zoning that restricted black settlement. Blacks were limited to purchasing property in South Central Los Angeles until 1947, and they remained discriminated against well into the 1960s, when only twenty thousand of three hundred thousand blacks lived outside the segregated area. Black population today remains concentrated in South Central Los Angeles.

Cultural Perspective

At Least Two Californias

The physical attributes and population of the two Californias differ: most of the water is in the north and most of the people are in the south. Richard Goldstein has said that Northern and Southern California are culturally divided. Each developed distinctive cultures and cuisines. Southern Californians worshiped the sun, the Beach Boys surfing culture, Hollywood-type "plastic people," and the automobile, earning it the moniker a "neon wasteland." Northern California found psychedelic solace with Jimi Hendrix and Janis Joplin and inaugurated the healthy and vegetarian California cuisine and the birth of the environmental movement.

Northern and Southern California cultures have influenced landscape patterns. Los Angeles initiated and defined sprawl, decentralization, and the clover-leaf system of highway off-ramps. Northern California's "dot-com" boom in Silicon Valley resulted in some of the priciest real estate in America, as small bungalow homes were replaced by "monster homes" of the new dot-com millionaires (photo 19.6).

Throughout its statehood, California has at times supported separating into two or three states. During the 1990s, an informal advisory vote was taken in Northern California, and two-thirds of the population living north of San Francisco voted to divide the state. In 2007, California considered dividing its electoral votes for president instead of the winner-take-all system giving all fifty-five votes to the leader. And in 2011, the Inland Empire of Southern California passed a resolution to secede from the rest of the state.

The most recent effort, called "Calexit," proposes dividing the state into East and West—with the liberal enclaves of the coast (San Francisco, Los Angeles) running the West and the more conservative Inland Empire, Sacramento Valley and Sierra Nevada foothills in the East. The group sponsoring the initiative hopes to include it on the 2018 ballot—although there is zero chance Congress would ever vote and allow this to happen. Nevertheless, the efforts are telling: it shows how disparate

PHOTO 19.6. Palo Alto, California. This very large home is a recent construction and covers most of the lot. It replaced a smaller, more modest house. When housing prices are extremely high and housing is limited, the value is in the land itself; it then becomes economically rational to demolish older, smaller housing and build larger to maximize profit and value.

Source: Lisa Benton-Short

are the fortunes within such a diverse state. On one side is the much-celebrated, postindustrial, "left-coast" California, beneficiary of the tech economy and strong property values. The other California, located in the state's interior, is still tied to basic industries like homebuilding, manufacturing, energy, and agriculture. It is populated largely by working- and middle-class people who, overall, earn roughly half that of those on the coast. California politics has been dominated by the left-coast influence of Silicon Valley and Bay Area progressives, leaving the interior feeling ignored and neglected.

Homes and Homelessness

Since the 1960s, the price of housing has made it difficult for ordinary people to purchase homes in the close-in metropolitan areas or on the coast. Living two hours from work is common but affordable. It is near impossible to find a three-bedroom-two-bath house in Northern or Southern California for under $250,000, and in Northern California the prices are closer to $1 million within fifty miles of most high-paying jobs. According to the California Association of Realtors, only 32 percent of household statewide can now afford to buy the median-priced, $496,000 home. In metro San Francisco, the median housing price is $800,000.

It is estimated that some twenty-five thousand people left Los Angeles between 2010 and 2015. Many of those leaving Los Angeles are lower-to-moderate income renters and house hunters who are most intensely feeling the brunt of high housing costs. Offering home affordability and an improving job market, Las Vegas has been by far the most popular destination for Angelenos relocating out of state; the city received about thirteen thousand former Los Angelenos.

Although California is a rich state, the wealth is unevenly distributed, and a widening gap separates the haves from the have-nots. The haves live in expensive homes, and the have-nots range from those living in small but still expensive apartments to the **homeless**. On any day in California, between 500,000 and 1.1 million people are homeless, many working but earning less than rent. Many were displaced in the late 1980s when federal institutions were closed, and people with mental illnesses, disabilities, or addictions were treated as "out-patients." Although the states were supposed to take over the services no longer provided by the federal government, few were able to afford to house those with disabilities. Federal housing officials blamed soaring rents and Congress' failure to fund affordable housing for a rise in homelessness in many cities including San Francisco, Oakland, San Diego, and Los Angeles.

Los Angeles has more than fifty-five thousand homeless, which includes a large number of homeless veterans and children. The number of homeless has increased 75 percent in the last five years. This is second only to New York City. Because of the year-round temperate climate more than 90 percent of the homeless live outdoors, in cars, tents, and encampments. Tent cities stretch from the Antelope Valley desert to the Santa Monica coast, but the nucleus of its homeless area is Skid Row, the largest in the nation, where people live either in shelters or on the street, often in cardboard boxes lined up along sidewalks and within sight of the affluent offices on Bunker Hill. (photo 19.7). The problem has become so acute and so visible that in 2016 voters in Los Angeles county approved a proposal to raise taxes to fund an enormous multibillion-dollar, ten-year program of housing and social services for the homeless.

Some homeless live in one-room SRO (single-room occupancy) hotels that provide rental assistance and communal bathrooms and kitchens. However, SROs and most affordable housing are increasingly difficult to find because of the rising cost of land. Developers have threatened Skid Row with

PHOTO 19.7. Los Angeles Skid Row. "Skid row" was originally a street in Seattle, Washington, named Skid Road, which was used to skid logs into the water. Over time, the road went into decline, and the term "skid row" became synonymous with a bad neighborhood.

redevelopment, such as converting the SROs into high-priced lofts. Some SROs are protected, having been purchased by non-profit agencies, but others could fall prey to developers, thereby making affordable housing even more difficult to find.

Population, Immigration, and Diversity

California is the most populous state and has been since the 1960s. Approximately one out of every eight Americans live in California. The population is overwhelmingly urban and coastal, living along the Pacific Plate section of the state. The state's racial composition continues to divide California's north and south. Hispanics are the fastest-growing group in California, but an overwhelming majority live in the south. The unprecedented influx of both Hispanic-Latino and Asian immigrants highlights the California demographic shift. Hispanics account for almost 50 percent of the population in Los Angeles County, while 35 percent of San Francisco's population is Asian. In Fremont, along the southeastern bay, more than 50 percent are of Asian ancestry.

California is also home to a large number of foreign born (27 percent versus 14 percent nationally). And cities are home to even larger numbers of foreign born. In Los Angeles, more than 35 percent are foreign born, coming primarily from Mexico and Central America, but also from around the world. In San Francisco, 35 percent are foreign born, with 35 percent from Asia—mainly China, India, and Korea. However, despite the diversity, most ethnic or racial groups tend to live near others who share their culture, and the state continues to be self-segregated.

The complexity of ethnicities in the state results in a widely divergent set of cultures and values. Hispanics number about fourteen million and continue to emigrate from Mexico and Central America. There is continued tension among the various cultural groups with different values. For example, the Hispanic community tends to favor traditional family values, including higher birthrates, which outweigh educational priorities. On the other hand, Chinese immigrants prioritize education for their children, and they are changing the San Francisco school system by promoting a diversity index for education to end discrimination.

Fremont has become one of the state's most diverse cities (137 languages are spoken in Fremont homes), but the city's immigrant experiences are different from those experienced by Los Angeles's immigrants, because most of Fremont's immigrants are affluent. Many Fremont residents are from India, and their festivals and Bollywood extravaganzas create near riots and mounds of trash, thereby becoming a source of community strife.

The most recent census shows **Hispanics** (or **Latinos**, depending on who is referring to them) population grew from 9 percent in 1960 to 39 percent today. The 2015 Census revealed that Latinos have passed whites as the largest ethnic group in California. California is now the first large state and the third overall—after Hawaii and New Mexico—without a white plurality.

This rapid shift in population composition has generated rising tension among white non-Hispanic Californians. In a special election in October 2004, Proposition 54 would have restricted the government from "classifying" (collecting and using) information on an individual's race, ethnicity, color, or national origin. The proposition failed to pass. Although

PHOTO 19.8. Fortress Living in Marina Del Rey. Homes in this oceanside community were built so the main entrance was from the garage, creating a very sterile environment. While "front doors" were on the other side of the buildings, they were seldom used.

some anti-immigrant efforts have occurred since, polls show the majority of Californians are in favor of protecting undocumented immigrants.

The changes in demographics have changed how people live in California. Los Angeles introduced **fortress living** to America, and it has diffused pandemic-like across the nation. The wealthy sought security and shelter from the perception of increased violence and rampant crime.

One response has been the rise of fortress-living or gated communities (photo 19.8). Gated communities are now common, and alarm systems or barred entrances are considered essential. Fear of "the other" has permeated both the psyche and the landscape. Gated communities simultaneously provide the illusion of safety and exclusivity.

Urban Trends

Ninety-five percent of California's population is urban. The two coastal metropolitan areas, one from the Mexican border to Santa Barbara and the other surrounding the San Francisco Bay, contain twenty-five million people, a majority of the state's wealthy, and approximately 70 percent of the state's population.

Most Californians define themselves in relation to the Los Angeles Basin or the Bay Area. However, the Central Valley is the fastest growing region within California (with about 6.5 million people in 2016). The Central Valley has become the state's affordable housing outlier, which explains its rapid growth.

Southern California Metropolitan Area

The Southern California Metropolitan Area is one of the largest in the world, both in population and in square miles; it extends almost continuously over 200 miles to the north from the Mexican border and another 150 miles inland to Palm Springs. Included within the conurbation are many city nodes; the largest and most identifiable is Los Angeles–Long Beach, followed by San Diego, Anaheim–Santa Ana, Riverside–San Bernardino, Oxnard–Ventura, and Santa Barbara–Santa Maria. All are interconnected with freeways and six major airports. It is among the most favored places in the nation to do business and to start companies.

Los Angeles
(2016 MSA 18.5 million)

Los Angeles, the second-largest city in America, occupies hundreds of miles of Mediterranean, semiarid land, whose dominant color is golden brown. Although green emerges for a short, glorious period after the winter rains, the city and the state would be brown without the elaborate water schemes.

Founded in 1781, Los Angeles was a small village situated on the ephemeral Los Angeles River. When California became a state, the village had a mere sixteen hundred people. Los Angeles grew slowly; by 1870, the population was only fifty-seven hundred. By 1930, the city had over a million people and was one of the largest in America.

Prior to World War II, Los Angeles County was California's leading fruit and vegetable producer, but suburban home tracts replaced the orchards and fields after the war. Today, there are few, if any, orange groves left.

Los Angeles has no major freshwater source. The growth of the city was due to the first aqueduct that brought water to the semiarid city in 1913. Later, the city began to import water from the Colorado River and Owens Valley. Water has supported the growth and has continued to be an important part of continued urban development, but it is also a political issue.

Los Angeles is the prototypical **polynucleated city**—a series of edge cities, each with its own downtown and shopping area. The metropolitan area includes eighty cities and five counties (Los Angeles, Orange, Ventura, San Bernardino, and Riverside), with half of California's population. The city's geography is a confusing network of eight-lane freeways, suburbs, beaches, ghettoes, ethnic communities, extreme affluence or poverty, and **alternative lifestyles**.

Los Angeles led the nation in agriculture until 1950, at which time it transformed into manufacturing aircraft, automobiles, and steel. Since the 1990s, manufacturing has been replaced with services, high-tech industry, electronics, a diverse service economy, the motion picture industry, computerized special effects, and a recent surge in digital media (including new shows through Netflix and Amazon).

Los Angeles is also recognized as an automobile capital because of its size, dependence on automobiles, and its general lack of public transportation. Freeways connect Los Angeles as a system of free highways, mostly built and completed by the early 1970s. Since that time, traffic has doubled, but few freeway miles have been added and the city has become known for its monumental traffic jams. Despite public opposition, the freeways have been recently augmented by toll roads; but many drivers refuse to use the toll roads. In the 1990s, a modern rail transit network was built suing many of the old transit rights-of-ways, decendants from an early twentieth century street car system. Today, the Metro system consists of six lines, serving ninety-three stations and about 360,000 riders daily (photo 19.9).

In 2015, Los Angeles released its first ever comprehensive sustainability plan, *pLAn*. Like many sustainability plans, Los Angeles has set short-term and long-term goals for the following areas:

- energy efficient buildings;
- affordable housing;
- waste and Landfills;
- climate;
- water;
- solar;
- preparedness and resiliency;
- environmental justice;
- air quality;
- green job; and
- transportation.

PHOTO 19.9. The Los Angeles Metro System.

Source: Lisa Benton-Short

To address issues of environmental justice, for example, the city passed an ordinance in 2016 requiring all city farmers' markets to accept food stamps in the form of Electronic Benefit Transfer (EBT). The number of farmers markets that accepted EBT went from 46 percent in 2015 to 96 percent in 2016. The city hopes this program will increase fresh food at farmers markets to more low-income residents and help to reduce food deserts.

San Diego
(2016 MSA 3.3 million)

San Diego, the nation's sixth-largest city, is located south of Los Angeles very near the Mexican border. Today, the peripheries of San Diego and Los Angeles melt into one conurbation. San Diego was the site of California's first mission (1769) and evolved into a pueblo during the Mexican regime (1834). When the first southern rail line was discussed, San Diego was the expected southern terminus, because of its natural harbor. However, the lack of a Peninsular Mountain pass forced the terminus north to Los Angeles, and San Diego settled as a military "Navy town." San Diego's naval fleet is the largest in the world, and the city's largest employer, adding $18 billion annually to the regional economy. The city is consistently listed as a top place to live in America (photo 19.11). The dry, cool climate has drawn many wealthy residents, who live in elite enclaves such as La Jolla.

BOX 19.5 ICONIC IMAGE: HOLLYWOOD

California is home to many iconic images: the Golden Gate Bridge, Disneyland, Orange Groves, surfboards, and missions. But one of the most recognized is the landmark Hollywood sign in Los Angeles (photo 19.10).

The sign was actually conceived as an outdoor ad campaign for a suburban housing development called "Hollywoodland" in 1923, but it has become a symbol of the entertainment industry and a beacon for wanna-be-movie stars.

The sign has been featured in hundreds of movies and television shows over the years—including *Sharknado*, *The Day After Tomorrow*, *Independence Day*, and the original *Muppet Movie*. The sign is also used by 20th Century Fox in its opening logo animation.

The Hollywood sign beckons: *This is a place where magic is possible, where dreams can come true.*

PHOTO 19.10. The Hollywood Sign in Los Angeles.
Source: iStock/Ershov_Maks

San Diego has its own identity, with an economy based on high-tech telecommunication, biotechnology, and tourism. The San Diego metropolitan area, like many of the largest cities in the West, is a polynucleated city with several core cities, including Chula Vista, Coronado, La Mesa, El Cajon, and National City.

San Diego has an extensive set of parks and protected areas that has boosted the tourist economy. Balboa park is an iconic San Diego destination; Mission Bay is a forty-six hundred acre aquatic playground of meandering shorelines, and a variety of waterways, inlets, and islets to explore. Tourism accounts for some $16 billion in the regional economy.

San Diego has both a sustainability plan and a climate action plan. Between 2010 and 2016, the city reduced its greenhouse gas emissions by 19 percent. Additionally, the city (along with private partners and other incentives) has allocated $128 million to climate action in 2018. It has also invested some $350,000 in sidewalks and public transit in low- and moderate-income.

In 2017, the city was ranked #1 in the country for solar rooftop installations, #1 for climate and carbon management, and #4 in clean technology leadership.

San José
(2016 MSA 1.9 million)

San José, at the southern extremity of the Bay Area peninsula, evolved in the shadow of San Francisco. In the 1950s, San José in the Santa Clara Valley was the nation's largest fruit and vegetable canning center, but in the 1980s, under the influence of Stanford University in nearby Palo Alto and the University of California at Berkeley across the bay, technology redefined the city and drew many new residents.

In 1939, Bill Hewlett and Dave Packard, who had met as students at Stanford, began a small technology enterprise in a garage. From these humble beginnings grew Silicon Valley, the nation's leading producer of semiconductors and software development. The archetype for America's new industry offered high salaries and campus-like office parks. Today, San José

PHOTO 19.11. San Diego.

Source: iStock/alancrosthwaite

anchors the wealthy enclave that spreads north into San Mateo County. Silicon Valley has become a magnet for the technologically educated. The San Jose metro area is also one of the most expensive places in America to live, with an average median home price of $717,000, twice that of the state average.

The county has worked at overcoming some of the more vexing problems of urban living, and it has become more sustainable. For example in Mountain View, just north of San José, a dying shopping center was rebuilt as a transit-oriented development (TOD) called the Crossings. A commuter rail line anchors the 540 compact housing units (30 units per acre) that are a mixed-use and walkable community. Such urban villages are visible on the landscape and represent a trend in sustainable planning.

San Francisco
(2016 MSA 4.6 million)

San Francisco became the first major metropolis after the Gold Rush and California's largest city until World War I. The Spanish established a presidio at the northern point of the San Francisco peninsula, near the entrance to the bay. The city's cosmopolitan feeling and setting, along with its recognition as one of the most sustainable cities, has made it a favorite city, highlighted by a well-known skyline featuring the Golden Gate Bridge and its steep streets and cable cars.

The city is surrounded on three sides by water—and although this limited its space to grow, it encouraged the development of a vibrant inner city with the second-most-dense population in the nation (after New York City). This density has led to effective public transportation; almost half of all San Franciscans do not take cars to work.

The city is the financial center for the state and the chief port for the Central Valley. San Francisco, one of the least industrialized cities in America, has a large financial and government workforce, and has become a center for biotechnology by housing the state's stem cell institute. More than half of the highly educated work force has at least a bachelor's degree. Like San Jose, San Francisco is one of the most expensive cities in California. With a median home price of $800,000 (more than twice that of the state), finding affordable housing is a significant issue for many.

The city has also been a birthplace of and supported various counterculture alternative lifestyles, including the City Lights Beat Generation, hippies, and a large LGBT (lesbian, gay, bisexual, and transsexual) population.

Long a pioneer in progressive environmental legislation, the city of San Francisco created its first sustainability plan in 1997. There have been many revised plans that include a range of practices and policies that make environmental accountability a hallmark of life in the Bay Area. In 2012, San Francisco was named the Greenest city in the United States and has continued to lead the way on sustainability and innovation.

East Bay Cities: Oakland, Berkeley, Richmond

The East Bay cities—Oakland, Berkeley, and Richmond—have an advantage San Francisco lacks: easy access into the interior valleys. East Bay growth was augmented with the 1936 opening of America's most traveled bridge, the Bay Bridge (photo 19.14). It was the first of eight bridges connecting the Bay Area. It partially collapsed during the 1989 Loma Prieta Earthquake and has since been rebuilt.

Oakland (pop 400,000), the Bay Area's workhorse, is a blue-collar city and the seventh-largest port in America. The city also has a radical political legacy based on a large black population (28 percent in 2017) that galvanized in the 1960s around the Black Panther movement.

Today Oakland is better known for its rising star in the green movement and a sustainability plan that promoted renewable energy, achieving zero waste in landfills, and building green buildings.

BOX 19.6   URBAN SUSTAINABILITY BEST PRACTICES: ZERO WASTE IN SAN FRANCISCO

Garbage is a challenge to sustainability. There are problems of collection and disposal and the environmental hazards associated with refuse. Plastics remain a problem for the environment. Unlike air and water pollution, solid waste—garbage—must be collected to be disposed of. Most of our garbage goes to landfills. But nearly all of what we throw away could be reused, recycled, or composted.

The good news is that material discarded in landfills peaked around 2005 and has declined as cities around the United States and Canada have implemented more effective recycling and composting programs. No city has done this more effectively than San Francisco.

In 2002, San Francisco pledged zero waste by 2020. Zero waste means that they send zero discards to the landfill or high-temperature destruction.

To achieve this ambitious goal, the city has passed series of ordinances designed to deal with solid waste in a variety of ways. In 2009, it passed a Mandatory Recycling and Composting Ordinance that requires everyone in San Francisco to separate recyclables, compostables, and landfill-bound trash. The city then launched its innovative "Fantastic Three" residential curbside

collection program that includes three bins—blue bins for recycling, green bins for composing (food scraps, yard trimmings, and soiled paper), and smaller black bins for trash (photo 19.12). Another ordinance requires every event held in San Francisco to offer recycling and composting at the event.

One of the less visible but important categories of waste encompasses all the debris produced by the construction industry. In 2006, the city passed an ordinance requiring the building trade to recycle at least two-thirds of its debris such as concrete, steel, and timber at a registered facility. Companies failing to comply run the risk of their registration being suspended for six months. At the same time, the city undertook to only use recycled materials for public works such as asphalting or gutters.*

The City's three bin system, policies, financial incentives, and extensive outreach to residents and businesses, helped San Francisco achieve the highest diversion rate—80 percent—of any major city in North America. San Francisco has shown that political determination and changing behaviors in how residents and business deal with garbage is effective. Whatever the results in 2020, San Francisco has set an example for other US cities to follow.

PHOTO 19.12. Trash, recycling, and composting bins help San Francisco to work toward its zero waste goals.

Source: iStock/joshuaraineyphotography

---

*Alexandre Pouchard. "San Francisco Closer to Turning Zero-Waste Ambition into Reality," *The Guardian*, June 17, 2014, at http://www.theguardian.com/environment/2014/jun/17/san-francisco-zero-waste-recycling-composting

BOX 19.7   NATIONAL PARKS: THE PRESIDIO

Nearly three square miles in area and twice the size of Central Park in New York City, the Presidio is nestled between the city of San Francisco and the Pacific Ocean. From 1776 until 1994, the Presidio guarded the Golden Gate as an Army post under Spanish, then Mexican, and then American flags.

The Presidio is a city within a city. The post has hundreds of buildings, including an officer's club, a bowling alley, a research hospital, warehouses, residences, a movie theater, horse stables, a museum, and a golf course.

The Presidio is also a natural park within a city. Monterey cypress and pines guard the ridge line from the strong Pacific winds and golden grass and Manzanita hug the side of the hills. The Presidio Forest spans six hundred acres and has hiking trails, vistas, beachfront promenades, enclaves of wildflowers, and grassy open spaces (photo 19.13).

In 1989, the Defense Department decided that the Presidio was obsolete. This set in motion its transfer to the National Park Service, which then began to envision its transformation from army post to national park. In 1994, the Presidio became a national park. But there were some that resented the inclusion of the Presidio, arguing it did not merit such a designation.

Despite more than a century of evolution and additions to the park system, Yellowstone and Yosemite continue to epitomize the national park ideal. This has been called the "Crown Jewel"

syndrome, a term that is reserved for a select number of national parks that embody ideals of pristine wilderness and monumental scenic vistas. The crown jewel syndrome has led to a national park hierarchy. At the top are the crown jewels (Yellowstone, Yosemite, and Grand Canyon), below them are the other "nature parks" (Everglades, Zion, Sequoia, and Badlands), and below those are the cultural parks (Independence Hall, Antietam battlefield, and historic sites such as Carl Sandburg's home). Below those, at the bottom of the hierarchy, are the urban parks such as the Presidio that don't quite fit either nature or culture parks. Being at the bottom can have implications for budget, postings, and general status within the Park Service.

Yet, urban national parks serve a crucial role in the national park system. They promote public use through their convenient access to residents and tourists. They are often reachable through public transportation. They are available and accessible to the urban poor, helping to introduce the national parks to many who might not otherwise get out to the "crown jewels." Consider this statistic: every year nineteen million people visit and use the Presidio; only 3.7 million visit Yosemite. Many Americans may not realize that there are 417 units in the national park system. Only a handful are the big wilderness parks. The Presidio reminds us that the national parks are more than just the crown jewels and that the urban parks play an important role within the park system.

PHOTO 19.13. Bicyclists and Walkers on Crissy Field at the Presidio, in San Francisco. Crissy Field was once a military airfield. Starting in 2001, it was transformed into a promenade with iconic views of the bay and Golden Gate Bridge. As an urban national park, the Presidio provides access to the metro areas 4.6 million residents, as well as tourists.

Source: iStock/DavidCallan

PHOTO 19.14. San Francisco Bay Bridges. The upper bridge in the picture is the famous Golden Gate, spanning the entrance to the bay and connecting northern California to the peninsula. In the center of the photo is the Bay Bridge, connecting the peninsula to the East Bay cities of Oakland, Berkeley, and Richmond. The dark area to the left of the Golden Gate is the Presidio.

Nearby, Berkeley (pop 121,000) is home to the famous and infamous flagship campus of the California university system, where dissent and protest characterized the 1960s. Berkeley is a wealthy city now, known for its continual influence from the university and its aging, esoteric hippies who continue to support healthy living. Berkeley was one of the first cities to adopt curbside recycling, convert its public transit fleet to biodiesel, and embrace solar power and green-collar jobs.

The Economy

The gross state product (GSP) for California in 2017 was $2.6 trillion, making it the sixth-largest economy in the world. The next-largest state economy, Texas, is only 60 percent of California's size. The economy is diverse and many of the state's largest companies are in banking, biotechnology, communications equipment and other technology hardware, health care, online retail, integrated oil and gas, movies and entertainment, semiconductors, software, and services (real estate, financial services, and tourism).

The Primary Sector

Agriculture

California is a farmer's paradise where almost any crop can thrive, but it capitalizes on highly profitable specialty crops. California is the largest producer of fruits, vegetables, nuts, nursery goods, and dairy; it ranks second in livestock but fifteenth in grains. Overall, four hundred crops are grown in the state, but its top twenty crops and livestock commodities account for 75 percent of state's gross farm income. California combines its long, sunny growing season, fertile soils, and water resources for high-value agricultural crops in several distinct agricultural districts. It is the largest producer of food in the United States yet has less than 4 percent of the farms.

Half of America's specialty crops are from irrigated California fields. The San Joaquin and Salinas/Monterey valleys are irrigated, predominantly by the Central Valley Project, which brings water from Northern California or the San Francisco Bay delta. The delta remains essential to agriculture and supplies almost 60 percent of California's water. Irrigation dependency is, however, an overarching problem plagued with inefficiency and salt and mineral buildup.

Irrigation has become a source of crop stabilization during the twenty-first century, because climate change has affected crops grown in specific locales. Highly evaporative irrigation techniques in the dry state are common because irrigated water cools the air, halts rising temperatures, and therefore decreases the chances of climatic instability.

The Agricultural Valleys   The elongated Central Valley stretches from the northern Sacramento Valley to the southern San Joaquin Valley. This alluvial plain is the largest irrigated area west of the Rocky Mountains. The Central Valley has half of the state's farmland and 75 percent of the irrigated land.

The San Joaquin Valley's year-round agricultural production features almonds, grapes, and dairy, but the Mediterranean climate requires irrigation. One of the largest challenges to dependence on irrigation water is to distribute it properly, or salinization can kill the soil.

PHOTO 19.15. Salinas Valley Harvest. California has been dependent on foreign workers to harvest its crops. Wages are low and turnover is high making this a volatile social issue.

The Sacramento Valley receives sufficient precipitation and therefore limits irrigation; only rice is wholly dependent on irrigation. The main crops are rice, almonds, tomatoes, sugar beets, wheat, hay, and prunes.

The Salinas Valley is cool, foggy, and damp, and among America's richest farmland. It grows a larger variety of vegetables than any other area in America. Many valley towns are identified with specific crops: Watsonville (strawberries), Castroville (artichokes), and Gilroy (garlic). Monterey County is known as the "salad bowl of America," because of its salad greens production, although production is heavily dependent on irrigation (photo 19.15).

Southern California's Oxnard Plain and Central Coast—Ventura, Santa Barbara, and San Luis Obispo counties—is used for agriculture, wetlands, and residential development. The coast produces celery, dry beans, strawberries, and bell peppers—but many areas have been replaced by residential sprawl since the 1980s.

Agricultural Production   Specialty Crops (Fruits, Vegetables, and Nuts). California ranks first in growing forty-eight different specialty crops, with 250 varieties of fruits, vegetables, and nuts. Agricultural production was centered in Southern California but, as property values rose, shifted into the Central Valley. Today most specialty crops are grown in the Central or Salinas valleys. Some crops are exclusive to California including almonds, artichokes, dates, figs, kiwifruit, olives, persimmons, pomegranates, pistachios, prunes, raisins, and walnuts (table 19.2).

TABLE 19.2. California's Contribution to Specialty-Crop Fruits and Vegetables

Crop	Percentage of national crop contribution
Almonds, Artichokes, Dates, Figs, Kiwifruit, Olives, Persimmons, Pomegranates, Pistachios, Prunes, Raisins, and Walnuts	98–100
Lemons	92
Tomatoes	98
Strawberries	80
Grapes	98
Avocados, Broccoli, and Cauliflower	90
Garlic and commercial garlic	98
Almonds	90

Grapes and Vineyards. California grows 88 percent of American raisin, table, and wine grapes and is the national leader in wine production. The cool temperatures and sloped ground of the Napa–Sonoma Valley are ideal wine-producing features. Table and raisin grapes prosper in the hot interior San Joaquin Valley.

During the 1990s, the number of wineries expanded in California's Central, Coastal, and Salinas valleys. Monterey County alone now has as many vineyard acres as Napa Valley, the growth fueled by tax-sheltered wealthy individuals who "returned to the land." The Santa Barbara, San Luis Obispo, and

Santa Ynez oak-covered hillsides were denuded and the oaks replaced with spindly new grapevines, prompting neighbors to complain about their ruined views. There are more than four thousand wineries in the state and the industry continues to flourish bringing in about $35 billion each year.

Orange Production. Spanish missionaries brought oranges to California in the 1700s, but groves began in earnest after the American annexation. Nearly all the trees were located in Southern California, especially in the Los Angeles Basin, where production grew after the introduction of aqueduct water in 1913. The late-nineteenth-century invention of the refrigerated railcar made it possible to ship perishables, such as the orange, over long distances. By 1920, California grew 75 percent of the nation's orange crop.

After World War II, the orange industry repositioned to Florida. California replaced orange groves with tract homes. As more houses were built and land prices escalated, farmland near urban areas became too expensive. Farmers sold their land and moved into the Central Valley, where land was about one-fifth the price they received for their Southland orange groves.

California oranges today are mostly in the southern Central Valley. Seventy-five percent of the oranges are navel oranges and are sold fresh, unlike Florida's Valencia oranges, which are raised for juice concentrate. Today, California is second to Florida in orange production (map l9.6).

Dairy. Since the 1980s, California has led the nation in production of milk, butter, ice cream, and mozzarella cheese. California milk production accounts for 20 percent of the state's total agricultural receipts. Tulare County is the largest dairy producer in America, and it accounts for 27 percent of all California milk production. This is followed by Merced, Kings, and Stanislaus Counties. Previously, the dairy industry was located farther south in the Los Angeles metropolitan area towns of Cerritos (formerly Dairy Valley) and Chino. As Los Angeles expanded, the dairy land became more valuable and was sold for development. The dairies relocated to the less populated and less expensive Central Valley (map 19.7).

California surpassed Wisconsin in milk production in 1993 and has remained the top milk producer since, accounting for 20 percent of all milk in the United States. Dairy, cheese,

MAP 19.6. Total Acres of Oranges, Other Than Valencia, 2012.

Source: USDA

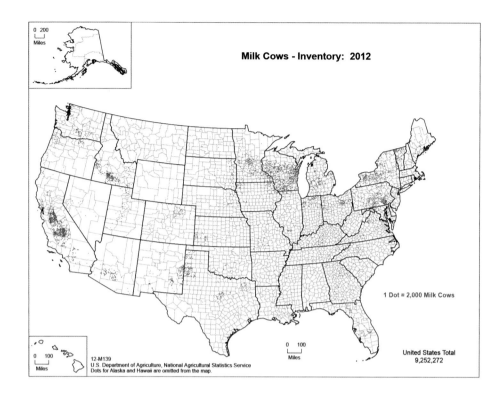

MAP 19.7 Milk Cows, 2012.
Source: USDA

yogurt, milk and butter, ice cream, and butter are all part of dairy production. Dairy farming is a leading agricultural commodity in California, producing $6.2 billion cash receipts from milk production in 2016. However, the diary industry has been struggling with low milk prices for many years.

California was able to dominate the market by establishing large dairy herds. Whereas the national average dairy herd size is 187 milk cow, California herds grew from an average of ninety-eight cows in 1969 to over seven hundred in 2003 and fouteen hundred by 2015.

California converts half of its fluid milk into producing one-sixth of the nation's cheese. About one quarter of all mozzarella cheese is made in California, and the state produces more than 160 million pounds of its native *queso del pais*, Monterey Jack.

Agricultural Exports*.* Although 80 percent of California's crops are consumed domestically, California is the nation's leading exporter of food. Currently, California's leading agricultural export products by value were almonds ($5 billion), dairy products ($1.6 billion), walnuts ($1.5 billion), wine ($1.5 billion), and pistachios ($850 million). The major export markets are Canada, the European Union, Japan, and China.

California agricultural exports account for 17 percent of all US exports. However, international trade agreements, such as the World Trade Organization (WTO) and the North American Free Trade Agreement (NAFTA), have made California crops less profitable. The trade agreements have opened up trade with other countries, but they have harmed local production.

Specialty crops lack federal subsidies, despite being almost 50 percent of the state's annual market value. This disadvantages specialty-crop farmers in comparison to the well-subsidized grain growers. The lack of subsidies allows other countries with reduced labor and land costs to gain market share in specialty crops. For example, government-supported Australian wine threatens the wine industry, and subsidized Chinese dehydrated garlic and onions threaten local growth.

Mineral Resources/Energy

Petroleum and Natural Gas   West Coast petroleum deposits in California are third in national oil and natural gas production. Leading producers are the Central Valley, Los Angeles Basin, and off Southern California's shore. In 1892, Edward Doheny drilled the first California wells in Los Angeles (photo 19.16) Later, wells were drilled at the seeping La Brea Tar Pits. Four of the top ten oil production facilities in America are in California, including untapped offshore reserves.

California offshore oil production is expensive and requires drilling in deep areas beyond the continental shelf. Although California produces oil, it consumes more than it produces. Controversies about increasing oil production, especially in the congested Los Angeles metropolitan area, focus on property values and the aesthetics of offshore drilling. Offshore oil leaks have caused concern and have resulted in increased regulations and drilling costs. Significant oil sands and shale in the basin may become important for future needs, as oil reserves decline and prices escalate. California is ranked third in the US in crude oil production Despite this, it must still import oil to meet its demands; 10 percent of oil comes from Alaska, 54 percent is imported from Saudi Arabia, Ecuador, and Colombia.

California provides for nearly 70 percent of its own electricity, but imports natural gas and hydropower. Hydropower

PHOTO 19.16. Oil Rigs in Huntington Beach, circa the 1940s. Oil rigs were once a common sight in many communities in Southern California.

Source: Courtesy of Orange County Historical Society, California

comes from the Pacific Northwest and 87 percent of California's natural gas production is from out-of-state facilities and delivered by the interstate natural gas pipeline.

Renewable Energy   Energy and population distribution continue to be unbalanced: population multiplies in Southern California, but new power plants are in the north. California has addressed its uneven energy system with progressive renewable energy plans. In 2002, the state established the California Renewable Portfolio Standard (RPS) to drive investment in clean energy. Subsequent amendments to the law have set increasingly ambitious targets. Today, the state is generating enough electricity from renewable sources to power more than five million homes, and that number is expected to nearly double by 2030. The state continues to meet its goals for renewable energy setting records in rooftop solar arrays, hydropower, and wind power generation. In 2015, the most recent RPS amendment requires all utilities in the state to source half of their electricity sales from clean, renewable sources—wind, solar, and geothermal by 2030. In 2017, a new amendment to the RPS sets the goal of 100 percent renewable energy by 2045; the bill passed the state Legislature. These ambitious goals mean growing investment in solar, wind, and other renewables.

Solar electricity production now contributes about 10 percent of California's total electricity. Additionally, California has instituted the California Solar Initiative, a financial incentive program that offers homeowners a tax rebate on top of a small federal tax credit. It is the most ambitious solar program in the nation.

And wind energy continues to grow rapidly. The size and diversity of the topography gives California several large wind energy sites that have been utilized by more than thirteen thousand wind turbines. In 2007, California received about 2.6 percent of the state's power from wind; by 2016 that had increased to nearly 7 percent. Additionally, hundreds of homes and farms are using smaller wind turbines to produce electricity. Geothermal has also seen growth and now produces about 6 percent of electricity generation with most of that based north of San Francisco.

The Secondary Sector

Although California was never a major manufacturing center, deindustrialization has nevertheless cost California manufacturing jobs. Since 1990, California has lost more than 40 percent of its manufacturing jobs.

While Northern California manufacturing is concentrated in technology-related industries, Southern California's manufacturing economy, with some eight hundred thousand workers, is more diverse. It includes low-tech industries such as apparel and food manufacturing, and high-tech businesses in aerospace parts and instruments, in computer and electronic components, and medical devices. Since 2000, Los Angeles lost 32 percent of its factory jobs, but still has 365,000 manufacturing workers who account for 9 percent of the county's employment. The outlook is bleak for fashion and textile manufacturing, but growth is predicted in manufacturing of medical devices, pharmaceuticals and sophisticated aerospace components.

Significant economic growth centers for the metropolitan area is the Los Angeles–Long Beach port. The port is the top container port in the US and receives about 43 percent of all cargo coming into the United States. Around $1.2 billion worth of cargo comes into the port each *day* and accounts for 8 percent of the GSP.

BOX 19.8 GLOBAL CONNECTIONS: TRADE NETWORKS AND PORTS

The busiest harbor in America and sixth largest in the world is the Los Angeles–Long Beach port. Los Angeles is the only major American city not built on a navigable waterway. The Los Angeles port at San Pedro was constructed twenty miles from the city center, after the annexation of land connecting to the port area.

When rail lines to the harbor area opened up trade in 1869, the ports were created by dredging the tidal marshes and mudflats. The harbor was completed and officially opened in 1907. Over time, the port has continuously been updated to meet new shipping requirements, such as late-twentieth-century **containerization**, which revolutionized freight handling. Containerization is a system of freight and cargo transfer that uses standard containers that can be loaded and sealed intact onto container ships, railroad cars, planes, and trucks.

Today the combined ports encompass seventy-five hundred acres of land, with forty-three miles of waterfront, twenty-seven passenger and cargo terminals, and 240 berths (photo 19.17). They handle two-thirds of the West Coast trade and act as a distribution center for the rest of the United States. Most of the containerized imports consist of furniture, auto parts, apparel, electronics, and plastics. In 2017, more than two thousand vessels unloaded a total cargo value of $292 billion. The port generated $59 million in revenue and employs some nine hundred thousand workers (direct and indirectly).

The American trade pattern has shifted during the late twentieth century, from one facing Europe to one facing Asia, and so the major ports are now on the West Coast. From 1970 to 2017, Asian imports into the port increased from 8 percent to 92 percent of the total goods brought in. The five largest trading partners are China ($137 billion) Japan ($39 billion) Vietnam ($15 billion), South Korea ($15 billion), and Taiwan ($12 billion).

The 2014 expansion of the Panama Canal has begun to shift shipping away from the West Coast and toward East Coast ports. Transfers by truck and rail are more expensive than container shipping, and easy access to the East Coast may decrease shipping to the West Coast.

PHOTO 19.17. The Port of Long Beach and Los Angeles. The Harbor is the busiest harbor in America and sixth largest in the world

Source: iStock/trekandshoot

The Tertiary Sector

Collectively California's tertiary sector drives economic growth in the state. Both Lockheed and Douglas aircraft industries were founded in California and were important defense industry employers in Southern California from the 1960s through 1970s; however, defense has shrunk to about 50 percent of its previous size, and in the process it eliminated many high-paying jobs.

However, many other services now contribute significantly to the state GSP. These jobs include the following:

- high technology (Silicon Valley and beyond);
- tourism;
- motion picture industry;
- aerospace; and
- education and health services.

For example, California's well-known technology sector includes a strong information industry, which employs 3 percent of the total private workforce and generates 8 percent of GSP. Well-known giants such as Google and Facebook are headquartered in California, and the San Francisco Bay area also supports a large startup community (photo 19.18).

A report in 2014 found that the aerospace industry is larger than both agriculture and Hollywood combined. California is responsible for 9 percent of the global market share in the aerospace industry. And the motion picture industry supports more than 2.4 million jobs nationwide.

The size and strength of the California economy mean that some of the world's largest companies are headquartered in the state, including Chevron, Apple, Hewlett-Packard, Intel, Google, Facebook, McKesson Corporation, and Wells Fargo & Company.

Tourism

California remains the nation's number one travel destination. Tourism is a $75 billion industry, the state's third-largest employer, and the fifth-largest contributor to the GSP. Growth in the travel industry continues, but it has had a negative impact on the environment and the quality of jobs.

California has long been a mecca for tourists. The state has several natural and human-made tourist destinations. The natural wonders include Yosemite, Death Valley, Big Sur, the many Sierra Nevada hiking and skiing areas, and expansive beaches. Many of these wonders are now crowded and restricted. Yosemite requires a reservation months to years in advance, and the beaches are contested grounds where wealthy residents no longer want the public on "their" beaches.

The most famous human-made attractions are Southern California's Disneyland, nearby Knott's Berry Farm, and the San Diego Zoo. In the Central Coast area, the Monterey Peninsula and its elite towns of Pebble Beach and Carmel are popular with the wealthy, while the Golden Gate Bridge, cable cars, and Chinatown beckon in San Francisco. Farther north is the wine country of Napa-Sonoma.

Informal Economy

Once the province of developing nations, the **informal economy** is expanding in the United States. About 28 percent of the Los Angeles and Bay Area economies runs outside of state-controlled economics. The informal economy includes low-skilled jobs that average $12,000 annually, paid in cash without taxes. Many are immigrants or undocumented workers, including small-scale vending, fruit/flower vendors, and subcontracted unskilled labor, such as immigrant laborers who gather each morning on hundreds of corners or in parking lots seeking temporary employment. The informal economy also hires undocumented workers in several industries, including the apparel industry, landscaping, construction, and restaurants. Estimates are that one in six construction workers is either off the books or misreported. Additionally, a growing segment of skilled workers unable to secure permanent positions are included in the informal economy.

In Los Angeles, the informal economy is visible everywhere. The workers are often Mexican or Central American Spanish-speaking immigrants with little education, who have no other way to earn a living. Informal economy wages are dishonest to laborers who are trapped in a system as the "working poor," and they are dishonest to tax-paying citizens. The informal economy is present in all the western states, and it is increasingly present in the fast-growing southeastern states where low-paying jobs demand low-cost labor.

The informal economy, though, encompasses more than immigrant laborers. Escalating taxes and slimmer profits have many legitimate firms turning to under-the-table cash employees. High technology, hit hard by outsourcing, uses unemployed people for temporary work, money the "employees" are happy to receive in an economy of fewer "good" jobs.

Several problems arise with the informal economy. Corporations can be heavily influenced by the short-term benefits of not paying workers' taxes. The informal economy brings the economy down in the long run, while short-term employees get trapped in the low-paying, temporary market and companies jeopardize long-term economic growth.

A Sustainable Future

You can live the California Dream, if you do not mind crowds, traffic, and insanely priced housing. Population growth and quality of life can be mutually exclusive; the more one grows, the more the other declines. The popular beach, mountain, and desert areas are crowded, and the crowds further impact environmental health. The US Census estimates that California in 2025 will have fifty million people. Architectural competitions garner ideas on how to house millions more in the Central Valley and still continue to grow California's agriculture, but is it possible?

Among the challenges to sustainability are the following:

- population growth;
- earthquakes, fires, and landslides;
- pollution and climate change;
- affordable housing;
- congestion and traffic; and
- numerous undocumented immigrants.

The good news is that California has a reputation for taking chances and being progressive. California did not wait for the federal government to finally admit to climate change and its damage, but instead passed the nation's strictest air pollution laws. In turn, these laws have influence beyond the state. For example automobile manufacturers have responded by developing electric and hybrid vehicles and low emission vehicles to meet the state standards, but these cars are available in all states. California has enacted legislation updating its appliance standards and building codes every three years as an important part of its sustainable credo. Oregon, Washington, and most states in the Atlantic Northeast have followed many of California's standards.

California is also a leader in renewable energy. Although other states sometimes feel energy initiatives are unprofitable, California is growing jobs based on being an incubator for clean-energy technologies, while reducing its energy impact.

The state is undertaking other sustainable projects, such as water recycling, and green buildings. The Tree People are an example of a Los Angeles group that supports a greener landscape by participating in planting restoration projects after fires. Tree plantings in the city absorb carbon dioxide and create oxygen, and they filter and collect water. Actions like these create more livable and sustainable cities.

Questions for Discussion

1. If the trend of the past decades continues, will the divide between haves and have-nots continue?

2. What precedent is there for Southern California to become effectively part of Mexico?

3. What are some of the social, political, and economic problems faced by multicultural California?

4. What is the direction of growth in California, and how might this play into the idea of two (or three?) Californias in the future?

5. How does the informal economy affect the state's economy?

6. Will California continue to be the number one producer of food? If not, where will the specialty crops come from? What are the advantages and disadvantages?

7. California has been at the leading edge of many cultural issues. Is California a harbinger of where the nation is headed in the long term in relation to diversity? Explain.

8. What impact have immigrants had on California's job market and on federal and state services?

9. What has California done to change energy production in the Intermontane? What effect will it have?

10. Explain the differences in water availability between Northern and Southern California.

11. Where is Silicon Valley located, and what factors led to its development?

Suggested Readings

Allen, J. P., and E. Turner. *The Ethnic Quilt: Population Diversity in Southern California*. Northridge, Calif.: Center for Geographical Studies, 1997.

Brechin, G. *Imperial San Francisco: Urban Power, Earthly Ruin*. Berkeley: University of California Press, 2006.

Chinn, T. W., ed. *A History of the Chinese in California: A Syllabus*. San Francisco, Calif.: Chinese Historical Society of America, 1969.

Conomos, T. J., ed. *San Francisco Bay: The Urbanized Estuary*. San Francisco, Calif.: American Association for the Advancement of Science, 1979.

Davis, M. *City of Quartz: Excavating the Future in Los Angeles*. New York: Vintage Press, 1992.

———. *Ecology of Fear*. New York: Vintage Press, 1998.

Godfrey, B. J. *Neighborhoods in Transition: The Making of San Francisco's Ethnic and Nonconformist Communities*. Berkeley: University of California Press, 1988.

Gumbrecht, B. *The Los Angeles River: Its Life, Death, and Possible Rebirth*. Baltimore, M.D.: Johns Hopkins University Press, 2001.

Guyton, B. *Glaciers of California: Modern Glaciers, Ice Age Glaciers, the Origin of Yosemite Valley, and a Glacier Tour in the Sierra Nevada*. Berkeley: University of California Press, 1998.

Haddad, B. *Rivers of Gold: Designing Markets to Allocate Water in California*. Washington, D.C.: Island Press, 2000.

Ito, K. *Issei: A History of Japanese Immigrants in North America*. Translated by Shinichiro Nakamura and Jean S. Gerard. Seattle, Wash.: Executive Committee for Publication of Issei, 1973.

Lopez-Garza, M., and D. Diaz, eds. *Asian and Latino Immigrants in a Restructuring Economy: The Metamorphosis of Southern California*. Stanford, Calif.: Stanford University Press, 2001.

McWilliams, C. *Southern California Country: An Island on the Land*. New York: Duell, Sloan, & Pearce, 1946.

Pellow, D., and L. Park. *The Silicon Valley of Dreams: Environmental Injustice, Immigrant Workers, and the High-Tech Global Economy*. New York: New York University Press, 2002.

Peters, G. L. *American Winescapes: The Cultural Landscapes of America's Wine Country*. Boulder, Colo.: Westview Press, 1997.

Reisner, M. *Cadillac Desert*. New York: Viking Penguin, 1986.

Saxenian, A. L. *Regional Advantage: Culture and Competition in Silicon Valley and Route 128*. Cambridge, Mass.: Harvard University Press, 1994.

Webber, H. *History and Development of the Citrus Industry*. Revised by Walter Reuther and Harry W. Lawton. University of California, Division of Agricultural Sciences, 1967, at http://lib.ucr.edu/agnic/webber/Vol1/Chapter1.htm.

Internet Sources

California Breathing, 2017. "Los Angeles County Asthma Profile," at https://www.cdph.ca.gov/Programs/CCDPHP/DEODC/EHIB/CPE/Pages/CaliforniaBreathing.aspx

California Department of Food and Agriculture. *California Agricultural Production Statistics*, at http://www.cdfa.ca.gov/statistics/

Nichols, Frederic H. "The San Francisco Bay and Delta: An Estuary Undergoing Change." *USGS Science for a Changing World*, at http://sfbay.wr.usgs.gov/general_factsheets/change.html

Los Angeles Almanac. *The Los Angeles Basin*, at http://www.laalmanac.com/geography/ge08e.htm

Los Angeles' Sustainability Plan, at http://plan.lamayor.org/about-the-plan/

San Diego's Sustainability report, at https://www.sandiego.gov/sites/default/files/final_capannualreport_pdf.pdf

U.S. Geological Survey. *Earthquake Hazards Program*, at http://earthquake.usgs.gov/

Kauai

1 Citizens of Moloka`i, still largely undeveloped, have fought a 200-home development.

6 Lāna`i, once the Pineapple Isle, is privately held, and there is talk of establishing wind farms and solar energy there.

Oahu

2 3

Honolulu

2 Honolulu, sometimes called the L.A. of the Pacific, is plagued with the same problems as other large cities.

Molokai

1

6

5

Maui

5 Lahaina, Maui, was the capital of the Hawaiian kingdom and then a whaling port.

3 Some Hawaiian natives, shut out of the land market, have taken to squatting.

Hawaii

Hilo

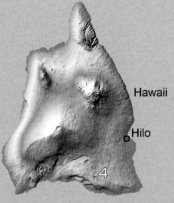

4

4 Some shores of Hawai`i, the youngest and most volcanically active island, continue to build with lava from Kilauea.

0   25   50 Miles

20
HAWAI`I
Aloha

Chapter Highlights

After reading this chapter, you should be able to:

- Label, map, and identify the major Hawaiian Islands
- Describe the climatic patterns on the islands and their relationship to the tourism industry
- Explain how Hawaiian natives have been impacted by their change of diet
- Describe Honolulu, its economy, and its issues
- Discuss how the islands were populated originally and the missionary impact on the islands
- Describe the economic evolution of Hawai`i from sandalwood to tourism and how it has impacted both the social equity and environment of the islands
- Discuss the importance of agriculture in the Hawaiian economy and how it has changed since 1950
- Describe the unique land ownership patterns on the islands
- Explain the importance of volcanics in shaping the islands

Terms

abyss
atoll

closed ecosystem
Great Mahele
Hawai`i Land Reform Act
pali

poi
seamount
shield cluster
shield volcano

taro
vog

Places

The Big Island: Hawai`i
Kaho`olawe

Kaua`i
Lāna`i
Maui

Moloka`i
Ni`ihau
O`ahu

Cities

Honolulu
   (2016 MSA 990,00)

Hilo
   (2016 MSA 43,200)

PHOTO 20.1. Surfboards at Waikiki Beach in Honolulu, Hawai`i.

Source: iStock/eddygaleotti

Introduction

Hawai`i is America's island paradise with an island lore of year-round tropical weather, treetop fruit, world-famous hula, and laid-back culture (photo 20.1). What more can one want? While still the perception of many, the island paradise of Hawai`i has been transformed into kitschy tourism and a tragic dichotomy between homelessness and uber-wealth. There are few affordable housing options and a rising homeless rate amid multimillion-dollar houses. Even ramshackle shacks on the friendly and most remote public isle, Moloka`i, are worth millions. Social injustice, housing inflation, island immigration, and environmental and water-related problems have resulted in an unsustainable environment.

Hawai`i has beckoned to westerners for centuries, first because of its isolated yet strategic location, then agriculturally, and finally as a tourist destination—all the while ignoring the rights of the native people. Keeping the islands pristine has proven impossible, but maintaining social and ecological integrity may be possible. Maintaining a **closed ecosystem**—one that recycles everything and wastes nothing—is an ideal goal on the isolated islands. Isolation should work to the island's advantage, but the ease of transportation and population growth has ended the isolation.

Since the 1960s, sandy beaches, big waves, and the perfect Waikīkī vacation have attracted visitors. Hawaiian tourist classifications range between the ultimate one-week budget honeymoon getaways to visits to exclusive resorts on entire islands. But tourism is a latecomer to the Hawaiian economy. Hawai`i became a tourist mecca after the invention of the commercial jet airplane, and after successive economies (sandalwood, whaling, ranching, and farming) had run their course and left their waste debris. Although the islands are amongst the wealthiest in the world, they are also home to the working homeless and the disenfranchised Native Hawaiian population, who still fight for a foothold on their island home.

The island archipelago may be paradoxically loved and suffocated to death simultaneously.

Physical Geography

Stretched from the Aleutian Trench to the Big Island, 132 volcanically formed islands, reefs, atolls, and shoals compose the fifteen-hundred-mile Hawaiian archipelago. The eight populated

BOX 20.1   ICONIC IMAGES: SURFS UP

Polynesians, the first inhabitants of Hawai`i, were surfing across the islands of the Pacific including Samoa and Tonga. When the Hawaiian Islands were first visited by British ships in 1767, the sailors recorded some of the first impressions of people surfing. In 1866, Mark Twain noted during his visit to the islands that surfing was the national pastime, for both men and women. A rich American eager to attract business to his resort at Redondo Beach in California employed George Freeth (1883–1919) to show off his surfing skills daily in front of the hotel on the beach. Freeth, an American born in O`ahu, is known as the father of modern surfing. He is credited with developing eight-foot surfing boards. His displays on the beach inaugurated surfing in California.

Since then surfing has gone global. But its modern origins and sentimental home are still in Hawai`i. The image of surfing seems to be permanently tethered to popular images of Hawai`i and the surfer is one of the "characters" of modern day Hawai`i (photo 20.2). The beaches are spectacular including Hookipa (Maui), Makaka Beach Park (O`ahu), Sunset Beach (O`ahu), Waimea Bay (O`ahu), and Ehukai Beach (O`ahu). There are many other surf beaches around the world but few as revered as in Hawai`i. The long offshore open water stretches allow winds to build up impressive cobalt blue waves that reach high into the sky.

PHOTO 20.2. Surfer Getting Barreled.
Source: iStock/EpicStockMedia

islands, the state of "Hawai`i," are the largest and youngest of the islands. Together they stretch four hundred miles end to end from the Big Island to Ni`ihau, and they have a total area about the size of New Jersey. The major islands include the following (listed from largest to smallest):

- Hawai`i (4,028 square miles)
- Maui (727 square miles)
- O`ahu (597 square miles)
- Kaua`i (552 square miles)
- Moloka`i (260 square miles)
- Lāna`i (141 square miles)
- Ni`ihau (72 square miles)
- Kaho`olawe (45 square miles)

The Hawaiian Islands are located in the Pacific Ocean about twenty-one hundred miles southwest of the US mainland and are the most remote islands in the world. The islands, ranging in latitude from 16°55'N to 23°N, are the only part of the United States south of the Tropic of Cancer. As part of the Hawaiian–Emperor Ridge Seamount, the islands extend in a wide arc between two eighteen-thousand-foot-deep Pacific **abysses** (the flat ocean floor found at the bottom of continental slopes). The still-growing chain was created over the past seventy million years.

The volcanic origins of the Hawaiian Islands are unusual because they are not at the edge of a tectonic plate where most volcanoes are found; they lie beneath a stationary hot spot in the mantle below the Pacific Plate. Molten magma

PHOTO 20.3. Field of Lava on Hawai`i's Big Island.
Source: iStock/Eachat

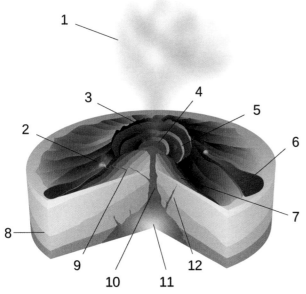

CHART 20.1. Diagram of a Hawaiian Eruption. (Key: 1. Ash plume. 2. Lava fountain. 3. Crater. 4. Lava lake. 5. Fumaroles. 6. Lava flow. 7. Layers of lava and ash. 8. Stratum. 9. Sill. 10. Magma conduit. 11. Magma chamber. 12. Dike.)
Source: Sémhur

melts the plate above the hot spot. The volcanoes become inactive as the plate moves past the hot spot, and then the hot spot repeats the process, forming the next island (chart 20.1). The older volcanoes on Kaua`i, for example, are extinct, cut off from the hot spot magma, while Big Island volcanoes are either still active (Kilauea) or inactive but not yet extinct.

Magma is lighter than the surrounding rock, so it rises through the mantle onto the seafloor and forms a basaltic **seamount**, which over geologic time rises through the mantle, the crust, and the ocean surface as a **shield volcano** island. The gentle-slope shield volcanoes are built by accretion of fluid lava flows. The complete cycle of volcano building and quiescence takes about six hundred thousand years—half the time rising from the ocean floor to sea level and half building the shield volcano (photo 20.3).

The plate inches southeast, so the northwest islands are the oldest. The basaltic volcanic peaks are some of the largest and highest mountains in the world, when counting both the underwater and above–sea level masses.

The smaller landmasses of the island chain lie to the northwest. The twenty-six Northwestern or Leeward Islands, from Kure (twelve hundred miles northwest of Honolulu) to Kaula (twenty miles west-southwest of Ni`ihau), are either the ring-like coral reef **atolls** or the summits of submarine volcanoes. These small islands abound in endemic insects, plants, and coral reefs and are a wintering area for migratory birds. During the past fifty years, the Northwestern Island waters have lost species to overfishing and erosion. To prevent further ecosystem losses, in June 2006, the Northwestern Islands were declared a national monument and became, at the time, the world's largest marine reserve known as Papahanaumokuakea Marine National Monument.

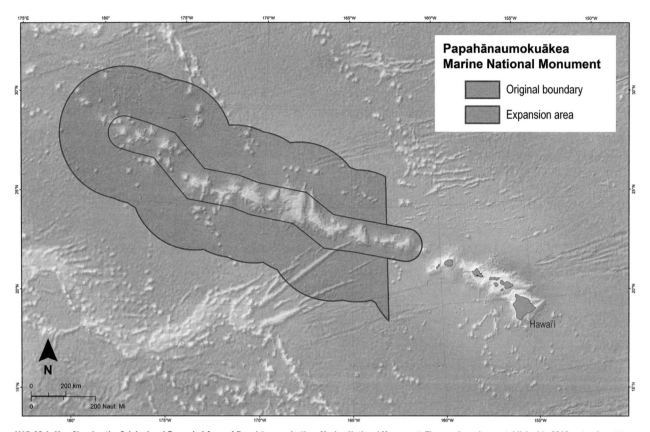

MAP 20.1. Map Showing the Original and Expanded Area of Papahānaumokuākea Marine National Monument. The new boundary, established in 2016, extends out to the US EEZ (shown in purple). The monument's original area is shown in blue.

It covers 140,000 square miles. Commercial activities are banned throughout the marine reserve (map 20.1). The Northwestern Islands are uninhabited, except for the minimally staffed crew from the US Fish and Wildlife Service on Midway Atoll. Prior to European contact, Hawaiians inhabited a few of these atolls for short periods of time, but generally the remote atolls and islands remained inviolate.

In 2016, President Obama quadrupled the size of Papahanaumokuakea Marine National Monument over half a million square miles, more than all the other US national parks combined.

The youngest and most volcanically active island is the Big Island of Hawai`i, although fifteen miles east of the Big Island a seamount is building. The seamount is called Loihi; it is already over ten thousand feet high but still three thousand feet below the ocean's surface. If Loihi continues to erupt, it may reach sea level in ten to twenty thousand years.

Lava flows have defined the unique shape of each volcanic island. Islands with multiple volcanoes, such as Hawai`i and Maui, are called volcanic **shield clusters**.

The prehistoric Hawaiian Islands were forested and teemed with more than eighty-seven hundred endemic flora and fauna species. The oldest inhabited island, Kaua`i, has been volcanically inactive in recorded history and has developed lush vegetation. The Big Island of Hawai`i, however, is bare where fresh lava has been deposited. The arrival of the Polynesians over the past fifteen hundred years brought new species to the islands, but it has been a major challenge to island vegetation and animals since the jet age, when invasive species were imported to the detriment of crops and the extinction of native species. The numerous jet-age invasive species threaten the economy, environment, and lifestyle of the islands.

Water

The islands are a mix of dry and very wet topographies arranged according to their seaward orientation. In the mountainous island interiors, surface water erodes and cuts into the lava, shaping canyons. Kaua`i, the oldest island, has the largest canyon, Waimea, and the most erosion, while younger Hawai`i has the least erosion because the basalt is porous and rain infiltrates the rock. Infrequent flash floods where the rock is less porous can be a natural hazard that simultaneously enriches the biological diversity.

Offshore water is warm and clear. Coral reefs—partially responsible for the famous surf on Hawaiian beaches—surround portions of the islands. Coral is home to more than five thousand species of fish, sea animals, and plants (photo 20.4). Sewage discharge and septic systems threaten the reefs and disrupt the coastal nutrient balance. The water off the

BOX 20.2   THE MAJOR HAWAIIAN ISLANDS

The individual islands from the north are: Kaua`i, Ni`ihau, O`ahu, Moloka`i, Lāna`i, Maui, Hawai`i, Kaho`olawe (map 20.2).

Kaua`i (2016 pop. 72,029)

About 5.5 million years ago, a single shield volcano shaped the oldest of the eight islands, Kaua`i. The verdant "Garden Isle" is the oldest inhabited island, the most ecologically diverse and the most eroded. It has three major physical attractions: Waimea Canyon—"the Grand Canyon of the Pacific"—the Na Pali coastline, and Mount Waialeale, one of the wettest places on Earth (more than 450 inches of rainfall annually).

The island is a popular tourist attraction and had approximately 1.1 million visitors in 2005. But the impact of tourists has affected natural flora biodiversity on Kaua`i. Pristine areas still exist within the deep valleys of the island, such as Wainiha, now a private nature reserve, but even these are being threatened with invasive species. The island now has a number of restoration sites where alien and invasive vegetation is being replaced with native plants, such as the overharvested maile vine used in lei making.

Ni`ihau (2016 pop. 130)

Ni`ihau is the "Forbidden Isle," a privately owned island eighteen miles southwest of Kaua`i. The Sinclair–Robinson family purchased the island from Kamehameha V in 1864 for $10,000 and remains the owners. Part of the original contract agreement was to preserve the Hawaiian language and culture. The island was a cattle and sheep ranch until 1999, when the ranch was shut down due to unprofitability. The closure of the ranch left the residents unemployed. They have since become subsistence farmers, fishers, and receive welfare. Most are Native Hawaiians and live a life that continues to preserve the native culture and language, and rejects most modern technology.

The island lies low on the horizon and does not catch the trade-wind rainfall, so it receives only about twelve inches of rain annually. The lack of rain often results in freshwater shortages, causing residents to occasionally evacuate for Kaua`i. While on Kaua`i, the Ni`ihau islanders have access to modern technology, but most choose to forgo it and return to Ni`ihau, even after the ranch was closed.

Until recently, only members of the owner's family, government officials, or invited guests have been allowed to visit the island. The owners have sought to maintain the culturally pristine and natural habitat, while at the same time finding economic viability. They have pursued, so far unsuccessfully, military contracts and have now allowed a select few to tour or hunt on the island. These tours respect the island residents' way of life by keeping them away from Western culture and tourism. Wild animals roam the island, such as an estimated six thousand feral pigs, which are a favorite hunting prize. The hunts are justified, since many of the pigs die during drought.

O`ahu (2016 pop. 992,605)

Two volcanoes, Waianae and Koolau, formed O`ahu. Lava created the Leilehua Plateau, the pineapple-growing agricultural region north of Honolulu. To the east of the plateau are the Waianae Mountains, which are part of the James Campbell Estate (leased to the Nature Conservancy) or part of the federally run military complex. To the west, the Koolau Mountains run the north-south extent of the island. Diamond Head to the south of Honolulu, visible from Waikīkī Beach, is an extinct volcano. The north shore of the island is called the surfing capital of the world, containing such famous beaches as Sunset, Waimea, and the Bonzai Pipeline. The big waves for surfing are due to winter storms and shallow reefs.

About 80 percent of the state's population resides in O`ahu. Honolulu, the largest urban and commercial area on all the islands, is complete with high rises, sprawl, and traffic. Its suburbs extend up the eastern side of the Koolau Mountain valleys to the northeast Ewa Plain and to Pearl Harbor, site of the Japanese attack on December 7, 1941, that brought the United States into World War II.

Moloka`i (2016 pop. 7,345)

Moloka`i is known as the "friendly isle", the most unspoiled and natural of the publicly held islands. Native Hawaiians constitute the majority of the population, and the Hawaiian language is evident in speech and signage. There are relatively few tourists. The island is dry on the leeward west end, and wet on the windward east end. The northern shore has the highest *pali* (cliffs) in the world, the "backside," dropping precipitously three thousand feet into the sea. The cliffs are the result of a tremendous landslide about 1.5 million years ago, after waves had undercut the shore for millions of years.

In the middle of Moloka`i's northern shore, thousands of feet below steep cliffs, is the remote Kalaupapa Peninsula, which was once a leper colony. In 1865, a law was passed criminalizing leprosy. Fear of the deforming and contagious disease caused the extreme measure of isolating the afflicted. By 1866, anyone showing signs of what they took to be the disease—and many with psoriasis or acne were misdiagnosed—were banished from their homes, taken to the waters off the peninsula, dumped in the ocean, and left to swim to shore and fend for themselves.

Father Damien arrived on Kalaupapa in 1873 and spent the rest of his life offering hope, help, and dignity to the exiles, before succumbing to the disease himself. More than eight

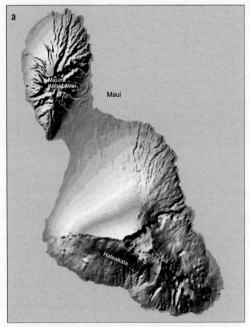

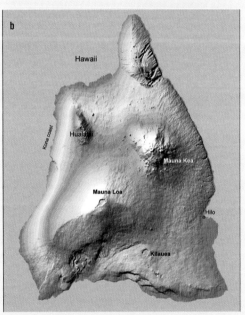

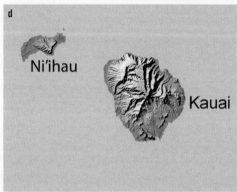

MAP 20.2. The Major Hawaiian Islands. (Maps not to scale.)

a. Maui is the second largest island (727 square miles) and is composed of two volcanoes and a Narrow Isthmus. At one time, the four islands Lāna`i, Kaho`olawe, Moloka`i, and Maui were one island called Maui Nui.

b. The Big Island (4,028 square miles) is composed of five volcanoes. The most active is Kileaua, which has been continually active since 1993.

c. O`ahu is the third-largest island (597 square miles) and houses about 75 percent of the state's population, most of whom live in Metro Honolulu. The North Shore is a world-famous surfing spot.

d. Kaua`i is the oldest of the islands and fourth largest (552 square miles). Ni`ihau is a privately held island inhabited by indigenous Hawaiians.

e. Moloka`i remains largely natural and inhabited by Hawaiian Natives. Kalaupapa was the infamous leper colony.

thousand were banished to the peninsula in the century of quarantine, before antibiotics arrested leprosy (Hansen's disease) in the 1940s. Today, a few of the exiles remain, now by choice, as it is often the only home they have ever known.

Maui (Maui County [includes Maui, Moloka`i, Lāna`i] 2016 pop. 152,062)

Maui is a remnant of a much bigger island that existed 1.2 million years ago. Maui Nui was perhaps 50 percent larger than the Big Island today. It was composed of Maui, Moloka`i, Lāna`i, and Kaho`olawe, but over time global sea-level change and volcano subsidence has submerged the saddles between the islands.

A narrow, low, fertile isthmus separates Maui's two volcanoes. On West Maui, Pu`u Kukui is considered extinct: The caldera is the present-day Iao Valley and has many incised valleys. East Maui has Hawai`i's third-largest shield volcano, Haleakala, which having last erupted in 1790 is still considered an active volcano. East Maui is less occupied than West Maui. The infamous and tortuous Hana–Piilani highway did not go completely around East Maui until the 1990s, and it is still partially gravel. West Maui is the more populated side and contains Lahaina, King Kamehameha's original island capital and an important whaling station. The first missionaries arrived at Lahaina.

The isthmus was an important producer of sugarcane, irrigated by an elaborate system originating in the wet, forested hillsides. Much of the remaining sugarcane grown on the islands is grown on thirty-seven thousand acres of the isthmus.

Lāna`i (2016 pop. 3,315)

Lāna`i is thirteen miles by eighteen miles—ninety-eight thousand acres—separated from Maui and Moloka`i by channels. Since 1917, the Dole pineapple plantation has run the Pineapple Island. It was a company island rather than a company town. Castle & Cooke—descendants of missionary families—purchased 98 percent of the island when the pineapple plantation closed. Castle & Cooke tried to convert the island to tourism but ran out of money, and David Murdock purchased Castle & Cooke in 1985. He also built and owns the two luxury resorts on the island. The three thousand residents, mostly people who worked on the pineapple plantation, now staff the resorts. There is no "real" Hawai`i on Lāna`i, only a hideout for the uber-wealthy. Bill Gates rented the entire island for his wedding. Microsoft cofounder Paul Allen has the largest private residence on the island.

Hawai`i (2016 pop. 196,428)

Hawai`i, the Big Island, is the youngest—four hundred thousand years old—and largest island in the archipelago. It contains two-thirds of state land and is larger than all the other islands combined. Eruptions from Kilauea add an additional forty-two acres annually. The Big Island also has the most climatic regions—from desert at Ka`u rainforest near Hilo to the snow-capped peak of Mauna Kea.

Five volcanoes (in order of age, oldest first) Kohala, Mauna Kea, Hualalai, Mauna Loa, and Kilauea, shape the island. The oldest, Kohala, is extinct. Mauna Kea is a dormant volcano that last erupted forty-five hundred years ago. Measured from its underwater base instead of sea level, Mauna Kea is taller than Mount Everest (33,476 feet from its base, 13,796 from sea level, compared to Mount Everest's 29,035 feet). Super-powered telescopes mounted atop Mauna Kea take advantage of the lack of atmospheric pollution. The Mauna Kea Observatory is also used by the National Oceanic and Atmospheric Administration (NOAA) as the research facility that monitors CO_2 since the 1950s. Hualalai last erupted around 1800 and may erupt again in the next hundred years. Mauna Loa (13,679 feet) is the world's largest active volcano and covers half of the island, and Kilauea is the world's most active volcano, continuously erupting since 1983.

Agriculture and tourism dominate the Big Island's economy. The twenty-mile Kona Coast on the leeward side of the island has excellent soils and climate supporting the only American-grown coffee. The mountain slopes of Haualalai and Mauna Loa provide the soil, precipitation, protective cover, and **vog** (**v**olcano + sm**og**), volcanic smog formed by the mixture of sulfuric dioxide and other pollutants, necessary to make good coffee. The Parker Ranch—150,000 acres between Mauna Kea and Kohala—is one of America's largest cattle ranches and Hawai`i's largest privately held ranch. The ranch is run by a charitable trust since 1992.

Kaho`olawe (uninhabited)

A small extinct volcano forms this island. The island was used as a penal colony (1826–1853), for ranching (1858–1952) and for bombing practice. In 1976, a Native Hawaiian group occupied the island and protested for the return of the island to Hawaiian sovereignty. In 1981, the entire island was declared historic and placed on the National Register. In 1990, the bombing halted but unexploded ordnance hinders occupation.

Sheep and goats overgrazed the land during the ranching period. Today, a native group protects environmental restoration and manages the island as a cultural reserve; eventually ownership will transfer to a sovereign Hawaiian nation. The US Navy has cleared part of the island of surface ordnance and removed goats. Revegetation programs are in place. In November 2003, Kaho`olawe was officially transferred from the US Navy to the state of Hawai`i.

PHOTO 20.4. Coral Reef off Moloka`i. Touching coral is a no-no while snorkeling, diving, or swimming in the ocean. Coral can be damaged, or they can die because of trampling or oils from human bodies.

sparsely settled islands is healthy, but overfishing, pollution, invasive algae, runoff, and human contact threaten the heavily populated islands.

Hawai`i has regularly faced drought. While drought affected the agricultural economy in the past, today water shortages threaten the increasingly large population. In heavily populated O`ahu, freshwater has been capped or diverted from flowing into the ocean, but this action has assaulted indigenous species ecosystems.

O`ahu

Access to freshwater has been an increased concern on O`ahu. The sugar crop consumed most of the water in the past, but today the major consumer is the growing population on the most populated island. Recent droughts have focused attention on the issue. Just north of Honolulu, water shortages threaten the island's fastest-growing region, the Ewa Plain. Groundwater once used for sugarcane fields is now being pumped at non-renewable rates, and the region has turned to reverse osmosis desalination (desal) as an answer.

Desal water is more expensive than groundwater, but the increased cost of groundwater drilling on the islands has made desal a reasonable possibility. A disadvantage is the amount of energy required to convert the saltwater. Opponents to desalination believe that conserving water may be more cost-effective before committing to the energy-intensive desalination process.

Currently, desalination is only being used as pilot projects in order to test several water resource alternatives to find the most cost-effective and energy-efficient method. The eleven million gallons of raw seawater required to produce five million gallons of desal water annually disrupts local ecosystems; this disruption has yet to be environmentally analyzed.

Maui

Maui faces water shortages in the near future because of urban population growth and competing agricultural claims. Because the water shortages and limited storage facilities are severe, Maui has been seeking help on water issues from sources outside Maui County.

One of the larger conflicts is between small traditional taro farmers and the much larger sugar and pineapple corporations. The starchy tuber **taro** is the traditional staple food, which few Hawaiians eat today due to the modern diet; however, the natives are more genetically disposed to taro, which has resulted in obesity. A few taro growers have been working to restore this significant element of the traditional Hawaiian diet, and therefore they are important on the island and for the native population. In 2003, Maui's Native Hawaiian taro farmers fought large corporate farmers and won continued water rights, although conserving water or efficient use remains problematic.

The major aquifer on Maui has reached 90 percent of its capacity; the county stopped issuing new permits, effectively ending new developments. Agriculture consumes 75 percent of the water, but escalating demands on water require more accountability of agricultural and urban water use. An additional issue with Maui water is the conversion of agricultural land to residential use. Former agricultural wells are now residential in use, but they are often contaminated with agricultural pesticides.

Climate

Hawai`i's tropical location is consistently warm throughout the year. The climate has little seasonality, but the trade winds and the mountainous topography have created a distinct rainfall

BOX 20.3 GEOSPATIAL TECHNOLOGIES: AN ATLAS OF RAINFALL

Geography professors at the university of Hawai`i and others collaborated to produce a rainfall atlas of Hawai`i. It is available online:
http://journals.ametsoc.org/doi/full/10.1175/ BAMS-D-11-00228.1

In chart 20.2, it is clear that there is distinct geography with most rainfall on the highest peaks and along the northeast coats. The rainfall reflects the pattern of the rain-bearing trade winds.

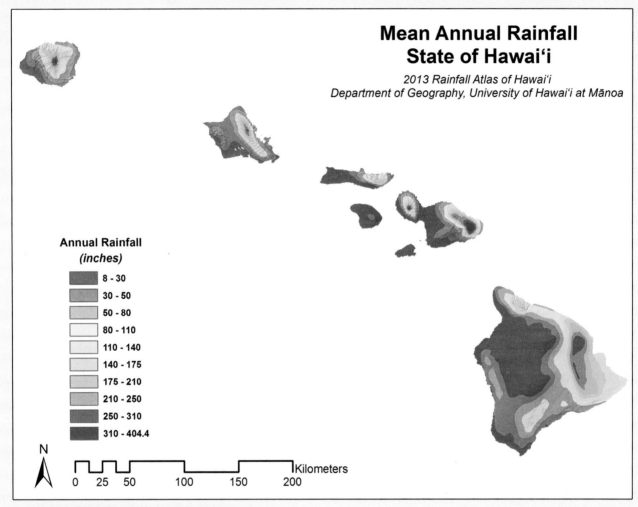

CHART 20.2. Mean Annual Rainfall in the State of Hawai`i.

Source: Giambelluca, T. W., Q. Chen, A. G. Frazier, J. P. Price, Y. L. Chen, P. S. Chu, J. K. Eischeid, and D. M. Delparte, D.M. "Online rainfall atlas of Hawai`i." *Bulletin of the American Meteorological Society* 94, no. 3 (2013): 313–16

pattern that determines the location of the Hawaiian tourism economy. Following the trade wind patterns, the windward (northeast) side of the islands receives plentiful rainfall, while the southwest leeward (protected from the wind and rain) side rainfall is scant. Tourist resorts are located on the dry leeward sides of the islands: for example, Honolulu and the Big Island's Kona Coast.

Average rainfall varies between the windward (four hundred inches in Kaua`i) and leeward (ten inches) sides, but it averages about twenty-five inches annually. The rainy season is between October and March. The warm air temperatures (85°F

in summer, 78°F in winter) are influenced by 74°F to 80°F water year-round.

At the higher elevations atop volcanoes, temperatures average 40°F. Rainfall is scant above three thousand feet on the Big Island mountains and on Maui's Haleakala, but both can and occasionally do receive snow.

The islands of Hawai`i are vulnerable to climate change. Warming of the surrounding seas harms the algae that protect corals, and leads to damaged coral reefs. Warming seas threaten ecosystems and native fish stocks. Climate change threatens economy of the islands.

BOX 20.4   CLIMATE CHANGE IN HAWAI`I

Hawai`i's climate is changing. In the last century, air temperatures have increased between 0.5°F and 1°F. A 2016 Environmental Protection Agency (EPA) report* noted that there are three ways in which climate change may impact Hawai`i:

1. *Warmer ocean temperatures*: The waters around Hawai`i are warming, which is harming Hawai`i's coral reefs and marine ecosystems. The El Niño Southern Oscillation ("El Niño") and other natural cycles cause ocean temperatures in the Pacific to fluctuate from year to year and from decade to decade. Even after accounting for these natural patterns, the waters around Hawai`i have been warming since the 1950s, with temperatures rising by several degrees from the ocean surface down to at least six hundred feet. Rising water temperatures can harm the algae that live inside corals. Because algae provide food for the coral, a loss of algae weakens corals and can eventually kill them. This process is commonly known as "coral bleaching," because the loss of the algae also causes the corals to turn white. Mass bleaching events are becoming more common, with documented cases in the north-western Hawaiian Islands in 1996 and 2002.

2. *Sea level rise and shoreline loss*: Since 1960, sea level has risen between two and eight inches relative to Hawai`i's shoreline. Sea level rise can make Hawai`i's existing coastal hazards—such as waves, hurricanes, tsunamis, and extreme tides—even worse. Additionally, rising sea level has accelerated coastal erosion, which has resulted in cliff collapse. Chronic erosion has affected more than 70 percent of Kaua`i and Maui's beaches over the last century.

3. *Water availability*: Rainfall in Hawai`i has been decreasing, but scientists do not know whether that trend will continue. El Niño will probably continue to dominate precipitation patterns from year to year in the tropical Pacific. Climate change-related increases in air temperatures will lead to more evaporation and more moisture in the air. As a result, the variability in El Niño-related precipitation is likely to increase, making rainfall predictions difficult. Although projections of future rainfall are uncertain, streams and rivers on the Hawaiian Islands have experienced a reduction in flow over the last century, resulting in less fresh water available for people and ecosystems. Additionally, increased drought may threaten taro and breadfruit, which are important traditional food sources for Hawai`i's native people.

---

*US Environmental Protection Agency (EPA), *What Climate Changes Means for Hawaii*, accessed 2017, http://19january2017snapshot.epa.gov/sites/production/files/2016-09/documents/climate-change-hi.pdf

Historical Geography and Settlement

Hawai`i was one of the last places in the Pacific to be settled. While Polynesians settled the South Pacific two thousand years ago, remote Hawai`i was settled much later. Two major Polynesian migrations occurred, first from the Marquesas (approximately 400 CE) and later from Tahiti (900–1000 CE), but smaller migrations continued through the fifteenth century. Researchers have theorized about the migration patterns.

Researchers have hypothesized that during El Niño events (which may have been prolonged during the 750–1250 CE Little Climatic Optimum) there were prevailing westerlies, which would have facilitated navigation. The Pacific migrations may also be part of a larger, world-scale pattern, similar to the tenth century Viking navigation to Newfoundland. The pattern fits the climatic record—a period of warmth, which would end with the Little Ice Age, when further oversea migrations were halted as storms advanced with colder climates.

By the mid-sixteenth century, the Spanish made regular runs between the Philippines and Mexico but missed the Hawaiian Islands. Captain James Cook stumbled upon Kaua'i in 1778 and named the islands in honor of his patron, the Earl of Sandwich. The Sandwich Islands were renamed the Hawaiian Islands in 1847.

Island life was transformed after the Europeans arrived, beginning with a scourge of sailor-spread venereal disease. Lacking immunity, many Hawaiians died. In the 1820s, the first missionaries arrived from New England. While the missionaries' moral code and religion conflicted with native beliefs, both the natives and the missionaries eventually compromised their positions. The natives accepted Christianity, and the missionary families often intermarried and therefore began acquiring land. Previously royals "owned" land, although it was shared and used by all. Europeans applied their ownership rules to the land, and the Hawaiians lost their previous rights to use land. Subsequent generations of the missionary families shifted their interests from religious conversion to socioeconomic conversion of the islands.

The missionary families' progeny became plantation owners, building economic empires that uprooted the natives, their culture, and their way of life. The reign of the last monarch, Queen Liliuokalani, sought to preserve and restore Hawaiian nationalism and sovereignty but threatened the nonnative sugar planters, who counted on the sugar crop and removal of tariffs to increase their profits.

Sugar was all the more lucrative for Hawai`i because it did not need refrigeration. Shipping the commodity to the United States was profitable and possible, but the tariffs to import the

PHOTO 20.5. Kapu: "No Trespassing" Sign on Moloka`i. Malama Ka`Aina is translated as "Care for the Land."

sugar into the United States were high. The white plantation owners instituted the last of several policies to shift power from the Hawaiians to the whites.

The islands were politically fragmented prior to the nineteenth century; each island was ruled by a different indigenous king until the unification reign of King Kamehameha I when Europeans reached the islands. The islands were then organized as a constitutional monarchy until 1893 when Queen Liliuokalani was deposed by foreign planters. In a bloodless coup, the planters overthrew the monarchy. After the queen was deposed in 1893, the Republic of Hawai`i was established; it lasted until 1898, when the United States annexed the islands as a coaling station for ships and the US government claimed more than 1.8 million acres of Hawaiian land for military use. Hawai`i was annexed despite opposition from Native Hawaiians and became a US territory in 1900. The plantation owners no longer had to pay tariffs.

In 1959, Hawai`i became the fiftieth state.

Native Hawaiians believe that the 1893 overthrow of the kingdom illegally expropriated their land and denied their rights. Today, Native Hawaiians support a sovereignty movement that would give them the same federal recognition as Native Americans. There are several sovereignty organizations that support a range of solutions, from restoring the monarchy to outright independence from outside rule (the United States). Included within the sovereignty movement are improved land rights for Native Hawaiians. The Hawaiian governor and senators recognize and promote Hawaiian sovereignty.

Cultural Perspectives

Kapu

Native Hawaiian laws prior to European contact revolved around *kapu*, a system of laws and regulations that separated the sacred from the common, the inferior classes from royalty, and men from women. Spatial segregation was common. Many *kapu* laws revolved around treatment of the chiefs, such as not having one's head higher, not gazing into a chief's eyes, and not wearing the royal red or yellow colored feathers. Other *kapu* taboos involved food: Women were forbidden to eat bananas, coconuts, or pork.

Since the foreigners did not practice *kapu* and did not suffer its consequences, King Kamehameha I was obligated in 1819 to end the *kapu* system. He did this by ceremonially eating the forbidden foods with women. The loss of the *kapu* taboos was instrumental in breaking the Hawaiian belief system and in their accepting Christianity.

Kapu, as used today on Hawai`i, often means "No trespassing," and it can be seen on signs forbidding entry into areas (photo 20.5).

Hawaiian Diet

The traditional Hawaiian diet was based on seafood and local foods—coconut, bananas, breadfruit, taro, and yams—some of which were imported during the initial Hawaiian migrations. The staples of the diet were fish and starches, such as **poi** (made from taro). The diet was low in fat, making the Hawaiians genetically predisposed to store fat for times of scarcity, which may

account for the disastrous effect of the current diet on the native population.

The current Native Hawaiian lifestyle and foods differ from the traditional and are reflected in the native body. Today, the Hawaiian native diet includes fatty, processed foods rich in white flour and sugar, which are poorly adapted to the native lifestyle or genetic disposition to store fat. A recent study found that one in four Hawaiian adults are obese, more than 60 percent of the obese are among the Native Pacific Islanders. Their lifespan is much shorter than that of the mainland population, due to high rates of diabetes, hypertension, stroke, and cardiovascular disease. For example, the prevalence of diabetes among the native population surpasses that of the rest of the US population. Hawaiians who eat a culturally appropriate traditional diet are healthier than when adopting a Western diet. Studies also reveal that Hawaiians today lack access to fresh produce and seafood, making a traditional diet difficult for natives to reclaim. Crossover foods, such as saimin, the Hawaiian version of Japanese ramen, have influenced the Hawaiian diet.

Hawaiian fast food is saimin—a ramen soup with fish stock and garnishes, such as scrambled eggs, tofu, green onions, fish, and meat. Spam is the most popular saimin garnish in Hawai`i.

Spam is Hawai`i's comfort food, and Hawaiians eat about six million cans annually, which equates to six cans per person. In fact, it is so popular that it is often stolen from grocery stores; many retailers have responded by putting the cans in plastic cases under lock and key. Spam became a popular imported food among Hawaiians during World War II, before refrigeration was common (Spam has a long shelf life). Spam can be served with saimin, musubi—similar to a sushi roll—and with

eggs and rice for breakfast (photo 20.6). The nutritional content of Spam, high in saturated fat and sodium, accounts for some of the native Hawaiian weight and health problems.

Land Ownership

Since the arrival of Europeans, Native Hawaiians, like American tribal indigenous, have lost control of their homelands. But unlike the Native Americans, the Hawaiians are not tribal and so have not been recognized as a nation and or granted the rights of the tribal indigenous. This has led to a prolonged debate about Hawaiian native rights, sovereignty, and land ownership.

Hawaiian royalty controlled all land, but it was used by all in a sustainable system of communal tenure. Fee-simple land was unknown, but commoners cultivated "their" land, and assumed a collective "ownership" in which inhabitants shared their production. Natural boundaries divided the land into narrow strips that reached from the mountaintops to the beach (*ahupua`a*), and presented each farmer a variety of land types and a degree of self-sufficiency. Oceanside land offered fish. The shallows were converted into fishponds, and the bottomlands into taro patches; the uplands were used for dryland crops, and the mountainside for wooded products.

During the first half of the nineteenth century many natives died after contact with European diseases, the subsistent economy evolved into one of international trade, royalty sought the imported luxuries brought by Europeans, and many natives were leaving their land and migrating to the thriving cities of Lahaina and Honolulu. All of these shifts were borne on the back of the commoner, whose place in society worsened. Pressure built to modify land tenure from the native feudal-like practice to Western ownership. Gradually, foreigners gained access to the land, at first through grants from the king, but later through intermarriage and laws.

In 1848, the Western missionaries convinced the king to enact the **Great Mahele** (land reform) that redistributed land ownership. Although the Great Mahele was meant to keep land out of the hands of foreigners, it resulted in severing the rights to land for the Hawaiians. Land went from communal "ownership" by the king and chiefs to a commodity of private ownership by Western land titles. Although provisions were made for granting land to native commoners, few were able to prove claims. Westerners imposed their legal structure on land ownership and made it even more difficult for Hawaiians to gain land access. Although westerners comprised less than two thousand people during the second half of the nineteenth century, they acquired the vast majority of Hawaiian lands. By 1893, foreigners controlled 90 percent of the land.

By the time Hawai`i became a state, fewer than one hundred people owned half the land, and Native Hawaiians owned only 4 percent. The huge plantation estates of deceased *haole* (Caucasian) owners were kept intact through trusts that effectively froze land ownership. Trust land remained with the trusts either as plantations or leased residential lots.

Most plantations are now gone and converted to residential lots and resort communities. The powerful estates and trusts have developed despite vigorous objections from local residents. Estates sell to politicians, who rezone the land from agricultural to resort (thereby increasing its value tremendously) and then flip the permitted land to developers for huge profits. During the beginning of the twenty-first century, several land deal corruption and injustice lawsuits have been filed.

The major estates have tried to maintain title to their property, lease it out long-term, and then renegotiate at much higher rates than the previous lease. Between 1950 and 1960, 80 percent of all residential land on O`ahu was leasehold. The leasehold practice slowed island development. Commercial development was stymied, because the estates would not sell the land and the costs of development were much higher than if the land was owned.

In 1967, the state legislature passed the **Hawai`i Land Reform Act**—allowing leasehold conversion to fee simple (full private ownership) based on market value. The reform act influenced the corporate development of Waikīkī. Corporations needed fee-simple ownership to amortize their high-rise investments. However, the act was unable to break the trusts on most residential land. Still the government and seventy-two private landowners owned 95 percent of all land (map 20.3; table 20.1). When long-term leases expired on suburban lots, the renegotiated leases escalated from $175 to $12,000–$18,000 annually for the land, excluding structures. Many longtime occupants who owned their houses could no longer afford the land rent and were forced to move.

Amended in 1975, the Land Reform Act stated that the breakup of the trusts attacked "certain perceived evils of concentrated property ownership." Thus ended the monopoly, because the large landowners were forced to convert the land to fee simple and sell to the inhabitants. The amendment allowed all residential lands to convert their leasehold, but courtroom battles still often decide land ownership conversion. Meanwhile, large developments of estate lands are still being pursued, often to the detriment of the native people, the land, and sustainable precepts.

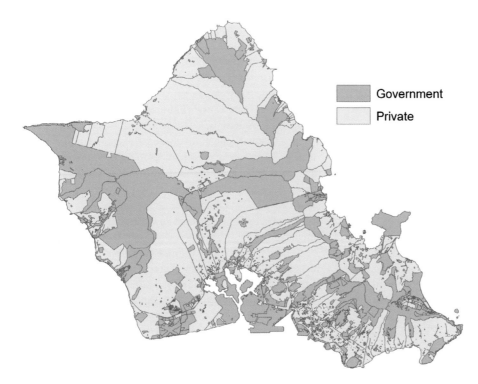

Government
Private

MAP 20.3. *Ahupua`a* Ownership of Land on O`ahu. Prior to European arrival, ownership was feudal in structure. It divided land in pie-shaped pieces from the tops of mountains to the sea. Many of the current landholdings still show the *ahupua`a* boundaries and divisions, but one-fifth of the land belongs to eight companies or estates, and the government remains a large landowner.

BOX 20.5   BIG LANDOWNERS

The state and federal government are the biggest landowners across the islands. But large private holding have long been part of the story. For decades land ownership was largely in the hands of the "Big Five" families, many descending from the missionary families: Castle & Cooke, Alexander & Baldwin, C. Brewer, Amfac, and Theo H. Davies and Co. Alexander & Baldwin were missionary families involved in sugarcane plantations and later in shipping and real estate. They are still involved in sugar cultivation and shipping and are still major landowners (table 20.1). The Robinson family obtained land early in 1864 when they purchased the entire island Ni`ihau for $10,000. Each of the companies has evolved:

The newly rich such as Larry Ellison and Steve Case, the owner of Grove Farm listed in table 20.1, who made their fortunes with the rise of the internet are only some of the recent uberwealthy buying up land in the island.

TABLE 20.1. Top Ten Landowners, 2012

Landowner	Holdings (acres)
State of Hawai`i	1,540,000
Federal Government	531,000
Bishop Estate (Kamehameha Schools)	363,000
Alexander & Baldwin	113,000
Parker Ranch	107,000
Larry Ellison	90,240
Moloka`i Ranch	58,000
Robinson Family (Kaua`i)	51,000
Robinson Family (Ni`ihau)	46,000
Grove Farm	36,000

Native Hawaiians have lost control of their islands. Congress first addressed the native loss of land in the Hawaiian Homes Commission Act of 1920, commonly called the Homestead Act, which promised ninety-nine-year homestead land leases for $1 annually to natives who had at least 50 percent Hawaiian blood. The act conveyed second-class land while still protecting the sugar barons' acreage. There was little support for building homes on the homestead land or for selling the land to others. A few Hawaiians retained ownership of good farmland as a *kuleana* (rights received upon the Great Mahele land reform), but many were unable to retain their rights through the years. Hence, both rural and urban homestead land was seldom awarded to the more than two hundred thousand eligible Hawaiians.

By the 1960s, the home commission and its lands were transferred from federal hands to the state. By 1975, less than 15 percent of the 190,000 acres of land controlled by homestead laws was leased to Native Hawaiians, and since that time land has been released so slowly that lawsuits have been filed claiming breaches of trust.

Homesteaded land is both rural and urban, and the demand varies for the two. Rural homesteaded land is meant to be farmed traditionally, but few Hawaiians still farm, and the forty-acre parcels are second-class farmland in undesirable areas. Few of the families granted parcels actually farm; instead, they lease it to larger plantations for stipends. On the other hand, the demand for Homestead Act urban land has thousands of applicants waiting up to fifty years to gain access, although building on the land is still onerously difficult: No mortgages are allowed and infrastructure is slow to develop. For example, in 1986 Big Island homesteaders were granted land, but they still lacked running water in 1999. They relied on hauling water and rainwater catchment.

The 50 percent blood requirement for the Homestead Act has bitterly divided the community. In 1999, a multiethnic group filed a lawsuit that challenged the Homestead Act on the basis of racial discrimination. The plaintiffs believe the homesteaded lands should benefit the entire population and not just Native Hawaiians. If won, it would shut out the Hawaiians who have been waiting for decades. The congressional Akaka Bill answered these lawsuits by giving Hawaiians the same protected status as Native Americans or Alaskan Natives. It failed to become law in the 111th Congress in 2009/2010. The issue of federal recognition of native Hawaiian remains contentious and unresolved.

Population, Immigration, and Diversity

In 1960, just after statehood, the total population of the islands was 633,000, which more than doubled to 1,428,557 in 2016. The indigenous population declined after Europeans arrived, and subsequently many other ethnic groups have arrived.

The island population was approximately three lakhs in 1788. By 1830, the population of pure Hawaiians had dropped to 130,000 and declined to 57,000 by 1872 before growing again. Today, there are perhaps eighty thousand pure Native Hawaiians, although about 250,000 claim Hawaiian blood.

Hawai`i's population is one of the most diverse in the United States. Diversity grew during the sugarcane era when there was a need for laborers, who were imported from China, Japan, the Philippines, and Portugal. Today, the state has 18 percent foreign born; another 16 percent are native-born Americans who have at least one immigrant parent. Foreign-born residents represent a vital share of the state's labor force in many sectors: more than 40 percent of workers in both the mining and agriculture industries are immigrants.

BOX 20.6 MOLOKA`I RANCH

Moloka`i Ranch, occupying the west end of the island emerged in 1897 when a business group bought up seventy thousand acres and leased another thirty thousand from the government. Over the years, a succession of owners and lessors controlled the ranch, raising cattle and growing pineapple. In the 1970s, about fourteen thousand acres were sold to developers for low-impact tourism and residential development; otherwise the ranch has remained intact. It covers 35 percent of the island and has twenty miles of coastline. In 2001, the ranch was sold again, this time to Singapore-based BIL International, with plans to build luxury developments for wealthy Chinese. The next year BIL purchased La`au Point and added it to the Moloka`i investment portfolio. By mid-2006, the company announced plans to build two hundred luxury home sites on La`au Point at the southwestern end of the island. Immediately a resistance movement arose. Almost every home on the island, total population less than seventy-five hundred, with the exception of those who work for the ranch, posted signs opposing the development (photo 20.7).

Moloka`i is the island least affected by development or tourism and is the only publicly held island where Native Hawaiians are the majority. The island residents are not wealthy. Their rights to land extend back sometimes to *ahupua`a*. They often live in small homes on the coast or have homesteaded in the interior. Unemployment has been a problem since the pineapple plantations closed in the 1980s. The residents feel that an invasion of wealthy tourists would ruin their lifestyle, create a rift between haves and have-nots, desecrate sacred lands, and

PHOTO 20.7. Opposition to La`au Development. Moloka`i residents were united in opposition to the development on Moloka`i Ranch. The island is the only publicly held island to remain "natural" and has a majority of Native Hawaiians, who saw the development as the end of their unique position on the islands.

also threaten an already scarce water supply for the agricultural homesteaders.

In 2008, facing stiff local resistance and a global recession impacting wealthy Asian households, the company closed the ranch. In 2017, it was on the market for $260 million.

Hawai`i is one of only four US states in which residents of European ancestry do not form a majority, and it is home to large Asian immigrant communities, including Filipino, Japanese, Chinese, and Koreans, and some Indians. The largest ethnic group (in 2016) is Asian with about 37 percent, whites (*haole*) 25 percent, Native Hawaiian (*Kanaka Maoli*) 10 percent, and Hispanic 10 percent, while blacks are 2 percent of the total population. The high degree of ethnic intermarriage is revealed in the almost 24 percent who identifies himself or herself as multiracial.

Most Native Hawaiians have mixed blood. Those who identify as Hawaiian are the poorest, have the worst health statistics (mortality, suicide, and disease), high dropout rate, highest unemployment rate, and highest incarceration rate. Only a few have gained the right to reclaim land.

Urban Trends

Honolulu
(2016 MSA 992,000)

Honolulu has been the primary city of the islands since 1872. Honolulu became the Pacific's largest city because of the good harbor on a dry, leeward coast with access to freshwater. Eight of the ten largest cities are on the Isle of O`ahu; most are suburbs to Honolulu. Three-quarters of all Hawaiian residents live in Honolulu County. The largest city off of O`ahu is Hilo on the Big Island. Hilo is one-eighth the size of Honolulu, at forty-three thousand.

Honolulu and Lahaina fought to be the dominant city during the nineteenth century. Lahaina was the capital and the center of whaling activity from 1840 to 1855, but by 1850 Honolulu replaced Lahaina as the capital.

Honolulu sprawls across the low-lying land from Waikīkī to Pearl Harbor and the Ewa Plain and then up the mountain valleys, where master-planned residential communities have replaced fields of sugarcane, taro, bananas, or rice. Many residents now favor a sustainable local produce economy that will halt further development in favor of agricultural land.

But today much of the land has been converted to dense urban use (photo 20.8)—the density exceeds sixty thousand per square mile in some parts of Honolulu—complete with urban problems, such as pollution and bumper-to-bumper traffic. Residents of sprawling bedroom towns spend three to four hours each day commuting to work in Honolulu. Gridlock is common.

PHOTO 20.8. Honolulu Skyline. Honolulu is the largest city in the islands, complete with high-rise canyons and monumental traffic problems.
Source: iStock/sorincolac

Honolulu has been called the New York of the Pacific and shares urban features, such as skyscrapers, traffic, and a wealthy population. One in eight Honolulu households is worth more than $1 million, excluding their home. The city has the tenth-highest number of millionaire families in the nation. The average cost of a home in Hawai`i is $650,000, well beyond the means of most.

In Honolulu, one in ten of the population lives below the poverty level, and several thousand are homeless. The homeless remain invisible to most tourists, removed from the tourist areas and parks, but a walk outside the tourist areas can reveal a seamier side to the city. Affordable housing is needed on the islands.

Waikīkī, Honolulu's main beach, receives the most tourism. The beach was a marshy wetland zone filled with rice paddies until hotels were able to own land and Waikīkī was drained and developed commercially. Today, high rises block any view of the beach, except along narrow tourist access points. The once-beckoning Hawaiian paradise is gone, replaced by high-end hotels offering wireless Internet service and a simulacrum of traditional Hawaiian culture, from surfboard rides to hula shows and ukulele lessons.

Honolulu's continued growth has caused environmental and planning problems that need repair. Honolulu has been recognized for some sustainable attributes, such as its air quality, local food, and agriculture.

In 2008, the city and state together created its first sustainability plan *Hawai`i 2050*. It is the most comprehensive statewide planning process in more than thirty years. The plan has prioritized the following nine goals to achieve by the year 2020:

1. increase affordable housing opportunities for households up to 140% of median income;
2. strengthen public education;
3. reduce reliance on fossil (carbon-based) fuels;
4. increase recycling, reuse, and waste reduction strategies;
5. develop a more diverse and resilient economy;
6. create a sustainability ethic;
7. increase production and consumption of local foods and products, particularly agriculture;
8. provide access to long-term care and elderly housing; and
9. preserve and perpetuate the "Kanaka Maoli" and island cultural values.

The Economy

After European contact, the island economy developed from 1800 to 1835 as a shipping stopover exporting fragrant sandalwood that was stripped from the forests until little remained. In the 1840s, Hawai`i was the headquarters for hundreds of whaling ships from New England that cruised the Pacific for two to four years at a time. By 1865, whales were becoming scarce and petroleum began replacing whale oil. But during the whaling era, Honolulu was established as the Pacific core city. *Haole* merchants controlled the land and set about consolidating the plantations that would become the next economy.

The agricultural domination of Hawai`i began in the pineapple and sugar plantations of the mid-nineteenth century, when big companies, especially the Big Five, gained control over the sugar industry. Pineapple and sugar agriculture were the state's leading economic activities from 1880 until statehood in 1959, a time when jet planes singlehandedly transformed the agricultural economy into the tourism economy. Tourism grew exponentially on the islands until it became the leading economic activity.

BOX 20.7   NATIONAL PARKS: THE USS ARIZONA MEMORIAL

The USS Arizona Memorial, at Pearl Harbor in Honolulu, Hawai`i, marks the final resting place of 1,102 of the 1,177 sailors and Marines killed on the USS Arizona during the Japanese attack on Pearl Harbor on December 7, 1941.

The Pearl Harbor area was designated a national historic landmark in 1964 for its strategic importance related to the US annexation of Hawai'i, and for the December 7, 1941, Japanese attack during World War II.

The memorial, built in 1962, is visited by more than two million people annually (photo 20.9).

It is only accessible by boat. The memorial design was constructed over the hull of the sunken battleship without touching it. The memorial has three main parts: entry, assembly room, and shrine. The central assembly room features seven large open windows on either wall and ceiling, to commemorate the date of the attack. Rumor says the twenty-one windows symbolically represent a twenty-one-gun salute or twenty-one Marines standing at eternal parade rest over the tomb of the fallen.

The memorial commemorates all those lost during the attack on Pearl Harbor and also serves as a symbol of peace and reminder of the healing that is still ongoing. It is also an active US military cemetery.

Every US Navy, Coast Guard, and Merchant Marine ship entering Pearl Harbor participates in the tradition of "manning the rails": personnel serving on these ships stand at attention at the ship's guard rails and salute the USS *Arizona* Memorial as their ship glides into port.

In 2008, an Executive Order established World War II Valor in the Pacific National Monument to tell the broader story of the Pacific War. These three sites include the USS Arizona Memorial, sites in the Aleutians Islands in Alaska and Newell, California.

PHOTO 20.9. The USS *Arizona* *Memorial* **in Pearl Harbor, Honolulu, Hawai`i.**

Source: iStock/HaizhanZheng

The Primary Sector

Agriculture

About one-tenth of island land is arable. But rich soil and a frost-free and ample rainfall environment enabled Hawai`i to grow tropical crops that are almost impossible to grow on the mainland. Agriculture, most importantly sugarcane and pineapples, was the leading Hawaiian economic sector until the 1960s.

Both sugarcane and pineapple production fell victim to high land and labor costs. Sugarcane all but disappeared as a crop in the 1970s, and in 2008, Del Monte pulled out of pineapple production. Dole and Maui pineapples are still producing, but pineapple is no longer among the top Hawaiian agricultural commodities.

Pineapple flourishes in the red volcanic soil; it requires less water than sugar and therefore no irrigation. The first European settlers found pineapple growing wild, but the variety grown today, Smooth Cayenne, was introduced in 1888. The pineapple industry grew under the direction of James Dole, cousin to Sanford Dole, president of the Republic of Hawai`i. After an initial investment in O`ahu, James purchased the island of Lāna`i in 1922 and established the largest pineapple plantation in the world, more than two hundred thousand acres. During the 1920s, Lāna`i produced up to 75 percent of the world's pineapples. But the Great Depression and cheaper Asian imports caused pineapple sales to decline, and the Dole family sold its holdings. By 2006, Hawai`i produced only 2 percent of the world's pineapples. Most pineapples are now grown in Thailand, the Philippines, Brazil, China, India, and Costa Rica.

In 1835, as the whaling industry waned, Europeans began sugarcane plantations. Cane requires abundant sunshine, water, and labor; however, ample water and labor were often unavailable. Both O`ahu and Maui improvised watering systems to grow the cane, and Chinese and Japanese laborers were imported to augment the native workforce.

Cane was grown on all the islands, but O`ahu took the lead in 1879, when James Campbell added artificial fertilizer and drilled for water on the dry plains of Ewa (near Pearl Harbor). Soon irrigated sugar was grown on the dry leeward sides of Maui and Kaua`i.

At one time, the plantations employed up to one-sixth of the native population, but as so many had died of European diseases, the plantation owners looked to Asia for laborers.

Although sugar was grown in the 1840s, it became a lucrative crop during the Civil War when the Union was unable to access sugar from the southern states. The 1876 Treaty of Reciprocity with the United States removed tariffs for sugar planters and gave the US military rights to Pearl Harbor. Rapid expansion of the industry followed, and westerners alienated most land for plantations. Sugar plantation profits were the underlying reason for the evolution of power from Hawaiians to the *haole* plantation owners.

Sugar production was highest from the end of World War II until the late 1980s. By 2003, sugar production had dropped from a 1970 high of 10.5 million tons to 2 million tons. As

a comparison, the major sugar producer in the world in the twenty-first century, Brazil, produced 22.75 million tons in 2003. Only Kaua`i and Maui still grow sugar. Sugar refineries during the twentieth century transferred from the plantation to the mainland in San Francisco Bay, California.

Sugar plantations were a boon to the economic wealth of the owners, but they destroyed the land. The sugar mills degraded forests, natural resources, and water. The mills are also a cause of air, water, and waste pollution.

In the 1880s, sugarcane replaced coffee as the primary Big Island crop, but small boutique coffee plantations have become popular investments in the twenty-first century. The distinct climate of the Kona coast of the Big Island is perfect for growing coffee. The coastal hills are the only region that receives more rain in summer than winter, and it is warmer and drier than other windward locations. Today, tiny independent coffee plantations are at the mercy of price fluctuations. There are about 650 small coffee farms that average three acres. A total of about thirty-five hundred acres produces about 3.8 million pounds annually. Today, coffee is mostly a tourist trade item centered on the small (two-by-twenty-mile) Kona district, along with a small plantation on Moloka`i.

Taro, the source for poi, arrived with the Polynesian migrations. But taro production and consumption almost halted during the plantation era. Recently, farmers returned to taro production in an effort to revive traditional and nutritious Hawaiian foods (photo 20.10).

Fishing

Traditionally, fish has been the dominant Hawaiian protein. Ancient Hawaiians used the coral reefs to build fish ponds— an early method of fish farming—where juvenile fish grew to full size and provided year-round food. The fish fed the

PHOTO 20.10. Taro Growing at Hanalei, Kaua`i. Taro has returned as a crop grown by native farmers on small plots of land. It is important within the traditional Hawaiian diet. The leaves are used to wrap meats and the root to make poi, the starch staple of the islands.
Source: L. Czaban

native population, but they were insufficient for large exports, although *haoles* developed an export economy.

Canneries complemented commercial fishing until the 1980s. After 1970 canneries closed, and the tuna market shifted from canned tuna to fresh fish. Complicating the fishery was confusion between the commercial fishery and the native fishery.

Natives are allowed traditional gathering and fishing rights, and many natives fish and sell a part of their catch to offset expenses or are obligated to share their catch with others. Living on islands, it would seem that Hawaiians should eat plenty of fish, but fish have become too expensive for many local residents. Fish have become the product of commercial deep-sea fishing expeditions rather than part of the Hawaiians' daily diet.

By the twenty-first century, overfishing along the major and northwestern islands has been a problem, and commercial enterprises are under increasing pressure to live within quotas, while management of fish stocks is failing. Commercial and tourist enterprises have limited access for the natives.

The Secondary Sector

Energy

Unlike mainland states, Hawai`i does not have access to fuel sources such as large rivers to produce hydropower. The islands do not have indigenous oil, natural gas, or coal resources. Such fuels need to be imported, which Hawai`i is heavily dependent on to meet its energy demand. This also makes energy a more expensive commodity.

Since 2000, the state has made reducing nonrenewable energy and diversifying renewables an important goal. In 2010, alternative sources accounted for 5 percent of the current energy source; today, nearly 26 percent of the energy used by customers of the Hawaiian Electric Companies come from renewable energy resources.

In 2004, lawmakers passed legislation to support alternative energy, with Maui endorsing and leading the program. From 2010 to 2015, Hawai`i's renewable energy use doubled, which further motivated the state to be even more progressive around renewable energy. In 2016, the state passed legislation that mandates that all of the state's electricity come from renewable sources no later than 2045, enacting the first hundred percent renewable energy standard in the United States.

Many of the islands now have a diversity of renewable energy sources. For example, nearly 40 percent of the electricity generated by Hawaiian Electric Light (the Big Island) was fueled by renewable resources, including wind, solar, biomass, biofuel, and hydro energy. On Maui, Maui Electric generated 25 percent from renewables; on O`ahu it was 11 percent.

One of the unique ways to create energy in Hawai`i is to take advantage of its lack of a continental shelf. Researchers are studying a process called ocean thermal energy conversion (OTEC) as an alternative way to produce electricity. OTEC uses the difference in temperature of cold seawater and the warm surface to cool buildings. In 2015, Hawai`i was the first US state to launch a power plant harnessing the deep ocean temperatures. It is a small prototype project, producing energy that can power about 120 Hawaiian homes for a year. Whether

PHOTO 20.11. Dukes Market in Waikiki, Honolulu. Duke's Market is a favorite spot for tourists shopping for nick knacks in Waikiki.
Source: iStock/jewhyte

BOX 20.8   GLOBAL CONNECTIONS: TOURISM

In 2017, nine million visitors came to Hawai`i. They spent $15.5 billion stimulating the local economy and providing $1.6 billion in state revenue. The tourist industry constitutes 21 percent of the entire economy. Hawai`i with its exotic image provides dreams and expectations for people all over the world including North America, Oceania, and Eurasia. Its distinct location means that the main sources of visitors are drawn from the United States, especially the western United States, as well as Japan (table 20.2). In coming years the number of Chinese visitors will no doubt rise substantially as the Hawaiian Tourism Authority actively promotes the islands as destinations for Chinese travelers.

TABLE 20.2. Tourists to Hawai`i, 2016

Region	Number of visitors (million)
US West	3.50
US East	1.80
Japan	1.48
Canada	0.51
Oceania	0.39
Korea	0.19
China	0.17
Europe	0.14

this technology can scale to produce enough energy for the island is not certain.

The Tertiary Sector

For many years, the defense budget ruled the Hawaiian economy, and the military was based in the strategic mid-Pacific location. Today, federal defense funding remains important but less than nondefense spending (civilian agencies, Social Security, Medicare, and federal retirement distributions). Overall military spending has accounted for about 10 percent of the state's gross state product (GSP) since the 1980s. The military presence has also declined from 33 percent in 1960 to 10 percent of the current total population.

Tourism

Statehood, jet travel, and tourism all merged in 1959. Hawai`i's mid-ocean location was difficult for tourists to reach prior to commercial air travel. Even in 1959, the air trip to the islands from the mainland was eight and a half hours in a prop plane, but the Big Five plantation owners saw the future of tourism. Even as the ink dried on the state constitution, they were already planning new resorts to replace the agricultural plantations. In a few years, inexpensive and faster air travel shaped the middle-class, bigger-is-better tourist industry based on mass marketing.

As plantations were replaced with destination resorts, the Big Five also transformed from local *haole* owners to diversified global concerns, as did most of the businesses on the islands. Local sugar and pineapple plantations were replaced by global business, little of it owned by Hawaiian residents. Tourism became the raison d'être for the islands.

In 1950, only forty thousand tourists came to the islands. Tourism grew from the 1970s average of about 1.5 million visitors annually to 9 million in 2016. Tourists spent more than $15.5 billion, which added $1.82 billion in state tax revenue (photo 20.11). Tourism employs 190,000 jobs.

Some companies pursue high-price tourism over mass tourism. Catering to the uber-wealthy is not new; before jet planes only the wealthy could afford island travel. The wealthy population provides more profit than the slim margins of discount travel. When the Japanese economy was healthy in the 1970s and 1980s, the Japanese were an important element in the tourist economy. Their average spending was three times the average *haole* mainlander. Fewer Japanese came, but they spent more money. On the other hand, mass tourism focuses on economies of scale that rely on slim economic margins, leaving no room for ecological or social considerations.

A tourist economy alone is problematic.

A Sustainable Future

Hawaiian environmental issues are a microcosm of the world situation. What is the carrying capacity of the islands? Only so many people can live on a limited land mass. Groups and individuals are beginning to invest in sustainable and renewable energy systems that address the environmental ills but still neglect the multiple societal ills on the islands.

The turn to tourism has proved successful and provided but only for the short term. The total dependence on tourism and fossil fuels is a questionable formula in the twenty-first century. The islands, and especially Honolulu, face the same urban ills as the rest of the nation—drugs, high crime rates, lack of good water, a growing prison population, and failing educational systems—as well as their own special ills. The islands' isolation from other landmasses, their reliance on imported food, and their dependence on tourism is unsustainable

The *Hawai`i 2050* Sustainability Plan listed the following challenges for a sustainable future:

- population growth on limited land;
- loss of traditional Kanaka Maoli culture;
- environmental damage;

- energy dependency;
- affordability—can the next generation afford to live on the islands?;
- quality of the oceans;
- vulnerability to climate change;
- deterioration of public infrastructure; and
- fragile island ecosystems.

A monumental island problem is the lack of room because of the growing population. Affordable housing and public infrastructure maintenance are only nominally addressed, and growth and congestion are seldom addressed for the good of all.

Native Hawaiians especially have suffered from this injustice because of past unjust policies and actions. Many Hawaiians believe that in the nineteenth century Native Hawaiian power was usurped. As a result, Native Hawaiian groups have formed activist organizations to claim sovereignty and to access land. The activist stance has had some small successes but has not returned them to their rightful place on the islands. Since the turn of the century, the homestead commission has adopted a master plan that accelerates native homestead settlement. The

return to the land, often emulating the traditional *ahupua`a* system, has created islands of hope and has reinvigorated the sense of place for the indigenous population, but becoming a central tourism destination has disrupted any sense of balance.

Modern transportation allows places like Hawai`i to be accessible to more people, but at the cost of dependence on tourism. Tourism provides almost one-third of all jobs in Hawai`i and more than one-quarter of the economy, but it is also a critical environmental issue. On the one hand, the islands seek to grow their tourist base, but on the other, tourism has caused and will continue to cause overcrowding, congestion, pollution, and water shortages.

However, many Hawaiians are working toward maintaining the native habitats and species unique to the locale by safeguarding water from pollution, developing renewable energy sources, and protecting land from thoughtless human encroachments (photo 20.12). Keeping the island's environment healthy necessitates a holistic approach and requires an honest examination of how Western ideas impact indigenous cultures. Maintaining the island paradise of the Aloha State requires supporting sustainability.

PHOTO 20.12. Wind Turbines near Upolu Point, Big Island, Hawai`i.
Source: iStock/Dmitri Kotchetov

Questions for Discussion

1. When was Hawaiʻi settled and from where did the first inhabitants migrate?

2. Who were the first Americans to settle in Hawaiʻi and what were their interests? How did their interests change over time?

3. What role has sugar played in the evolution of Hawaiʻi?

4. How has the economy of Hawaiʻi changed since World War II? What were important factors in the change?

5. How can tourism be maintained at a sustainable cost to the environment?

6. What is the basis of claims for independence by Native Hawaiians? How does their status differ from that of Native Americans?

7. Should Native Hawaiians be treated like Native Americans and be given special status and opportunities? Why or why not?

8. How has land ownership affected the distribution of wealth and population on the islands?

9. What are the problems Hawaiʻi faces in achieving sustainability? How does tourism play into these problems?

10. In what ways has the state been making advances in sustainability?

Suggested Readings

Allen, H. G. *The Betrayal of Liliuokalani, Last Queen of Hawaiʻi, 1838–1917*. Honolulu, Hawaiʻi: Mutual Publishing, 1982.

Budnick, R. *Stolen Kingdom: An American Conspiracy*. Honolulu, Hawaiʻi: Aloha Press, 1992.

Carlquist, S. *Hawaiʻi: A Natural History*. Lawai, Kauaʻi, Hawaiʻi: National Tropical Botanical Garden, 1994.

Coffman, T. *Nation Within: The Story of America's Annexation of the Nation of Hawaiʻi*. Kaneohe, Hawaiʻi: Tom Coffman/Epicenter, 1998.

Cuddihy, L. W., and C. P. Stone. *Alteration of Native Hawaiian Vegetation: Effects of Humans, their Activities and Introductions*. Honolulu: University of Hawaiʻi Cooperative National Park Resources Studies Unit, 1990.

Eyre, D. L. *By Wind, by Wave: An Introduction to Hawaiʻi's Natural History*. Honolulu, Hawaiʻi: Bess Press, 2000.

Finney, Ben R. "Anomalous Westerlies, El Niño, and the Colonization of Polynesia." *American Anthropologist* 87, no. 1 (March 1985): 9–26.

Fuchs, L. H. *Hawaiʻi Pono: A Social History*. San Diego, Calif.: Harcourt Brace Jovanovich, 1984.

Haas, M., ed. *Multicultural Hawaiʻi: The Fabric of a Multiethnic Society*. New York: Garland, 1998.

Herman, R. D. K. "The Aloha State: Place Names and the Anti-Conquest of Hawaiʻi." *Annals of the Association of American Geographers* 89, no. 1 (March 1999): 76–102.

Hulten, J. J. "Land Reform in Hawaiʻi." *Land Economics* 42, no. 2 (May 1966): 235–40.

Jones, S. B. "Geography and Politics in the Hawaiian Islands." *Geographical Review* 28, no. 2 (April 1938): 193–213.

Ladefoged, T. N. "Spatial Similarities and Change in Hawaiian Architecture: The Expression of Ritual Offering and Kapu in Luakini Heiau, Residential Complexes, and Houses." *Asian Perspectives: Journal of Archaeology for Asia and the Pacific* 37, no. 1 (Spring 1998): 59–73.

Levy, N. M. "Native Hawaiian Land Rights." *California Law Review* 63, no. 4 (July 1975): 848–85.

Mlot, C. "In Hawaiʻi, Taking Inventory of a Biological Hot Spot." *Science* 269, no. 5222 (July 21, 1995): 322–23.

Morgan, J. *Hawaiʻi: A Geography*. Boulder, Colo.: Westview Press, 1983.

Osorio, J. K. K. *Dismembering Lahui: A History of the Hawaiian Nation to 1887*. Honolulu: University of Hawaiʻi Press, 2002.

Pooley, S. G. "Hawaiʻi's Marine Fisheries: Some History, Long-Term Trends, and Recent Developments." *Marine Fisheries Review* 55, no. 2 (Spring 1993): 7–19.

Silva, N. K. *Aloha Betrayed: Native Hawaiian Resistance to American Colonialism*. Durham, N.C.: Duke University Press, 2004.

Spickard, P., J. L. Rondilla, and D. Hippolite Wright, eds. *Pacific Diaspora: Island Peoples in the United States and across the Pacific*. Honolulu: University of Hawaiʻi Press, 2002.

Taylor, F. J., D. W. Eyre, and E. M. Welty. *From Land and Sea: The Story of Castle and Cooke of Hawaiʻi*. San Francisco, Calif.: Chronicle Books, 1976.

Tayman, J. *The Colony: The Harrowing True Story of the Exiles of Molokaʻi*. New York: Scribner, 2006.

Trask, H. *From a Native Daughter: Colonialism and Sovereignty in Hawaiʻi*. Monroe, Maine: Common Courage, 1993.

Wang, C., L. Abbott, A. K. Goodbody, and W. Hui. "Ideal Body Image and Health Status in Low-Income Pacific Islanders." *Journal of Cultural Diversity* 9, no. 1 (Spring 2002): 12–22.

Woodcock, D. W., ed. *Hawaiʻi: New Geographies*. Honolulu: Department of Geography, University of Hawaiʻi-Manoa, 1999.

Wooden, W. S. *Return to Paradise: Continuity and Change in Hawaiʻi*. Lanham, MD: University Press of America, 1995.

Internet Sources

Hawaii's Sustainability Plan, at http://www.oahumpo.org/wp-content/uploads/2013/02/Hawaii2050_Plan_FINAL.pdf

Hawaii's renewable energy, at https://www.hawaiianelectric.com/clean-energy-hawaii/clean-energy-facts/renewable-energy-sources.U.S. Geological Survey. "Vog: A Volcanic Hazard," May 29, 1996, at http://hvo.wr.usgs.gov/volcanowatch/1996/96_05_29.html

U.S. Geological Survey. "Once a Big Island, Maui County Now Four Small Islands," April 10, 2003, at http://hvo.wr.usgs.gov/volcanowatch/2003/03_04_10.html

Economic Research Service. State Fact Sheet: Hawaiʻi, at http://www.ers.usda.gov/StateFacts/HI.htm

Spam (read more about stolen spam), at https://www.washingtonpost.com/news/morning-mix/wp/2017/10/19/spam-heists-in-hawaii-prompt-retailers-to-put-the-wildly-popular-mystery-meat-in-locked-cases/?utm_term=.9ea0ffb6da5c

Glossary

Note: Numbers in brackets following the definitions indicate the chapter where the term appears.

Aboriginal: In Canada, a person identified with a North American Indian, Métis, or Inuit group. [18]

abyss: The flat ocean floor found at the bottom of continental slopes. [20]

acculturation: Modification in a culture by adopting outside cultural traits. [16]

agglomeration: A concentration of economic activities in an industrial sector in a geographic area. [13]

aging in place: Living in one's longtime home as one ages. Said of the farming population in the Midwest and Great Plains. [14]

agribusiness: Agriculture based on commercial principles and advanced technology. Also, huge commercial farms owned by large and often vertically integrated corporations. [14]

allophone: An immigrant whose mother tongue or home language is neither English nor French. This term is used this way in Quebec. [4]

alluvial fan: A fan-shaped deposit of sediment located at the base of a mountain. [16]

alternative lifestyle: A mode or style of conducting one's life that is considerably removed from the generally perceived norm. [19]

Anglophone: An English-speaking person, especially in a region where two or more languages are spoken. (See **Francophone**.) [4]

antebellum: The period before a war; in the United States, before the Civil War. [9]

anthracite: Hard coal with high carbon content. Anthracite was mined in nineteenth-century Scranton, Pennsylvania, but little remains today. [8]

anthropocentric: Interpreting the world exclusively in terms of human values and experiences. Finding humans as the center of the universe, and basing all one's actions on furthering only human interests. [2]

Appalachian Regional Commission (ARC): Federal–state partnership formed in 1963 to increase jobs, improve infrastructure, and increase health care and education in Appalachia. [8]

aquifer: A permeable rock layer through which groundwater flows easily. [3]

archipelago: Any sea or broad sheet of water interspersed with many islands or with a group of islands. [18]

Army Corps of Engineers: Part of the US Army responsible for engineering services, including planning and design of infrastructure such as bridges, levees, and construction of military facilities. [11]

arroyo (*Sp.* "dry creek"): A steep-sided gully or wash that fills with water after a heavy rain. Found in semiarid to arid areas. [16]

artesian spring: A spring that emits water from underground pressure. [10]

assimilation: The loss of all ethnic traits and complete blending into the host society. [8]

atoll: A low coral reef that surrounds an interior body of water called a lagoon. Atolls form around the fringes of sunken volcanoes. [20]

baby boom: The generation of people born after World War II (from 1945 until 1964). [4]

badlands: Lands eroded by wind and water into small gullies stripped of vegetation and soil. Areas having intricately dissected topography resulting from fluvial erosion and characterized by high drainage density and steep, mostly barren side slopes with narrow interfluvial ridges. [14]

bald: Bare mountaintop. Especially in the Ozarks and Appalachians. [12]

Bald Knobbers: Vigilantes in the Ozarks during 1883–1889. They retaliated against marauders in the area by killing them, but it got out of hand and many murders were committed. [12]

bank: A shoal; a shallow area that is an extension of the continental shelf before it drops abruptly down the continental slope to the ocean floor. Fish can be abundant on the banks. [6]

barrier island: A long, narrow, sandy island separated from the mainland by a shallow lagoon or wetland, which protects the mainland from the open ocean. A sand body that is essentially parallel to the shore, the crest of which is above normal high-water level. For example, the string of islands along the shore of North Carolina known as the Outer Banks. [9]

basalt: A dense, fine-grained, dark-gray igneous rock, which breaks through the crust of the earth and erupts on the surface before solidifying as lava. [3]

basement rock: The crust of the earth below sedimentary deposits, often of Precambrian age. [7]

basin: A low area of land, generally surrounded by mountains. [16]

Basque: People from the western Pyrenees who moved to the Intermontane and practiced their native sheep raising. [16]

batholith: A large body of igneous rock, usually granite, that has been exposed by erosion of the overlying rock. [15]

bayou: A small, sluggish stream that cuts through the low, swampy land of a delta. [11]

Beltway: A high-speed highway that encircles or skirts an urban area. For example, the highway surrounding Washington, D.C. [7]

Bible Belt: Those sections of the United States, especially in the South and Midwest, where Protestant fundamentalism is widely practiced. [12]

bioaccumulation: Accumulation of toxic substances in lower food chains, then consumed by higher levels and increasing the amount of toxins. For example, humans at the top of the food chain eat contaminated fish that have high levels of mercury, and intake is faster than the rate of excretion. [17]

biome: A major regional biotic community consisting of plants, animals, and the prevailing climate. Terrestrial biomes include desert, grassland, tropical rainforest, deciduous and coniferous forests, and tundra. [3]

biomimicry: The process of emulating nature to design and produce products, systems, and buildings. [18]

bioregion (or **ecoregion**): A place defined by life-forms; a life-territory. An ecologically and geographically defined area that shares climate and geology, the main factors determining the distribution of plants and animals in the area. [1]

bioswale: A bioswale is a landscape element designed to concentrate or remove debris and pollution out of surface runoff water. A bioswale consists of a swaled drainage course with gently sloped sides which can be filled with vegetation or lined with rocks to slow down the velocity of stormwater runoff. Most bioswales will be placed on a slope such as the side of a roadway. Bioswales are beneficial in protecting surface water and local waterways from excessive pollution from stormwater runoff. [10]

birthrate: Number of people born as a percentage of the total population in any given period of time. [4]

bituminous: Second-hardest coal after anthracite. It is primarily used for making coke for use in steel making, and for burning in power plants. Bituminous coal accounts for an overwhelming percentage of the coal presently mined. Most comes from the Appalachian mines. [8]

blackwater rivers: Dark-water rivers found in the southern United States. They flow through swamps and wetlands and are colored by the tannins from decaying vegetation. [9]

bog: A peat-accumulating wetland that has no significant inflows or outflows and supports acid-loving mosses, particularly sphagnum, and heaths that may develop into peat. Water comes mostly from precipitation. Some shrubs (heath family) and evergreens grow in bogs. Minnesota's peatland region in the north-central part of the state has many examples of bogs. [3]

boll weevil: A beetle that feeds on and devastates cotton crops. An infestation of boll weevils in the 1920s ended cotton production in many southern states. [9]

boom and bust town: Town characterized by large jumps in population over a five- to ten-year construction period, after which the population settles to a lower level associated with the completed activities, such as mining or power plant operation. [15]

boreal forest (or **taiga**): High- to mid-latitude biome dominated by coniferous forest. Predominant vegetation of this biome is various species of spruce, fir, pine, and cedar. [3]

borough: An administrative unit of a city. In this book, borough is used in relation to New York City and the five boroughs (counties) that make up the city. [7]

bosque: Mesquite-cottonwood riparian forests found along the flood plains in Texas and the southwestern United States. Their presence is welcome in the semiarid to arid region. [11]

BosWash: That part of the east coast that is within the area of metropolitan Boston to Washington, D.C., megalopolis. [7]

break-in-bulk point: A place where goods are moved from one mode of transportation to another. Transfer point where goods change mode of transportation. For example, unloading goods from a ship and transferring to trucks. [5]

brewis: National food dish of Newfoundland made of hard bread (hard tack) and salt fish (cod). [6]

British North America Act (1867): Established the Dominion of Canada and gave the Canadian government the right to make their own laws. [5]

broiler chickens: Reared for meat rather than for eggs. The broiler industry began in the late 1950s, when strains were selectively bred for meat production. In 2001, in the United States, there were 8.4 billion broilers produced, with an average live weight of 5.06 pounds. [12]

brownfield: Any real property that has been contaminated by a hazardous substance, solid waste, or pollutant and is hampered for redevelopment because of cost and liability concerns. [13]

Brundtland Report: is also called Our Common Future: Report of the World Commission on Enviroment and Development was published 1987. The report placed environmental issues firmly on the international political agenda and discussed the environment and development as a single issue. The Brundtland Report laid the groundwork for the convening of the 1992 Earth Summit and the adoption of Agenda 21, the Rio Declaration and to the establishment of the Commission on Sustainable Development. The Brundtland Report also defined sustainable development as "development that meets the needs of the present without compromising the ability of future generations to meet their own needs." Today, that definition remains the most widely used. [2]

Bureau of Land Management (BLM): Agency of the US Department of the Interior that oversees the management of public land, such as national forests. [15]

bush: Land remote from settlement. Said of Alaska outside of the Pacific borderland. [18]

butte: Isolated hill or mountain with steep sides, smaller than a mesa. [16]

cache: A specially designed container placed outside to store and keep food safe from animals. [18]

Cajun: A member of a group of people with an enduring cultural tradition, whose French Catholic ancestors established permanent communities in Louisiana and Maine after being expelled from Acadia in the late eighteenth century. [11]

caldera (*Sp.* "cauldron"): A basin-shaped volcanic depression, at least a mile in diameter. Formed when a large volume of magma is removed from beneath a volcano, resulting in the ground subsiding or collapsing into the emptied space. Such large depressions are typically formed by the subsidence of volcanoes. Crater Lake occupies the best-known caldera in the Cascades. [3]

caliche (or **hardpan**): Crust or layer of hard subsoil encrusted with calcium carbonate, occurring in arid or semiarid regions like the Great Plains in the United States. Term used in Oklahoma. [14]

Canadien: A Canadian of French descent. [5]

canebrake: Riverbottom in interior plateau and southern Appalachia overgrown with cane. Most has been cleared for agricultural use. [8]

canyon: A narrow, deep, steep-sided opening in the earth's surface with steep cliff walls, cut into the earth by running water; a gorge. In the United States, the most famous is the Grand Canyon, carved by the Colorado River over the past 60 million years and located mainly in northern Arizona. [16]

cap and trade: Emissions trading system to control greenhouse gas emissions, where total emissions are limited, or capped. [5]

cape: Land projecting out into a body of water. For example, Cape Cod, Cape Hatteras. [9]

capelin: Small fish that is very abundant on the coasts of Greenland, Iceland, Newfoundland, and Alaska. It is used as bait for cod. Similar to anchovies, smelt, or herring. [6]

carbon cycle: Carbon circulating through the biosphere, geosphere, atmosphere, and hydrosphere. Among the most complex of biogeochemical cycles. [3]

caribou: Seasonally migrating reindeer native to North America. Many Native communities are dependent on the caribou for their subsistence. [18]

Carolina bay: Oval-shaped depressions along the Atlantic coast. Vary from a few acres to square miles. Trend northwest to southeast and appear in groups. Vary between marsh and lake-like. Named for bay trees often found in the bays. [9]

carpetbagger: A Northerner who relocated to the South for financial or political advantage after the Civil War. [9]

carrying capacity: The number of people that an area can support given the quality of the natural environment and the level of technology of the population. [2]

center of population: Demographic term; calculated by finding the balance point for population, where an equal number live north-south-east-west of the given point. The center of population has steadily been moving southwest with each census. [7]

center pivot irrigation (CPI): A self-propelled irrigation method that uses sprinkler systems mounted on wheels. CPI irrigates a circular area and is more water efficient than older irrigation, but is dependent on fossil fuel to run the water pumps. [14]

chain migration: An individual or small group migration to foreign soil, influencing others, especially family and friends, to migrate with them in a channelized diffusion of movement. [11]

chaparral ecosystem: A Mediterranean natural plant community featuring the drought-hardy woody chaparral shrub. The ecosystem is subject to frequent intense wildfires. [19]

Chinese Exclusion Act (1882): Policy of prohibiting immigration of Chinese laborers to the United States. From the time of the US acquisition of California in 1848, there had been a large influx of Chinese laborers to the Pacific coast. They were encouraged to immigrate because of the need for cheap labor and were employed largely in the building of transcontinental railroads. [19]

chinook (*Salishan language,* "snow eater"): A strong, dry, warm wind that blows from the Rocky Mountains onto the Great Plains, usually in winter and spring. Chinooks can result in temperature increases of 35°F–40°F in fifteen minutes. [14]

Clean Water Act (CWA) (1972): The basic federal statute governing all aspects of water quality protection in the United States. [8]

clear-cut: A forest harvesting technique that cuts all trees in an area at one time. [17]

climate change: Changes in long-term trends in the average climate, such as changes in average temperatures. Most scientists today agree that we are in a period of climate change and that it is human induced. [3]

closed ecosystem: An ecosystem that does not rely on exchange of matter outside its system to exist. The waste products of one species are used by another, so there is no waste or pollution. Used to define Earth itself or smaller isolated units, such as Hawai`i. [20]

coastal plain: Low areas of Earth that have been eroded nearly level or formed of flat-lying sediments. In the United States, located along the Atlantic Ocean and Gulf of Mexico. [9]

cod (or **codfish**): Any of various marine fishes of the family *Gadidae*, especially *Gadus morhua*, an important food fish of northern Atlantic waters, especially Newfoundland Grand Banks, until 1992 when the fishery was closed. [6]

colonia (*Sp.* "community"): A residential area in Texas along the border region that often lacks infrastructure such as potable water, sewers, or electricity. [11]

Colorado River Compact (1922): Agreement among the states in the Colorado River Basin, allocating the river waters between the states. [16]

Columbia Basin Project: A 1930s program to irrigate dryland-farming areas of the Columbia Basin. The centerpiece was Grand Coulee Dam. [16]

Combined statistical area: A Combined Statistical Area (CSA) is composed of adjacent metropolitan statistical area (MSA) and the smaller, micropolitan statistical areas that surround the MSA. Micropolitian statistical areas are an uban cluster with a population of at least 10,000 but fewer than 50,000 people and are geographically removed from larger cities. Generally, a CSA is geographically larger than the MSA, but the economic or social linkages may be weaker than in an MSA. [7]

community-supported agriculture (CSA): A way for the public to create a relationship with a farm and receive a weekly basket of produce. [13]

concentrated animal feeding operations (CAFOs): A farm housing at least one thousand animal units. [9]

Confederation: (1) The union of the British North American colonies of New Brunswick, Nova Scotia, Quebec, and Ontario (Province of Canada), brought about on July 1, 1867, under the name Dominion of Canada. (2) The federal union of all the Canadian provinces and territories, the most recent addition being Newfoundland in 1949. [5]

containerization: Standard-sized (twenty feet by forty feet), reusable receptacles that can accommodate smaller cartons or cases in a single shipment, designed for efficient handling of cargo. Containerization has become the dominant mode of shipping and trucking in the past thirty years. Shipping containers can be transferred to trucks without reloading, be simply placed on trucks, and moved to their next destination. [19]

continental climate: Inland areas have greater temperature extremes. Coastal regions have fewer extremes. Water holds warmth, while land loses warmth more quickly. [3]

continental divide: A drainage divide on a continent where each side of the divide drains into a different ocean or sea; specifically, the crest of the Rocky Mountains, which divides the rivers of North America into those that flow east and those that flow west. [15]

continental glaciation: An ice sheet covering a large part of a continent. [3]

continental shelf: The part of the sea floor that slopes gently down from the continents, the shallowest part of the ocean. [3]

contract farmer: A farmer who contracts with a vertically integrated conglomerate to grow or produce a crop or livestock to the company's specifications. The farmer owns the land and livestock buildings, but the company owns the crops or animals and provides all feed or nutrients. [9]

coquina: A soft limestone composed of fragments of shell and coral, found especially in Florida. Used as a vernacular building stone. [10]

cordillera: An extensive chain of mountains or mountain ranges, especially the principal mountain system of a continent, often referring to the system of mountain chains near the border of a continent. For example, the western cordillera within the United States includes the Rocky Mountains, Sierra Nevada, and the Cascade ranges. [15]

Corridor: The densely populated and industrialized areas of Ontario and Quebec, aka Inner Canada. [5]

cotton gin: Patented in 1784 by Eli Whitney; removed seeds from the blossoms. It sparked an explosion in Southern cotton production and fostered the associated expansion of racial slavery throughout the region. [9]

coulee: Large, abandoned meltwater channels. A gorge formed by glacial meltwaters or a stream that is now dry. A term primarily used in the northwestern United States. [16]

cove: Small, oval-shaped, smooth-floor valley in a woodland area. Used especially in the Appalachians. [8]

cracker: A poor white person who settled in the southern uplands. Often used in a disparaging way, but sometimes with pride, as in the excellent *Ecology of a Cracker Childhood* by Janisse Ray. [9]

Creole: A language, culture, and group of people located in the New Orleans area. Creoles may be a mixture of Spanish, French, and African American blood. [11]

Crown Land: In Canada, areas that belong to the Crown, similar to government-owned lands in the United States. About 89 percent of all land in Canada is Crown Land, which is divided between federal and provincial. [5]

Crow Rate: A subsidy offered to the Canadian Pacific Railway by the Canadian government. It enabled the railroad to expand westward and thereby reduced the transportation costs for prairie farmers. [14]

cuesta: A ridge bounded by a gentle slope on one side and an escarpment on the other. [11]

cultural adaptation: Changing one's culture is response to a new environment. [1]

cultural hearth: A nuclear area within which an advanced and distinctive set of culture traits, ideas, and technologies develops and from which there is diffusion of those characteristics and the cultural landscape features they imply. The area from which the culture of a group diffused. Source areas from which radiated ideas and innovations that changed the world beyond. [5]

cultural preadaptation: Possessing adaptive traits prior to migration. Said of Ukrainian immigrants from the steppes who migrated to the plains and prairies. They were culturally preadapted to the harsh climate regimes and therefore able to survive. [6]

death rate: The ratio of total deaths to total population over a specified period of time. [4]

Deindustrialization: Deindustrialization is a process of social and economic change caused by the elminiation or reduction of industrial capacity or activity in a country or region, especially heavy industry or manufacturing industry. Deindustrialization involves a decrease in the relative size and importance of the industrial sector in an economy. [4]

delta: A body of alluvium, nearly flat and fan-shaped (where the Greek letter delta Δ originates), at the mouth of a river where it enters a body of water. The alluvium is formed from deposited sediment carried by the body of water. Two major deltas in the United States are the Mississippi and Sacramento–San Joaquin deltas. [11]

Dene: The Athabaskan-speaking peoples of northwest Canada and inland Alaska, considered as a group. [18]

desalination: Removing the salts from water to make it drinkable. [19]

dome mountain: Formed when tectonic forces lift the Earth's crust into a broad bulge or dome. The dome is raised above its surroundings, so erosion will occur, and as a result of erosion, peaks and valleys are formed. For example, the Black Hills in South Dakota. [3]

Dominion Lands Act: The Canadian homesteader act of 1872, meant to bring farmers onto the Canadian prairie. [14]

drainage basin: The area of land drained by a river and its tributaries to a common outlet. [3]

drowned rivers: Ancient river mouths and valleys resulting from rising sea level over the past twelve thousand years. Found on the coastal plains of continents. [7]

dryland farming: Farming without irrigation, found in semiarid grassland areas. Dryland farming results in unpredictable crop and livestock production. Uses drought-tolerant crops. For example, the growing of sorghum in the Great Plains. [14]

eco-industry: Companies providing goods and services for environmental protection. A more exacting definition: a cradle-to-cradle closed-loop industrial park linked to minimize its ecological footprint, in which the waste of one industry is the resource for another. [8]

ecological balance: A state of dynamic equilibrium within a community of organisms in which genetic, species, and ecosystem diversity remain relatively stable, subject to gradual changes through natural succession. [16]

ecological footprint: A measure of human demand on the Earth's ecosystems and natural resources. [2]

ecology: The scientific study of relations of living organisms with each other and their physical surroundings. [1]

ecoregion (or **bioregion**): A relatively large unit of land and water defined by the influences of shared climate and geology, the main factors determining the distribution of plants and animals in the area. [1]

ecosystem (or **ecological system**): An interconnected geographic area including all the living organisms (people, plants, animals, and microorganisms), their physical surroundings (such as soil, water, and air), and the natural cycles that sustain them. Ecosystems can be small scale (a small area in detail such as a single stand of aspen) or large scale (a large area such as an entire watershed including hundreds of forest stands across many different ownerships). [1]

ecotone: A transition zone between two ecosystems. [1]

embayment: A coastline recess forming a sediment-filled, low-lying basin or bay. The most prevalent US embayment is the Mississippi Embayment, which reaches to Cairo, Illinois. [11]

environmental justice: When poor communities are given equal protection from industrial and waste facilities. [2]

equalization payment: In Canada, a partial redistribution of wealth from the wealthier provinces to the less wealthy. In the past, Ontario was a wealthy province, but the lagging economy made Ontario in 2010 a "have-not" province, which received an equalization payment, while Newfoundland became for the first time a "have" province, which contributed to equalization. [5]

erosion: The wearing away of land by water, wind, waves, ice, and other agents. [3]

escarpment: A long cliff or steep slope separating two comparatively level or more gently sloping surfaces and resulting from erosion or faulting. [5]

estuary: A semienclosed coastal body of water where seawater and fresh water mix; a drowned river mouth. Estuaries and tidal creeks fluctuate and are nutrient-rich ecosystems. [11]

ethanol: A colorless volatile flammable liquid, C_2H_5OH, synthesized or obtained by fermentation of sugars and starches. In the United States, ethanol is created largely from corn; however, in Brazil sugar cane is the source of ethanol. [13]

eutrophication: Waters rich in organic nutrients in which algae proliferate. Leads to extinction of other organisms and possible ecosystem collapse. [11]

Exclusive Economic Zone (EEZ): A maritime zone beyond and adjacent to the territorial sea, the maximum being two hundred nautical miles from land. The coastal state has sovereign rights for the purpose of exploring, exploiting, conserving, and managing natural resources, both living and nonliving, of the seabed, subsoil, and the subjacent waters, and with regard to other activities, for the economic exploitation and exploration of the zone. The previous limit was twelve miles, but in the 1970s, most of the major fishing nations agreed to adopt a two-hundred-mile economic zone in order to preserve fish stocks, which even then were in serious decline. Fishing on the high seas was limited to a very few nations, primarily the former Soviet Union and Japan. Unfortunately, the two-hundred-mile limit has not had the desired effect; the Grand Banks were closed in 1992 and remain closed in 2011. [6]

Exodusters (exodus + dust as in Dust Bowl): Former slaves who fled the South for Kansas in 1879. They chose Kansas because it was the home of abolitionist John Brown, and the state was reputed to be progressive and tolerant. Several all-black towns, such as Nicodemus, still exist in the state. [14]

exotic stream: In the drier plateau section of the United States, a stream that carries water, something otherwise unknown—or exotic—into this arid environment. [16]

external costs (or **negative externalities**): Disadvantageous impacts paid for by the consumer for the actions of firms and individuals. For example, the environmental and social costs of the current economic system, where these external costs are passed on to the consumer. [2]

fall line: The line in the United States along which the coastal plain meets the harder rock piedmont. The drop from the rock to the sandy coastal plain is marked by waterfalls and rapids. [7]

family farm: Independently operated enterprise providing the main source of income for the family. Family farms once served as the social and economic foundation for rural communities. They provided both social capital and clientele for local businesses. Family farms declined steeply in the late twentieth century due to technologic change, low commodity prices, vertical integration, and globalization. [13]

fault: A feature of Earth's crust created by the breaking and movement of rock layers below the surface. [3]

fault-block mountain: Mountain created either by the uplift or subsidence of land between faults. The land may be uplifted on one side and depressed on the other, resulting in a tilted fault block. For example, in the United States, the Sierra Nevada and the Basin and Range. [3]

fish farm: A commercial facility in which fish are raised for food. [17]

fish ladder: A series of shallow steps down which water is allowed to flow; designed to permit salmon to circumvent artificial barriers such as power dams as the salmon swim upstream to spawn. [17]

fjord: A long, narrow arm of the sea resulting from the drowning of a glaciated valley. [3]

flake: A frame or platform for drying fish or produce. Used in Newfoundland to dry cod. [6]

flash flood: A sudden local flood due to heavy rain, especially in desert areas. [16]

flatwoods: A pine forest wetland that is drier than a pocosin. Found along the southeastern coastal plain. [11]

folded mountain: The most common type of mountain. Created by tectonic plates pushing against each other, which creates intense pressure. Therefore, the only direction for these mountains to move is up. When two plates move away from each other, they create a rift valley in between them. Sometimes, if plates collide, one plate will force the other under itself and create a folded mountain. Folded mountains are mainly composed of limestone and shale. For example, the Appalachians in the United States. [3]

fortress living: Living isolated from others in a socioeconomically segregated, gated community. [19]

Francophone: A French-speaking person, especially in a region where two or more languages are spoken. Very common term in Quebec. (See **Anglophone**.) [4]

Frontier Thesis (or **the Turner thesis**): Famous thesis about settlement of the American West, delivered on July 12, 1893, at the annual meeting of the American Historical Association, by Frederick Jackson Turner. He first presented his thesis in the now famous paper "The Significance of the Frontier in

American History." The Turner thesis was this: The settlement of the West by white people—"the existence of an area of free land, its continuous recession, and the advance of American settlement westward"—was the central story of American history. [14]

frost-freeze cycles: Swelling and shrinking of ground due to changes in temperature over the year. [14]

Gadsden Purchase (1853): A purchase from Mexico to settle a question as to the limits of the Mexican Cession of 1848. James Gadsden negotiated for the acquisition of nineteen million acres of additional land and the settlement of the claims. The territory acquired lies in the states of Arizona and New Mexico and was purchased with the intent of building a southern transcontinental rail line through the Gila River tributary watershed. [16]

Geechee: An African American on the Sea Islands of Georgia who speaks Gullah. (See **Gullah.**) [9]

General Agreement on Tariffs and Trade (GATT) (1947): Trade agreement by the United Nations to facilitate international trade. Precursor to the World Trade Organization (WTO). [5]

genetically modified organism (GMO): An organism whose genetic material has been deliberately altered. [13]

geography: The spatial and temporal analysis of human and natural systems and their interrelation across scales. [1]

geothermal spring: A spring heated by thermal vents in Earth's crust. [12]

ghost town: A town that once flourished but is deserted today, usually because of depletion of a nearby resource such as gold or silver. [15]

glacial drift: Mass of rocks and finely ground material carried by a glacier, then deposited when the ice melted. [3]

glacial erratic: A rock transported by a glacier or glacial event that deviates from the size and composition of the surrounding landscape. [16]

glacier: A large mass of snow that accumulates and becomes granular and compact through settling and recrystallization. A thick mass of ice moving slowly across Earth's surface. [3]

global warming: The increase in average Earth temperature, based on greenhouse gas emissions, and at least partially human induced. This term is now replaced by climate change because of irregular temperature fluctuations over the short term. Long-term indications now show an overall global warming. [3]

globalization: Globalization involves the increasing connections of different parts of the world. It refers to expansion of economic, political, and cultural processes to the point that they become global in scale and impact. The process of globalization produces outcomes that vary across places and states. [4]

Golden Horseshoe: Densely populated and industrialized region of Ontario, centered on the west end of Lake Ontario. [5]

Gold Rush: The discovery of gold in California in 1848 (the "gold standard" for this term). However, there have been many gold rushes, mostly notably in the Klondike, the Yukon, and Alaska. [19]

grass banking: Mutually beneficial grazing management involving rotational grazing, in order to protect and restore grasslands. [16]

grassland: Land dominated by grasses, rather than trees or shrubs; prairie. [14]

Great Mahele: Land redistribution in Hawai`i in the 1830s that allowed commoners to hold private title to land. [20]

Great Migration: The movement of millions of African Americans from 1910 to 1970 from the South to the Northeast and Midwest. They were escaping Jim Crow racism and pursuing jobs in the manufacturing industries. [11]

greenhouse gases (GHGs): Gases that contribute to the greenhouse effect by absorbing infrared radiation produced by solar warming of the Earth's surface. Major GHGs include carbon dioxide (CO_2), methane (CH_4), nitrous oxide (NO_2), and water vapor. Elevated levels of GHGs have been observed in the recent past and are related, at least in part, to human activities such as burning fossil fuels. [3]

Green Mountain Boys: Vermont's militia during the period of the Vermont Republic. Led by Ethan Allen, the group protected their land titles when given to New York. [6]

Green Revolution: In the 1960s, an effort to ostensibly end world hunger and feed a rapidly growing world population. The Rockefeller Foundation put one of their scientists, Norman Borlaug, to work on ways to increase the yield of food grains. [13]

groundwater: Fresh water found beneath Earth's surface and beyond the root zone in tiny spaces between rock and soil. [3]

Gullah: A group of isolated African Americans brought over as slaves who were located on the Sea Islands off South Carolina. They developed their own form of English dialect, which has been disparaged. [9]

habitant (*Fr.*): An early inhabitant of French Canada, who worked the land as a renter for the *seigneur*. [5]

haboob: An intense dust storm, with winds up to thirty miles per hour, which often precedes summer monsoon rains in the Sonoran Desert. [16]

hammock: A hardwood- and evergreen-forested area rising slightly above a flat plain. Tropical hammocks are found in southern Florida. [10]

hatchery: A place where eggs (especially fish eggs) are hatched under artificial conditions. [17]

Hawai`i Land Reform Act (1967): A law that allowed lessees to buy fee interest in leased land formerly held by trusts. [20]

headwater stream: Smallest streams for river systems, often ephemeral. [8]

hillbilly: A term used disparagingly of a backwoods person, especially in the Ozarks or Appalachia. [12]

Hispanic: A US citizen or resident of Latin American or Spanish descent. Though often used interchangeably in American English, *Hispanic* and *Latino* are not identical terms, and in certain contexts the choice between them can be significant. [19]

hogback: A sharp crested ridge protruding from the surrounding area. [15]

holistic system: The process of how things influence one another within a whole. Looking at nature as an interconnected whole of interrelated ecosystems, which include humans as part of the biotic life community. [1]

homeless: Individuals who lack a fixed, regular, and adequate nighttime residence. [19]

Homestead Act (An Act to Secure Homesteads to Actual Settlers on the Public Domain): A law passed in 1862 to encourage settlers to move west to settle less desirable land. It became law on January 1, 1863, and allowed anyone to file for a quarter-section of free land (160 acres). The land was "proved up" and yours at the end of five years, if you had built a house on it, farmed a portion, and lived there. [14]

hurricane: A severe tropical cyclone originating in the equatorial regions of the Atlantic Ocean, the Caribbean Sea, or eastern regions of the Pacific Ocean, traveling north, northwest, or northeast from its point of origin, and involving strong winds and heavy rains. [11]

Hutterites: Members of an Anabaptist sect originating in Moravia and now living communally in the prairies of Canada and the northwest United States. [14]

hypoxia (literally, "low oxygen"): Condition created when coastal waters or estuaries become polluted by nutrient overload, creating a lack of oxygen. The most direct result is fish kills, which lead to habitat loss and loss of ecological biodiversity. Hypoxia is evident throughout the coastal water of the United States, for example, Tampa Bay and the Chesapeake, but the largest zone is spring and summer in the Gulf of Mexico west of the mouth of the Mississippi River. [11]

ice age: A time of widespread glaciation. (See **Pleistocene**.) [3]

ice road: Canadian winter road made of frozen water over permafrost. Used to haul supplies to far northern areas. [18]

imagineer: A word formed by Disney, combining *imagine* and *engineering*. Imagineers were the creative force behind the building of the Disney theme parks. [10]

Indian Removal Act (1830): Legislation that forced Native Americans to relinquish their lands east of the Mississippi in exchange for land in Oklahoma, where they were forced to move. President Andrew Jackson pushed this act through, after years of divesting Native Americans of their land. [13]

industrial ecology: The network of all industrial processes as they may interact and live off each other, not only in the economic sense, but also in the sense of direct use of each other's material and energy wastes. [9]

informal economy: Economic activity that is neither taxed nor monitored by the government. Typical in developing economies but also prevalent in portions of the US economy with substantial numbers of immigrants. [19]

Inner Canada: The densely populated and industrialized areas of Ontario and Quebec, aka the Corridor. [5]

Inuit: Native people of Arctic Alaska and Canada. Once called Eskimos ("eaters of raw flesh") by the nearby Algonquian tribes; this term is considered offensive. [18]

island arc: A chain of volcanic islands or mountains formed by plate tectonics, as an oceanic tectonic plate subducts under another tectonic plate along an oceanic trench. The Aleutian Islands are an island arc. [18]

isostatic rebound: The upward movement of Earth's crust following isostatic depression (common after glaciation). [18]

Jim Crow laws: Statutes enacted by Southern states and municipalities, beginning in the 1880s, that legalized segregation between blacks and whites. After years of legal suits, sit-ins, and boycotts, the Civil Rights Act of 1964, the Voting Rights Act of 1965, and the Fair Housing Act of 1968 finally ended the legal sanctions to Jim Crow. [11]

karst: A landscape characterized by the presence of caves, springs, sinkholes, and losing streams, created as groundwater dissolves soluble rock such as limestone or dolomite. [3]

kettle: A steep-sided, bowl-shaped depression commonly without surface drainage; usually formed by a large detached block of stagnant ice that had been partially or wholly buried in the drift. A depression formed as buried ice melted and overlying sediments collapsed. [13]

keystone species: A species that has a major influence on the structure of an ecosystem. When a keystone species is threatened, the entire ecosystem may collapse. Prairie dogs are a keystone species in the prairies. Animals depend on the prairie dogs as a food source or for their habitat. Salmon are a keystone species in coastal ecosystems. [17]

kudzu: A vine native to China and Japan but imported into the United States; originally planted for decoration, for forage, or as a ground cover to control erosion. It now grows wild in many parts of the southeastern United States. Known as "the plant that ate the South." [9]

lagoon: An excavated, diked, or walled structure or combination of structures designed for the treatment or storage of manure. In many states, lagoons must be designed and constructed in compliance with Natural Resources Conservation Service specifications. [9]

lahar: Landslide or mudflow of volcanic fragments down a volcano. Lahars have occurred in the Puget Sound area. [17]

lake effect: The effect of any lake, especially the Great Lakes, in modifying the weather in nearby areas. During the winter, lake effect causes heavy snowfall on the leeward side of the lake. During the growing season, lake effect extends the season, making it ideal for growing crops not usually associated with the area, such as on the east side of Lake Michigan or the east side of Lake Ontario, or between Lakes Ontario and Erie. [13]

Land Ordinance of 1785: Establishment of a system for surveying and subdividing public land outside the states, while raising money for the federal government after the Revolutionary War. Passed by the Congress of the Articles of Confederation, the statute provided for the surveying of blocks of land thirty-six square miles each, to be known as townships. Each township was to set aside one section for public education and schools, with each section containing 640 acres. [13]

land trust: Land sold to conservation groups to keep it preserved in its present use. Grazing land and farmland in danger of development are often preserved as land trusts. [15]

la raza (*Sp.*, "the race"): Refers to the Latino presence in the United States and working to protect and preserve the culture. Often used in the expression *Viva la raza* ("Long live the race"), most specifically the re-takeover of southwestern states. [16]

Latino: Refers more exclusively to persons or communities of Latin American origin. (See **Hispanic**.) [19]

Law of the Indies: Spanish guidelines set by the king of Spain to instruct colonists how to design newly settled towns. Part of the design was a layout with a central plaza. [15]

Leadership in Energy and Environmental Design (LEED): A green building rating system. [7]

levee: A ridge of earth along a river that hinders flooding. [11]

lichen: Organism consisting of a symbiotic joining of a species of fungi and a species of algae. [18]

life cycle analysis: Analysis of the environmental impacts of a good or service. Identifies the energy, material, and waste flows of a product. [2]

lignite: Low-grade coal. Brown coal. Lithified accumulations of organic debris. [8]

limestone: Sedimentary rock composed of carbonate minerals, especially calcium carbonate. Limestone is formed from deposition of shells, coral, and other marine organisms that accumulated on shallow sea floors. [12]

liquefaction: The transformation of soil from a solid state to a liquefied state due to pressure and stress. Said of soil in earthquake-prone areas with deep sediment and little surface bedrock. [19]

locks: A part of a waterway enclosed by gates, used to raise or lower boats from one water level to another. [5]

loess: Glacial material transported and deposited by wind, consisting primarily of silt-size particles. [13]

long lot: Land division system giving access to a transportation artery (river or road) for a maximum number of farms while still living in a linear neighborhood village. The early French government tried to transplant a vestigial form of feudalism, the seigneurial system, to its possessions in Canada. The long-lot system of land division associated with seigneuries remains vividly imprinted on the landscapes of North America that were settled by French-speaking people. Long lots can be found in many parts of Canada, where the French influence is strong, and near Detroit (for the same reason). [5]

losing stream: A surface stream that loses water to the subsurface through bedrock openings. Often found in karst topography or arid areas. [12]

Lower Canada: The southern, mainly French-speaking portion of Quebec from 1791 until 1841, when it was reunited with Upper Quebec to form the present-day province of Quebec. [5]

Loyalist: One who maintains loyalty to an established government, political party, or sovereign, especially during war or revolutionary change. Said of those who remained loyal to Britain during the American Revolution, many of whom moved to Canada. [5]

Main Street: The Corridor of Canada in the densely populated St. Lawrence Valley of Quebec and Great Lakes of Ontario. [5]

maîtres chez nous (*Fr.*): "Masters of our own house." Rallying cry in Quebec during the Quiet Revolution, as the Québécois attempted to master their own economic destiny. [5]

managed use: Organized handling of forest property to provide optimum use. However, *optimum* can be defined by whoever is using the term, an environmentalist or a logger, for example. [17]

mangrove: A type of exposed-root tree or shrub that grows in tidal estuaries or salt marshes. [10]

Manifest Destiny: The nineteenth-century doctrine that the United States had the right and duty to expand throughout the North American continent. This view justified Jefferson's Louisiana Purchase from France, the claim to thousands of square miles in the heart of the continent that were inhabited solely by Indian nations. He was thus planting the American way of life on the continent. [16]

Mardi Gras (*Fr.*, "Fat Tuesday"): The last day before Lent, when many foods are given up for the season. Celebrated in many southern cities, especially New Orleans and other cities in Louisiana. [11]

marine climate: A climate strongly influenced by an oceanic environment, found on islands and the windward shores of continents. Characterized by small daily and yearly temperature ranges and high relative humidity. [17]

maritime influence: The movement onshore of prevailing westerly wind systems from the ocean, which moderates summer and winter temperature extremes. [6]

maroon: Escaped slave who hid out in the Dismal Swamp area of Albemarle and Chesapeake bays. [9]

marsh: A fresh, brackish, or saltwater wetland, vegetated mostly by herbaceous plants that grow up out of the water (emergent plants). Marshes are frequently or continually flooded and are often found at the edges of rivers, creeks, ponds, and lakes, in isolated depressions, and along the Atlantic, Pacific, and Gulf coasts. [3]

meander: A curve or loop in a river. There is a relationship between the amount of meander and the gradient of a river; the less steep the more meander. But gradient is not the only variable in the amount of meanders in a river. [14]

Mediterranean climate: A climate characterized by moist, mild winters and hot, dry summers. [3]

Megalopolis: The region that contains the coastal area between Boston and Washington, D.C., so named by Jean Gottman in the 1950s. The most densely populated area in America, containing about 17 percent of the total population. [7]

melting pot: A place where immigrants of different cultures or races form an integrated society by assimilating socially. [11]

mesa (*Sp.*, "table"): An isolated, relatively flat-topped natural elevation, usually more extensive than a butte and less extensive than a plateau. [16]

Métis: A general term that refers to Canadians descended from North American Indians and Europeans; descendants of French explorers, fur traders, and settlers, and native North American peoples. [14]

metropolitan area: Metropolitan Areas or Metropolitan Statistical Areas (MSA) are defined by the US Census as urban areas with a core area of at least 50,000 residents and economic links to surrounding counties. [4]

Mexican Cession of 1848: Stemming from the Treaty of Guadalupe. The United States acquired a large tract of land, including what is now California, Nevada, Utah, most of Arizona, and parts of New Mexico, Colorado, and Wyoming. [16]

migration: Leaving one's native country to settle in another land. [4]

milkshed: A region producing milk for a specific community. Usually located near the community, due to the perishable nature of milk. [6]

Mining Law of 1872: Federal law in the United States that authorizes mining for minerals on publicly held land. [15]

mission: One of three settlement types used by the Spanish to settle California. The missions were built between 1769 and 1833, and they are some of the oldest buildings in California. The mission was the religious outpost, used to raise agricultural goods. (See also **presidio** and **pueblo**.) [19]

monadnock: An isolated hill or mountain of resistant rock rising above eroded lowlands. [6]

moonshine: Illegally distilled liquor, especially in Appalachia and the American South. Named because of the time of day the spirits were distilled and transported. [8]

Moraine: A ridge of rocks, gravel, and sand deposited along the margins of a glacier or ice sheet. [3]

mountaintop removal (MTR): Strip-mining on steroids; removal of large portions of mountains to access coal layers beneath the overburden. Destroys communities, ecosystems, and causes flooding and loss of biodiversity. [8]

muskeg: A large expanse of permafrost peatlands or bogs and fens filling in with vegetation, and sometimes containing stunted trees, especially black spruce. Peatlands are common to Canada, Alaska, and Siberia. Minnesota has the largest peatland areas in the lower forty-eight states, located in the north central part of the state. [18]

National Policy: Canadian economic program since 1879, based on protectionist high tariffs on manufactured goods and opposed to free trade. [5]

natural increase: Growth in population by births over deaths. The difference between the number of persons added due to births over a period of time, minus the number of persons who die. Expressed as increase or decrease per 1,000: ([births – deaths] / population) × 1,000. [4]

New Homestead Act: Act being considered by Congress to repopulate the dying towns of the Great Plains. The bill focuses on small businesses and entrepreneurs, and it provides incentives such as free land, tax credits, and venture capital. [14]

New South: The abolition of slavery failed to provide African Americans with political or economic equality, and it took a long, concerted effort to end segregation. The New South has evolved into a manufacturing region, and high-rise buildings crowd the skylines of such cities as Atlanta and Little Rock. [9]

new urbanism: A return to traditional neighborhood design with walkable cities, deemphasizing cars and building community. Often with houses based on 1920–1930 designs. For example, Celebration, Florida. [10]

nonpoint source pollution: Pollution from diffuse sources; not from a single identifiable source. [3]

nonrenewable resource: A natural resource that cannot be renewed as quickly as it is consumed. Many minerals are nonrenewable, but the resources most commonly referred to in this regard are fossil fuels. [2]

North American Free Trade Agreement (NAFTA): Formed in January 1994, between Canada, the United States, and Mexico. The world's largest free trade area, whose major objective is to eliminate trade barriers. [5]

North Atlantic Ocean Conveyor: A marine circular flow that is brought about by changes in seawater density. Increased salinity results in increased density, and water sinks. When water has decreased salinity, the density falls and can cause climatic changes. [6]

oil sands: Bituminous or tar sands that are a mixture of sand, water, and extremely heavy crude oil. Oil sands in Alberta, Canada, are among the world's largest. [18]

old growth: Mature ecosystem of forest with the associated plants and animals. [17]

open pit mine: A type of mine that uncovers ore by digging a large hole. The largest active open pit mine is the Bingham Canyon Mine near Salt Lake City. [16]

open-range ranching: A cattle- or sheep-ranching area characterized by a general absence of fences. [14]

orographic precipitation: Patterns that result when moist air encounters a topographic barrier and is forced to rise over it; for example, the increase in precipitation with elevation on the windward slopes of a mountain range and the rain shadow on the leeward side. The Front Range (leeward) of the Rocky Mountains is affected by orographic precipitation. [3]

Outer Canada: The part of Canada that is not in the Corridor or Inner Canada, therefore anything outside the St. Lawrence and Great Lakes basins. [5]

outport: Small seaside village in Newfoundland that lives off the fisheries. In 1949, there were approximately fourteen hundred of these villages, most with populations under two hundred. In 2005, there were about four hundred outports. [6]

overburden: Material covering a mineral seam or bed that must be removed before the mineral can be removed in strip mining or mountaintop removal. [8]

oxbow lake: A crescent-shaped lake lying alongside a winding river. Created over time as erosion and deposits of soil change the river's course, leaving the lake as a remnant of a meander. [11]

pali: Hawaiian word for steep hills or cliffs. [20]

panhandle: A narrow arm of land attached to a larger region or state. A classic example is the Oklahoma panhandle, which literally looks like a panhandle, versus the panhandle of Nebraska, which is far wider and not as obvious physically. [14]

park: A high-altitude, wide, grassy open valley in the Rocky Mountains, surrounded by wooded mountains. [15]

peat: Any wetland that accumulates partially decayed plant matter. The softest and most polluting coal. [8]

pedalfer: Soil rich in alumina and iron and deficient in carbonates, found in and characteristic of humid regions. [3]

pedocal: A soil of semiarid and arid regions that is rich in calcium carbonate and lime. [3]

Pennsylvania Dutch: A misnomer for Germans (*Deutsch*) who settled inland from Philadelphia. [7]

permafrost: A permanently frozen layer of soil. [18]

petroleum: Unprocessed oil after extraction; a complex mixture of hydrocarbons. [11]

phytoplankton: A microscopic plant that lives in the sea. It is at the bottom of the food chain. [6]

Piedmont: An area of plains and low hills at or near the foot of a mountain region. In the United States, the Piedmont is a rolling plateau region inland from the coastal plain, east and south of the Appalachian Mountains. [9]

Pittsburgh Plus: A form of spatial price discrimination based on oligopolistic (monopoly) collusion. The mill price at one location determines the delivered price at all locations, regardless of the location of the plant from which delivery is actually made. (It was used in the marketing of steel in the United States, especially in the Birmingham-Chattanooga-Atlanta triangle.) [8]

plantation agriculture: The system of agricultural production begun with slaves working sugar plantations established in the Eastern Mediterranean by leaders of the Crusades in the twelfth century. In the 1540s, the Portuguese introduced sugar plantations and African slavery to Brazil. By the nineteenth century, plantation slavery had spread throughout the New World. Virtually all plantation societies shared certain characteristics: (1) they relied on forced labor, most often African slaves; (2) they were organized to export a single cash crop (sugar, tobacco, rice, indigo, cotton) to a distant, usually European, market; and (3) although they were organized as capitalist enterprises, their owners sought to control not only the labor of their work force, but every aspect of their lives. By the time plantation agriculture reached North America in the seventeenth century, most English planters were fully aware of how essential African slave labor had been to every profitable plantation economy in the Caribbean and South American countries. [9]

platform: Sedimentary deposits covering basement rock. [3]

playa: A temporary, high-salinity lake that evaporate quickly and leaves behind an alkali flat or salt pan. [16]

Pleistocene: A period in geologic history (basically the last one million years) when ice sheets covered large sections of Earth's land surface not now covered by glaciers. [3]

pocosin: A type of wetlands along the Atlantic coastal area. Pocosins are heavily vegetated with shrubs and pine. The transition from pocosins to a drier wetland is called the flatwoods. [3]

poi: Staple of the native Hawaiian diet, made from pounding and cooking taro root. [20]

point source pollution: Pollution from a single identifiable source of air, water, heat, light, or noise. For example, a pipe dumping chemicals into a river. [3]

polder: An area protected from incoming waters. Polders often imply an area at or below sea level surrounded by dikes to prevent the intrusion of river water and/or seawater. Usually there is an extensive drainage system to lower the water table within the polder. Excess water is pumped from the polder. Seen in North America in the Annapolis Valley of Nova Scotia settled by Acadians. [6]

polynucleated city: A metropolitan area with several city cores. A polynucleated city is usually dependent on fossil fuel transport, especially automobiles. [19]

portage: Carrying boats and supplies overland between navigable waterways. [5]

postindustrial economy: An economy that gains its basic character from economic activities developed primarily after manufacturing grew to predominance. Most notable would be quaternary economic patterns. [6]

potlatch: A ceremonial feast of the natives of the northwest coast of North America, especially the Kwakiutl, entailing the public distribution of property. The host and his relatives lavishly distributed gifts to invited guests, who were expected to accept any gifts offered with the understanding that at a future time they were to reciprocate in kind. Property was destroyed by its owner in a show of wealth that the guests would later attempt to surpass. Potlatch was outlawed in 1884 due to the destruction of property and reinstated in 1951; by that time, the destruction of property was no longer practiced. [17]

prairie: A region of grassland and fertile soil. The French gave the name to the open space of the Midwest when they first saw it. [13]

Precambrian: The geologic time period preceding six hundred million years ago. [3]

precipitation: The discharge of water, in a liquid or solid state, out of the atmosphere, generally onto a land or water surface. It is the common process by which atmospheric water becomes surface or subsurface water; it includes rainfall, snow, hail, and sleet, and is therefore a more general term than rainfall. [3]

presidio (*Sp.*): A military post. One of the three types of settlements in Spanish California. For example, the Presidio of Monterey. (See also **mission, pueblo.**) [19]

primary sector: That portion of a region's economy devoted to the extraction of basic materials (e.g., mining, lumbering, agriculture). [4]

prior appropriation: The commodification of water; when water rights are unconnected to land ownership and can be sold or mortgaged like other property. The first person to use a quantity of water from a water source for a beneficial use has the right to continue to use that quantity of water for that purpose. Subsequent users can use the remaining water for their own beneficial purposes provided that they do not impinge on the rights of previous users. [14]

privateer: A privately owned warship or captain authorized by a country's government. Sir Francis Drake was a privateer for Queen Elizabeth I of England. [6]

pueblo (*Sp.*, "town or village"): A type of Indian village constructed by some tribes in the southwestern United States. A large community dwelling, divided into many rooms, up to five stories high, and usually made of adobe. Pueblos were the original Spanish towns in California, including Los Angeles and San Jose. [19]

pulpwood: Timber ground up and reconstituted into paper, flake board, and other similar products. [11]

push and pull factors: A migration theory that suggests that circumstances at the place of origin (such as poverty and unemployment) repel or push people out of that place to other places that exert a positive attraction or pull (such as a high standard of living or job opportunities). [11]

quaternary sector: That portion of a region's economy devoted to informational and idea-generating activities (e.g., basic research, universities and colleges, and news media). [6]

Québécois nationalism: A "distinct society" maintaining French language and seeking independence from Canada as separatists. Formed after the Quiet Revolution. [5]

Quiet Revolution: Period of Quebec history (1950–1965) of social transformation from a backward, rural, religious (Roman Catholic), and agrarian society to one more modern, urban, industrial, and secular. This led to increased nationalism and even a vote (unsuccessful) on the separation of Quebec from Canada. [5]

"Rain follows the plow": Debunked nineteenth-century theory of climatology that human habitation, in particular, agriculture, effected a permanent change in the climate of arid and semi-arid regions, making these regions more humid. Popular past belief in the Great Plains. [14]

rain shadow: Reduction of precipitation commonly found on the leeward (downwind) side of a mountain. [3]

rancho: A large grazing farm where horses and cattle are raised; distinguished from *hacienda*, a cultivated farm or plantation. Found in pre-US California. [19]

range war: Conflicts in the western United States between ranchers and farmers, or cattle ranchers and sheep ranchers, that often escalated to violence. In the twenty-first century, the range wars continue, but now are often between ranchers and environmentalist groups. [14]

***rang* system:** Land division; French for range or row of farm lots (concession). Also, a road that runs beside or through a concession. In Quebec, the rows of farm lots were originally along water and, as the waterside filled up, were arranged back from the water in rows, as *rang* 2, *rang* 3, and so on. [5]

Reciprocity Treaty of 1854: Agreement between the United States and Canada to reduce tariffs on goods. Also known as the Elgin–Marcy Treaty. Repealed in 1866. [5]

Reconstruction: The period (1865–1877) during which the states that had seceded to the Confederacy were controlled by the federal government before being readmitted to the Union. [9]

Redlining: The practice of denying or limiting financial services to certain neighborhoods based on racial or ethnic composition without regard to the residents' qualifications or creditworthiness. The term "redlining" refers to the practice of using a red line on a map to delineate so-called bad-risk neighborhoods on a city map and then use the map as the basis for determining loans. Redlining was legal from 1934 to 1968. A consequence of this has been to perpetuate housing segregation in many US cities. [13]

redneck: Disparaging term for poor whites who live in the South. A redneck has no need to impress and is seemingly at peace with the world, not a part of the rat race. [9]

reductionist: An approach to understanding the nature of complex things by reducing them to the interactions of their parts, or to simpler or more fundamental components. The belief that a complex system is nothing but the sum of its parts. [1]

redwater river: A river in the South that is colored due to the red-colored sediment load. [9]

region: A way to interpret Earth's surface. An area having characteristics that distinguish it from other areas. A territory of interest to people, for which one or more distinctive traits or a pattern are used as the basis for its identity. For example, the Midwestern region was largely one that was glaciated during the last ice age, remains flat, and contains many water features. Areas that are adjacent have a different landscape pattern because they were not glaciated or have other characteristics that differ from the Midwest. [1]

renewable resource: A natural resource such as sunlight, wind, tides, and geothermal heat, which are naturally replenished and therefore practically inexhaustible. [2]

replacement level: The mean number of births per woman necessary to assure the long-term replacement of a population for a given mortality level. [4]

resettlement: The period in Newfoundland when three hundred outports were moved or abandoned to larger outports. Lasted from approximately 1950 to 1972, during the premiership of Joey Smallwood. [6]

resource hinterland: A region outside the core that provides the core with resources. Typically not an affluent region in the twentieth century, but possibly more affluent as resource commodities grow rare in the twenty-first century. [6]

rift valley: A valley formed by the sinking of land between two faults. Evident in the St. Lawrence lowlands, and in the Rio Grande rift valley extending from Mexico into Colorado. [5]

right-to-work state: States where employees can decide whether or not to join a union. There are twenty-two right-to-work states, mostly in the South and West. [9]

riparian rights: The rights of an owner of land bordering on a river, lake, bayou, or sea that relate to water use, ownership of the shore, right of ingress and egress, accretions, and so on. Riparian rights are allocated to all owners of water frontage land. Rooted in English common law and used in the eastern United States. [9]

Royal Proclamation of 1763: In Canada, determined Aboriginal title and allowed for self-governance of the indigenous population. [5]

rural: Outside of metropolitan urban areas. Redefined in 2003 in the United States as 75 percent of the land and 17 percent of the population. In Canada, 20 percent of the population are rural. [4]

Rust Belt: the Rust Belt includes parts of the northeastern and midwestern United States that are characterized by declining industry, aging factories, and a declining population. The Rust Belt begins in western New York and traverses west through Pennsylvania, West Virginia, Ohio, Indiana, and the Lower Peninsula of Michigan, ending in northern Illinois, eastern Iowa, and southeastern Wisconsin. Parts of New England are also included. The region was home to economies that were dominant in industry and were once known as the Manufacturing Belt, or Steel Belt." The term Rust Belt refers to the deindustrialization, or economic decline of the industrial heartland, especially the steel- and automobile-producing regions. The term also captures the consequences of deindustrialization such as population loss and urban decay. The term Rust Belt was introduced in the 1980s and has since been used not only to describe the area of the United States, but also the international equivalents such as the Ruhr area of Germany. [4]

salt dome: A vertical cylinder of salt. There are about five hundred underground salt domes in the Gulf Coast region, stretching from Mexico to the Florida panhandle. [11]

saw-grass: Tall, sharp-serrated grass found along the coastal area of eastern America. [10]

scabland: A flat region with exposed lava rock, a thin layer of soil, and sparse vegetation. Usually cut through with channels. Part of the eastern Washington landscape. [16]

seamount: An underwater mountain rising from the ocean floor and having a peaked or flat-topped summit below the surface of the sea. [20]

secondary sector: That portion of a region's economy devoted to the processing of basic materials extracted by the primary sector. [4]

Second Great Awakening: The early-nineteenth-century Christian religious revival that emphasized evangelism and lay ministers. The revival spread from the "burned-over district" of upstate New York, through the eastern half of the United States. [8]

seigneur (*Fr.*): A feudal lord who owned a large estate by grant from the king of France. Applicable in Quebec. [5]

seigneurie (*Fr.*): In the old French regime in Quebec, a tract of land granted by the Crown, usually as a reward for services rendered to the Crown or to a friend of the authorities. It was expected and usually a condition of the grant, that the *seigneur* would encourage settlement on the lands in his *seigneurie*. In general, the land was not sold but rather leased in perpetuity, and each settler had to pay an annual rent. When land was sold or transferred for a fee, it was the improvements on the land, the buildings, and so on that were sold, not the land itself. The feudal elements of this system quickly became irrelevant in the New World, where land was available in abundance for tenants who felt oppressed and wanted to move. The seigneurial system was abolished in Quebec in the mid-1850s, and the settlers (*habitants*) then had the opportunity to purchase the land outright. [5]

seismic line: A clearing made in dense boreal woods for geologic drilling and dynamiting. Interferes with wildlife migrations, habitat, and safety. [18]

sharecropper: An agricultural tenant who pays for use of the land with a predetermined share of the crop rather than with a cash rent. [11]

shield: A broad area of very old rocks above sea level. Usually characterized by thin, poor soils and low population densities. [3]

shield cluster: Island composed of more than one shield volcano. For example, in the Hawaiian islands, Hawai`i and Maui. [20]

shield volcano: A gently sloping volcano in the shape of a flattened dome, built almost exclusively of lava flows. [20]

short sea shipping: Promoting the use of waterways to ease traffic congestion on national highways. Commercial waterborne transportation that does not transit an ocean. It is an alternative form of commercial transportation that utilizes inland and coastal waterways to move commercial freight from major domestic ports to its destination. [6]

shut-in: A river confined in a deep, narrow, water-sculpted gorge or channel. Common in the Ozarks. [12]

sinkhole (or sink): A rounded depression in the landscape, formed when an underground cavity collapses. Sinks may be a sheer vertical opening into a cave, or a shallow depression of many acres. [10]

slough: A swamp or shallow lake in the northern or midwestern United States, or a slowly flowing, shallow swamp or marsh in the southeastern United States. [10]

smart growth: A set of policies governing transportation and planning of cities away from sprawl and favoring quality-of-life issues. Smart growth cities advocate compact land use, walkability, bicycle-friendliness, and mixed-use housing. [6]

smog: Mixture of particulate matter and chemical pollutants in the lower atmosphere, usually over urban areas. [19]

sod house: First houses built on the Great Plains in the nineteenth century, out of the only building material available: sod. [14]

specialty crop: Any agricultural crop except wheat, feed grains, oil seeds, cotton, rice, peanuts, and tobacco. Mostly orchard fruit and vegetable agriculture. [19]

sprawl: Unplanned and uncontrolled spreading of urban development on undeveloped land. [4]

spring: A natural discharge of water from a rock or soil to the surface. [12]

steppe: A vast semiarid, grass-covered plain, as found in southeast Europe, Siberia, and central North America. [14]

stratovolcano: A steep-sided, often symmetrical cone volcano composed of alternating layers of lava flows, ash, and pyroclastic material (from volcanic explosion or ejection), which tend to erupt explosively. Also known as a conical or composite volcano. For example, Mount St. Helens, Washington. [17]

strip-mining (or surface mining): The type of mining in which soil and rock are stripped away by large machines to get at coal or other minerals buried just beneath the surface structures. [8]

subbituminous: Coal that is softer than bituminous and harder than lignite. Has a lower percentage of sulfur and therefore has become the favored coal since the Clean Air Act of 1970. Found predominately in the Powder River Basin. [8]

subregion: A portion of a larger region that shares its major characteristics but has a specific identity, which can be geographical, geological, cultural, or economic. A subregion of the Pacific Northwest is the glacially formed Puget Trough, which is between the Coastal and Cascade mountains. [1]

subsidence: A sinking of Earth's crust due to underground excavations. Subsidence is prevalent along the Gulf Coast and in Florida. [11]

subsidy: Monetary assistance granted by a government to a person or group in support of an enterprise regarded as being in the public interest. The average farmer subsidy in the United States is $16,000, mainly in the form of tax reductions and low water prices. [14]

subsistence economy: A way of life prevalent in the North and in Alaska, sometimes used as synonymous with "living off the land." For Natives it is nothing less than a cultural, spiritual, and social way of life that relies on hunting, fishing, and gathering, as well as sharing of resources and dissemination of information across generational lines. Not a cash economy. [18]

suitcase farmer: A farmer who puts beef cattle to pasture for several months while pursuing leisure or other ventures, returning after several months to share in the profit. [14]

Sun Belt: The southern tier of the United States, focused on Florida, Texas, Arizona, and California, and extending as far north as Virginia. The term gained wide use in the 1970s, when the economic and political impact of the nation's overall shift in population to the South and West became conspicuous. [4]

Surface Mining Control and Reclamation Act (SMCRA) (1977): Act stating a need for balance between protection of the environment and agricultural productivity and the nation's need for coal as an essential source of energy. Provisions include the return of land to its original contour and condition; prime farmland cannot be mined unless it can be restored to an equivalent or higher level of yield. [8]

sustainability: Living on Earth while maintaining a balance of all natural ecosystems, including humans. Recognizing that resources are limited, so that they are sustained throughout time and for future generations. [1]

sustainable development: Development that meets the needs of the present without compromising the needs of future generations. Seen as the guiding principle for long-term global development, sustainability consists of three pillars: economic development, social development, and environmental protection. [2]

sustainable development goals: In 2015, the United Nations launched the Sustainable Development Goals (SDGs). There are seventeen goals that cover a range of environmental, economic and social issues. [2]

sustainable geography: The study of human and physical landscapes that together create the ecological landscape, one that links the physical and the human and is dynamically balanced to remain healthy and thriving over the long term. [1]

sustainable hazard mitigation: The viewing of disasters from a broad perspective and connecting the issues of disasters to other problems. The ability to tolerate and overcome damage, diminished productivity, and reduced quality of life from an extreme event without significant outside assistance. To be done sustainably, it must improve environmental quality, people's quality of life, and local resilience; it must enhance local economies and create community. [11]

sustainable yield: The amount of a naturally self-reproducing community, such as trees or fish, that can be harvested without diminishing the ability of the community to sustain itself. [11]

swamp: A wetland type, vegetated mostly by trees and shrubs; often associated with rivers, slow streams, or isolated depressions. [3]

syncretism: A form of cultural encounter in which the traditions entailed are fused into a novel emergent, whose meanings and symbolic expressions are in some respects different from either of the original singular traditions. [18]

taiga (or **boreal forest**): A moist, subarctic coniferous forest that begins where the tundra ends and is dominated by spruces and firs. [3]

tariff: A tax imposed by one country on imports from other countries. This could be to favor one's own goods. [5]

taro: A starchy tuber that was the staple plant for the native Hawaiian diet. Currently being resurrected as a crop to help improve the Hawaiian native diet. [20]

technopole: One form of enterprise zone, the mine and foundry of the informational economy. For example, Silicon Valley. [7]

Tennessee Valley Authority (TVA): A series of dams along the Tennessee River created to manage water resources in a region devastated by the Depression. Authorized in 1933, it was built to control floods, promote land conservation, and provide electrical service. [8]

territory: In Canada, an administrative division created and controlled by federal law. A territory therefore does not have the same rights and privileges as a province. [18]

tertiary sector: That portion of a region's economy devoted to service activities (e.g., transportation, retail and wholesale operations, insurance). [4]

thaw lake: A bog or marshy pond formed when permafrost melts. The ground beneath the lake remains frozen and prevents the water from draining away. [18]

thermal inversion: An inversion of the normal pattern of air being warmer near the surface of Earth. In thermal inversion, a mass of cold air is trapped below a mass of warmer air, creating the condition called smog. [19]

thermohaline circulation: Circulation in a large body of water caused by changes in water density brought about by variations in water temperature and salinity. Cold, salty water is heavier than warmer, less saline water and will sink into the deep ocean. [6]

three Es: Sustainability is often defined as a balance of the three E's: the environment, the economy, and social equity. [2]

tidal bore: A high wave (often dangerous) caused by tidal flow (as by colliding tidal currents or in a narrow estuary). Tidal bores form when an incoming tide rushes up a river, developing a steep forward slope due to resistance to the tide's advance by the river, which is flowing in the opposite direction. The river changes its direction of flow, flowing over the outgoing river water. [6]

tidewater: The area east of the fall line along the South Atlantic coast. In colonial America, the Tidewater was a region around Chesapeake Bay. [9]

tornado: A high-speed rotating column of air, usually occurring in the Great Plains or Midwest where warm and cold fronts meet. [14]

total fertility rate (TFR): The average number of children a woman will bear during her childbearing years. Developed countries have much lower TFRs than lesser developed countries, although TFRs are dropping in most lesser developed countries. [4]

township and range system: The system started by the US government in the late 1780s, by which the land northwest of the Ohio River was divided into sections and offered to people who agreed to farm. [13]

trace: A path or trail made by animals and/or humans. [8]

tragedy of the commons: The exploitation of a common resource when competing parties share it, each pursuing their own interest. Term originated by Garrett Hardin, originally in relation to English common fields but now applied to many common areas, such as the ocean and fisheries. [6]

Trail of Tears: Forced march of Cherokee Nation and other tribes in the 1830s, from Georgia to Oklahoma territory. More than four thousand are estimated to have died on the march. [11]

transhumance: The seasonal movement of people and animals in search of pasture. Commonly, winters are spent in snow-free lowlands and summers in the cooler uplands. [15]

transit-oriented development (TOD): A mixed-use development designed to be easily accessed by public transportation. [7]

transmountain diversion: Moving water from an area that is not as needy to an area with high population growth that lacks sufficient water. [15]

trawler (or **factory freezer**): A type of ocean ship from which fish are caught, then processed, frozen, and stored on board. [6]

Treaty of Guadalupe Hidalgo (1848): The treaty that ended the Mexican-American War and ceded to the United States California, Nevada, Utah, and parts of Colorado, Arizona, New Mexico, and Wyoming for $15 million. [19]

Treaty of Paris (1763): The treaty that ended the French and Indian War. England gained all French lands in North America, except two small islands off Newfoundland. Beginning of overseas British Empire. [5]

tree line: The latitude or the elevation on mountain slopes above which trees cannot grow. [15]

triangular trade: Trade between three ports, each receiving what it needs and sending what it produces in a closed loop. In the eighteenth- and nineteenth-century United States, the most famous was the shipment of tobacco and sugar to England, manufactured goods (textiles) to Africa, and slaves to America. [9]

triple bottom line: A calculation of financial, environmental, and social performance. Often referred to as "profits, planet, and people," which together form a more viable option toward sustainability goals than the conventional bottom line, which is profit alone. [2]

trophic cascade: An ecological process that starts at the top of a food chain and trickles down to the bottom. [15]

tundra: A treeless area between the icecap and the tree line of Arctic regions, having permanently frozen subsoil and supporting low-growing vegetation such as lichens, mosses, and stunted shrubs. [3]

unintended consequences: Outcomes that are not (or are not limited to) the results originally intended. Unintended consequences have been tied to the hubris humans have about their control of nature and its often undesirable consequences. [1]

Upper Canada: A historical region and province of British North America, roughly coextensive with southern Ontario, Canada. It was formed in 1791 and joined Lower Canada in 1841. [5]

urban: Characteristic of the city or city life. In the United States, an area is considered urban when it has more than twenty-five hundred people. In Canada, urban areas are those over one thousand people. [4]

urban village: A planning concept that features medium-density settlement, mixed uses, walkability, and a dependence on public transit. [13]

urbanization: Urbanization is defined as the complex process of urban growth in demographic, social, political, behavioral, and economic terms. Urbanization is the process by which an increasing percentage of a population lives in cities and suburbs. This process is often linked to industrialization and modernization and refers to the movement from rural to urban areas and the social reorganization that occurs as a result. The United States and most European nations began to urbanize in the 19th century. [4]

vernacular: Originally a linguistic term connoting the common speech of a people. It has been adopted by architectural historians to identify the common buildings of ordinary people that characterize a place or region. A vernacular cultural region is one recognized by the inhabitants. For example, Little Italy or a BBQ region in the South. [5]

vertical integration: The joining of companies engaged in different but related businesses. Often, a variety of businesses that create a product from raw material to final product. In the food industry, it is the control of multiple aspects of production, including animal production, processing, distribution, and marketing. In the pork industry, known as "birth to bacon." [9]

vertical zonation: Distribution of organisms, vegetation, and soils by altitude. [15]

vog: A portmanteau word of *volcanic* and *fog*. A form of volcanic smog on the big island of Hawai`i. The vog is a benefit for growing coffee on the Kona coast, but it also has respiratory health issues. [20]

volcanic mountain: Formed when molten rock, or magma deep within the Earth, erupts and piles up on the surface. Volcanic mountains are usually made of basalt and rhyolite. [3]

volcanic plug: Landforms created when lava hardens within the vent of an active volcano. Erosion may remove surrounding rock and produce distinctive landforms. For example, Devil's Tower in northwestern Wyoming. [14]

water gap: Deep valleys with water, such as rivers or streams, running through mountainous areas. The Appalachian region has many water and wind (dry) gaps. For example, Delaware Water Gap. [8]

watershed: A divide that separates neighboring drainage basins. In the United States, the term is used synonymously with drainage basin. [1]

water table: The level where ground is saturated with water. [14]

wetland: A transitional zone of waterlogged land that is usually between a dryland and water body. Wetlands include swamps, marshes, sloughs, bogs, and similar areas. They are important wildlife habitat and nurseries, as well as important filtration areas for water. [3]

wind gap: Notch in a mountain ridge, a dry water gap, where water once flowed. [8]

windmill: Traditionally used in dry areas of the United States to provide shallow groundwater for cattle and household use. [14]

wind turbine: Machine that converts wind energy into electricity. [3]

xerophytic: A plant adapted to living in an arid habitat; a desert plant. [3]

yeoman: Freeholder of lower status—conservative, family oriented, and holding communal values—who owned and worked his own farm. Thomas Jefferson idealized the independent yeoman farmer as the symbol of agrarian virtues for the United States. [9]

Index

arroyo, 370
artesian spring, 207
artificial lakes, 25, 228, 258
asbestos, 77
Asian carp, 64
Asian population, 43–46; in California, 467; in Canadian Corridor, 68–70; in Florida, 213; in Hawai`i, 500; in Intermontane, 387; in Megalopolis, 214–125; in Midwest, 287
Aspen, Colorado, 347–348, 350, 362
Aspenization, 350
assimilation, 166
asthma, 248, 259, 265, 445, 459–460
Astor, John Jacob, 406
Astoria, Oregon, 402–403, 406
Atchafalaya River, 230, 249
Athabasca glacier, 344
Athabascan tribe, 378, 429, 435, 438–440
Atlanta, Georgia, 43, 47, 50, 177–178, 182, 184–190, 194–196
Atlantica, 102, 107–108
Atlantic Canada, 108
Atlantic City, New Jersey, 115, 137, 251
atoll, 486, 488–489
Austin, Moses, 235
Austin, Stephen, 235
Austin, Texas, 242, 245–247
auto production, 78, 251

baby boom, 41
badlands, 309–310, 473
Bailey, Robert G., 4
Bakersfield, California, 459
Bakken Formation, 322, 332–334
Balcones Escarpment, 228, 242, 244–245, 251, 262, 312
bald, 257, 261
Bald Knobbers, 257, 261
Baltimore, Maryland, 50, 114, 116, 124, 132, 136–137, 386
Banff National Park, 7, 63, 362
bank, 85
banking services, 52, 79, 131, 137–138, 156, 160, 185–186, 195, 218, 221, 237, 288, 360, 474
barbeque, 181–182, 241
barrier island, 27, 35, 118, 123, 172, 174–176, 178, 203, 208, 212, 216, 218, 227–228, 230, 232
basalt, 21, 368–369, 488–489
basement rock, 114
basin, 4, 21, 23
Basin and Range, 5, 7, 23, 37, 311, 355, 368–371, 373, 377–378, 388, 391–392, 454–456, 459
Basque(s), 378, 380–381
batholith, 310, 343–344, 358
Bay of Fundy, 89–90, 93, 97, 100, 106

bayou(s), 27, 226–227, 238–239, 247
BBQ, 181–182
beaches, dredging, 202, 207–208, 280
beaver, 37, 63, 340–341, 349, 424
beetles, 347, 432
Bell, Harold Wright, 271
Beltway, 134
Bend, Oregon, 381, 387
Bentonville, Arkansas, 264, 269–270
Beotuks, 90
Berendt, John, 189
Bering Sea, 37, 425, 429, 431–432, 434, 446
Berkeley, California, 470–472, 474
Bible Belt, 263
bicycling, 188, 292, 294
Big Five, 499, 501, 505
Bighorn River, 340
Big Island, 486–489, 491–494, 499–500, 503–504, 506
Big Spring, 258
Big Thompson Project, 346
bioaccumulation, 403, 449
biofuel, 297–298, 331, 356, 363, 504
biome, 37, 204
biophysical carrying capacity, 14
bioregion, 4. See also ecoregion(s)
bioswale, 118, 131, 215
Birmingham, Alabama, 5, 50, 156–157
Birmingham Civil Rights National Monument, 157
birthrate(s), 42, 44–46, 65, 79, 94, 98, 381, 436, 440, 467
Bitterroot Mountains, 23, 344, 356
bituminous, 149
Black Belt: in Alabama, 227; in Chicago, 290; in Gulf Coastal Plains, 226–227, 237, 239, 241, 246, 251
Black Hills, 5, 23, 310
Black Mesa, 378
blacks, 42–43; in Appalachia, 155; in California, 465; in Florida, 214, 217; in Great Plains, 318; in Gulf Coastal Plains, 237–241, 250; in Hawai`i, 500; in Megalopolis, 134; in Midwest, 290, 292; in South Atlantic, 183–184, 186, 189
Black Swamp, 278, 284, 288
blackwater rivers, 177
blasting, 164
BLM. See Bureau of Land Management
Bloomberg, Michael, 34
bluegrass, 147, 155, 159; Kentucky Bluegrass, 161
Blue Ridge Province, 144–145
blues, 228, 239–241
bog, 27–28
boll weevil, 189, 191–192, 240–241, 246–247
boom and bust town(s), 350–351, 356, 360, 391
Boone, Daniel, 151

borders, 5–6, 76, 177, 381
boreal forest, 20, 32, 37, 85, 300, 309, 347, 425, 427, 430–432, 434, 437, 446. See also taiga
borough(s), 128–129, 131
bosque, 228
Boston, Massachusetts, 50, 84, 114, 123–126, 137–139
Boston Mountains, 257
BosWash, 114
Boulder, Colorado, 340, 343, 353–355, 362, 364
braided rivers, 430
Branson, Missouri, 263–264, 270–271
break-in-bulk point, 60, 70, 116
brewis, 98
brine, 301, 456
British Columbia, 6, 22–23, 31, 42–43, 46, 53, 59, 62, 75, 78–79, 105, 309, 319, 341, 344, 349 353, 356–358, 360, 398–400, 405, 407–410, 412–413, 415–420, 424–425, 429, 434, 440
British North America Act, 62
broiler chicken, 267
Bronx, 115, 127, 129–130, 136
Brooklyn, 115, 120, 128–130
Brooks Range, 23, 341, 344, 347, 427, 437, 444
brownfield, 101, 131, 158, 286
Brundtland Report, 12
buffalo, 284, 300, 308–309, 311, 316–319, 321, 408
buffalo soldiers, 318
Bureau of Land Management (BLM), 350, 390
bush pilots, 448
butte, 371
Butte, Montana, 360

cache, 434
Cades Cove, 147
CAFOs. See concentrated animal feeding operations
Cahokia, 228, 234, 284
Cairo, Illinois, 228, 230, 242, 244, 264, 282–283
Cajun(s), 94, 226, 235, 238, 247
caldera, 25, 400, 402, 492
Caldwell, Erskine, 184
Calgary, Alberta, 47, 50, 318 323–327, 444
caliche, 315
California: climate, 457–459; cultural perspectives, 465–467; economy, 474–481; historical geography and settlement, 463–465; physical geography, 454–456; smog, 459; urban trends, 468–473; water, 456
Callenbach, Ernest, 398
Calomel, 239

Calusa, 211
Campbell, James, 490, 503
Canada: climate regions, 30; economic trends, 51–53; ecoregions, 8; historical geography and settlement, 41–43; immigration, 45–48; physical geography, 19–40; population trends, 44–45; regions, 4–6; urban trends, 49–51; territories, 58–59
Canadian Aboriginals, 42, 62, 65–66, 319, 407, 435–437
Canadian Corridor: climate, 62; cultural perspectives, 66–67; economy, 75–79; historical geography and settlement, 62–66; immigration and diversity, 67–70; physical geography, 58–60; population, 67; urban trends 70–75; water, 60–62
Canadian Prairie: climate, 315; cultural perspectives, 320–321; economy, 327–331; historical geography and settlement, 319–320; physical geography, 309–310; urban trends, 324–327; water, 312–315
Canadian Rockies, 327, 340–345, 349, 360
Canadian Shield, 58–60, 66, 73, 77, 79, 85, 87, 276, 280, 300, 309, 319, 425, 427–430
Canadien, 66
canebrake, 147, 151, 161
Canmore, Alberta, 344
Cannery Row, Monterey, California, 40
canola, 321, 329, 331, 412
canyon, 368
Canyonlands, 371
CAP. See Central Arizona Project
cap and trade, 79
cape, 174
Cape Cod, 22, 84, 91, 103, 107, 114, 122, 137–138, 172
capelin, 104
Cape May, 115
capitalism, 123, 179; green capitalism, 160
carbon cycle, 33
carbon dioxide, 22, 32–34, 203, 207, 259, 291, 297, 332, 363, 411, 427, 481
carbon sink, 427, 433, 446
caribou, 86, 426–427, 430, 444, 449
Carlsbad Caverns, 311
Carolina bay, 176
carpetbagger(s), 189
carpet industry, 195; sustainable carpet, 194
carrying capacity, 7, 14–15, 342, 505
Carson, Kit, 349
Carson Sink, 374
Cartier, Jacques, 60
Cascade Mountains, 23–24, 374, 398–401
casinos: in Appalachia, 166; in Gulf Coastal Plains, 226, 241, 251–252; in Intermontane, 378, 384–385, 392; in Midwest, 302
Castro, Fidel, 214

Castro Street, San Francisco, 48–49
Catawba River, 178
catfish, 181, 248–249
Catskills, 147, 166
cattle, 35, 147, 160, 184, 211, 215, 218–219, 228, 240–241, 288, 298, 309, 311, 313, 317–319, 321, 324, 327, 329–333, 357, 370, 383, 389–390, 464, 490, 492, 500
cattle ticks, 240
CCC. See Civilian Conservation Corps
Celebration, Florida, 216–217
census metropolitan area (CMA), 50
center of population, 214
center pivot irrigation (CPI), 311, 314, 328
Central Arizona Project (CAP), 374–375
Central City, Colorado, 360
Central Coast, 465, 475, 480
Central Lowlands, 5, 21, 256, 276–77, 283, 298, 310
Central Texas Uplift, 312
Central Valley, 454–456, 458, 464, 468, 474–477, 481
CERP. See Comprehensive Everglades Restoration Plan
chain migration, 238, 263, 285
Champlain, Samuel de, 70
Champlain Sea, 60
Channeled Scablands, 21, 368–369
chaparral ecosystem, 454
Chapel Hill, North Carolina, 185
Charleston, South Carolina, 174, 185–187, 192, 195–196
Charleston, West Virginia, 158
Charlotte, North Carolina, 34, 50, 184–186
Chattahoochee River, 177–178
Chattanooga, Tennessee, 160, 167
cheatgrass, 389–390
chemical industry: in Appalachia, 148; in Gulf Coastal Plains, 249–251
Chemical Valley, 148
Cherokee, 145, 151, 236–237
Chesapeake Bay, 115–120, 132, 135–136, 189, 248
Cheyenne, Wyoming, 353
Chicago, Illinois, 43, 48, 50, 264, 276, 280, 285, 287–291, 300–301, 303, 329, 444, 446
Chickasaw, 234
China, 40, 60, 76, 78–79, 161, 173, 191, 246, 270, 298, 300, 302, 321, 418, 477, 479, 503
Chinese Exclusion Act, 464
Chinese immigrants, 40, 43, 46–48, 73; in California, 467; in Canadian Corridor, 125; in Great Plains, 322; in Hawai`i, 499; in Intermontane, 383; in Megalopolis, 134; in Midwest, 287, 292; in Ozarks, 263; in Pacific Northwest, 409–410
chinook, 315

Chinook tribe, 405
chip mills, 159, 162, 269–271
Choctaw, 234
Chugach Mountains, 440–441
Churchill, Manitoba, 428–429
Cincinnati, Ohio, 50, 147, 284, 287, 294
cities. See under urban
city, definition of, 50
citrus, 209, 216–218, 388
Civilian Conservation Corps (CCC), 166
Clean Air Act, 13, 162, 167
Clean Water Act (CWA), 12–13, 29, 89, 117–120, 148, 163, 280–281
Clear Creek, Colorado, 359
clear-cut(ing), 93, 269, 343, 416–417
Cleveland, Ohio, 12, 52, 151, 278, 281, 291–292, 294, 302
climate change, 12–13, 19, 32–35; and Appalachia, 149, 152; and arctic region, 424, 426–428, 430–434, 441, 449; and California, 474, 481; and Canadian Corridor, 58, 61–63, 65; and Chesapeake Bay, 118–119; and Great Plains, 317, 332, 334; and Gulf Coastal Plains, 231, 234, 245; and Florida, 202, 207–208, 210, 218, 220, 222; and Hawai`i, 494–495, 506; and Intermontane, 376, 387, 389, 393; and Megalopolis, 114, 117, 120–121, 126–127; and Midwest, 280; and North Atlantic Provinces, 92, 100, 104; and Ogallala Aquifer, 317; and Ozarks, 259, 261, 269–270; and Pacific Northwest, 403, 405–406, 411–412, 415, 419; and permafrost, 433; and Rocky Mountains, 347–348, 354; and sea level rise, 35; and snowpack, 346; and South Atlantic, 174, 178–179, 186, 188
climate regions, 30–31
closed ecosystem, 486
CMA. See census metropolitan area
Coachella Valley, California, 373, 388–389
coal, 32–34, 149; in Appalachia, 144–145, 147–149, 151, 153–154, 156, 160–167; in Canadian Corridor, 62, 74, 78; in Great Plains, 331, 333–334; in Intermontane, 372, 388; in Megalopolis, 131–132, 136; in Midwest, 297; in North Atlantic Provinces, 100, 105; in Rocky Mountains, 351, 353; in South Atlantic, 178, 196
coal ash, 151, 164
Coal River Mountain Watch, 167
coal sludge, 167
coastal plain, 172, 174–175, 177–178, 185, 202
Coastal Prairie, 228
Coastal Range, 399–400, 454–455, 458–459
Coast Mountains, 399–400
cod, 84, 93, 95, 99, 102–104, 442, 446
coffee, 418, 492, 403

forests/forestry, *(continued)*
219, 256–261, 265, 268–269, 271,
308–310, 312, 315, 370–371, 434, 440,
443, 446, 455, 461–462, 473, 489, 492,
501, 503; boreal, 20, 37, 425, 427,
430–432, 437; in Gulf Coastal Plains,
227, 246, 248; in Megalopolis, 114–115,
118, 124, 135; in Midwest, 276–279, 284,
296, 300; in Pacific Northwest, 398–400,
403–404, 409, 416–417, 420; in Rocky
Mountains, 342–344, 347, 349–350, 353,
356, 360. *See also* logging
Fort Collins, Colorado, 353–356, 363
Fort McMurray, 98, 427, 440, 442, 445–446
fortress living, 467–468
49th Parallel, 5, 29, 62, 321, 344, 349,
377, 406
fossil fuels, 15, 22, 32–33, 74, 195, 258,
294, 296–297, 328–329, 331, 362, 393,
416, 505
Four Corners, 343, 372, 375, 378–379
fracking, 165, 332, 334
francophone, 42, 58, 66–68, 79, 98
Fraser River, 25, 345, 400, 402, 412, 419
Fremont, John C., 349, 380
French and Indian Wars, 151
freshwater, 21–23, 27–29, 60, 65, 89–90,
92, 118, 176, 205–207, 229, 231, 276,
279–281, 303, 388, 399, 419, 427, 429,
456, 458, 468, 490, 493, 500
Fresno, California, 459
Frobisher, Martin, 442
Frontenac Axis, 58–59, 66, 87
Front Range, 323, 340–341, 345–346, 350,
353, 362
fruits, 77, 135–136, 218, 228, 246, 250, 331,
349, 356, 388, 416, 457, 474–475

Gadsden Purchase, 377
galena lead, 267
Galveston Bay, 228
gangs, 385
Garreau, Joel, 4
gas, 21, 34, 122, 187, 297, 378, 474, 477,
504; in Alaska and Arctic, 427, 433, 435,
443–446, 449; in Great Plains, 332–334;
in Gulf Coastal Plains, 229–230,
243–244, 246, 249–250; in North
Atlantic Provinces, 29, 100–101, 105;
in Pacific Northwest, 404; in Rocky
Mountains, 343, 353, 360, 362.
See also natural gas
GDP (gross domestic product), 45, 50, 52,
79, 99, 106, 322, 360
Geechee, 180–181
gender, 48, 105
General Agreement on Tariffs and Trade
(GATT), 76
genetically modified organism (GMO), 240,
296, 298, 328–329

geography, definition, 3, 19; Smith and
Thompson, 249
geology, 22, 116, 144, 202, 454–455
Georges Banks, 91, 95
geothermal power, 392, 449
geothermal spring(s), 257–259
Gershwin, George, 181
GHG. *See* greenhouse gases
ghost town(s), 350–351, 439, 447
ginseng, 356–357
glacial drift, 21, 399
glacial erratic, 369
glaciation, 21, 85, 428; eras of, 117, 147; and
Great Lakes, 276, 278; and Great Plains,
312; maximum extent of, 22
glacier(s), 7, 21–23, 25, 35, 85, 90, 114, 122,
276–277, 308, 316, 344–345, 348, 350,
399–400, 404, 406, 424–426, 429, 432, 448
Glacier Bay, 447
Glacier National Park, 348
global warming, 35, 178, 317, 412, 426,
433–434
GMO. *See* genetically modified organism
gold, 43, 53, 151, 179, 192, 203, 211, 242,
399, 403, 407, 412; in Alaska and Yukon,
424, 429–430, 435, 439–441, 443; in
California, 377, 380, 387–388, 391, 406,
464, 471; in Great Plains, 310, 331; in
Rocky Mountains, 343, 350–351, 358–360
Gold Coast, 203, 212
Golden Gate Bridge, 458, 470–471,
473–474, 480
Golden Horseshoe, 53, 66–67, 69, 77–78
Gold Rush, 360, 377, 380, 399, 403–406,
429, 435, 443, 464, 471
Gondwana, 21
Gottman, Jean, 50, 114
government, 6, 12–13, 16–17, 29, 34, 48,
59, 62, 64–66, 68, 71–72, 74, 76, 78,
103–105, 108, 114, 127, 130, 132,
134–135, 137, 144, 152, 156, 158, 163,
173, 181, 184–186, 194–195, 214,
219–220, 243, 248, 252, 264, 284, 310,
318–319, 321, 324, 328, 349, 358, 360,
378, 384, 386–387, 390–392, 407, 412,
417, 419, 464, 466–467, 471, 477, 481,
490, 496, 498–500; in Alaska and Arctic,
424–425, 431, 433, 435–436, 440–441,
444, 446–447; and renewable energy, 79,
138, 334; and water, 120, 188, 281, 289,
346, 403, 406
grain elevators, 132, 323
Grand Banks, 75, 85, 90–92, 102–105, 123
Grand Canyon, 7, 205, 345, 368, 371–372,
391–392, 473, 490
Grand Coulee Dam, 373
grass banking, 391, 393
grassland, 4–5, 35, 37–38, 172, 203, 218,
228, 238, 257, 259, 261, 276, 279, 284,
308–309, 311, 369–371, 455, 461

Grassland Foundation, 332
gray stormwater infrastructure, 118
gray wolves, 37, 342
grazing, 144, 203, 218, 230, 265, 311,
317–318, 329, 332, 353, 357, 383,
389–391, 398, 426
Great American Desert, 311, 317–318
Great Basin, 25, 368–370, 374, 376, 383
Great Divide Basin, 343
Great Harbour Deep, 93
Great Lakes, 7, 22, 24–25, 27–28, 58, 60–62,
64–66, 71, 73, 75, 78, 90, 104, 126, 157,
231, 234, 248, 277–285, 287–288,
300–301, 303, 319–320, 446
Great Lakes Lowlands, 58–60, 66, 70
Great Mahele, 498–499
Great Migration, 151, 238
Great Plains, 4–5, 8, 37–38, 45, 75, 228, 298,
308, 327–330, 332–333, 340, 343, 391;
climate, 27, 35, 314–316, 318,
345–346; climate change and, 317;
cultural perspectives, 42, 320–321;
historical geography and settlement,
41–42, 244, 264, 322–324, 355; physical
geography, 21, 257–258, 308–309,
311–313, 370
Great Salt Lake, 369, 374, 387–388
Great Smoky Mountains, 144–145, 148, 162,
166–167
Great Valley, 123, 144–145, 180
green building, 72, 118, 139, 217, 243,
245–246, 252, 415, 471, 481; in
Midwest, 291
green stormwater infrastructure, 118
greenhouse effect, 34, 317
greenhouse gases (GHG); 32–33, 100, 122,
354, 387, 433, 445; California and, 470;
emissions, 33–34, 58, 61, 79, 108, 127,
134, 138, 188, 194–195, 222, 246, 292,
326–327, 356, 386, 406, 412, 415, 420,
441–442
Green Mountain Boys, 95
Green Mountains, 86, 95, 106
Green Revolution, 296, 328
Grey, Zane, 370
gross domestic product (GDP), 45, 50, 52,
79, 99, 106, 322, 360
ground, 32, types of, 35, 212, 369, 433–434
groundwater, 23–24, 27–29, 73, 148, 151,
165, 176, 193–194, 203, 207, 215, 240,
244, 247, 258, 267, 308–309, 312–313,
315, 329, 341, 358, 360, 374, 384, 391,
456, 493
Gulf Coastal Plains, 21, 37, 215; climate,
228–234; cultural perspectives, 239–241;
historical geography and settlement,
234–239; physical geography, 226–228
Gulf of Mexico, 21, 25, 29–30, 32, 89, 177,
207, 231–232, 312, 315, 321, 374; dead
zones in, 247

Gulf Stream, 89, 90
Gullah, 174–175, 180–181
Gypsum Hills, 311–312

habitant(s), 64
haboob, 375–376
Haida, 404–405, 435, 437
hail, 315
Halifax, Nova Scotia, 99–100, 103, 127, 442
Hamilton, Alexander, 132
Hamilton, Ontario, 70, 78, 300
hammock, 203–204, 206
Harper, Stephen, 66
Hart, John Fraser, 246
hatchery, 249, 415
Hawai`i: climate, 493–495; cultural
    perspectives, 496–499; historical
    geography and settlement, 495–496;
    physical geography, 486–493
Hawai`i Land Reform Act, 498
Hawken, Paul, 194
Hayden, Ferdinand, 249
HBC. *See* Hudson's Bay Company
headwater stream, 164
health care, 356
Hemingway, Ernest, 212
hemp, 77, 161
herding, 184, 378
Hetch-Hetchy, 456
Hewlett, Bill, 470
Hiassen, Carl, 222
Hibernia oil field, 105
high-fructose corn syrup (HFCS), 329
Highland Rim, 147
High Plains, 298, 308–311, 319, 328, 331,
    343, 352; aquifer, 313–314
hillbilly, 159, 256, 262–263
Hill Country, 235, 237, 312
Hispanics, 15, 43, 99, 124, 128, 155,
    242, 244, 269, 322, 324, 353, 440;
    in California, 467; in Florida,
    213–214, 216–217; in Hawai`i, 500; in
    Intermontane, 378, 380–381, 385–387;
    in South Atlantic, 184–186, 195
Hmong population, 263–264, 287
hogbacks, 341, 370
hog farming, 106, 193–194, 299
hollers, 152, 155, 240, 257, 266
Holocene, 21
homeless, 247, 295, 355, 415, 466, 486, 501
Homestead Act, 316, 318–319, 323, 499
homesteading, 259, 284, 309, 499–500, 506
Honolulu, 486, 488, 490–491, 493–494, 497,
    500–502, 504–505
Hood Canal, 403–404
Hoover Dam, 373, 384
Hopewell, 151, 284
Hopi, 349, 375, 377–379
horse farms, 147, 161
hot spot, 23, 369, 487–488

Hot Springs, Arkansas, 257–259,
    268–269, 400
Houston, Texas, 48, 50, 74, 128, 186, 226,
    228, 235, 237, 242–245, 251, 324, 348
Hudson, Henry, 115
Hudson River, 25, 87, 106, 114, 117, 127,
    129, 166
Hudson River Valley, 123, 126, 146
Hudson's Bay Company (HBC), 349, 406,
    424, 435
Huguenots, 155, 211, 215, 234
Humboldt River, 25, 374, 377
hunting: 66, 86, 90, 105, 151, 158, 205, 211,
    238, 241, 250–251, 260, 262, 265, 284,
    316–317, 340, 349–350, 353, 360, 362,
    407, 490; in Alaska and Arctic, 424, 432,
    434–436, 439; in South Atlantic, 179
hurricane(s): 28, 30, 37–38, 92, 100, 120,
    122, 348, 434, 495; definition of, 210;
    in Florida, 202, 204, 207, 209–211, 214,
    216, 218–220; in Gulf Coastal Plains,
    226, 229, 231–235, 243, 245, 248–249,
    251; in South Atlantic, 178, 186, 194
Hutcheson Memorial Forest, 115
Hutterites, 320, 322
hydraulic fracturing, 165, 286, 332, 334
hydrocarbon(s), 228
hydropower, 21, 61, 117, 124, 138, 148,
    152, 177, 270, 504; in Arctic Canada,
    78; in California, 477–478; in Pacific
    Borderland, 402, 415, 419, 430
hyperdiverse, 47, 70
hypoxia, 117, 138, 231, 331, 403–404

ice age(s), 21–22, 25, 37, 41, 60, 92, 117, 175,
    277–279, 312, 316, 349, 368, 428, 495;
    and Appalachia, 144
icebergs, 87, 90–92, 105
icefields, 344–345
ice road, 429, 448–449
igloos, 434, 436–437
IISD. *See* International Institute for
    Sustainable Development
Iliamna Lake, 430
imagineer, 216–217
immigration, 39, 41–46, 48, 98–99, 153–156,
    184, 213, 234, 241, 263, 285–288, 327, 353,
    381, 383, 388, 407, 409–410, 440, 486, 499;
    in California, 63, 65–68, 464–465, 467; in
    Canada, 319–322; in Megalopolis, 130,
    134. *See also* migration
Immigration Nationality Act, 45
Imperial Valley, California, 373–374
Indian Removal Act, 151, 284
indigenous populations, 42, 436
indigo, 123, 179–180, 189, 192, 246
industrial ecology, 194
Industrial Revolution, 52, 65, 89, 103,
    105–106, 117, 125–126, 157, 166, 180,
    280, 288, 300

informal economy, 480–481
infrastructure, 15, 29, 72, 99, 102–103,
    105, 108, 118, 131, 138, 174, 178–181,
    184–185, 189, 196, 206, 210, 215,
    230–231, 241, 245, 251, 264, 279, 283,
    288, 291, 297, 347, 360, 362, 378, 382,
    387, 411, 415, 420, 433–434, 441–442,
    446, 449, 499, 506; need for investment
    in, 62, 138, 434
Inner Canada, 58–59, 76
Innuitian Mountains, 428
Inside Passage, 398–399, 403–404, 425,
    446–447
interdisciplinary studies, geography as, 3
Interior Plateau, 8, 144, 147, 151, 159, 161,
    344, 360
Intermontane, 7–8, 22, 25, 30–31, 309,
    367–393; climate, 37, 374–375; cultural
    perspectives, 378–381; historical
    geography and settlement, 316, 375–377;
    physical geography, 343, 368–374
International Institute for Sustainable
    Development (IISD), 332
International Monetary Fund, 76
International Northeast Economic Region
    (AINER), 107–108
Intracoastal Waterway, 208
Inuit, 42, 87, 105, 410, 428, 432, 434–440,
    442, 449
Inupiaq, 434
Inuvialuit, 440
invasive species, 38, 62, 64–65, 79, 87,
    205–207, 282, 309, 362, 389, 398,
    489–490; Asian carp, 64; in Great
    lakes, 64; kudzu, 173–174; nutria,
    230, 238
Iowa, 28, 42, 277–278, 280, 287,
    297–300, 333
Iqaluit, 431, 440–441
iron, 27, 35, 62, 78, 176, 312; in Midwest,
    300–301; in Ozarks, 257, 264, 268
Iroquoian Confederacy, 62, 151
irrigation, 37, 202, 231, 247, 258, 311,
    313–314, 317–318, 328, 332, 345–346,
    357, 502; in California, 328, 456, 458,
    474–475; in Intermontane, 37, 372–373,
    385, 388–389, 392
island arc, 425
isolation, and Appalachia, 152–153
isostatic rebound, 428

Jackson, Andrew, 234
Jacksonville, Florida, 174, 181, 202–203,
    212, 215–216
James Bay Project, 430
Jamestown, Virginia, 179, 189
Jefferson, Thomas, 132, 265, 310
jet stream, 29
Jim Crow laws, 42, 184, 217, 239–241, 318
Jones Act, 448

plateaus, 22, 86, 143, 144, 147, 148, 152, 156, 256, 268, 284, 341, 343, 344, 368, 370, 388, 427

platform, 19, 20, 103, 202, 230, 249, 348, 513, 518

playa, 367, 369, 518

Pleistocene, 19, 21, 22, 202, 276, 278, 369, 387, 399, 450, 515, 518

pocosin, 19, 27, 176, 513, 518

point source pollution, 19, 29, 39, 65, 118–20, 145, 267, 270, 281, 517

polar bears, 429, 436

polder, 83, 94, 518

pollution, 12, 13, 15, 16, 19, 24, 27–29, 37, 52, 53, 61, 65, 79, 89, 105, 108, 117, 119–122, 135, 138, 145, 148. 159, 160, 164, 166–68, 177, 187, 193, 194, 196, 198, 203, 207, 213, 215, 231, 244, 248, 250, 256, 267, 270, 271, 280, 281, 288, 296, 300, 303, 304, 312, 313, 317, 331, 332, 340, 351, 360, 361, 372, 383, 386, 387, 398, 399, 4012, 404, 412, 413, 420, 442, 445, 446, 459, 472, 481, 492, 493, 500, 503, 506, 510, 511, 517, 518. *See also* air pollution; water pollution

polynucleated city, 453, 468, 470, 518

population, 14–17, 29, 31, 38, 41–53, 509, 510–514, 516–22; Alaska and Arctic, 423, 424, 435, 436, 438–42, 454; Appalachia, 145, 152–156, 161, 162, 166, 168; California, 455, 456, 460, 463, 465, 467, 468, 471, 478, 481; Canadian Corridor, 58, 59, 64–73, 76–80; Florida, 201, 202, 205–8, 211–20; Great Plains, 317, 321–24, 328, 332, 334; Gulf Coastal Plains, 226, 237, 239–44, 247, 251; Hawai`i, 486, 490, 491, 493, 497, 499–507; Intermontane, 368, 369, 372, 374, 376, 381, 385–88, 392, 394; Megalopolis, 114, 115, 117, 119, 121–25, 127–139; Midwest, 275, 280–96, 303; North Atlantic Provinces, 84, 85, 90–92, 95, 96, 98–100, 103, 106, 108, 109; Ozarks, 262–64, 270, 271; Pacific Northwest, 397, 398, 400–10, 412, 419, 420; Rocky Mountains, 339, 340, 345, 346, 350–55, 362; South Atlantic, 172, 178–81, 184–88, 196;

portage, 57, 60, 518

Portland, Maine, 50, 83, 100, 103, 124

Portland, Oregon, 363, 369, 387, 397, 398, 400–402, 405–407, 410–14, 419, 420

postindustrial economy, 518; in California, 446; in Intermontane, 392; in Megalopolis, 114; in Midwest, 301, 303; in North Atlantic Provinces, 83, 108; in Pacific Northwest, 413

potlatch, 397, 406, 407, 518

Potomac River, 12, 117, 118, 132, 134, 148, 176–78

poultry farming, 267

pounding, 95

poverty, 12, 14, 17, 42, 518; in Appalachia, 154, 155, 166; in California, 468; in Canadin Corridor, 70; in Gulf Coastal Plains, 226, 234, 241, 247, 251; in Hawai`i, 510; in Intermontane, 378, 380; in Megalopolis, 128, 130, 132; in Midwest, 284, 291; in Ozarks, 263, 266; in Rocky Mountains, 353; in South Atlantic, 195, 196

Powder River Basin, 62, 149, 162, 307, 520

Powell, John Wesley, 318, 332, 349, 371

power plants, coal-burning, 33, 78, 122, 145148, 151, 162, 246

prairie, 5, 22, 31, 37, 45, 66, 75, 77, 85, 89, 144, 151, 225, 228, 245, 257, 275–77, 282–84, 288, 308, 309–16, 318–24, 326–35, 352, 427, 434, 512, 514, 515, 518

Prairie Peninsula, 5, 275, 277, 284

Prairie provinces, 309, 319, 322, 324

Precambrian, 19, 21, 144, 145, 308, 510, 518

presidio(s), 453, 463, 464, 471, 473, 474, 516, 518

primary industry/sector, 51–52; in Alaska and Arctic, 423, 442, 446, 449; in Appalachia, 160; in Canadian Corridor, 76, 78; in Gulf Coastal Plains, 251; in Hawai`i, 502; in Megalopolis, 123, 135; in Midwest, 294; in North Atlantic Provinces, 85, 102, 108; in Ozarks, 265; in Pacific Northwest, 415, 416, 419; in Rocky Mountains, 356, 360; in South Atlantic, 189, 218

Prince Edward Island (PEI), 62, 84, 85, 94, 97, 98, 106, 108

Princeville, North Carolina, 178

Prince William Sound, 423

prior appropriation, 177, 307, 374, 518

privateer, 83, 94, 518

Prohibition, 71, 153, 82

Prospect, Nova Scotia, 102

Providence, Rhode Island, 113, 125, 136

Prudhoe Bay, 423, 435, 443, 444, 448, 449

pueblo, 377, 393

Pueblo, Colorado, 313, 353, 360

Pueblo tribe, 355, 375, 377

Puget Sound, 22, 35, 75, 397–404, 406, 410, 411, 416, 419, 420, 515

pulpwood, 225, 248, 518

purple loosestrife, 64

push/pull factors, and migration, 45, 53, 65, 225, 238, 518

quality of life, 14, 35, 110, 126, 131, 151, 166, 245, 250, 263, 271, 327, 353, 380, 386, 398, 410–12, 419, 420, 481, 520

quaternary sector, 83, 106, 388, 518

Quebec, 7, 23, 25, 27, 42, 43, 44–46, 50, 58–60, 62, 63, 65–73, 76, 79, 80, 86, 87, 94, 95, 107, 109, 282, 319, 427, 428, 430, 431, 435, 509, 511–13, 515, 516, 518, 519

Quebec City, Quebec, 50, 57, 60, 66–68, 70–73, 77, 79, 80

Québécois nationalism, 57, 66, 68, 518

Queen Charlotte Basin, 398–99, 404

Queens, 115, 128–30, 138

Quiet Revolution, 57, 66–68, 80, 516, 518

railroads, 132, 136, 155, 156, 161, 189, 241, 247, 248, 256, 268, 279, 324, 350, 377, 511

"Rain follows the plow," 307, 316, 318, 518

rain shadow, 19, 29–31, 149, 315, 327, 340, 343, 345, 347, 357, 370, 374, 388, 404, 458, 459, 517, 518

Raleigh-Durham, North Carolina, 171, 185

ramps, 152, 465

ranchers/ranching, 235, 298, 307–309, 311, 317–19, 322, 332 –34, 327, 336, 340, 343, 353, 356, 357, 360, 362, 363, 367, 368 378, 379, 388–91, 393, 455, 518

rancho, 453, 464

range war, 307, 318, 518

rang system, 57, 64, 65, 518

Raton Mesa and Basin, 307, 309, 312

Ray, Janisse, 184, 512

Reciprocity Treaty of 1854, 57, 75, 503, 518

Reconstruction, 171, 175, 183, 225, 234, 252, 261, 519

recycling, 15, 35, 51, 79, 85, 108, 130, 139, 160, 186, 224, 264, 363, 385, 386, 415, 456, 472, 474, 481, 501

redneck, 171, 184, 189, 519

Red River, 6

Red River Valley, 22

reductionist, 519

redwater river, 171, 177, 519

redwood, 454

Regina, Sasketchewan, 308, 324

religion, 68, 123, 153, 255, 256, 263, 377, 439, 495

renewable resource(s), 11, 14, 15, 17, 103, 296, 504, 519

replacement level, 41, 44, 46, 519

Research Triangle, 171, 185, 195

reservations, 42, 211, 284, 302, 317, 319, 353, 378, 379

resettlement, 83, 93, 519

resource hinterland, 83, 102, 108, 308, 328, 519

rice, 189, 192, 241, 246, 457, 475, 497, 500, 501, 520

Richmond, California, 471

Richmond, Virginia, 50, 171, 176, 183, 185, 196

Rideau Canal, 74, 75

Ridge and Valley Province, 132, 144, 145

Riel, Louis, 319

rift valley, 57, 60, 513, 519

right-to-work states, 195, 250, 519

Ring of Fire, 38, 397, 398, 423, 425
Rio Grande, 6, 25, 227, 231, 311, 312, 345, 371, 374, 375, 388
Rio Grande Plain, 225, 228
Rio Grande Valley, 242, 244, 246, 247, 519
riparian rights, 171, 177, 328, 519
Riverwalk, San Antonio, 225, 244, 246
rock walls, New England, 96
Rocky Mountain Trench, 339, 344, 345
Rodinia, 21, 262
Roosevelt, Franklin D., 148, 465
Roosevelt, Teddy, 310
round barn, 286
Roundup, 298
Royal Proclamation of 1763, 57, 65, 66, 407, 519
Ruark, Justin, 262
Rupert's Land, 307, 319
Russell Cave, 151
Rust Belt, 41, 52, 53, 158, 288, 519

Sacramento, California, 25, 50, 400, 455–456, 459, 464, 474
Sacramento Valley, 465, 475
Safe Drinking Water Act, 165
saimin, 497
St. Anthony Falls, 292, 296
St. Augustine, Florida, 42, 180, 211–213, 215–216, 218
St. Francois Mountains, 256–257
St. John, New Brunswick, 86–87, 89, 92, 94, 99–100, 106
St. John's, Newfoundland, 98–101, 103–104
St. Lawrence Lowlands, 58–60, 62, 77, 87
St. Lawrence River, 25, 58–63, 66, 70–71, 77, 85, 90, 92
St. Lawrence Seaway, 60–62, 64–65, 71, 100, 137
St. Louis, Missouri, 228, 235, 264–265, 268, 287, 298, 317
Salinas Valley, 454, 456, 475
salmon, 89, 358, 376, 402–403, 405–408, 415, 418–419, 430, 432, 435, 440, 446
salt, 18, 27, 29, 90, 92, 117–118, 148, 152, 158, 174, 176, 203–204, 206, 210, 227, 229–231, 258, 300–301, 311, 374, 406, 456–458, 474, 493
salt dome, 228
salt flats, 371, 374
Salt Lake, 353, 369, 374, 380, 388
Salt Lake City, Utah, 353, 380, 384, 387, 391–392
salt lakes, 25, 374
salt licks, 300
Salton Sea, 373
Salvage, Newfoundland, 93
San Andreas Fault, 21, 460–461
San Antonio, Texas, 27, 50, 228, 235, 242, 244–246, 312, 334

Sand Hills, 309, 311, 321, 328, 445
San Diego, California, 34, 50, 234, 376, 442, 454, 456–457, 459, 463, 466, 468–471
San Francisco, California, 30, 38, 43, 47–50, 373, 385, 412, 442, 457–458, 460, 463–468, 471–474, 480
San Francisco Bay, 35, 457, 454–458, 503
San Joaquin Valley, 474–475
San Jose, California, 50, 235, 463, 470–471
Santa Fe, New Mexico, 42, 353, 355–356, 381
Santa Fe Trail, 312–313, 377
Savannah, Georgia, 176–177, 185, 187–189, 203
saw-grass, 203, 205–206
scabland, 368–369
scrubbers, 122, 151
Sea Island cotton, 192
Sea Islands, 172, 174–175, 177, 180–181, 195, 202
sea level rise, 35, 38, 100, 114, 117, 119–120, 174, 178–179, 202, 208, 210, 220, 495
seamount, 487–489
Seattle, Washington, 34, 47, 50, 52, 72, 398–401, 403, 405–407, 410–412, 415–416, 418–420, 426, 435, 447–448, 466
Second Great Awakening, 153, 256
secondary sector, 52; and California, 478–479; and Canadian Corridor, 77–79; and Chesapeake Bay, 118–119; and Gulf Coastal Plains, 250–251; and Hawai`i, 504; and Megalopolis, 136–137; and Midwest, 301; and North Atlantic Provinces, 106; and Ozarks, 269; and South Atlantic, 195
segregation, 157, 166, 189, 195, 226, 239–241, 247, 290, 496
seigneur, 64
seigneurie, 64–65
seismic line, 446
Seminoles, 211
separatism, in Quebec, 59, 68, 70
Seward Peninsula, 434, 439–440
Shaker Square, 294
sharecropper(s), 189, 237–238, 246
Shenandoah Valley, 161
shield, 20–21
shield cluster, 489
shield volcano(es), 23, 488, 490, 492
shipbuilding, 84, 95, 98, 123–124, 135, 411, 448
Shishmaref, 434
short sea shipping, 103, 108
Shoshone, 316, 353, 387
shrimping, in Gulf Coastal Plains, 248–249
Sierra Nevada, 22–23, 368–370, 374, 377, 399, 454–456, 459, 465, 480
Silicon Valley, 74, 79, 196, 465–466, 470–471, 479

silver, 280, 343, 350–351, 358–360, 377, 388
single-room occupancy (SRO) hotels, 466
sinkhole(s), 25, 147, 203, 207, 210, 256–258, 260, 265, 374
sinks, 374
Sioux, 178, 260, 310, 316, 333, 349
skiing, 106, 347, 350, 354, 360–362, 381, 387, 480
slough, 204, 206
Smallwood, Joey, 93
smart growth, 103, 215
SMCRA. *See* Surface Mining Control and Reclamation Act
Smith, Jedediah, 349
smog, 354–355, 387, 459–460
Snake River Plain, 368–369, 373, 388
social carrying capacity, 14
sod buildings, 320
sod house, 320–321, 437, definition of, 320
sod igloo, 436–437
soils, 22, 24, 35
solar energy, 73, 79, 125, 135, 148, 185, 222, 321, 331, 347, 356, 363, 386–387, 392, 437, 468, 474, 470, 478, 504
Sonoran Desert, 344, 368–371, 375
sorghum, 152, 249, 260, 314, 328
South Atlantic: climate, 178; cultural perspectives, 180–184; economy, 188–195; historical geography and settlement, 178–180; physical geography, 172–175; population, immigration, 184–185; urban trends, 185–188; water, 176–178
South Coast, 455
Southern California conurbation, 456, 468–469
Southern Rockies, 341, 343, 345–346, 349, 351, 353, 355, 358, 362
soybeans, 192, 298, 300, 331
space program, 220
Spam, 497
specialty crop(s), 77, 202, 218, 389, 456, 474–475, 477
Spokane, Washington, 27, 353, 369, 381, 383, 387–388
sprawl, 50, 62, 73–75, 100, 124, 135–136, 138, 147, 185–188, 195–196, 214, 218, 244, 264–265, 270–271, 301, 324, 349, 353, 355, 362, 383–384, 387, 398, 411, 413, 419–420, 460–461, 465, 475, 490–500
spruce bark beetles, 432
SRO. *See* single-room occupancy hotels
Staten Island, 115, 120, 128–129
steel, 52, 70, 78, 132, 135, 149, 156–160, 189, 285, 288, 301, 448, 458
steppe, 5, 30, 32, 322, 399
storm water, 164, 210, 215, 281, 403
stratovolcano(es), 23, 398, 400
straw bale buildings, 321

urban trends: in Alaska and Arctic, *(continued)* 123–135; in Midwest, 287–294; in Northern New England, 99–102; in Ozarks, 264–265; in Pacific Northwest, 410–415; in Rocky Mountains, 353–356; in South Atlantic, 185–188

urban village, 471

Utes, 349, 377–378

valley fill, 163

Vancouver, British Columbia, 43, 46–48, 50, 52, 68, 72, 86, 320, 345, 398–402, 406–408, 410, 412- 415, 419–420, 442, 448

Vancouver Island, 31, 404, 408

vegetables, 77, 90, 98, 135–136, 218, 228, 246, 260, 356, 457, 474–475

vegetation, 4–5, 35–38

Vermont, 45, 84, 86, 95, 99–101, 103, 106–108, 117, 184, 361

vernacular, 67

vertical integration, 193, 301, 361

vertical zonation, 346–347

Viburnum Trend, 268

Victoria, British Columbia, 412, 414, 419

Ville de Quebec, 67, 70–71

Vinland, 92

vog, 492

volatile organic compounds (VOCs), 79, 459

volcanic mountain, 23

volcanic plug, 311

volcanoes, 21, 23, 398, 400–401, 425–426, 428, 487–489, 491–492

Voting Rights Act, 241

Wabash Valley, 262

Walmart, 263–265, 269–270

Walton, Sam, 269

Wampanoags, 122

Washington, D.C., 16, 30, 47, 50, 114, 188, 124, 132–137, 139, 178

Washington, George, 132, 175, 310

wastewater, 118, 151, 178, 215, 281, 288, 332, 386, 403

water: in Appalachia, 148; in California, 456–457; in Canadian Corridor, 60–62;

in Florida, 207–209; in Great Plains, 312–314; in Gulf Coastal Plains, 228–231; in Hawai`i, 489–493; in Intermontane, 371–373; in Megalopolis, 117–120; in Midwest, 279–283; in North Atlantic Provinces, 89–90; in Ozarks, 258–259; in Pacific Borderland, 429–430; in Pacific Northwest, 400–403; in Rocky Mountains, 345–346; in South Atlantic, 176–178. *See also* irrigation

water gap, 148

water pollution, 12, 15, 27–29; in Appalachia, 148, 150, 159, 164; in Florida, 213; in Great Plains, 317, 331–332; in Midwest, 280, 296, 300, 303; in Ozarks, 256, 270–271; in Pacific Northwest, 398, 402, 420; in South Atlantic

watersheds, 4, 6–7, 23–24, 29; Great Lakes, 58, 277

water table, 27, 35, 193, 207, 240, 298, 309, 369, 374

water transfers, 345–346

water wars, 29; Great Plains and, 311; Intermontane and, 393; South Atlantic and, 177–179

Welch, Thomas, 259

Welland Canal, 61–62

Welty, Eudora, 226

West Gulf Coastal Plain, 228

West Virginia, 144–145, 147; climate change, 152; coal and, 162–163; population, 154–155, 158–159

wetland(s), 21, 27–28, 35, 37; in Artic Slope, 427–429; in California, 458; in Florida, 202, 205–207; in Great Plains, 309 in Gulf Coastal Plains, 227–230, 233, 243, 251; losses of, 229–230; in Megalopolis, 117–118, 122; in Midwest, 277–280, 282; in South Atlantic, 174

wheat, 135, 260, 286, 294, 296, 309, 313–315, 319–321, 324, 328–329, 388–389

Whiskey Rebellion, 153

whitebark pine, 347

Whitehorse, 427, 429, 440–441

White Mountains: in Appalachia, 23–24; in North Atlantic, 85, 106

Willamette Valley, 369, 377, 398, 405–406, 411, 416

Williams, Danny, 98

wind, 10, 29

wind gap, 148

windmill, 27, 109, 308, 312, 332, 334

wind power: in Appalachia, 148; in California, 478; in Canadian Corridor, 78; in Great Plains, 332–335; in Internmontane, 387, 392; in Megalopolis, 135; in Midwest, 302; in New York City, 117; in North Atlantic Provices, 100, 108; in South Atlantic, 196

wind turbine(s), 10, 108, 148, 196, 246, 333–335, 478, 506

wineries, 60, 161, 357, 388, 416, 475–476

Winnipeg, Manitoba, 324, 332

wolves, 37, 342, 348

Works Progress Administration (WPA), 166

World Trade Organization (WTO), 76, 192, 218, 411, 477

Wright, Frank Lloyd, 393

Wyoming Basin, 343, 353, 377, 408

xeriscaping, 385, 457

xerophytic, 37, 370, 454

Yankee, 96, 99

yellow fever, 186, 239

Yellowhead Pass, 344

Yellowknife, 427, 431, 440–441, 443

Yellowstone Lake, 345

Yellowstone National Park, 7, 38, 342–343, 345

yeoman, 180, 184, 189

Yosemite, 7, 473, 480

Young, Brigham, 380

Youngstown, Ohio, 288

Yucca Mountain, 369–370

Yukon, 341, 344, 424, 426–427, 429, 434–437, 440–441, 449

Yukon River, 25, 427, 429, 434–435

Yup'ik, 434, 438

zebra mussel, 64

zinc, 257, 267–268, 350, 358–360, 443

About the Authors

Lisa Benton-Short is professor of geography at the George Washington University, Washington, D.C. She is an urban geographer with an interest in the dynamics of the urban environment from many angles, including urban sustainability, planning and public space, monuments and memorials, urban national parks, globalization, and immigration. Her regional specialty is in the United States. She has published eight books and numerous articles.

John Rennie Short is professor of geography and public policy at the University of Maryland, Baltimore County. He is an expert on urban issues, environmental concerns, globalization, political geography, and the history of cartography. He has studied cities around the world and lectured around the world to a variety of audiences. Dr. Short is the author of forty books and numerous papers in academic journals and has received awards from the National Science Foundation, the Environmental Protection Agency, the National Geographic Society, and the Social Science Research Council.

Chris Mayda (d. 2016) was professor of geography and sustainability at Eastern Michigan University.